CHILTON BOOK COMPANY

REPAIR MANUAL

DATSUN/NISSAN
1200 ·210
SENTRA
1973-88

All U.S. and Canadian models of DATSUN 1200, 210 ●
NISSAN Sentra

President GARY R. INGERSOLL
Senior Vice President, Book Publishing and Research RONALD A. HOXTER
Vice President and General Manager JOHN P. KUSHNERICK
Editor-in-Chief KERRY A. FREEMAN, S.A.E.
Managing Editor DEAN F. MORGANTINI, S.A.E.
Senior Editor RICHARD J. RIVELE, S.A.E.
Senior Editor W. CALVIN SETTLE, JR., S.A.E.
Editor JOHN BAXTER

CHILTON BOOK COMPANY
Radnor, Pennsylvania
19089

CONTENTS

SAFETY NOTICE

Proper service and repair procedures are vital to the safe, reliable operation of all motor vehicles, as well as the personal safety of those performing repairs. This book outlines procedures for servicing and repairing vehicles using safe, effective methods. The procedures contain many NOTES, CAUTIONS and WARNINGS which should be followed along with standard safety procedures to eliminate the possibility of personal injury or improper service which could damage the vehicle or compromise its safety.

It is important to note that repair procedures and techniques, tools and parts for servicing motor vehicles, as well as the skill and experience of the individual performing the work vary widely. It is not possible to anticipate all of the conceivable ways or conditions under which vehicles may be serviced, or to provide cautions as to all of the possible hazards that may result. Standard and accepted safety precautions and equipment should be used during cutting, grinding, chiseling, prying, or any other process that can cause material removal or projectiles.

Some procedures require the use of tools specially designed for a specific purpose. Before substituting another tool or procedure, you must be completely satisfied that neither your personal safety, nor the performance of the vehicle will be endangered.

Although the information in this guide is based on industry sources and is as complete as possible at the time of publication, the possibility exists that the manufacturer made later changes which could not be included here. While striving for total accuracy, Chilton Book Company cannot assume responsibility for any errors, changes, or omissions that may occur in the compilation of this data.

PART NUMBERS

Part numbers listed in this reference are not recommendations by Chilton for any product by brand name. They are references that can be used with interchange manuals and aftermarket supplier catalogs to locate each brand supplier's discrete part number.

SPECIAL TOOLS

Special tools are recommended by the vehicle manufacturer to perform their specific job. Use has been kept to a minimum, but where absolutely necessary, they are referred to in the text by the part number of the tool manufacturer. These tools can be purchased, under the appropriate part number, from Kent-Moore Corporation, 29784 Little Mack, Roseville, Michigan 48066. For Canada, contact Kent-Moore of Canada, Ltd., 2395 Cawthra Mississauga, Ontario, Canada L5A 3P2 or an equivalent tool can be purchased locally from a tool supplier or parts outlet. Before substituting any tool for the one recommended, read the SAFETY NOTICE at the top of this page.

ACKNOWLEDGMENTS

Chilton Book Company expresses appreciation to the Nissan Motor Corporation in U.S.A., Gardena, California 90247, and Devon Datsun, Devon, Pennsylvania, for their assistance in the preparation of this book.

Chilton's Repair Manual: Datsun/Nissan 1200, 210, Sentra 1973–88
ISBN 0-8019-7850-5 pbk.
Library of Congress Catalog Card No. 87-47921

General Information and Maintenance

HOW TO USE THIS BOOK

Chilton's Repair Manual for the Dastun/Nissan 1200, 210 and Sentrais intended to help you learn more about the inner workings of your vehicle and save you money on its upkeep and operation.

The first two chapters will be the most used, since they contain maintenance and tune-up information and procedures. Studies have shown that a properly tuned and maintained truck can get at least 10% better gas mileage than an out-of-tune truck. The other chapters deal with the more complex systems of your truck. Operating systems from engine through brakes are covered to the extent that the average do-it-yourselfer becomes mechanically involved. This book will not explain such things as rebuilding the differential for the simple reason that the expertise required and the investment in special tools make this task uneconomical. It will give you detailed instructions to help you change your own brake pads and shoes, replace spark plugs, and do many more jobs that will save you money, give you personal satisfaction, and help you avoid expensive problems.

A secondary purpose of this book is a reference for owners who want to understand their truck and/or their mechanics better. In this case, no tools at all are required.

Before removing any bolts, read through the entire procedure. This will give you the overall view of what tools and supplies will be required. There is nothing more frustrating than having to walk to the bus stop on Monday morning because you were short one bolt on Sunday afternoon. So read ahead and plan ahead. Each operation should be approached logically and all procedures thoroughly understood before attempting any work.

All chapters contain adjustments, maintenance, removal and installation procedures, and repair or overhaul procedures. When repair is not considered practical, we tell you how to remove the part and then how to install the new or rebuilt replacement. In this way, you at least save the labor costs. Backyard repair of such components as the alternator is just not practical.

Two basic mechanic's rules should be mentioned here. One, whenever the left side of the truck or engine is referred to, it is meant to specify the driver's side of the truck. Conversely, the right side of the truck means the passenger's side. Secondly, most screws and bolt are removed by turning counterclockwise, and tightened by turning clockwise.

Safety is always the most important rule. Constantly be aware of the dangers involved in working on an automobile and take the proper precautions. (See the section in this chapter Servicing Your Vehicle Safely and the SAFETY NOTICE on the acknowledgement page.)

Pay attention to the instructions provided. There are 3 common mistakes in mechanical work:

1. Incorrect order of assembly, disassembly or adjustment. When taking something apart or putting it together, doing things in the wrong order usually just costs you extra time; however, it CAN break something. Read the entire procedure before beginning disassembly. Do everything in the order in which the instructions say you should do it, even if you can't immediately see a reason for it. When you're taking apart something that is very intricate (for example, a carburetor), you might want to draw a picture of how it looks when assembled at one point in order to make sure you get everything back in its proper position. (We will supply exploded views whenever possible). When making adjustments, especially tune-up adjustments, do them in order; often, one adjustment affects another, and you cannot expect even satisfac-

tory results unless each adjustment is made only when it cannot be changed by any order.

2. Overtorquing (or undertorquing). While it is more common for over-torquing to cause damage, undertorquing can cause a fastener to vibrate loose causing serious damage. Especially when dealing with aluminum parts, pay attention to torque specifications and utilize a torque wrench in assembly. If a torque figure is not available, remember that if you are using the right tool to do the job, you will probably not have to strain yourself to get a fastener tight enough. The pitch of most threads is so slight that the tension you put on the wrench will be multiplied many, many times in actual force on what you are tightening. A good example of how critical torque is can be seen in the case of spark plug installation, especially where you are putting the plug into an aluminum cylinder head. Too little torque can fail to crush the gasket, causing leakage of combustion gases and consequent overheating of the plug and engine parts. Too much torque can damage the threads, or distort the plug which changes the spark gap.

There are many commercial products available for ensuring that fasteners won't come loose, even if they are not torqued just right (a very common brand is Loctite®). If you're worried about getting something together tight enough to hold, but loose enough to avoid mechanical damage during assembly, one of these products might offer substantial insurance. Read the label on the package and make sure the products is compatible with the materials, fluids, etc. involved before choosing one.

3. Crossthreading. This occurs when a part such as a bolt is screwed into a nut or casting at the wrong angle and forced. Cross threading is more likely to occur if access is difficult. It helps to clean and lubricate fasteners, and to start threading with the part to be installed going straight in. Then, start the bolt, spark plug, etc. with your fingers. If you encounter resistance, unscrew the part and start over again at a different angle until it can be inserted and turned several turns without much effort. Keep in mind that many parts, especially spark plugs, used tapered threads so that gentle turning will automatically bring the part you're treading to the proper angle if you don't force it or resist a change in angle. Don't put a wrench on the part until its's been turned a couple of turns by hand. If you suddenly encounter resistance, and the part has not seated fully, don't force it. Pull it back out and make sure it's clean and threading properly.

Always take your time and be patient; once you have some experience, working on your truck will become an enjoyable hobby.

TOOLS AND EQUIPMENT

Naturally, without the proper tools and equipment it is impossible to properly service your vehicle. It would be impossible to catalog each tool that you would need to perform each or any operation in this book. It would also be unwise for the amateur to rush out and buy an expensive set of tool on the theory that he may need on or more of them at sometime.

The best approach is to proceed slowly gathering together a good quality set of those tools that are used most frequently. Don't be misled by the low cost of bargain tools. It is far better to spend a little more for better quality. Forged wrenches, 10 or 12 point sockets and fine tooth ratchets are by far preferable to their less expensive counterparts. As any good mechanic can tell you, there are few worse experiences than trying to work on a truck with bad tools. Your monetary savings will be far outweighed by frustration and mangled knuckles.

Begin accumulating those tools that are used most frequently; those associated with routine maintenance and tune-up.

In addition to the normal assortment of screwdrivers and pliers you should have the following tools for routine maintenance jobs:

1. SAE (or Metric) or SAE/Metric wrenches-sockets and combination open end-box end wrenches in sizes from $\frac{1}{8}''$ (3 mm) to $\frac{3}{4}''$ (19 mm) and a spark plug socket ($\frac{13}{16}''$ or $\frac{5}{8}''$ depending on plug type).

If possible, buy various length socket drive extensions. One break in this department is that the metric sockets available in the U.S. will all fit the ratchet handles and extensions you may already have ($\frac{1}{4}''$, $\frac{3}{8}''$, and $\frac{1}{2}''$ drive).

2. Jackstands for support.

3. Oil filter wrench.

4. Oil filler spout for pouring oil.

5. Grease gun for chassis lubrication.

6. Hydrometer for checking the battery.

7. A container for draining oil.

8. Many rags for wiping up the inevitable mess.

In addition to the above items there are several others that are not absolutely necessary, but handy to have around. these include oil dry, a transmission funnel and the usual supply of lubricants, antifreeze and fluids, although these can be purchased as needed. This is a basic list for routine maintenance, but only your personal needs and desire can accurately determine you list of tools.

The second list of tools is for tune-ups. While the tools involved here are slightly more sophisticated, they need not be outrageously expensive. There are several inexpensive tach/dwell meters on the market that are every bit as good

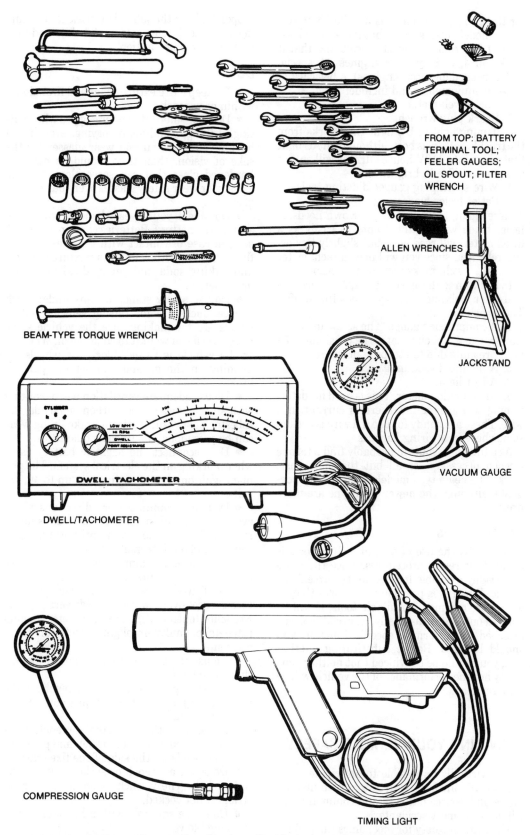

FROM TOP: BATTERY TERMINAL TOOL; FEELER GAUGES; OIL SPOUT; FILTER WRENCH

ALLEN WRENCHES

JACKSTAND

BEAM-TYPE TORQUE WRENCH

DWELL TACHOMETER

DWELL/TACHOMETER

VACUUM GAUGE

COMPRESSION GAUGE

TIMING LIGHT

You need only a basic assortment of hand tools and test instruments for most maintenance and repair jobs

for the average mechanic as a $100.00 professional model. Just be sure that it goes to a least 1,200-1,500 rpm on the tach scale and that it works on 4, 6, 8 cylinder engines. (A special tach is needed for diesel engines). A basic list of tune-up equipment could include:

1. Tach/dwell meter.
2. Spark plug wrench.
3. Timing light (a DC light that works from the truck's battery is best, although an AC light that plugs into 110V house current will suffice at some sacrifice in brightness).
4. Wire spark plug gauge/adjusting tools.
5. Set of feeler blades.

Here again, be guided by your own needs. A feeler blade will set the points as easily as a dwell meter will read well, but slightly less accurately. And since you will need a tachometer anyway. . . well, make your own decision.

In addition to these basic tools, there are several other tools and gauges you may find useful. These include:

1. A compression gauge. The screw-in type is slower to use, but eliminates the possibility of a faulty reading due to escaping pressure.
2. A manifold vacuum gauge.
3. A test light.
4. An induction meter. This is used for determining whether or not there is current in a wire. These are handy for use if a wire is broken somewhere in a wiring harness.

As a final not, you will probably find a torque wrench necessary for all but the most basic work. The beam type models are perfectly adequate, although the newer click type are more precise.

Special Tools

Normally, the use of special factory tools is avoided for repair procedures, since these are not readily available for the do-it-yourself mechanic. When it is possible to preform the job with more commonly available tools, it will be pointed out, but occasionally, a special tool was designed to perform a specific function and should be used. Before substituting another tool, you should be convinced that neither your safety nor the performance of the vehicle will be compromised.

SERVICING YOUR VEHICLE SAFELY

It is virtually impossible to anticipate all of the hazards involved with automotive maintenance and service but care and common sense will prevent most accidents.

The rules of safety for mechanics range from "don't smoke around gasoline" to "use the proper tool for the job." The trick to avoiding injuries is to develop safe work habits and take every possible precaution.

Do's

● Do keep a fire extinguisher and first aid kit within easy reach.

● Do wear safety glasses or goggles when cutting, drilling, grinding, or prying, even if you have 20/20 vision. If you wear glasses for the sake of vision, then they should be made of hardened glass that can serve also as safety glasses, or wear safety glasses over your regular glasses.

● Do shield your eyes whenever you work around the battery. Batteries contain sulphuric acid; in case of contact with the eyes or skin, flush the area with water or a mixture of water and baking soda and get medical attention immediately.

● Do use safety stands for any under-truck service. Jacks are for raising vehicles; safety stands are for making sure the vehicle stays raised until you want it to come down. Whenever the vehicle is raised, block the wheels remaining on the ground and set the parking brake.

● Do use adequate ventilation when working with any chemicals. Like carbon monoxide, the asbestos dust resulting from brake lining wear can be poisonous in sufficient quantities.

● Do disconnect the negative battery cable when working on the electrical system. The primary ignition system can contain up to 40,000 volts.

● Do follow manufacturer's directions whenever working with potentially hazardous materials. Both brake fluid and antifreeze are poisonous if taken internally.

● Do properly maintain your tools. Loose hammerheads, mushroomed punches and chisels, frayed or poorly grounded electrical cords, excessively worn screwdrivers, spread wrenches (open end), cracked sockets, slipping ratchets, or faulty droplight sockets can cause accidents.

● Do use the proper size and type of tool for the job being done.

● Do when possible, pull on a wrench handle rather than push on it, and adjust your stance to prevent a fall.

● Do be sure that adjustable wrenches are tightly adjusted on the nut or bolt and pulled so that the face is on the side of the fixed jaw.

● Do select a wrench or socket that fits the nut or bolt. The wrench or socket should sit straight, not cocked.

● Do strike squarely with a hammer. Avoid glancing blows.

● Do set the parking brake and block the

drive wheels if the work requires that the engine be running.

Don't's

• Don't run an engine in a garage or anywhere else without proper ventilation – EVER! Carbon monoxide is poisonous; it takes a long time to leave the human body and you can build up a deadly supply of it in your system by simply breathing in a little every day. You may not realize you are slowly poisoning yourself. Always use proper vents, window, fans or open the garage door.

• Don't work around moving parts while wearing a necktie or other loose clothing. Short sleeves are much safer than long, loose sleeves and hard-toed shoes with neoprene soles protect your toes and give a better grip on slippery surfaces. Jewelry such as watches, fancy belt buckles, beads or body adornment of any kind is not safe working around a truck. Long hair should be hidden under a hat or cap.

• Don't use pockets for toolboxes. A fall or bump can drive a screwdriver deep into your body. Even a wiping cloth hanging from the back pocket can wrap around a spinning shaft or fan.

• Don't smoke when working around gasoline, cleaning solvent or other flammable material.

• Don't smoke when working around the battery. When the battery is being charged, it gives off explosive hydrogen gas.

• Don't use gasoline to wash your hands; there are excellent soaps available. Gasoline may contain lead, and lead can enter the body through a cut, accumulating in the body until you are very ill. Gasoline also removes all the natural oils from the skin so that bone dry hands will such up oil and grease.

• Don't service the air conditioning system unless you are equipped with the necessary tools and training. The refrigerant, R-12, is extremely cold and when exposed to the air, will instantly freeze any surface it comes in contact with, including your eyes. Although the refrigerant is normally non-toxic, R-12 becomes a deadly poisonous gas in the presence of an open flame. One good whiff of the vapors from burning refrigerant can be fatal.

• Don't ever use a bumper jack (the jack that comes with the vehicle) for anything other than changing tires! If you are serious about maintaining your truck yourself, invest in a hydraulic floor jack of at least 1½ ton capacity. It will pay for itself many times over through the years.

NOTE: *Datsun special tools referred to in this guide are available through Kent-Moore*

Corporation, 29784 Little Mack, Roseville, Michigan 48066. For Canada, contact Kent-Moore of Canada, Ltd., 2395 Cawthra Mississauga, Ontario, Canada L5A 3Ps.

HISTORY

The first Datsun automobile was built in 1914, a small 10 horsepower car with motorcycle fenders. The original name of the company, D.A.T., was derived from the last initials of the company's three main financial backers. A sports-type two seater was produced in 1918 and called the "son of D.A.T.", which later evolved into Datsun. Throughout the 1920's and 1930's the Datsun automobile looked like the English Austin after which it was closely patterned, while the company also began to branch out into the truck market. The year 1933 saw the formation of Nissan Motor Company, and was also the first year Datsuns were exported.

Following the end of World War II (in which Nissan produced military vehicles and aircraft engines), the company managed to resume truck and passenger car production. It wasn't until 1960 that the first Datsun was imported into the United States; since then, Datsun has moved up into second place in imported car sales. The company's introduction of the Sentra model (under the Nissan badge) in 1982 moved Nissan into the forefront of the fuel mileage competition for gasoline-engined cars.

This guide covers all Datsun 1200, B210, and 210 coupes, sedans, hatchbacks and station wagons from 1973 to 1982 (the "A Series" models) as well as the Nissan Sentra.

SERIAL NUMBER IDENTIFICATION

Chassis

The chassis serial number is stamped into the firewall. The chassis number is also located on a dashboard plate which is visible through the windshield. The vehicle identification number is broken down as follows:

• The first 3 digits are "JN1" – Nissan passenger vehicle; or "1N4" – U.S.A. produced passenger vehicle.

• The next letter refers to the type of engine in use. For example, "P" refers to the E16i gasoline engine and "S" refers to the CD17 diesel.

• The third letter refers to the model – for example, "B" refers to the Sentra.

• The fourth space is filled by a number referring to the model.

• The fifth space refers to the body type.

- Next comes the restraint system – "S" for Standard and "Y" for four wheel drive.
- The seventh space is occupied by a check digit (this keeps anyone from creating a fictitious serial number based on this basic information).
- Next comes the model year – for example, "J" for 1988.
- The ninth space contains a letter referring to the manufacturing plant.
- The final block contains the 6 digit sequential serial or "chassis" number for the actual vehicle.

Vehicle Identification Plate

The vehicle identification plate is attached to the firewall. This plate gives the vehicle model, engine displacement in cubic centimeters (cc), SAE horsepower rating, wheelbase, engine number, and chassis number.

Engine

All 1200, B210, and 210 series engines are classified as A Series engines. Sentra gasoline engines are E-series. The Sentra diesel engines are CD series. The engine number is stamped on the right side top edge of the cylinder block on all A-series models. On Sentra Gasoline engines the engine number is stamped on the flywheel housing below the No. 4 spark plug. On the diesel it is located on the front/upper portion of the flywheel housing right at the rear of the block. This serial number is preceded by the engine model code.

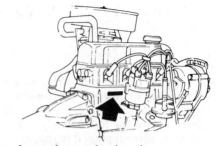

A-series engine number location

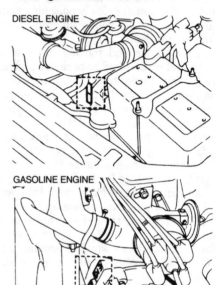

DIESEL ENGINE

GASOLINE ENGINE

Sentra engine serial number location

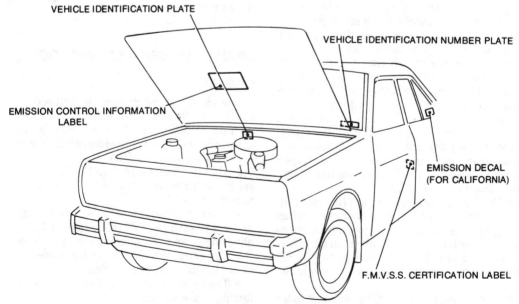

VEHICLE IDENTIFICATION PLATE

VEHICLE IDENTIFICATION NUMBER PLATE

EMISSION CONTROL INFORMATION LABEL

EMISSION DECAL (FOR CALIFORNIA)

F.M.V.S.S. CERTIFICATION LABEL

General vehicle identification locations, all models

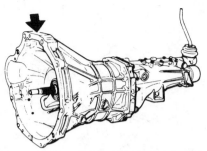

A-series manual transmission number location

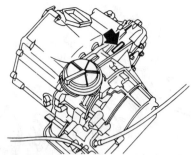

Sentra automatic transaxle number location

Manual Transmission Number

The manual transmission serial number is stamped on the front upper face of the transmission bell housing (case).

Automatic Transmission Number

Automatic transmission serial numbers are found on a plate attached to the right-hand side of the transmission case.

Manual Transaxle Number

The Sentra manual transaxle serial number is attached to the clutch withdrawal lever on the upper end of the transaxle.

Automatic Transaxle Number

The Sentra automatic transaxle serial number label is attached to the upper face of the transaxle case.

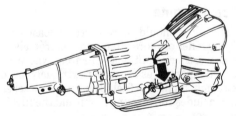

Automatic transmission number location, A-series

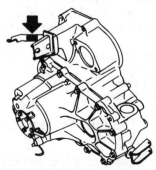

Sentra manual transaxle number location

ROUTINE MAINTENANCE

Air Cleaner

All Datsuns/Nissans covered in this guide are equipped with a disposable paper cartridge air cleaner element. At every tuneup, or sooner if the car is operated in a dusty or smoggy area, undo the wing nut, remove the housing top, and withdraw the element. Check the element. Replace the filter if it is extremely dirty. Loose dust can sometimes be removed by striking the filter against a hard surface several times or by blowing through it with compressed air. The filter should be replaced every 24,000 miles. Before installing either the original or a replacement filter, wipe out the inside of the air cleaner housing with a clean rag or paper towel. Install the paper air cleaner filter, seat the top cover on the bottom housing, and tighten the wing nut.

NOTE: *Some flat, cartridge, type air cleaner elements have the word "UP" printed on them. Be sure the side with "UP" on it faces up.*

Air Induction Valve Filter

This filter is located in the air cleaner of the later model 210 Datsuns and Sentra. Replace it when you replace your air filter element by removing the screws which attach the valve filter case, and remove the filter case. Install the new

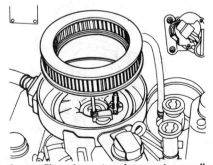

Air cleaner filter element replacement—gasoline engine

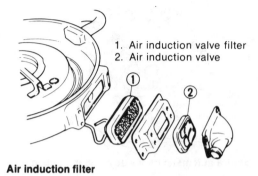

1. Air induction valve filter
2. Air induction valve

Air induction filter

filter, paying attention to which direction the valve is facing so that exhaust gases will not flow backwards through the system.

Fuel Filter

REPLACEMENT

Gasoline Engine

CARBURETED MODELS

The fuel filter on all carbureted models is a disposable plastic unit. It's located on the right inner fender. The filter should be replaced at least every 24,000 miles. A dirty filter will starve the engine and cause poor running.

1. Locate fuel filter on right-side of the engine compartment.
2. Disconnect the inlet and outlet hoses from the fuel filter. Make certain that the inlet hose (bottom) doesn't fall below the fuel tank level or the gasoline will drain out.
3. Pry the fuel filter from its clip and replace the assembly.
4. Replace the inlet and outlet lines; secure the hose clamps to prevent leaks.
5. Start the engine and check for leaks.

FUEL INJECTED MODELS

1. Make sure the ignition switch is off. Pull the fuel pump fuse out of the fuse panel. This is located in the top row, fourth fuse from the right. Start the engine and allow it to idle until

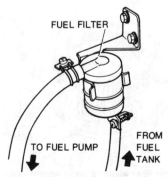

FUEL FILTER

TO FUEL PUMP

FROM FUEL TANK

Typical fuel filter, carbureted models

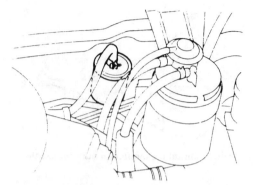

The high pressure fuel filter used on fuel injected models

it stalls. Finally, crank the engine for a few seconds – until it no longer tries to fire. Turn off the ignition switch.
2. Place a metal container under the filter to catch spilled fuel. Note the routing of the fuel hoses. Loosen the hose clamps and carefully pull the hoses off the filter.
3. Loosen the clamp that retains the filter. Remove the filter.
4. Install the filter in reverse order. Make sure the hoses are installed fully over the bulged areas of the filter fittings and that the clamps are a short distance inside the ends of the hoses. *Make sure the clamps are tightened snugly. Make sure to remove the metal fuel container from the area. Allow any additional fuel to evaporate thoroughly.*
5. Install the fuel pump fuse. Start the engine and operate it for a few minutes, checking for leaks.

Diesel Engine

The filter should be replaced at least every 30,000 miles or more often under extremely adverse weather conditions or in areas where ambient temperatures are either extremely low or extremely high. The fuel filter on the diesel engine includes the priming pump and the fuel filter sensor.

1. Remove the fuel filter sensor and drain the fuel into an appropriate container.
2. Unscrew the fuel filter and discard.
3. Install the fuel filter sensor to the new fuel filter.
4. Hand tighten the fuel filter to the priming pump.
5. Bleed the fuel system as outlined in the following proceedure.

Bleeding The Fuel System (Diesel Engine)

NOTE: *Air should be bled out of the fuel system when the injection pump is removed or*

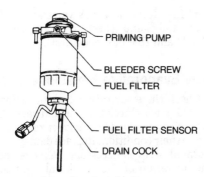

PRIMING PUMP

BLEEDER SCREW

FUEL FILTER

FUEL FILTER SENSOR

DRAIN COCK

Fuel filter assembly—diesel engine

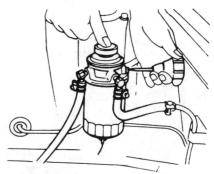

Loosen the priming pump vent screw by turning counterclockwise with a screwdriver

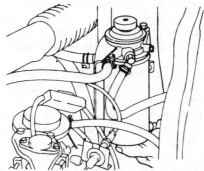

When installing the fuel filter, hand tighten only

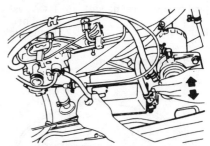

Prime the priming pump and check for an air bubble at the hose end

the fuel system is repaired. This is also required if the fuel tank has been completely emptied.

1. Loosen the air vent screw or cock.

2. Move the priming pump up and down until no further air bubbles come out of the air vent screw or cock, then tighten the air vent screw or cock.

3. Disconnect the fuel return hose on the pump side, then install a suitable hose on the pump side.

4. Prime the priming pump to make sure that a bubble does not appear at the hose end and connect the return hose.

NOTE: *If the engine does not operate smoothly after it has started, race it two or three times. If the engine does not start, loosen the injection tubes at the nozzle side and crank the engine until fuel overflows from the injection tubes. Tighten the injection tube flare nuts.*

Draining Water From The Fuel System (Diesel Engine)

If the filter warning light illuminates and a chime sounds (on models so equipped) while the engine is running, drain any water that is in the fuel filter.

1. Disconnect the harness connector at the bottom of the fuel filter assembly.

2. Place a container under the fuel filter, then loosen the drain cock 4 or 5 turns to drain the water.

NOTE: *If the water does not drain sufficiently move the priming pump up and down.*

3. After draining the water completely, close the drain cock and reconnect the harness connector.

4. Bleed the air from the fuel system as outlined earlier.

Positive Crankcase Ventilation Valve

This valve feeds crankcase blow-by gases into the intake manifold to be burned with the normal air/fuel mixture. The PCV valve should also be replaced every 24,000 miles. The PCV filter, located inside the air cleaner canister, should be replaced every 24,000 miles or more frequently under dusty or smoggy conditions. Make sure that all PCV connections are tight. Check that the connecting hoses are clear and not clogged. Replace any brittle or broken hoses.

To replace the valve, which is located in the intake manifold directly below the carburetor:

1. Squeeze the hose clamp with pliers and remove the hose.

2. Using a wrench, unscrew the PCV valve and remove the valve.

3. Disconnect the ventilation hoses and flush with solvent.

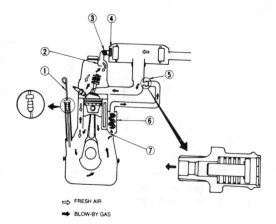

⇨ FRESH AIR

➡ BLOW-BY GAS

1. Seal type oil level gauge
2. Baffle plate
3. Flame arrester
4. Filter

5. P.C.V. valve
6. Steel net
7. Baffle plate

Typical PCV valve location

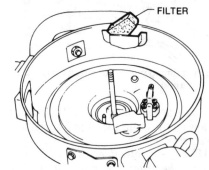

FILTER

PCV filter location in top of air cleaner

4. Install the new PCV valve and replace the hoses and clamp (check to make sure they are pliable and free of cracks first).

Fuel Evaporative Emissions System

Check the evaporation control system every 12,000 miles. Check the fuel and vapor lines for proper connections and correct routing according to their condition. Replace damaged or deteriorated parts as necessary. Remove and check the operation of the check valve on pre-1975 models in the following manner:

1. With all the hoses disconnected from the valve, apply air pressure to the fuel tank side of the valve. The air should flow through the valve and exit the crankcase side of the valve. If the valve does not behave in the above manner, replace it.

2. Apply air pressure to the crankcase side of the valve. Air should not pass to either of the two outlets.

3. When air pressure is applied to the carburetor side of the valve, the air should pass through to exit out the fuel tank and/or the crankcase side of the valve.

NOTE: *On 1975 and later models, the flow guide valve is replaced with a carbon filled canister which stores fuel vapors until the engine is started and the vapors are drawn into the combustion chambers and burned.*

To check the operation of the carbon canister purge control valve, disconnect the rubber hose between the canister control valve and the T-fitting, at the T-fitting. Apply vacuum to the

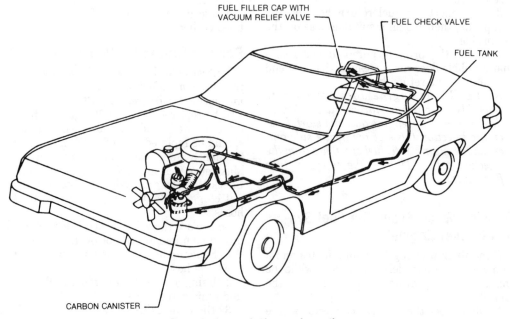

FUEL FILLER CAP WITH
VACUUM RELIEF VALVE

FUEL CHECK VALVE

FUEL TANK

CARBON CANISTER

Evaporative emissions schematic

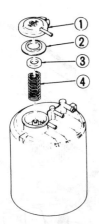

1. Cover
2. Diaphragm
3. Retainer
4. Diaphragm spring

1975 and later carbon canister fuel evaporative emissions system

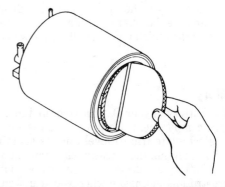

The carbon canister has a replaceable filter in the bottom

hose leading to the control valve. The vacuum condition should be maintained indefinitely. If the control valve leaks, remove the top cover of the valve and check for a dislocated or cracked diaphragm. If the diaphragm is damaged, a repair kit containing a new diaphragm, retainer, and spring is available and should be installed. The carbon canister has an air filter in the bottom of the canister. The filter element should be checked once a year or every 12,000 miles;

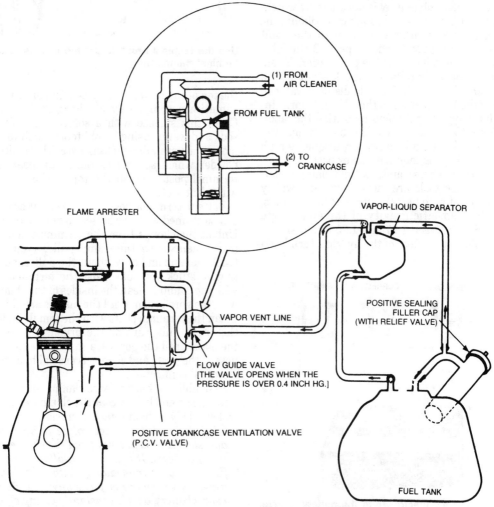

1973–74 check valve fuel evaporative emissions system

more frequently if the car is operated in dusty areas. Replace the filter by pulling it out of the bottom of the canister and installing a new one.

Battery

The battery in your Datsun is located in the engine compartment. Keep an eye on the battery electrolyte (fluid) level and its specific gravity. A few minutes occasionally spent monitoring battery condition is worth saving hours of frustration and hassle when your car won't start due to a dead battery. Use only distilled water (available in most supermarkets and hardware stores) to top up the battery, as tap water in many areas contains harmful chemicals and minerals.

Note that 1987 models only utilize a maintenance-free battery. This type of battery requires much less maintenance than standard units. However, you should occasionally check that the electrolyte level is adequate by watching the side of the see-through case. Should the level in one or more cells drop to the point where water must be added, peel off the label covering the cell caps at the perforation. Then, pry the plugs for cells that are low out with a dull, small prying device. Add distilled water to bring the level *just* up to the "MAX" mark. Install the plugs tightly and reposition the label.

Four tools that will make battery maintenance easier are a hydrometer, a squeeze bulb filler (syringe or common turkey baster), a battery terminal brush and a battery clamp puller. All of these tools are inexpensive and widely available at auto parts stores, hardware stores, etc. The specific gravity of the electrolyte should be between 1.27 and 1.20 (often shown by a color on the float of the hydrometer). Keep

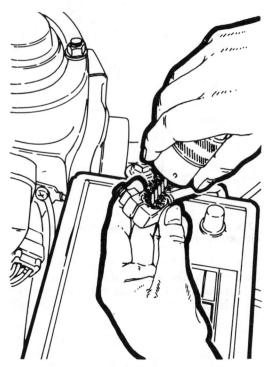

Use the terminal brush to get the insides of the terminal clamps shiny

the top of the battery clean, as a film of dirt can sometimes completely discharge a battery. Clean this surface with a solution of baking soda and water, using an old toothbrush to remove the crystallized electrolyte (the whitish powder which sometimes builds up near the terminal posts). Flush the top of the battery with clear water.

Battery terminal posts and terminal clamps can be cleaned with the battery terminal brush. Unbolt the clamps from the terminals and remove them using the clamp puller (you can twist them up and off without the puller, but if they're stuck you may twist the terminal off with the clamp). Clean the insides of the clamps with the wire brush, until the insides are shiny. Clean the terminal posts with the female end of the brush unit, turning the brush around on the posts until the posts are shiny. The cleanliness of the posts and clamps is crucial to a good electrical connection.

Assemble the battery wire clamps to the terminal posts and lightly coat the clamps with petroleum jelly to help retard corrosion.

CAUTION: *Battery electrolyte is an acid, and should be kept away from the skin, especially the eyes. If it is accidentally splashed, flush the area immediately with cold, clean water. Never smoke or place any open flame near a battery, as it is constantly giving off an explosive gas while charging.*

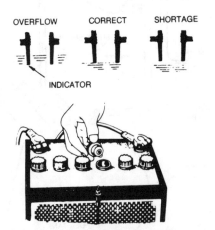

OVERFLOW   CORRECT   SHORTAGE

INDICATOR

Make sure the electrolyte in the battery is level with the bottoms of the filler holes

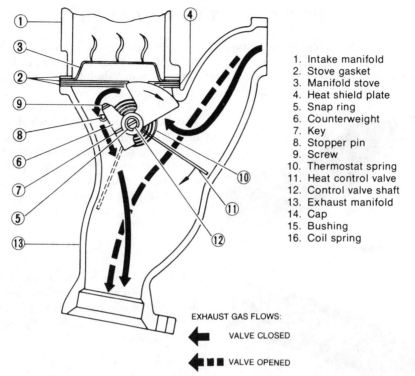

1. Intake manifold
2. Stove gasket
3. Manifold stove
4. Heat shield plate
5. Snap ring
6. Counterweight
7. Key
8. Stopper pin
9. Screw
10. Thermostat spring
11. Heat control valve
12. Control valve shaft
13. Exhaust manifold
14. Cap
15. Bushing
16. Coil spring

EXHAUST GAS FLOWS:

◀ VALVE CLOSED

◀ ■ ■ VALVE OPENED

Heat control valve (early fuel evaporative system) A-series engine

Heat Control Valve

The heat control valve, or Early Fuel Evaporative System, is a thermostatically operated valve found in the exhaust manifold of 1200, B210 and early 210 models. It closes when the engine is warming up to direct hot exhaust gases to the intake manifold, in order to pre-heat the incoming fuel/air mixture. If it sticks shut, the result will be frequent stalling during warmup, especially in cold or damp weather. If it sticks open, the result will be a rough idle after the engine is warm.

The heat control valve should be checked for free operation every six months or 6,000 miles. Simply give the counterweight a twirl (engine cold) to make sure that no binding exists. If the valve sticks, apply a heat control solvent (usually available in spray cans) to the ends of the shaft. This type of solvent is available in most auto parts stores. Sometimes lightly rapping the end of the shaft with a hammer (engine hot) will break it loose. If this fails, the components will have to be removed from the car for repair.

NOTE: *The 1980 and later 210 engines do not use the heat control valve.*

Belts

INSPECTION

Check the belts driving the fan, air pump, air conditioning compressor, and the alternator for cracks, fraying, wear, and tension every 6,000 miles. It is recommended that the belts be replaced every 24 months or 24,000 miles. Belt deflection at the midpoint of the longest span between pulleys should not be more than $^{1}/_{16}$″ with 22 lbs. of pressure applied to the belt. Check belt tension when the engine is cold or has been off for at least 30 minutes.

ADJUSTING AND REPLACEMENT

To adjust the tension on all components except the air conditioning compressor, power steering pump, and some late model air pumps, loosen the pivot and mounting bolts of the component which the belt is driving, then, using a wooden lever, pry the component toward or away from the engine until the proper tension is achieved.

CAUTION: *Never tighten power steering pump, air conditioning compressor, and air pump belts by prying the pump or compressor away from the engine. Damage to the component will result. Also, do not overtighten belts—shaft bearings on the various components will wear out unusually fast.*

Tighten the component mounting bolts securely. If a new belt is installed, recheck the tension after driving about 1,000 miles.

NOTE: *The replacement of the inner belt on multi-belted engines may require the removal of the outer belts.*

HOW TO SPOT WORN V-BELTS

V-Belts are vital to efficient engine operation—they drive the fan, water pump and other accessories. They require little maintenance (occasional tightening) but they will not last forever. Slipping or failure of the V-belt will lead to overheating. If your V-belt looks like any of these, it should be replaced.

Cracking or weathering

This belt has deep cracks, which cause it to flex. Too much flexing leads to heat build-up and premature failure. These cracks can be caused by using the belt on a pulley that is too small. Notched belts are available for small diameter pulleys.

Softening (grease and oil)

Oil and grease on a belt can cause the belt's rubber compounds to soften and separate from the reinforcing cords that hold the belt together. The belt will first slip, then finally fail altogether.

Glazing

Glazing is caused by a belt that is slipping. A slipping belt can cause a run-down battery, erratic power steering, overheating or poor accessory performance. The more the belt slips, the more glazing will be built up on the surface of the belt. The more the belt is glazed, the more it will slip. If the glazing is light, tighten the belt.

Worn cover

The cover of this belt is worn off and is peeling away. The reinforcing cords will begin to wear and the belt will shortly break. When the belt cover wears in spots or has a rough jagged appearance, check the pulley grooves for roughness.

Separation

This belt is on the verge of breaking and leaving you stranded. The layers of the belt are separating and the reinforcing cords are exposed. It's just a matter of time before it breaks completely.

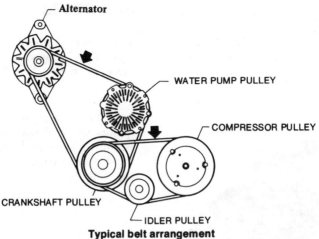

Typical belt arrangement

Belt tension adjustments for the factory installed air conditioning compressor and power steering pump are made at the idler pulley. The idler pulley is the smallest of the three pulleys. At the top of the slotted bracket holding the idler pulley there is a bolt which is used to either raise or lower the pulley. To free the bolt for admustment, it is necessary to loosen the lock nut in the face of the idler pulley. After adjusting the belt tension, tighten the lock nut in the face of the idler pulley.

NOTE: *Some 1980 and later California Datsuns/Nissans come equipped from the factory with special fan belts which, if loose, generate friction heat by slipping and shrink, taking up the slack. If your car is new or has low mileage on it, it may still have this type of belt(s) on it. The optical air conditioning drive belt is adjusted in a similar manner.*

Extra belts, especially alternator drive belts, should be part of your car's emergency equipment particularly if the brunt of your mileage is driven on the highway. Along with the new belts should be any tools (wrenches, wooden prybars, etc.) needed to install the belts while out on the road.

Air Conditioning System

SAFETY WARNINGS

The compressed refrigerant used in the air conditioning system expands into the atmosphere at a temperature of -21.7°F or lower. This will freeze any surface, including your eyes, that it contacts. In addition, the refrigerant decomposes into a poisonous gas in the presence of flame. Further, the refrigerant nor-mally produces high pressure in the system, especially when it is running.

For these reasons, any repair work to an air conditioning system should be left to a professional. Do not, under any circumstances, attempt to loosen or tighten any fittings or perform any work other than that outlined here.

SYSTEM INSPECTION

Checking for Oil Leaks

Refrigerant leaks show up as oily areas on the various components because the compressor oil is transported around the entire system along with the refrigerant. Look for oil spots on all the hoses and lines, and especially on the hose and tubing connections. If there are oily deposits, the system may have a leak, and you should have it checked by a qualified repairman.

NOTE: *A small area of oil on the front of the compressor is normal and no cause for alarm.*

Checking the Compressor Belt

Inspect the belt carefully for glazing on the V surfaces, which indicates slippage (there should be a slight crosshatch or fabric appearance), cracks (which usually start at the center) or any other damage, including being too stretched to permit a tight adjustment. Replace the A/C belt if there is any sign at all of damage, as this belt carries a great deal of load.

On most air conditioning installations, the compressor is mounted directly to the block or cylinder head and remains in the same position regardless of the belt adjustment. An idler pulley is held in place by an adjusting bolt and a lock nut. To adjust the belt, all that is necessary is to loosen the locknut, turn the adjusting bolt double nuts, and retighten the locknut.

HOW TO SPOT BAD HOSES

Both the upper and lower radiator hoses are called upon to perform difficult jobs in an inhospitable environment. They are subject to nearly 18 psi at under hood temperatures often over 280°F., and must circulate nearly 7500 gallons of coolant an hour—3 good reasons to have good hoses.

A good test for any hose is to feel it for soft or spongy spots. Frequently these will appear as swollen areas of the hose. The most likely cause is oil soaking. This hose could burst at any time, when hot or under pressure.

Swollen hose

Cracked hoses can usually be seen but feel the hoses to be sure they have not hardened; a prime cause of cracking. This hose has cracked down to the reinforcing cords and could split at any of the cracks.

Cracked hose

Weakened clamps frequently are the cause of hose and cooling system failure. The connection between the pipe and hose has deteriorated enough to allow coolant to escape when the engine is hot.

Frayed hose end (due to weak clamp)

Debris, rust and scale in the cooling system can cause the inside of a hose to weaken. This can usually be felt on the outside of the hose as soft or thinner areas.

Debris in cooling system

Check the belt tension by depressing the belt in the center of its longest span with your thumb. It should depress approximately $7/16''$. If the tension is incorrect, loosen the locknut. Then, turn the adjusting bolt via the two nuts until tension is correct. Hold the adjusting bolt in position as you tighten the locknut. Recheck the tension to make sure it has not changed. Readjust if necessary.

Checking Refrigerant Level

The first order of business when checking the sight glass is to find it. It will be in the head of the receiver/drier. In some cases, it may be covered by a small rubber plug designed to keep it clean. Once you've found it, remove the cover, if necessary, wipe it clean and proceed as follows:

1. With the engine and the air conditioning system running, look for the flow of refrigerant through the sight glass. If the air conditioner is working properly, you'll be able to see a continuous flow of clear refrigerant through the sight glass, with perhaps an occasional bubble at very high outside temperatures.

2. Cycle the air conditioner on and off to make sure what you are seeing is a pure stream of liquid refrigerant. Since the refrigerant is clear, it is possible to mistake a completely discharged system for one that is fully charged. Turn the system off and watch the sight glass. If there is refrigerant in the system, you'll see bubbles during the off cycle. Also, the lines going into and out of the compressor will be at radically different temperatures (be careful about touching the line going forward to the condenser, which is in front of the radiator, as it will be very hot). If the bubbles disappear just after you start the compressor, there are no bubbles when the system is running, and the

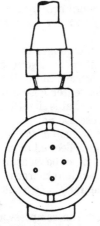

The air conditioner sight glass. Here is how the sight glass will look if there are just a few bubbles.

air flow from the unit in the car is cold, everything is O.K.

3. If you observe bubbles in the sight glass while the system is operating, the system is low on refrigerant. You may want to charge it yourself, as described later. Otherwise, have it checked by a professional.

4. If all you can see in the sight glass is oil streaks, this is an indication of trouble. This is true because there is no liquid refrigerant in the system (otherwise, the oil would mix with the refrigerant and would be invisible). Most of the time, if you see oil in the sight glass, it will appear as a series of streaks, although occasionally it may be a solid stream of oil. In either case, it means that part of the charge of refrigerant has been lost.

USING THE BAR GAUGE MANIFOLD

WARNING: *Refrigerant work is usually performed by highly trained technicians. Improper use of the gauges can result in a leakage of refrigerant liquid, damage to the compressor, or even explosion of a system part. The do-it-yourselfer must be very careful to insure that he proceeds with extreme care and understands what he is doing before proceeding. The best insurance for safety is a complete understanding of the system and proper techniques for servicing it. A careful study of a complete text such as CHILTON'S GUIDE TO AIR CONDITIONING SERVICE AND REPAIR, book part No. 7580, is the best insurance against either dangerous or system-damaging problems.*

To use the bar gauge manifold, follow the procedures outlined below.

1. It is first necessary to clear the manifold itself of air and moisture, especially if the fittings have been left open. You should follow this procedure, unless you know that the hoses and gauge manifold have recently been bled with refrigerant and capped off tightly. Otherwise, you may actually force air and moisture into the system when you are testing or charging it. Begin with both the service valves on the refrigerant gauge set *closed*.

   a. First, tap a can of refrigerant. To do this, first unscrew the tap's cutting tool all the way. Turn the rotatable locking lever so it leaves one side of the collar assembly open. Then, slide the tap onto the top of the can so the collar tabs fit over the rim that runs around the top of the can. Turn the locking lever so that it secures the collar. Then, turn the cutting tool all the way down to tap the can.

   b. Remove any plugs that may be present and then screw the *center* hose to the screw fitting on top of the tap. Now, slightly loosen

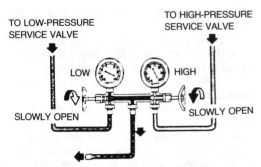

TO LOW-PRESSURE
SERVICE VALVE

TO HIGH-PRESSURE
SERVICE VALVE

LOW   HIGH

SLOWLY OPEN

SLOWLY OPEN

Connections for the bar gauge manifold

the plugs in the ends of the other two lines.

c. Sit the can of refrigerant down right side up on a flat surface. *Make sure the can does not get pulled up off the surface as you work, or you could be splattered by liquid refrigerant.* Then, open the tap by unscrewing the tapping tool handle all the way. Crack both of the bar gauge manifold valves just a little-- just until you hear a slight hiss at the plug at the end of the hose on either side. Allow the refrigerant to enter the system until you are sure it has reached the ends of the hoses (30 seconds). Tighten the plugs at the bottom of the hoses and then *immediately* turn off both manifold valves.

2. Using a wrench if the cap has flats, uncap the low and high pressure, Schrader valve type fittings for the system. The low pressure fitting is located on the suction port of the compressor. In a typical mounting of the unit with the ports facing the front of the car, this is the lower port. You'll find that there is a line connecting with this port that comes from the evaporator (located behind the cowl). The high pressure fitting is located on the muffler, which, in turn is located on the line coming out of the commpressor and heading toward the condenser. There is a low pressure gauge on the left side of the manifold, which shows pressures up to about 100 psi *and* vacuum. Connect the line on this side to the low pressure side of the system. The gauge on the right or high pressure side of the manifold reads only pressure and, typically, the scale goes up to 500 psi. or higher.

On many newer systems, the threads on high and low pressure Schrader valves are of different sizes to prevent improper hookup.

If you have an older set of gauges, you can get an adapter or a different hoses that will convert your gauges to the new thread sizes. Consult a heating, air conditioning and refrigeration supply source.

WARNING: *When making connections, start the threads carefully and, once you are sure they are not crossthreaded, turn the fitting as fast as you can in order to avoid getting*

sprayed by refrigerant. Sometimes the Schrader valve will open early--before the fitting is tight, and this will cause a little refrigerant to be sprayed out.

3. Use of the gauges once they are bled and installed typically includes reading high and low side pressures with both valves closed, charging the system with the low side valve cracked partly open, and discharging it with both valves partly open. Refer to the section just below on "Charging the System" for specifics.

4. To disconnect the gauges, turn the fittings as quickly as possible so as to close the Schrader valves as quickly as possible. Note that liquid refrigerant and oil may be sprayed out for a short time as this is done, especially on the low pressure side. Turn the fittings by reaching down from above, as liquid will be sprayed out underneath the gauge connection. Less refrigerant will be sprayed out on the high side if the connection is broken a few minutes after the system is turned off. Cap the open ends of the gauges immediately. If, for any reason, the ends are left open for a minute or two, repeat the bleeding procedure above. Tightly cap the system openings right away.

DISCHARGING THE SYSTEM

NOTE: *Fluorocarbon refrigerants like that used in car air conditioners damage the upper atmosphere, destroying its ability to screen off dangerous solar radiation. For this reason, air conditioning service shops will soon be required to use special charging/evacuating stations to condense and recover refrigerants rather than releasing them to the atmosphere. While these environmental regulations may not apply to the do-it-yourselfer, you may wish to have your system discharged by a professional equipped to recover the refrigerant if you are concerned about the environment.*

1. Connect the gauges to the high and low sides of the system, as described above. Do not connect a refrigerant can to the center hose.

2. Insert the center hose into a glass bottle with an opening that is slightly larger in diameter than the hose. *Do not attempt to cap or seal the opening in the top of the bottle in any way.* This bottle will collect oil discharged from the system so that it can be measured and replaced when the system is recharged. Make sure you keep the bottle upright to avoid spilling any of this oil out.

3. Make sure the compressor is turned off and remains off throughout the procedure. Crack the low side manifold valve until refrigerant gas is expelled at a steady, moderate rate.

Don't open the valve all the way, or too much refrigerant oil will be expelled from the system.

4. As refrigerant pressure drops and the gas begins to be expelled only very slowly, open the low side manifold valve more and more to compensate and keep the refrigerant moving out of the system.

5. Once *all* the pressure is discharged, slowly open the high side service valve, repeating Steps 3 and 4 until the system is clear. Close it after any pressure has escaped.

6. Disconnect the gauges and recap the openings. Retain the bottle of oil. If you have the system evacuated and recharged by a professional, give him the bottle of oil. He will measure the amount it contains and replace it with a like amount.

CHARGING THE SYSTEM

WARNING: *Charging the system can prove to be very dangerous. You must satisfy yourself that you are fully aware of all risks before starting. Although most systems use a high pressure cutoff switch for the compressor, overcharging the system, attempting to charge it when it contains air, or charging it when there is inadequate cooling of the condenser could cause dangerous pressures to develop if this switch should fail. Overcharging could also damage the compressor.*

The safest way to charge the system is with a set of gauges installed and reading both low and high side pressures so that you can monitor pressures throughout the procedure. It is best to refer to a text on refrigeration and air conditioning first, so that you understand what will happen. Using the simple hose sold for do-it-yourself charging of the system can be safe, provided three precautions are taken:

a. Make sure the system has been completely evacuated by a professional with a good vacuum pump. Eliminating air and the moisture that it contains from within the system is a vital step toward maintaining safe pressures during the charging process and ensuring reliable and effective operation later.

b. Charge the system with precisely the amount of refrigerant it is specified to use *and no more.* Consult the label on the compressor. Purchase the right number of cans. You can precisely estimate what percentage of a can has been charged into the system by noting the frost line on the can.

c. Run the engine at a moderate speed during charging (not too fast), valve the refrigerant into the system at a controlled rate, and keep a fan blowing across the condenser at all times.

Charge the system by following these steps:

1. Make sure the system has been completely evacuated with a good vacuum pump. This should be done with gauges connected and the pump must be able to create a vacuum of 28-29 in.Hg near sea level. Lower this specification one in.Hg for each 1,000 feet above sea level at your location.

2. Connect the gauges as described above, including tapping in a new can of refrigerant. If you are using a gaugeless hose that is part of a charging kit, follow the directions on the package; in any case, make sure to hook up the hose to the low pressure side of the system--to the accumulator or POA valve.

3. Situate a fan in front of the condenser and use it to blow air through the condenser and radiator throughout the charging process.

4. Unless the system has a sight glass, get the exact refrigerant capacity off the compressor label. Make sure you have only the proper number of cans available to help avoid unnecessary overcharge.

5. It will speed the process to place the cans, top up, in warm water. Use a thermometer and make sure the water is *not over 120°F*. You will need to warm the water as the process goes on. Monitor the temperature to make sure it does not go too high, as warm water will almost immediately create excessive pressure inside the can—pressure that will not be reflected in gauge readings. Make sure the cans *always* stay top up. This requires a lot of attention because as the cans run low on refrigerant, they begin to float and may turn upside down. Charging the system with the can upside down may cause liquid refrigerant to enter the system, damaging the compressor. If the bar gauge manifold or charging line suddenly frosts up, check the position of the can immediately and rectify it, if necessary!

6. Start the process with the engine off. Open the charging valve (if you are using a kit) or the low side bar gauge manifold valve slightly until the pressures equalize. Then, close the charging valve or bar gauge manifold back off. Place an electric fan in front of the condenser. Then, start the engine and run it at idle speed or just very slightly above. Turn the blower to the lowest speed. Then, turn the air conditioner on in the normal operating mode. If the system has no refrigerant in it, the low pressure cutout switch on the compressor will keep it from starting until some pressure is created in the system.

7. If you're working with a charging kit, follow the manufacturer's instructions as to how far to open the charging valve. If you're working with a bar gauge manifold, and the system has a lot of refrigerant in it (you're just topping it off) follow the rest of this step. Otherwise,

skip to 8. Note the operating pressure (the average if the compressor is cycling). Then, open the manifold valve until system low side pressure rises 10 psi. Throughout the charging procedure, maintain this pressure by opening or closing the valve to compensate for changes in the temperature of the refrigerant can. Also, keep your eye on the high side pressure and make sure it remains at a moderate level (usually less than 200 psi).

8. Gradually open the valve on the suction (left) side of the bar gauge manifold, as you watch the low side gauge. Allow the pressure to build until the compressor comes on and runs continuously. Keep permitting it to rise until it reaches 40 psi. Then, carefully control the position of the valve to maintain this pressure. You will have to change the position of the valve to compensate for cooling of the refrigerant can and surrounding water and to help empty the can.

9. When the first can runs out of refrigerant, close off the manifold valve or charging line valve. Tap in a new can, immerse it in liquid, keeping it right side up, and then open the charging line valve if you're working without gauges. If you are working with gauges, open the valve on the tap and then open the low side manifold valve as described in Step 8 to maintain the pressure as before.

10. Continue with the process until the last can is hooked up. Measure in a fraction of a can, if necessary, by watching the frost line on the can and stopping appropriately. Watch for the time when bubbles just disappear from the sight glass. If you're just topping off the system, stop charging just after this occurs. Otherwise, this is a sign that you should expect the system to be completely charged and find that you have just about measured the right amount of refrigerant in. Be ready to stop charging! If you're just topping off the system, turn off the charging valve or low side manifold valve and then run the system with the fan on high and the engine accelerated to about 1,500 rpm to check the charge. If bubbles appear, charge the system slightly more until just after all the bubbles disappear.

11. When charging is complete, turn off the manifold or charging line valves and any valve on the can. Disconnect the low side line *at the suction line and not at the gauges*, grabbing the connection from above, watching for liquid refrigerant that may spray out, and unscrewing the connection as fast as you can. Turn off the engine and allow the pressure on the high side to drop until it stabilizes. Then, disconnect the high side gauge connection (if necessary) as quickly as possible. Cap both system openings and all gauge openings as soon as possible.

Windshield Wipers

Intense heat from the sun, snow and ice, road oils and the chemicals used in windshield washer solvent combine to deteriorate the rubber wiper refills. The refills should be replaced about twice a year or whenever the blades begin to streak or chatter.

WIPER REFILL REPLACEMENT

Normally, if the wipers are not cleaning the windshield properly, only the refill has to be replaced. The blade and arm usually require replacement only in the event of damage. It is not necessary (except on new Tridon® refills) to remove the arm of the blade to replace the refill (rubber part), though you may have to position the arm higher on the glass. You can do this by turning the ignition switch on, and operating the wipers. When they are positioned where they are accessible, turn the ignition switch off.

There are several types of refills and your car could have any kind, since aftermarket blades and arms may not use exactly the same type refill as the original equipment.

Most Trico® styles use a release button that is pushed down to allow the refill to slide out of the yoke jaws. The new refill slides in and locks in place. Some Trico® refills are removed by locating where the metal backing strip or the refill is wider. Insert a small screwdriver blade between the frame and metal backing strip. Press down to release the refill from the retaining tab.

The Anco® style is unlocked at one end by squeezing 2 metal tabs, and the refill is slid out of the frame jaws. When the new refill is installed, the tabs will click into place, locking the refill.

The polycarbonate type is held in place by a locking lever that is pushed downward, out of the groove in the arm, to free the refill. When the new refill is installed, it will lock in place automatically.

The Tridon® refill has a plastic backing strip with a notch about an inch from the end. Hold the blade (frame) on a hard surface so that the fram is tightly bowed. Grip the tip of the backing strip and pull up while twisting counterclockwise. The backing strip will snap out of the retaining tab. Do this for the remaining tabs until the refill is free of the arm. The length of these refills is molded into the end and they should be replaced with identical types.

No matter which type of refill you use, be sure that all of the frame claws engage the refill. Before operating the wipers, be sure that no part of the metal frame is contacting the windshield.

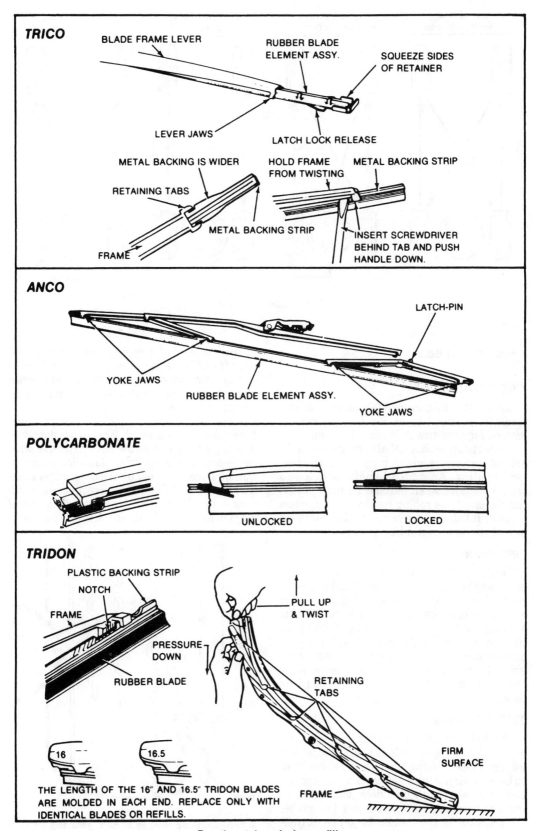

TRICO

BLADE FRAME LEVER

RUBBER BLADE
ELEMENT ASSY.

SQUEEZE SIDES
OF RETAINER

LEVER JAWS

LATCH LOCK RELEASE

METAL BACKING IS WIDER

HOLD FRAME
FROM TWISTING

METAL BACKING STRIP

RETAINING TABS

METAL BACKING STRIP

FRAME

INSERT SCREWDRIVER
BEHIND TAB AND PUSH
HANDLE DOWN.

ANCO

LATCH-PIN

YOKE JAWS

RUBBER BLADE ELEMENT ASSY.

YOKE JAWS

POLYCARBONATE

UNLOCKED

LOCKED

TRIDON

PLASTIC BACKING STRIP

NOTCH

FRAME

PULL UP
& TWIST

PRESSURE
DOWN

RUBBER BLADE

RETAINING
TABS

FIRM
SURFACE

16

16.5

THE LENGTH OF THE 16″ AND 16.5″ TRIDON BLADES
ARE MOLDED IN EACH END. REPLACE ONLY WITH
IDENTICAL BLADES OR REFILLS.

FRAME

Popular styles of wiper refills

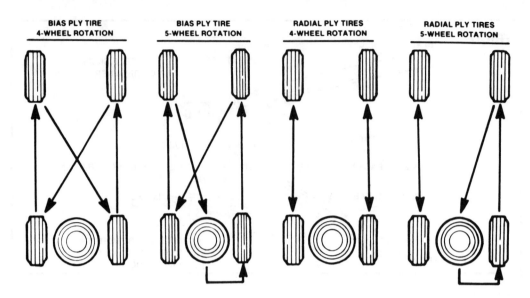

Tire rotation patterns

Tires and Wheels

TIRE ROTATION

Rotating the tires every 6,000 miles or so will result in increased tread life. Use the correct pattern for your tire switching. Most automotive experts agree that radial tires are better all around performers, giving longer wear and better handling. An added benefit which you should consider when purchasing tires is that radials haved less rolling resistance and, when properly inflated, can give up to a 10% increase in fuel economy over a bias-ply tire.

TIRE DESIGN

Never mix bias tires and radials, or vice versa, as this can cause serious handling problems. Always replace tires in sets of four or five when switching tire types and never substitute a belted tire for a bias-ply, a radial for a belted tire, etc. An occasional pressure check and periodic rotation can make your tires last much longer than a neglected set, while maintaining the safety margin which was designed into them.

TIRE INFLATION

Check the air pressure in your tires every few weeks. Make sure that the tires are cool, as you will get a false reading when the tires are heated because air pressure increases with temperature. A decal (usually on a door jamb or inside the glove compartment) tells you the proper tire pressure for the standard equipment tires. Naturally, when you replace tires you will want

to get the correct tire pressures for the new ones from the dealer or manufacturer. It pays to buy a tire pressure gauge to keep in the car, since those at service stations are usually inaccurate or broken.

While you are checking the tire pressure, take a look at the tread. The tread should be wearing evenly across the tire. Excessive wear in the center of the tread could indicate over-inflation. Excessive wear on the outer edges could indicate underinflation. An irregular wear pattern is usually a sign of incorrect front wheel alignment or wheel balance. A front end that is

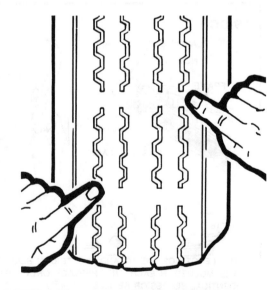

When bands appear as shown, your tire tread is below 1/16 inch. Tire should be replaced

out of alignment will usually pull the car to one side of a flat road when the steering wheel is released. Incorrect wheel balance will produce vibration in the steering wheel, while unbalanced rear wheels will result in floor or trunk vibration.

CARE OF SPECIAL WHEELS

Normal appearance maintenance of aluminum wheels includes frequent washing and waxing. However, you *must be careful to avoid*

the use of abrasive cleaners. Failure to heed this warning will cause the protective coating to be damaged.

The special coating may be abraded by repeated washing of the car in an automatic car wash using certain types of brushes. Once the finish abrades, it will provide less protection and normal exposure to either caustic cleaners or road salt will cause the process to continue. If the wheel reaches the point where it requires refinishing, it must be specially prepared and

Troubleshooting Basic Wheel Problems

Problem	Cause	Solution
The car's front end vibrates at high speed	• The wheels are out of balance • Wheels are out of alignment	• Have wheels balanced • Have wheel alignment checked/adjusted
Car pulls to either side	• Wheels are out of alignment • Unequal tire pressure • Different size tires or wheels	• Have wheel alignment checked/adjusted • Check/adjust tire pressure • Change tires or wheels to same size
The car's wheel(s) wobbles	• Loose wheel lug nuts • Wheels out of balance • Damaged wheel • Wheels are out of alignment • Worn or damaged ball joint • Excessive play in the steering linkage (usually due to worn parts) • Defective shock absorber	• Tighten wheel lug nuts • Have tires balanced • Raise car and spin the wheel. If the wheel is bent, it should be replaced • Have wheel alignment checked/adjusted • Check ball joints • Check steering linkage • Check shock absorbers
Tires wear unevenly or prematurely	• Incorrect wheel size • Wheels are out of balance • Wheels are out of alignment	• Check if wheel and tire size are compatible • Have wheels balanced • Have wheel alignment checked/adjusted

Troubleshooting Basic Tire Problems

Problem	Cause	Solution
The car's front end vibrates at high speeds and the steering wheel shakes	• Wheels out of balance • Front end needs aligning	• Have wheels balanced • Have front end alignment checked
The car pulls to one side while cruising	• Unequal tire pressure (car will usually pull to the low side) • Mismatched tires • Front end needs aligning	• Check/adjust tire pressure • Be sure tires are of the same type and size • Have front end alignment checked
Abnormal, excessive or uneven tire wear See "How to Read Tire Wear"	• Infrequent tire rotation • Improper tire pressure • Sudden stops/starts or high speed on curves	• Rotate tires more frequently to equalize wear • Check/adjust pressure • Correct driving habits
Tire squeals	• Improper tire pressure • Front end needs aligning	• Check/adjust tire pressure • Have front end alignment checked

Tire Size Comparison Chart

| "Letter" sizes | | | Inch Sizes | Metric-inch Sizes | | |
"60 Series"	"70 Series"	"78 Series"	1965–77	"60 Series"	"70 Series"	"80 Series"
		Y78-12	5.50-12, 5.60-12 6.00-12	165/60-12	165/70-12	155-12
		W78-13	5.20-13	165/60-13	145/70-13	135-13
		Y78-13	5.60-13	175/60-13	155/70-13	145-13
			6.15-13	185/60-13	165/70-13	155-13, P155/80-13
A60-13	A70-13	A78-13	6.40-13	195/60-13	175/70-13	165-13
B60-13	B70-13	B78-13	6.70-13	205/60-13	185/70-13	175-13
			6.90-13			
C60-13	C70-13	C78-13	7.00-13	215/60-13	195/70-13	185-13
D60-13	D70-13	D78-13	7.25-13			
E60-13	E70-13	E78-13	7.75-13			195-13
			5.20-14	165/60-14	145/70-14	135-14
			5.60-14	175/60-14	155/70-14	145-14
			5.90-14			
A60-14	A70-14	A78-14	6.15-14	185/60-14	165/70-14	155-14
	B70-14	B78-14	6.45-14	195/60-14	175/70-14	165-14
	C70-14	C78-14	6.95-14	205/60-14	185/70-14	175-14
D60-14	D70-14	D78-14				
E60-14	E70-14	E78-14	7.35-14	215/60-14	195/70-14	185-14
F60-14	F70-14	F78-14, F83-14	7.75-14	225/60-14	200/70-14	195-14
G60-14	G70-14	G77-14, G78-14	8.25-14	235/60-14	205/70-14	205-14
H60-14	H70-14	H78-14	8.55-14	245/60-14	215/70-14	215-14
J60-14	J70-14	J78-14	8.85-14	255/60-14	225/70-14	225-14
L60-14	L70-14		9.15-14	265/60-14	235/70-14	
	A70-15	A78-15	5.60-15	185/60-15	165/70-15	155-15
B60-15	B70-15	B78-15	6.35-15	195/60-15	175/70-15	165-15
C60-15	C70-15	C78-15	6.85-15	205/60-15	185/70-15	175-15
	D70-15	D78-15				
E60-15	E70-15	E78-15	7.35-15	215/60-15	195/70-15	185-15
F60-15	F70-15	F78-15	7.75-15	225/60-15	205/70-15	195-15
G60-15	G70-15	G78-15	8.15-15/8.25-15	235/60-15	215/70-15	205-15
H60-15	H70-15	H78-15	8.45-15/8.55-15	245/60-15	225/70-15	215-15
J60-15	J70-15	J78-15	8.85-15/8.90-15	255/60-15	235/70-15	225-15
	K70-15		9.00-15	265/60-15	245/70-15	230-15
L60-15	L70-15	L78-15, L84-15	9.15-15			235-15
	M70-15	M78-15				255-15
		N78-15				

Note: Every size tire is not listed and many size comparisons are approximate, based on load ratings. Wider tires than those supplied new with the vehicle, should always be checked for clearance.

then coated with an enamel clearcoat. This is an extremely lengthy process and every step must be performed in precisely the right way. Special protective gear must be worn to protect the person performing the refinishing operation from the solvents in the cleaners and coatings. We therefore suggest that you have a professional paint shop perform the work for best and safest results.

FLUIDS AND LUBRICANTS

Oil and Fuel Recommendations

Your Datsun/Nissan is designed to operate on regular low lead or lead-free fuel. The octane ratings are listed on the inside of the fuel filler door, but these need only be checked when traveling outside of the United States. Should you find the regular gasoline available, say in Mexico, to be of too low an octane, mix a 50/50 regular leaded-to-unleaded Premium ratio. This will give your car the lead it needs (if designed to run on leaded gas) and also the octane it needs. 1975 California cars and all 1976 and later models will run happily on the unleaded gasoline available in the United States. Make sure you don't *ever* use anything but unleaded in any of these catalytic converter-equipped models. Even a tank or two of leaded fuel will destroy the converter's effectiveness. This will result in a dirty-running car that will fail any required emissions test; it may very well cause operating problems due to clogging of the exhaust system.

Oil must be selected with regard to the antici-

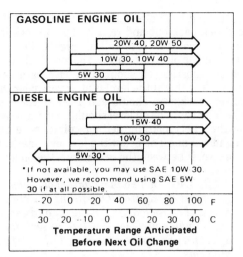

Engine oil viscosity chart for 1973–86 vehicles

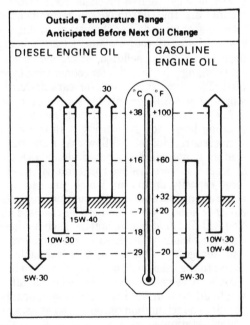

Engine oil viscosity chart for 1987–88 vehicles

pated temperatures during the period before the next oil change. Using the applicable chart, select the oil viscosity for the lowest expected temperature and you will be assured of easy cold starting and sufficient engine protection. The oil you pour into your Datsun/Nissan equipped with a gasoline engine should have the designation SF marked on the top of its container. Or in combination with other categories, for example, SF/CC. In diesel engine equipped cars, use oils with the designations SE/CC, SF/CC, SE/CD, SF/CD or CD.

SYNTHETIC OIL

There are many excellent synthetic and fuel-efficient oils currently available that can provide better gas mileage, longer service life, and in some cases better engine protection. These benefits do not come without a few hitches, however — the main one being the price of synthetic oils, which is three or four times the price per quart of conventional oil.

Synthetic oil is not for every car and every type of driving, so you should consider your engine's condition and your type of driving. Also, check your car's warranty conditions regarding the use of synthetic oils.

Both brand new engines and older, high mileage engines are the wrong candidates for synthetic oil. The synthetic oils are so slippery that they can prevent the proper break-in of new engines; most manufacturers recommend that you wait until the engine is properly broken in (5,000) until using synthetic oil. Older engines with wear have a different problem with synthetics: they use (consume during operation) more oil as they age. Slippery synthetic oils get past these worn parts easily. If your engine is using conventional oil, it will use synthetics much faster. Also, if your car is leaking oil past old seals you'll have a much greater leak problem with synthetics.

Consider your type of driving. If most of your accumulated mileage is high speed, highway type driving, the more expensive synthetic oils may be of benefit. Extended highway driving gives the engine a chance to warm up, accumulating less acids in the oil and putting less stress on the engine over the long run. Under these conditions, the oil change interval can be extended (as long as your oil filter can last the extended life of the oil) up to the advertised mileage claims of the synthetics. Cars with synthetic oils may show increased fuel economy in highway driving, due to less internal friction. However, many automotive experts agree that 50,000 miles is too long to keep any oil in your engine.

Cars used under harder circumstances, such as stop-and-go, city type driving, short trips, or extended idling, should be serviced more frequently. For the engines in these cars, the much greater cost of synthetic or fuel-efficient oils may not be worth the investment. Internal wear increases much quicker on these cars, causing greater oil consumption and leakage.

NOTE: *The mixing of conventional and synthetic oils is not recommended. If you are using synthetic oil, it might be wise to carry two or three quarts with you no matter where you drive, as not all service stations carry this type of lubricant.*

Engine

OIL LEVEL CHECK

The oil level should be checked frequently — at every gas stop or at the longest at every second gas stop. Note that long trips in hot weather may cause an engine which uses very little oil to suddenly consume a small amount. Note also that springtime weather and the rapid rise in temperature it brings often results in a drop in oil level as accumulated moisture is suddenly evaporated out of the oil. Be especially careful to check oil frequently under these circumstances.

The best time to check oil is after the car has been sitting all night. Under these conditions, the dipstick will usually give an accurate reading without even wiping it off. If the car is sitting on a grade, the angle of the crankcase will cause the dipstick to give a false reading. *Make sure the car is sitting on a level surface!*

If you have been driving, turn the engine off and allow it to sit for five minutes so as much as possible of the oil circulating in the engine will drain back into the crankcase, giving an accurate reading (checking the level too early could result in overfilling of the crankcase).

Pull the stick out and read the level. If the line representing the oil level is not sharp and clear, wipe the stick thoroughly with a clean rag or paper towel. Then, reinsert the stick until it

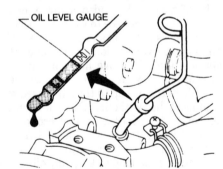

Oil level gauge location—gasoline engine

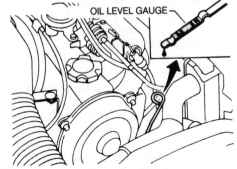

Oil level gauge location—diesel engine

is stopped by the seal around its top. Pull the dipstick back out and read it. The oil dipstick has two marks on it to indicate high and low oil level. If the oil is at or below the low level mark on the dipstick, oil should be added as necessary. Note that if the level is at or very near the lower mark, you should add 1 quart through the filler cap. The oil level should be maintained in the safety margin, neither going above the high level mark or below the low level mark. If the level is between the two marks, the oil level is o.k.

WARNING: *Don't add a quart of oil unless a full quart is required. Overfilling the crankcase will cause foaming of the oil and consequent engine problems, including seal damage and, in some engines, valve lifter problems.*

OIL AND FILTER CHANGE

The mileage figures given in your owner's manual are the Datsun/Nissan recommended intervals for oil and filter changes assuming average driving. If your Datsun/Nissan is being used under dusty, polluted, or off-road conditions, change the oil and filter sooner than specified. The same thing goes for cars driven in stop-and-go traffic or only for short distances.

Always drain the oil after the engine has been running long enough to bring it to operating temperature. Hot oil will flow easier and more contaminants will be removed along with the oil than if it were drained cold. You will need a large capacity drain pan, which you can purchase at any store which sells automotive parts. Another necessity is containers for the used oil. You will find that plastic bottles, such as those used for bleach or fabric softener, make excellent storage jugs. One ecologically desireable solution to the used oil disposal problem is to find a cooperative gas station owner who will allow you to dump your used oil into his tank or take the oil to a reclamation center (often at garages and gas stations).

Datsun/Nissan recommends changing both the oil and filter during the first oil change and the filter every other oil change thereafter. For the small price of an oil filter, it's cheap insurance to replace the filter at every oil change. One of the larger filter manufacturers points out in its advertisements that not changing the filter leaves one quart of dirty oil in the engine. This claim is true and should be kept in mind when changing your oil.

To change your oil:

1. Run the engine until it reaches normal operating temperature.

2. Jack up the front of the car and support it on safety stands if necessary to gain access to the filter.

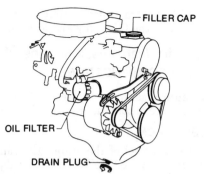

FILLER CAP

OIL FILTER

DRAIN PLUG

Oil filler, drain and filter locations. All engines similar

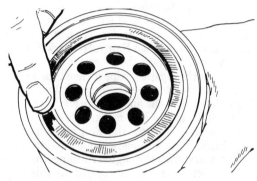

Apply a light coat of oil to the rubber gasket on the oil filter before installing it

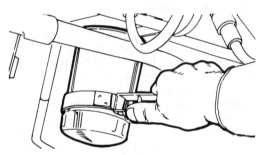

A strap wrench will make oil filter removal easier. Do not install a filter with a strap wrench

3. Slide a drain pan of at least 6 quarts capacity under the oil pan.

4. Loosen the drain plug. Turn the plug out by hand. By keeping an inward pressure on the plug as you unscrew it, oil won't escape past the threads and you can remove it without being burned by hot oil. Use a rag to unscrew the plug.

5. Allow the oil to drain completely and then install the drain plug. *Don't overtighten the plug,* or you'll be buying a new pan or a self-tapping replacement plug for buggered threads.

6. Using the oil filter strap wrench, remove the oil filter. As the filter unscrews the final turn, level it as you pull it off the engine block.

Keep in mind the filter is still filled with about a quart of dirty, hot oil.

7. Empty the old filter into the drain pan and dispose of the filter.

8. Using a clean rag, wipe off the filter adapter on the engine block. Be sure that the rag doesn't leave any lint which could clog an oil passage.

9. Coat the rubber gasket on the new filter with a wipe of fresh oil. Spin it onto the engine by hand; when the filter begins to snug up against the mounting surface give it another ½-¾ turn. *Do not turn it any more* or you'll ruin the gasket and the filter will leak.

10. Refill the engine with the correct amount of fresh oil. See the Capacities chart.

11. Crank the engine over several times and then start it. If the oil pressure indicator light doesn't go out or the pressure gauge shows zero, shut the engine down and find out what's wrong.

12. If the oil pressure is OK and there are no leaks, shut the engine off and lower the car.

Manual Transmission/Transaxle/ Transfer Case

FLUID RECOMMENDATIONS

Use API GL-4 for transmissions/transaxles and API GL-5 for transfer cases and differentials. Use the viscosity recommendations shown in the illustration.

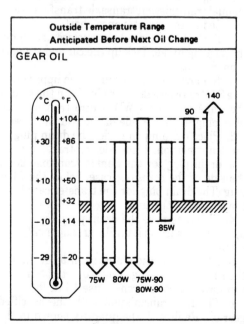

Use these viscosity recommendations in selecting oil for manual transmission, transaxles, transfer cases, and differentials

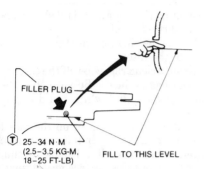

FILLER PLUG

$\widehat{T}$ 25–34 N·M
(2.5–3.5 KG-M,
18–25 FT-LB)

FILL TO THIS LEVEL

Transmission oil should be level with the bottom of the filler plug on manual transmissions

FLUID LEVEL CHECK

Manual Transmission/Transaxle/Transfer Case

Check the level of the lubricant in the transmission, manual transaxle or transfer case every 3,000 miles. The lubricant level should be even with the bottom of the filler hole. Hold in on the filler plug when unscrewing it. When you are sure that all of the threads of the plug are free of the transmission case, move the plug away from the case slightly. If lubricant begins to flow out of the transmission, then you know it is full. If not, add the proper viscosity and type gear oil as necessary. It is recommended that these lubricants be changed as specified in the Maintenance Intervals Chart.

DRAIN AND REFILL

Change the transmission lubricant in your manual transmission/transaxle/transfer case as specified in the maintenance chart:

1. Park the car on a level surface and apply the parking brake. Jack up the car and support it on stands.

2. Remove the oil filler plug (the upper one). The Sentra transaxle filler plug is on the side of the transaxle. The 4 WD Sentra transfer case filler plug in on the side of the transfer case.

3. Place a drain pan under the drain plug in the transmission, transaxle, or transfer case. The drain plug for the Sentra transaxle is on the side of the transaxle case, below the filler plug. The drain plug for the transfer case is on the bottom of the unit.

4. Slowly remove the drain plug keeping an upward pressure on it until you can quickly pull it out.

5. Allow all of the old gear oil to drain and then replace the plug. Don't overtighten it (if you have a torque wrench, use 15 ft. lbs.

6. Fill the transmission with the specified gear oil. Refill with the quantity shown in the Capacities chart. An oil suction gun or squeeze bulb filler (turkey baster) are handy for this chore and can be used for the rear axle, too (ex-

cept on the Sentra, which is front wheel drive).

7. Replace the filler plug and lower the car.

Automatic Transmission/Transaxle

FLUID RECOMMENDATIONS

Datsun/Nissan recommends the use of Dexron® type automatic transmission fluid

LEVEL CHECK

Check the level of the automatic transmission fluid every 2,000 miles. There is a dipstick at the right rear of the engine under the hood. It has a scale on each side, one for COLD and the other for HOT. The transmission is considered hot after 15 miles of highway driving.

Park the car on a level surface with the engine running. Shift into Drive, then each reduced-gear range, then Neutral or Park. Set the handbrake and block the wheels.

Remove the dipstick, wipe it clean, then reinsert it firmly. Remove the dipstick and check the fluid level on the appropriate scale. The level should be at the Full mark.

If the level is below the Full mark, add or DEXRON® type automatic transmission fluid as necessary, with the engine running, through the dipstick tube. *Do not overfill*, as this may cause the transmission to malfunction and damage itself.

DRAIN AND REFILL

1. The transmission should be warm but not too hot. Place a drain pan under the transmission or transaxle. Remove the drain plug from the transaxle case and allow the fluid to drain.

2. If changing the fluid on a rear drive transmission, loosen all the pan attaching bolts two or three turns. Then, remove the pan bolts from the rear and both sides up to the front corner bolts. Gently pry the rear of the pan away from the case and tilt it downward slowly so most of the fluid will drain. Then support the pan while removing the remaining bolts. Lower the pan and tip it to remove the remaining flu-

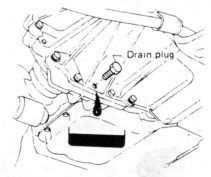

Drain plug

The drain plug for automatic transaxles

id. Wipe the inside of the pan. Remove all traces of gasket material from the transmission and pan sealing surfaces with a flat but dull object.

3. Install the drain plug on transaxles and torque to 10-13 ft. lbs. On transmissions install the pan and a new gasket and install the bolts finger tight. Then, torque in 2 equal stages, alternately and evenly, to 4 ft. lbs.

4. Refill the transmission with just a bit less than the specified refill capacity of Dexron® fluid. Start the engine and run the transmission, putting the selector lever in every position for a few seconds. Then, recheck the fluid level and adjust it up to the specified level.

PAN AND FILTER SERVICE

1. On cars with conventional rear drive transmissions, remove the pan as described above. On Sentras, remove the pan guard. Drain the fluid as described above. Then, remove the pan by remnoving all the attaching bolts and then gently prying the pan at one corner down and then removing it. Screw all traces of gasket material from both pan and transmission or transaxle case.

2. Remove all the strainer attaching bolts and pull the strainer off the transmission or transaxle.

3. Install the new strainer, torqing the bolts alternately and evenly to 2.2-2.5 ft. lbs. on transmissions and 5.1-6.5 on transaxles.

4. Install the pan with a new gasket. Torque the bolts alternately and evenly in 2 stages to 4-5 ft. lbs. Refill the transmission with fluid as described above.

Transfer Case

Since the procedures are almost identical and fluid recommendations are identical, transfer case fluid recommendations, checks and changes are included above with the Manual Transmission/Transaxle procedure.

Rear Axle

FLUID RECOMMENDATIONS

Use SAE 90W gear oil.

LEVEL CHECK

Check the rear axle lubricant on the 1200, B210 and 210 cars every 6,000 miles. Remove the filler plug in the axle housing. The lubricant should be up to the bottom of the filler hole with the vehicle resting on a level surface. Add the recommended fluid as necessary to bring the lubricant up the proper level.

DRAIN AND REFILL

Change the gear oil in the rear axle every 36,000 miles as follows:

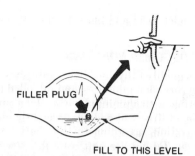

FILLER PLUG

FILL TO THIS LEVEL

Checking rear axle oil level, 1200, B210 and 210. Fill to the level of the filler plug hole

1. With the car on a level surface, jack up the rear and support it with stands.

2. Slide a drain pan under the drain plug, remove the plug, and allow the oil to drain out.

3. Install the drain plug, but don't overtighten it. Remove the filler plug.

4. Refill the rear axle with SAE 90 gear oil up to the level of the filler plug. A kitchen turkey baster is useful here in adding the oil. Also, some oil brands come in plastic bottles with useful built-in spouts.

Cooling System

Your Datsun/Nissan's internal combustion gasoline engine generates power by the controlled explosion of a mixture of gasoline and air in the combustion chamber of each cylinder. The piston of each cylinder is at the top of its upward travel when this explosion occurs. The explosion (ignition) forces the piston downward, turning the crankshaft and creating mechanical energy. But not all of the force of the ignited fuel mixture is expended in forcing the piston downward; some heat is released, from the combustion, from the friction of the piston and piston rings moving up and down against the inside of the cylinder bore, and from the movement of the engine's other internal parts. The job of the cooling system is to effectively remove that heat from the engine before it raises

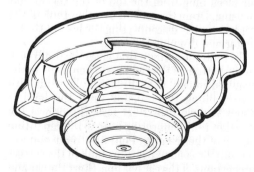

Check the rubber gasket on the cap when checking the coolant level

the cylinder head and block temperatures too greatly.

FLUID RECOMMENDATIONS

Use a quality Ethylene-Glocol antifreeze containing corrosion inhibitors and intended to be compatible with aluminum parts. Make sure to mix the antifreeze at a 50-50 or slightly higher concentration, according to the chart on the container. *Do not use antifreeze full strength. Do not use plain water (except for a short period in an emergency).*

LEVEL CHECK

Check the coolant level every time you change the oil. Check for loose connections and signs of deterioration of the coolant hoses. Maintain the coolant level 3″ below the level of the filler neck when the engine is cold. Add a mixture of 70/30% to 50/50% water to ethylene glycol antifreeze as necessary. See "Draining the Cooling System" below for radiator cap removal cautions and radiator draining.
Never add cold water to an overheated engine while the engine is not running; this can cause the engine block to crack. Run the engine until it reaches normal operating temperature after filling the radiator to make sure that the thermostat has opened and all air is bled from the system.

DRAINING THE COOLING SYSTEM

To drain the cooling system, allow the engine to cool down *before attempting to remove the radiator cap.* Turn the heater on all the way. Wrap a heavy rag or cloth around the cap to avoid burns, and turn it just enough until it hisses. This removes the pressure from the radiator; wait until the hissing stops and the cap can be turned freely to the first lock before removing the cap. Then turn the cap past the lock (by depressing it slightly) and remove it. After removing the cap, drain the radiator by unscrewing the petcock or drain plug at the bottom of the radiator. On the diesel, remove the air bleed plug from the top of the thermostat housing. Drain the coolant overflow tank (if the car has one) by disconnecting the hose at the radiator and draining the tank.

To refill the system, first close the drain cock in the bottom of the radiator. Then, pour in the required amount of antifreeze. Follow this with water, filling the radiator until the level is about ½″ below the filler neck. Reconnect the overflow tank connecting hose to the cap fitting on top of the radiator. Pour antifreeze and water into the coolant overflow tank in the correct proportions, if the car has one. Start the car and idle it. Until it reaches operating temperature. When all air has been bled from the system on

the diesel, reinstall the bleed plug. On gas engine cars, wait until the thermostat opens (warm water begins flowing through the top of the radiator and the level stops dropping). Then, fill the radiator to ½″ below the filler neck on cars without an overflow tank and all the way to the top of the radiator on cars with an overflow tank. Install the cap securely.

FLUSHING AND CLEANING THE SYSTEM

Drain and refill the system as described above, using plain water. Allow the engine to run a few minutes past the point where the thermostat opens to thoroughly mix the coolant remaining in the block with the freshly added water. Then, stop the engine and drain the system. Repeat this procedure 6-8 times or until the water draining out is practically clear. Then, fill it with fresh antifreeze and water as described above.

If the system is slightly clogged, it is possible to use a cleaner the is available at auto supply stores. Usually, the system is drained and refilled with fresh water mixed with the cleaner. Then, after the engine is run for a time, the system is flushed as described above. Make sure to follow all package directions thoroughly! If the system is severely clogged, it may be necessary to remove the radiator as described in Chapter 3 and have it cleaner chemically at a radiator shop.

COOLANT HOSE REPLACEMENT

Remove the radiator cap, unscrew the drain petcock or plug, and drain the radiator into a clean pan if you are going to use the old coolant. Disconnect the hose clamps and remove the hose by either cutting it off or twisting it to break its seal on the radiator and engine coolant inlets. Radiator hoses should always be pliable. Any hose that feels brittle or hard should be replaced, as this condition indicates the hose could split anytime (usually when you are miles from any service facility). When installing the new hose, do not overtighten the hose clamps or you might slice the hose underneath. Refill the

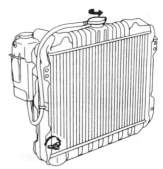

Radiator drain petcock location

radiator, run the engine with the radiator cap on and recheck the coolant level.

NOTE: *As with your extra belts, you should carry extra radiator hoses if you plan to travel long distances, or if your normal mileage is on the highway. Don't forget whatever tools you may need to remove the hose clamps and hoses.*

Brake and Clutch Master Cylinder

FLUID RECOMMENDATIONS

NOTE: *The clutch in your 1200, B210 or 210 model Datsun is operated hydraulically, employing a system much the same as the hydraulic brake system in the car.*

Both systems use a DOT 3 type brake fluid. The Sentra does not have a hydraulic clutch.

LEVEL CHECK

Check the levels of brake fluid in the brake and clutch master cylinder reservoirs every 3,000 miles. The fluid level should be maintained to a level not below the bottom line marked on the outside of the reservoirs and not above the top line. Any sudden decrease in the level in any of the three reservoirs (two for the brakes and one for the clutch) indicates a probable leak in that particular system. The system must be check thoroughly and any leak corrected.

To add fluid, clean the area around the cap thoroughly to prevent dirt from getting into the system. Then, remove the cap, add fresh fluid, and immediately and tightly replace the cap. Cap the can of fluid you are using tightly too, as

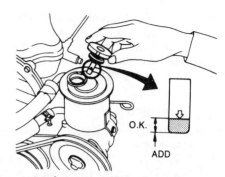

Power steering reservoir check

brake fluids draw moisture out of the air very rapidly, and fluids containing moisture will damage the system.

Power Steering Pump

FLUID RECOMMENDATIONS

Use Dexron® automatic transmission fluid only.

LEVEL CHECK

Check the fluid level in the reservoir by observing the dipstick when the fluid is cold. Add fluid as necessary to bring the level into the proper range on the dipstick. DO NOT OVERFILL.

Steering Gear

FLUID RECOMMENDATIONS

Use a lubricant intended for use in manual steering boxes.

LEVEL CHECK

Check the level of the lubricant in the steering gearbox every 12,000 miles. If the level is

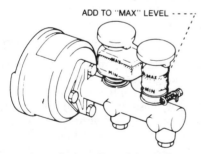

Brake master cylinder, all models similar

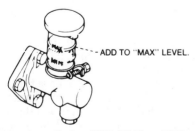

Clutch master cylinder, 1200, B210 and 210

💧 : CHECK FLUID LEAKS.

🥄 : ADD FLUID.

When topping up steering gearbox, check these areas for leaks

low, check for leakage. An oily film is not considered a leak; solid grease must be present. Change the lubricant every 36,000 miles. The lubricant is added and checked through the filler plug hole in the top of the steering gear.

Chassis Greasing

Datsun/Nissan doesn't install lubrication fittings (grease nipples) in lube points on the steering linkage or suspension. You can buy metric threaded fittings to grease these points or use a pointed, rubber end tip on your grease gun. Lubricate all joints equipped with a plug every 24,000 miles. When greasing, keep the grease gun as square with the fitting as possible, or grease will just squeeze out around the fitting instead of inside the fitting. Replace the plugs after lubrication.

Body Lubrication

At every oil change, lubricate door, hatch, and hood hinges with engine oil. Lubricate latches with a white grease.

Front Wheel Bearings

ADJUSTMENT

1200, B210 210

NOTE: *The Sentra, a front wheel drive vehicle, has pressed bearings, which are not adjustable on the front wheels. The factory procedures for wheel bearing adjustment is of little use to the owner/mechanic unless very well equipped, since it involves the use of a spring scale, an inch-pound torque wrench, and a foot-pound torque wrench. If you wish to work on the complex front wheel bearings used on front drive cars, refer to Chapter 7. For the following procedure, you will only need a foot-pound torque wrench.*

1. Jack up the car and safely support it with jackstands.
2. Remove the bearing dust cap and the cot-

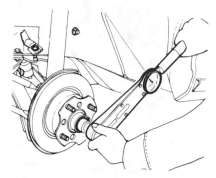

Tightening the hub nut with a torque wrench during wheel bearing adjustment

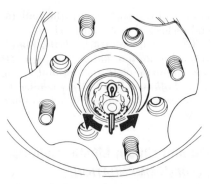

Split and spread the cotter pin

ter pin. Discard the cotter pin, as you will be replacing it with a new one.

3. Torque the spindle nut to 16-18 ft. lbs. on the 1200; 18-22 ft. lbs. on the B210, and 22-25 ft. lbs. on the 210 sedan and wagon.
4. Spin the wheel hub a few times to seat the bearing, then check the torque on the nut again.
5. Loosen the nut about 60 degrees on all models except the 210. Loosen the 210 nut about 90 degrees.
6. Install the adjusting cap and a new cotter pin. You may have to loosen the nut a bit to allow the cotter pin holes to align, but do not loosen the nut beyond 15 degrees.
7. Reinstall the tire and wheel, and rotate the entire assembly. There should be no roughness or binding. Grasp the top of the tire and move it in and out. The play should be negligible. If there is excessive play, the wheel bearings must be retightened. If roughness persists, check the condition of the wheel bearings for nicks, pitting and damage.
8. Install the cap and lower the car from the stands.

REMOVAL, PACKING, AND INSTALLATION

It is important to remember that wheel bearings, although basically very durable, are subject to many elements that can quickly destroy them. Grit, misalignment, and improper preload are especially brutal to any roller bearing assembly. And like any bearing (ball, roller, needle, etc.), lubrication is extremely important.

1. Loosen the lug nuts on the wheel you intend to fix. Jack up the car and safely support it with jackstands.
2. Remove the wheel and tire. Remove the brake drum or brake caliper, following the procedure(s) in this chapter.
3. It is not necessary to remove the drum or disc from the hub. The outer wheel bearing will come off with the hub. Simply pull the hub and disc or drum assembly toward you and off the spindle. (Follow hub removal procedures for

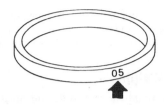

Sentra wheel bearing spacer size number

Packing wheel bearing with grease

Sentra). Be sure to catch the bearing before it falls to the ground.

4. From the inner side of the hub, remove the inner grease seal, and lift the inner bearing from the hub. Discard the grease seal, as you will be replacing it with a new one.

5. Clean the bearings carefully in solvent, and allow them to air dry (or blow them out with compressed air, if available). You risk leaving bits of lint in the races if you dry them with a rag. Clean the grease caps, nuts, spindle, and the races in the hub thoroughly, and allow the parts to dry.

6. Inspect the bearings carefully. If they show any signs of wear (pitting, cracks, scoring, brinelling, burns, etc.), replace them along with the bearing cups in which they run in the hub. Do not mix old and new parts; you won't regret replacing everything if the parts look marginal.

7. If the cups are worn at all, remove them from the hub, using a brass rod as a drift. Use care not to damage the cup seats with the drift.

8. If the old cups were removed, install the new inner and outer cups into the hub, using either a tool made for the purpose, or a socket or piece of pipe of a large enough diameter to press on the outside rim of the cup only.

CAUTION: *Be careful not to cock the bearings in the hub. If they are not fully seated, the bearings will be impossible to adjust properly.*

9. Pack the inside of the hub and cups with grease. Pack the inside of the grease cap while you're at it, but do not install the cap into the hub.

10. Pack the inner bearing with grease. Place a large glob of grease into the palm of one hand and push the inner bearing through it with a sliding motion. The grease must be forced through the side of the bearing and in between each roller. Continue until the grease begins to ooze out the other side through the gaps between the rollers; the bearing must be completely packed with grease. Install the inner bearing into its cup in the hub, then press a new grease seal into place over it.

11. Install the hub and rotor or drum assembly onto the spindle. Pack the outer bearing with grease in the same manner as the inner bearing, then install the outer bearing into place in the hub.

12. Apply a thin coat of grease to the washer and the threaded portion of the spindle, then loosely install the washer and adjusting nut. Refer to the bearing preload adjustment above and adjust the bearings to complete the procedure.

Rear Wheel Bearings (Front Wheel Drive Cars)

SENTRA

1982-86

NOTE: *To perform this procedure, a spring scale is required.*

1. Raise the rear of the vehicle and support it securely. Remove the wheel. Release the parking brake.

2. Pry off the hub cap and its O-ring. Then, pry the ends of the cotter pin straight and remove it.

3. Unscrew and remove the bearing adjusting nut and the bearing retaining nut. Hold the wheel bearing outer race in the brake drum with the thumbs and slide the outer bearing, drum, and washer.

4. Remove the grease seal and inside bearing inner race.

5. Thoroughly pack wheel bearing *(not Multipurpose)* grease into both bearings. Then, position the inside bearing into the hub. Coat the sealing lips of a new grease seal with the same grease and install it.

6. Grease: the threaded portion of the wheel spindle; the surface of the bearing retaining nut that contacts the bearing; and the surface of the bearing washer which contacts the bearing.

7. Then, install the hub and drum onto the spindle, and install the outside bearing, bearing retaining washer and bearing retaining nut.

8. Torque the wheel bearing retaining nut with a torque wrench to 29-33 ft. lbs. Turn the hub back and forth several times to seat the bearings.

9. Again, torque the retaining nut to 29-33 ft. lbs. Install the adjusting cap. If any of the slots align with the hole in the spindle, install a

Checking rear wheel bearing preload with a spring scale on 1982–86 Sentra

new cotter pin. If not, tighten the cap as much as 15 degrees farther until a slot aligns with the spindle hole. Install the cotter pin and bend back the ends fully.

10. Turn the hub and feel for axial play. It should be zero. Use the spring scale to start the drum turning via one of the wheel studs, holding the scale so it remains at 90 degrees to the centerline of the drum. Starting torque should be 3.1 lb. or less. Otherwise, it is necessary to repeat the adjustment to ensure that bearing preload (how tightly it is assembled) is not excessive.

INSPECTION

1987-88 Models

The rear wheel bearings used on the latest front drive cars are part of the rear axle spindle. They are not disassembled and repacked with grease periodically. They can be disassembled and replaced only as a major machine shop operation.

You *can*, however inspect them as follows if there is any question about their condition:

1. Raise the vehicle and support it securely. Remove the rear wheel. Spin the brake drum to make sure it turns smoothly.

2. Check the tightening torque of the wheel bearing locknut. It should be 137-188 ft. lbs.

3. If there is any doubt about the bearing's condition, mount a dial indicator to the rear suspension, zero it with the stem against the brake drum and the drum forced all the way inboard. Then, work the drum outward. End play should be 0.0020″ or less. Otherwise, the bearings require replacement.

Trailer Towing

GENERAL RECOMMENDATIONS

Factory trailer towing packages are available on most cars. However, if you are installing a trailer hitch and wiring on your car, there are a few thing that you ought to know. Note that you should always increase tire pressures to 4 lbs. over the normal pressure specified for the vehicle when towing a trailer. Always use a safety chain in case the hitch breaks or comes apart.

Trailer Weight

Trailer weight is the first, and most important, factor in determining whether or not your vehicle is suitable for towing the trailer you have in mind. The horsepower-to-weight ratio should be calculated. The basic standard is a ratio of 35:1. That is, 35 pounds of GVW for every horsepower.

To calculate this ratio, multiply you engine's rated horsepower by 35, then subtract the weight of the vehicle, including passengers and luggage. The resulting figure is the ideal maximum trailer weight that you can tow. One point to consider: a numerically higher axle ratio can offset what appears to be a low trailer weight. If the weight of the trailer that you have in mind is somewhat higher than the weight you just calculated, you might consider changing your rear axle ratio to compensate.

Hitch Weight

There are three kinds of hitches: bumper mounted, frame mounted, and load equalizing.

Bumper mounted hitches are those which attach solely to the vehicle's bumper. Many states prohibit towing with this type of hitch, when it attaches to the vehicle's stock bumper, since it subjects the bumper to stresses for which it was not designed. Aftermarket rear step bumpers, designed for trailer towing, are acceptable for use with bumper mounted hitches.

Frame mounted hitches can be of the type which bolts to two or more points on the frame, plus the bumper, or just to several points on the frame. Frame mounted hitches can also be of the tongue type, for Class I towing, or, of the receiver type, for classes II and III.

Load equalizing hitches are usually used for large trailers. Most equalizing hitches are welded in place and use equalizing bars and chains to level the vehicle after the trailer is hooked up.

The bolt-on hitches are the most common, since they are relatively easy to install.

Check the gross weight rating of your trailer. Tongue weight is usually figured as 10% of gross trailer weight. Therefore, a trailer with a maximum gross weight of 2,000 lb. will have a maximum tongue weight of 200 lb. Class I tarilers fall into this category. Class II trailers are those with a gross weight rating of 2,000-3,500 lb., while Class III trailers fall into the 3,500-6,000 lb. category. Class IV trailers are those over 6,000 lb. and are for use with fifth wheel trucks, only.

When you've determined the hitch that you'll need, follow the manufacturer's installation instructions, exactly, especially when it comes to fastener torques. The hitch will subjected to a lot of stress and good hitches come with hardened bolts. Never substitute an inferior bolt for a hardened bolt.

Wiring

Wiring the car for towing is fairly easy. There are a number of good wiring kits available and these should be used, rather than trying to design your own. All trailers will need brake lights and turn signals as well as tail lights and side marker lights. Most states require extra marker lights for overly wide trailers. Also, most states have recently required back-up lights for trailers, and most trailer manufacturers have been building trailers with back-up lights for several years.

Additionally, some Class I, most Class II and just about all Class III trailers will have electric brakes.

Add to this number an accessories wire, to operate trailer internal equipment or to charge the trailer's battery, and you can have as many as seven wires in the harness.

Determine the equipment on your trailer and buy the wiring kit necessary. The kit will contain all the wires needed, plus a plug adapter set which included the female plug, mounted on the bumper or hitch, and the male plug, wired into, or plugged into the trailer harness.

When installing the kit, follow the manufacturer's instructions. The color coding of the wires is standard throughout the industry.

One point to note, some domestic vehicles, and most imported vehicles, have separate turn signals. On most domestic vehicles, the brake lights and rear turn signals operate with the same bulb. For those vehicles with separate turn signals, you can purchase an isolation unit so that the brake lights won't blink whenever the turn signals are operated, or, you can go to your local electronics supply house and buy four diodes to wire in series with the brake and turn signal bulbs. Diodes will isolate the brake and turn signals. The choice is yours. The isolation units are simple and quick to install, but far more expensive than the diodes. The diodes, however, require more work to install properly, since they require the cutting of each bulb's wire and soldering in place of the diode.

One final point, the best kits are those with a spring loaded cover on the vehicle mounted socket. This cover prevents dirt and moisture from corroding the terminals. Never let the vehicle socket hang loosely. Always mount it securely to the bumper or hitch.

Trailer and Tongue Weight Limits for your Datsun/Nissan

● Never tow a trailer weighing more than 1,000 lbs.

● Never tow the trailer if the tongue load exceeds 10% of the total weight of the trailer. If necessary, shift the load inside the trailer to bring the tongue weight within the standard.

● Never allow the combined weight of vehicle and trailer to exceed the GVWR as listed on the F.M.V.S.S. Certification Label.

PUSHING AND TOWING

All Datsun/Nissan 1200, B210, 210 and Sentra models with manual transmissions can be push started, except 1976 and later California cars, and all other cars with catalytic converters, as push starting may damage the converter. All models equipped with automatic transmissions, including Sentra, may NOT be push started.

Before starting, check to make sure that the bumpers of both vehicles are aligned as much as possible. An old tire placed between the bumpers of the two vehicles makes a good cushion against damage to either car. Make sure that all electrical components are turned off (headlights, heater, etc.). Turn the ignition switch on, push in the clutch pedal and place the shift lever in third gear. Give the driver of the push vehicle the signal to go; at about 15 mph, signal the driver to fall back, depress the accelerator pedal and release the clutch pedal slowly (check to be certain the ignition switch is on). The engine should start.

You can perform the same procedure as above, but without a push car, if you are within access to a long hill (devoid of traffic, of course). In either situation, it is not advisable to tow-start your Datsun/Nissan for fear of ramming the towing vehicle when the engine starts.

Both manual and automatic 1200, B210, and 210 Datsun/Nissans may be towed for short distances and at speeds no more than 20 mph. NEVER tow a Sentra model with automatic transmission with the front (drive) wheels touching the ground. If the car must be towed a long distance, it should be done with either the drive wheels off the ground or the driveshafts disconnected. Sentra manual transaxle models should be towed with their drive (front) wheels off the ground to avoid transaxle damage. If this is not possible, place the transaxle in neutral and make sure the ignition switch is NOT in the LOCK position. Restrict towing an automatic transmission car to a distance of less than 20 miles. Any towing of a manual transmission

JUMP STARTING A DEAD BATTERY

The chemical reaction in a battery produces explosive hydrogen gas. This is the safe way to jump start a dead battery, reducing the chances of an accidental spark that could cause an explosion.

Jump Starting Precautions

1. Be sure both batteries are of the same voltage.
2. Be sure both batteries are of the same polarity (have the same grounded terminal).
3. Be sure the vehicles are not touching.
4. Be sure the vent cap holes are not obstructed.
5. Do not smoke or allow sparks around the battery.
6. In cold weather, check for frozen electrolyte in the battery.
7. Do not allow electrolyte on your skin or clothing.
8. Be sure the electrolyte is not frozen.

Jump Starting Procedure

1. Determine voltages of the two batteries; they must be the same.
2. Bring the starting vehicle close (they must not touch) so that the batteries can be reached easily.
3. Turn off all accessories and both engines. Put both cars in Neutral or Park and set the handbrake.
4. Cover the cell caps with a rag—do not cover terminals.
5. If the terminals on the run-down battery are heavily corroded, clean them.
6. Identify the positive and negative posts on both batteries and connect the cables in the order shown.
7. Start the engine of the starting vehicle and run it at fast idle. Try to start the car with the dead battery. Crank it for no more than 10 seconds at a time and let it cool off for 20 seconds in between tries.
8. If it doesn't start in 3 tries, there is something else wrong.
9. Disconnect the cables in the reverse order.
10. Replace the cell covers and dispose of the rags.

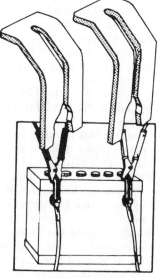

Side terminal batteries occasionally pose a problem when connecting jumper cables. There frequently isn't enough room to clamp the cables without touching sheet metal. Side terminal adaptors are available to alleviate this problem and should be removed after use.

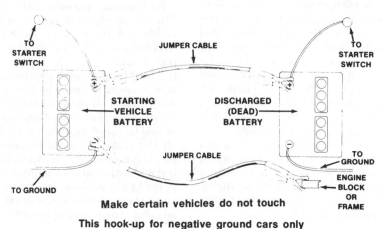

TO STARTER SWITCH

JUMPER CABLE

TO STARTER SWITCH

STARTING VEHICLE BATTERY

DISCHARGED (DEAD) BATTERY

JUMPER CABLE

TO GROUND

ENGINE BLOCK OR FRAME

TO GROUND

Make certain vehicles do not touch

This hook-up for negative ground cars only

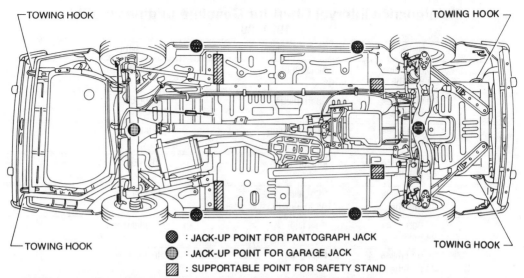

TOWING HOOK

TOWING HOOK

TOWING HOOK

TOWING HOOK

⬤ : JACK-UP POINT FOR PANTOGRAPH JACK

⬤ : JACK-UP POINT FOR GARAGE JACK

▨ : SUPPORTABLE POINT FOR SAFETY STAND

Jacking and towing locations, 210. 1200 and B210 models similar except they use the rear spring shackles as tow hooks. Sentra has single central tow hook on each end.

car over 50 miles should be done with the driveshaft disconnected.

JUMP STARTING A DEAD BATTERY

Jump starting a dead battery is a procedure that should be known to every car owner (see illustration). Make sure the cars are not touching, the cables are not crossed, and the clamps connected positive-to-positive and negative-to-negative. You should carry a set of good quality jumper cables in your car at all times.

JACKING

NEVER use the bumper jack—the jack supplied with the car—for anything other than changing tires. If you are serious about performing your own maintenance, invest in a 1 ½ ton hydraulic floor jack and (at least) two sturdy jackstands. A hydraulic jack will pay for itself very quickly in safety, time saved and overall utility.

ALWAYS chock the wheels when changing a tire or working beneath the car. This cannot be overemphasized. CLIMBING UNDER A CAR SUPPORTED BY ONLY A JACK IS EXTREMELY DANGEROUS.

Maintenance Interval Chart for Gasoline Engines
1973–80

Interval	Item	Service
7,500 miles 6 months	Engine oil and filter	Replace
15,000 miles 12 months	Valve clearance	Adjust
15,000 miles 12 months	Carb idle speed & mixture	Adjust
30,000 miles 24 months	Carburetor choke	Clean/inspect
7,500 miles 6 months	Drive belts	Inspect/adjust
30,000 miles 24 months	Air filter	Replace

Maintenance Interval Chart for Gasoline Engines (cont.)
1973–80

Interval	Item	Service
30,000 miles 24 months	Air cleaner	Inspect
30,000 miles 24 months	Spark plugs	Replace
15,000 miles 12 months	Ignition timing	Adjust
30,000 miles 12 months	Ignition wires	Inspect
30,000 miles 24 months	PCV filter, Air induction valve filter	Replace
30,000 miles 24 months	Fuel filter	Replace
30,000 miles 24 months	Fuel lines	Inspect
30,000 miles 24 months	Engine coolant	Replace

1981–83

Interval	Item	Service
7,500 miles 6 months	Engine oil and filter	Replace
15,000 miles 12 months	Valve clearance	Adjust
15,000 miles 12 months	Carb idle speed	Adjust
30,000 miles 24 months	Carburetor choke	Clean/inspect
30,000 miles 24 months	Drive belts	Inspect/adjust
30,000 miles 24 months	Air filter	Replace
30,000 miles 24 months	Air cleaner	Inspect
30,000 miles 24 months	Spark plugs	Replace
15,000 miles 12 months	Ignition timing	Adjust
30,000 miles 12 months	Ignition wires	Inspect
30,000 miles 24 months	PCV filter, Air induction valve filter	Replace
30,000 miles 24 months	Fuel filter	Replace
30,000 miles 24 months	Fuel lines	Inspect
30,000 miles 24 months	Engine coolant	Replace
30,000 miles 24 months	Exhaust oxygen sensor	Inspect

Note: Perform these services at 1,000 miles, also.

Maintenance Interval Chart for Gasoline Engines *(cont.)*
1984–86

Interval	Item	Service
7,500 miles 6 months	Engine oil and filter	Replace
15,000 miles 12 months	Valve clearance	Adjust
15,000 miles 12 months	Carb idle speed	Adjust
30,000 miles	Idle speed control filter	Replace
30,000 miles	Vacuum control modulator valve filter	Replace
30,000 miles 24 months	Carburetor choke	Clean/inspect
30,000 miles 24 months	Drive belts	Inspect/adjust
30,000 miles	Air filter	Replace
30,000 miles 24 months	Air cleaner	Inspect
30,000 miles 24 months	Spark plugs	Replace
15,000 miles 12 months	Ignition timing	Adjust
24 months (inspect every 30,000 miles, also—1984 models only)	Ignition wires	Inspect
30,000 miles 24 months	PCV filter, Air induction valve filter	Replace
30,000 miles 24 months	Fuel filter	Replace
30,000 miles 24 months	Fuel lines	Inspect
30,000 miles 24 months	Engine coolant	Replace
30,000 miles 24 months	Exhaust oxygen sensor	Inspect

1987

Interval	Item	Service
7,500 miles 6 months	Engine oil and filter	Replace
15,000 miles 12 months	Valve clearance	Adjust
60,000 miles	Engine timing belt	Replace
15,000 miles 12 months	Carb idle speed	Adjust
30,000 miles	Idle speed control filter	Replace
30,000 miles	Vacuum control modulator valve filter	Replace
30,000 miles 24 months	Carburetor choke	Clean/inspect

Maintenance Interval Chart for Gasoline Engines (cont.)
1987

Interval	Item	Service
30,000 miles 24 months	Drive belts	Inspect/adjust
30,000 miles	Air filter	Replace
30,000 miles 24 months	Air cleaner	Inspect
30,000 miles 24 months	Spark plugs	Replace
15,000 miles 12 months	Ignition timing	Adjust
24 months (inspect every 30,000 miles, also—1984 models only)	Ignition wires	Inspect
30,000 miles 24 months	PCV filter, Air induction valve filter	Replace
30,000 miles 24 months	Fuel filter	Replace
30,000 miles 24 months	Fuel lines	Inspect
30,000 miles 24 months	Engine coolant	Replace
30,000 miles 24 months	Exhaust oxygen sensor	Inspect

1988

Interval	Item	Service
7,500 miles 6 months	Engine oil and filter	Replace
15,000 miles 12 months	Valve clearance	Adjust
60,000 miles	Engine timing belt	Replace
15,000 miles 12 months	Carb idle speed	Adjust
30,000 miles 24 months	Carburetor choke	Clean/inspect
30,000 miles 24 months	Drive belts	Inspect/adjust
30,000 miles	Air filter	Replace
30,000 miles 24 months	Air cleaner	Inspect
30,000 miles 24 months	Spark plugs	Replace
15,000 miles 12 months	Ignition timing	Adjust
24 months (inspect every 30,000 miles, also—1984 models only)	Ignition wires	Inspect
30,000 miles 24 months	PCV filter, Air induction valve filter	Replace
30,000 miles 24 months	Fuel filter	Replace

Maintenance Interval Chart for Gasoline Engines (cont.)
1988

Interval	Item	Service
30,000 miles 24 months	Fuel lines	Inspect
30,000 miles 24 months	Engine coolant	Replace
30,000 miles 24 months	Exhaust oxygen sensor	Inspect

Maintenance Interval Chart for Diesel Engines
1983

Interval	Item	Service
5,000 miles 6 months	Engine oil and filter	Replace
30,000 miles	Air filter	Replace
30,000 miles 24 months	Fuel filter	Replace
30,000 miles 24 months	Fuel lines, all hoses	Inspect
15,000 miles 12 months	Drive belts	Inspect
15,000 miles 12 months	Valve clearance	Adjust
15,000 miles	Injection nozzle tips	Remove/inspect
30,000 miles 24 months	Engine coolant	Replace
30,000 miles 24 months	Engine idle speed	Adjust
30,000 miles	Injection timing	Inspect/adjust
60,000 miles	Timing belts	Replace

Chassis Maintenance Chart

Interval	Item	Service
15,000 miles	Brake pads, discs drums and linings	Inspect
15,000 miles 12 months	Brake lines and hoses	Inspect
30,000 miles 24 months	Brake fluid	Replace (1973–84 only)
15,000 miles	Transmission, Transaxle, Transfer case fluid level	Inspect
15,000 miles 12 months	Steering gear, linkage, driveshafts & boots	Inspect
15,000 miles 12 months	Power steering lines, hoses	Inspect
15,000 miles 12 months	Exhaust system	Inspect
15,000 miles 12 months	Locks, hinges, hood latch	Inspect
30,000 miles 24 months	Front wheel bearings (through 1986 only)	Repack

Capacities

Year	Model	Engine Crankcase (qts)		Transmission (pts)			Drive Axle (pts)	Gas Tank (gals)	Cooling System (qts)
		With Filter	Without Filter	4-Spd	5-Spd	Automatic (total capacity)			
1973	1200	3.6	2.6	2.5	—	11.8	1.8	10/10.5 (sedan)	5.2
1974	B-210	3.45	—	2.5	—	11.8	1.8	11.5	5.5
1975	B-210	4.2	3.7	2.7	—	11.4	1.89	11.5	6.25 ①
1976–78	B-210	3.8	3.4	2.75	3.6	11.8	1.8	11.5	6.25 ①
1979–82	210	3.5	3.0	②	2.5	11.8	1.8	13.25	5.25
1982–85	Sentra	4.1	3.6	4.8	5.75	13.1	—	13.25	5.0 ③
1984–85	Sentra Diesel	4.4	3.75	4.8	5.75	12.75	—	13.25 ④	7.4
1986	Sentra	3.375	3.0	4.875	5.75	12.75	—	13.25 ④	5.0 ③
1986	Sentra Diesel	4.25	3.375	4.875	5.75	12.75	—	13.25 ④	5.0 ③
1987	Sentra	3.375	2.9	—	5.75	13.25	—	13.75	9.75
1987	Sentra Diesel	4.0	3.5	—	5.75	13.25	—	13.75	6.875
1988	Sentra	3.375	3.0	5.75	5.815	13.25	—	13.25 ⑤	4.6 ⑥

① Automatic transmission: 6 qts.
② A12A 2.5 pts.; A14, A15 2.75 pts.
③ Automatic transmission: 5.625 qts.
④ MPG Model: 10⅝ gals.
⑤ 12.375 with 4 WD
⑥ 4.625 with automatic transmission

Engine Performance and Tune-Up

2

TUNE-UP PROCEDURES

The tune-up is a routine maintenance operation which is essential for the efficient and economical operation, as well as the long life, of your car's engine. The interval between tune-ups is a variable factor which depends upon the way you drive your car, the conditions under which you drive it (weather, road type, etc.) and the type of engine installed in your car. Manufacturer's recommended tune-up intervals should be followed if possible, but it is generally correct to say that no car should be driven more than 12,000 miles between tune-ups, especially in this age of emission controls and fuel shortages. Cars driven extremely hard or under severe weather conditions should be tuned at closer intervals.

The replacement parts involved in a tune-up include spark plugs, air filter, distributor cap, ignition points (if equipped), rotor, and spark plug wires. In addition to these parts and the adjustments involved in properly adapting them to your engine, there are several adjustments of other parts involved in completing the job. Included in these adjustments are carburetor, idle speed and air/fuel mixture, ignition timing, and valve clearance adjustments.

This chapter gives specific procedures on how to tune-up your 1200, B210 or 210 model Nissan, or your Nissan Sentra. It is intended to be as complete as possible. Use the accompanying troubleshooting chart to diagnose minor engine operation problems.

Tune up time is also a good time to look around the engine compartment for potential problems, such as fuel and oil leaks, cracking or hard radiator or heater hoses, loose or frayed belts, loose wire connections, etc.

CAUTION: *When working around a running engine, always be certain there is plenty of ventilation. Make sure the transmission is in Neutral (unless otherwise specified) and the parking brake is fully applied. Always keep hands, hair, and clothing away from the fan, hot manifolds and radiator. Remove any jewelry or neckties. When the engine is running, do not grasp the ginition wires, distributor cap or coil wire, as a shock in excess of 20,000 volts may result. Whenever working around the distributor, even if the engine is not running, make sure that the ignition is switched off. Removing or disturbing the distributor cap on an electronic ignition system with the ignition switch "on" can often cause the system to fire.*

For 1973-79 models, Nissan recommends a tune-up, including distributor points (unless equipped with electronic ignition), and spark plugs every 12,000 miles. In 1980 and on later models, Nissan and Nissan have been using a new, more durable spark plug in all models sold in the United States. Also, the exclusive use of unleaded gas as well as high energy ignition increase spark plug life. Nissan recommends that the new plugs be replaced every 30,000 miles or 24 months, whichever comes first. (Of course, the Nissan plugs can be replaced with quality spark plugs from any major manufacturer). Certain Canadian 1980 and later Nissans still use the conventional 12 month, 12,000 mile plugs. Even though the manufacturer suggests such a long life span for the spark plugs on these models, it would be wise to remove, clean, inspect, and regap them every 12,000 miles.

Spark Plugs

A typical spark plug consists of a metal shell surrounding a ceramic insulator. A metal electrode extends downward through the center of the insulator and protrudes a small distance. Located at the end of the plug and attached to the side of the outer metal shell is the side electrode. The side electrode bends in at a 90″ angle so that its tip is even with, and parallel to, the

Tune-Up Specifications

When analyzing compression test results, look for uniformity among cylinders, rather than specific pressures.

Year	Model	Spark Plug Type	Spark Plug Gap (in.)	Distributor Point Dwell (deg)	Distributor Point Gap (in.)	Ignition Timing (deg) MT	Ignition Timing (deg) AT	Fuel Pump Presure (psi)	Idle Speed (rpm) MT	Idle Speed (rpm) AT	Valve Clearance In	Valve Clearance Ex
1973	1200	BP5-ES	.034	49–55	.020	5B @ 700	5B @ 600	2.6	800	650	0.010 cold / 0.014 hot	0.010 cold / 0.014 hot
1974	B210	BP5-ES	.033	49–55	.020	5B @ 800	5B @ 650	3.4	800	650	0.014 hot	0.014 hot
1975	B210 (Federal)	BP5-ES	.033	49–55	.020	10B	10B	3.8	700	650	0.014 hot	0.014 hot
1975	B210 (California)	BP6-ES	.033	Electronic	(1)	10B	10B	3.8	750	650	0.014 hot	0.014 hot
1976	B210 (Federal)	BP5-ES	.033	44–55	.020	10B	10B	3.8	700	650	0.014 hot	0.014 hot
1976	B210 (California)	BP5-ES	.033	Electronic	(1)	10B	10B	3.8	700	650	0.014 hot	0.014 hot
1977	B210 (Federal)	BP5-ES	.041	49–55	.020	10B	8B	3.8	700	650	0.014 hot	0.014 hot
1977	B210 (California)	BP5-ES	.041	Electronic	(1)	10B	10B	3.8	700	650	0.014 hot	0.014 hot
1978	B210 (except FU)	BP5-ES	.041	Electronic	(1)	10B	8B (2)	3.9	700	650	0.014 hot	0.014 hot
1978	B210 (FU model)	BP5-EQ	.047	Electronic	(1)	5B	—	3.9	700	—	0.014 hot	0.014 hot
1979	210	BP5-ES (6)	.041 (7)	Electronic	(1)	10B (3)(5)	8B (3)	3.8	700	650	0.014 hot	0.014 hot
1980	210	BP5-ES	.041	Electronic	(1)	10B (2)	8B	3.8	700	650	0.014 hot	0.014 hot
1981–82	210	BP5-ES11, BP5-ES11	.041	Electronic	(1)	5B (8)	5B	3.8	700	650	0.014 hot	0.014 hot
1982	Sentra	BPR5ES-11	.041	Electronic	(1)	4A	6A	3.8	750	650	0.011 hot	0.011 hot
1983	Sentra	BPR5ES-11 (9)	.041 (10)	Electronic	(1)	5A (11)	5A	3.8	750	650	0.011 hot	0.011 hot
1984–86	Sentra	BPR5ES-11 (9)	.041 (10)	Electronic	(1)	15B (12)	8B (12)	3.8	800 (13)	650	0.011 hot	0.011 hot
1987	Sentra	BPR5ES-11	.041	Electronic	—	7B	7B	15	800	700 (14)	0.011 hot	0.011 hot
1988	Sentra	BPR5ES-11	.041	Electronic	—	7B	7B	15	800	700	0.011 hot	0.011 hot

NOTE: Emission control requires a very precise approach to tune-up. Timing and idle speed are peculiar to the engine and its application, rather than to the engine alone. Data for the particular application is on a sticker in the engine compartment on all late models. If the sticker disagrees with this chart, use the sticker figure. The results of any adjustment or modifications should be checked with a CO meter. On many 1980 cars, CO levels are not adjustable.

EFI: electronic fuel injection

NOTE: FU models are Hatchbacks with 5-speed transmissions sold in the U.S.A. except for California

① Electronic ignition—reluctor (air) gap: 0.008–0.016 in. (1975–78); 0.012–0.020 in. (1979–84)

② A14, A15 engine: 8B

③ California models: 5B

④ California: 10B

⑤ FU model: 5B

⑥ FU model: BP-5EQ

⑦ FU model: 0.043–0.051 in.

⑧ A12A with M/T, 10B; Canada 10B

⑨ Canada: BPR5ES

⑩ Canada: .033

⑪ M.P.G. Model: 2A

⑫ Calif. & Canada: 5A

⑬ Calif. & Canada: 750

⑭ Set in Drive, handbrake applied.

⑮ Injected engines—14, carbureted—2.8–3.8

Diesel Engine Tune-Up Specifications

Year Model	Engine Displacement cu. in. (cc)	Warm Valve Clearance (in.)		Injection Pump Setting (deg)	Injection Nozzle Pressure (psi)		Idle Speed (rpm)	Compression Pressure (psi)
		In	Ex		New	Used		
'83–'85	102 (1680)	0.008–0.012	0.016–0.020	See Text	1,920–2,033	1,778–1,920	750	455 ①
'86	102 (1680)	0.008–0.012	0.016–0.020	0.0370–0.0012 ③	1,920–2,033	1,778–1,920	750 ④	448 ②
'87	102 (1680)	0.008–0.012	0.016–0.020	0.0370–0.0012 ③	1,920–2,033	1,778–1,920	700	448 ②

NOTE: The underhood specification sticker often reflects tune-up specification changes made in production. Sticker figures must be used if they disagree with those in this chart.
① At 200 rpm
② Minimum—284
③ Pump plunger lift. See text
④ Automatic transmission—670 in Drive

tip of the center electrode. The distance between these two electrodes (measured in thousandths of an inch) is called the spark plug gap. The spark plug in no way produces a spark but merely provides a gap across which the current can arc. The coil produces anywhere from 20,000 to 40,000 volts, which travels to the distributor where it is distributed through the spark plug wires to the spark plugs. The current passes along the center electrode and jumps the gap to the side electrode, and, in so doing, ignites the air/fuel mixture in the combustion chamber.

Spark plug life and efficiency depend upon the condition of the engine and the temperatures to which the plug is exposed. Combustion chamber temperatures are affected by many factors such as compression ratio of the engine, air/fuel mixtures, exhaust emission equipment, and the type of driving you do. Spark plugs are designed and classified by number according to the heat range at which they will operate most efficiently.

SPARK PLUG HEAT RANGE

Spark Plug heat range is actually quite simple: the amount of heat the plug absorbs is determined by the length of the lower insulator. The longer the insulator (or the farther it extends into the engine), the hotter the plug will operate; the shorter the insulator the coller it will operate. A plug that absorbs little heat and remains too cool will quickly accumulate deposits of oil and carbon since it is not hot enough to burn them off. This leads to plug fouling and consequently to misfiring. A plug that absorbs too much heat will have no deposits, but, due to the excessive heat, the electrodes will burn away quickly and in some instance, preignition

may result. Preignition takes place when plug tips get so hot that they glow sufficiently to ignite the fuel/air mixture before the actual spark occurs. This early ignition will usually cause a pinging during low speeds and heavy loads. In severe cases, the heat may become high enough to start the fuel/air mixture burning throughout the combustion chamber rather than just to the front of the plug as in normal operation. At this time, the piston is rising in the cylinder making its compression stroke. The burning mass is compressed and an explosion results, forcing the piston back down in the cylinder while it is still trying to go up. Obviously, something must go, and it does: pistons are often damaged.

The general rule of thumb for choosing the correct heat range when picking a spark plug is: if most of your driving is long distance high speed travel, use a colder plug; if most of your driving is stop and go, use a hottter plug. Factory installed plugs are, of course compromise

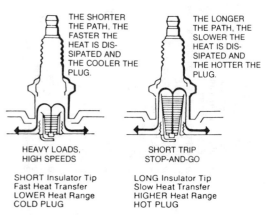

THE SHORTER THE PATH, THE FASTER THE HEAT IS DISSIPATED AND THE COOLER THE PLUG.

THE LONGER THE PATH, THE SLOWER THE HEAT IS DISSIPATED AND THE HOTTER THE PLUG.

HEAVY LOADS, HIGH SPEEDS

SHORT TRIP STOP-AND-GO

SHORT Insulator Tip
Fast Heat Transfer
LOWER Heat Range
COLD PLUG

LONG Insulator Tip
Slow Heat Transfer
HIGHER Heat Range
HOT PLUG

Spark plug heat range

Troubleshooting Engine Performance

Problem	Cause	Solution
Hard starting (engine cranks normally)	• Binding linkage, choke valve or choke piston	• Repair as necessary
	• Restricted choke vacuum diaphragm	• Clean passages
	• Improper fuel level	• Adjust float level
	• Dirty, worn or faulty needle valve and seat	• Repair as necessary
	• Float sticking	• Repair as necessary
	• Faulty fuel pump	• Replace fuel pump
	• Incorrect choke cover adjustment	• Adjust choke cover
	• Inadequate choke unloader adjustment	• Adjust choke unloader
	• Faulty ignition coil	• Test and replace as necessary
	• Improper spark plug gap	• Adjust gap
	• Incorrect ignition timing	• Adjust timing
	• Incorrect valve timing	• Check valve timing; repair as necessary
Rough idle or stalling	• Incorrect curb or fast idle speed	• Adjust curb or fast idle speed
	• Incorrect ignition timing	• Adjust timing to specification
	• Improper feedback system operation	• Refer to Chapter 4
	• Improper fast idle cam adjustment	• Adjust fast idle cam
	• Faulty EGR valve operation	• Test EGR system and replace as necessary
	• Faulty PCV valve air flow	• Test PCV valve and replace as necessary
	• Choke binding	• Locate and eliminate binding condition
	• Faulty TAC vacuum motor or valve	• Repair as necessary
	• Air leak into manifold vacuum	• Inspect manifold vacuum connections and repair as necessary
	• Improper fuel level	• Adjust fuel level
	• Faulty distributor rotor or cap	• Replace rotor or cap
	• Improperly seated valves	• Test cylinder compression, repair as necessary
	• Incorrect ignition wiring	• Inspect wiring and correct as necessary
	• Faulty ignition coil	• Test coil and replace as necessary
	• Restricted air vent or idle passages	• Clean passages
	• Restricted air cleaner	• Clean or replace air cleaner filler element
	• Faulty choke vacuum diaphragm	• Repair as necessary
Faulty low-speed operation	• Restricted idle transfer slots	• Clean transfer slots
	• Restricted idle air vents and passages	• Clean air vents and passages
	• Restricted air cleaner	• Clean or replace air cleaner filter element
	• Improper fuel level	• Adjust fuel level
	• Faulty spark plugs	• Clean or replace spark plugs
	• Dirty, corroded, or loose ignition secondary circuit wire connections	• Clean or tighten secondary circuit wire connections
	• Improper feedback system operation	• Refer to Chapter 4
	• Faulty ignition coil high voltage wire	• Replace ignition coil high voltage wire
	• Faulty distributor cap	• Replace cap
Faulty acceleration	• Improper accelerator pump stroke	• Adjust accelerator pump stroke
	• Incorrect ignition timing	• Adjust timing
	• Inoperative pump discharge check ball or needle	• Clean or replace as necessary
	• Worn or damaged pump diaphragm or piston	• Replace diaphragm or piston

Troubleshooting Engine Performance (cont.)

Problem	Cause	Solution
Faulty acceleration (cont.)	• Leaking carburetor main body cover gasket	• Replace gasket
	• Engine cold and choke set too lean	• Adjust choke cover
	• Improper metering rod adjustment (BBD Model carburetor)	• Adjust metering rod
	• Faulty spark plug(s)	• Clean or replace spark plug(s)
	• Improperly seated valves	• Test cylinder compression, repair as necessary
	• Faulty ignition coil	• Test coil and replace as necessary
	• Improper feedback system operation	• Refer to Chapter 4
Faulty high speed operation	• Incorrect ignition timing	• Adjust timing
	• Faulty distributor centrifugal advance mechanism	• Check centrifugal advance mechanism and repair as necessary
	• Faulty distributor vacuum advance mechanism	• Check vacuum advance mechanism and repair as necessary
	• Low fuel pump volume	• Replace fuel pump
	• Wrong spark plug air gap or wrong plug	• Adjust air gap or install correct plug
	• Faulty choke operation	• Adjust choke cover
	• Partially restricted exhaust manifold, exhaust pipe, catalytic converter, muffler, or tailpipe	• Eliminate restriction
	• Restricted vacuum passages	• Clean passages
	• Improper size or restricted main jet	• Clean or replace as necessary
	• Restricted air cleaner	• Clean or replace filter element as necessary
	• Faulty distributor rotor or cap	• Replace rotor or cap
	• Faulty ignition coil	• Test coil and replace as necessary
	• Improperly seated valve(s)	• Test cylinder compression, repair as necessary
	• Faulty valve spring(s)	• Inspect and test valve spring tension, replace as necessary
	• Incorrect valve timing	• Check valve timing and repair as necessary
	• Intake manifold restricted	• Remove restriction or replace manifold
	• Worn distributor shaft	• Replace shaft
	• Improper feedback system operation	• Refer to Chapter 4
Misfire at all speeds	• Faulty spark plug(s)	• Clean or replace spark plug(s)
	• Faulty spark plug wire(s)	• Replace as necessary
	• Faulty distributor cap or rotor	• Replace cap or rotor
	• Faulty ignition coil	• Test coil and replace as necessary
	• Primary ignition circuit shorted or open intermittently	• Troubleshoot primary circuit and repair as necessary
	• Improperly seated valve(s)	• Test cylinder compression, repair as necessary
	• Faulty hydraulic tappet(s)	• Clean or replace tappet(s)
	• Improper feedback system operation	• Refer to Chapter 4
	• Faulty valve spring(s)	• Inspect and test valve spring tension, repair as necessary
	• Worn camshaft lobes	• Replace camshaft
	• Air leak into manifold	• Check manifold vacuum and repair as necessary
	• Improper carburetor adjustment	• Adjust carburetor
	• Fuel pump volume or pressure low	• Replace fuel pump
	• Blown cylinder head gasket	• Replace gasket
	• Intake or exhaust manifold passage(s) restricted	• Pass chain through passage(s) and repair as necessary
	• Incorrect trigger wheel installed in distributor	• Install correct trigger wheel

Troubleshooting Engine Performance (cont.)

Problem	Cause	Solution
Power not up to normal	• Incorrect ignition timing	• Adjust timing
	• Faulty distributor rotor	• Replace rotor
	• Trigger wheel loose on shaft	• Reposition or replace trigger wheel
	• Incorrect spark plug gap	• Adjust gap
	• Faulty fuel pump	• Replace fuel pump
	• Incorrect valve timing	• Check valve timing and repair as necessary
	• Faulty ignition coil	• Test coil and replace as necessary
	• Faulty ignition wires	• Test wires and replace as necessary
	• Improperly seated valves	• Test cylinder compression and repair as necessary
	• Blown cylinder head gasket	• Replace gasket
	• Leaking piston rings	• Test compression and repair as necessary
	• Worn distributor shaft	• Replace shaft
	• Improper feedback system operation	• Refer to Chapter 4
Intake backfire	• Improper ignition timing	• Adjust timing
	• Faulty accelerator pump discharge	• Repair as necessary
	• Defective EGR CTO valve	• Replace EGR CTO valve
	• Defective TAC vacuum motor or valve	• Repair as necessary
	• Lean air/fuel mixture	• Check float level or manifold vacuum for air leak. Remove sediment from bowl
Exhaust backfire	• Air leak into manifold vacuum	• Check manifold vacuum and repair as necessary
	• Faulty air injection diverter valve	• Test diverter valve and replace as necessary
	• Exhaust leak	• Locate and eliminate leak
Ping or spark knock	• Incorrect ignition timing	• Adjust timing
	• Distributor centrifugal or vacuum advance malfunction	• Inspect advance mechanism and repair as necessary
	• Excessive combustion chamber deposits	• Remove with combustion chamber cleaner
	• Air leak into manifold vacuum	• Check manifold vacuum and repair as necessary
	• Excessively high compression	• Test compression and repair as necessary
	• Fuel octane rating excessively low	• Try alternate fuel source
	• Sharp edges in combustion chamber	• Grind smooth
	• EGR valve not functioning properly	• Test EGR system and replace as necessary
Surging (at cruising to top speeds)	• Low carburetor fuel level	• Adjust fuel level
	• Low fuel pump pressure or volume	• Replace fuel pump
	• Metering rod(s) not adjusted properly (BBD Model Carburetor)	• Adjust metering rod
	• Improper PCV valve air flow	• Test PCV valve and replace as necessary
	• Air leak into manifold vacuum	• Check manifold vacuum and repair as necessary
	• Incorrect spark advance	• Test and replace as necessary
	• Restricted main jet(s)	• Clean main jet(s)
	• Undersize main jet(s)	• Replace main jet(s)
	• Restricted air vents	• Clean air vents
	• Restricted fuel filter	• Replace fuel filter
	• Restricted air cleaner	• Clean or replace air cleaner filter element
	• EGR valve not functioning properly	• Test EGR system and replace as necessary
	• Improper feedback system operation	• Refer to Chapter 4

plugs, since the factory has no way of knowing what sort of driving you do. It should be noted that most people never have occasion to change their plugs from a factoryrecommended heat range, but if you spend most of your driving on the highway or around town, you may want to try a set of cooler or hotter than normal spark plugs and run them until the next tune up. Then check the condition of the plugs, comparing them to the color photos in the center of this book.

REMOVAL AND INSTALLATION

1. Grasp the spark plug boot and pull it straight out. Don't pull on the wire. If the boot(s) are cracked, replace them.
2. Place the spark plug socket firmly on the plug. Turn the spark plug out of the cylinder head in a counterclockwise direction.

NOTE: *The Nissan cylinder head is aluminum, which is easily stripped. Remove plugs only when the engine is cold.*

Removal should not be difficult, but if it is loosen the plug only slightly and drip penetrating oil onto the threads. Allow the oil time enough to work and then unscrew the plug. Proceeding in this manner will prevent damaging the threads in the cylinder head. Be sure to keep the socket straight to avoid breaking the ceramic insulator.

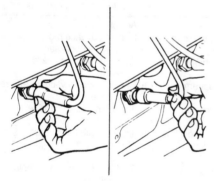

Correct method of removing spark plug wires on left. Pulling the wire instead of the boot on the right is incorrect

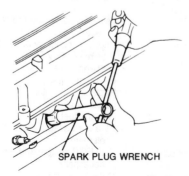

SPARK PLUG WRENCH

Keep the plug socket square on the spark plug

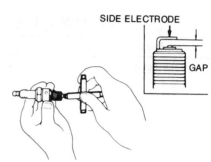

SIDE ELECTRODE

GAP

Check the spark plug gap with a wire gauge

3. Continue and remove the remaining spark plugs.
4. Inspect the plugs using the "color center" section illustrations and then clean or discard them according to condition.

New spark plugs come pregapped, but always double check the setting. The recommended spark plug gap is listed in the "Tune-UP Specifications" Chart. Use a spark plug wire gauge for checking the gap. The wire should pass through the electrode with just a slight drag. Avoid adjusting the plug gap with a flat-bladed feeler gauge; a false reading could result. Using the electrode bending tool on the end of the gauge, bend the side electrode to adjust the gap. Never attempt to adjust the center electrode. Lightly oil the threads of the replacement plug and install it hand-tight. It is a good practice to use a torque wrench to tighten the spark plugs on any car and especially on the Nissan, since the head is aluminum. Torque the spark plugs to 14-22 ft. lbs. Install the ignition wire boots firmly on the spark plugs.

Spark Plug Wires

Visually inspect the spark plug cables for burns, cuts, or any breaks in the insulation. Check the spark plug boots and the rubber nipples on the distributor and coil for the same. Any damaged wiring must be replaced.

If there is no obvious physical damage to the wires, check them for excessive resistance with an ohmmeter:

1. Remove the distributor cap and leave the wires connected to the cap.

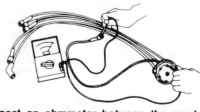

Connect an ohmmeter between the spark plug terminal (in boot) and the electrode inside the cap to check spark plug cable resistance

2. Connect one lead of the ohmmeter to the corresponding electrode inside the cap and the other lead to the spark plug terminal (remove it from the spark plug for the test).

3. Replace any wire that shows over 50,000Ω (resistance should not run over 35,000Ω and 50,000Ω should be considered the outer limits of acceptability).

Test the coil wire by connecting the ohmmeter between the center contact in the cap, and either of the primary terminals at the coil. If the total resistance of the coil and cable is more than 25,000Ω, remove the cable from the coil and check the resistance of the cable alone. If the resistance is higher than 15,000Ω, replace the cable.

It should be remembered that wire resistance is a function of length. The longer the cable the greater the resistance. Thus, if your cables are longer than factory originals, their resistance could be greater.

When installing a new set of spark plug cables, replace the calbes one at a time so there will be no mixup. Start by replacing the longest cable first. Install the boot firmly over the spark plug. Route the wire exactly the same as the original. Insert the nipple firmly into the tower on the distributor cap. Repeat the process for each cable.

Firing Orders

To avoid confusion, replace the spark plug wires one at a time.

Breaker Points and Condenser

NOTE: *Nissan California B210 models manufactured in 1975-77, and all 1978 and later B210, 210 and Sentra models are*

A-series engines

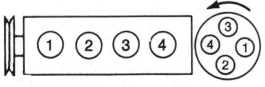

E-series (Sentra) engines

equipped with electronic, breakerless ignition systems. The 1200 series and the non-California B210 models prior to 1978 have the point type ignition systems. The following section covers maintenance procedures for these points systems.

INSPECTION OF THE POINTS

1. Disconnect the high tension wire from the top of the distributor and the coil.

2. Remove the distributor cap by prying off the spring clips on the sides of the cap.

3. Remove the rotor from the distributor shaft by poulling it straight up. Examine the condition of the rotor. If it is cracked or the metal tip is excessively worn or burned, it should be replaced. Clean the tip with fine emery paper.

4. Pry open the contacts of the points with a screwdriver and check the condition of the contacts. If they are excessively worn, burned or pitted, they should be replaced.

5. If the points are in good condition, adjust them and replace the rotor and the distributor cap. If the points need to be replaced, follow the replacement procedure given below.

REMOVAL AND INSTALLATION

1. Remove the coil high tension wire from the top of the distributor cap. Remove the distributor cap and place it out of the way. Remove the rotor from the distributor shaft by pulling up.

NOTE: *A magnetic screwdriver or one with a holding (locking) mechanism is very handy here and for all ignition work. Most screws used for points and other distributor assemblies are very small, hard to handle, and easily dropped. A locking or magnetic screwdriver makes removal and installation of these screws safer and much easier. A screw dropped into a distributor body usually means having to remove the entire distributor to retrieve the screw.*

2. Remove the condenser from the distributor body. Remove the points assembly attaching screws and then remove the points. A magnetic screwsriver or one with a holding mechanism will come in handy here. After the points are removed, wipe off the cam and apply new cam lubricant. If you don't the points will wear out in a few thousand miles.

3. Slip the new set of points onto the locating dowel and install the screws that hold the assembly onto the plate. Don't tighten them all the way yet, since you'll only have to loosen them to set the point gap.

4. Install the new condenser on single point models and attach the condenser lead to the points.

5. Set the point gap and dwell (see the following sections).

DWELL ADJUSTMENT WITH A FEELER GAUGE

1. If the contact points of the assembly are not parallel, bend the stationary contact so that they make contact across the entire surface of the contacts. Bend only the stationary bracket part of the point assembly; not the movable contact.

2. Turn the engine until the rubbing block of the points is on one of the high points of the distributor cam. You can do this by either turning the ignition switch to the start position and releasing it quickly ("bumping" the engine) or by using a wrench on the bolt which holds the crankshaft pulley to the crankshaft.

3. Place the correct size feeler gauge between the contacts (see the Tune-Up Chart). Make sure that it is parallel with the contact surfaces.

4. Loosen both contact plate attaching screws just enough that the contact plate and points gap can be adjusted with the adjusting screw.

5. While holding the feeler gauge in one hand between the points contacts, insert a screwdriver into the eccentric adjusting screw with the other hand. Turn the adjusting screw to either increase or decrease the gap to the proper setting. When the correct gap is found, there should be a moderate drag on the feeler gauge as you pass it through both contacts.

6. Tighten both contact plate attaching screws while still holding the feeler gauge between the contacts. Turn the engine through

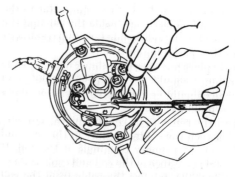

Turn eccentric screw to get correct point gap. Feeler gauge should slide between the contacts with a slight drag

one complete revolution until the points are at maximum "open" again. Recheck the gap; when you are stisfied with it, make sure both contact plate screws are secure.

7. Replace the rotor and distributor cap, and the high tension wire which connects the top of the distributor and the coil. Make sure that the rotor is firmly seated all the way onto the distributor shaft and that the tab of the rotor is aligned with notch in the shaft. Align the tab in the base of the distributor cap with the notch in the distributor body. Make sure that the cap is firmly seated on the distributor and that the retainer clips are in place. Make sure that the end of the high tension wire is firmly placed in the top of the distributor and the coil.

Dwell Adjustment with a Dwell Meter

The dwell angle or cam angle is the number of degrees that the distributor cam rotates while the points are closed. There is an inverse relationship between dwell angle and point gap. Increasing the point gap will decrease the dwell angle and vice versa. Checking the dwell angle with a meter is a far more accurate method of measuring point opening than the feeler gauge method.

After setting the point gap to specification with a feeler gauge as described above, check the dwell angle with a meter. Attach the dwell meter according to the manufacturer's instruction sheet. The negative lead is grounded and the positive lead is connected to the primary wire terminal which runs from the coil to the distributor. Start the engine, let it idle and reach operating temperature, and observe the dwell on the meter. The reading should fall within the allowable range (see Tune Up spec chart). If it does not, the gap will have to be reset or the breaker points will have to be replaced.

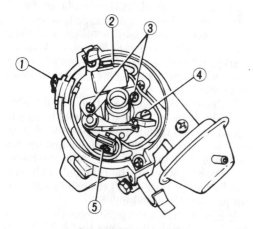

1. Primary lead terminal
2. Ground lead wire
3. Set screw
4. Adjuster
5. Screw

Adjusting screws and lead connections, points type distributor

Here's how to check and adjust dwell angle:

1. Adjust the points with a feeler gauge as previously described.

2. Connect the dwell meter to the ignition circuit as according to the manufacturer's instructions. One lead of the meter is connected to a ground and the other lead is connected to the distributor post on the coil. An adapter is usually provided for this purpose.

3. If the dwell meter has a set line on it, adjust the meter to zero the indicator.

4. Start the engine.

NOTE: *Be careful when working on any vehicle while the engine is running. Make sure that the transmission is in Neutral and that the parking brake is applied. Keep hands, clothing, tools and the wires of the test instruments clear of the rotating fan blades.*

5. Observe the reading on the dwell meter. If the reading is within the specified range, turn off the engine and remove the dwell meter.

NOTE: *If the meter does not have a scale for 4 cylinder engines, multiply the 8 cylinder reading by two.*

6. If the reading is above the specified range, the breaker point gap is too small. If the reading is below the specified range, the gap is too large. In either case, the engine must be stopped and the gap adjusted in the manner previously covered.

After making the adjustment, start the engine and check the reading on the dwell meter. When the correct reading is obtained, disconnect the dwell meter.

7. Check the adjustment of the ignition timing.

Nissan Electronic Ignition

In 1975, in order to comply with California's tougher emissions laws, Nissan introduced electronic ignition systems for all models sold in that state. Since that time, the Datsun/Nissan electronic ignition system has undergone a metamorphosis from a standard transistorized circuit (1975-1978) to an Integrated Circuit system (IC), 1979-88. Some Canadian 210's with the A12A engine continued to use the points type ignition system.

The electronic ignition system differs from the conventional breaker points system in form only; its function is exactly the same: to supply a spark to the spark plugs at precisely the right moment to ignite the compressed gas in the cylinders and create mechanical movement.

Located in the distributor, in addition to the normal rotor used to conduct the spark to the wires and plugs is a spoked rotor (reluctor). This part fits on the distributor shaft where the breaker points cam is found on nonelectronic

ignitions. The rotor (reluctor) revolves with the top rotor and shaft and, as it passes a pickup coil inside the distributor body, breaks a high flux phase which occurs while the space between the reluctor spokes passes the pickup coil. This allows current to flow to the pickup coil. Primary ignition current is then cut off by the electronic ignition unit, allowing the magnetic field in the ignition coil to collapse, creating the spark which the distributor passes on to the spark plug.

The 1979-86 IC ignition system uses a ring-type pickup coil which surrounds the reluctor instead of the single post type pickup coil on earlier models.

1987-88 models are equipped with a different means of generating the distributor signal. The reluctor and pickup coil are replaced by a rotor plate and crank angle sensor. The rotor plate is machined with slits that break and then restore a beam of light (a light emitting diode is situated above the plate and a photo-sensitive diode is located underneath). There are 360 slits in the plate to generate an engine speed signal and 4 slits to generate 180° crank angle signals.

When the slits in the rotor plate break and then restore the beam of light, the photo diode generates rough pulses. Then, a wave forming circuit located in the base of the distributor converts these pulses to clear on-off pulses. The Electronic Control Unit, a microcomputer, then utilizes these signals, in combination with others, to generate the actual on-off signal that controls the ignition coil and fires the ignition.

Because no points or condenser are used, and because dwell is determined by the electronic unit, no adjustments are necessary. Ignition timing is generally checked in the usual way (be careful to check for slight variations depending on model and engine), but unless the distributor is disturbed it is not likely to ever change very much.

Service consists of inspection of the distributor cap, rotor, and ignition wires, replacing

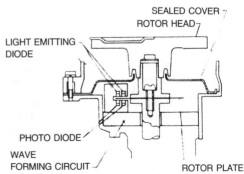

Cross-section of the Crank Angle Sensor used with 1987–88 electronic ignition systems

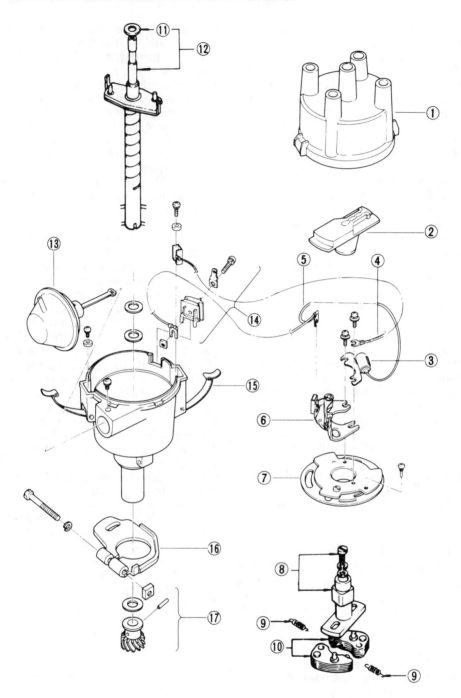

1. Cap	7. Breaker plate	13. Vacuum control assembly
2. Rotor	8. Cam assembly	14. Terminal assembly
3. Condenser	9. Governor spring	15. Clamp
4. Ground wire	10. Governor weight	16. Retaining plate
5. Lead wire	11. Thrust washer	17. Gear set
6. Breaker points	12. Shaft assembly	

Exploded view of points type distributor

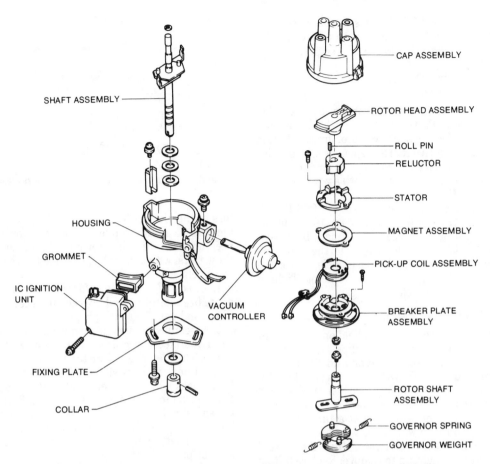

SHAFT ASSEMBLY

CAP ASSEMBLY

ROTOR HEAD ASSEMBLY

ROLL PIN

RELUCTOR

STATOR

HOUSING

MAGNET ASSEMBLY

GROMMET

PICK-UP COIL ASSEMBLY

IC IGNITION
UNIT

VACUUM
CONTROLLER

BREAKER PLATE
ASSEMBLY

FIXING PLATE

ROTOR SHAFT
ASSEMBLY

COLLAR

GOVERNOR SPRING

GOVERNOR WEIGHT

IC (electronic) ignition distributor, 1979 and later A-series. Sentra unit similar

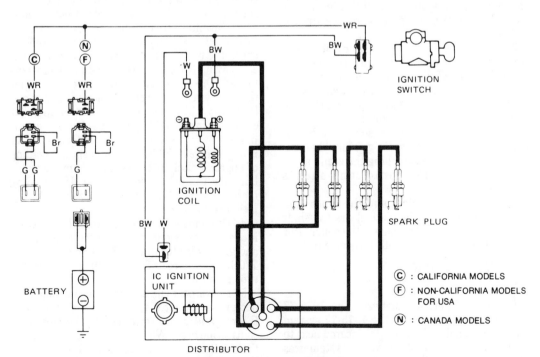

WR

BW

BW

IGNITION
SWITCH

C

N

F

WR

W

WR

Br

Br

G G

G

IGNITION
COIL

SPARK PLUG

BW W

BATTERY

IC IGNITION
UNIT

Ⓒ : CALIFORNIA MODELS

Ⓕ : NON-CALIFORNIA MODELS
     FOR USA

Ⓝ : CANADA MODELS

DISTRIBUTOR

1979–80 IC ignition system. 1980 210 shown

when necessary. These parts can be expected to last at least 40,000 miles. In addition, the reluctor air gap should be checked periodically.

ADJUSTMENTS

Reluctor Air Gap

1. Remove the cap and rotor as described below under "Parts Replacement". Use a non-magnetic feeler gauge (wood or brass). Rotate the engine until a reluctor spoke is aligned with the pick-up coil (either bump the engine around with the starter, or turn it with a wrench on the crankshaft pulley bolt).

2. The gap should measure 0.008-0.016″ through 1978, or 0.012-0.020″ for 1979 and later. Adjustment, if necessary, is made by loosening the pickup coil closer to or farther from the reluctor. On 1979 and later models, center the pickup coil (ring) around the reluctor. Tighten the screws and recheck the gap.

PARTS REPLACEMENT

1. The distributor cap is held on by two clips or two screws. Release the clips or remove the screws with a screwdriver and lift the cap straight up and off, with the wires attached. Inspect the cap for cracks, carbon tracks, or a worn center contact. Replace it if necessary, transferring the wires one at a time from the old cap to the new.

2. Pull the ignition rotor (not the spoked reluctor) straight up to remove. Replace it if its contacts are worn, burned, or pitted. Do not file the contacts. To replace, press it firmly onto the shaft. It only goes on one way, so be sure it is fully seated.

3. Inspect the wires for cracks or brittleness. Replace them one at a time to prevent crosswiring, carefully pressing the replacement wires into place. The cores of electronic wires are more susceptible to breakage than those of standard wires, so treat them gently.

4. If the crank angle sensor must be replaced, first remove the sealing cover. Then, remove the two screws attaching the crank angle sensor to the electronic components underneath.

5. Slide the rotor plate and the sensor upward together. Once the plate clears the shaft and the sensor clears the edge of the distributor body, separate them. Install in reverse order.

TROUBLESHOOTING

1975-78

The main differences between the 1975-77 and 1978 systems are: (1) the 1975-77 system uses an external ballast resistor located next to the ignition coil, and (2) the earlier system uses a wiring harness with individual eyelet connec-

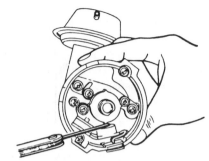

Checking air gap, electronic ignition distributors

tors to the electronic unit, while the later system uses a multiple plug connector. You will need an accurate voltmeter and ohmmeter for these tests, which must be performed in the order given.

1. Check all connections for corrosion, looseness, breaks, etc., and correct if necessary. Clean and gap the spark plugs.

2. Disconnect harness (connector or plug) from the electronic unit. Turn the ignition switch On. Set the voltmeter to the DC 50v range. Connect the positive (+) voltmeter lead to the back/white wire terminal, and the negative (–) lead to the black wire terminal. Battery voltage should be obtained. If not, check the black/white and black wires for continuity; check the battery terminals for corrosion; check the battery state of charge.

3. Next, connect the voltmeter (+) lead to the blue wire and the (–) lead to the black wire. Battery voltage should be obtained. If not, check the blue wire for continuity; check the ignition coil terminals for corrosion or looseness; check the coil for continuity. On 1975-77 models, leaving the ballast resistor-to-coil wires attached. On 1978 models, disconnect the ignition coil wires. Connect the leads of an ohmmeter to the ballast resistor outside terminals (at each end) for 1975-77, and to the two coil terminals for 1978. With the ohmmeter set in the X1 range, the 1975-78 B210 should show a reading of approximately 0Ω. The maximum allowable limit for the 0Ω models is 1.8Ω. If a reading higher than the limit is received, replace the ignition coil assembly.

4. Disconnect the harness from the electronic control unit. Connect an ohmmeter to the red and green wire terminals. Resistance should be 720Ω. If far more or far less, replace the distributor pick-up coil.

5. Disconnect the anti-diesling solenoid connector (see Chapter 4). Connect a voltmeter to the red and green terminals of the electronic control harness. When the starter is cranked, the needle should deflect slightly. If not, replace the distributor pick-up coil.

6. Reconnect the ignition coil and the electronic control unit. Leave the anti-dieseling solenoid wire disconnected. Unplug the high tension lead (coil to distributor) from the distributor and hold it ⅛-½″ from the cylinder head with a pair of insulated pliers and a heavy glove. When the engine is cranked, a spark should be observed. If not, check the lead, and replace if necessary. If still no spark, replace the electronic control unit.

7. Reconnect all wires.

1976-77: connect the voltmeter (+) lead to the blue electronic control harness connector and the (–) lead to the black wire. The harness should be attached to the control unit.

1978: connect the voltmeter (+) lead to the (–) terminal of the ignition coil and the (–) lead to ground.

As soon as the ignition switch is turned On, the meter should indicate battery voltage. If not, replace the electronic control unit.

1979-86

1. Make a check of the power supply circuit. Turn the ignition OFF. Disconnect the connector from the top of the IC unit. Turn the ignition ON. Measure the voltage at each terminal of the connector in turn by touching the probe of the positive lead of the voltmeter to one of the terminals, and touching the probe of the negative lead of the voltmeter to a ground, such as the engine. In each case, battery voltage should be indicated. If not, check all wiring, the ignition switch, and all connectors for breaks, corrosion, discontinuity, etc., and repair as necessary.

2. Check the primary windings of the ignition coil. Turn the ignition OFF. Disconnect the harness connector from the negative coil terminal. Use an ohmmeter to measure the resistance between the positive and negative coil terminals. If resistance is 0.84-1.02Ω (1.04-1.27Ω on the Sentra) the coil is OK. Replace it if far from this range.

If the power supply, circuits, wiring, and coil are in good shape, check the IC unit and pick-up coil, as follows:

3. Turn the ignition OFF. Remove the distributor cap and ignition rotor. Use an ohmmeter to measure the resistance between the two terminals of the pick-up coil, where they attach to the IC unit. Measure the resistance by reversing the polarity of the probes. If approximately 400Ω are indicated, the pick-up coil is OK, but the IC unit is bad and must be replaced. If other than 400Ω are measured, go to the next Step.

4. Be certain the two pin connector to the IC unit is secure. Turn the ignition ON.

Measure the voltage at the ignition coil negative terminal. Turn the ignition OFF.

CAUTION: *Remove the tester probe from the coil negative terminal before switching the ignition OFF, to prevent burning out the tester.*

If zero voltage is indicated, the IC unit is bad and must be replaced. If battery voltage is indicated, proceed.

5. Remove the IC unit from the distributor:

a. Disconnect the battery ground (negative) cable.

b. Remove the distributor cap and ignition rotor.

c. Disconnect the harness connector at the top of the IC unit.

d. Remove the two screws securing the IC unit to the distributor.

e. Disconnect the two pick-up coil wires from the IC unit.

CAUTION: *Pull the connectors free with a pair of needlenosed pliers. Do not pull on the wires to detach the connectors.*

f. Remove the IC unit.

6. Measure the resistance between the terminals of the pick-up coil. It should be approximately 400Ω. If so, the pick-up coil is OK, and the IC unit is bad. If not approximately 400Ω, the pick-up coil is bad and must be replaced.

7. With a new pick-up coil installed, install the IC unit. Check for a spark at one of the spark plugs (see Chapter 10). If a good spark is obtained, the IC unit is OK. If not, replace the IC unit.

1987-88

1. If the engine runs, check ignition timing as described below. If this does not resolve the problem, remove the spark plugs and check for burning or fouling. Clean/replace as appropriate.

2. If the engine will not start or if checking the timing and plugs fails to resolve the problem, devise a means to conduct current out of the spark plug end of one of the plug wires and to a metal probe of some sort. An easy method of doing this is to cut the lower half of the threads and side electrode off an old spark plug while leaving the center electrode and insulator intact. Unplug the carburetor or injector solenoid connector. Then, hold this probe *with a pair of pliers with insulated handles* about ¼″ away from the block. Have someone crank the engine and watch for spark. If there is no spark, continue with the tests below.

3. Remove the high tension cables and check them with an ohmmeter. Resistance must be 30,000Ω or less.

4. While a special testing unit is required to confirm problems in the crank angle sensor, you can utilize the self-diagnosing system in the

Electronic Control Unit to get a preliminary indication that this is or is not the problem. To do this, proceed as follows:

a. Unclamp the Electronic Control Unit from its mount under the passenger's seat, leaving it securely plugged. Start the engine and drive the car for about 10 minutes to warm it up fully. If the problem is not doubtful ignition with rough running but a no-start condition, perform the test (Steps b through d) after cranking the engine for 10 seconds or so.

b. Insert a screwdriver into the side of the E.C.U. Watch the inspection lamps located on the top of the unit near the diagnostic mode selector hole and then turn the diagnostic mode selector all the way to the right.

c. Note the pattern that is flashed. A faulty crank angle sensor signal is indicated by Code 11. Code 11 is indicated if the red lamp (on the left) and green lamp (on the right) each blink once.

d. After the lamps have flashed the code three times, turn the diagnostic mode selector all the way the other way—counterclockwise. Make sure the lights then flash Code 44, which is four reds and four greens, indicating normal E.C.M. operation. Then, turn the ignition switch off and install the E.C.U. back under the passenger seat.

If the inspection lamps indicate a faulty crank angle sensor, take the car to a repair shop equipped with a logic probe so the crank angle sensor may be definitely determined to be faulty. If necessary, it can then be replaced as described above under "Parts Replacement".

5. Measure the voltage across the battery terminals (red lead to +, of course) with the ignition switch off. Voltage should be 11.5-12.5 volts. If below 11.5 volts, repair the battery or charging system as described in Chapter 3.

6. Check the voltage across the battery terminals with the engine cranking (have someone crank the engine while you check the reading). Voltage must be 9.6 volts. Otherwise, repair the battery or charging system as described in Chapter 3.

7. Remove the distributor cap. Check the resistance between the terminal for the center (coil-to-distributor) terminal and each of the terminals for the wires going to the cylinders. Resistance must be 50Ω or less. Check also for carbon deposits and cracks. Replace the cap if any of these deficiencies are noted.

8. Disconnect the coil high tension lead. Note locations and then disconnect the (+) and (–) primary terminals of the coil. Make sure the coil is near room temperature (68° F.). Connect an ohmmeter between the high tension connection and the (–) primary terminal. Resistance must be 8,200-12,400Ω. Replace the coil if resistance is not within this range.

9. Check the resistance of the coil primary circuit by connecting the ohmmeter between the two primary connections. Resistance must be 0.84-1.02Ω. Replace the coil if resistance is not within this range.

Ignition Timing

Ignition timing is an important part of the tune-up. It is always adjusted after the points are gapped (dwell angle changed), since altering the dwell affects the timing. It should also be checked to compensate for timing belt or gear wear on engines with electronic ignition at the interval specified in the Maintenance Chart. Three basic types of timing lights are available, the neon, the DC, and the AC powered. Of the three, the inductive DC light is the most frequently used by professional tuners. The bright flash put out by the DC light makes the timing marks stand out on even the brightest of days. Another advantage of the DC light is that you don't need to be near an electrical outlet. Neon lights are available for a few dollars, but their weak flash makes it necessary to use them in a fairly dark work area. One neon light lead is attached to the spark plug and the other to the plug wire. The DC light attaches to the spark plug and the wire with an adapter and two clips

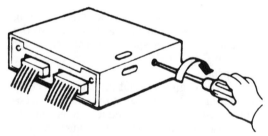

Rotating the Diagnostic Mode Selector to the right to read the diagnostic codes from the inspection lamps

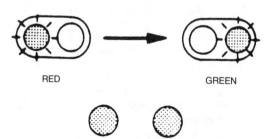

RED   GREEN

The inspection lamp appearance in reading out Code 11 (faulty crank angle sensor)

attached to the battery posts for power. The AC unit is similar, except that the power cable is plugged into a hous outlet.

CAUTION: *When performing this or any other operation with the engine running, be very careful of the alternator belt and pulleys. Make sure that your timing light wires don't interfere with the belt.*

Ignition timing is the measurement, in degrees of crankshaft rotation, of the point at which the spark plugs fire in each of the cylinders. It is measured in degrees before or after Top Dead Center (TDC) of the compression stroke. Ignition timing is adjusted by turning the distributor body in the engine.

Ideally, the air/fuel mixture in the cylinder will be ignited by the spark plug just before the piston passes TDC of the compression stroke. If this happens, the piston will be beginning its downward motion of the power stroke just as the compressed and ignited air/fuel mixture begins to develop a considerable amount of pressure. The expansion of the air/fuel mixture then forces the piston down on the power stroke and turns the crankshaft.

Because it takes time for the mixture to burn, the spark plug must fire a little before the piston reaches TDC. Otherwise, the mixture will not be burned completely early enough in the downstroke and the full power of the explosion will not be used by the engine.

The timing measurement is given in degrees of crankshaft rotation before the piston reaches TDC (BTDC). If the setting for the ignition timing is 5° BTDC (5B), the spark plug must fire 5° before each piston reaches TDC. This only holds true, however, when the engine is at idle speed.

As the engine speed increases, the pistons go faster. The spark plugs have to ignite the fuel even sooner if it is to be completely ignited when the piston reaches TDC. To do this, the distributor has a means to advance the timing of the spark as the engine speed increases. This is accomplished by centrifugal weights within the distributor and a vacuum diaphragm, mounted on the side of the distributor. It is necessary to disconnect the vacuum line from the diaphragm when the ignition timing is being set.

If the ignition is set too far advanced (BTDC), the ignition and expansion of the fuel in the cylinder will occur too soon and there will be excessive temperature and pressure. This causes engine ping. If the ignition spark is set too far retarded, after TDC (ATDC), the piston will have already passed TDC and started on its way down when the fuel is ignited. This will cause the piston to be forced down for only a portion of its travel and creates less pressure in the cyl-

inder, resulting in poor engine performance and lack of power.

The timing is best checked with a timing light. This device is connected in series (or through induction) with the No. 1 spark plug. The current which fires the spark plug also causes the timing light to flash.

The timing marks are located at the front crankshaft pulley and consist of a notch on the crankshaft pulley and a scale of degrees of crankshaft rotation attached to the front cover.

When the engine is running, the timing light is aimed at the marks on the flywheel pulley and the pointer.

IGNITION TIMING ADJUSTMENT

NOTE: *Nissan does not give ignition timing adjustments for 1980 and later California Nissans and Nissans. The procedure has been discontinued.*

1. Set the dwell to the proper specification on cars with ignition points.

2. Locate the timing marks on the crankshaft pulley and the front of the engine.

3. Clean off the timing marks so that you can see them (the numbers correspond to degrees before and after Top Dead Center).

4. Use chalk or white paint to color the mark on the crankshaft pulley and the mark on the scale which will indicate the correct timing when aligned with the notch on the crankshaft pulley.

5. Attach a tachometer to the engine (some dwell meters have a tachometer built in).

6. Attach a timing light to the engine, according to the manufacturer's instructions.

7. Leave the vacuum line connected to the distributor vacuum diaphragm on all models except 1979 210 wagons equipped with the A15 engine and automatic transmission, and all 1980 and later 210's and Sentra. Plug disconnected vacuum hoses with golf tees. On Canadian 210 models and Sentra, disconnect the air induction hose from the air cleaner, and cap or plug the air pipe. On 1987 and '88 Sentras with Electronic Injection, disconnect the throttle sensor electrical harness connector.

8. Check to make sure that all of the wires clear the fan and then start the engine. Allow the engine to reach normal operating temperature.

9. Adjust the idle to the correct rpm setting.

10. Aim the timing light at the timing marks. If the marks that you put on the pulley and the engine are aligned when the light flashes, the timing is correct. Turn off the engine and remove the tachometer and the timing light. If the marks are not in alignment, proceed with the following steps:

11. Turn off the engine.

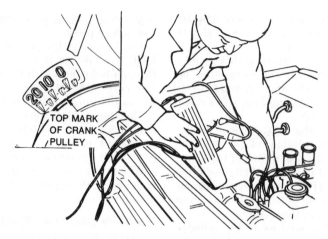

Checking ignition timing with timing light. Timing marks shown at left

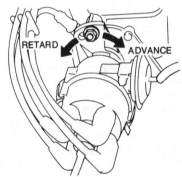

Sentra (E-series) distributor timing adjustment showing adjusting locknut

12. Loosen the distributor lockbolt just enough so that the distributor can be turned with a little effort.

13. Start the engine. Keep the wires of the timing light clear of the fan.

14. With the timing light aimed at the pulley and the marks on the engine, turn the distributor in the direction of rotor rotation to retard the spark, and in the opposite direction of rotor rotation to advance the spark.

15. Align the marks on the pulley and the engine with the flashes of the timing light.

16. Tighten the distributor holddown bolt when proper timing is found. Recheck the timing after tightening the lockbolt to make sure it has not changed; if necessary, reset it.

17. Stop the engine and restore all vacuum hoses and electrical connectors to their normal condition.

Valve Lash

Valve adjustment determines how far the valves enter the cylinder and how long they stay open and closed.

If the valve clearance is too large, part of the lift of the camshaft will be used in removing the excessive clearance. Consequently, the valve will not be opening as far as it should, it will start to open too late and will close too early. This condition has two effects: the valve train components will emit a tapping sound as they take up the excessive clearance and as the valves slam shut, and the engine will peform poorly because the valves don't open fully and allow the proper amount of gases to flow into and out of the engine.

If the valve clearance is too small, the intake valves and the exhaust valves will open too far and they will not fully seat on the cylinder head when they close. When a valve seats itself on the cylinder head, it does two things: it seals the combustion chamber so that none of the gasses in the cylinder escape and it cools itself by transferring some of the heat it absorbs from the combustion in the cylinder to the cylinder head and to the engine's cooling system. If the valve clearance is too small, the engine will run poorly because of the gases escaping from the combustion chamber. The valves will also become overheated and will warp, since they cannot transfer heat unless they are touching the valve seat in the cylinder head.

Valve adjusting shim

NOTE: *While all valve adjustments must be made as accurately as possible, it is better to have the valve adjustment slightly loose than slightly tight, as a burned valve may result from overly tight adjustments.*

This holds true for valve adjustments on most engines.

VALVE ADJUSTMENT

All Except Sentra

1. Run the engine until it reaches normal operating temperature. Oil temperature, not water temperature, is critical to valve adjustment. With this in mind, make sure the engine is fully warmed up since this is the only way to make sure the parts have reached their full expansion. Generally speaking, this takes around fifteen minutes. After the engine has reached normal operating temperature, shut it off.

2. Purchase a new valve cover gasket before removing the valve cover. The new silicone gasket sealers, available in tubes, are just as good or better if you can't find a gasket. Remove valve cover.

3. Note the location of any hoses or wires which may interfere with valve cover removal, disconnect them and move them aside. Then, remove the bolts which hold the valve cover in place.

4. After the valve cover has been removed, the next step is to get the number one piston at TDC on the compression stroke. There are at least two ways to do it; you can bump the engine over with the starter or turn it over by using a wrench on the front pulley attaching bolt. The easiest way to find TDC is to turn the engine over slowly with a wrench (after first removing no. 1 plug) until the piston is at the top of its stroke and the TDC timing mark on the crankshaft pulley is in alignment with the timing mark pointer. Make sure transmission is in Neutral and battery ground cable is disconnected. At this point, the valves for No. 1 cylinder should be checked.

NOTE: *Make sure both valves are closed with the valve springs up as high as they will go. An easy way to find the compression stroke is to remove the distributor cap and see toward which spark plug lead the rotor is pointing. If the rotor points to number one spark plug lead, number one cylinder is on its compression stroke. When the rotor points to number two spark plug lead, number two cylinder is on its compression stroke, etc.*

5. With no. 1 piston at TDC of the compression stroke, check the clearance on valves Nos. 1, 2, 3, and 5 (counting from the front to the rear).

6. To adjust the clearance, loosen the locknut with a wrench and turn the adjuster with a screwdriver while holding the locknut. The correct size feeler gauge should pass with a slight drag between the rocker arm and the valve stem.

7. Turn the crankshaft one full revolution to position the no. 4 piston at TDC of the compression stroke. Adjust valves nos. 4, 6, 7, and 8 in the same manner as the first four.

8. Replace the valve cover.

Sentra Gasoline Engine

1. Start engine and run it until normal operating temperature has been reached (usually after about fifteen minutes). Turn off the engine.

2. Remove air cleaner securing bolts, disconnect air cleaner hoses and remove air cleaner.

3. Remove the valve rocker cover.

4. Rotate the crankshaft pulley until TDC of the compression stroke of No. 1 cylinder is found (see valve adjustment procedure for the 1200/B210 series for more details on finding TDC).

5. With the No. 1 piston at Top Dead Center on its compression stroke, adjust valve clearance of valves 1, 2, 3 and 6 (see valve arrangement diagram). Adjust the valve by loosening the rocker adjusting screw locknut, inserting the proper feeler gauge between the rocker and the end of the valve stem, and turning the adjusting screw until the specified clearance (0.011″) is obtained. After adjustment, tighten

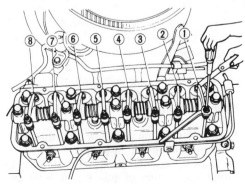

Adjusting A-series valve clearances

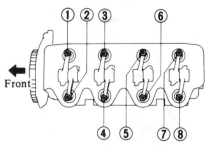

Sentra gasoline engine valve arrangement

the locknut and recheck the clearance (the feeler gauge should drag slightly but should not be tight).

6. Set the No. 4 cylinder at TDC of its compression stroke and adjust valve clearance of valves 4, 5, 7 and 8.

7. Replace the rocker cover, using a new gasket. Replace the air cleaner assembly.

Sentra Diesel Engine

1. Run the engine to normal operating temperature.

2. Shut off the engine and remove the valve cover.

3. Turn the crankshaft until #1 piston is at TDC of the compression stroke.

4. The folloiwing valves may now be adjusted:

#1 intake and exhaust
#2 intake
#3 exhaust

5. Measure the clearance between the cam lobe and the lifter. Valve clearance should be adjusted one valve at a time. Adjustment is made by removing or adding shims in the lifter. Lifters are removed or added, not at TDC, nut ¼ turn PAST TDC, in the normal direction of the rotation. A special tool, Nissan #KV11102600 is used. The tool should be inserted from the injector nozzle side of the head. The lifter has a cutout portion to aid in removing the shim. Turn the lifter so that this cutout

A-series mixture screw. Note limiter tab

is on the nozzle side. The shim should be stamped with their size, in millimeters. If, when you measure the clearance, you find that an adjustment is needed, remove the shim, note what size it is and determine what size you need to correct the gap.

Intake: 0.008-0.012"
Exhaust: 0.016-0.020"

6. Turn the crankshaft until #4 piston is at TDC compression. The following valves may now be adjusted:

#2 exhaust
#3 intake
#4 intake and exhaust

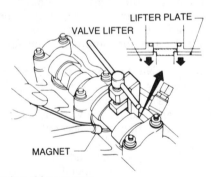

Inserting shim magnet

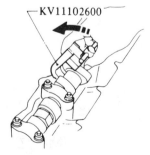

Special tool for adjusting valves

Idle Speed And Mixture Adjustment
GASOLINE ENGINES

Carburetor

EXCEPT NON-CALIFORNIA CARBURETOR-EQUIPPED 1987 MODELS

NOTE: *1980 and later model Nissans require a CO Meter to adjust their mixture ratios, therefore no procedures concerning this adjustment are give. Also, many model Nissans have a plug over their mixture control screw. It is suggested that on these models mixture adjustment be left to a qualified technician.*

1. Start the engine and allow it to run until it reaches normal operating temperature.

2. Allow the engine idle speed to stabilize by running the engine at idle for at least two minutes.

3. If you have not done so already, check and adjust the ignition timing to the proper setting.

4. Shut off the engine and connect a tachometer.

5. Disconnect and plug the air hose between the three way connector and the check valve, if equipped. On 1980-86 models, disconnect the air induction hose to the air cleaner and plug the pipe. With the transmission in Neutral, check the idle speed on the tachometer. If the reading is correct, continue on to Step 6 for 1973-79 Nissans. On 1987 California/Canada models, idle the engine for 2 minutes; then race the engine to 2,500 rpm three times, then check idle speed. For 1980 and later, and certain California models, proceed to step 10 below if the idle is correct. If the idle is not correct, for all 1200, B210 and 210 models, turn the idle speed adjusting screw clockwise with a screwdriver to increase idle speed or counterclockwise to decrease it, until the proper idle speed is achieved. On Sentra, turn the throttle adjusting screw.

6. With the automatic transmission in Drive (wheels blocked and parking brake on) or the manual transmission in Neutral, turn the mixture screw out until the engine rpm starts to drop due to an overly rich mixture (transmission placed in Drive in order to put a load on the engine for this procedure).

CAUTION: *While making the idle adjustments on automatic transmission cars (transmission in "Drive"), DO NOT race the engine, or even raise the rpm above those engine speeds recommended. The parking brake and wheel chocks cannot be expected to hold the car in this situation, and injury and/or damage will most certainly occur. Before racing the engine, place the transmission in Neutral, make sure the parking brake is firmly applied and the wheels chocked.*

7. Turn the adjusting screw until just before the rpm starts to drop due to an overly lean mixture. Turn the mixture screw in until the idle speed drops 60-70 rpm with manual transmission, or 15-25 rpm with automatic transmission (in Drive) for 1975-76 B210; 35-45 rpm with manual transmission or 10-20 rpm with automatic for 1977-78 B210, 1979 210. If the mixture limiter cap will not allow this adjustment, remove it, make the adjustment, and reinstall it. Go on to step 10 for all 1975-79 models.

8. On 1973-74 models, turn the mixture screw back out to the point midway between the two extreme positions where the engine began losing rpm to achieve the fastest and smoothest idle.

9. Adjust the curb idle speed to the proper specification, on 1973-74 models, with tidle speed adjusting screw.

10. Install the air hose. If the engine speed increases, reduce it with the idle speed screw until a smooth idle as listed in the Tune-Up specifications chart is achieved.

CARBURETOR-EQUIPPED 1987 NON-CALIFORNIA MODELS

1. Start the engine and run it until it reaches operating temperature. Block the wheels if the car has an automatic transmission. Make sure the parking brake is tightly engaged.

2. Open the hood. Make sure the engine has run at least two minutes past the point where it reached operating temperature according to the temperature gauge.

3. Turn the engine off and disconnect the vacuum control modulator harness connector. Connect a tachometer. Make sure wires are away from any moving parts.

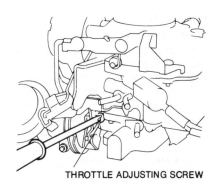

THROTTLE ADJUSTING SCREW
Throttle adjusting screw, Sentra carburetor

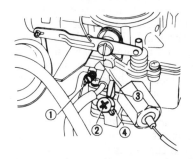

1. Throttle adjusting screw
2. Idle adjusting screw
3. Idle limiter cap
4. Stopper

Carburetor adjusting screws, A-series engines

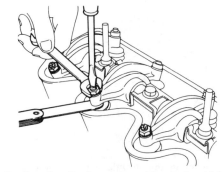

Adjusting the Sentra valves. There should be a slight drag on the feeler gauge

4. Start the engine back up. Then, race it to 2,500 rpm three times. Allow it to return to idle.

5. Put the transmission in Drive if the car has an automatic. Check idle speed with a tach. It should be 750 – manual transmission and 625 in Drive – automatic transmission. If not, adjust the throttle adjusting screw on the carburetor.

6. Turn the engine off an reconnect the vacuum control modulator harness connector.

7. Start the engine up and repeat the racing procedure of Step 4. Put the transmission in Drive if the car has an automatic. Read the idle speed. It should be 800 rpm on manual transmission cars and 700 on automatics. If not, the Electronic Control Unit or vacuum control modulator requires diagnosis and repair.

Fuel Injected Engines

1. Start the engine and idle it until it reaches operating temperature. Install a tachometer. Turn all accessories off. Chock the wheels securely if the car has an automatic transmission and apply the parking brake. The front wheels must be straight ahead to avoid abnormal power steering pump load. Open the hood and make sure the engine runs for 2 more minutes.

2. Shut the engine off. Disconnect the throttle sensor harness connector. Start the engine back up.

3. Race the engine to 2,500 rpm three times. Then, allow it to return to idle speed.

4. If the car has an automatic transmission, put it in "Drive". Check the idle speed and adjust it via the throttle body throttle adjusting screw to 750 rpm for manual transmission cars and 670 for automatics, if necessary. Note that it is necessary to looen the locknut with a small wrench to turn the screw, and then relock the adjusting screw.

5. Turn the engine off and reconnect the throttle sensor harness connector. Then, start the engine, repeat the racing procedure of Step 3 and return the engine to idle speed. Put the car into Drive if it has an automatic transmssion. Check idle speed. It should be 800 rpm with manual transmisslon and 700 with an automatic. If the idle speed was adjusted correctly in Step 4 and is now incorrect, it will be necessary to have the E.C.U. and related system diagnosed.

DIESEL ENGINE

NOTE: *A special tachometer compatible with diesel engines will be required for this procedure. A normal tachometer will not work.*

1. Make sure all electrical accessories are turned off.

2. The automatic transmission (if so equipped) should be in "D" with the parking brake on and the wheels blocked.

3. Start the engine and run it until it reaches the normal operating temperature.

4. Attach the diesel tachometer's pickup to the No. 1 injection tube.

NOTE: *In order to obtain a more accurate reading of the idle speed, you may wish to remove all the clamps on the No. 1 injection tube.*

5. Run the enigne at about 2,000 rpm for two minutes under no-load conditions.

6. Slow the engine down to idle speed for about 1 min. and then check the idle.

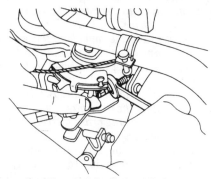

Loosen the idle screw locknut while holding the control lever—diesel engine

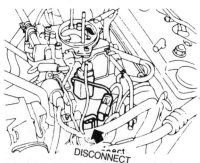

Disconnecting the throttle sensor harness connector to set idle speed on 1987–88 fuel injected models

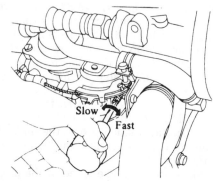

Idle speed adjusting screw—diesel engines

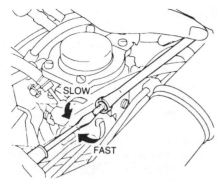

CD17 idle speed adjustment except 1987

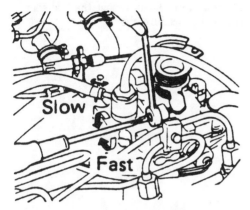

Adjusting idle speed on the 1987 CD17

7. If the engine is not idling at the proper speed, turn it off and disconnect the accelerator wire from the injection pump control lever.

NOTE: *It is not necessary to disconnect the accelerator wire on the CD17.*

8. Move the control lever to the full acceleration side, and then loosen the idle screw lock nut while still holding the control lever.

9. Start the engine again and turn the adjusting screw until the proper idle is obtained. Stop the engine.

10. Tighten the idle adjusting screw locknut while still holding the control lever to the full acceleration side and then connect the accelerator wire.

IDLE MIXTURE ADJUSTMENT

Carbureted Cars

NOTE: *Idle mixture is adjusted on carbureted cars only, and then only by using a "CO meter"—an expensive engine testing device used typically by well-equipped repair shops in the repair of emission system problems. Before attempting to adjust CO, make sure there are no vacuum system leaks, tuning problems (idle speed, ignition timing, spark plug condition or gap problems), or engine operating problems such as burned or misadjusted*

valves. *It is possible that, if your car idles roughly in the absence of any of these problems, the cost of having the CO adjusted can be reduced by following the procedure given here.*

1. Remove the carburetor from the engine as described in Chapter 5.

2. Locate the mixture adjustment plug located to the right of and below the idle speed screw. Find a drill that is *considerably smaller* than the diameter of the orifice in the carburetor casting into which the plug is mounted.

3. Drill *very cautiously* and slowly. Feel for the point where the drill *just* penetrates the inner end of the plug. *Don't drill farther, or the carburetor mixture screw will be damaged.*

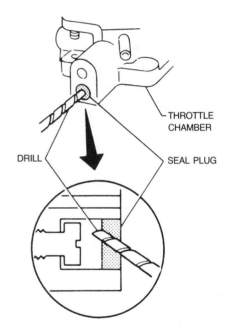

Drilling out the mixture adjusting plug (carburetor-equipped engines)

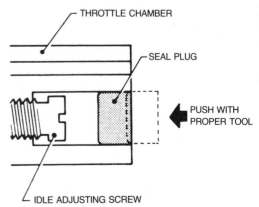

Install the plug into the mixture adjusting screw orifice so it is just slightly inside the bore

4. Once you have drilled through the plug, use a less brittle metal object that will fit through the hole in the plug to pry it out of the carburetor orifice. Carefully clean all metal shavings out of the bore so the mixture screw threads will not be damaged.

5. Install the carburetor back onto the car. Make sure all vacuum lines are securely connected.

6. Have the person adjusting the CO with the required equipment follow these procedures:

a. Run the engine until it is hot. Then, shut it off.

b. Disconnect the air/fuel ratio solenoid harness connector. Disconnect the air induc-tion hose from the air cleaner and plug or cap the hose.

c. Start the engine and race it three times to 2,500 rpm. Then, allow it to idle.

d. Insert the CO meter probe 16″ into the tailpipe. Read the CO. If necessary, adjust the mixture screw to obtain 4-6% for California and Canadian cars and 2-4% for 49 States cars.

7. Tap a new seal plug squarely into the car-buretor bore with an object with a perfectly flat front. The object should be just slightly smaller than the bore.

8. Restore all disconnected hoses and electri-cal connectors. Then, repeat the idle speed ad-justment procedure above.

ENGINE ELECTRICAL

Ignition Coil

TESTING

Testing the coil is a simple operation. All you need is an ohmmeter and an understanding of how the meter probes should be connected (make sure the ignition switch is turned off). Make sure to set the ohmmeter to an appropriate scale. To test the primary circuit, connect the probes between the two primary terminals of the coil. To test the secondary circuit, connect the probes between the inner conducting surfaces of the coil secondary tower and the *negative (–)* primary terminal. If either reading is outside specifications, replace the coil:

• Primary resistance: 1973-81 — 0.84-1.02Ω; 1982-85 — 1.04-1.-27Ω; 1986-88 — 0.84-1.02Ω.

• Secondary resistance: 1973-81 — 200-12,400Ω; 1982-85 — 7,300-11,000Ω; 1986-88 — 8,200-12,400Ω.

Distributor Ignitor or Crank Angle Sensor

REMOVAL AND INSTALLATION

1. The distributor cap is held on by two clips or two screws. Release the clips or remove the screws with a screwdriver and lift the cap straight up and off, with the wires attached.

2. Pull the ignition rotor (not the spoked reluctor) straight up to remove.

NOTE: *Performing this repair requires working with small parts in a confined space. Look the job over. It may be better to remove the distributor, as described just below, in order to make it easier to complete the work without losing any parts.*

3. To replace the IC ignition unit on reluctor type distributors:

a. First use two small, dull prying devices

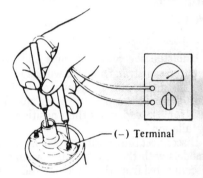

(–) Terminal

To test the coil secondary circuit, position the ohmmeter probes as shown

to work the reluctor off the distributor shaft. Pry evenly and simultaneously to do this. Make sure to catch the roll pin and save it with the reluctor.

b. Note their routing and then unplug the two electrical connectors for the ignitor unit. Pull the grommet out of the side of the distributor for additional working space and to keep the wires out of the way.

c. Remove the mounting screws and remove the ignitor and the two spacers.

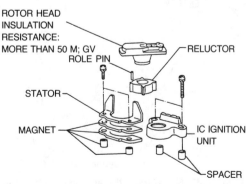

ROTOR HEAD
INSULATION
RESISTANCE:
MORE THAN 50 M; GV
ROLE PIN
RELUCTOR
STATOR
MAGNET
IC IGNITION UNIT
SPACER

Exploded view of reluctor, IC ignitor and related components of the reluctor type distributor

d. Install in reverse order.

4. To install a new crank angle sensor:

a. First remove the sealing cover. Unplug the harness connector, if it has not already been unplugged in removing the distributor. Then, remove the two screws attaching the crank angle sensor to the electronic components underneath.

b. Slide the rotor plate and the sensor upward together. Once the plate clears the shaft and the sensor clears the edge of the distributor body, separate them. Install in reverse order. Make sure to install the reluctor roll pin so as to hold the reluctor in the proper position relative to the distributor shaft.

Distributor

REMOVAL

All models

1. Unfasten the retaining clips and lift the distributor cap straight up. It will be easier to install the distributor if the wiring is not disconnected from the cap. If the wires must be removed from the cap, mark their positions to aid in installation.

2. Disconnect the distributor wiring harness. On models with the reluctor, the wiring must be disconnected from the reluctor itself and the grommet pulled out of the side of the distributor body. On the latest models, with the crank angle sensor, disconnect the harness at the multiprong plug.

3. Disconnect the vacuum lines from the vacuum advance/retard mechanisms, if there are any.

4. Note the position of the rotor in relation to the base. Scribe or paint a mark on the base of the distributor and on the engine block (on the end of the head on Sentra) so the marks can be lined up for reinstallation. Align the marks with the direction the metal tip of the rotor is pointing.

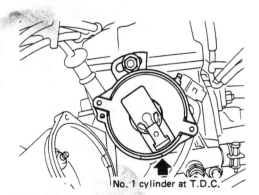

On the 1987–88 Sentra, if the engine crankshaft is turned to Top Dead Center, the rotor and the marks on the distributor body will align as shown

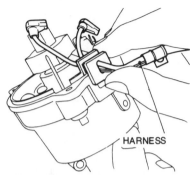

Disconnecting the distributor wiring harness on distributors with a reluctor

5. Remove the bolt(s) which hold(s) the distributor to the engine.

6. Lift the distributor assembly from the engine on the A-series engines. On Sentra, pull the distributor straight out from the end of the head.

INSTALLATION

1. Lightly lubricate the distributor shaft with engine oil and insert the shaft and assembly into the engine. Line up the mark on the distributor and the one on the engine with the metal tip of the rotor. Make sure that the vacuum advance diaphragm is pointed in the same direction as it was pointed originally. This will be done automatically if the marks on the engine and the distributor are lined up with the rotor.

2. Install the distributor holddown bolt and clamp. Leave the bolt loose enough so that you can turn the distributor with a slight amount of effort.

3. Connect the primary wire to the coil or reconnect the electrical connector. Install the distributor cap on the distributor housing. Secure the distributor cap with the spring clips.

4. Install the spark plug wires, if removed. Make sure that the wires are pressed all the way into the top of the distributor cap and firmly onto the spark plug.

5. Adjust the point dwell and set the ignition timing (see Chapter 2 "Tune-Up").

NOTE: *If the crankshaft has been turned or the engine disturbed in any manner (i.e., disassembled and rebuilt) while the distributor was removed, or if the marks were not drawn, it will be necessary to initially time the engine. Follow the procedure given below.*

INSTALLATION – ENGINE DISTURBED

1. It is necessary to place the No. 1 cylinder in the firing position to correctly install the distributor. To locate this position, the ignition timing marks on the crankshaft front pulley are used.

2. Remove the No. 1 cylinder spark plug. Turn the crankshaft until the piston in the no. 1 cylinder is moving up on the compression stroke. This can be determined by placing your thumb over the spark plug hole and feeling the air being forced out of the cylinder. Stop turning the crankshaft when the timing marks that are used to time the engine on the front pulley are aligned.

3. Oil the distributor housing lightly where the distributor bears on its mounting flange. Oil the distributor drive gear on A-series engines.

4. Install the distributor so that the rotor, which is mounted on the shaft, points toward the No. 1 spark plug terminal tower position when the cap is installed. Of course, you won't be able to see the direction in which the rotor is pointing if the cap is on the distributor, so lay the cap on the top of the distributor. Make a mark on the side of the distributor housing just below the No. 1 spark plug terminal. Make sure that the rotor points toward that mark when you install the distributor.

5. When the distributor shaft has reached the bottom of the hole, move the rotor back and forth slightly until the driving gear on the end of the shaft enters the slots cut in the end of the oil pump shaft and the distributor assem.... slides down into place.

6. When the distributor is correctly installed, the breaker points (if equipped) should be in such a position that they are just ready to break contact with each other. On electronic ignition distributors, the reluctor tooth will be very close to approaching the stator pole. This is accomplished by rotating the distributor body after it has been installed in the engine. Once again, line up the marks that you made before the distributor was removed from the engine.

7. Install the distributor holddown bolt.

8. Install the spark plug into the No. 1 spark plug hole and continue from Step 3 of the preceding distributor installation procedure.

ALTERNATOR PRECAUTIONS

To prevent damage to the alternator and regulator, the following precautionary measures must be taken when working with the the electrical system.

1. Never reverse battery connections; make sure positive is attached to positive, and negative to negative.

2. Booster batteries for starting must be connected properly. Make sure that the positive cable of the booster battery is connected to the

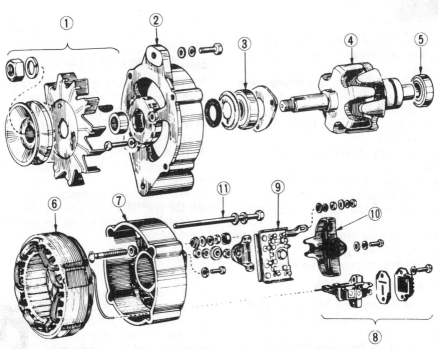

1. Pulley assembly
2. Front cover
3. Front bearing
4. Rotor
5. Rear bearing
6. Stator
7. Rear cover
8. Brush assembly
9. Diode set plate assembly
10. Diode cover
11. Through-bolt

Exploded view of 1200 and B210 alternator

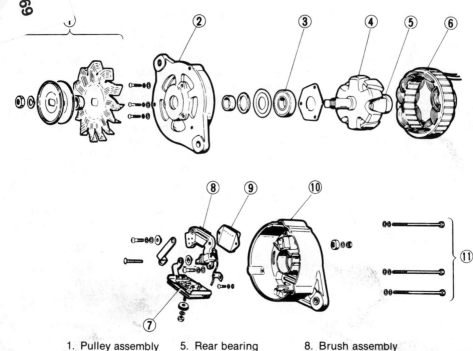

1. Pulley assembly
2. Front cover
3. Front bearing
4. Rotor
5. Rear bearing
6. Stator
7. Diode (Set plate) assembly
8. Brush assembly
9. IC voltage regulator
10. Rear cover
11. Through bolt

210 and Sentra-type integral regulator alternator

positive terminal of the battery that is getting the boost. This applies to both negative and ground cables.

3. Disconnect the battery cables before using a fast charger; the charger has a tendency to force current through the diodes in the opposite direction for which they are designed. This burns out the diodes.

4. Never use a fast charger as a booster for starting the vehicle.

5. Never disconnect the voltage regulator while the engine is running.

6. Do not ground the alternator output terminal.

7. Do not operate the alternator on an open circuit with the field energized.

8. Do not attempt to polarize an alternator.

REMOVAL AND INSTALLATION

1. Disconnect the negative battery terminal.

2. Disconnect the two lead wires and connector from the alternator.

3. Loosen the drive belt adjusting bolt and remove the belt.

4. Unscrew the alternator attaching bolts and remove the alternator from the vehicle.

5. Install the alternator in the reverse order of removal.

Regulator

REMOVAL AND INSTALLATION

NOTE: *1978 and later models are equipped with integral regulator alternators. Since the regulator is part of the alternator, no adjustments are possible or necessary on these models.*

1. Disconnect the negative battery terminal.

2. Disconnect the electrical lead connector of the regulator.

3. Remove the two mounting screws and remove the regulator from the vehicle.

4. Install the regulator in the reverse order of removal.

ADJUSTMENT

1. Adjust the voltage regulator core gap by loosening the screw which is used to secure the contact set on the yoke, and move the contact up or down as necessary. Retighten the screw. The gap should be 0.6-1.0mm.

2. Adjust the point gap of the voltage regulator coil by loosening the screw used to secure the upper contact and move the upper contact up or down. The gap for 1973-76 1200 and B210 models is 0.3-0.4mm. The point gap for all oth-

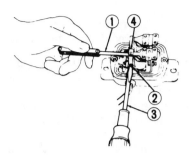

1. Feeler gauge 3. Phillips screwdriver
2. Screw 4. Upper contact

Adjusting voltage regulator point gap

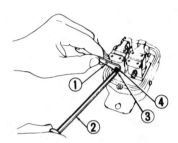

1. Wrench 3. Adjusting screw
2. Phillips screwdriver 4. Locknut

Adjusting the regulated voltage, voltage regulator models

er models with separate regulators is 0.35-0.45mm.

3. The core gap and point gap on the 0.8-1.0mm and the point gap adjusted to 0.4-0.6mm.

4. The regulated voltage is adjusted by loosening the locknut and turning the adjusting screw clockwise to increase, or counterclockwise to decrease the regulated voltage. The voltage should be between 14.3-15.3 volts at 68°F.

Battery

Refer to Chapter One for details on battery maintenance.

REMOVAL AND INSTALLATION

1. Disconnect the negative (ground) cable from the terminal, and then the positive cable. Special pullers are available to remove the cable clamps, if they seem stuck.

NOTE: *To avoid sparks, always disconnect the ground cable first, and connect it last.*

2. Remove the battery holddown clamp.

3. Remove the battery, being careful not to spill the acid.

NOTE: *Spilled acid can be neutralized with a baking soda/water solution. If you somehow*

Alternator and Regulator Specifications

Model	Year	Alternator Identification Number	Rated Output @ 5000 RPM	Output @ 2500 RPM (not less than)	Brush Length	Brush Spring Tension (oz)	Regulated Voltage
1200	1973	LT135-138	35	14	0.571	8.80–12.32	14.3–15.3
B210	1973–74	LT135-13B	35	14	0.571	8.99–12.17	14.3–.5.3
		LT150-05 ③	50	28	0.571	8.99–12.17	14.3–15.3
B210	1975–76	LT150-19	50	37.5	0.295	9.0–12.2	14.3–15.3
B210	1977	LT150-26	50	37.5	0.295	9.0–12.2	14.3–15.3
B210	1978	LT150-36 ①	50	40	0.295	9.0–12.2	14.3–15.3
210	1979–80	LR150-36 ①	50	40	0.295	8.99–12.17	14.4–15.0
210	1981–82	LR150-99 ② ①	50	40	0.28	8.99–12.17	14.4–15.0
Sentra Gasoline	1982–86	LR150-125B ①	50	42	0.28	8.99–12.17	14.4–15.0
Sentra Diesel	1984–86	LR150-402	50	42	0.28	6.35–12.70	14.4–15.0
		LR160-401	60	50	0.28	6.35–12.70	14.4–15.0
Sentra Diesel	1987	LR170-404	60	56	0.236	6.35–12.70	14.1–14.7
Sentra Gasoline	1987	A5T41592	60	50	0.31	10.93–15.7	14.1–14.7
	1987–88	LR160-715	57	48	0.276	9.88–14.11	14.1-14.7

① Uses integral voltage regulator
② LR150-99B in 1982
③ Optional

get acid into your eyes, flush it out with lots of water and get to a doctor.

4. Clean the battery posts thoroughly before reinstalling, or when installing a new battery.

5. Clean the cable clamps, using a wire brush, both inside and out.

CAUTION: *Make absolutely sure that the battery is connected properly (positive to positive, negative to negative)! Reversed polarity can burn out your alternator and regulator in a matter of seconds.*

6. Install the battery and the holddown clamp or strap. Connect the positive, and the negative cable (see "Note" above). Do not hammer the cables onto the terminal posts. The assembled terminals should be coated lightly (externally) – with petroleum jelly or grease to help prevent corrosion. There are also felt washers impregnated with an anti-corrosion substance which are slipped over the battery posts before installing the cables; these are available in most auto parts stores.

Starter

Datsun began using a gear reduction starter in 1978 and later Canadian models. The differences between the gear reduction and conventional starters are: the gear reduction starter has a set of ratio reduction gears while the conventional starter does not; the brushes on the gear reduction starter are located on a plate behind the starter drive housing, while the conventional starter's brushes are located in its rear cover. The extra gears on the gear reduction starter make the starter pinion gear turn at about half the speed of the starter, giving the starter twice the turning power of a conven-

Note the wire locations before removing the starter

tional starter. There is no difference in removal and installation procedures between the two.

REMOVAL AND INSTALLATION

1. Disconnect the negative battery cable from the battery.

2. Disconnect the starter wiring at the starter, taking note of the positions for correct reinstallation.

3. Remove the bolts attaching the starter to the engine and remove the starter from the vehicle.

4. Install the starter in the reverse order of removal.

SOLENOID REMOVAL AND INSTALLATION

1. Disconnect the battery negative cable. Note routing and then disconnect all starter wiring.

2. Note the location of the solenoid on top of the starter motor itself. If there is plenty of room, you can remove the solenoid with the starter mounted on the engine. Otherwise, remove the starter from the engine as described above.

3. Remove the two through bolts from the starter front housing or gear case. Slide the solenoid to the rear slightly and grasp the shims which are mounted between the solenoid and front housing or gear case to keep them with the assembly. Then, pull the solenoid assembly upward and to the rear so as to disengage the front end of the solenoid plunger from the shift lever. Once the plunger is free, remove the solenoid assembly.

4. To install the solenoid, first position the shims against the front of the unit, carefully lining up the through-bolt holes in them with those in the front of the solenoid body. If necessary, turn the plunger so the slot will fit over the vertical top of the shift lever, which is located in the front housing or gear case. Then, work the unit into position with the front end of the plunger near the top of the opening in the gear case or front housing.

5. Position the opening in the front of the plunger over the shift lever and then lower the assembly so as to engage the plunger with the lever. Then, position the shims and solenoid so all bolt holes will line up.

6. Install the through bolts and washers from in front of the gear case or front housing, if necessary turning the shims and solenoid assembly to line up the holes more perfectly. Torque the through bolts alternately and evenly to about 5 ft. lbs.

7. If necessary, reinstall the starter. Then, install the main battery cable and the two ignition cables, each to its correct terminal. Make sure the terminals are clean, and install the

nuts and washers securely. Connect the battery negative cable and test the starter.

OVERHAUL

Non-Reduction Gear Type

1. With the starter out of the vehicle, remove the bolts holding the solenoid to the top of the starter and remove the solenoid as described above.

2. To remove the brushes, remove the two thru-bolts, and the two rear cover attaching screws. Remove the dust cover, the retaining clip, and thrust washers (make sure to retain these carefully). Then, remove the rear cover.

3. Disconnect the electrical leads, lift up the brush spring with a wire hook and remove the brushes.

4. Remove the shift lever spring and then remove the shift lever from the front gear case.

5. Separate the gear case from the yoke housing. Then, pull the yoke off the armature. Inspect the dust cover in the gear case and replace it if it is cracked or brittle.

6. Remove the pinion stop washer C-clip by prying it out of the groove with a screwdriver and then sliding it off the shaft. Slide the return spring off the shaft. Slide the pinion stop washer off the shaft.

7. Slide the starter drive pinion off the armature shaft.

8. Check the drive pinion for an ineffective one-way clutch: the pinion must rotate freely on its splined center in one direction and lock tightly immediately when turned the other way. Check it also for teeth that are worn or broken. Replace the assembly if there are problems in either area.

9. Install the drive pinion onto the armature shaft by sliding it into position, engaging the internal, helical splines with those on the shaft. Slide and rotate the pinion into position. Install the return spring.

10. Slide the pinion stop washer onto the shaft. Install a new C-clip so it rests securely in the groove all the way around.

11. Inspect the lengths of the brushes with a small ruler. Inspect the brush spring tension with a spring scale. If under specifications, if the brush mounting plate is bent, or if the brushes do not slide freely, replace the brush assembly.

12. Insert the front end of the armature shaft into the front gear case. Assemble the yoke over the armature shaft, putting the through-bolt holes in the horizontal position and lining them up with those in the front gear case. Assemble the shift lever and spring into the cover.

13. Pull the brushes upward with a wire hook and work the brush holder assembly and brushes over the commutator. Release the wire

hook and then connect the electrical connectors.

14. Install the rear cover over the armature shaft and yoke assembly, aligning all the boltholes. Install the through bolts and cover bolts.

15. Install the thrust washers, E-clip and dust cover.

16. Install the solenoid as described above. Wire the primary connectors to the solenoid without connecting the large field connector. Then, energize the solenoid for a short time (30 seconds or less) while you measure the distance between the front of the pinion gear and the inside of the gear case. Clearance must be 0.30-2.5mm. If not, change the solenoid mounting shims to correct the clearance (thicker shims increase the clearance).

17. Install the starter as described above.

Reduction Gear Type

1. Remove the starter. Remove the solenoid.

2. Remove the dust cover. Pry the E-ring off with a small, blunt instrument. Remove the thrust washers. Remove the through bolts, brush holder setscrews, and the rear cover. The rear cover can be pried off with a small, blunt

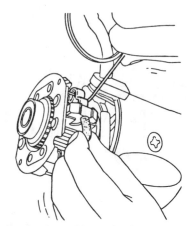

Lift brush spring with a wire hook and remove brush on non-reduction starters

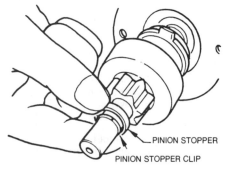

Pinion stopper removal

PINION STOPPER

PINION STOPPER CLIP

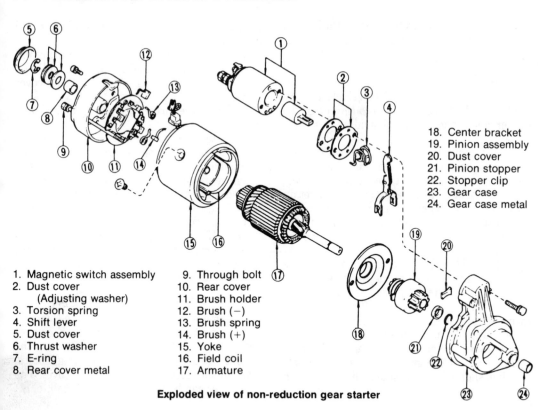

18. Center bracket
19. Pinion assembly
20. Dust cover
21. Pinion stopper
22. Stopper clip
23. Gear case
24. Gear case metal

1. Magnetic switch assembly	9. Through bolt
2. Dust cover	10. Rear cover
(Adjusting washer)	11. Brush holder
3. Torsion spring	12. Brush (−)
4. Shift lever	13. Brush spring
5. Dust cover	14. Brush (+)
6. Thrust washer	15. Yoke
7. E-ring	16. Field coil
8. Rear cover metal	17. Armature

Exploded view of non-reduction gear starter

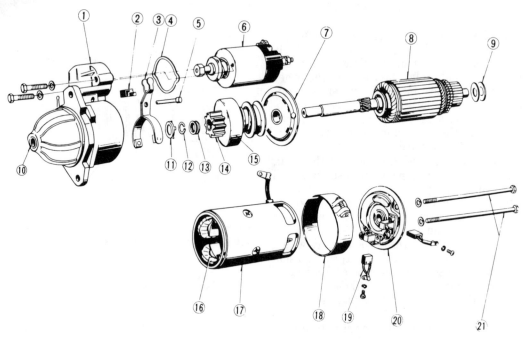

1. End housing	8. Armature	15. Overrunning clutch
2. Dust cover	9. Thrust washer	16. Field coil
3. Lever	10. Bushing	17. Yoke
4. Dust cover	11. Stop washer	18. Brush cover
5. Pin	12. Stop clip	19. Brush
6. Solenoid	13. Pinion retainer	20. Rear cover
7. Center bracket	14. Pinion	21. Through-bolt

Exploded view of 1200 and B210 starter

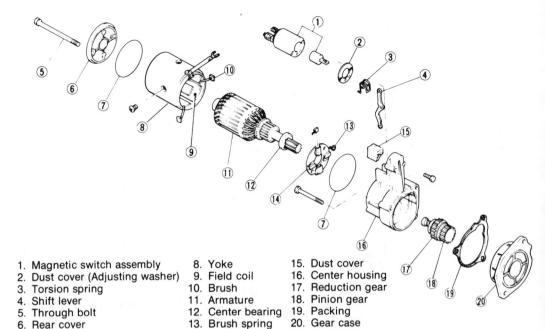

1. Magnetic switch assembly
2. Dust cover (Adjusting washer)
3. Torsion spring
4. Shift lever
5. Through bolt
6. Rear cover
7. O-ring
8. Yoke
9. Field coil
10. Brush
11. Armature
12. Center bearing
13. Brush spring
14. Brush holder
15. Dust cover
16. Center housing
17. Reduction gear
18. Pinion gear
19. Packing
20. Gear case

Gear reduction starter

instrument, but be careful not to damage the O-ring.

3. Lift the brush spring and hold it against the side of the negative brush (at the top) to separate the brush from the commutator. The positive brush is insulated from the brush holder, and its lead wire is connected to the field coil in the yoke. Remove the positive brush from the brush holder by lifting the brush spring upward. Then, remove the brush holder from the commutator.

4. Remove the yoke from the armature and front gear case. Then, remove the armature and the shift lever from the front gear case.

5. Slide the pinion-retaining stop washer toward the rear. Then, carefully pry the C-clip out of the groove in the forward direction and work it off the shaft. Finally, slide the washer off the armature shaft followed by the pinion assembly.

6. Pry the E-clip off the idler gear shaft. Then, remove the dust cover and drive the idler gear shaft out of the gear housing toward the rear by gently tapping the end with a hammer and dull punch.

7. Inspect the commutator surface. It may be sanded very lightly with No. 500-600 sandpaper. If there is a great deal of wear or roughness, it should be taken to an electrical shop and machined. Ideally, the armature and field coils should be taken to an electrical shop and subjected to a number of continuity tests to verify that insulation and conductors are in good shape.

8. Inspect the length of each brush. Replace any that are worn beyond limits. The new brush must be soldered onto the field coil in the yoke. This work should be performed by a competent auto-electrical shop. Test the brush springs for tension and replace, if necessary.

9. Check the drive pinion for an ineffective one-way clutch: the pinion must rotate freely on its splined center in one direction and lock tightly immediately when turned the other way. Check it also for teeth that are worn or broken. Replace the assembly if there are problems in either area.

10. Apply multipurpose grease sparingly to the following parts:

● The frictional surface of the pinion.
● The wearing surfaces of the shift lever.
● The solenoid plunger where it slides mechanically.
● The armature bearing surfaces in the front gear case and rear cover.

11. Then, install the idler gear into the gear housing with the flange facing the rear. Insert the shaft with the E-clip groove facing to the rear and tap it into the housing from the rear. Install the E-clip onto the idler gear shaft. Install the dust cover.

12. Install the pinion gear onto the armature shaft, followed by the retaining washer. Work the C-clip onto the shaft and into the groove. Then, work the washer back over the C-clip.

13. Carefully position the armature into the front gear case with the flange on the idler gear

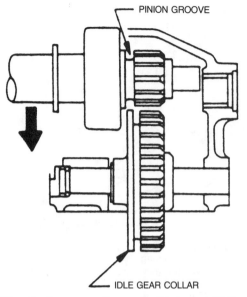

PINION GROOVE

IDLE GEAR COLLAR

Align the flange or collar on the idler gear with the groove on the pinion gear when assembling the armature into the front gear case on the reduction gear starter

fitting into the groove at the rear of the pinion gear.

14. Install the shift lever and dust cover. Install the yoke over the armature with the through-bolt holes aligned.

15. Install the brush holder around the commutator. Install the negative brush (at the top) so it rests against the commutator. Install the positive brush into the brush holder by lifting the brush spring upward.

16. Install the through bolts, brush holder setscrews, and the rear cover. Install the thrust washers and the E-ring. Install the dust cover.

17. Install the solenoid as described above. Energize the solenoid primary terminals by connecting them to the battery with a jumper wire and mark the position of the front of the idler gear. Then, measure the position of the front of the gear when it is pulled forward all the way by hand and its center rests against the housing. This dimension must be 0.3-2.5mm. If necessary, change the number/thickness of the shims under the solenoid to bring the dimension within specifications.

Battery and Starter Specifications

All cars use 12 volt, negative ground electrical systems

Year	Model	Battery Amp Hour Capacity	Lock Test Amps	Lock Test Volts	Lock Test Torque (ft. lbs.)	No Load Test Amps	No Load Test Volts	No Load Test RPM	Brush Spring Tension (oz)	Min Brush Length (in)
1973	1200	45	420	6.3	6.5 MT	60	12	7,000	56	0.26
					7.2 AT	60	12	6,000	29	0.37
1974–78	B210	60	420	6.3	6.5	60	12	7,000	49–64	0.47
			—	—	—	60	12	6,000 ①	29	0.37
			—	—	—	100 RG	12	4,300 RG	56–70	0.43
1979–82	210	60	—	—	—	60	11.5	7,000	50–64	0.47
						100 RG	11	3,900	56–70	0.43
1982–86	Sentra Gasoline	60/70 ②	—	—	—	60	11.5	7,000	50–64	0.43
1984–86	Sentra Diesel	70/80	—	—	—	<100	11.5	>3,900	56–70	0.43
1987	Sentra MT	60/65 ③	—	—	—	<100	11	>3,900	56–70	0.43
	Gasoline AT ④					<70	11	>1,800	64–78	0.47
	AT ⑤					<70	11.5	>1,800	50–90	0.453
1987	Sentra Diesel	80	—	—	—	<140	11	>3,900	96–116	0.35
1988	Sentra ⑥	60/65 ③	—	—	—	<60	11.5	>7,000	—	0.43
	Sentra ⑦					<100	11	>3,900	56–70	0.43
	Diesel ⑧					<70	11.5	>1,800	50–90	0.453

MT: Manual Transmission
AT: Automatic Transmission
RG: Reduction gear type starter (Canada)
① 1974 Automatic Transmission models only
—: Not recommended
② 1982–83: 30A U.S.A. MPG model; 65A Canada

③ 1987–88 30A Standard USA; 65A USA option, Canada
④ Hitachi
⑤ Mitsubishi
⑥ California
⑦ Manual trans, 49 states
⑧ Auto trans and 4 wd

18. Install the starter into the car and reconnect the battery.

ENGINE MECHANICAL

Design

The "A Series" engines used in the 1200, B210 and 210 models covered in this book are all members of the same "family". The A12, A12A, A13, A14 and A15 series of engines are all water cooled, inline, overhead valve, four cylinder powerplants. All of these engines utilize a cast iron block and an aluminum cylinder head. Camshafts in these engines are placed high in the block, allowing for short pushrods, which in turn means low valve train reciprocating weight and higher engine speeds. The A12 through A15's also have in common a five main bearing crankshaft. The engines differ mainly in displacement, which becomes greater as the number after the "A" prefix becomes greater (A12's are 1200 cubic centimeters, A13's 1300 and so on).

The "E series" engines used in the Nissan Sentra depart significantly in engine design from the "A series engines. The Sentra E15 and E16 engine utilizes a single overhead camshaft and "hemi"combustion chambers. Distributor drive on the "E" series engines also departs from its Datsun cousins, and follows proven European practice of driving the distributor directly off of the overhead cam.

In 1984, an all new overhead cam, 4-cylinder diesel was introduced. This lightweight diesel displaces 1680cc and is designated the CD17.

Engines are referred to by model designation codes throughout this book. Use the "General Engine Specifications" table in this chapter for the identification of engines by model and displacement.

Engine Overhaul Tips

Most engine overhaul procedures are fairly standard. In addition to specific parts replacement procedures and complete specifications for your individual engine, this chapter also is a guide to accept rebuilding procedures. Examples of standard rebuilding practice are shown and should be used along with specific details concerning your particular engine.

Competent and accurate machine shop services will ensure maximum performance, reliability and engine life.

In most instances it is more profitable for the do-it-yourself mechanic to remove, clean and inspect the component, buy the necessary parts and deliver these to a shop for actual machine work.

On the other hand, much of the rebuilding work (crankshaft, block, bearings, piston rods, and other components) is well within the scope of the do-it-yourself mechanic.

TOOLS

The tools required for an engine overhaul or parts replacement will depend on the depth of your involvement. With a few exceptions, they will be the tools found in a mechanic's tool kit (see Chapter 1). More in-depth work will require any or all of the following:

- a dial indicator (reading in thousandths) mounted on a universal base
- micrometers and telescope gauges
- jaw and screw-type pullers
- scraper
- valve spring compressor
- ring groove cleaner
- piston ring expander and compressor
- ridge reamer
- cylinder hone or glaze breaker
- Plastigage®
- engine stand

Use of most of these tools is illustrated in this chapter. Many can be rented for a one-time use from a local parts jobber or tool supply house specializing in automotive work.

Occasionally, the use of special tools is called for. See the information on Special Tools and Safety Notice in the front of this book before substituting another tool.

INSPECTION TECHNIQUES

Procedures and specifications are given in this chapter for inspecting, cleaning and assessing the wear limits of most major components. Other procedures such as Magnaflux® and Zyglo® can be used to locate material flaws and stress cracks. Magnaflux® is a magnetic process applicable only to ferrous materials. The Zyglo® process coats the material with a fluorescent dye penetrant and can be used on any material Check for suspected surface cracks can be more readily made using spot check dye. The dye is sprayed onto the suspected area, wiped off and the area sprayed with a developer. Cracks will show up brightly.

OVERHAUL TIPS

Aluminum has become extremely popular for use in engines, due to its low weight. Observe the following precautions when handling aluminum parts:

• Never hot tank aluminum parts (the caustic hot tank solution will eat the aluminum.

• Remove all aluminum parts (identification tag, etc.) from engine parts prior to the tanking.

• Always coat threads lightly with engine oil or anti-seize compounds before installation, to prevent seizure.

• Never over-torque bolts or spark plugs especially in aluminum threads.

Stripped threads in any component can be repaired using any of several commercial repair kits (Heli-Coil®, Microdot®, Keenserts®, etc.).

When assembling the engine, any parts that will be frictional contact must be prelubed to provide lubrication at initial start-up. Any product specifically formulated for this purpose can be used, but engine oil is not recommended as a prelube.

When semi-permanent (locked, but removable) installation of bolts or nuts is desired, threads should be cleaned and coated with Loctite® or other similar, commercial non-hardening sealant.

REPAIRING DAMAGED THREADS

Several methods of repairing damaged threads are available. Heli-Coil® (shown here), Keenserts® and Microdot® are among the most widely used. All involve basically the same principle—drilling out stripped threads, tapping the hole and installing a prewound insert—making welding, plugging and oversize fasteners unnecessary.

Two types of thread repair inserts are usually supplied—a standard type for most Inch Coarse, Inch Fine, Metric Course and Metric Fine thread sizes and a spark lug type to fit most spark plug port sizes. Consult the individ-

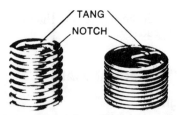

Standard thread repair insert (left) and spark plug thread insert (right)

Drill out the damaged threads with specified drill. Drill completely through the hole or to the bottom of a blind hole

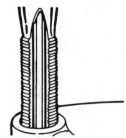

With the tap supplied, tap the hole to receive the thread insert. Keep the tap well oiled and back it out frequently to avoid clogging the threads

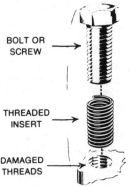

Damaged bolt holes can be repaired with thread repair inserts

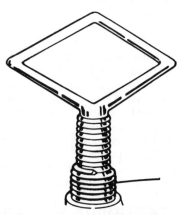

Screw the threaded insert onto the installation tool until the tang engages the slot. Screw the insert into the tapped hole until it is ¼–½ turn below the top surface. After installation break off the tang with a hammer and punch

ual manufacturer's catalog to determine exact applications. Typical thread repair kits will contain a selection of prewound threaded inserts, a tap (corresponding to the outside diameter threads of the insert) and an installation tool. Spark plug inserts usually differ because they require a tap equipped with pilot threads and a combined reamer/tap section. Most manufacturers also supply blister-packed thread repair inserts separately in addition to a master kit containing a variety of taps and inserts plus installation tools.

Before effecting a repair to a threaded hole, remove any snapped, broken or damaged bolts or studs. Penetrating oil can be used to free frozen threads; the offending item can be removed with locking pliers or with a screw or stud extractor. After the hole is clear, the thread can be repaired, as follows:

Checking Engine Compression

A noticeable lack of engine power, excessive oil consumption and/or poor fuel mileage measured over an extended period are all indicators of internal engine war. Worn piston rings, scored or worn cylinder bores, blown head gaskets, sticking or burnt valves and worn valve seats are all possible culprits here. A check of each cylinder's compression will help you locate the problems.

As mentioned in the Tools and Equipment section of Chapter 1, a screw-in type compression gauge is more accurate that the type you simply hold against the spark plug hole, although it takes slightly longer to use. It's worth it to obtain a more accurate reading. Follow the procedures below for gasoline and diesel engined trucks.

Gasoline Engines

1. Warm up the engine to normal operating temperature.
2. Remove all spark plugs.
3. Disconnect the high tension lead from the ignition coil.
4. On fully open the throttle either by operating the carburetor throttle linkage by hand or by having an assistant floor the accelerator pedal.
5. Screw the compression gauge into the no.1 spark plug hole until the fitting is snug.

NOTE: *Be careful not to crossthread the plug hole. On aluminum cylinder heads use extra care, as the threads in these heads are easily ruined.*

6. Ask an assistant to depress the accelerator pedal fully on both carbureted and fuel injected trucks. Then, while you read the compression

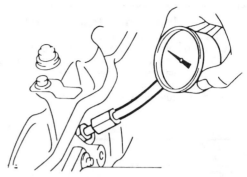

The screw-in type compression gauge is more accurate

gauge, ask the assistant to crank the engine two or three times in short bursts using the ignition switch.

7. Read the compression gauge at the end of each series of cranks, and record the highest of these readings. Repeat this procedure for each of the engine's cylinders. Compare the highest reading of each cylinder to the compression pressure specification in the Tune-Up Specifications chart in Chapter 2. The specs in this chart are maximum values.

A cylinder's compression pressure is usually acceptable if it is not less than 80% of maximum. The difference between each cylinder should be no more than 12-14 pounds.

8. If a cylinder is unusually low, pour a tablespoon of clean engine oil into the cylinder through the spark plug hole and repeat the compression test. If the compression comes up after adding the oil, it appears that the cylinder's piston rings or bore are damaged or worn. If the pressure remains low, the valves may not be seating properly (a valve job is needed), or the head gasket may be blown near that cylinder. If compression in any two adjacent cylinders is low, and if the addition of oil doesn't help the compression, there is leakage past the head gasket. Oil and coolant water in the combustion chamber can result from this problem. There may be evidence of water droplets on the engine dipstick when a head gasket has blown.

Diesel Engines

Checking cylinder compression on diesel engines is basically the same procedure as on gasoline engines except for the following:

1. A special compression gauge adaptor suitable for diesel engines (because these engines have much greater compression pressures) must be used.
2. Remove the injector tubes and remove the injectors from each cylinder.

NOTE: *Don't forget to remove the washer underneath each injector; otherwise, it may get lost when the engine is cranked.*

Standard Torque Specifications and Fastener Markings

In the absence of specific torques, the following chart can be used as a guide to the maximum safe torque of a particular size/grade of fastener.

- There is no torque difference for fine or coarse threads.
- Torque values are based on clean, dry threads. Reduce the value by 10% if threads are oiled prior to assembly.
- The torque required for aluminum components or fasteners is considerably less.

U.S. Bolts

SAE Grade Number	1 or 2			5			6 or 7		
Number of lines always 2 less than the grade number.									
Bolt Size (Inches)—(Thread)	Maximum Torque			Maximum Torque			Maximum Torque		
	Ft./Lbs.	Kgm	Nm	Ft./Lbs.	Kgm	Nm	Ft./Lbs.	Kgm	Nm
¼ — 20	5	0.7	6.8	8	1.1	10.8	10	1.4	13.5
— 28	6	0.8	8.1	10	1.4	13.6			
5/16 — 18	11	1.5	14.9	17	2.3	23.0	19	2.6	25.8
— 24	13	1.8	17.6	19	2.6	25.7			
3/8 — 16	18	2.5	24.4	31	4.3	42.0	34	4.7	46.0
— 24	20	2.75	27.1	35	4.8	47.5			
7/16 — 14	28	3.8	37.0	49	6.8	66.4	55	7.6	74.5
— 20	30	4.2	40.7	55	7.6	74.5			
½ — 13	39	5.4	52.8	75	10.4	101.7	85	11.75	115.2
— 20	41	5.7	55.6	85	11.7	115.2			
9/16 — 12	51	7.0	69.2	110	15.2	149.1	120	16.6	162.7
— 18	55	7.6	74.5	120	16.6	162.7			
5/8 — 11	83	11.5	112.5	150	20.7	203.3	167	23.0	226.5
— 18	95	13.1	128.8	170	23.5	230.5			
¾ — 10	105	14.5	142.3	270	37.3	366.0	280	38.7	379.6
— 16	115	15.9	155.9	295	40.8	400.0			
7/8 — 9	160	22.1	216.9	395	54.6	535.5	440	60.9	596.5
— 14	175	24.2	237.2	435	60.1	589.7			
1 — 8	236	32.5	318.6	590	81.6	799.9	660	91.3	894.8
— 14	250	34.6	338.9	660	91.3	849.8			

Metric Bolts

Relative Strength Marking	4.6, 4.8			8.8		
Bolt Markings						
Bolt Size Thread Size x Pitch (mm)	Maximum Torque			Maximum Torque		
	Ft./Lbs.	Kgm	Nm	Ft./Lbs.	Kgm	Nm
6 x 1.0	2–3	.2–.4	3–4	3–6	.4–.8	5–8
8 x 1.25	6–8	.8–1	8–12	9–14	1.2–1.9	13–19
10 x 1.25	12–17	1.5–2.3	16–23	20–29	2.7–4.0	27–39
12 x 1.25	21–32	2.9–4.4	29–43	35–53	4.8–7.3	47–72
14 x 1.5	35–52	4.8–7.1	48–70	57–85	7.8–11.7	77–110
16 x 1.5	51–77	7.0–10.6	67–100	90–120	12.4–16.5	130–160
18 x 1.5	74–110	10.2–15.1	100–150	130–170	17.9–23.4	180–230
20 x 1.5	110–140	15.1–19.3	150–190	190–240	26.2–46.9	160–320
22 x 1.5	150–190	22.0–26.2	200–260	250–320	34.5–44.1	340–430
24 x 1.5	190–240	26.2–46.9	260–320	310–410	42.7–56.5	420–550

Torque Specifications
All readings in ft. lbs.

Engine Model	Cylinder Head Bolts	Main Bearing Bolts	Rod Bearing Bolts	Crankshaft Pulley Bolt	Flywheel to Crankshaft Bolts	Manifolds Intake	Manifolds Exhaust
A12	40–43	36–43	23–28	108–116	47–54	7–10	7–10
A13	51–54	36–43	23–27	108–145	54–61	7–10	7–10
A12A, A14, A15	51–54	36–43	23–27	108–145	58–65 ①	11–14	11–14
E15	51–54 ②	36–43	23–27	83–108	58–65	12–15	12–15
E16	51–54 ③	36–43	23–27	83–108 ④	58–65	12–15	12–15
CD17	72–80	33–40	23–27	90–98	72–80	13–16	13–16

① 1975–77 A14: 54–61 ft. lbs.
② Second (final) torquing. First torque to 29–33 ft. lbs.
③ This is done in a complex sequence—see text
④ 1987–88—80–94

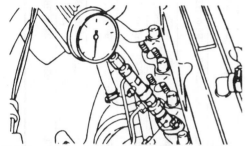

Diesel engines require a special compression gauge adaptor

3. When fitting the compression gauge adaptor to the cylinder head, make sure the bleeder of the gauge (if equipped) is closed.

4. When reinstalling the injector assemblies, install new washers underneath each injector.

Engine

REMOVAL AND INSTALLATION

All A-series Models

NOTE: *The engine and transmission are removed together and then separated when out of the car.*

1. Mark the location of the hinges on the bottom of the hood with a scribe or grease pencil for later installation. Unbolt and remove the hood.

2. Disconnect the battery cables.

3. Drain the coolant from the radiator, and drain the automatic transmission fluid.

CAUTION: *When draining the coolant, keep in mind that cats and dogs are attracted by the ethylene glycol antifreeze, and are quite likely to drink any that is left in an uncovered* container or in puddles on the ground. This will prove fatal in sufficient quantity. Always drain the coolant into a sealable container. Coolant should be reused unless it is contaminated or several years old.

4. Remove the radiator and radiator shroud after disconnecting the automatic transmission coolant tubes (if equipped).

5. Remove the air cleaner.

6. Remove the fan and pulley.

7. Disconnect:
   a. Water temperature gauge wire.
   b. Oil pressure sending unit wire.
   c. Ignition distributor primary wire.
   d. Starter motor connections.
   e. Fuel hose.
   f. Alternator leads.
   g. Heater hoses.
   h. Throttle and choke connections.

Engine I.D. Table

Vehicle	Number of Cylinders	Displacement cu. in. (cc)	Type	Engine Model Code
1200	4	71.5 (1171)	OHV	A12
B210	4	78.59 (1288)	OHV	A13
	4	85.24 (1397)	OHV	A14
210	4	75.5 (1237)	OHV	A12A
	4	85.3 (1397)	OHV	A14
	4	90.8 (1488)	OHV	A15
Sentra	4	90.8 (1488)	OHC	E15
	4	97.6 (1597)	OHC	E16
	4	102.5 (1680)	OHC	CD17

NOTE: OHV is Overhead Valve
OHC is Overhead Cam

General Engine Specifications

Year	Model	Type (model)	Engine Displacement Cu In. (cc)	Fuel System Type	Horsepower (SAE) @ rpm	Torque @ rpm (ft. lbs.)	Bore x Stroke (in.)	Compression Ratio	Normal Oil Pressure (psi)
1973	1200 Sedan 1200 Coupe	OHV 4 (A12)	71.5 (1171)	2 bbl	69 @ 6000	70 @ 4000	2.87 x 2.76	8.5:1	54–60
1974	B210 Sedan, Coupe	OHV 4 (A13)	78.6 (1288)	2 bbl	75 @ 6000	77 @ 3600	2.87 x 3.03	8.5:1	43–50
1975	B210 Sedan, Coupe	OHV 4 (A14)	85.24 (1397)	2 bbl	78 @ 6000	75 @ 4000	3.09 x 3.03	8.5:1	43–50
1976–78	B210	OHV 4 (A14)	85.2 (1397)	2 bbl	80 @ 6000	83 @ 3600	2.99 x 3.03	8.5:1	43–50
1979–82	210, 210 MPG	OHV 4 (A12A)	75.5 (1237)	2 bbl	58 @ 5600	67 @ 3600	2.95 x 2.75	8.5:1	43–50
		OHV 4 (A14)	85.3 (1397)	2 bbl	65 @ 5600	75 @ 3600	2.99 x 3.03	8.5:1 ①	43–50
		OHV 4 (A15)	90.8 (1488)	2 bbl	67 @ 5200	80 @ 3200	2.99 x 3.23	8.9:1	43–50
1982–83	Sentra	OHC 4 (E15)	90.8 (1488)	2 bbl	67 @ 5200	85 @ 3200	2.99 x 3.23	9.0:1	43–50
1983–86	Sentra	OHC 4 (E16)	97.45 (1597)	2 bbl	69 @ 5200	92 @ 3200	2.99 x 3.465	9.4:1	43–57
	Sentra Diesel	OHC 4 (CD17)	102.5 (1680)	Diesel	55 @ 4800	104 @ 2800	3.15 x 3.29	22.2:1	43–57
1987	Sentra	OHC 4 (E16)	97.45 (1597)	2 bbl	70 @ 5000	92 @ 2800	2.99 x 3.23	9.0:1	43–57
	Sentra	OHC 4 (E16)	97.45 (1597)	EFI	71 @ 5000	94 @ 2800	2.99 x 3.23	9.011	43–57
	Sentra Diesel	OHC 4 (CD17)	102.5 (1680)	Diesel	55 @ 4800	104 @ 2800	3.15 x 3.29	21.8	50–64
1988	Sentra	OHC 4 (E16)	97.45 (1597)	EFI	71 @ 5000	94 @ 2800	2.99 x 3.23	9.0:1	43–57

Crankshaft and Connecting Rod Specifications

All measurements in inches

Engine Model	Crankshaft					Connecting Rod Bearings		
	Main Brg Journal Dia	Main Brg Oil Clearance	Shaft End-Play	Thrust on No.	Journal Dia	Oil Clearance	Side Clearance
A12 (1200)	1.9671–1.9668	0.001–0.002	0.002–0.006	3	1.7701–1.7706	0.001–0.002	0.007–0.012
A13	1.966–1.967	0.0008–0.002	0.002–0.006	3	1.7701–1.7706	0.0008–0.002	0.008–0.012
A14 (1975–78)	1.966–1.967	0.008–0.002	0.002–0.006	3	1.7701–1.7706	0.0008–0.002	0.008–0.012
A12A, A14, A15 (1979–1982)	1.9663–1.9671	0.001–0.0035	0.002–0.0059	3	1.7701–1.7706	0.0012–0.0031	0.004–0.008
E15	1.9663–1.9671	0.0012–0.0030	0.002–0.0071	3	1.5730–1.5738	0.0012–0.0024	0.004–0.014
E16 through 1986	1.9663–1.9671	0.0012–0.0030 ①	0.0020–0.0071	3	1.5370–1.5378	0.0012–0.0024	0.0040–0.0146
E16 1987–88	1.9661–1.9671	0.0012–0.0022 ②	0.0020–0.0071 ③	3	1.5730–1.5738	0.0004–0.0017	0.004–0.0146
CD17 through 1986	2.0847–2.0852	0.0015–0.0026	0.0020–0.0071	3	1.7701–1.7706	0.0009–0.0026	0.0115–0.0125
CD17 1987	2.0847–2.0850	0.0015–0.0026	0.0020–0.0071	3	1.7701–1.7706	0.0013–0.0026	0.012

① #2, 3, 4: 0.0012–0.0036
② #2, 4: 0.0012–0.0036
③ 1988—0.0020–0.0065

Piston and Ring Specifications
All measurements in inches

Engine Model	Piston-to-Bore Clearance	Ring Gap			Ring Side Clearance		
		Top Compression	Bottom Compression	Oil Control	Top Compression	Bottom Compression	Oil Control
A12 1973	0.001–0.002	0.008–0.014	0.008–0.014	0.012–0.035	0.002–0.003	0.002–0.003	0.002–0.003
A13	0.001–0.002	0.008–0.014	0.008–0.014	0.012–0.035	0.002–0.003	0.002–0.003	—
A14 1975–78	0.0009–0.002	0.008–0.014	0.008–0.014	0.012–0.035	0.002–0.003	0.001–0.002	Combined ring
A12A, A14, A15 1979–82	0.0010–0.0018	0.008–0.014	0.008–0.014	0.012–0.035	0.002–0.003	0.001–0.002	Combined ring
E15	0.0009–0.0017	0.0079–0.0138	0.0059–0.0118	0.0118–0.0354	0.0016–0.0029	0.0012–0.0025	0.0020–0.0057
E16 through 1987	0.0009–0.0017	0.0079–0.0138	0.0059–0.0118	0.0118–0.0354	0.0016–0.0029	0.0012–0.0025	0.0020–0.0057
E16 1988	0.0009–0.0017	0.0079–0.0118	0.0059–0.0098	0.0079–0.0236	0.0016–0.0029	0.0012–0.0025	0.0002–0.0070
CD17 through 1986	0.0020–0.0028	0.0079–0.0138	0.0079–0.0138	0.0118–0.0177	0.0008–0.0024	0.0016–0.0031	0.0012–0.0028
CD17 1987	0.0010–0.0018	0.0079–0.0091	0.0079–0.0091	0.0118–0.0130	0.0008–0.0024	0.0016–0.0031	0.0012–0.0028

Valve Specifications

Model	Seat Angle (deg)	Spring Test Pressure lbs @ in.	Free Length (in.)	Stem-to-Guide Clearance (in.)		Stem Diameter (in.)	
				Intake	Exhaust	Intake	Exhaust
A12, A13, A14 (1973–78)	45°	52.7 @ 1.52	1.83	0.0006–0.0018	0.0016–0.0028	0.3138–0.3144	0.3128–0.3134
A12A, A14 A15 (1979–82)	45°30′	52.7 @ 1.19	1.83	0.0006–0.0018	0.0016–0.0028	0.3138–0.3144	0.3128–0.3134
E15	45°	51.66 @ 1.543	1.83	0.0008–0.0020	0.0018–0.0030	0.2744–0.2750	0.2734–0.2740
E16	45°	51.66 @ 1.543	1.83	0.0008–0.0020	0.0018–0.0030	0.2744–0.2750	0.2734–0.2740
CD17	45°30′	①	②	0.0008–0.0020	0.0016–0.0028	0.2742–0.2748	0.2734–0.2740

① Inner: 19.2 @ 1.417
   Outer: 33.7 @ 1.555
② Inner: 1.7008
   Outer: 1.8268

i. Engine ground cable.
j. Thermal transmitter wire.
k. Wire to fuel cut-off solenoid.
l. Vacuum cut solenoid wire.
NOTE: *A good rule of thumb when disconnecting the rather complex engine wiring of today's cars is to put a piece of masking tape on the wire and on the connection you removed the wire from, then mark both pieces of tape 1,2,3, etc. When replacing wiring, simply match the pieces of tape.*
CAUTION: *On models with air conditioning, it is necessary to remove the compressor and the condenser from their mounts. DO NOT ATTEMPT TO UNFASTEN ANY OF THE AIR CONDITIONER HOSES. See chapter one for additional warnings.*

8. Disconnect the power brake booster hose from the engine.
9. Remove the clutch operating cylinder and return spring.
10. Disconnect the speedometer cable from the transmission. Disconnect the backup light switch and any other wiring or attachments to the transmission.
11. Disconnect the column shift linkage. Re-

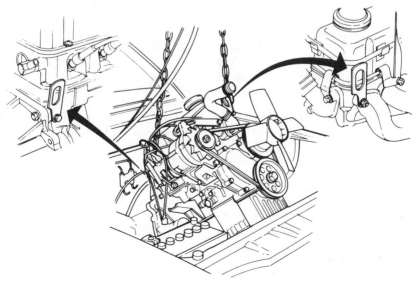

Removing the A-series engine. All engines removed in a similar manner, except Sentra which is removed sideways

Gearshift lever removal: 1200, B210. 210 similar

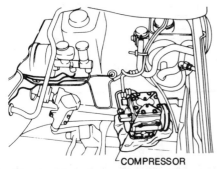

—COMPRESSOR

Secure A/C compressor to the inside of the fender or frame when removing engine on all models

move the floorshift lever. On 1200 and B210 models, remove the boot, withdraw the lock pin, and remove the lever from inside the car.

12. Detach the exhaust pipe from the exhaust manifold. Remove the front section of the exhaust manifold.

13. Mark the relationship of the driveshaft flanges with a centerpunch or scribe and remove the driveshaft. The marks are matched up later during installation; the driveshaft must be installed in the same relationship as it was removed.

14. Place a jack under the transmission. Remove the rear crossmember, keeping the jack underneath just enough for support. On 1200 and B210 models, remove the rear engine mounting nuts. Remove the front engine mount bolts from all models.

15. Attach a strong (heavy chain or heavy rope in good condition) lifting sling to the lifting eyelets on the engine. Run the sling through both eyelets, and then through a suitable pulley or other lifting device.

NOTE: *Make sure that whatever will be supporting the engine as you pull it out of the car will be able to support the weight of both engine and transmission. Many children's swing sets are not sturdy enough for this and are not recommended. Engine lifting tripods are available at any equipment rental shop, and are designed for this work.*

16. Drape a heavy cloth across the grille of the car. This will protect and cushion the grille, crossmember and engine from any damage. Slowly lift the engine up and out of the car. It is helpful to have at least two people working on this job, especially to help the transmission clear its tunnel and engine compartment. When the engine is out of the car, do not rest the weight of the entire unit on the oil pan. Be careful not to alter the length of the buffer rod on those cars so-equipped.

17. To install: Lower the engine carefully into the engine compartment with the transmission angled downward. Make sure the tranmssion will fit squarely into the transmission tunnel in the body. Then, carefully lower the assembly while leveling it off until it sits in its normal position and the various mounts line up.

18. Install and tighten the front engine mounting bolts. On 1200 and B210 models, install the rear engine mounting nuts. Install the rear crossmember, making sure the jack will continue to support the transmission until it is securely in place and the bolts are torqued. Then, remove the jack from under the transmission.

19. Remove the lifting sling and, if the car has a buffer rod, rebolt it into position securely. If the buffer rod length has not been altered, it should still be correct.

20. Attach the driveshaft to the transmission output flange, according to the marks made during removal. The driveshaft *must* be installed in the same relationship as it was removed.

21. Install the front section of the exhaust manifold. Attach the exhaust pipe to the exhaust manifold.

22. On 1200 and B210 models, install the shift lever inside the car, install the lockpin and then the boot. On other cars, reconnect the column-type shift linkage. Connect the backup light switch and any other wiring or attachments to the transmission. Connect the speedometer cable to the transmission.

23. Install and connect the clutch operating cylinder and return spring. Bleed the system as describe in Chapter 7. Connect the power brake booster hose to the engine.

24. Install the air conditioning compressor as described later in this chapter.

25. Install/connect, according to markings made earlier:

    a. Water temperature gauge wire.
    b. Oil pressure sending unit wire.
    c. Ignition distributor primary wire.
    d. Starter motor connections.
    e. Fuel hose.
    f. Alternator leads.
    g. Heater hoses.
    h. Throttle and choke connections.

i. Engine ground cable.
j. Thermal transmitter wire.
k. Wire to fuel cut-off solenoid.
l. Vacuum cut solenoid wire.
26. Install the cooling fan and pulley.

27. Install the air cleaner.
28. Install the radiator and radiator shroud. Connect the automatic transmission coolant tubes (if the car is equipped with an automatic transmission).

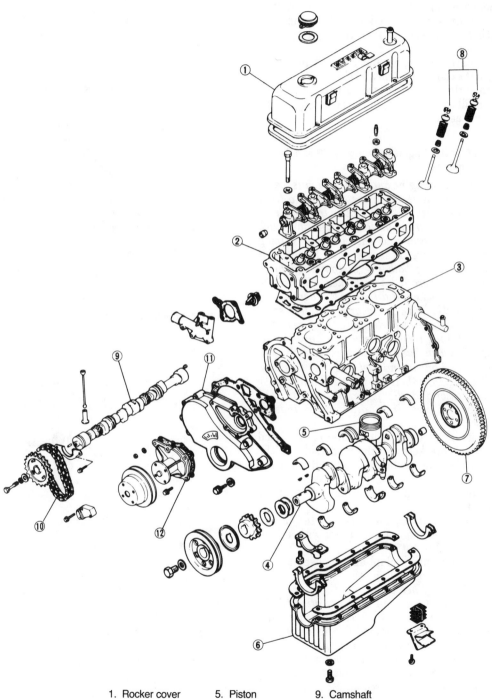

1. Rocker cover	5. Piston	9. Camshaft
2. Cylinder head	6. Oil pan	10. Timing chain
3. Cylinder block	7. Flywheel	11. Front cover
4. Crankshaft	8. Valve parts	12. Water pump

A series engine components

29. Bolt the hood into position with bolt loose. Then, align the hood with the marks made earlier and final tighten the bolts.

30. Connect the battery cables.

31. Refill the radiator with coolant. Refill the automatic transmission with the specified amount of fluid. If engine oil has been drained, replace the oil filter and refill the crankcase with the specified amount and type of lubricant.

32. Start the engine and check it for leaks. Bleed the cooling system and chedk its fluid level after the engine has cooled back off. Check and refill the fluid level in the automatic transmission as necessary.

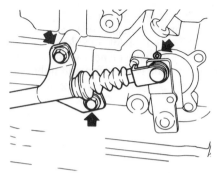

Sentra transaxle linkage attaching points

Sentra E-Series Engines Through 1986 and Sentra Diesel Engines

NOTE: *The engine and transaxle must be removed as a unit. Since the Sentra is a front wheel drive car, this is a fairly involved procedure. It is very important to label and mark all cables, hoses and vacuum lines during this procedure. Masking tape works well here. Marking both the disconnected hose, etc., and where it was attached will help to avoid the "where did that go?" later.*

CAUTION: *Be sure the car is on a flat, solid surface with the wheels chocked before beginning. Do not remove the engine until the exhaust system has cooled off completely; you will avoid burns and fuel line fires this way. Also, when unbolting the air conditioner compressor and idler pulley mount, DO NOT disconnect any air conditioning fittings or hoses.*

1. Scribe or draw a line around the hood mounting brackets on the underside of the hood, to facilitate installation later. Remove the hood.

2. Remove battery and battery support bracket.

3. Remove air cleaner and related hoses. Plug the air horn of the carburetor with a clean rag to keep dirt out.

4. Drain engine coolant and remove radiator with the radiator cooling fan.

CAUTION: *When draining the coolant, keep in mind that cats and dogs are attracted by the ethylene glycol antifreeze, and are quite likely to drink any that is left in an uncovered container or in puddles on the ground. This will prove fatal in sufficient quantity. Always drain the coolant into a sealable container. Coolant should be reused unless it is contaminated or several years old.*

5. Remove the power steering pump, if equipped.

6. Unbolt the air conditioner compressor and

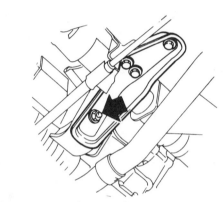

Sentra rear engine mount

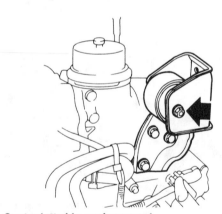

Sentra left side engine mount

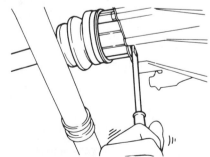

Removing Sentra halfshaft. Use care not to damage the grease seal

idler pulley bracket from the cylinder block, observing the "Caution" above. Remove the compressor drive belt and hold the compressor unit upright, attached to the car with a wire or rope.

7. Disconnect the exhaust header pipe from the exhaust manifold.

8. Disconnect the manual transaxle control rod link support rod from the transaxle.

9. Disconnect the automatic transaxle control linkage from the transaxle.

10. Remove the lower ball joint. Do not reuse the nuts once they have been removed. Replace them with new nuts.

11. Drain the transaxle gear oil or fluid.

12. Disconnect the right and left halfshafts from the transaxle.

NOTE: *When drawing out the halfshafts, it is necessary to loosen the strut head bolts so the struts can be rocked outward. Be careful not to damage the grease seal on the transaxle side.*

13. Disconnect the clutch cable.

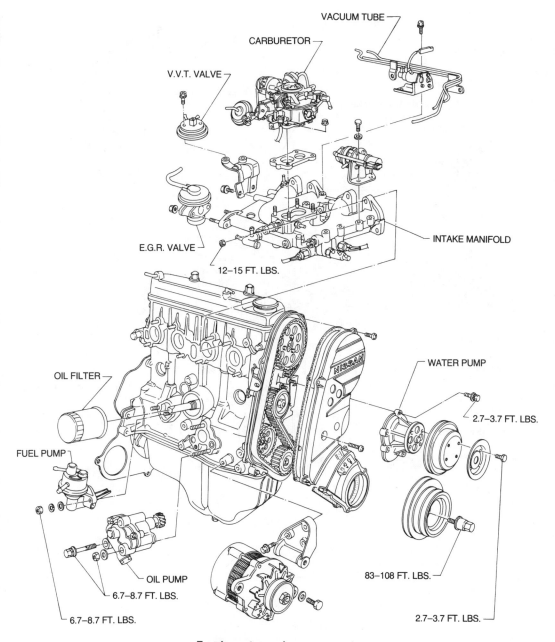

E series outer engine components

14. Remove the speedometer cable with the pinion from the transaxle. Plug the hole from which the pinion gear was removed with a clean rag to keep out dirt.

15. Disconnect the accelerator cable.

16. Disconnect any vacuum and air hoses between the engine and vehicle body. Disconnect all cables, wires and harness connectors.

17. Disconnect the fuel hoses from the fuel pump.

18. Attach a suitable sling to the lifting eyelets on the engine.

19. Unbolt the engine mounts, and lift the engine up and away from the car. The Transaxle can now be separated from the engine.

INSTALLATION

1. Install the engine with transaxle attached. When installing, make sure that the brake lines, brake master cylinder, etc., do not interfere with the engine and transaxle. Also make sure that the air conditioning compressor and power steering pump (if equipped) are securely out of the way when lowering the engine. Care-

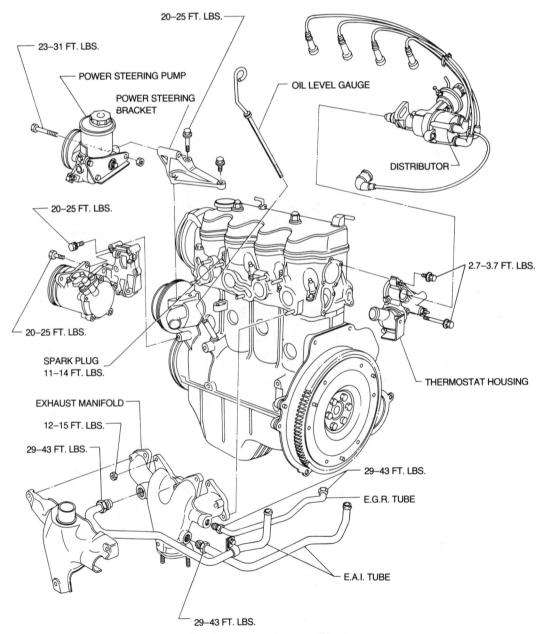

E series outer engine components

fully work the engine/transaxle assembly into position. Then, install all mounting through bolts. Tighten the engine mount bolts, making sure there is some clearance in the rubber insulator. Remove the lifting sling and crane.

2. Connect the fuel hoses to the fuel pump. Connect all cables, wires, and herness connectors. Connect the vacuum and air hoses that run from the body to the engine assembly.

3. Connect and adjust the accelerator cable.

4. Remove the rag from the transaxle and install the speedometer drive pinion gear. Reconnect the speedometer cable.

5. Reconnect the clutch cable and adjust it as described in Chapter 7.

6. Make sure the splined ends of the halfshafts are clean and then reinsert them into the transaxle. When they are securely locked in place, retorque the strut nuts where the tops of the struts are fastened to the body. Refer to Chapter 7 for additional details.

7. Install new transaxle fluid of the specified type and of the amount specified in Chapter 1.

8. Install both ball joints with new nuts and torque them as described in Chapter 9.

9. Connect the automatic transmission control linkage to the transaxle. If the car has a manual transmission, connect the control rod link support rod to the transaxle.

10. Connect the header pipe to the exhaust manifold.

11. Bolt the air conditioner compressor and idler pulley bracket to the cylinder block, observing the "Caution" above. Install the compressor drive belt.

12. Install the power steering pump, if the car has power steering. Refill the pump with approved fluid.

13. Install the radiator and cooling fan, and reconnect the fan electrical connector. Refill the cooling system with 50/50 ethylene glycol/water mix.

14. Remove the rag installed into the air horn or throttle body and install the air cleaner and related hoses.

15. Install the battery support bracket and the battery. When you are sure that all electrical connections are safely reconnected, reconnect the battery cables.

16. Install the hood with bolts loose. Align it with the marks made earlier and then torque the bolts. Start the engine, check for leaks, bleed the cooling system, and recheck and if necessary refill all fluid reservoirs.

1987-88 Sentra E Series Engines

1. Scribe the hood hinge locations on the bottom of the hood and then remove it. Disconnect the negative battery cables. Drain the cooling system, engine oil pan, and transaxle. Raise the vehicle about two feet off the ground and support it securely via major body members. Remove both front wheels.

CAUTION: *When draining the coolant, keep in mind that cats and dogs are attracted by the ethylene glycol antifreeze, and are quite likely to drink any that is left in an uncovered container or in puddles on the ground. This will prove fatal in sufficient quantity. Always drain the coolant into a sealable container. Coolant should be reused unless it is contaminated or several years old.*

The EPA warns that prolonged contact with used engine oil may cause a number of skin disorders, including cancer! You should make every effort to minimize your exposure to used engine oil. Protective gloves should be worn when changing the oil. Wash your hands and any other exposed skin areas as soon as possible after exposure to used engine oil. Soap and water, or waterless hand cleaner should be used.

2. Remove both front water shields. Refer to Chapter 9 and remove both front brake calipers without disconnecting the brake hoses.

3. Refer to Chapter 8 and disconnect Left and Right side transverse link and tie rod ball joints. Then, remove the two bolt/nut combinations on either side that retain the knuckles to the struts.

4. Gently pry the driveshafts out of either side of the transaxle, being careful not to damage the grease seals. Suspend the inner driveshaft ends on wire.

5. Locate a lifting crane and run a cable and hooks to the engine lifting hooks. Support the engine securely.

6. Remove the transaxle support rod bolt from the crossmember that runs underneath it.

7. Remove the crossmember that supports the transaxle and engine. Disconnect the exhaust pipe.

8. Remove the bolt that connects the front engine mounting buffer rod to the body.

9. Remove the air cleaner. Label and then, disconnect all wires, multiple connectors, and hoses. If the car has air conditioning, remove the compressor *without disconnecting refrigerant hoses* as described later in this chapter.

10. Lift the engine slightly and then disconnect all the engine mounts by removing the through-bolts. Remove the engine/transaxle assembly from the car, being *very cautious to avoid contacting the body and especially brake system metal tubing and the master cylinder.*

11. To install the engine, first lower it into position very cautiously and slowly to avoid contacting any body/engine compartment parts. Line up all engine mounts precisely and then install the through-bolts.

12. If necessary, install the air conditioning compressor. Reconnect the wires, multiple connectors and hoses disconnected above.

13. Install the air cleaner.

14. Install the bolt that connects the front engine mounting buffer rod to the body. Reconnect the exhaust pipe with new gaskets.

15. Install the crossmember that supports the engine/transaxle unit. Install the bolt that attaches the transaxle support rod to the crossmember.

16. Make sure the driveshaft splines are clean. Carefully reinsert them into the sides of the transaxle case, making sure not to damage the seals.

17. Install the steering knuckles onto the struts, torquing the bolts/nuts to 72-87 ft. lbs.

18. Reconnect the transverse link and tie rod ball joints torquing bolts to 43-54 ft. lbs. and 22-29 ft. lbs. respectively.

19. Install the brake calipers as described in Chapter 9. Torque the mounting bolts to 40-47 ft. lbs. Install the front watershields.

20. Resinstall the wheels. Lower the car to the ground and install and tension the belts. Refill all fluid levels. Start the engine and check for leaks. Refill the automatic transaxle when hot. Bleed the cooling system, allow the engine to cool, and refill it.

Rocker or Cam Cover

REMOVAL AND INSTALLATION

The pushrod engines used in the Datsuns covered in this manual use stamped steel rocker covers retained by six small bolts located on the outside edge of the cover. The overhead cam engines use cast alumium rocker covers retained by studs and nuts. Prior to removing either type of cover, buy a new gasket; in the case of cast alumnum covers used with studs, buy new stud seals as well.

To remove the cover:

1. Remove the air cleaner. Label and remove all hoses and wires that cross over the cover.

2. Remove the cover mounting bolts or stud nuts and washers. If a stamped cover is difficult to remove, you can bump one end. Cast covers

are usually removed easily after the seals are screwed or gently pried out with a soft instrument.

3. Replace the gasket and remount the cover in position. Install through bolts in stamped covers just finger tight. On cast covers, insert new seals and then install the washers and nuts, tightening just finger tight.

4. Tighten the retaining bolts on stamped covers gently, going around the cover from side to side and end to end in several stages. Torque the retaining nuts on cast covers in two stages, ging back and forth. First torque to 17-35 in. lbs. and then to 35-51 in. lbs.

Rocker Shaft

REMOVAL AND INSTALLATION

A12, A12A, A13, A14, A15 Engines

1. Remove the rocker cover.

2. Loosen the rocker adjusting bolts and push the adjusting screws away from the pushrods.

3. Unbolt and remove the rocker shaft assembly.

4. To install, reverse the above. Tighten the rocker shaft bolts to 14-18 ft. lbs. in a circular sequence. Adjust the valves.

NOTE: *Both the intake and the exhaust valve springs are the uneven pitch type. That is, the springs have narrow coils at the bottom and wide coils at the top. The narrow coils (painted white) must be the side making contact on the cylinder head surface.*

E-Series Engines

1. Remove the rocker cover.

2. Loosen each rocker adjusting locknut and screw slightly.

3. Unbolt the rocker shaft assembly and remove from the head.

4. Reverse the procedure for installation, torquing the rocker shaft bolts to 12-15 ft. lbs. Adjust the valves.

NOTE: *Make sure that the oil holes in the ends of the rocker shaft face downward when the rocker shaft is installed. Also, be sure that the cutout in the center retainer of the rocker shaft faces toward the exhaust manifold side when installed.*

Thermostat

REMOVAL AND INSTALLATION

All Engines

1. Drain the engine coolant into a clean container so that the coolant remaining in the engine block is below the thermostat housing.

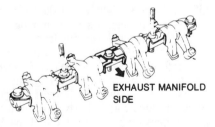

EXHAUST MANIFOLD SIDE

Make sure cutout on Sentra rocker shaft faces exhaust manifold

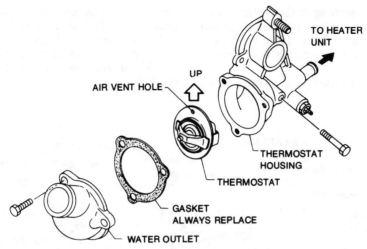

TO HEATER UNIT

UP

AIR VENT HOLE

THERMOSTAT HOUSING

THERMOSTAT

GASKET
ALWAYS REPLACE

WATER OUTLET

E-series thermostat and housing

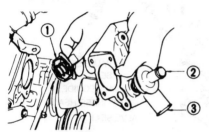

1. Thermostat 2. Air check valve 3. Water outlet
A-series thermostat removal

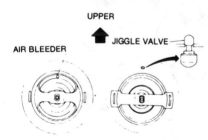

UPPER

JIGGLE VALVE

AIR BLEEDER

1980 A-series thermostat: place jiggle valve toward top

Save the drained coolant for use again, if it is still a fresh mixture.

CAUTION: *When draining the coolant, keep in mind that cats and dogs are attracted by the ethylene glycol antifreeze, and are quite likely to drink any that is left in an uncovered container or in puddles on the ground. This will prove fatal in sufficient quantity. Always drain the coolant into a sealable container. Coolant should be reused unless it is contaminated or several years old.*

2. Disconnect the upper radiator hose at the water outlet.

3. Loosen the two securing nuts and remove the water outlet, gasket, and the thermostat from the thermostat housing.

4. Install the thermostat in the reverse order of removal, using a new gasket with sealer and with the thermostat spring toward the inside of the engine.

Intake Manifold

REMOVAL AND INSTALLATION

1. Remove the air cleaner assembly together with all of the attending hoses.

2. Disconnect the throttle linkage and fuel and vacuum lines from the carburetor.

3. The carburetor or throttle body can be removed from the manifold at this point or can be removed as an assembly with the intake manifold. If there is plenty of room, remove the entire assembly; if clearances are tight, remove the carburetor or throttle body first.

4. Disconnect the intake and exhaust manifold from each other on the A series engines unless you are removing both. Loosen the intake manifold attaching nuts, working from the two ends toward the center, and then remove them.

5. Remove the intake manifold from the engine.

6. Install the intake manifold as follows: Note that it is vitally important to use new gaskets and that late model E series engines use four separate ones.

7. Install the manifold over the retaining studs and then install all retaining nuts finger tight.

8. Note the torque figure on the appropriate chart. Then, begin torquing the manifold nuts

to $\frac{1}{3}$ that figure, starting at the center and alternating, top and bottom, outward until you torque the outermost bolts. Then, repeat the procedure at $\frac{2}{3}$ the torque rating; and finally at the full rating.

9. Install bolts linking the manifolds on those engines that use them. Install the carburetor or throttle body if necessary.

10. Reconnect throttle linkage and adjust it if necessary. Reconnect the fuel lines. Install the air cleaner and hoses. Start the engine and check for leaks.

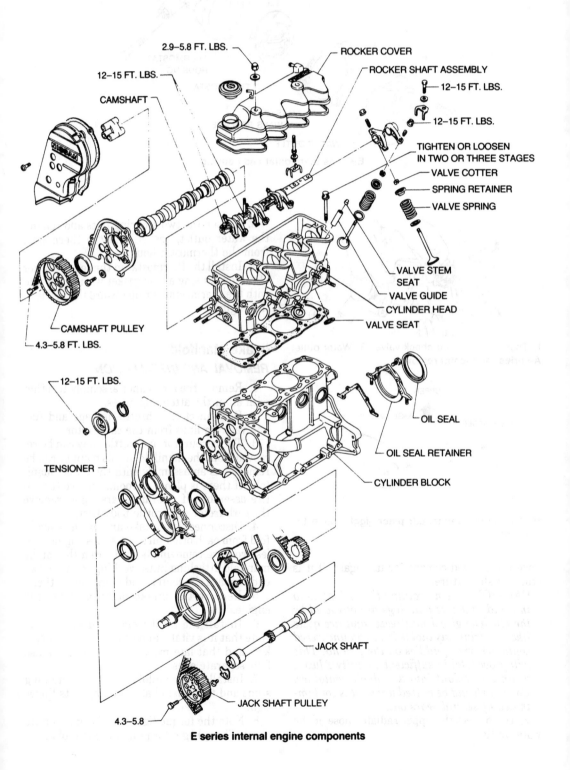

E series internal engine components

Exhaust Manifold
REMOVAL AND INSTALLATION

1. Remove the air cleaner assembly, if necessary for access. Remove the heat shield, if present.

2. Disconnect the exhaust pipe from the exhaust manifold. Disconnect the intake manifold from the exhaust manifold (A-series engines only) unless you are removing both.

3. Remove all temperature sensors, air induction pipes and other attachments from the manifold. Disconnect the EAI and EGR tubes from their fittings on the E series manifolds.

4. Loosen and remove the exhaust manifold attaching nuts and remove the manifold from the engine.

5. Install the exhaust manifold in the reverse order of removal.

Air Conditioner Compressor
REMOVAL AND INSTALLATION

CAUTION: *Refer to Chapter 1 and familiarize yourself with the warnings and cautions covering refrigeration work there. Refrigeration is a highly skilled trade and it is extremely dangerous to work on refrigeration components unless you have a complete understanding of what is happening and are properly equipped. Above all, do not attempt to disconnect any refrigerant lines until all the refrigerant has been discharged from the system.*

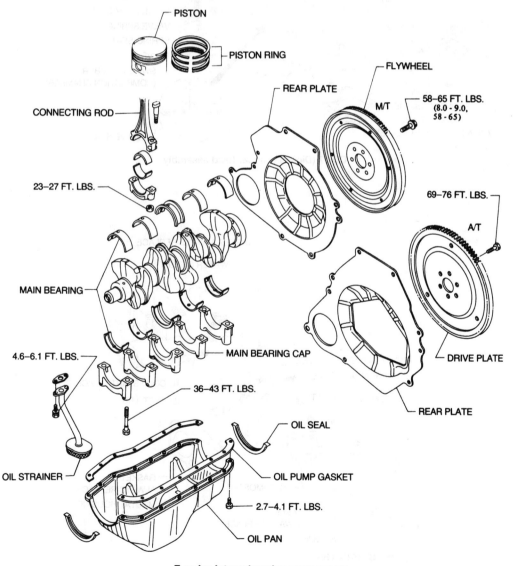

E series internal engine components

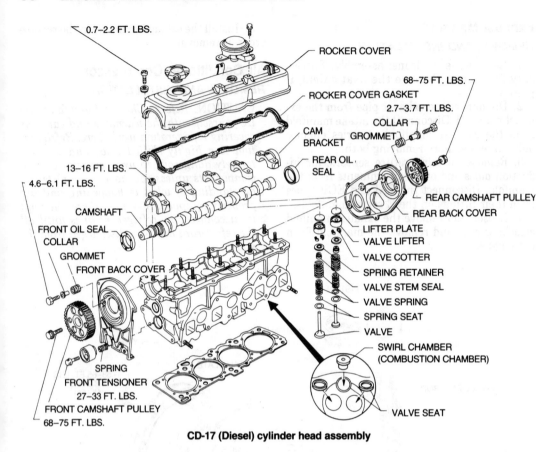

0.7–2.2 FT. LBS.

ROCKER COVER

68–75 FT. LBS.

ROCKER COVER GASKET

2.7–3.7 FT. LBS.

COLLAR
GROMMET
CAM
BRACKET

13–16 FT. LBS.

4.6–6.1 FT. LBS.

REAR OIL
SEAL

CAMSHAFT

REAR CAMSHAFT PULLEY

FRONT OIL SEAL
COLLAR

REAR BACK COVER

GROMMET

LIFTER PLATE
VALVE LIFTER

FRONT BACK COVER

VALVE COTTER

SPRING RETAINER

VALVE STEM SEAL

VALVE SPRING

SPRING SEAT

VALVE

SWIRL CHAMBER
(COMBUSTION CHAMBER)

SPRING

FRONT TENSIONER

27–33 FT. LBS.

FRONT CAMSHAFT PULLEY

68–75 FT. LBS.

VALVE SEAT

CD-17 (Diesel) cylinder head assembly

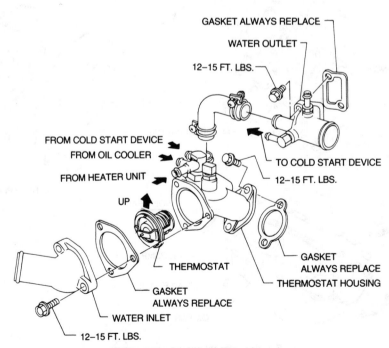

GASKET ALWAYS REPLACE

WATER OUTLET

12–15 FT. LBS.

FROM COLD START DEVICE

FROM OIL COOLER

TO COLD START DEVICE

FROM HEATER UNIT

12–15 FT. LBS.

UP

THERMOSTAT

GASKET
ALWAYS REPLACE

GASKET
ALWAYS REPLACE

THERMOSTAT HOUSING

WATER INLET

12–15 FT. LBS.

CD-17 (Diesel) thermostat assembly

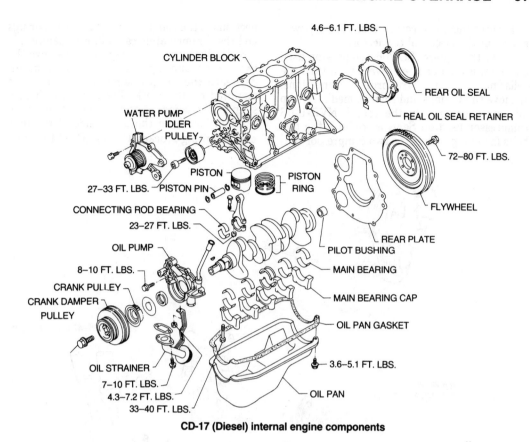

4.6–6.1 FT. LBS.

CYLINDER BLOCK

REAR OIL SEAL

REAL OIL SEAL RETAINER

WATER PUMP
IDLER
PULLEY

72–80 FT. LBS.

PISTON

PISTON
RING

27–33 FT. LBS.   PISTON PIN

FLYWHEEL

CONNECTING ROD BEARING

23–27 FT. LBS.

REAR PLATE

PILOT BUSHING

OIL PUMP

MAIN BEARING

8–10 FT. LBS.

MAIN BEARING CAP

CRANK PULLEY

CRANK DAMPER
PULLEY

OIL PAN GASKET

OIL STRAINER

3.6–5.1 FT. LBS.

7–10 FT. LBS.
4.3–7.2 FT. LBS.
33–40 FT. LBS.

OIL PAN

CD-17 (Diesel) internal engine components

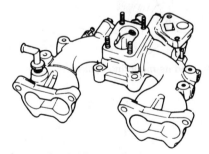

A-series engine intake manifold

A-series engine exhaust manifold

Removing the A-series intake and exhaust manifolds as a unit

1. If possible, run the compressor for a few minutes to normalize system oil distribution. Then, completely discharge the refrigerant from the system as described in Chapter 1.

2. Procure a supply of refrigerant oil, appropriate O-rings for the compressor fittings, and effective caps or plugs.

3. Loosen the compressor belt adjusting locknut, located in the center of the idler pulley. Turn the adjusting bolt (accessible from below) to remove the belt tension. Then, remove the belt.

4. Disconnect the compressor clutch power supply at the electrical connector.

5. On the square, SC-206 compressor used on 210's, use an open-end wrench to turn the collar nuts off the two compressor connections. Remove the O-rings and then immediately cap all four openings. On the round, NVR-140S compressor used on Sentras, remove the two bolts fastening each of the two compressor con-

nections to the compressor, remove the O-rings and then immediately cap all four openings.

6. On both types of compressor, remove the two lower mounting bolts, accessible from underneath the compressor mounting bracket mounted on the block. Then, on the SC206, support the compressor and remove the large through bolt from the upper side of the unit and mounting bracket. On the NVR140S, sup-

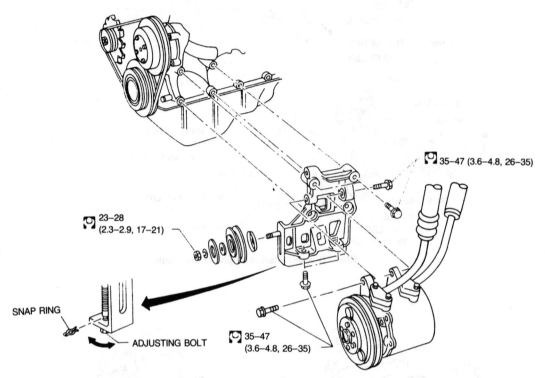

The NVR 140S compressor used on Sentra and its mounting system

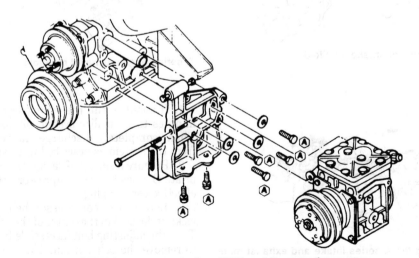

The SC206 compressor used on B210 and its mounting system

port the unit and remove the two bolts from the upper compressor mounts, and then remove the unit.

7. The compressor oil should be checked for condition and quantity if a lot of refrigerant has leaked from the system. Drain the oil and measure the amount. The SC206 holds 139-219ml and the NVR140S holds 89ml. If there are any metal chips in the oil, replace it with fresh refrigerant oil that has been kept in a sealed container. Use Suniso 5GS oil or equivalent.

8. Install the unit in reverse order—by first supporting it from below so the boltholes in the upper mounting ears line up with those in the upper mount, and install the through-bolts. Then, install the lower bolts. Torque all bolts to 27-35 ft. lbs.

9. Install new O-rings coated with clean refrigerant oil into the connections. Remove all caps and make the connections, torquing to 33-36 ft. lbs. on the SC206 and 108-120 in. lbs. on the NVR 140 S.

10. Reconnect the clutch electrical connector. Install and tighten the V-belt.

11. Have the system completely evacuated with a vacuum pump at a refrigeration shop. Charge the system with refrigerant as described in Chapter 1 or have it charged by a refrigeration mechanic.

Radiator

REMOVAL AND INSTALLATION

NOTE: *On some models it may be necessary to remove the front grille.*

1. Drain the engine coolant into a clean container.

CAUTION: *When draining the coolant, keep in mind that cats and dogs are attracted by the ethylene glycol antifreeze, and are quite likely to drink any that is left in an uncovered container or in puddles on the ground. This will prove fatal in sufficient quantity. Always drain the coolant into a sealable container. Coolant should be reused unless it is contaminated or several years old.*

2. Disconnect the upper and lower radiator hoses and the expansion tank hose.

3. Disconnect the automatic transmission oil cooler lines after draining the transmission. Cap the lines to keep dirt out of them.

4. If the fan has a shroud, unbolt the shroud and move it back, hanging it over the fan.

5. Remove the radiator mounting bolts and the radiator.

6. Installation is the reverse of removal. Fill the automatic transmission to the proper level. Fill the cooling system.

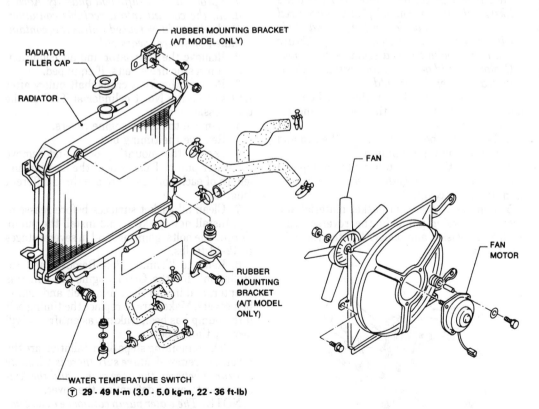

RUBBER MOUNTING BRACKET (A/T MODEL ONLY)

RADIATOR FILLER CAP

RADIATOR

FAN

FAN MOTOR

RUBBER MOUNTING BRACKET (A/T MODEL ONLY)

WATER TEMPERATURE SWITCH
Ⓣ 29 - 49 N·m (3.0 - 5.0 kg-m, 22 - 36 ft-lb)

Sentra radiator and fan assembly, others similar

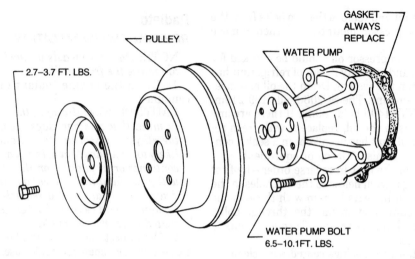

E series water pump

Water Pump
REMOVAL AND INSTALLATION

All Engines, exc. Diesel

1. Drain the engine coolant into a clean container.

CAUTION: *When draining the coolant, keep in mind that cats and dogs are attracted by the ethylene glycol antifreeze, and are quite likely to drink any that is left in an uncovered container or in puddles on the ground. This will prove fatal in sufficient quantity. Always drain the coolant into a sealable container. Coolant should be reused unless it is contaminated or several years old.*

2. On the A-series, loosen the four bolts retaining the fan shroud t the radiator and remove the shroud.

3. Loosen the belt, then remove the ran and pulley from the water pump hub.

4. Remove the bolts retaining the pump and remove the pump together with the gasket from the front cover.

5. Remove all traces of gasket material and install the water pump in the reverse order with a new gasket and sealer. Tighten the bolts uniformly.

A-series engine water pump removal

CD 17 Diesel

1. Disconnect the negative battery cable. Drain the cooling system.

CAUTION: *When draining the coolant, keep in mind that cats and dogs are attracted by the ethylene glycol antifreeze, and are quite likely to drink any that is left in an uncovered container or in puddles on the ground. This will prove fatal in sufficient quantity. Always drain the coolant into a sealable container. Coolant should be reused unless it is contaminated or several years old.*

2. Remove the alternator and air conditioning compressor drive belts, if equipped.

3. Remove the front crankshaft pulley after first setting the No. 1 cylinder at TDC on the compression stroke.

4. Remove the front engine covers.

5. Remove the timing belt.

6. Loosen the mounting bolts and remove the water pump. Take note of the location and length of each bolt, as there are three different lengths.

7. Clean all gasket surfaces before reassembly. Install new gaskets, and install the pump. Torque the bolts, going around in several stages to 12-14 ft. lbs.

8. Refer to "Timing Belt Removal and Installation" for the CD17 engine later in this chapter, and install the timing belt and timing belt covers. Make sure to replace the timing belt if the pump has been leaking, as antifreeze will destroy timing belts.

9. The remaining steps of installation are the reverse of removal. *Make sure there is adequate clearance between the hose clamp and the timing cover to avoid deforming the cover.*

NOTE: *The water pump cannot be disassembled and must be replaced as a unit. Inspect*

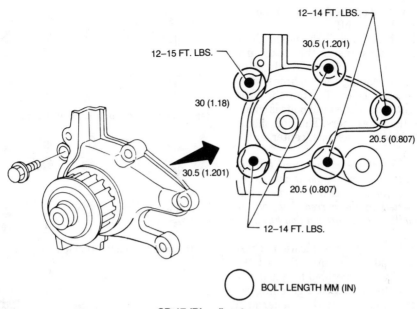

BOLT LENGTH MM (IN)

CD-17 (Diesel) water pump

the timing belt for wear or damage and re-place if necessary.

Cylinder Head

REMOVAL AND INSTALLATION

A-Series Overhead Valve Engines

NOTE: *To prevent distortion or warping of the cylinder head, allow the engine to cool completely before removing the head bolts. Also, do not pry the head off of the block. If the head seems stuck, tap lightly around the lower perimeter of the head with a rubber mallet to loosen head from the block.*

1. Drain the coolant.

CAUTION: *When draining the coolant, keep in mind that cats and dogs are attracted by the ethylene glycol antifreeze, and are quite likely to drink any that is left in an uncovered container or in puddles on the ground. This will prove fatal in sufficient quantity. Always drain the coolant into a sealable container. Coolant should be reused unless it is contaminated or several years old.*

2. Disconnect the battery ground cable.

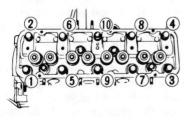

A-series cylinder head bolt loosening sequence

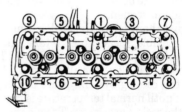

A-series cylinder head torque tightening sequence

3. Remove the upper radiator hose. Remove the water outlet elbow and the thermostat.

4. Remove the air cleaner, carburetor, rocker arm cover, and both manifolds.

5. Remove the spark plugs.

6. Disconnect the temperature gauge connection.

7. Remove the head bolts and remove the head and rocker arm assembly together. Rap the head with a mallet to loosen it from the block. Remove the head and discard the gasket.

8. Remove the pushrods one by one, marking them with the tape to keep them in order.

9. Make sure that head and block surfaces are clean. Check the cylinder head surface with a straightedge and a feeler gauge for flatness. If the head is warped more than 0.1mm, it must be trued. If this is not done, there will probably be a leak. The block surface should also be checked in the same way. If the block is warped more than 0.1mm, it must be trued (machined flat).

10. Install a new head gasket. Most gaskets have a TOP marking. Make sure that the prop-

er head gasket is used on the A12 so that no water passages are blocked off.

11. Install the head. Install the pushrods in their original locations. Install the rocker arm assembly. Loosen the rocker arm adjusting screws to prevent bending the pushrods when tightening the head bolts. Tighten the head bolts finger tight. One of the head bolts is smaller in diameter than the others. This bolt should be inserted in hole number one, center in the illustration.

CAUTION: *The above mentioned bolt is thinner than the others because it acts as the oil passageway for the rocker components. It must be inserted in the correct hole or the valve train will seize up after a few hundred miles.*

12. Refer to the Torque Specifications chart for the correct head bolt torque. Tighten the bolts to one third of the specified torque in the order shown in the head bolt tightening sequence illustration. Torque the rocker arm mounting bolts to 15-18 ft. lbs.

13. Tighten the bolts to two thirds of the specified torque in sequence.

14. Adjust the valve to the cold setting.

15. Reassemble the engine. Intake and exhaust manifold bolt torque for 1200 A12 engines is 84-120 in. lbs., for all others 11-14 ft. lbs. Fill the cooling system. Start the engine and run it until normal temperature is reached. Remove the rocker arm cover. Torque the bolts in sequence once more. Check the valve clearance.

16. Retorque the head bolts after 600 miles of driving. Check the valve clearance after torquing, as this may disturb the setting.

E-series Overhead Cam Engines

NOTE: *Make sure engine is cold before removing head: An aluminum head is prone to warpage if removed while warm.*

1. Crank the engine until the No. 1 piston is at Top Dead Center on its compression stroke (No. 1 valves both closed). Disconnect the negative battery cable. Drain the cooling system and remove the air cleaner assembly.

CAUTION: *When draining the coolant, keep in mind that cats and dogs are attracted by the ethelyne glycol antifreeze, and are quite likely to drink any that is left in an uncovered container or in puddles on the ground. This will prove fatal in sufficient quantity. Always drain the coolant into a sealable container. Coolant should be reused unless it is contaminated or several years old.*

2. Remove the alternator.

3. Number all spark plug wires as to their respective cylinders and remove the distributor, with all wires attached.

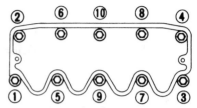

Head loosening sequence, Sentra gasoline

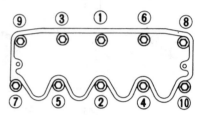

Sentra gasoline head torquing sequence

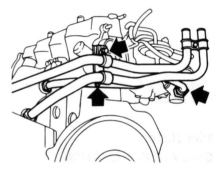

Disconnect EGR (upper) and EAI tubes on Sentra

4. Remove the EAI pipes bracket and EGR tube at the right (EGR valve) side. Disconnect the same pipes on the front (exhaust manifold) side from the manifold.

5. Remove the exhaust manifold cover and the exhaust manifold, taking note that the center manifold nut has a different diameter than the other nuts.

6. Remove the air conditioning compressor bracket and the power steering pump bracket (if equipped).

7. Label and disconnect the carburetor or throttle body injector throttle linkage, fuel line, and all vacuum and electrical connections.

8. Remove the intake manifold with carburetor or throttle body.

9. Remove the water pump drive belt and pulley. Remove the crankshaft pulley.

10. Remove the rocker (valve) cover.

11. Remove the upper and lower dust cover on the camshaft timing belt shroud.

12. With the shroud removed, the cam sprocket, crankshaft sprocket, jackshaft sprocket, tensioner pulley, and toothed rubber timing belt are in front of you.

13. Mark the relationship of the camshaft sprocket to the timing belt and the crankshaft

sprocket to the timing belt with paint or a grease pencil. This will make setting everything up during reassembly much easier if the engine is disturbed during assembly.

14. Remove the belt tensioner pulley.

15. Mark an arrow on the timing belt showing direction of engine rotation, as the belt wears a certain way and should be replaced the way it was removed. Slide the belt off the sprockets.

16. Loosen the cylinder head bolts in the order shown in the illustration, in several stages. Then remove them.

17. Carefully remove the cylinder head from the block, pulling the head up evenly from both ends. If the head seems stuck, DO NOT pry it off. Tap lightly around the lower perimeter of the head with a rubber mallet to help break the joint. Label all head bolts with tape or magic marker, as they must go back in their original positions.   .

18. Thoroughly clean both the cylinder block and head mating surfaces. Avoid scratching either.

19. Turn the crankshaft and set No. 1 cylinder at TDC on its compression stroke. This causes the crankshaft timing sprocket mark to be aligned with the cylinder block cover mark.

20. Align the camshaft sprocket mark with the cylinder head cover mark. This causes the valves for No. 1 cylinder to position at TDC on the compression stroke.

21. Place a new gasket on the cylinder block.

22. On 1983 engines: Install the cylinder head on the block and tighten the bolts in two stages: first to 29-33 ft. lbs. on all bolts, then go around again and torque them all up to 51-54 ft. lbs. After the engine has been warmed up, check all bolts and re-torque if necessary. On 1984-88 engines, install the head on the block. Coat all bolt threads and seats with a very light coating of engine oil and install washers; then start the bolts (note that bolts labeled "A" are 95mm long; "B" are 110mm long; and "C" are 80mm long.

   a. Torque the bolts to 22 ft. lbs. in the specified order.

   b. Torque the bolts to 51 ft. lbs. in the specified order.

   c. Loosen all bolts completely in the specified order for loosening them.

   d. Torque all bolts to 22 ft. lbs. in the specified order.

   e. Torque all bolts to 51-54 ft. lbs. in the specified order. If you have an angled wrench, do not torque the bolts past 22 ft. lbs. but, instead, torque Bolts A 45 degrees, Bolts B 55 degrees, and Bolts C 40 degrees farther, following the sequence.

23. Install the timing belt and tensioner pulley as described below in the Timing Belt Removal and Installation procedure.

24. Install the timing belt cover as described later in this chapter. Install the cam cover as described earlier.

25. Install the crankshaft pulley. Install the water pump pulley and belt.

26. Install the intake manifold with carburetor or throttle body.

27. Connect the carburetor or throttle body injector throttle linkage, fuel line, and all vacuum and electrical connections.

28. Install the air conditioning compressor bracket and the power steering pump bracket (if equipped). Install the air conditioning compressor as described above and the power steering pump as described in Chapter 8.

29. Install the exhaust manifold and the exhaust manifold cover, taking note that the center manifold nut has a different diameter than the other nuts.

30. Install the EAI pipes bracket and EGR tube cna connect them at the right (EGR valve) side. Connect the same pipes on the front (exhaust manifold) side of the manifold.

31. Install the distributor and all ignition wires, connecting them according to their previous markings.

32. Install the alternator. Reconnect the battery. Refill the cooling system. Start the engine. When it is warm, set the ignition timing and adjust the valves. After the engine has cooled, refill the cooling system.

CD 17 Diesel

1. Drain the coolant and disconnect the battery.

CAUTION: *When draining the coolant, keep in mind that cats and dogs are attracted by the ethylene glycol antifreeze, and are quite likely to drink any that is left in an uncovered container or in puddles on the ground. This will prove fatal in sufficient quantity. Always drain the coolant into a sealable container. Coolant should be reused unless it is contaminated or several years old.*

2. Disconnect the exhaust pipe.

3. Set the No. 1 cylinder at TDC on the com-

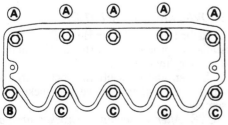

Angle torque bolts according to their letter code on the E16 engine

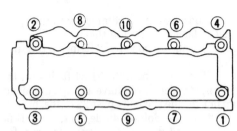

CD17 headbolt loosening sequence

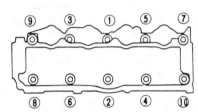

CD17 torque sequence

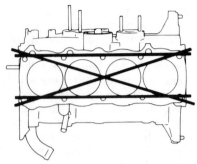

Check the cylinder head for warpage

pression stroke. Tag and disconnect all hoses and electrical connections.

4. Remove the valve timing belt on the camshaft pulley side of the engine.

5. Remove the rear engine cover.

6. Remove the injection pump timing belt.

7. Loosen the injection pump pulley and remove it with a suitable puller.

8. Tag and removal the fuel injection lines from the injectors.

9. Remove the camshaft (valve) cover and loosen the cylinder head bolts in the reverse of the torque sequence given in this section.

10. Remove the cylinder head, with the manifolds still attached. If the head will not budge, tap around the head-to-block mating surface with a rubber mallet. The manifolds can be removed on a bench.

11. Head gaskets are selected by measuring the piston projection. See "Piston and Connecting Rod" for an application chart. Clean and inspect the head as described below. Then, once the proper gasket has been selected, install the gasket and head.

12. Lightly oil the head bolt threads and underside of the heads and install with washers. Torque the head bolts as follows:

   a. Torque all the bolts in the sequence shown to 29 ft. lbs.

   b. Torque all the bolts in the sequence shown to 72-79 ft. lbs.

   c. Loosen all the bolts completely.

   d. Torque all the bolts in the sequence shown to 29 ft. lbs.

   e. If you do not have an angle type wrench, torque all the bolts in the sequence shown to 72-79 ft. lbs. If you do have an angle wrench, turn each bolt, in the sequence shown, 82-87 degrees farther.

13. Adjust the valves as described in Chapter 2. Install the cam cover as described above.

14. Install the injection lines as described in Chapter 5.

15. Install the injection pump drive pulley. Then, install the pump timing belt as described later in this chapter.

16. Install the rear timing belt cover.

17. Install the front engine timing belt and belt cover.

18. Connect all hoses and electrical connections according to the tags made earlier.

19. Connect the exhaust pipe. Refill the cooling system. Connect the battery. Start the engine and check for leaks.

CLEANING AND INSPECTION

Using a wire brush, clean the carbon from the cylinder head, then check it for cracks and flaws.

Make sure that the cylinder head and the block surfaces are clean. Check the cylinder head surface for flatness, using a straightedge and a feeler gauge. If the cylinder head and/or the block are warped more than 0.1mm, it must be trued by a machine shop; if this is not done, there will probably be a compression or water leak.

Valves and Springs

VALVE ADJUSTMENT

NOTE: *For valve adjustment procedures refer to Valve Lash in Chapter 2.*

REMOVAL AND INSTALLATION

1. Refer to the Cylinder Head, Removal and Installation procedures in this section and remove the cylinder head.

2. Loosen and back off the rocker arm adjusting screws, then remove the rocker arm assembly.

NOTE: *After removing the rocker arm assembly (E-series), remove the spring retainers and the rocker arms from the shaft(s) (be sure to keep the parts in order), then reinstall the rocker arm shaft.*

3. Using the spring compression tool No. ST12070000 (A-series), No. KV101072S0 (E-series), No. KV101092S0 (CD-series) compress the valve springs. Remove the valve keeper, then slowly relieve the spring pressure. Remove the springs, the valve seals and the valves.

4. To install, use new oil seals and reverse the removal procedures. On the CD-series engines use tool No. KV10107900 and drive in the valve seal until it contacts the guide and set the valve lifter plate so that the mark faces the valve lifter side. Tighten the rocker shaft bolts to 14-18 ft. lbs. on the A-series engines; 13-15 ft. lbs. on E-series engines, in a circular sequence. Adjust the valves. (See the procedure in Chapter 2).

NOTE: *On most engines, the intake/exhaust valve springs are the uneven pitch type. That is, the springs have narrow coils at the bottom and wide coils at the top. The narrow coils (painted white) must be the side making contact on the cylinder head surface.*

INSPECTION

Before the valves can be properly inspected, the stem, the lower end of the stem, the entire valve face and head must be cleaned. An old valve works well for chipping carbon from the valve head, a wire brush, a gasket scraper or a putty knife can be used for cleaning the valve face and/or the area between the face and the lower stem. DO NOT scratch the valve face during cleaning. Clean the entire stem with a rag soaked in thinners to remove all of the varnish and gum.

Thorough inspection of the valves requires the use of a micrometer and a dial indicator. If these instruments are not available, the parts should be taken to a reputable machine shop for inspection. Refer to the Valve Specifications chart, for the valve stem and stem-to-guide specifications.

Using a dial indicator, measure the inside diameter of the valve guides at their bottom, midpoint and top positions, at 90° apart. Subtract the valve stem measurement; if the clearance exceeds that listed in the specifications chart under Stem-to-Guide Clearance, replace the valve(s).

Check the top of each valve for pitting and unusual wear due to improper rocker adjustment, etc. The stem tip can be ground flat if it is worn but no more that 0.5mm can be removed; if this limit must be exceeded to make the tip flat and square, then the valve must be replaced. If the valve stem tips are ground, make sure that the valve is fixed securely into the jig,

so that the tip contacts the grinding wheel squarely at exactly 90°.

REFACING

Valve refacing should only be handled by a reputable machine shop, as the experience and equipment needed to do the job are beyond that of the average owner/mechanic. During the course of a normal valve job, refacing is necessary when simply lapping the valves into their seats will not correct the seat and face wear. When the valves are reground (resurfaced), the valve seats must also be recut, again requiring special equipment and experience.

CHECK SPRINGS

1. Place the valve spring on a flat, clean surface, next to a square.

2. Measure the height of the spring and rotate it against the edge of the square to measure the distortion (out-of-roundness). If the spring height between springs varies or the distortion exceeds more than 1.6mm, replace the spring(s). The valve spring squareness should not exceed: 2.2mm (outer - gasoline engine), 2.1mm (outer - diesel engine) or 1.9mm (inner).

3. A valve spring tester is needed to test the spring pressure. Compare the tested pressure with the pressures listed in the Valve Specifications chart in this section.

Valve Seats
INSPECTION

Check the valve seat inserts for evidence of pitting or excessive wear at the valve contact surface. Because the cylinder head must be machined to accept the new seat inserts, consult an engine specialist or machinist about this work.

REMOVAL AND INSTALLATION

CAUTION: *To prevent damaging the other cylinder head components, completely disassemble the head.*

1. The old valve seat can be removed by machining it from the head or by heating the head in an 302-320°F (150-160°C) oil bath, then driving it from the head with a punch.

NOTE: *When removing the valve insert, be careful not to damage the cylinder head surface.*

2. Select a valve insert replacement and check the outside diameter, then ream the cylinder head recess at room temperature.

3. Heat the cylinder head to 302-320°F (150-160°C) in an oil bath, then press in the new valve seat, until it seats in the recess.

CUTTING THE SEATS

1. Allow the cylinder head to cool to room temperature. Using a valve seating tool kit, cut a new valve contact surface on the valve seat.

NOTE: *When repairing the valve seat, make sure that the valve and the guide are in good condition; if wear is evident, replace the valve and/or the guide, then correct the valve seat.*

2. To complete the operation, use valve grinding compound and lap the valve to the seat.

3. To install the removed components, reverse the removal procedures.

Valve Guides

REMOVAL AND INSTALLATION

1. Using a 2-ton press or a hammer and a suitable driving tool, drive the old valve guide from the cylinder head, in the rocker cover to combustion chamber direction.

NOTE: *Heating the cylinder head to 302-320°F (150-200°C) will facilitate the operation.*

2. Using the Valve Guide Reamer tool KV11081000 (A series) or ST11081000 (E series) engines, ream the valve guide hole.

3. Using a new valve guide, press it into the cylinder head and ream the guide hole with the proper size reamer.

4. Using a valve seating tool kit, cut a new valve contact on the valve seat.

5. To install the removed components, reverse the removal procedures.

KNURLING

Valve guides which are not excessively worn or distorted may in some cases, be knurled rather than reamed. Knurling is a process in which metal inside the valve guide bores is displaced and raised (forming a very fine cross-hatch pattern), thereby reducing clearance. Knurling also provides for excellent oil control. The possibility of knurling rather than reaming the guides should be discussed with a machinist.

Oil Pan

REMOVAL AND INSTALLATION

All Engines Except E-Series

To remove the oil pan it will be necessary to unbolt the motor mounts and jack the engine with a lifting sling and crane to gain clearance. Drain the oil, remove the attaching screws, and remove the oil pan and gasket. Install the oil pan in the reverse order with a new gasket, tightening the screws to 4-7 ft. lbs.

CAUTION: *The EPA warns that prolonged contact with used engine oil may cause a*

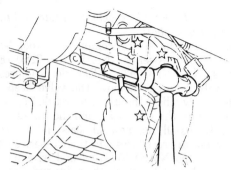

Cutting the seal on E-Series oil pans using sealer in place of a gasket

number of skin disorders, including cancer! You should make every effort to minimize your exposure to used engine oil. Protective gloves should be worn when changing the oil. Wash your hands and any other exposed skin areas as soon as possible after exposure to used engine oil. Soap and water, or waterless hand cleaner should be used.

E-Series Engines

1. Raise the vehicle and support it securely. Drain the engine oil.

2. Remove the right side splash and lower covers.

3. Remove the center crossmember.

4. Disconnect the front exhaust pipe.

5. Install a lifting sling and crane over the engine to securely support it. Then, disconnect the engine torque buffer rod. Remove its brackets.

6. Disconnect the engine mounts and remove the mounting brackets for clearance. Then raise the engine as necessary for clearance to remove the pan.

7. On E Series engines built through 1986, remove the attaching bolts, pull the pan down and remove gaskets. On 1987-88 models, first remove the bolts. Then use a seal cutter, which is a sharp, bladed device which is rested against the pan and can be slid along it. Insert the blade of the cutter between the oil pan and block, gently tapping it inward with a hammer. Then, tap the side of the cutter with a hammer to cut the sealer bond used in place of a gasket all around the oil pan.

8. Scrape all traces of either gasket material or sealer from both the pan and the sealing surface on the bottom of the block. Then, replace the gasket. On pans using sealer, use "Genuine Liquid Gasket" or equivalent, cut the tube so the nozzle opening is one size larger than the smallest opening. Lay a bead 4-5mm in diameter along the groove in the pan. At boltholes, run the sealer bead around the bolthole to the

inside, so the center of the bead will lay about 7mm inside the center of the bolthole.

9. On all pans, replace the grooved front and rear end seals. Raise the pan into position. Tighten the bolts very gently all around. Then, torque them to 35-51 in. lbs. on cars using gaskets and 55-73 in. lbs. on 1987-88 cars using sealer.

10. Connect the exhaust pipe.

11. Lower the engine and install mounting brackets and through bolts. Install the center crossmember and transaxle bolt. Install the splash shield and covers. Install the drain plug and refill the oil pan. Start the engine and check for leaks.

Oil Pump

The oil pump is mounted externally on the engine, this eliminates the need to remove the oil pan in order to remove the oil pump. The oil pump is actually part of the oil filter mounting bracket.

REMOVAL AND INSTALLATION

1973 and Later All A Series Models

1. Drain the engine oil and remove oil filter. CAUTION: *The EPA warns that prolonged contact with used engine oil may cause a number of skin disorders, including cancer! You should make every effort to minimize your exposure to used engine oil. Protective gloves should be worn when changing the oil.*

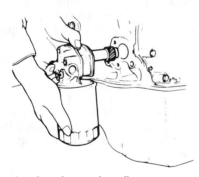

Removing A-series engine oil pump

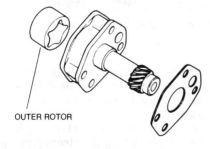

OUTER ROTOR

Exploded view of A-series engine oil pump

Wash your hands and any other exposed skin areas as soon as possible after exposure to used engine oil. Soap and water, or waterless hand cleaner should be used.

2. Remove the front stabilizer bar if it is in the way of removing the oil pump (if equipped).

3. Remove the splash shield.

4. Remove the oil pump body with the drive spindle assembly.

5. Install the oil pump in the reverse order of removal, after removing any traces of the old gasket and installing a new gasket.

6. Make sure the pump mounting bolts are tight. Install the oil filter to the oil pump. Check the oil level mark on the dipstick and add oil if necessary. Start the engine and check for leaks.

E-Series Engines

1. Loosen the alternator lower bolts.

2. Remove the alternator belt and adjusting bar bolt. Move the alternator aside so there is ample room to work.

3. Disconnect the oil pressure gauge harness.

4. If necessary, remove the oil filter from the engine to give proper access to the oil pump bolts.

5. Unbolt the oil pump from the engine block and remove.

6. If the oil pump gasket is worn, replace it. Install the oil pump, making sure all bolts are tight. You may have to turn the pump body slightly when inserting the pump drive gear into the block, in order to properly engage the drive gear with its drive gear on the engine jackshaft.

CD 17 Diesel

1. Remove the valve timing belt as described later in this chapter.

2. Drain the oil and remove the oil pan. CAUTION: *The EPA warns that prolonged contact with used engine oil may cause a number of skin disorders, including cancer! You should make every effort to minimize*

Removing oil pressure gauge harness from oil pump, E-series

your exposure to used engine oil. Protective gloves should be worn when changing the oil. Wash your hands and any other exposed skin areas as soon as possible after exposure to used engine oil. Soap and water, or waterless hand cleaner should be used.

3. The oil pump is bolted to the front of the engine block, at the front of the crankshaft. Loosen the mounting bolts and remove the oil pump assembly.

NOTE: Remove the crankshaft key to avoid damage to the oil seal on the pump.

4. Remove the oil pump rear cover and check gear clearance using a feeler gauge. Body-to-outer gear clearance should be 0.1-0.2mm; outer gear-to-crescent clearance should be 0.2-0.3mm.

5. Replace the oil seal in the pump by carefully prying it out. Coat the new seal liberally with clean engine oil before installation. Install the crankshaft key.

6. Install the pump to the block, using a new gasket and torquing the bolts to 9-12 ft. lbs. Replace the oil pan, applying sealer to the four corners of the oil pan and use a new oil pan gasket. Install the drain plug and refill the pan with oil.

7. Replace the timing belt as described later. Start the engine and check for leaks.

Timing Chain Cover
REMOVAL AND INSTALLATION

A12, A12A, A13, A14, A15 Overhead Valve Engines

1. Remove the radiator. Loosen the alternator adjustment and remove the belt. Loosen the air pump adjustment and remove the belt on engines with the air pump system.

CAUTION: When draining the coolant, keep in mind that cats and dogs are attracted by the ethylene glycol antifreeze, and are quite likely to drink any that is left in an uncovered container or in puddles on the ground. This will prove fatal in sufficient quantity. Always drain the coolant into a sealable container. Coolant should be reused unless it is contaminated or several years old.

2. Remove the fan and water pump.

3. Bend back the locktab from the crankshaft pulley nut. Remove the nut by affixing a heavy wrench and wrapping the wrench with a hammer. The nut must be unscrewed in the opposite direction of normal engine rotation. Pull off the pulley.

4. It is recommended that the oil pan be removed or loosened before the front cover is removed.

5. Unbolt and remove the timing chain cover.

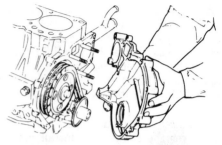

Removing the A-series engine timing cover

When removing the A-series engine timing cover it is necessary to loosen or remove the oil pan

6. Replace the crankshaft oil seal in the cover. Most models use a felt seal.

7. Apply sealant to both sides of the timing cover gasket. Install the timing chain cover. Front cover bolt torque is 4 ft. lbs.

8. Install the oil pan. Oil pan bolt torque is 4 ft. lbs.

9. Install the crankshaft pulley and pulley nut.

10. Install the water pump with a new gasket. Water pump bolt torque is 84-120 in. lbs.

11. Install the air pump, alternator, and radiator. Install and adjust the belts. Refill the oil pan and cooling system. Start the engine and check for leaks.

Timing Belt Cover and Seal
REMOVAL AND INSTALLATION

E-series Overhead Cam Engines

1. Loosen the air conditioner belt and remove.

2. Loosen the alternator adjusting bolt, and remove the alternator belt. Unbolt the alternator mounting bracket and remove the alternator.

3. Remove the power steering belt (if equipped) by loosening the steering pump adjusting bolt.

4. Remove the water pump pulley.

5. Rotate the engine until it is at TDC No. 1 firing position. Remove the crankshaft pulley.

6. Support the engine securely with a jack and block of wood under the oil pan. Then, unbolt the mount that sits in front of the timing belt cover. Unbolt and remove the bracket that interferes with timing belt cover removal.

7. Loosen and remove the eight bolts securing the timing cover and remove the cover.

8. Remove the timing belt as described below. Then, slide the lower timing belt sprocket off the crankshaft.

9. Gently pry the seal out of the front of the block, *avoiding contact with the crankshaft so the sealing surface of the crank will not be scratched.*

10. Apply clean engine oil to the lip of the new seal. Insert it squarely into the opening until it sits at the same depth as the old seal.

11. Install the cover with new seals. Torque the belt cover bolts to 32-44 in. lbs. Install the mounting bracket onto the block. Torque the bolts to 29-40 ft. lbs. Then, reinstall the through bolt and nut for the mount. Remove the jack and block from under the oil pan.

12. Install the crankshaft pulley. Install the water pump pulley. Torque the crank pulley

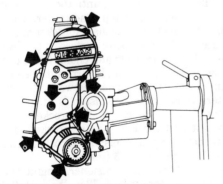

Upper and lower dust retaining bolts

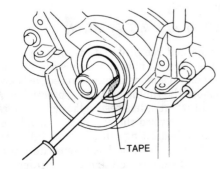

Carefully pry out the front oil seal

bolt to 83-108 ft. lbs.; the water pump pulley bolt to 32-44 in. lbs.

13. Install the power steering belt. Install the alternator and alternator/water pump drive belt.

14. Install the air conditioner belt. Adjust all accessory drive belts.

CD 17 Engine

1. Disconnect the negative battery cable. Drain the cooling system and then remove the radiator together with the upper and lower radiator hoses.

CAUTION: *When draining the coolant, keep in mind that cats and dogs are attracted by the ethylene glycol antifreeze, and are quite likely to drink any that is left in an uncovered container or in puddles on the ground. This will prove fatal in sufficient quantity. Always drain the coolant into a sealable container. Coolant should be reused unless it is contaminated or several years old.*

2. Remove the fan, fan coupling and fan pulley. Using a gear puller, remove the crankshaft damper pulley.

3. Remove the power steering pump, bracket and idler pulley.

4. Support the engine securely with a jack and block of wood under the oil pan. Then, unbolt the mount that sits in front of the timing belt cover. Unbolt and remove the bracket that interferes with timing belt cover removal.

5. Remove the front belt cover. Remove the valve timing belt (see "Timing Belt and Camshaft" removal in this chapter).

6. Remove the front oil seal by taping the end of a thin prybar or old screwdriver, and carefully pry the old seal out from around the end of the crankshaft. Do not scratch the shaft with the prybar.

7. Coat a new seal with clean engine oil. Slide it onto the crankshaft end and back into place in the front of the block. Use a small drift to evenly drive the seal back until it seats in position.

8. Follow the "Timing Belt and Camshaft" removal and installation procedure and install the timing belt.

9. Install front timing belt cover and install all attaching bolts.

10. Install the engine mounting bracket. Reconnect the engine mount. Remove the jack and block of wood from under the oil pan.

11. Install the power steering pump as described in Chapter 8.

12. Install the crankshaft damper pulley. Install the fan, fan coupling and fan pulley.

13. Install the radiator and hoses. Refill the cooling system. Connect the battery.

Timing Chain and Camshaft
REMOVAL AND INSTALLATION
A12, A12A, A13, A14, A15 Overhead Valve Engines

NOTE: *It is recommended that this operation be done with the engine removed from the vehicle.*

1. Remove the timing chain cover.
2. Unbolt and remove the chain tensioner.
3. Remove the camshaft sprocket retaining bolt.
4. Pull off the camshaft sprocket, easing off the crankshaft sprocket at the same time. Remove both sprockets and chain as an assembly. Be careful not to lose the shim and oil slinger from behind the crankshaft sprocket.
5. Remove the distributor, distributor drive spindle, pushrods, and valve lifters. Number all parts with tape.

NOTE: *The lifter cannot be removed until the camshaft has been removed.*
Remove the oil pump and pump driveshaft.

6. Unbolt and remove the camshaft locating plate.

A-series engine camshaft locating plate correctly installed

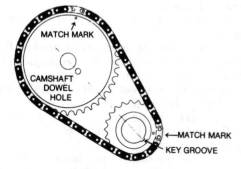

A-series engine timing mark alignment

7. Remove the camshaft carefully. This will be easier if the block is inverted to prevent the lifters from falling down.
8. The camshaft bearings can be pressed out and replaced. They are available in undersizes, should it be necessary to regrind the camshaft journals.
9. Reinstall the camshaft. If the locating plate has an oil hole, it should be to the right of the engine. The locating plate is marked with the word LOWER and an arrow. Locating plate bolt torque is 36-48 in. lbs. Be careful to engage the drive pin in the rear end of the camshaft with the slot in the oil pump driveshaft.
10. Camshaft endplay can be measured after temporarily replacing the camshaft sprocket and securing bolt. The standard endplay specifications for the A12 engine are 0.025-0.076mm with a service limit (largest allowable endplay limit) of 0.1mm. The A12A, A13, A14 and A15 engines have standard endplay specifications of 0.1-0.2mm with a service limit of 0.1mm. If the endplay is excessive, replace the locating plate. New plates are available in several sizes. Bolt the correct camshaft retaining plate into position.
11. If the crankshaft or camshaft has been replaced, install the sprockets temporarily and make sure that they are parallel. Adjust by shimming under the crankshaft sprocket.
12. Turn the crankshaft until the keyway and the No. 1 piston is at top dead center. The oil slinger behind the crankshaft sprocket must be replaced with the concave surface to the front. Assemble the sprockets and chain. If the chain and sprocket installation is correct, the sprocket marks must be aligned between the shaft centers when the No. 1 piston is at top dead center. Install the camshaft sprocket to the camshaft and the crankshaft sprocket to the crankshaft. Engine camshaft sprocket retaining bolt torque is 33-36 ft. lbs.
13. Install the chain tensioner. Engine chain tensioner bolt torque is 48-72 in. lbs. Install the timing chain cover as described above.

Timing Belt
REMOVAL AND INSTALLATION

Timing belt removal and installation procedures are covered in conjunction with the camshaft removal and installation procedure below. To remove the timing belt alone, proceed up to the point where it has been removed. Then, refer to steps toward the end of the installation procedure beginning with belt installation. Since the diesel engine has a separate timing belt at the rear which drives the injection pump, that procedure is covered here.

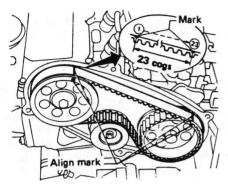

Aligning the timing marks for the injection pump drive belt on the CD17 diesel

CD17 Diesel

1. Remove the rear timing belt cover. Rotate the engine until the No.1 cylinder is at TDC on the compression stroke. At this position, the TDC mark on the front pulley will be aligned and the timing marks on the two rear timing belt sprockets will be at about the 1 O'clock position.

2. Loosen the tensioner lockbolt, use a thin probe to turn the tensioner pulley (the small pulley located under the belt) on its mounting cam so it is in the lowest possible position. Then, tighten the lockbolt to hold it there.

3. Remove the timing belt. Install the new belt with the two marks (lines on the outer surface) aligned with the round marks on the front surfaces of the two sprockets. If reusing an old belt and the marks show signs of wear, put marks 23 notches apart (the distance between where the two timing marks on the tops of the sprockets should go).

4. Loosen the tensioner locknut and allow spring tension to keep the tensioner in position. Turn the engine crankshaft two times *in the normal direction of rotation.*

5. *Holding the tensioner in position to keep it from turning on its cam,* torque the tensioner locknut to 12-15 ft. lbs.

6. Install the rear timing belt cover.

Camshaft and Timing Belt

REMOVAL AND INSTALLATION

E-series Overhead Cam Engines

1. Removal of the cylinder head from the engine is optional. However, the camshaft must slide into the bearings from the end of the cylinder head. To gain clearance without removing the head, it will be necessary to remove the engine. Crank the engine until the No. 1 piston is at Top Dead Center on its compression stroke.

2. Follow the "Timing Belt Cover" removal procedure and remove the cover. Mark the relationship of the camshaft sprocket to the timing

belt and the crankshaft sprocket to the timing belt with paint or grease pencil. This will make setting everything up during reassembly much easier, if the engine is disturbed during assembly.

3. Remove the distributor.

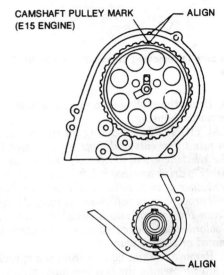

Camshaft and crankshaft sprocket alignment marks, E-series engine

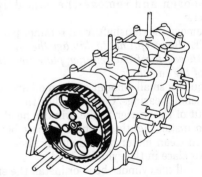

Remove three cam sprocket bolts and pull off sprocket, E-series

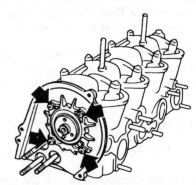

E-series front camshaft retainer screws

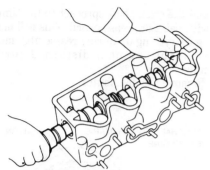

Use care in removing camshaft from head, E-series

4. Drain the cooling system and remove the thermostat housing.

CAUTION: *When draining the coolant, keep in mind that cats and dogs are attracted by the ethylene glycol antifreeze, and are quite likely to drink any that is left in an uncovered container or in puddles on the ground. This will prove fatal in sufficient quantity. Always drain the coolant into a sealable container. Coolant should be reused unless it is contaminated or several years old.*

5. Remove the timing belt from the sprockets, after loosening the belt tensioner pulley.

6. Remove the rocker cover and remove the rocker shaft assembly.

7. Loosen and remove the cam drive sprocket.

8. Remove the camshaft front retainer plate. NOTE: *Be careful not to damage the oil seal lip between the front retainer plate and the end of the camshaft.*

9. Squirt a small amount of clean oil around the camshaft bearings. Carefully slide the camshaft out of the carrier in the cylinder head.

10. To install, lightly oil the camshaft bearings with clean motor oil and slowly slide the cam into place in the cylinder head.

11. Install the cylinder head or install the engine back into the car. Install the camshaft front retainer plate on the cylinder head. Install a new oil seal. Check the camshaft end-play. If it is worn past the limit of 0.4mm, either the camshaft or the retainer plate or both must be replaced.

12. Install the cam drive sprocket. Tighten the camshaft drive sprocket to 51-69 in. lbs. Then, install the valve rocker assembly as described above.

12. Install the timing belt as described above. Check the valve timing after all sprockets and timing belt are installed.

13. Install the thermostat housing with a new gasket.

14. Install the distributor. Install the timing belt cover as described above.

15. Adjust the valves, and adjust all drive belts. Refill the cooling system, if necessary.

CD 17 Diesel

NOTE: *The camshaft is normally removed with the cylinder head removed from the engine. Follow the procedure below for timing belt removal, then follow the "Cylinder Head Removal" procedure earlier in this section; the camshaft removal procedure follows timing belt removal. The injection pump has its own belt drive and is covered later in this section.*

1. Support the engine with a jack and remove the right side engine mount, then jack the engine up to allow working clearance.

2. Set the No. 1 cylinder at TDC on its compression stroke.

3. Remove the alternator and air conditioning compressor (if equipped) drive belts.

4. Using a puller, remove the crankshaft damper pulley.

5. Loosen the tensioner pulley and set it to the "free" position. Remove the idler pulley.

6. Remove the crankshaft pulley with the timing belt. Remove the injection pump timing belt as described below.

7. Check the belt for damage, missing teeth, wear or saturation with oil or grease. If damage is evident or if you are in doubt as to the belt's condition, replace the belt.

NOTE: *Do not bend, twist or turn the timing belt inside out. Do not allow the belt to come into contact with any grease, oil or solvents.*

8. Remove the cylinder head and manifolds.

9. Remove the camshaft bearing caps and check the clearance with Plastigage®. Do not turn the camshaft. If the bearing clearance exceeds 0.1mm replace the bearing caps, camshaft or cylinder head.

10. After checking clearances, remove the bearing caps and remove the camshaft with both oil seals. Have the camshaft runout and lobe height checked; if worn beyond specification, replace the camshaft.

NOTE: *There are two different diameter seals used on the camshaft front and rear. Be sure to use the correct seal when installing. (The front seal has an arrow on the outer edge facing clockwise; the rear seal arrow points counterclockwise). If you are replacing the oil*

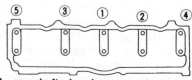

CD17 camshaft bearing cap torque sequence

seals without removing the camshaft, remove the pulleys and carefully pry the seals out using a small pry bar or an old screwdriver covered with tape. Use care not to scratch the camshaft, cylinder head or bearing cap.

11. To install the camshaft, first lubricate all bearing surfaces with clean engine oil. Install the camshaft bearing caps and torque, in the sequence illustrated, to 13-16 ft. lbs. Before installing the oil seals, lubricate with clean engine oil. Reinstall the cylinder head and check valve clearances; adjust if necessary.

12. Install the crankshaft and camshaft timing sprockets. Torque the camshaft timing sprocket bolt to 68-75 ft. lbs. Install the timing belt assembly in the reverse order of removal. Align the marks on the timing belt with those on the camshaft and crankshaft pulleys. When tensioning the belt, loosen the tensioner bolt and turn the crankshaft two times in its normal rotating direction, then tighten the tensioner while holding it. Do not allow the tensioner to rotate when tightening, and NEVER turn the engine against its normal rotating direction.

13. Install the timing belt cover as described above. Install the injection pump timing belt as described below. Install the crankshaft damper as described in that procedure.

14. Install the alternator and air conditioning compressor (if equipped) drive belts.

15. Reconnect all engine mounts and mounting brackets securely and remove the supporting jack.

Camshaft

INSPECTION

Place the camshaft on a set of V-blocks, supported by the outermost bearing surfaces. Place a dial micrometer, with it's finger resting on the center bearing surface, then turn the camshaft to check the bearing runout; the runout should not exceed 0.1mm, if it does exceed the limit, replace the camshaft.

Check the camshaft bearing surfaces (in the engine) with an internal micrometer and the bearing surfaces (of the camshaft) with a micrometer.

Jack Shaft

REMOVAL AND INSTALLATION

E-Series Engine

1. Refer to the Timing Belt and/or Chain, Removal and Installation procedures in this section and remove the timing belt.

2. Pull the crankshaft sprocket from the crankshaft. Remove the jackshaft sprocket bolts, then separate the sprocket from the jackshaft.

3. Remove the lower locating plate from the cylinder block. Remove the jackshaft and the crankshaft oil seals from the locating plate.

4. Remove the jackshaft locating plate, then pull the shaft out through the front of the cylinder block.

5. Check the jackshaft bearing diameters (in the cylinder block) with an internal micrometer and the bearing diameters (of the jackshaft) with a micrometer; the clearance should not exceed 0.15mm, if it does exceed the limit, replace the jackshaft bearings.

6. Use a hammer and a brass drift to remove and install the jackshaft bearings in the cylinder block.

NOTE: *Be sure to align the oil hole in the bearing with the hole in the cylinder block. After installation, check the bearing clearances. Using sealant, install a new welch plug into the cylinder block.*

7. In installation, use new oil seals and gaskets and observe the following torques: Torque, the oil pump bolts to 69-86 in. lbs., the tensioner pulley bolts to 12-15 ft. lbs., the timing cover bolts to 30-48 in. lbs., and the crankshaft pulley bolt to 83-108 ft. lbs.. First, lubricate all bearing surfaces. Then, carefully slide the jackshaft into the block.

8. Install the jackshaft locating plate and install the mounting bolts.

9. Install the lower locating plate to the cylinder block. Coat the seal lips with clean engine oil and install the jackshaft and the crankshaft oil seals into the locating plate.

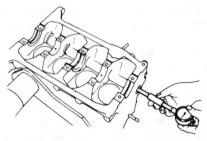

Checking the jackshaft bearing diameters with an internal micrometer

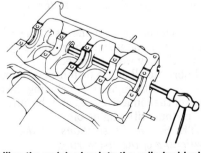

Installing the welch plug into the cylinder block

10. Install the sprocket onto the jackshaft. Install the jackshaft sprocket bolts and torque to 78-108 in. lbs. Install the crankshaft sprocket onto the crankshaft.

11. Refer to the Timing Belt Removal and Installation procedures in this section and install and adjust the timing belt.

12. Adjust the drive belt tensions.

Pistons and Connecting Rods

REMOVAL AND INSTALLATION

It is recommended that the engine be removed from the vehicle and mounted on an engine stand, before removing the pistons and connecting rods from the engine.

1. Refer to the Cylinder Head Removal and Installation procedures in this section and remove the cylinder head.

2. Using a ridge reamer tool, remove the carbon buildup and metal ridge worn into the top of the cylinder wall.

3. Drain the lubricant from the engine. Invert the engine on the stand, then remove the oil pan, the oil strainer and the pickup tube.

CAUTION: *The EPA warns that prolonged contact with used engine oil may cause a number of skin disorders, including cancer! You should make every effort to minimize your exposure to used engine oil. Protective gloves should be worn when changing the oil. Wash your hands and any other exposed skin areas as soon as possible after exposure to used engine oil. Soap and water, or waterless hand cleaner should be used.*

4. Position the piston to be removed at the bottom of its stroke, so that the connecting rod bearing cap can be easily reached.

5. Remove the connecting rod bearing cap nuts and the cap and the lower half of the bearing. Cover the rod bolts with lengths of rubber tubing to protect the cylinder walls when the rod and piston assembly is driven out.

6. Push the piston/connecting rod assembly, out through the top of the cylinder block with a length of wood or a wooden hammer handle.

CAUTION: *When removing the piston/connecting rod assembly, be careful not to scratch the cylinder wall with the connecting rod.*

7. Keep all of the components from each cylinder together and install them in the cylinder from which they were removed.

8. Lubricate all of the piston/connecting rod components with engine oil, including the bearing face of the connecting rod and the outer face of the pistons with engine oil.

NOTE: *See the illustrations for the correct positioning of the piston rings.*

9. Turn the crankshaft until the rod journal

of the particular cylinder you are working on is brought to the TDC position.

10. Clamp the piston/ring assembly into a ring compressor, the notched mark or number (on the piston head) must face the front of the engine and the oil hole (on the side of the connecting rod) must face the right side of the engine; push the piston/connecting rod assembly into the cylinder bore until the big bearing end of the connecting rod seats on the rod journal of the crankshaft.

CAUTION: *Use care not to scratch the cylinder wall with the connecting rod.*

11. Push down on the piston/connecting rod assembly, while turning the crankshaft (the connecting rod rides around on the crankshaft rod journal), until the crankshaft rod journal is at the BDC (bottom dead center) position.

12. Align the mark on the connecting rod bearing cap with that on the connecting rod and torque the connecting rod bearing cap bolts to the torque shown in the specifications chart.

13. To complete the installation, install the oil pan, invert the engine, and install the cylinder head. Then, install the engine into the car, and refill the oil pan and the cooling system. Start the engine and check for leaks.

CLEANING AND INSPECTION

Clean the piston after removing the rings (refer to Piston Ring Replacement), by scraping the carbon from the top of the piston (DO NOT scratch the piston surface). Use a broken piston ring or a ring cleaning tool, to clean out the ring grooves. Clean the entire piston with solvent and a brush (NOT a wire brush).

With the piston thoroughly cleaned, place both compression rings on each piston. Using a feeler gauge, check the side clearance of the piston rings. If the side clearance is too large, replace the piston; if the side clearance is too small, cut the land areas a little larger.

Using a feeler gauge to check the ring end gap, lubricate the cylinder wall, then (using an inverted piston) drive the new ring(s) approximately 25-50mm below the top of the cylinder bore.

NOTE: *If the ring gap is too small, carefully remove the rings and file the ends until the proper gap is acquired.*

PISTON PIN REPLACEMENT

The piston pin, the piston and the connecting rod are held together as an assembly, by pressing piston pin into the connecting rod. An arbor press and a special pin removing stand tool No. ST13040000 (1973-78), KV10105300 (1979-81), or KV10107400 (1982 and later), are used for removing and installing the piston pin.

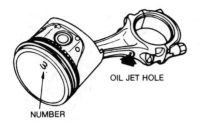

Piston and rod positioning—A-series engines

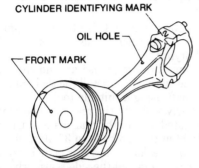

Piston and rod positioning, E-series

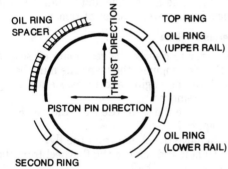

Ring positioning, E-series

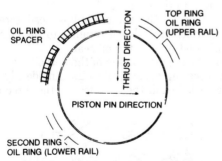

Piston ring placement—A-series engines

NOTE: *The piston pin should slide smoothly into the piston, using hand pressure, at room temperature.*

IDENTIFICATION AND POSITIONING

The pistons are marked with a notch or a number stamped on the piston head. When installed in the engine the notch or number

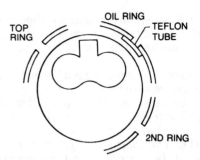

Space CD17 ring gaps 120° apart when installing piston

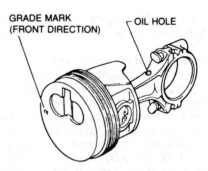

CD17 piston identification marks

markings must be facing the front of the engine.

The connecting rods are installed in the engine with the oil hole facing the right side of the engine.

NOTE: *It is advisable to number the pistons, connecting rods and bearing caps in some manner so that they can be reinstalled in the same cylinder, facing in the same direction from which they are removed.*

PISTON RING REPLACEMENT

A piston ring expander is necessary for removing and installing the piston rings (to avoid damaging them). When the rings are removed, clean the ring grooves using an appropriate ring groove cleaning tool, using care not to cut too deeply. Use solvent to thoroughly remove all of the carbon and varnish deposits.

When installing the rings, make sure that the stamped mark on the ring is facing upwards. Install the bottom rings first, then the upper ones last. Be sure to use a ring expander, to keep from breaking the rings.

ROD BEARING REPLACEMENT

The connecting rod side clearance and the big-end bearing inspection should be performed while the rods are still installed in the engine. Determine the clearance between the connecting rod sides and the crankshaft, using a feeler gauge. If the side clearance is below the minimum tolerance, have a machine shop correct the tolerance; if the clearance is excessive, substitute an unworn rod and recheck the clearance.

To check the connecting rod big-end bearing clearances, remove the rod bearing caps one at a time. Using a clean, dry shop rag, thoroughly clean all of the oil from the crank journal and the bearing insert in the cap.

NOTE: *The Plastigage® gauging material you will be using to check the clearances is soluble in oil; therefore any oil on the journal or bearing could result in an incorrect reading.*

Lay a strip of Plastigage® across the bearing insert. Reinsert the bearing cap and retorque to specifications.

Remove the rod cap and determine the bearing clearance by comparing the width of the now flattened Plastigage® to the scale on the Plastigage® envelope. The journal taper is determined by comparing the width of the strip near its ends. Rotate the crankshaft 90° and retest, to determine the journal eccentricity.

CAUTION: *DO NOT rotate the crankshaft with Plastigage® installed, for an incorrect reading will result.*

If the clearances are not within the tolerances, the bearing inserts must be replaced with ones of the correct oversize or undersize and/or the crankshaft must be ground. If installing new bearing inserts, make sure that the tabs fit correctly into the notch of the bearing cap and rod. Lubricate the face of each insert before installing them onto the crankshaft.

Rear Main Oil Seal

REPLACEMENT

A Series And CD 17 (Diesel) Engines

In order to replace the rear main oil seal, the rear main bearing cap must be removed. Removal of the rear main bearing cap requires the use of a special rear main bearing cap puller. Also, the oil seal is installed with a special crankshaft rear oil seal drift. Unless these or similar tools are available to you, it is recommended that the oil seal be replaced by a Datsun/Nissan service center or an independent mechanic experienced in working on these cars.

1. Remove the engine and transmission assembly from the vehicle.
2. Remove the transmission from the engine. Remove the oil pan.
3. Remove the clutch from the flywheel.
4. Remove the flywheel from the crankshaft.
5. Except on the CD 17, remove the rear main bearing cap together with the bearing cap side seals.
6. Remove the rear main oil seal from

Installing A-series rear oil seal using drift

around the crankshaft. On the CD 17, pry the old seal from around the crankshaft with a small prybar.

7. Apply lithium grease around the sealing lip of the oil seal and install the seal around the crankshaft using a suitable tool.

8. Apply sealer to the rear main bearing cap as indicated, install the rear main bearing cap, and tighten the cap bolts to 33-40 ft. lbs.

9. Apply sealant to the rear main bearing cap side seals and install the side seals, driving the seals into place with a suitable drift.

10. Assemble the engine and install it in the vehicle in the reverse order of removal.

E-Series Engines

In order to replace the rear main oil seal in the E series engines, the transaxle must be removed, or the engine and transaxle assembly must be removed.

1. Remove the transaxle from the car. Refer to Chapter 7.

2. Remove the clutch from the flywheel.

3. Unbolt and remove the flywheel from the end of the crankshaft.

4. Unbolt the two bolts attaching the oil seal retainer to the oil pan.

5. Remove the three Phillips head screws that attach the oil seal retainer to the engine block, and remove the oil seal.

6. During installation of the new oil seal, apply a coating of clean oil to the outside edge of the seal. Install the new seal in the direction

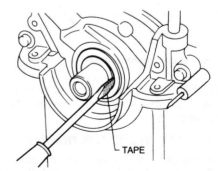

Prying out the oil seal on the CD-17 series engine using a suitable tool

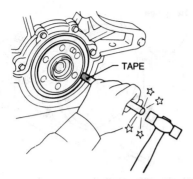

Drive in the new oil seal—CD-17 series engines

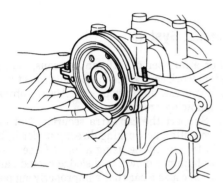

Installing E-series rear oil seal retainer

that the dust seal lip faces (to the outside of the crankcase). Coat the mating shaft with clean oil also, when installing the oil seal retainer, to prevent scratches and a folded lip.

7. Install the retainer and the three retaining screws fastening it to the block and the two bolts attaching it to the oil pan.

8. Install the flywheel onto the end of the crankshaft and torque the retaining bolts as described below. Install the clutch and transaxle as described in Chapter 7.

Crankshaft and Main Bearings

REMOVAL AND INSTALLATION

1. Refer to the Piston and Connecting Rod, Removal and Installation procedures, in this section and remove the connecting rod bearings from the crankshaft.

NOTE: *It may not be necessary to remove the piston/connecting rod assemblies from the cylinder block.*

2. On the A-series engine, remove the timing chain and the flywheel from the engine. On the E-series engine, remove the jackshaft sprocket, the crankshaft sprocket, the front side rear timing plate, then the clutch/flywheel assembly (manual transmission) or driveplate (automatic transmission), the rear oil seal retainer and the rear plate.

3. Check the crankshaft thrust clearance (end play) before removing the crankshaft from the engine block. Using a pry bar, pry the crankshaft forward to the extent of its travel and measure the clearance at the No. 3 main bearing. Pry the crankshaft rearward to the extent of its travel and measure the clearance on the other side of the bearing.

NOTE: *If the clearance is greater than specified, the thrust bearing must be replaced. When removing the crankshaft bearing caps, be sure to keep the bearing together with the caps, unless new bearings are going to be installed.*

4. Remove the crankshaft bearing caps, the cap bearings and the crankshaft from the engine.

5. To install, check the clearances with the Plastigage® method, as described just below, and then replace the bearings (if necessary). Lubricate both the bearing wear surfaces and all crankshaft wear surfaces thoroughly with clean engine oil. Torque the crankshaft bearing cap bolts to specification.

NOTE: *When torquing the main bearing caps, start with the center bearing and work towards both ends at the same time.*

6. On the A-series engine, replace the timing chain and the flywheel onto the engine. On the E-series engine, install the rear oil seal retainer and rear plate and then the clutch/flywheel assembly or driveplate (automatic transmission). Install the front side rear timing plate, crankshaft sprocket and jackshaft sprocket.

7. On the E-Series engine , install the timing belt as described above.

8. On all engines, Refer to the Piston and Connecting Rod, Removal and Installation procedures, in this section and install the connecting rod bearings from the crankshaft. Perform the remaining steps of engine assembly and installation as detailed there.

CLEANING AND INSPECTION

The crankshaft inspection and servicing should be handled exclusively by a reputable machinist, for most necessary procedures require a dial indicator, fixing jigs and a large micrometer; also machine tools, such as: crankshaft grinder. The crankshaft should be throughly cleaned (especially the oil passages), Magnafluxed (to check for minute cracks) and the following checks made: Main journal diameter, crank pin (connecting rod journal) diameter, taper, out-of-round and run-out. Wear, beyond the specification limits, in any of these areas means the crankshaft must be reground or replaced.

MAIN BEARING CLEARANCE CHECK AND REPLACEMENT

Checking the main bearing clearances is done in the same manner as checking the connecting rod big-end clearances.

1. With the crankshaft installed, remove the main bearing cap. Clean all of the oil from the bearing insert (in the cap and the crankshaft journal), for the Plastigage® material is oil-soluble.

2. Lay a strip of Plastigage® across the full width of the bearing cap and install the bearing cap, then torque the cap to specifications.

NOTE: *DO NOT rotate the crankshaft with the Plastigage® installed.*

3. Remove the bearing cap and compare the scale on the Plastigage® envelope with the flattened Plastigage® material in the bearing. The journal taper is determined by comparing the width of both ends of the Plastigage® material. Rotate the crankshaft 90° and retest, to determine eccentricity.

4. Repeat the procedure for the remaining bearings. If the bearing journal and insert appear to be in good shape (with no unusual wear visible) and are within tolerances, no further main bearing service is required. If unusual wear is evident and/or the clearances are outside specifications, the bearings must be replaced and the cause of their wear determined.

Flywheel and Ring Gear

REMOVAL AND INSTALLATION

1. Refer to Chapter 7 and remove the automatic transmission or transaxle and torque converter, or the manual transmission/transaxle and clutch.

2. If there is doubt about the condition of the flywheel, locate a dial indicator on the outer surface. Force the crankshaft all the way forward; then, zero the indicator. Turn the crankshaft smoothly without forcing it rearward. Note the total indication reading. It should be 0.15mm or less. Otherwise, the flywheel requires replacement.

3. To replace the flywheel, support it securely with a jack. Then, remove the bolts and remove it from the rear of the crankshaft.

4. Place the new flywheel in position and support it securely, rotating it if necessary and shifting it up and down to line up all boltholes.

5. Install the flywheel bolts and torque in three stages to the torque specified in the Torque Specifications Chart.

RING GEAR REPLACEMENT

The ring gear is integral with the flywheel. If it is damaged due to starter misuse or mechanical problems, replace the flywheel assembly.

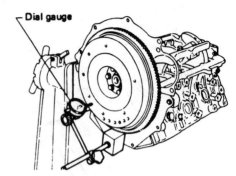

Checking flywheel runout

Exhaust System

For a number of different reasons, exhaust system work can be the most dangerous type of work you can do on your car. Always observe the following precautions:

1. Support the car extra securely. Not only will you often be working directly under it, but you'll frequently be using a lot of force -- say, heavy hammer blows, to dislodge rusted parts. This can cause a car that's improperly supported to shift and possibly fall.

2. Wear goggles. Exhaust system parts are always rusty. Metal chips can be dislodged, even when you're only turning rusted bolts. Attempting to pry pipes apart with a chisel makes chips fly even more frequently.

3. If you're using a cutting torch, keep it at a great distance from either the fuel tank or lines. Stop what you're doing and feel the temperature of fuel bearing pipes or the tank frequently. Even slight heat can expand or vaporize the fuel, resulting in accumulated vapor or even a liquid leak near your torch.

4. Watch where your hammer blows fall. You could easily tap a brake or fuel line when you hit an exhaust system part with a galncing blow. Inspect all lines and hoses in the area where you've been working before driving the car.

Special Tools

A number of special exhaust system tools can be rented from auto supply houses or local stores that rent special equipment. A common one is a tail pipe expander, designed to enable you to join pipes of identical diameter.

It may also be quite helpful to use solvents designed to loosen rusted bolts or flanges. Soaking rusted parts the night before you do the job can speed the work of freeing rusted parts considerably. Remember that these solvents are often flammable. Apply them only after the parts are cool.

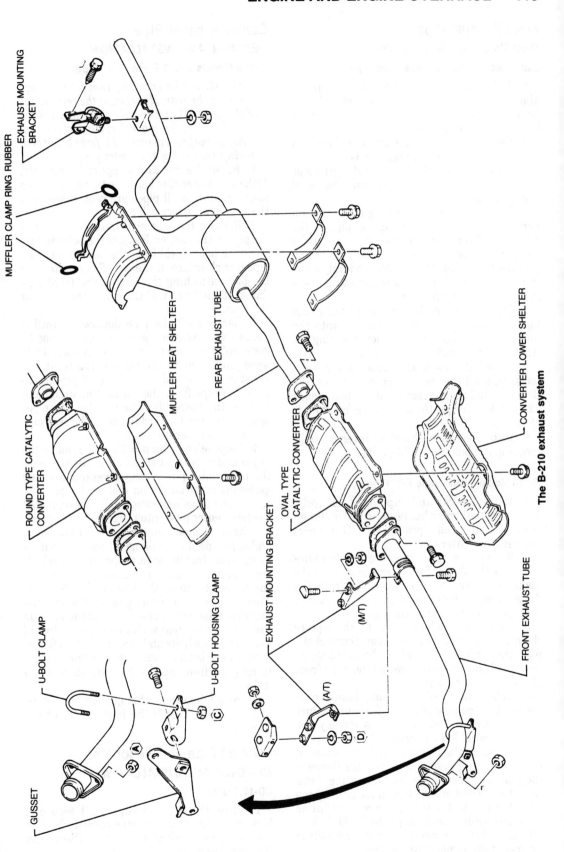

The B-210 exhaust system

Front Exhaust Pipe
REMOVAL AND INSTALLATION
Sentra Models with 2-Piece Front Pipe

1. Raise the car and support it securely. Make sure the engine has been turned off for an hour or more so all pipes are cool. Disconnect the negative battery cable.

2. Remove the bolts fastening the clamps to the head shields. Remove the two bolts fastening the two halves of the heat shield together at the rear. Remove the upper and lower halves of the heat shield.

3. Remove the three attaching nuts from underneath the flange fastening the pipe to the manifold. Then, remove the nuts and bolts from the flange at the rear of the pipe. Then, pull the pipe down at the front and out at the rear. Remove gaskets and any gasketing material left on sealing flanges.

4. Install a new gasket onto the front of the pipe. Install the pipe by inserting it into the muffler pipe (at its rear) and then inserting the front up into the exhaust manifold.

5. Install the bolts and nuts at the rear, torquing until the spring located between the flanges is fully compressed and the bolts reach 12-15 ft. lbs. Torque the nuts at the front to 14-19 ft. lbs.

6. Install the heat shield in reverse order, torquing the bolts to 36-72 in. lbs.

B-210 Models with Single Front Pipe

1. Raise the car and support it securely. Make sure the engine has been turned off for an hour or more so all pipes are cool. Disconnect the negative battery cable.

2. Remove the three attaching nuts from underneath the flange fastening the pipe to the manifold. Then, remove the bolts from the flange (connecting to the front of the catalytic converter) at the rear of the pipe.

3. Remove the bolts connecting the pipe to the mounting bracket at the rear. Support the pipe from underneath. Unbolt the pipe bracket from the body mounting bracket near the front of the pipe. Remove the pipe.

4. Unbolt the U-bolt type clamp located near the front of the pipe and transfer it to the new pipe or replace it. Remove gaskets and any gasketing material left on sealing flanges.

5. To install the pipe, first insert the pipe at the front, install a new gasket over the flange at the rear, and install the rear mounting bolts. Install the front mounting nuts and tghten them to 14-19 ft. lbs. Install the rear mounting bolts and washers and torque to 23-31 ft. lbs.

6. Install bracket mounting nuts and bolts in reverse of the removal procedure.

Center Exhaust Pipe
REMOVAL AND INSTALLATION
Sentra Models with 2-Piece Front Pipe

WARNING: *The catalytic converter is supported at the rear. However, if the rear flange of this pipe will not readily separate from the front flange of the converter, support the converter at the front to prevent it from being bent during removal of the center pipe.*

1. Raise the car and support it securely. Make sure the engine has been turned off for an hour or more so all pipes are cool. Disconnect the negative battery cable.

2. Remove the bolt attaching the center of the pipe to the hanger. Remove the bolts and remove the heat shield from the forward exhaust pipe (for clearance at the rear flange). Remove the bolts attaching the pipe to the front pipe flange at the front and the converter flange at the rear.

3. Gently shift the pipe downward until it clears the converter flange. If this cannot be done easily because the pipe is frozen at its forward joint, remove the nuts at the front (exhaust manifold) end of the forward pipe, separate that pipe from the exhaust manifold and remove the assembly. Then, twist the pipes apart or tap the forward flange of the rear pipe rearward to separate them.

4. Remove the clamp bolts and remove the upper and lower heat shields. Install them onto the new center pipe. Remove gaskets and any gasketing material left on sealing flanges.

5. If the pipes separated easily above, install the new center pipe onto the front pipe (inserting the front pipe into its center) at the front, and then line up the flange at the rear with a new gasket. Install the nuts and bolts loosely. If they did not separate above, assemble them at the center, torquing the bolts to 12-15 ft. lbs. Then, connect the front pipe at the exhaust manifold flange with a new gasket.; then line up the flange at the rear with a new gasket. Install the rear flange bolts and torque to 12-15 ft. lbs. If they have been loosened, torque the nuts attaching the front pipe to the manifold to 14-19 ft.lbs.

6. Install the support hanger bolt and torque to 9-12 ft. lbs. Install the heat shield for the front pipe.

Exhaust Pipe and Resonator
REMOVAL AND INSTALLATION
CD-17 Diesel

1. Raise the car and support it securely. Make sure the engine has been turned off for an hour or more so all pipes are cool. Disconnect the negative battery cable.

2. Support the rear section of the exhaust system. Support the front section also.

3. Remove the nuts from the exhaust manifold retaining studs. Remove the nuts from the rear of the flange at the rear of the resonator (at about the middle of the system).

4. Remove the bolt from the top of the hanger located just forward of the resonator.

5. Pull the front of this section of the exhaust system down and off the exhaust manifold. Pull the rear out of the rear section (you may need to have a helper hold the rear section in place to do this.

6. Install new gaskets at the front and rear of the system, making sure exhaust pipe holes and boltholes line up.

7. Raise the assembly into position and insert the rear studs through the flange at the front of the rear pipe. Raise the front and install it so the studs at the bottom of the exhaust manifold fit through the flange on the front of the pipe. Instals the nuts onto the exhasut manifold studs first; then onto the flange at the rear of the resonator. Torque the manfiold stud nuts to 20-27 ft. lbs. and the resr stud nuts to 23-31 ft. lbs.

8. Inspect the rubber hanger and replace it if necessary. Install the hanger bolt to the body, torquing to 78-102 in. lbs.

Catalytic Converter
REMOVAL AND INSTALLATION
Sentra

1. Raise the car and support it securely. Make sure the engine has been turned off for an hour or more so all pipes are cool. Disconnect the negative battery cable.

2. On models equipped with an Air Injection Valve tube connecting at the rear of the converter, unbolt and disconnect the tube at the converter. If necessary for clearance, disconnect the tube at the forward end and remove it.

3. Support the converter. Then, remove the bolts from the flanges at front and rear.

4. Disconnect the converter at the flanges front and rear. It may be helpful to pry gently at the crack between the halves of flanged connections to do this. When the converter is free, remove it and unbolt and remove the top and bottom halves. Remove gaskets and any gasketing material left on sealing flanges.

5. Bolt the halves of the heat shield onto the new converter. Install new gaskets front and rear, put the converter into position and support it.

6. Install the bolts at either end and torque to 23-31 ft. lbs.

7. Install the A.I.V. tube, line it and a new

gasket up with the flange on the rear of the converter, install the bolts and torqu to 51-69 in. lbs.

B-210 and Other Models with a Single Front Exhaust Pipe

1. Raise the car and support it securely. Make sure the engine has been turned off for an hour or more so all pipes are cool. Disconnect the negative battery cable.

2. Break all four converter mounting bolts (two at the front flange and two at the rear) loose by putting a wrench on each and turning it half a turn. Then, support the converter from underneath. Then, remove the two mounting bolts from the front flange.

3. Disconnect the two rubber hangers from the heat shield on top of the muffler. Move the support to the pipe behind the converter. Then, lower the converter and muffler assembly.

4. Complete removal of the two rear converter flange mounting bolts. Pull the converter forward and off the rear mounting flange.

5. Remove the four mounting bolts holding the top and bottom halves of the converter heat shields together and pull the heat shields off the converter. Remove gaskets and any gasketing material left on sealing flanges.

6. Install the heat shields onto the new converter, torquing the bolts to 55-73 in. lbs. Install the gasket onto the rear flange, insert the nipple of the rear exhaust pipe into the rear of the converter, line up the boltholes, and install the bolts finger tight.

7. Raise the assembly and line up the boltholes in the forward flange. Install the bolts and washers finger tight.

8. Reinstall the rubber muffler hangers. Torque all four converter mounting bolts to 23-31 ft. lbs.

Rear Exhaust Pipe and Muffler
REMOVAL AND INSTALLATION

1. Raise the car and support it securely. Make sure the engine has been turned off for an hour or more so all pipes are cool. Disconnect the negative battery cable.

2. Support the catalytic converter and the muffler. Remove the bolts from the rear of the catalytic converter. On the Sentra, unbolt the hangers at the rear exhaust pipe (1) and the muffler (2).

3. On B-210 and other cars with an integral muffler and rear pipe remove the two rubber hangers from the muffler heat shield and the nut and washer from the mounting bracket welded to the rear pipe.

4. Remove the muffler and rear exhaust pipe

assembly. On the Sentra (both gas and diesel), the muffler's front pipe fits inside an expanded section of the rear exhaust pipe. On these cars, remove the nuts and disassemble and remove the U-clamp. Then, twist the muffler while pulling it out of the rear exhaust pipe to separate the two. If the two are badly corroded together, it may help to apply solvents to the joint; to tap the pipe forward or, if the exhaust tube is bad and the muffler is being saved, to carefully chisel the pipe off the muffler. If the two are very badly corroded together, the best procedure may be to simply replace both parts.

5. On the B-210, remove the four retaining bolts and remove the muffler heat shield from the top of the muffler and the two straps from underneath. Install these parts onto the new muffler, torquing the forward bolts to 26-43 in. lbs. and the rear bolts to 69-104 in. lbs. Remove gaskets and any gasketing material left on sealing flanges.

6. On Sentras, line the muffler and pipe up at the right angle, cover the outside diameter of the mufler pipe with an exhaust system sealer, and then insert the muffler into the pipe. Assemble the U-clamp around the muffler rear exhaust pipe with the U-bolt on top, install the nuts and torque to 12-15 ft. lbs.

7. Inspect all non-metal hangers and unbolt and replace any that are defective. Hang the assembly to the underside of the car in reverse order. Install a new gasket for the flange on the front of the exhaust pipe. On B-210s, insert the rear exhaust pipe nipple into the rear of the converter. On Sentras, align the gasket and pipe flange and converter flange boltholes and then install the bolts and washers. Torque the bolts to 23-31 ft. lbs.

Emission Controls

EMISSION CONTROLS

There are three types of automotive pollutants; crankcase fumes, exhaust gases and gasoline evaporation. The equipment that is used to limit these pollutants is commonly called emission control equipment.

Crankcase Emission Controls

OPERATION

The crankcase emission control equipment consists of a positive crankcase ventilation valve (PCV), a closed or open oil filler cap, and hoses to connect this equipment. When the engine is running, a small portion of the gases which are formed in the combustion chamber during combustion leak by the piston rings and enter the crankcase. Since these gases are under pressure they tend to escape from the crankcase and enter into the atmosphere. If these gases were allowed to remain in the crankcase, they would contaminate the engine oil and cause sludge to build up. If the gases are allowed to escape into the atmosphere, they would pollute the air, as they contain unburned hydrocarbons. The crankcase emission control equipment recycles these gases back into the engine combustion chamber where they are burned.

Crankcase gases are recycled in the following manner: while the engine is running, clean filtered air is drawn into the crankcase through the carburetor air filter and then through a hose leading to the rocker cover. As the air passes through the crankcase it picks up the combustion gases and carries them out of the crankcase, up through the PCV valve and into the intake manifold. After they enter the intake manifold they are drawn into the combustion chamber and burned.

The most critical component in the system is the PCV valve. This vacuum controlled valve regulates the amount of gases which are recycled into the combustion chamber. At low engine speeds the valve is partially closed, limiting the flow of gases into the intake manifold. As engine speed increases, the valve opens to admit greater quantities of the gases into the intake manifold. If the valve should become blocked or plugged, the gases will be prevented from escaping from the crankcase by the normal route. Since these gases are under pressure, they will find their own way out of the crankcase. This alternate route is usually a weak oil seal or gasket in the engine. As the gas escapes by the gasket, it also creates an oil leak. Besides causing oil leaks, a clogged PCV valve also allows these gases to remain in the crankcase, promoting the formation of sludge in the engine. Since the valve admits some fresh air to the intake manifold, it can also cause mixture problems if it should become stuck open because of sludge inside. In this case, a bad valve could be indicated by rough engine idle.

The above explanation and the troubleshooting procedure which follows applies to all engines with PCV systems.

SERVICE

Testing

Check the PCV system hoses and connections, to see that there are no leaks; then replace or tighten, as necessary.

To check the valve, remove it and blow through both of its ends. When blowing from the side which goes toward the intake manifold, very little air should pass through it. When blowing from the crankcase (valve cover) side, air should pass through freely. Also, pull the hose off of the valve, leaving it installed in the intake manifold. Start the engine and allow it to idle. There should be a strong vacuum so that if the valve is touched with a finger, it is drawn tightly against it.

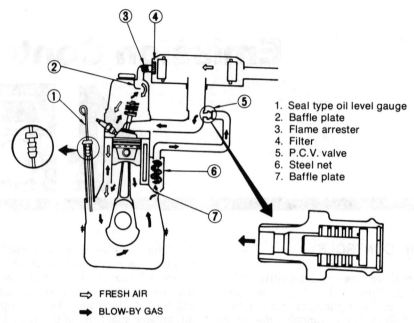

1. Seal type oil level gauge
2. Baffle plate
3. Flame arrester
4. Filter
5. P.C.V. valve
6. Steel net
7. Baffle plate

⇨ FRESH AIR

➡ BLOW-BY GAS

Crankcase emissions control system, A-series. E-series similar

Replace the valve with a new one, if the valve fails to function as outlined.

NOTE: *Do not attempt to clean or adjust the valve; replace it with a new one.*

PCV Valve Removal and Installation

To remove the PCV valve, simply loosen the hose clamp and remove the valve from the manifold-to-crankcase hose. Then, unscrew it from the intake manifold. Install the PCV valve in the reverse order of removal. Tighten the valve gently—it will seal completely with a slight amount of torque.

PCV Filter Removal and Installation

Replace the PCV filter inside the air cleaner when you replace the PCV valve, or more frequently if operating in dusty or smoggy conditions.

Evaporative Emission Control System

When raw fuel evaporates, the vapors contain hydrocarbons. To prevent these nasties from escaping into the atmosphere, the fuel evaporative emission control system was developed.

There are two different evaporative emission control systems used on Datsuns.

The system used through 1974 consists of a sealed fuel tank, a vapor-liquid separator, a flow guide (check) valve, and all of the hoses connecting these components, in the above or-

der, leading from the fuel tank to the PCV hose, which connects the crankcase to the PCV valve.

In operation, the vapor formed in the fuel tank passes through the vapor separator, onto the flow guide valve and the crankcase. When the engine is not running, if the fuel vapor pressure in the vapor separator goes above 0.4 in. Hg., the flow guide valve opens and allows the vapor to enter the engine crankcase. Otherwise the flow guide valve is closed to the vapor separator while the engine is not running. When the engine is running, and a vacuum is developed in the fuel tank or in the engine crankcase and the difference of pressure between the relief side and the fuel tank or crankcase becomes 2 in. Hg., the relief valve opens and allows ambient air from the air cleaner into the fuel tank or the engine crankcase. This ambient air replaces the vapor within the fuel tank or crankcase, bringing the fuel tank or crankcase back into a neutral or positive pressure range.

The system used on 1975 and later models consists of sealed fuel tank, vapor-liquid separator (certain models only), vapor vent line, carbon canister, vacuum signal line and a canister purge line.

In operation, fuel vapors and/or liquid are routed to the liquid/vapor separator or check valve where liquid fuel is directed back into the fuel tank as fuel vapors flow into the charcoal filled canister. The charcoal absorbs and stores the fuel vapors when the engine is not running or is at idle. When the throttle valves in the carburetor (or air intakes for fuel injection) are opened, vacuum from above the throttle valves

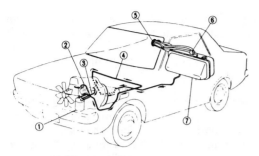

1. Carbon canister
2. Vacuum signal line
3. Canister vent line
4. Vapor vent line
5. Fuel filler cap with vacuum relief valve
6. Fuel check valve
7. Fuel tank

Evaporative emission control system schematic

Applying vacuum to carbon canister

is routed through a vacuum signal line to the purge control valve on the canister. The control valve opens and allows the fuel vapors to be drawn from the canister through a purge line and into the intake manifold and the combustion chambers.

On 1985 and later models, the system is cut off by a Thermostatic Vacuum Valve or a solenoid operated by the E.C.C.S. system (carburetors) or the E.C.U. (fuel injection). If a Thermostatic Vacuum Valve is used, it should consistently cut off vacuum to the purge control valve at lower engine temperatures. The electronically controlled systems will also cut off the vacuum to the purge control valve under various engine operating conditions. In either case, however, if there is vacuum to the Purge Control Valve under cold engine operating conditions, or, if vacuum is never applied to the Vacuum Cut Solenoid Valve operated by the electronics, the Thermostatic Vacuum Switch or associated vacuum lines may be defective.

INSPECTION AND SERVICE

Check the hoses for proper connections and damage. Replace as necessary. Check the vapor separator tank for fuel leaks, distortion and dents, and replace as necessary. If there is never any vacuum to the Purge Control Valve, or if it is supplied vacuum continuously (even when the engine is cold) refer the problem to a qualified technician. Diagnosis of the E.C.C.S. system or the E.C.U. function are beyond the scope of a do-it-yourself book.

Flow Guide Valve – Through 1974

Remove the flow guide valve and inspect it for leakage by blowing air into the ports in the valve. When air is applied from the fuel tank side, the flow guide valve is normal if the air

passes into the check side (crankcase side), but not into the relief side (air cleaner side). When air is applied from the check side, the valve is normal if the passage of air is restricted. When air is applied from the relief side (air cleaner side), the valve is normal if air passes into the fuel tank side or into the check side.

Carbon Canister and Purge Control Valve – 1975 and Later

To check the operation of the carbon canister purge control valve, disconnect the rubber hose between the canister control valve and the T-fitting, at the T-fitting. Inhale air on the hose leading to the control valve. Make sure there are no leaks. If the control valve leaks, remove the top cover of the valve and check for a dislocated or cracked diaphragm. If the diaphragm is damaged, a repair kit containing a new diaphragm, retainer, and spring is available and should be installed.

The carbon canister has an air filter in the bottom of the canister. The filter element should be checked once a year or every 12,000 miles; more frequently if the car is operated in dusty areas. Replace the filter by pulling it out of the bottom of the canister and installing a new one.

REMOVAL AND INSTALLATION

Removal and installation of the various evaporative emission control system components consists of disconnecting the hoses, disconnecting any electrical connectors, loosening retaining screws, and removing the part which is to be replaced or checked. Install in the reverse order. When replacing hose, make sure that it is fuel and vapor resistant.

Spark Timing Control System

The spark timing control system has been used in different forms on Datsuns since 1972. The first system, Transmission Controlled Spark System (TCS) was used on most Datsuns through 1979. This system consists of a thermal vacuum valve, a vacuum switching valve, a high gear detecting switch, and a number of vacuum hoses. Basically, the system is designed to retard full spark advance except when the car is in high gear and the engine is at normal operating temperature. At all other times, the spark advance is retarded to one degree or another.

The 1980-83 Spark Timing Control System replaces the TCS system. The major difference is that it works solely from engine water temperature changes rather than a transmission-mounted switch. The system includes a thermal vacuum valve, a vacuum delay valve, and attendant hoses. It performs the same function as the earlier TCS system; to retard full spark advance at times when high levels of pollutants would otherwise by given off.

On 1984 and later models the ignition timing is controlled by the central electronic control unit adjusting the engine operating conditions: as the best ignition timing in each driving condition and is determined by the electric signal calculated in the unit.

The information signals (used to determine the engine timing) are received from the water temperature, the engine rpm, the engine load and etc. The electronic control unit sends signals to the power transistor (of the ignition coil) and controls the ignition timing.

The distributor is equipped with a sensor and a signal rotor plate (photo-electric), which detects the position of the crankshaft and sends a signal to the control unit to control the various operations. The signal rotor plate has 360 (at 1° intervals) slots surrounding the outer edge (for detecting the rpm and ignition timing control) and 4 (at 90° intervals) slots on a inner circle (for detecting the piston TDC). When the signal rotor plate cuts the light signal between the Light Emitting Diode (LED) and the Photo Diode, an alternate voltage is created and sent to the control unit.

INSPECTION AND ADJUSTMENTS

Through 1983

Normally the TCS and Spark Timing Control systems should be trouble-free. However, if you suspect a problem in the system, first check to make sure all wiring (if so equipped) and hoses are connected and free from dirt. Also check to make sure the distributor vacuum advance is working properly. If everything appears all right, connect a timing light to the engine and make sure the initial timing is correct. On vehicles with the TCS system, run the engine until it reaches normal operating temperature, and then have an assistant sit in the car and shift the transmission through all the gears slowly. If the system is functioning properly, the tim-

ing will be 10 to 15 degrees advanced in high gear (compared to the other gear positions). If the system is still not operating correctly, you will have to check for continuity at all the connections with a test light.

To test the Spark Timing Control System, connect a timing light and check the ignition timing while the temperature gauge is in the "cold" position. Write down the reading. Allow the engine to run with the timing light attached until the temperature needle reaches the center of the gauge. As the engine is warming up, check with the timing light to make sure the ignition timing retards. When the temperature needle is in the middle of the gauge, the ignition timing should advance from its previous position. If the ignition timing does not change, replace the thermal vacuum valve.

1984 and Later

The ignition timing is automatically controlled by the control unit and adjustment is unnecessary. The system requires extremely complex and specialized test equipment and procedures. Thus, its diagnosis and repair are well beyond the scope of do-it-yourself repairs. The latest models (1987-88) have a self diagnosing capability which may help you to at least partially discover and confirm the source of a problem. Refer to the section dealing with troubleshooting the electronic ignition in Chapter 2 for the specific procedure.

Early Fuel Evaporation System

The Early Fuel Evaporation System is used on the A-series engines. The system's purpose is to heat the air/fuel mixture when the engine is below normal operating temperature. The 1973-79 engines use a system much akin to the old style exhaust manifold heat riser. The only adjustment necessary is to occasionally lubricate the counterweight, with a spray-type heat riser lubricant. Other than that, the system should be trouble-free.

The 1980 and later engines use coolant water instead of exhaust gas heat to pre-warm the fuel mixture. This system should be trouble-free.

Throttle Opener Control System (TOCS)

The Throttle Opener Control System (TOCS) used on the A-series engines (except 1980 and later California cars) and Canadian Sentras is designed to reduce hydrocarbon emissions during coasting conditions.

During coasting, high manifold vacuum prevents the complete combustion of the air/fuel mixture because of the reduced amount of air.

This condition will result in a large amount of hydrocarbon (HC) emissions. Enriching the air/fuel mixture for a short time (during the high vacuum condition) will reduce the emission of the HC. However, enriching the air/fuel mixture with only the mixture adjusting screw will cause poor engine idle or invite an increase in the carbon monoxide (CO) content of the exhaust gases.

The TOCS system used on the 1980 and later A-series non-California cars and Canadian Sentras consists of a servo diaphragm, vacuum control valve, throttle opener solenoid valve, speed detecting switch and amplifier (on manual transmission models). Automatic transmission models use the speed detecting switch and amplifier. At the moment when manifold vacuum increases, as during deceleration, the vacuum control valve opens to transfer the manifold vacuum to the servo diaphragm chamber, and the carburetor throttle valve opens slightly. Under this condition, the proper amount of fresh air is sucked into the combustion chamber, resulting in a more thorough ignition and more complete burning of the HC in the exhaust gases.

ADJUSTMENT – TOCS

1. Connect a tachometer to the engine.
2. Connect a quick-response vacuum gauge to the intake manifold.
3. Disconnect the solenoid valve electrical leads.
4. Start and warm up the engine until it reaches normal operating temperature.
5. Adjust the idle speed to the proper specification (see Tune Up Specifications chart).
6. Raise the engine speed to 3,000-3,500 rpm under no-load (transmission in Neutral or Park), then allow the throttle to snap closed quickly. Take notice as to whether or not the engine rpm returns to idle speed and if it does, how long the fall in rpm is interrupted before it reaches idle speed.

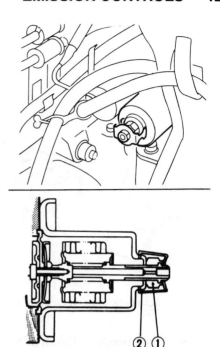

1. Adjusting nut   2. Lock spring
TOCS location and adjustment

Connect a quick response vacuum gauge to intake manifold when checking Throttle Opener Control System (TOCS)

Adjusting the TOCS pressure

At the moment the throttle is snapped shut at high engine rpm, the vacuum in the intake manifold reaches between −23.6 in. Hg. or above, then gradually decreases to idle level.

The pressure of the TOCS while operating should be −22.05 ± 0.79 in. Hg.

Turning the adjusting screw clockwise raises the vacuum level. Turning the screw counterclockwise lowers the vacuum level.

NOTE: *When adjusting the TOCS, turn the adjusting nut in or out with the lock spring in place. Always set the lock spring properly to prevent changes in the set pressure.*

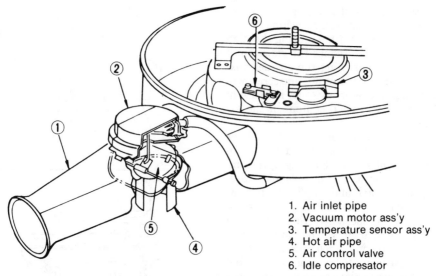

1. Air inlet pipe
2. Vacuum motor ass'y
3. Temperature sensor ass'y
4. Hot air pipe
5. Air control valve
6. Idle compresator

Automatic temperature controlled air cleaner, B210 and 210. Sentra similar

Automatic Temperature Controlled Air Cleaner

The rate at which fuel is drawn into the airstream and atomized (the process where the liquid gasoline is changed into a very fine mist) in the carburetor varies with the temperature of the air with which the fuel is being mixed. Because your car operates in a wide range of air temperatures, this air/fuel ratio cannot be held constant for efficient fuel combustion. Cold air drawn into the engine causes a denser and leaner air/fuel mixture and inefficient fuel atomization, and thus, more hydrocarbons in the exhaust gas. Hot air drawn into the engine causes a richer air/fuel mixture and, although there is more efficient atomization, there will still be excess hydrocarbons in the exhaust gases.

Although the throttle body fuel injection system used on the latest models does not require air preheating to keep the mixture ratio correct, it is still used. This is because keeping the air at a consistent temperature helps the atomization process and helps evaporate fuel that lays in the intake manifold. Thus, slighly rough running problems, especially when the engine is cold, may be due to a malfunction in this system.

The automatic temperature controlled air cleaner is designed so that the temperature of the ambient air being drawn into the engine is automatically controlled, to hold the temperature of the air and, consequently, the fuel/air ratio at a constant rate for efficient fuel combustion.

A temperature sensing vacuum switch controls vacuum applied to a vacuum motor operating a valve in the intake snorkle of the air cleaner. When the engine is cold or the air being drawn into the engine is cold, the vacuum motor opens the valve, allowing air heated by the exhaust manifold to be drawn into the engine. As the engine warms up, the temperature sensing unit partially or fully shuts off the vacuum applied to the vacuum motor. This allows the valve to close as far as necessary to reduce or completely shut off the heated air and allow more cooler, outside (under hood) air to be drawn into the engine. If the temperature reaches the maximum setting for the temperature sensing vacuum switch, only unheated air will be introduced.

TESTING

When the air around the temperature sensor of the unit mounted inside the air cleaner housing reaches 100°F, the sensor should block the flow of vacuum to the air control valve vacuum motor. When the temperature around the temperature sensor is below 100°F, the sensor should allow vacuum to pass into the air valve vacuum motor thus blocking off the air cleaner snorkle to under hood (unheated) air.

When the temperature around the sensor is above 118°F, the air control valve should be completely open to under hood air.

If the air cleaner fails to operate correctly, check for loose or broken vacuum hoses. If the hoses are not the cause, replace the vacuum motor in the air cleaner.

Exhaust Gas Recirculation (EGR)

The EGR system is used on all 1974 and later B210 and 210 model Datsuns and Nissan Sentras. Exhaust gas recirculation is used to reduce combustion temperatures in the engine, thereby reducing the oxides of nitrogen emissions.

An EGR valve is mounted on the center of the intake manifold. The recycled exhaust gas is drawn into the bottom of the intake manifold riser portion through the exhaust manifold heat stove and EGR valve. A vacuum diaphragm is connected to a timed signal port at the carburetor flange.

As the throttle valve is opened, vacuum is applied to the EGR valve vacuum diaphragm. When the vacuum reaches about 2 in. Hg. the diaphragm moves against spring pressure and is in a fully up position at 8 in. Hg. of vacuum. As the diaphragm moves up, it opens the exhaust gas metering valve which allows exhaust gas to be pulled into the engine intake manifold. The system does not operate when the engine is idling because the exhaust gas recirculation would cause a rough idle.

On 1975 and later models, a thermal vacuum valve inserted in the engine thermostat housing controls the application of the vacuum to the EGR valve. When the engine coolant reaches a predetermined temperature, the thermal vacuum valve opens and allows vacuum to be routed to the EGR valve. Below the predetermined temperature, the thermal vacuum valve closes and blocks vacuum to the EGR valve.

All 1978-80 B210 and 210 models have a B.P.T. (Back Pressure Transducer) valve installed between the EGR valve and the thermal vacuum valve. The B.P.T. valve monitors exhaust pressure in order to control, through its diaphragm, carburetor throttle vacuum applied to the EGR valve. The diaphragm opens and closes an air bleed, which is connected into the EGR vacuum line. High pressure results in higher levels of exhaust recirculation, because the diaphragm is raised, closing off the air bleed, and allowing more vacuum to reach and open the EGR valve. Thus, the amount of recir-

E-series EGR location on side of intake manifold

culated exhaust gas varies with exhaust pressure.

The 1980 California 210 and all 1981 and later carbureted U.S. 210s and Nissan Sentras use a V.V.T. valve (venturi vacuum transducer) in place of the B.P.T. valve. The V.V.T. monitors exhaust pressure and carburetor vacuum in order to activate the diaphragm which controls the throttle vacuum applied to the EGR control valve. This system expands the operating range of the EGR unit, as well as increasing the EGR flow rate as compared to the B.P.T. unit.

The latest models (1987-88), when equipped with electronic fuel injection, use an EGR & Canister Purge Solenoid Valve to activate the EGR system and canister purge only when: vehicle speed exceeds 6 mph; and engine temperature exceeds 140° F.

Many 1975 and later Datsuns are equipped with an EGR warning system which signals via a light in the dashboard that the EGR system may need service. The EGR warning light should come on every time the starter is engaged as a test to make sure the bulb is not blown. The system uses a counter which works in conjunction with the odometer, and lights the warning signal after the vehicle has traveled a pre-determined number of miles.

To reset the counter, which is mounted in the engine compartment, remove the grommet installed in the side of the counter and insert the tip of a small screwdriver into the hole. Press down on the knob inside the hole. Reinstall the grommet.

TESTING

Pre-1975

Check the operation of the EGR system as follows:

1. Visually inspect the entire EGR control system. Clean the mechanism free of oil and dirt. Replace any rubber hoses found to be cracked or broken.

2. Make sure that the EGR solenoid valve is properly wired.

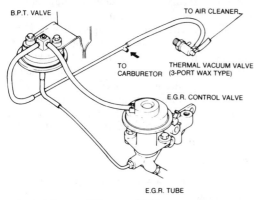

1980 210 Thermal Vacuum Valve

3. Increase the engine speed from idling to 2,000-3,500 rpm. The plate of the EGR control valve diaphragm and the valve shaft should move upward as the engine speed is increased.

4. Disconnect the EGR solenoid valve electrical leads and connect them directly to the vehicle's 12 volt electrical supply (battery). Race the engine again with the EGR solenoid valve connected to a 12 volt power source. The EGR control valve should remain stationary.

5. With the engine running at idle, push up on the EGR control valve diaphragm with your finger. When this is done, the engine idle should become rough and uneven.

6. Inspect the two components of the EGR system as necessary in the following manner:

a. Remove the EGR control valve from the intake manifold.

b. Apply 4.7-5.1 in. Hg. of vacuum to the EGR control valve by sucking on a tube attached to the outlet on top of the valve. The valve should move to the full up position. The valve should remain open for more than 30 seconds after the application of vacuum is discontinued and the vacuum hose is blocked.

c. Inspect the EGR valve for any signs of warpage or damage.

d. Clean the EGR valve seat with a brush and compressed air to prevent clogging.

e. Connect the EGR solenoid valve to a 12 volt DC power source and notice if the valve clicks when intermittently electrified. If the valve clicks, it is considered to be working properly.

f. Check the EGR temperature sensing switch by removing it from the engine and placing it in a container of water together with a thermometer. Connect a self-powered test light to the two electrical leads of the switch.

g. Heat the container of water.

h. The switch should conduct current when the water temperature is below 77°F (25°C) and stop conducting current when the water reaches a temperature somewhere between 88-106°F (31-41°C). Replace the switch if it functions otherwise.

1975 and Later

1. Remove the EGR valve and apply enough vacuum to the diaphragm to open the valve.

2. The valve should remain open for over 30 seconds after the vacuum is removed.

3. Check the valve for damage, such as warpage, cracks, and excessive wear around the valve and seat.

4. Clean the seat with a brush and compressed air and remove any deposits from around the valve and port (seat).

5. To check the operation of the thermal vac-

uum valve, remove the valve from the engine and apply vacuum to the ports of the valve. The valve should not allow vacuum to pass.

6. Place the valve in a container of water with a thermometer and heat the water. When the temperature of the water reaches 134°-145°F (56-63°C), remove the valve and apply vacuum to the ports; the valve should allow vacuum to pass through it.

7. To test the B.P.T. valve installed on some 1978 and later models, disconnect the two vacuum hoses from the valve. Plug one of the ports. While applying pressure to the bottom of the valve, apply vacuum to the unplugged port and check for leakage. If any exists, replace the valve.

8. To test the check valve installed in some 1978 and later models, remove the valve and blow into the side which connects to the EGR valve. Air should flow. When air is applied in the other side, air flow resistance should be greater. If not, replace the valve.

9. To check the V.V.T. valve which replaces the B.T.P. valve on some 1980 and later models, disconnect the top and bottom center hoses and apply a vacuum to the top hose. Check for leaks. If a leak is present, replace the valve.

Mixture Ratio Rich-Lean and EGR Large-Small Exchange Systems

1980 California and all 1981 and later models; California Sentra

These systems control the air-fuel mixture ratio and the amount of recirculated exhaust gas (manual transmission models only) in accordance with the engine coolant temperature and speed of the car. The systems consist of a vacuum switching valve, a power valve, a speed detecting switch amplifier and a water temperature switch.

When the coolant temperature is above 122°F and the car is traveling at least 40 mph, the vacuum switching valve is on and acts to lean down the fuel mixture. It also allows a small amount of EGR to be burned on manual transmission cars. When the coolant temperature is above 122°F but the vehicle is traveling less than 40 miles per hour, the vacuum switching valve is off and allows the mixture to richen. It also allows a large amount of EGR to be burned in manual transmission models. When coolant temperature is below 122°F the vacuum switching valve is always on and acts to lean down the fuel mixture.

TESTING

1. Warm the engine up to operating temperature.

2. Shut off the engine and jack up the drive

wheels of the vehicle just far enough that they clear the ground.

CAUTION: *Make sure the front wheels are chocked when raising the rear end of the car. When you have jacked the car to the desired height, support it with jackstands. DO NOT get in the car and attempt the following procedure with the car on a jack.*

3. Start the engine and shift the transmission into HIGH (top) gear and maintain the indicated speed above 50 mph.

4. Pinch the hose running from the vacuum switching valve to the air cleaner and see if the engine speed decreases and operates erratically.

5. Shift the transmission into the next lowest gear and run the indicated speed lower than 30 mph.

6. Disconnect the vacuum hose running between the vacuum switching valve and the power valve, by detaching it at the power valve and blocking its open end with your finger. The engine should operate erratically. If the expected engine reaction in both of these tests does not happen, check all wiring connections and hoses for breaks and blockage.

E.C.U. Controlled EGR & Canister Purge Control Solenoid Valve (1987-88 Models)

TESTING

NOTE: *To perform these tests, you will need a voltmeter and an ohmmeter.*

If the car consistently gives poor operation when warming up that clears up when the engine gets hot; or if it idles and accelerates poorly and straightens out as soon as it picks up speed, test this valve as follows:

1. Disconnect the E.C.U. 20-pin harness connector. Then turn on the ignition switch. Check for voltage between Terminal 7 of the E.C.U. and ground by connecting a voltmeter between the terminal and ground (+ to Terminal 7). There should be 12 volts. If there is no voltage, skip to Step 3. Otherwise, proceed with the next step.

2. Disconnect the solenoid harness connector.

a. Using an ohmmeter, test for continuity (zero Ω resistance) between terminal "b" of the solenoid valve harness connector on the harness side and terminal 7 of the E.C.U. If there is no continuity, the harness should be repaired.

b. Check for continuity between the terminals of the solenoid valve side of the harness connector. There should be practically 0 Ω resistance. If not, replace the valve. If there is continuity, then energize the valve by run-

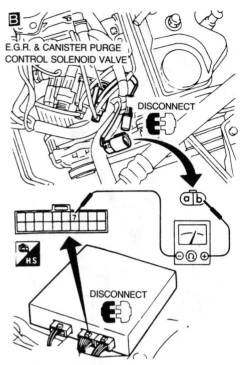

Terminal 7 of the E.C.U. harness connector and Terminal "b" of the solenoid harness connector

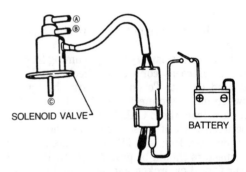

Test the opening of the EGR vacuum solenoid valve by energizing it with the battery as shown. Then, blow through the labeled ports as directed in the text.

ning a jumper to one side from the battery + terminal and grounding the other terminal. With the valve energized, you should be able to blow air through the top connector ("A") on the valve and out the bottom connector ("C"). With the voltage disconnected, you should be able to blow air into the lower connection on top of the valve ("B") and out the connector on the bottom ("C"). If the valve fails either test, replace it.

c. Check for continuity between the other solenoid harness connector prong ("A") and the battery. Connect an ohmmeter between these two points. Repair the harness, ignition

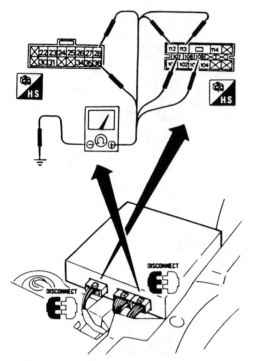

To test the ground circuit of the E.C.U., test the resistance between each of the connectors shown and ground

switch, appropriate fuse, or fusible link "G" as necessary.

3. If there is battery voltage coming from the E.C.U. harness connector, check the E.C.U. ground circuit. To do this, turn the ignition switch off. Disconnect the 15 and 16 pin connectors from the E.C.U. Then, check resistance between each of these terminals and ground: 28; 36; 107; 109; 112; 113. Resistance at *all* the connectors should be practically 0Ω. If not, repair frayed or broken wiring in the harness.

4. If these tests fail to uncover the problem, have a mechanic familiar with electronic system testing perform an E.C.U. input/output signal inspection test.

Air Injection System

It is difficult for an engine to completely burn the air/fuel mixture through the normal combustion in the combustion chambers. Under certain operating conditions, unburned fuel is exhausted into the atmosphere. Air injection is one answer to the pollution problem of unburned exhaust gases.

The air injection system used on 1975-80 B210 and 210 Datsuns is designed so that ambient air, pressurized by a belt-driven air pump, is injected through the injection nozzles into the exhaust ports near each of the four exhaust valves. The exhaust gases are at high tempera-

tures and ignite when brought into contact with the oxygen. The unburned fuel is then burned in the exhaust ports and manifold.

California B210 models began utilizing a secondary system in 1976 consisting of an air control valve which limits injection of secondary air and an emergency relief valve which controls the supply of secondary air. This system protects the catalytic converter from overheating. In 1977 through 1980, the function of these two valves was taken by a single combined air control (C.A.C.) valve.

All engines with the air pump system have a series of minor alterations to accomodate the system. These are:

1. Special close-tolerance carburetor. Most engines require a slightly rich idle mixture adjustment.

2. Distributor with special advance curve. Ignition timing is retarded about 10° at idle in most cases.

3. Cooling system changes such as larger fan, higher fan speed, and thermostatic fan clutch. This is required to offset the increase in temperature caused by retarded timing at idle.

4. Faster idle speed.

5. Heated air intake on some engines.

The only periodic maintenance required on the air pump system is replacement of the air filter element and adjustment of the drive belt.

TESTING

Air Pump

If the air pump makes an abnormal noise and cannot be corrected without removing the pump from the car, the following check is the only one the owner/mechanic should make. Disassembly of the pump and replacement of any internal parts requires (in most cases) special tools, and knowledge generally outside the realm of the owner/mechanic. Major pump problems should be handled by a professional.

Check belt tension on the air pump drive belt. There should be about ¼ in. play in the belt at its center point; too tight a belt will wear out the pump bearings quickly (and cause a noise), and a belt too loose will slip around on the pulley (causing the pump to operate inefficiently).

Turn the pump pulley ¾ of a turn in the clockwise direction and ¼ of a turn in the counterclockwise direction. If the pulley is binding and if rotation is not smooth, this could indicate a defective bearing.

Check Valve

Remove the check valve from the air pump discharge line. Test it for leakage by blowing air into the valve from the air pump side and from the manifold side. Air should only pass through

Air pump (arrow)

the valve from the air pump side if the valve is functioning normally. A small amount of air leakage from the manifold side can be overlooked. Replace the check valve if it is found to be defective.

Anti-Backfire Valve

Disconnect the rubber hose connecting the mixture control valve with the intake manifold and plug the hose. If the mixture control valve is operating correctly, air will continue to blow out the mixture control valve for a few seconds after the accelerator pedal is fully depressed (engine running) and released quickly. If air continues to blow out for more than five seconds, replace the mixture control valve.

Air Pump Relief Valve

Disconnect the air pump discharge hose leading to the exhaust manifold. With the engine

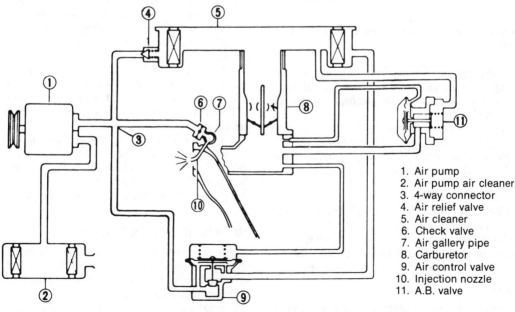

1. Air pump
2. Air pump air cleaner
3. 4-way connector
4. Air relief valve
5. Air cleaner
6. Check valve
7. Air gallery pipe
8. Carburetor
9. Air control valve
10. Injection nozzle
11. A.B. valve

Air injection system schematic—typical

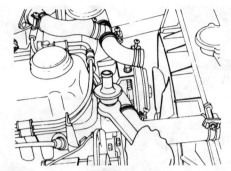

Air pump system check valve

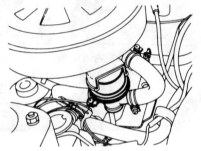

Removing anti-backfire (AB) valve, 210. Sentra location similar

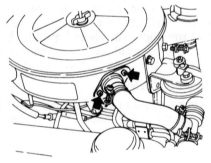

Removing air pump relief valve, B210 and 210 to 1980

running, restrict the air-flow coming from the pump. The air pump relief valve should vent the pressurized air to the atmosphere if it is working properly.

NOTE: *When performing this test do not completely block the discharge line of the air pump as damage may result if the relief valve fails to function properly.*

Air Injection Nozzles

Check around the air manifold for air leakage with the engine running at 2,000 rpm. If air is leaking from the eye joint bolt, retighten or replace the gasket. Check the air nozzles for restrictions by blowing air into the nozzles.

Hoses

Check and replace hoses if they are found to be weakened or cracked. Check all hose connec-

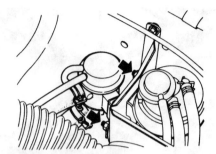

Combined Air Control valve mounting, California models

tions and clips. Be sure that the hoses are not in contact with other parts of the engine.

Emergency Air Relief Valve

1. Warm up the engine.
2. Check all hoses for leaks, kinks, improper connections, etc.
3. Run the engine up to 2000 rpm under no load. No air should be discharged from the valve.
4. Disconnect the vacuum hose from the valve. This is the hose which runs to the intake manifold. Run the engine up to 2000 rpm. Air should be discharged from the valve. If not, replace it.

Combined Air Control Valve

1. Check all hoses for leak, kinks, and improper connections.
2. Thoroughly warm up the engine.
3. With the engine idling, check for air discharge from the relief opening in the air cleaner case.
4. Disconnect and plug the vacuum hose from the valve. Air should be discharged from the valve with the engine idling. If the disconnected vacuum hose is not plugged, the engine will stumble.
5. Connect a hand operated vacuum pump to the vacuum fitting on the valve and apply 7.8-9.8 in.Hg of vacuum. Run the engine speed up to 3000 rpm. No air should be discharged from the valve.
6. Disconnect and plug the air hose at the check valve, with the conditions as in the preceding step. This should cause the valve to discharge air. If not, or if any of the conditions in this procedure are not met, replace the valve.

Air Induction System (A.I.S.)

The air induction system (A.I.S.) is designed to send secondary air to the exhaust manifold, utilizing a vacuum caused by exhaust pulsation in the exhaust manifold.

The exhaust pressure in the exhaust manifold usually pulsates in response to the opening

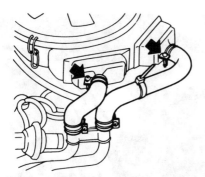

Sentra Air Induction connections. A-series similar

and closing of the exhaust valves. As a result, it decreases below atmospheric pressure periodically.

If a secondary air intake is opened to the atmosphere under vacuum conditions, secondary air can be drawn into the exhaust manifold in proportion to the vacuum. Therefore, the A.I.S. system reduces carbon monoxide (CO) and HC emissions in exhaust gases.

The A.I.S. system has been used in conjunction with the air injection (air pump) system in B210 and 210 Datsuns from the mid 1970s up until 1979. In 1980, only the California model 210s used both systems together, the air pump having been dropped from the non-California cars. The 1981 and later model 210s and Nissan Sentras use just the A.I.S. system, as they employ no air pump.

1987-88 Sentras disable the Air Induction System under certain operating conditions. While this system will usually not produce any engine operating problems, the vehicle may exhibit high hydrocarbon or CO emissions in a state emissions certification test. Should this occur, you may want to make a few simple checks of the air induction control valve, a vacuum actuated shutoff valve for the system located under the air induction valve. You can also test the Air Induction Control Solenoid Valve, which acutates the Air Induction Control Valve.

NOTE: *To perform these tests, you will need a hand vacuum pump, an ohmmeter, a voltmeter and jumper wires that will reach the battery.*

1. Disconnect the hose at the outlet of the air induction valve body. Attempt to blow air into the valve and to draw air out of it. No airflow should exist. Otherwise, the Air Induction Control Valve requires replacement.

2. Disconnect the vacuum hose from the Air Induction Control Valve vacuum diaphragm on the bottom of the valve. Apply a vacuum to the valve. Now, repeat the attempt to blow air into and draw it out of the air induction valve. It

should be possible to draw air out and impossible to blow it in. If air cannot be drawn out, replace the air induction valve. If it will not flow in either direction, replace the Air Induction Control Valve. If all tests are passed, proceed with Step 3.

3. Remove the E.C.U. from under the seat. Turn the ignition switch off. Disconnect the E.C.U. 20-prong (center) connector.

4. Turn the ignition switch on. Then, use a voltmeter to check for voltage between terminal 15 (as shown in the illustration) of the connector and ground. If there is voltage, check the E.C.U. ground circuit as described in the E.C.U. Controlled EGR & Canister Purge Control Solenoid Valve Tests (Step 3) above. If that fails to resolve the problem, first check the connections for bending or damage and then have a professional mechanic familiar with electronics test the E.C.U. input/output signal. If there is no voltage, proceed with the next step.

5. Disconnect the connector to the A.I.V. Solenoid Valve harness connector. Use an ohmmeter and test for continuity between the "b" terminal of the solenoid valve connector and terminal 15 of the E.C.U. If there is no continuity, repair the harness or have it repaired and, if necessary, have the E.C.U. tested further. If there is continuity, proceed with Step 4.

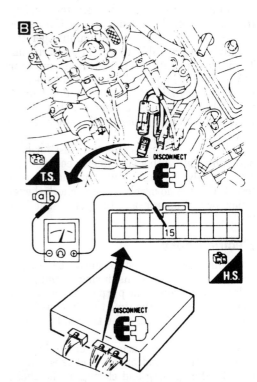

Testing the A.I.V. Solenoid Valve function of the E.C.U.

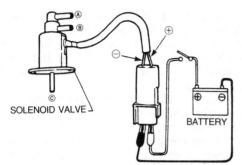

Testing the Air Induction Control Valve Solenoid Valve

6. Disconnect the electrical connector for the Air Induction Control Valve Solenoid Valve (linked through its vacuum line to the Air Induction Control Valve). Use an ohmmeter between the two terminals on the solenoid valve side of the connector to test for continuity. If there is infinite resistance, replace the Solenoid Valve. If not, proceed with the tests below.

7. Label and then disconnect the vacuum lines from the Air Induction Control Valve Solenoid Valve. If necessary for clearance, dismount the valve. Attempt to blow air into the lower connector of the solenoid valve ("B") and feel near the bottom connector ("C") to see if air flows out. With the valve de-energized, if there is no airflow, replace the valve.

8. Jumper the positive battery terminal to the terminal of the Solenoid Valve Connector marked "+" on the illustration. Jumper the negative battery cable to the other terminal. Then, blow air into the top vacuum connector ("A") while feeling for air to come out the connector just below it ("B"). Air must flow from A to B. This is the most common failure of the valve and will disable the A.I.V. system. If the valve fails this test, replace it.

9. If the valve passes this test, test for harness continuity with an ohmmeter between the solenoid valve harness connector and the battery. If there is no problem there, check the ignition switch, appropriate fuse, or fusible link "G".

Electric Choke

Gasoline engines produce most of their hydrocarbon (HC) emissions during warmup and at low rpm running. The purpose of the electric choke is to shorten the time the choke is in operation, thus shortening the time of the greatest HC output.

An electric heater warms the bimetal spring (typical spring found on most chokes) which controls the opening and closing of the choke valve. The heater begins to heat as soon as the engine starts.

Electric choke (arrow)

Catalytic Converter

This system is used on all 1975 (California) and later models. In addition to the air injection system, EGR and the engine modifications, the catalyst further reduces pollutants. Through catalytic action, it changes residual hydrocarbons and carbon monoxide the the exhaust gas into carbon dioxide and water before the exhaust gas is discharged into the atmosphere.

NOTE: *Only unleaded fuel must be used with catalytic converters; lead in fuel will quickly pollute the catalyst and render it useless.*

The emergency air relief valve is used as a catalyst protection device. When the temperature of the catalyst goes above maximum operating temperature, the temperature sensor signals the switching module to activate the emergency air relief valve. This stops air injection into the exhaust manifold and lowers the temperature of the catalyst.

Certain late 1970's catalyst equipped models have a floor temperature warning system which emits a warning if the catalytic converter or engine becomes overly hot or malfunctions, causing floor temperature to rise.

Vacuum Hoses of Emission Control System

1982 AND LATER SENTRA

The following show the various color coding for connecting emission control vacuum hoses and air hoses for carbureted Sentras. Careful attention should be paid to the proper location and hook-up of the hoses.

Yellow: Vacuum line to distributor
White: Vacuum line for EGR system
Green: Manifold vacuum line

Pink: Atmospheric pressure
Blue: Venturi vacuum line to VVT valve

Oxygen Sensor

REMOVAL AND INSTALLATION

NOTE: *Make sure the engine and exhaust system have had plenty of time to cool thoroughly before attempting to work on the exhaust gas sensor.*

1. Allow the engine to cool thoroughly. Disconnect the electrical connector for the exhaust gas sensor.

2. Unscrew the sensor from the manifold with an open-end wrench.

3. Coat the threads of the new sensor with a compound designed to prevent seizing of exhaust system components (compounds are available that are specifically formulated for this application).

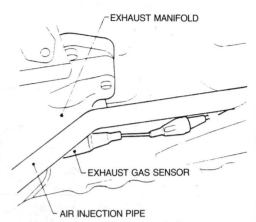

Location of the exhaust gas sensor

4. Install the new sensor, torquing it gently. Reconnect the electrical connector.

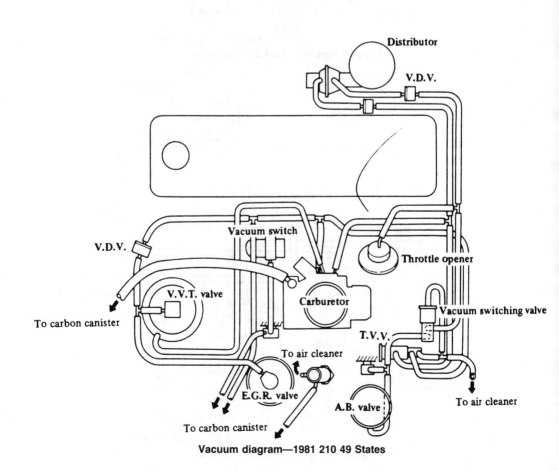

Vacuum diagram—1981 210 49 States

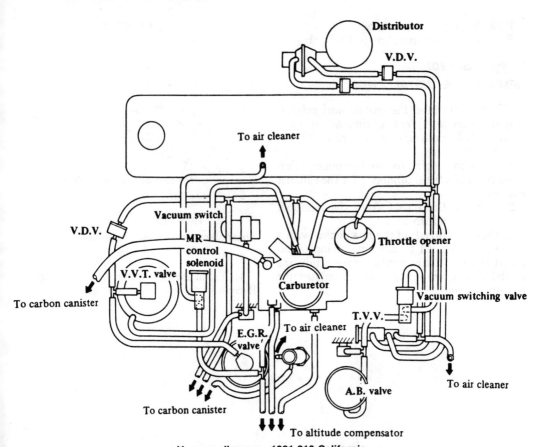

Vacuum diagram—1981 210 California

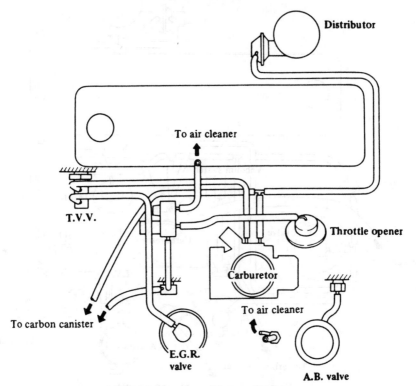

Vacuum diagram—1981 210 Canada

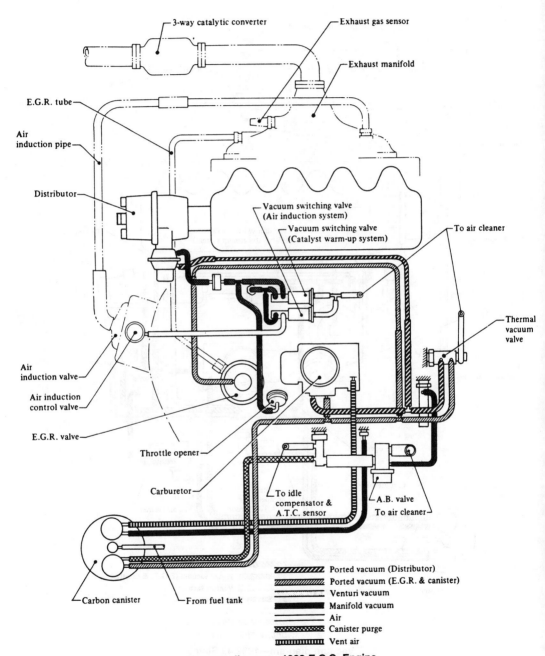

Vacuum diagram—1982 E.C.C. Engine

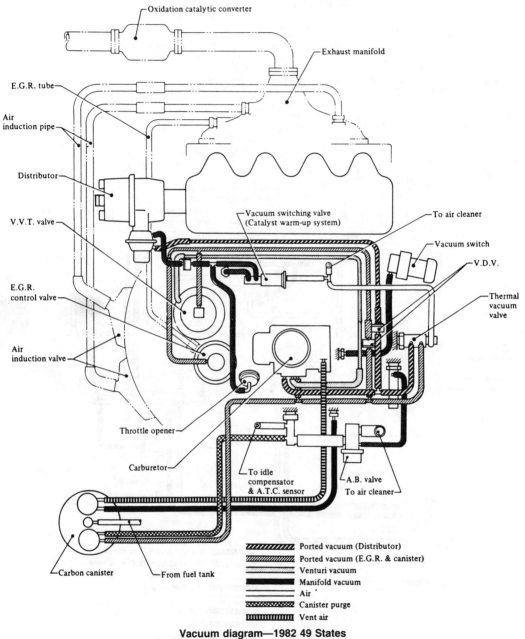

Vacuum diagram—1982 49 States

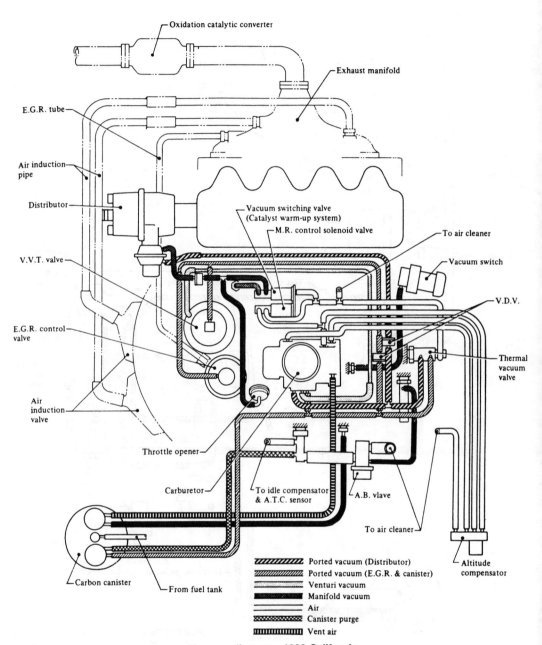

Oxidation catalytic converter

Exhaust manifold

E.G.R. tube

Air induction pipe

Distributor

Vacuum switching valve
(Catalyst warm-up system)

M.R. control solenoid valve

To air cleaner

Vacuum switch

V.V.T. valve

V.D.V.

E.G.R. control valve

Thermal vacuum valve

Air induction valve

Throttle opener

Carburetor

To idle compensator
& A.T.C. sensor

A.B. vlave

To air cleaner

Altitude compensator

Carbon canister

From fuel tank

Ported vacuum (Distributor)

Ported vacuum (E.G.R. & canister)

Venturi vacuum

Manifold vacuum

Air

Canister purge

Vent air

Vacuum diagram—1982 California

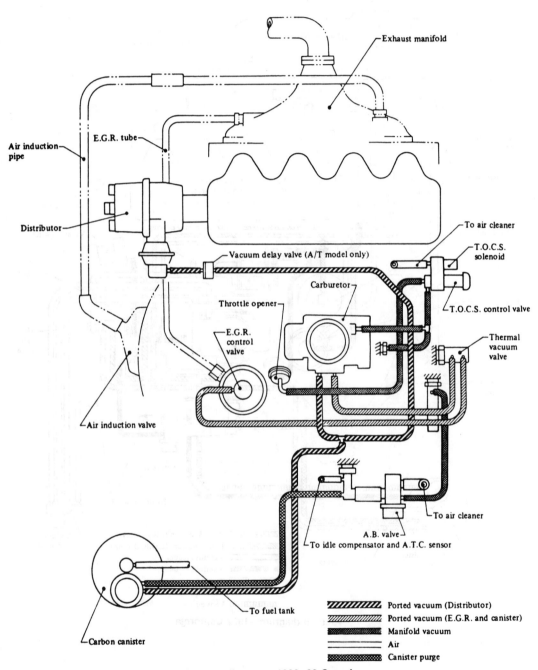

Vacuum diagram—1982–83 Canada

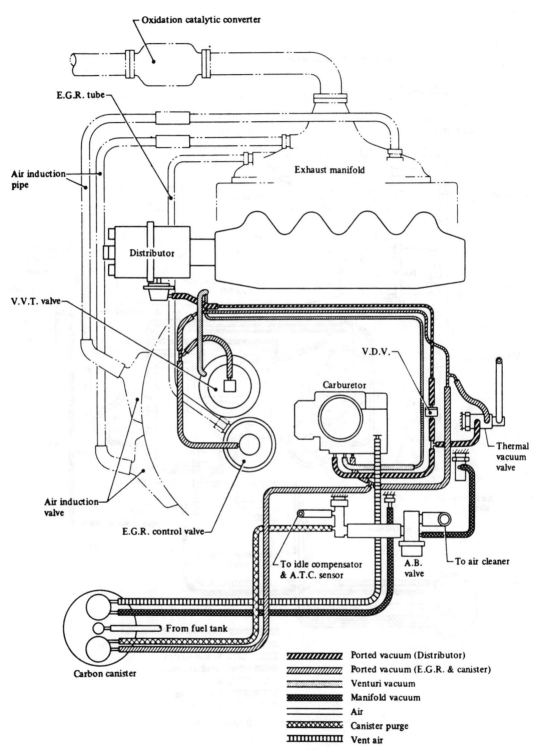

Vacuum diagram—1983 49 States

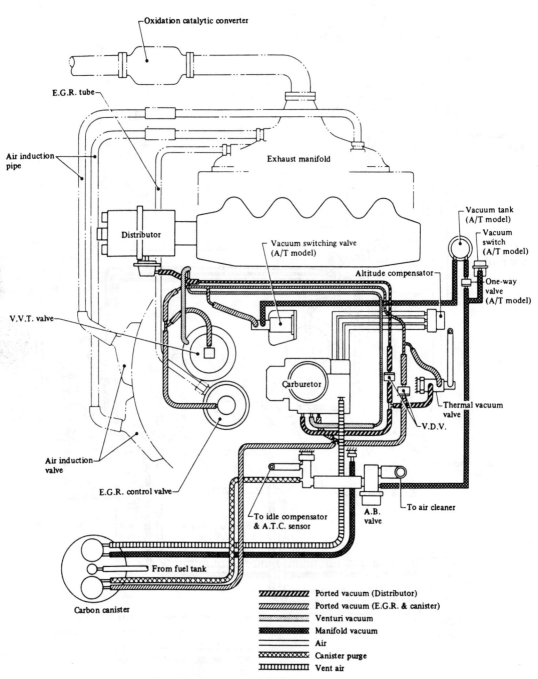

Oxidation catalytic converter

E.G.R. tube

Air induction
pipe

Exhaust manifold

Vacuum tank
(A/T model)

Distributor

Vacuum switching valve
(A/T model)

Vacuum
switch
(A/T model)

Altitude compensator

One-way
valve
(A/T model)

V.V.T. valve

Carburetor

Thermal vacuum
valve

V.D.V.

Air induction
valve

E.G.R. control valve

To idle compensator
& A.T.C. sensor

A.B.
valve

To air cleaner

From fuel tank

Carbon canister

Ported vacuum (Distributor)
Ported vacuum (E.G.R. & canister)
Venturi vacuum
Manifold vacuum
Air
Canister purge
Vent air

Vacuum diagram—1983 High Altitude

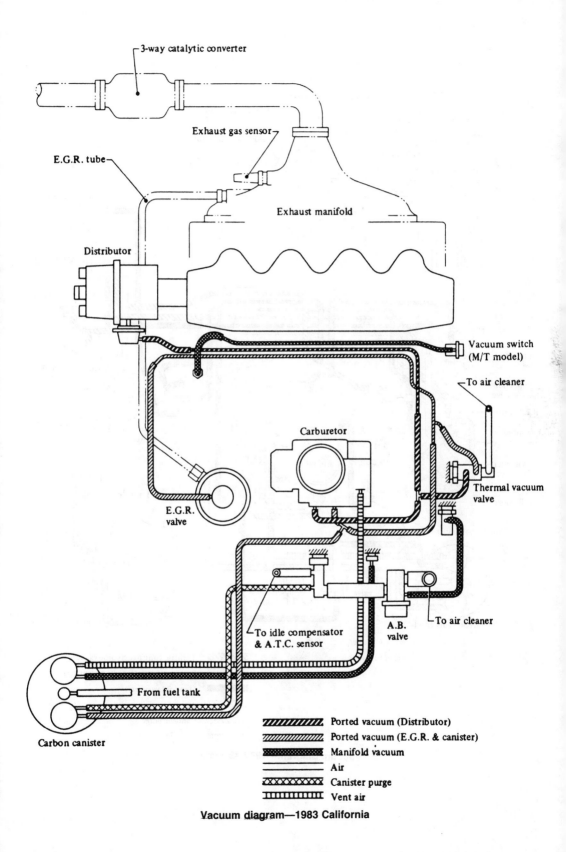

3-way catalytic converter

Exhaust gas sensor

E.G.R. tube

Exhaust manifold

Distributor

Vacuum switch
(M/T model)

To air cleaner

Carburetor

Thermal vacuum
valve

E.G.R.
valve

To idle compensator
& A.T.C. sensor

A.B.
valve

To air cleaner

From fuel tank

Carbon canister

/////////	Ported vacuum (Distributor)
/////////	Ported vacuum (E.G.R. & canister)
▓▓▓▓▓▓	Manifold vacuum
————	Air
XXXXXXX	Canister purge
ⅢⅢⅢⅢⅢ	Vent air

Vacuum diagram—1983 California

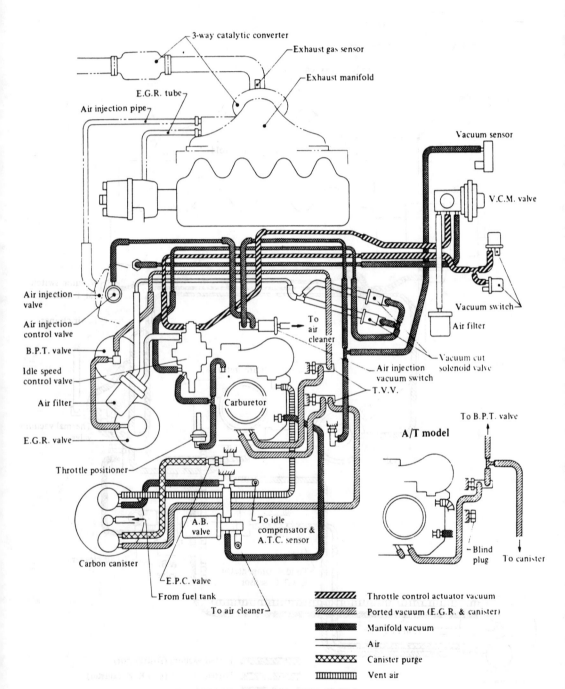

Vacuum diagram—1984 49 States

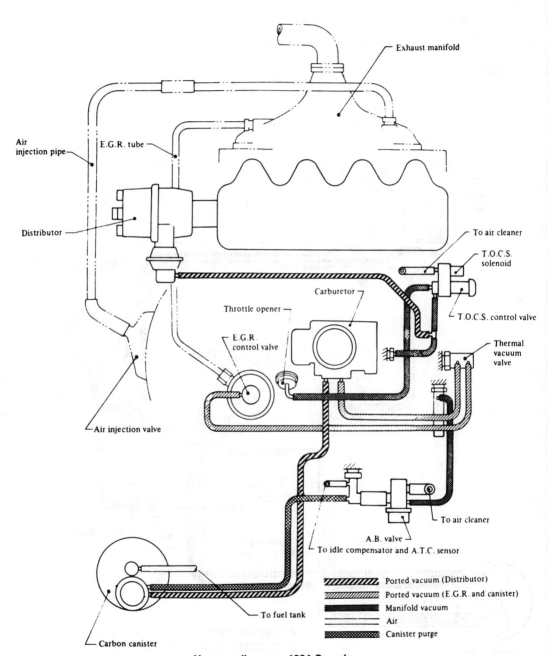

Exhaust manifold

Air injection pipe

E.G.R. tube

Distributor

To air cleaner

T.O.C.S. solenoid

T.O.C.S. control valve

Throttle opener

Carburetor

E.G.R. control valve

Thermal vacuum valve

Air injection valve

To air cleaner

A.B. valve

To idle compensator and A.T.C. sensor

Ported vacuum (Distributor)
Ported vacuum (E.G.R. and canister)
Manifold vacuum
Air
Canister purge

To fuel tank

Carbon canister

Vacuum diagram—1984 Canada

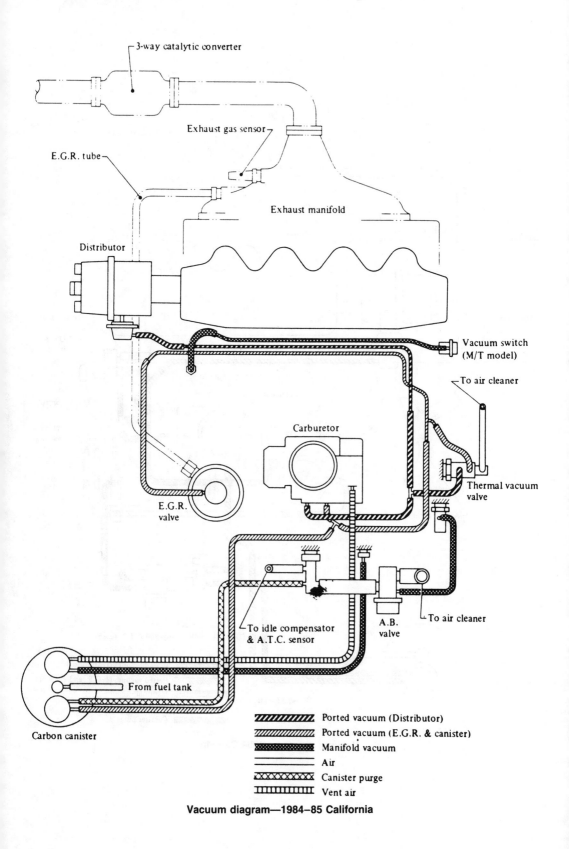

3-way catalytic converter

Exhaust gas sensor

E.G.R. tube

Exhaust manifold

Distributor

Vacuum switch (M/T model)

To air cleaner

Carburetor

Thermal vacuum valve

E.G.R. valve

To idle compensator & A.T.C. sensor

A.B. valve

To air cleaner

From fuel tank

Carbon canister

/////////	Ported vacuum (Distributor)
//////////	Ported vacuum (E.G.R. & canister)
▓▓▓▓▓▓	Manifold vacuum
—————	Air
XXXXXXXX	Canister purge
⊓⊓⊓⊓⊓⊓⊓	Vent air

Vacuum diagram—1984–85 California

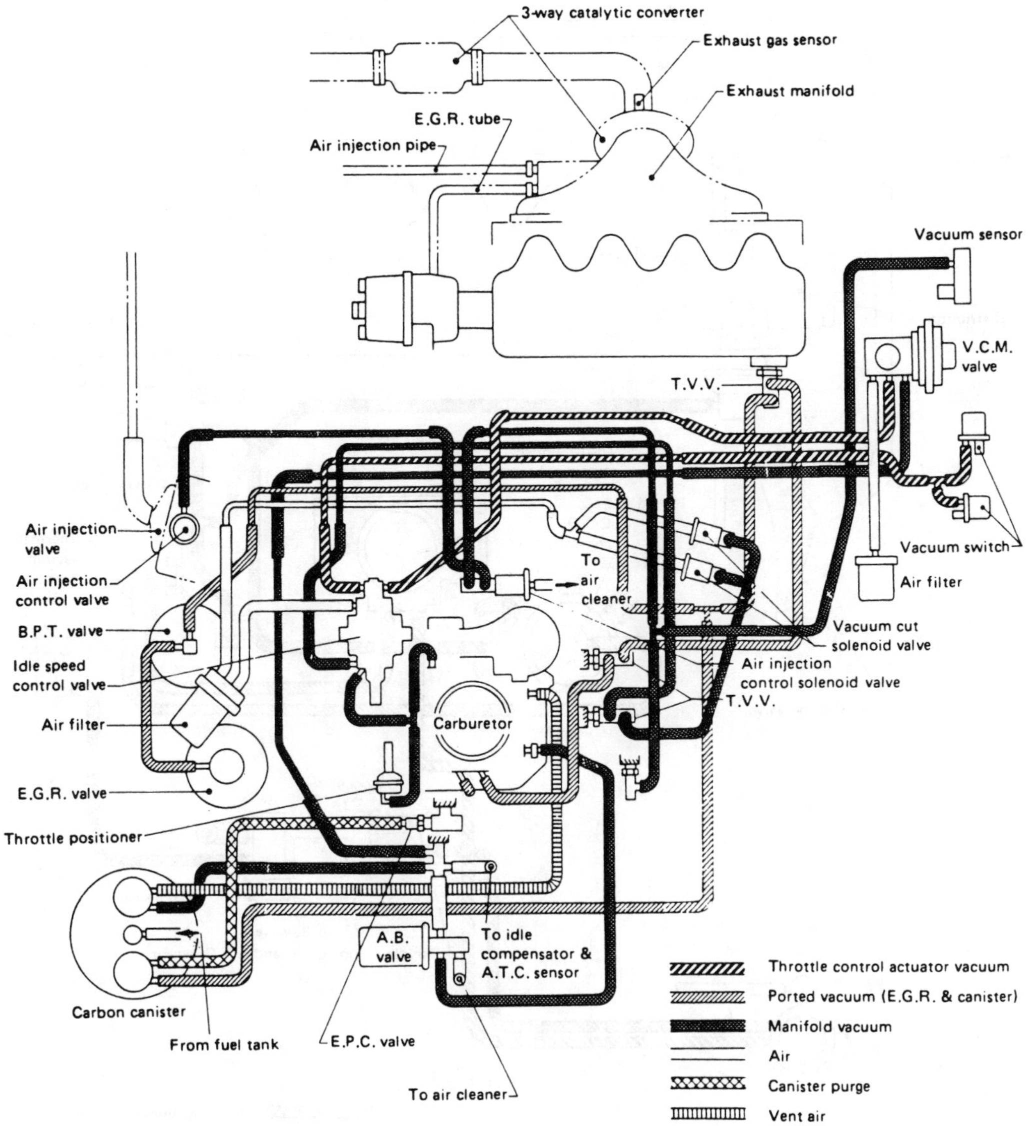

3-way catalytic converter

Exhaust gas sensor

Exhaust manifold

E.G.R. tube

Air injection pipe

Vacuum sensor

V.C.M. valve

T.V.V.

Vacuum switch

Air filter

Air injection valve

Air injection control valve

To air cleaner

B.P.T. valve

Idle speed control valve

Air filter

Carburetor

Vacuum cut solenoid valve

Air injection control solenoid valve

T.V.V.

E.G.R. valve

Throttle positioner

Carbon canister

From fuel tank

A.B. valve

To idle compensator & A.T.C. sensor

E.P.C. valve

To air cleaner

▨▨▨	Throttle control actuator vacuum
▨▨▨	Ported vacuum (E.G.R. & canister)
▬▬▬	Manifold vacuum
───	Air
⨯⨯⨯	Canister purge
ⅢⅢⅢ	Vent air

Vacuum diagram—1985 49 States

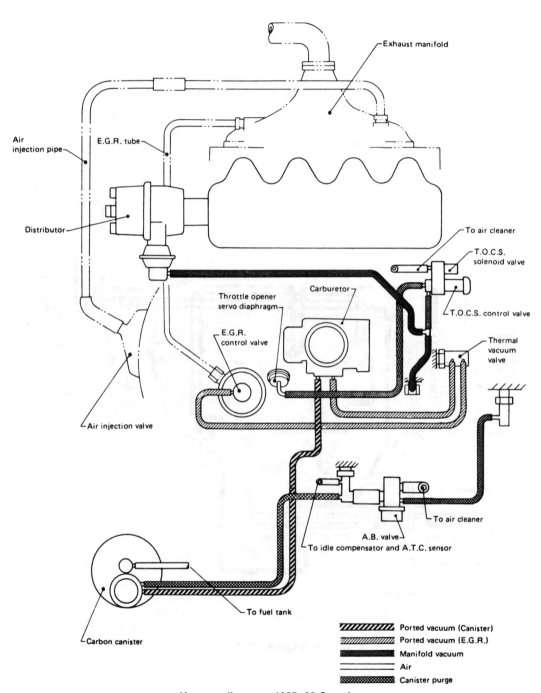

Exhaust manifold

Air
injection pipe

E.G.R. tube

Distributor

To air cleaner

T.O.C.S.
solenoid valve

T.O.C.S. control valve

Throttle opener
servo diaphragm

Carburetor

E.G.R.
control valve

Thermal
vacuum
valve

Air injection valve

To air cleaner

A.B. valve

To idle compensator and A.T.C. sensor

To fuel tank

Carbon canister

Ported vacuum (Canister)
Ported vacuum (E.G.R.)
Manifold vacuum
Air
Canister purge

Vacuum diagram—1985–86 Canada

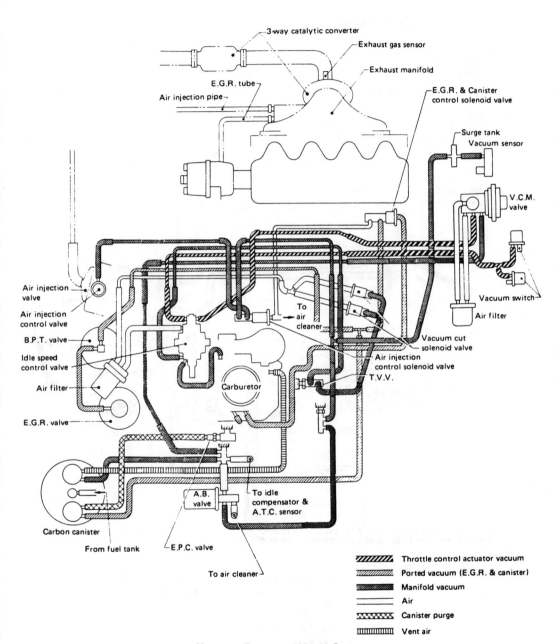

Vacuum diagram—1986 49 States

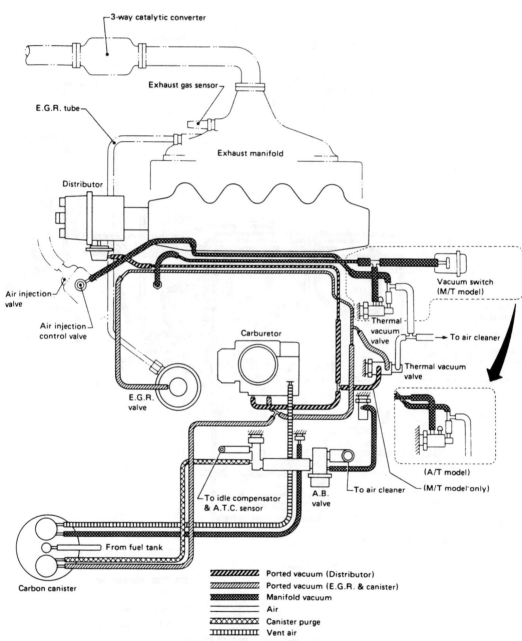

- 3-way catalytic converter
- Exhaust gas sensor
- E.G.R. tube
- Exhaust manifold
- Distributor
- Air injection valve
- Air injection control valve
- Carburetor
- E.G.R. valve
- Vacuum switch (M/T model)
- Thermal vacuum valve
- To air cleaner
- Thermal vacuum valve
- (A/T model)
- (M/T model only)
- To idle compensator & A.T.C. sensor
- A.B. valve
- To air cleaner
- From fuel tank
- Carbon canister

▨▨▨▨▨	Ported vacuum (Distributor)
▨▨▨▨▨	Ported vacuum (E.G.R. & canister)
▩▩▩▩▩	Manifold vacuum
─────	Air
✕✕✕✕✕	Canister purge
⊤⊤⊤⊤⊤	Vent air

Vacuum diagram—1986 California

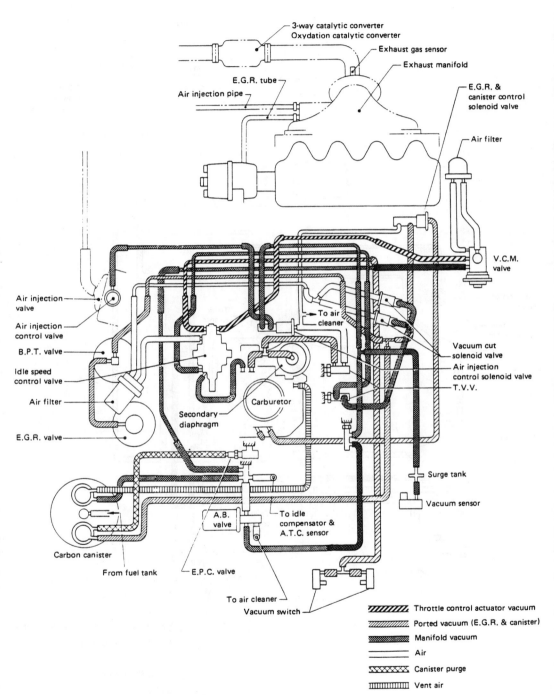

3-way catalytic converter
Oxydation catalytic converter

Exhaust gas sensor

Exhaust manifold

E.G.R. tube

Air injection pipe

E.G.R. & canister control solenoid valve

Air filter

V.C.M. valve

Air injection valve

Air injection control valve

B.P.T. valve

Idle speed control valve

Air filter

E.G.R. valve

Secondary diaphragm

Carburetor

To air cleaner

Vacuum cut solenoid valve

Air injection control solenoid valve

T.V.V.

Surge tank

Vacuum sensor

Carbon canister

From fuel tank

E.P.C. valve

A.B. valve

To idle compensator & A.T.C. sensor

To air cleaner

Vacuum switch

Throttle control actuator vacuum

Ported vacuum (E.G.R. & canister)

Manifold vacuum

Air

Canister purge

Vent air

Vacuum diagram—1987 E16S 49 States

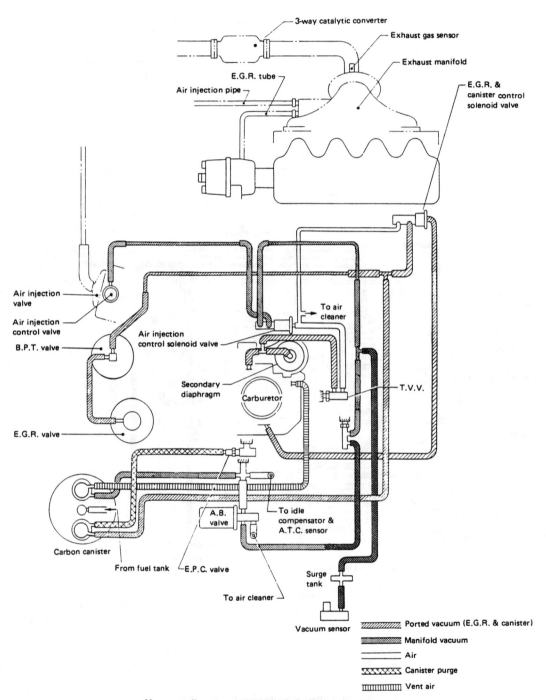

Vacuum diagram—1987 E16S California and Canada

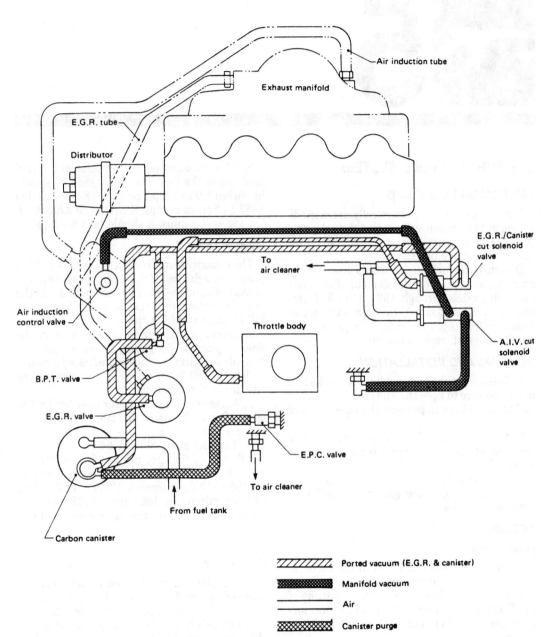

Air induction tube

Exhaust manifold

E.G.R. tube

Distributor

To air cleaner

E.G.R./Canister cut solenoid valve

Air induction control valve

Throttle body

A.I.V. cut solenoid valve

B.P.T. valve

E.G.R. valve

E.P.C. valve

To air cleaner

From fuel tank

Carbon canister

Ported vacuum (E.G.R. & canister)

Manifold vacuum

Air

Canister purge

Vacuum diagram—1987–88 All Engines with E.C.C.S.

Fuel System

CARBURETED FUEL SYSTEM

Mechanical Fuel Pump

The fuel pump is a mechanically operated diaphragm-type pump driven by the fuel pump eccentric on the camshaft. It is mounted on the side of the engine block.

Design of the fuel pump permits disassembly, cleaning, and repair or replacement of defective parts on models through 1981. On all Sentra models (1982 and later), the pump cannot be disassembled. If it fails either the pressure or the volume test, replace the unit.

REMOVAL AND INSTALLATION

1. Disconnect the two fuel lines from the fuel pump. Be sure to keep the line leading from the fuel tank up high to prevent the excess loss of fuel.
2. Remove the two fuel pump mounting nuts and remove the fuel pump assembly from the side of the engine.
3. Install the fuel pump in the reverse order of removal, using a new gasket and sealer on the mating surface.

TESTING

Pressure Test

1. Disconnect the line between the carburetor and the pump at the carburetor.
2. Connect a rubber hose to each open end of the T-connector, and connect this connector-hose assembly between carburetor and fuel pump.
NOTE: *Locate this T-connector as close to the carburetor as possible.*
3. Connect a suitable pressure gauge to the opening of the T-connector, and fasten the hose between the carburetor and T-connector securely with a hose clamp.
4. Start the engine and run at various speeds.

5. The pressure gauge indicates static fuel pressure in the line. The gauge reading should be within 3.0 to 3.9 psi on pre-1982 pumps. On 1982-84 Sentra pumps, it should be 2.8-3.8 psi. On 1985-87 pumps, it should be 2.8-3.8 psi.

Capacity Test

The capacity test is conducted on cars built in years through 1984 if the static pressure of the pump is ok and there is still reason to doubt the pump's performance (i.e. poor acceleration at full throttle and high rpm).

1. Disconnect the pressure gauge from the line. In place of the gauge, install a container suitable to collect the fuel (a graduated container works well here, as you can measure the amount of fuel immediately).
2. Make sure the carburetor float bowl is full of gas. Start the engine and run at about 1,000 rpm for one minute.
3. The fuel pump should deliver 450cc (15.2 US fl. oz.) of fuel per minute for all 1973-81 1200, B210 and 210 models. The delivery rate for 1982 210 fuel pumps is 1300cc (44.0 U.S. fl. oz.) per minute at 1000 rpm; 1982 and later Sentra pumps deliver the same amount at 600 rpm.

Carburetor

The carburetor used on all models is a two-barrel downdraft type with a low speed (primary) side and a high speed (secondary) side.

All models have an electrically operated anti-dieseling solenoid. As the ignition switch is turned off, the valve is energized and shuts off the supply of fuel to the idle circuit of the carburetor.

All 1984 and later U.S.A. carbureted models are equipped with the E.C.C. System (Electronic Controlled Carburetor). The E.C.C control unit consists of a microcomputer, connectors for signal input and output and power supply,

CHILTON'S
FUEL ECONOMY
& TUNE-UP TIPS

55 WAYS TO IMPROVE FUEL ECONOMY

Tune-up • Spark Plug Diagnosis • Emission Controls

Fuel System • Cooling System • Tires and Wheels

General Maintenance

CHILTON'S FUEL ECONOMY & TUNE-UP TIPS

Fuel economy is important to everyone, no matter what kind of vehicle you drive. The maintenance-minded motorist can save both money and fuel using these tips and the periodic maintenance and tune-up procedures in this Repair and Tune-Up Guide.

There are more than 130,000,000 cars and trucks registered for private use in the United States. Each travels an average of 10-12,000 miles per year, and, and in total they consume close to 70 billion gallons of fuel each year. This represents nearly ⅔ of the oil imported by the United States each year. The Federal government's goal is to reduce consumption 10% by 1985. A variety of methods are either already in use or under serious consideration, and they all affect you driving and the cars you will drive. In addition to "down-sizing", the auto industry is using or investigating the use of electronic fuel delivery, electronic engine controls and alternative engines for use in smaller and lighter vehicles, among other alternatives to meet the federally mandated Corporate Average Fuel Economy (CAFE) of 27.5 mpg by 1985. The government, for its part, is considering rationing, mandatory driving curtailments and tax increases on motor vehicle fuel in an effort to reduce consumption. The government's goal of a 10% reduction could be realized — and further government regulation avoided — if every private vehicle could use just 1 less gallon of fuel per week.

How Much Can You Save?

Tests have proven that almost anyone can make at least a 10% reduction in fuel consumption through regular maintenance and tune-ups. When a major manufacturer of spark plugs sur-

TUNE-UP

1. Check the cylinder compression to be sure the engine will really benefit from a tune-up and that it is capable of producing good fuel economy. A tune-up will be wasted on an engine in poor mechanical condition.

2. Replace spark plugs regularly. New spark plugs alone can increase fuel economy 3%.

3. Be sure the spark plugs are the correct type (heat range) for your vehicle. See the Tune-Up Specifications.

Heat range refers to the spark plug's ability to conduct heat away from the firing end. It must conduct the heat away in an even pattern to avoid becoming a source of pre-ignition, yet it must also operate hot enough to burn off conductive deposits that could cause misfiring.

The heat range is usually indicated by a number on the spark plug, part of the manufacturer's designation for each individual spark plug. The numbers in bold-face indicate the heat range in each manufacturer's identification system.

Manufacturer	Typical Designation
AC	R **45** TS
Bosch (old)	WA **145** T30
Bosch (new)	HR **8** Y
Champion	RBL **15** Y
Fram/Autolite	**41**5
Mopar	P-**62** PR
Motorcraft	BRF-**42**
NGK	BP **5** ES-15
Nippondenso	W **16** EP
Prestolite	14GR **5** 2A

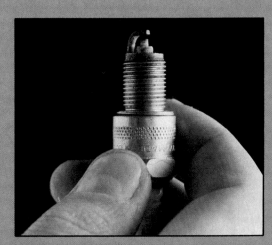

Periodically, check the spark plugs to be sure they are firing efficiently. They are excellent indicators of the internal condition of your engine.

On AC, Bosch (new), Champion, Fram/Autolite, Mopar, Motorcraft and Prestolite, a higher number indicates a hotter plug. On Bosch (old), NGK and Nippondenso, a higher number indicates a colder plug.

4. Make sure the spark plugs are properly gapped. See the Tune-Up Specifications in this book.

5. Be sure the spark plugs are firing efficiently. The illustrations on the next 2 pages show you how to "read" the firing end of the spark plug.

6. Check the ignition timing and set it to specifications. Tests show that almost all cars have incorrect ignition timing by more than 2°.

veyed over 6,000 cars nationwide, they found that a tune-up, on cars that needed one, increased fuel economy over 11%. Replacing worn plugs alone, accounted for a 3% increase. The same test also revealed that 8 out of every 10 vehicles will have some maintenance deficiency that will directly affect fuel economy, emissions or performance. Most of this mileage-robbing neglect could be prevented with regular maintenance.

Modern engines require that all of the functioning systems operate properly for maximum efficiency. A malfunction anywhere wastes fuel. You can keep your vehicle running as efficiently and economically as possible, by being aware of your vehicle's operating and performance characteristics. If your vehicle suddenly develops performance or fuel economy problems it could be due to one or more of the following:

PROBLEM	POSSIBLE CAUSE
Engine Idles Rough	Ignition timing, idle mixture, vacuum leak or something amiss in the emission control system.
Hesitates on Acceleration	Dirty carburetor or fuel filter, improper accelerator pump setting, ignition timing or fouled spark plugs.
Starts Hard or Fails to Start	Worn spark plugs, improperly set automatic choke, ice (or water) in fuel system.
Stalls Frequently	Automatic choke improperly adjusted and possible dirty air filter or fuel filter.
Performs Sluggishly	Worn spark plugs, dirty fuel or air filter, ignition timing or automatic choke out of adjustment.

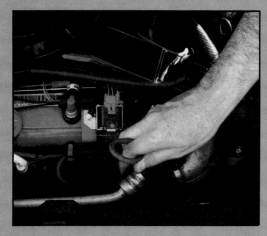

Check spark plug wires on conventional point type ignition for cracks by bending them in a loop around your finger.

Be sure that spark plug wires leading to adjacent cylinders do not run too close together. (Photo courtesy Champion Spark Plug Co.)

7. If your vehicle does not have electronic ignition, check the points, rotor and cap as specified.

8. Check the spark plug wires (used with conventional point-type ignitions) for cracks and burned or broken insulation by bending them in a loop around your finger. Cracked wires decrease fuel efficiency by failing to deliver full voltage to the spark plugs. One misfiring spark plug can cost you as much as 2 mpg.

9. Check the routing of the plug wires. Misfiring can be the result of spark plug leads to adjacent cylinders running parallel to each other and too close together. One wire tends to pick up voltage from the other causing it to fire "out of time".

10. Check all electrical and ignition circuits for voltage drop and resistance.

11. Check the distributor mechanical and/or vacuum advance mechanisms for proper functioning. The vacuum advance can be checked by twisting the distributor plate in the opposite direction of rotation. It should spring back when released.

12. Check and adjust the valve clearance on engines with mechanical lifters. The clearance should be slightly loose rather than too tight.

SPARK PLUG DIAGNOSIS

Normal

APPEARANCE: This plug is typical of one operating normally. The insulator nose varies from a light tan to grayish color with slight electrode wear. The presence of slight deposits is normal on used plugs and will have no adverse effect on engine performance. The spark plug heat range is correct for the engine and the engine is running normally.

CAUSE: Properly running engine.

RECOMMENDATION: Before reinstalling this plug, the electrodes should be cleaned and filed square. Set the gap to specifications. If the plug has been in service for more than 10-12,000 miles, the entire set should probably be replaced with a fresh set of the same heat range.

Oil Deposits

APPEARANCE: The firing end of the plug is covered with a wet, oily coating.

CAUSE: The problem is poor oil control. On high mileage engines, oil is leaking past the rings or valve guides into the combustion chamber. A common cause is also a plugged PCV valve, and a ruptured fuel pump diaphragm can also cause this condition. Oil fouled plugs such as these are often found in new or recently overhauled engines, before normal oil control is achieved, and can be cleaned and reinstalled.

RECOMMENDATION: A hotter spark plug may temporarily relieve the problem, but the engine is probably in need of work.

Incorrect Heat Range

APPEARANCE: The effects of high temperature on a spark plug are indicated by clean white, often blistered insulator. This can also be accompanied by excessive wear of the electrode, and the absence of deposits.

CAUSE: Check for the correct spark plug heat range. A plug which is too hot for the engine can result in overheating. A car operated mostly at high speeds can require a colder plug. Also check ignition timing, cooling system level, fuel mixture and leaking intake manifold.

RECOMMENDATION: If all ignition and engine adjustments are known to be correct, and no other malfunction exists, install spark plugs one heat range colder.

Carbon Deposits

APPEARANCE: Carbon fouling is easily identified by the presence of dry, soft, black, sooty deposits.

CAUSE: Changing the heat range can often lead to carbon fouling, as can prolonged slow, stop-and-start driving. If the heat range is correct, carbon fouling can be attributed to a rich fuel mixture, sticking choke, clogged air cleaner, worn breaker points, retarded timing or low compression. If only one or two plugs are carbon fouled, check for corroded or cracked wires on the affected plugs. Also look for cracks in the distributor cap between the towers of affected cylinders.

RECOMMENDATION: After the problem is corrected, these plugs can be cleaned and reinstalled if not worn severely.

MMT Fouled

APPEARANCE: Spark plugs fouled by MMT (Methycyclopentadienyl Maganese Tricarbonyl) have reddish, rusty appearance on the insulator and side electrode.

CAUSE: MMT is an anti-knock additive in gasoline used to replace lead. During the combustion process, the MMT leaves a reddish deposit on the insulator and side electrode.

RECOMMENDATION: No engine malfunction is indicated and the deposits will not affect plug performance any more than lead deposits (see Ash Deposits). MMT fouled plugs can be cleaned, regapped and reinstalled.

High Speed Glazing

APPEARANCE: Glazing appears as shiny coating on the plug, either yellow or tan in color.

CAUSE: During hard, fast acceleration, plug temperatures rise suddenly. Deposits from normal combustion have no chance to fluff-off; instead, they melt on the insulator forming an electrically conductive coating which causes misfiring.

RECOMMENDATION: Glazed plugs are not easily cleaned. They should be replaced with a fresh set of plugs of the correct heat range. If the condition recurs, using plugs with a heat range one step colder may cure the problem.

Ash (Lead) Deposits

APPEARANCE: Ash deposits are characterized by light brown or white colored deposits crusted on the side or center electrodes. In some cases it may give the plug a rusty appearance.

CAUSE: Ash deposits are normally derived from oil or fuel additives burned during normal combustion. Normally they are harmless, though excessive amounts can cause misfiring. If deposits are excessive in short mileage, the valve guides may be worn.

RECOMMENDATION: Ash-fouled plugs can be cleaned, gapped and reinstalled.

Detonation

APPEARANCE: Detonation is usually characterized by a broken plug insulator.

CAUSE: A portion of the fuel charge will begin to burn spontaneously, from the increased heat following ignition. The explosion that results applies extreme pressure to engine components, frequently damaging spark plugs and pistons.

Detonation can result by over-advanced ignition timing, inferior gasoline (low octane) lean air/fuel mixture, poor carburetion, engine lugging or an increase in compression ratio due to combustion chamber deposits or engine modification.

RECOMMENDATION: Replace the plugs after correcting the problem.

Photos Courtesy Champion Spark Plug Co.

EMISSION CONTROLS

13. Be aware of the general condition of the emission control system. It contributes to reduced pollution and should be serviced regularly to maintain efficient engine operation.

14. Check all vacuum lines for dried, cracked or brittle conditions. Something as simple as a leaking vacuum hose can cause poor performance and loss of economy.

15. Avoid tampering with the emission control system. Attempting to improve fuel econ-

FUEL SYSTEM

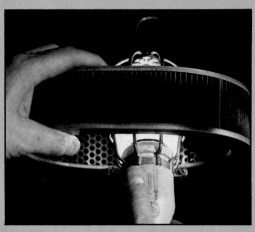

Check the air filter with a light behind it. If you can see light through the filter it can be reused.

Extremely clogged filters should be discarded and replaced with a new one.

18. Replace the air filter regularly. A dirty air filter richens the air/fuel mixture and can increase fuel consumption as much as 10%. Tests show that 1/3 of all vehicles have air filters in need of replacement.

19. Replace the fuel filter at least as often as recommended.

20. Set the idle speed and carburetor mixture to specifications.

21. Check the automatic choke. A sticking or malfunctioning choke wastes gas.

22. During the summer months, adjust the automatic choke for a leaner mixture which will produce faster engine warm-ups.

COOLING SYSTEM

29. Be sure all accessory drive belts are in good condition. Check for cracks or wear.

30. Adjust all accessory drive belts to proper tension.

31. Check all hoses for swollen areas, worn spots, or loose clamps.

32. Check coolant level in the radiator or expansion tank.

33. Be sure the thermostat is operating properly. A stuck thermostat delays engine warm-up and a cold engine uses nearly twice as much fuel as a warm engine.

34. Drain and replace the engine coolant at least as often as recommended. Rust and scale

TIRES & WHEELS

38. Check the tire pressure often with a pencil type gauge. Tests by a major tire manufacturer show that 90% of all vehicles have at least 1 tire improperly inflated. Better mileage can be achieved by over-inflating tires, but never exceed the maximum inflation pressure on the side of the tire.

39. If possible, install radial tires. Radial tires deliver as much as 1/2 mpg more than bias belted tires.

40. Avoid installing super-wide tires. They only create extra rolling resistance and decrease fuel mileage. Stick to the manufacturer's recommendations.

41. Have the wheels properly balanced.

omy by tampering with emission controls is more likely to worsen fuel economy than improve it. Emission control changes on modern engines are not readily reversible.

16. Clean (or replace) the EGR valve and lines as recommended.

17. Be sure that all vacuum lines and hoses are reconnected properly after working under the hood. An unconnected or misrouted vacuum line can wreak havoc with engine performance.

---

23. Check for fuel leaks at the carburetor, fuel pump, fuel lines and fuel tank. Be sure all lines and connections are tight.

24. Periodically check the tightness of the carburetor and intake manifold attaching nuts and bolts. These are a common place for vacuum leaks to occur.

25. Clean the carburetor periodically and lubricate the linkage.

26. The condition of the tailpipe can be an excellent indicator of proper engine combustion. After a long drive at highway speeds, the inside of the tailpipe should be a light grey in color. Black or soot on the insides indicates an overly rich mixture.

27. Check the fuel pump pressure. The fuel pump may be supplying more fuel than the engine needs.

28. Use the proper grade of gasoline for your engine. Don't try to compensate for knocking or "pinging" by advancing the ignition timing. This practice will only increase plug temperature and the chances of detonation or pre-ignition with relatively little performance gain.

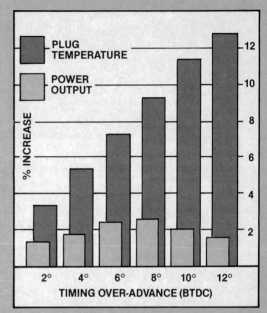

Increasing ignition timing past the specified setting results in a drastic increase in spark plug temperature with increased chance of detonation or preignition. Performance increase is considerably less. (Photo courtesy Champion Spark Plug Co.)

---

that form in the engine should be flushed out to allow the engine to operate at peak efficiency.

35. Clean the radiator of debris that can decrease cooling efficiency.

36. Install a flex-type or electric cooling fan, if you don't have a clutch type fan. Flex fans use curved plastic blades to push more air at low speeds when more cooling is needed; at high speeds the blades flatten out for less resistance. Electric fans only run when the engine temperature reaches a predetermined level.

37. Check the radiator cap for a worn or cracked gasket. If the cap does not seal properly, the cooling system will not function properly.

---

42. Be sure the front end is correctly aligned. A misaligned front end actually has wheels going in differed directions. The increased drag can reduce fuel economy by .3 mpg.

43. Correctly adjust the wheel bearings. Wheel bearings that are adjusted too tight increase rolling resistance.

Check tire pressures regularly with a reliable pocket type gauge. Be sure to check the pressure on a cold tire.

Check the fluid levels (particularly engine oil) on a regular basis. Be sure to check the oil for grit, water or other contamination.

A vacuum gauge is another excellent indicator of internal engine condition and can also be installed in the dash as a mileage indicator.

44. Periodically check the fluid levels in the engine, power steering pump, master cylinder, automatic transmission and drive axle.

45. Change the oil at the recommended interval and change the filter at every oil change. Dirty oil is thick and causes extra friction between moving parts, cutting efficiency and increasing wear. A worn engine requires more frequent tune-ups and gets progressively worse fuel economy. In general, use the lightest viscosity oil for the driving conditions you will encounter.

46. Use the recommended viscosity fluids in the transmission and axle.

47. Be sure the battery is fully charged for fast starts. A slow starting engine wastes fuel.

48. Be sure battery terminals are clean and tight.

49. Check the battery electrolyte level and add distilled water if necessary.

50. Check the exhaust system for crushed pipes, blockages and leaks.

51. Adjust the brakes. Dragging brakes or brakes that are not releasing create increased drag on the engine.

52. Install a vacuum gauge or miles-per-gallon gauge. These gauges visually indicate engine vacuum in the intake manifold. High vacuum = good mileage and low vacuum = poorer mileage. The gauge can also be an excellent indicator of internal engine conditions.

53. Be sure the clutch is properly adjusted. A slipping clutch wastes fuel.

54. Check and periodically lubricate the heat control valve in the exhaust manifold. A sticking or inoperative valve prevents engine warm-up and wastes gas.

55. Keep accurate records to check fuel economy over a period of time. A sudden drop in fuel economy may signal a need for tune-up or other maintenance.

and an exhaust gas sensor monitor lamp. The control unit senses and controls various carburetor operations.

On all non-California models instead of the choke valve and fast idle cam of a conventional carburetor, this system utilizes a duty-controlled solenoid valve for fuel enrichment and an idle speed control actuator (ISCA) for the basic controls. These devices are controlled according to the engine speed , amount of intake air, and objective engine speed. Also, the air-fuel ratio and ignition timing are controlled according to the engine water temperature, atmospheric pressure, vehicle speed and transaxle

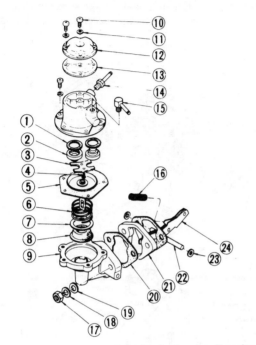

1. Packing
2. Valve assembly
3. Retainer
4. Screw
5. Diaphragm assembly
6. Diaphragm spring
7. Retainer
8. Diaphragm assembly
9. Complete-body lower
10. Screw
11. Washer-spring
12. Fuel pump cap
13. Cap gasket
14. Connector-inlet
15. Connector-outlet
16. Rocker arm spring
17. Nut
18. Washer-spring
19. Washer-plain
20. Gasket
21. Spacer
22. Rocker pin
23. Spacer
24. Rocker arm

A-series fuel pump. E-series similar type

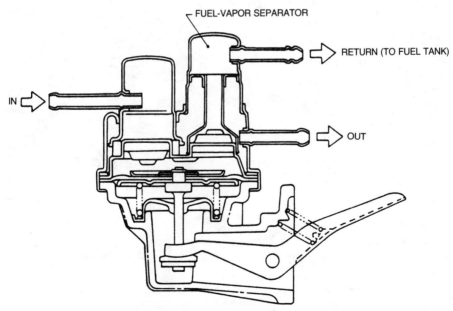

Non-rebuildable fuel pump used on 1982 and later Sentras

gear position. In addition, this system controls the ignition timing and the idle speed according to applied electric loads such as a cooler, thereby achieving better emission control, fuel economy etc.

On California models the carburetor is equipped with an air-fuel ratio control on-off valve instead of a power valve. This on-off valve opens or closes the compensating air bleed and main jet to compensate for rich/lean air-fuel ratio, depending on varying conditions, such as acceleration, deceleration, low coolant temperature, low voltage, etc. These varying conditions are detected by various sensors which transmit corresponding signals to provide air-fuel ratio compensation.

ADJUSTMENTS

Tnrottle Linkage Adjustment

On all models, make sure the throttle is wide open when the accelerator pedal is floored.

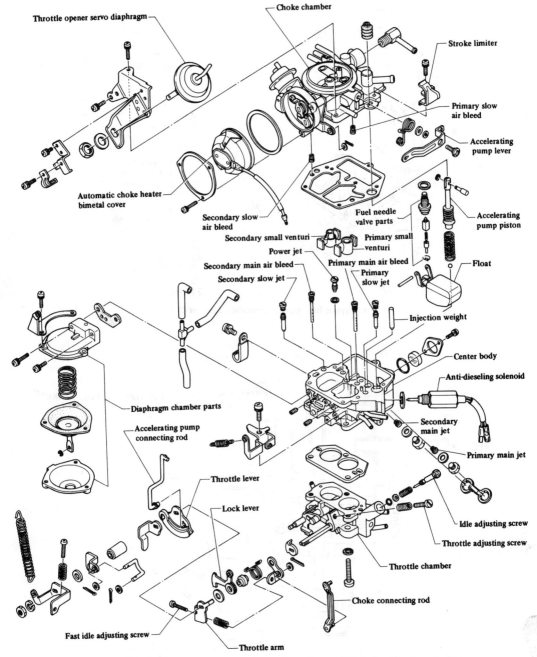

Exploded view '82 210 carburetor. Other A-series and E-series Sentra similar

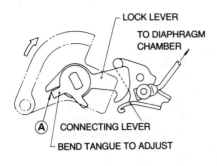

LOCK LEVER

TO DIAPHRAGM CHAMBER

(A) CONNECTING LEVER

BEND TANGUE TO ADJUST

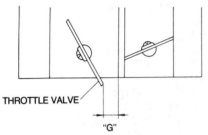

THROTTLE VALVE

"G"

Interlock opening adjustment

Some models have an adjustable accelerator pedal stop to prevent strain on the linkage.

Primary And Secondary Throttle Valve Interlock Opening Adjustment

With the carburetor removed from the engine, turn the throttle arm until the adjusting plate comes in contact with the lock lever at point "A" and Check clearance "G". Clearance should be 6.3mm.

Dashpot Adjustment

NOTE: *This adjustment does not apply to 1984-86 non-California U.S.A. models*
A dashpot is used on carburetors of all cars with automatic transmissions and many late model manual transmission models. The dashpot slowly closes the throttle on automatic transmissions to prevent stalling and serves as an emission control device on all late model vehicles.

The dashpot should be adjusted to contact the throttle lever on deceleration. Contact should occur, for pre-1984 models at approximately 2,000-2,300 rpm for all models of the A-series and E16 Automatics engines, and 2,300 to 2,500 rpm for all E15 series engines. On 1987 models, it should occur at 1,800-2,600 rpm.

NOTE: *Before attempting to check the dashpot adjustment, make sure the idle speed, timing and mixture adjustments are correct.*

If the dashpot does not contact the throttle lever at the proper speed, the carburetor must be removed from the engine and the dashpot adjusting screw must be turned to change the dashpot adjustment. The dashpot adjusting

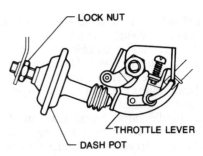

LOCK NUT

THROTTLE LEVER

DASH POT

Dashpot adjustment

screw is located on the throttle lever that contacts the dashpot. To do this:

1. Invert the carburetor. Use a drill (consult the conversion chart in back of this book) of 0.13-0.17mm diameter on 1984 and earlier models and of 0.54-0.74mm on 1987 models. Insert the drill between the edge of the throttle valve that is normally lower and the throttle bore to set the throttle opening and measure the clearance.

2. Adjust the dashpot adjusting screw until it just touches the end of the dashpot at the throttle clearance (opening) determined with the appropriate drill.

Float Level Adjustment

The fuel level is normal if it is within the lines on the window glass of the float chamber (or the

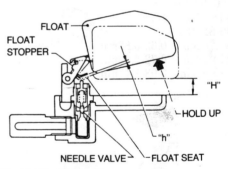

FLOAT

FLOAT STOPPER

"H"

HOLD UP

"h"

NEEDLE VALVE   FLOAT SEAT

Float level adjustment

Close-up of float level sight window

sight glass) when the vehicle is resting on level ground and the engine is off.

If the fuel level is outside the lines, remove the float housing cover. Have an absorbent cloth under the cover to catch the fuel from the fuel bowl. Adjust the float level by bending the needle seat on the float.

The needle valve should have an effective stroke of about 1.5mm. When necessary, the needle valve stroke can be adjusted by bending the float stopper.

NOTE: *Be careful not to bend the needle valve rod when installing the float and baffle plate, if removed.*

Fast Idle Adjustment

NOTE: *This adjustment does not apply to non-California U.S.A. models.*

MODELS UP TO 1986

1. With the carburetor removed from the engine, place the adjusting screw on the upper step of the fast idle cam and measure the clearance between the throttle valve and the wall of the throttle valve chamber at the center of the valve. Check it against the following specifications:

1973 1200, 1974-76 B210
  MT: 0.80-0.88mm
  AT: 1.07-1.17mm
1977-78 B210
  MT: 0.73-0.87mm
  AT: 1.00-1.14mm
1979-82 210
  A12 engine: 0.63-0.80mm
  A14 engine: 0.72-0.89mm
  A15 engine: 0.98-1.17mm

1982-86 Sentra
  MT: 0.80-0.87mm
  AT: 1.07-1.14mm
NOTE: *MT is Manual Transmission; AT is Automatic Transmission.*

2. Install the carburetor on the engine.

3. Start the engine and check the fast idle rpm at operating temperature, and the adjusting screw on the second step of the fast idle cam.

1973 1200, 1974 B210
  MT: 1,720-2.050 rpm
  AT: 2,650-2,950 rpm
1975-76 B210
  MT: 2,450-2,650 rpm
  AT: 2,700-2,900 rpm
1977-78 B210
  MT: 1,900-2,700 rpm
  AT: 2,400-3,200 rpm
1980 and later 210 w/A12, 14
  49s: 2,400-3,200 rpm
  Cal.: 2,300-3,100 rpm
1980 and later 210 w/A15
  MT: 2,300-3,100 rpm
  AT: 2,700-3,500 rpm
1982-83 Sentra E15
  49s: 2,400-3,200 rpm
  Cal.: 2,300-3,100 rpm
  Canada MT: 1,900-2,700 rpm
  Canada AT: 2,400-3,200 rpm
1984-86 Sentra E16
  49s: Not adjustable
  Cal. MT: 2,600-3,400 rpm
  Cal. AT: 2,900-3,700 rpm
  Canada MT: 1,900-2,700 rpm
  Canada AT: 2,400-3,200 rpm

4. To adjust the fast idle speed, turn the fast

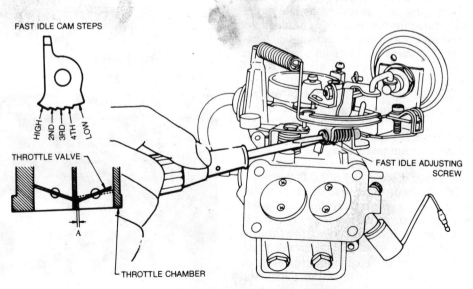

FAST IDLE CAM STEPS

HIGH 2ND 3RD 4TH LOW

THROTTLE VALVE

A

THROTTLE CHAMBER

FAST IDLE ADJUSTING SCREW

Fast idle adjustment, all models similar

idle adjusting screw counterclockwise to increase the speed; clockwise to decrease the speed.

1987 CALIFORNIA AND CANADA MODELS

1. Make sure the engine has been run until it is at operating temperature and that it is in proper tune. Turn the engine off. Then, open the throttle slightly and close the choke manually all the way. Hold the choke in this position and then release the throttle.

2. Install a tachometer and then start the engine. Adjust the fast idle speed screw to obtain 1,800-2,600 rpm with manual transmission-equipped cars and 2,100-2,900 rpm (in neutral) on automatic transmission cars.

Automatic Choke Adjustment

NOTE: *This adjustment does not apply to 1984 and later non-California U.S.A. models*

1. With the engine cold, make sure the choke is fully closed (press the gas pedal all the way to the floor and release).

2. Check the choke linkage for binding. The choke plate should be easily opened and closed with your finger. If the choke sticks or binds, it can usually be freed with a liberal application of a spray-type carburetor cleaner made for the purpose. A couple of quick squirts on the linkage and choke plate normally does the trick. If not, the carburetor will have to be disassembled for repairs.

3. The choke is correctly adjusted when the index mark on the choke housing (notch) aligns with the center mark on the carburetor body. If the setting is incorrect, loosen the three screws clamping the choke body in place and rotate the choke cover left or right until the marks align. Tighten the screws carefully to avoid cracking the housing.

Choke Unloader Adjustment

NOTE: *This adjustment does not apply to 1984 and later non-California U.S.A. models, nor to 1987 California/Canada models.*

1. Close the choke valve completely.

2. Hold the choke valve closed by stretching a rubber band between the choke piston lever and a stationary part of the carburetor.

3. Open the throttle lever fully.

4. Adjust the gap between the choke plate and the carburetor body to:

1973-77 A-series engines: 2.00mm

1978-80 A-series engines: 2.36mm

1978 and later: Non-Cal. 5 speed hatchback, 210, B210 and 1980 and later Canada manual trans. A12A: 2.17mm

1982-83 E-series engines: 2.36mm

1984-86 E-series engines: 3.00mm

REMOVAL AND INSTALLATION

1. Remove the air cleaner.

2. Disconnect the fuel and vacuum lies from the carburetor.

3. Remove the throttle lever.

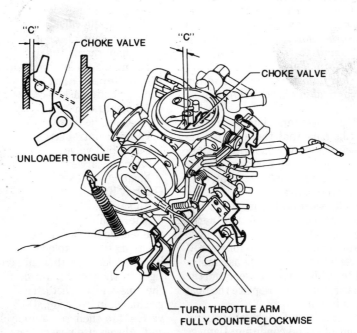

Adjusting choke unloader gap "C" to specifications

4. Remove the four nuts and washers retaining the carburetor to the manifold.

5. Lift the carburetor from the manifold.

6. Remove and discard the gasket used between the carburetor and he manifold.

7. Install the carburetor in the reverse order of removal, using a new carburetor base gasket.

OVERHAUL

Efficient carburetion depends greatly on careful cleaning and inspection during overhaul, since dirt, gum, water, or varnish in or on the carburetor parts are often responsible for poor performance.

Overhaul your carburetor in a clean, dust-free area. Carefully disassemble the carburetor, referring often to the exploded views. Keep all similar and look-alike parts segregated during disassembly and cleaning to avoid accidental interchange during assembly. Make a note of all jet sizes.

When the carburetor is disassembled, wash all parts (except diaphragms, electric choke units, pump plunger, and any other plastic, leather, fiber, or rubber parts) in clean carburetor solvent. Do not leave parts in the solvent any longer than is necessary to sufficiently loosen the deposits. Excessive cleaning may remove the special finish from the float bowl and choke valve bodies, leaving these parts unfit for service. Rinse all parts in clean solvent and blow them dry with compressed air to allow them to air dry. Wipe clean all cork, plastic, leather, and fiber parts with a clean, lint-free cloth.

NOTE: *Carburetor solvent is available in various sized solvent cans, which are designed with a removable small parts basket in the top. The carburetor choke chamber and body, and all small parts can be soaked in this can until clean. These solvent cans are available at most auto parts stores, and are quite handy for soaking other small engine parts.*

Blow out all passages and jets with compressed air and be sure that there are no restrictions or blockages. Never use wire or similar tools to clean jets, fuel passages, or air bleeds. Clean all jets and valves separately to avoid accidental interchange.

Check all parts for wear or damage. If wear or damage is found, replace the defective parts. Especially check the following:

1. Check the float needle and seat for wear. If wear is found, replace the complete assembly.

2. Check the float hinge pin for wear and the float(s) for dents or distortion. Replace the float if fuel has leaked into it.

3. Check the throttle and choke shaft bores for wear or an out-of-round condition. Damage or wear to the throttle arm, shaft, or shaft bore will often require replacement of the throttle body. These parts require a close tolerance of fit; wear may allow air leakage, which could affect starting and idling.

NOTE: *Throttle shafts and bushings are not included in overhaul kits. They can be purchased separately.*

4. Inspect the idle mixture adjusting needles for burrs or grooves. Any such condition requires replacement of the needle, since you will not be able to obtain a satisfactory idle.

5. Test the accelerator pump check valves. They should pass air one way but not the other. Test for proper seating by blowing and sucking on the valve. Replace the valve if necessary. If the valve is satisfactory, wash the valve again to remove breath moisture.

6. Check the bowl cover for warped surfaces with a straightedge.

7. Closely inspect the valves and seats for wear and damage, replacing as necessary.

8. After the carburetor is assembled, check the choke valve for freedom of operation.

Carburetor overhaul kits are recommended for each overhaul. These kits contain all gaskets and new parts to replace those that deteriorate most rapidly. Failure to replace all parts supplied with the kit (especially gaskets) can result in poor performance and a leaky carburetor later.

Some carburetor manufacturers supply overhaul kits of three basic types: minor repair; major repair; and gasket kits. Basically, they contain:

Repair Kits:
All gaskets
Float needle valve
Volume control screw
All diaphragms
Spring for the pump diaphragm

Major Repair Kits:
All jets and gaskets
All diaphragms
Float needle valve
Volume control screw
Pump ball valve
Main jet carrier
Float

Gasket Kits:
All gaskets

After cleaning and checking all components, reassemble the carburetor, using new parts and referring to the exploded view. When reassembling, make sure that all screws and jets are tight in their seats, but do not overtighten as the tips will be distorted. Tighten all screws gradually in rotation. Do not tighten needle valves into their seats; uneven jetting will result. Always use new gaskets. Be sure to adjust the float level when reassembling.

Carburetor Specifications

Year	Model	Vehicle Model	Carb Model	Main Jet # Primary	Main Jet # Secondary	Main Air Bleed # Primary	Main Air Bleed # Secondary	Slow Jet # Primary	Slow Jet # Secondary	Float Level (in.)	Power Jet #
1973	A12	1200	DCH 306-4 ① DCH 306-5 ②	95	140	80	80	43 ③	50 ③	0.709 0.748	60
1974	A13	B210	DCH 306-6 ① DCH 306-7 ②	140	145	65	80	43 ④	50 ④	0.709 0.748	55
1975	A14 (Federal)	B210	DCH 306-10 ① DCH 306-14 ②	102	150	95	80	45	50	0.75	45
	A14 (California)	B210	DCH 306-11 ① DCH 306-15 ②	104	150	95	80	45	50	0.75	43
1976–77	A14 (Federal)	B210	DCH 306-10A ① DCH 306-14A ②	102	145	95	80	45	50	0.75	45
1978	A14 (Federal)	B210	DCH 306-60 ① DCH 306-14 ②	104	145	110 95	80	45	50	0.75	48 40
	A14 (California)	B210	DCH 306-11 ① DCH 306-15 ②	105 104	145	95	80	45	50	0.75	40 48
	A14 (FU Model)	B210	DCH 306-37	107	145	65	60	46	50	0.75	48
1979	A14, A15 (Federal)	210	DCH 306-60E ① DCH 306-68 ②	106 105	145	110 95	80	45	50	0.75	43
	A14, A15 (California)	210	DCH 306-61 ① DCH 306-63 ②	107	145	95	80	45	50	0.75	43
	A14 (FU Model)	210	DCH 306-67	107	145	65	60	46	50	0.75	48
1980	A14, A15 (Federal)		DCH 306-100 ① DCH 306-101 ②	107	143	65	60	45	50	0.75	43
	A12A (Federal)		DCH 306-105	95	138	65	60	45	50	0.75	35
	A14, A15 (California)		DCH 306-110 ① DCH 306-111 ②	107	145	80	80	45	50	0.75	38
	A12A (California)		DCH 306-15	94	145	95	80	45	50	0.75	38

Carburetor Specifications (cont.)

Year	Model	Carb Model	Main Jet # Primary	Main Jet # Secondary	Main Air Bleed # Primary	Main Air Bleed # Secondary	Slow Jet # Primary	Slow Jet # Secondary	Float Level (in.)	Power Jet #
1980 (cont.)	A12A (Canada)	DCH 306-70 ①	96	140	70	60	43	50	0.75	50
	A14, A15 (Canada)	DCH 306-60 ① DCH 306-12 ②	104	145	110 95	80	45	50	0.75	48 50
1981	A12A (Federal)	DCR 306-100	105	125	95	80	45	50	0.75	35
	A14, A15 (Federal)	DCR 306-104 ① DCR 306-101 ① DCR 306-102 ②	115	125	80	80	45	50	0.75	35
	A12A (California)	DCR 306-110	103	125	60	80	45	50	0.75	35
	A15 (California)	DCR 306-111 ① DCR 306-112 ②	114	125	60	80	45	50	0.75	35
	A12A ⑤ (Canada)	DCR 306-120	100	145	70	80	43	50	0.75	35
	A15 ⑤ (Canada)	DCR 306-121 ① DCR 306-122 ②	100	145	70	80	43	70	0.75	35
1982	A12A (Federal)	DCR 306-106	105	125	95	80	45	50	0.75	35
	A14 ② (MPG)	DCR 306-109	117	125	80	80	45	50	0.75	35
	A15 (Federal)	DCR 306-107 ① DCR 306-108 ②	115 116	125	80	80	45	50	0.75	35
	A12A (California)	DCR 306-116	103	125	60	80	45	50	0.75	35
	A15 (California)	DCR 306-117 DCR 306-118	115 116	125	80	80	45	50	0.75	35
1982–83	E15 (Federal)	DCR 306-132 ① DCR 306-133 ②	117 115	125 125	60 60	80 80	45 45	50 50	N.A.	38 38

Year	Application	Part Number									
	E15 (California)	DCR 306-142 ① DCR 306-143 ②	115 114	125 125	80 80	80 80	45 45	50 50	N.A.	38 35
	E15 (Canada)	DCR 306-152 ① DCR 306-153 ②	100 100	130 130	70 70	60 60	43 43	80 80	N.A.	40 40
	E15 (MPG)	DFP 306-2	98	135	60	80	43	55	N.A.	—
	A12A (Canada)	DCH 306-70 ①	96	140	70	60	43	50	0.75	50
	A14, A15 (Canada)	DCH 306-60 ① DCH 306-12 ②	104	145	110 95	80	45	50	0.75	48 50
1981	A12A (Federal)	DCR 306-100	105	125	95	80	45	50	0.75	35
	A14, A15 (Federal)	DCR 306-104 ① DCR 306-101 ① DCR 306-102 ②	115	125	80	80	45	50	0.75	35
	A12A (California)	DCR 306-110	103	125	60	80	45	50	0.75	35
	A15 (California)	DCR 306-111 ① DCR 306-112 ②	114	125	60	80	45	50	0.75	35
	A12A ⑤ (Canada)	DCR 306-120	100	145	70	80	43	50	0.75	35
	A15 ⑤ (Canada)	DCR 306-121 ① DCR 306-122 ②	100	145	70	80	43	70	0.75	35
1982	A12A (Federal)	DCR 306-106	105	125	95	80	45	50	0.75	35
	A14 ② (MPG)	DCR 306-109	117	125	80	80	45	50	0.75	35
	A15 (Federal)	DCR 306-107 ① DCR 306-108 ②	115 116	125	80	80	45	50	0.75	35
	A12A (California)	DCR 306-116	103	125	60	80	45	50	0.75	35
	A15 (California)	DCR 306-117 DCR 306-118	115 116	125	80	80	45	50	0.75	35

Carburetor Specifications (cont.)

Year	Model	Vehicle Model	Carb Model	Main Jet #		Main Air Bleed #		Slow Jet #		Float Level (in.)	Power Jet #
				Primary	Secondary	Primary	Secondary	Primary	Secondary		
1982–83	E15 (Federal)		DCR 306-132 ①	117	125	60	80	45	50	N.A.	38
			DCR 306-133 ②	115	125	60	80	45	50		38
	E15 (California)		DCR 306-142 ①	115	125	80	80	45	50	N.A.	38
			DCR 306-143 ②	114	125	80	80	45	50		35
	E15 (Canada)		DCR 306-152 ①	100	130	70	60	43	80	N.A.	40
			DCR 306-153 ②	100	130	70	60	43	80		40
	E15 (MPG)		DFP 306-2	98	135	60	80	43	55	N.A.	—
1984	E16 (Federal)	Man. Trans.	DFE2832-1	90	105	80	70	43	65	0.47	—
		Auto. Trans.	DFE2832-2	82	105	110	70	45	65	0.47	—
	(Calif.)	all	all	91	130	110	60	43	65	0.47	—
	(Canada)	all	all	100	135	110	60	180	100	0.47	35
1985	E16 (Federal)	Man. Trans.	DFE2832-5	90	105	80	70	43	65	0.47	—
		Auto. Trans.	DFE2832-6	82	105	110	70	45	65	0.47	—
	(Calif.)	all	all	91	130	110	60	43	65	0.47	—
	(Canada)	all	all	100	135	110	60	43	65	0.47	35
1986	E16 (Calif.)	Man. Trans.	DFC328-3	91	130	110	60	43	80	0.650–0.689	—
		Auto. Trans.	DFC328-4	91	130	110	60	43	80	0.650–0.689	—
	E16 (Federal)	Man. Trans.	DFE2832-11	90	115	80	70	43	65	0.650–0.689	—
		Auto. Trans.	DFE2832-12	82	115	110	70	45	65	0.650–0.689	—

Year	Model	Transmission	Carburetor								
	E16 (Canada)	Man. Trans.	DCZ328-11	100	135	110	60	43	80	0.650–0.689	—
		Auto. Trans.	DCZ328-12	100	135	110	60	43	80	0.650–0.689	—
1987	E16S (Calif & Canada)	Man. Trans.	DRC328-11	87	130	100	60	43	80	0.650–0.689	—
		Auto. Trans.	DFC328-12	87	130	100	60	43	80	0.650–0.689	—
	E16S (Federal)	Man. Trans.	DFE2832-21	90	105	80	70	43	65	0.650–0.689	—
		Auto. Trans.	DFE2832-22	82	105	110	70	45	65	0.650–0.689	—

NOTE: FU models are 5-speed Hatchbacks sold in the United States except California.
① Manual transmission
② Automatic transmission
③ Slow jet air bleed: Primary #215, Secondary #100
④ Slow jet air bleed: Primary #240, Secondary #100
⑤ 1982 Canada carburetors same specs and models as 1981

GASOLINE FUEL INJECTION SYSTEM

NOTE: *This book contains very basic testing and service procedures for your car's fuel injection system. More comprehensive testing and diagnosis procedures may be found in* CHILTON'S GUIDE TO FUEL INJECTION AND FEEDBACK CARBURETORS, *book part No. 7488, available at your local retailer.*

Electric Fuel Pump

REMOVAL AND INSTALLATION

CAUTION: *Make sure all sources of ignition are removed from the area of the fuel tank and that the area is very well ventilated! Failure to observe this precaution could result in fire or explosion!*

1. Disconnect the negative battery cable. Release the fuel system pressure as described just below under Fuel Pump Testing. Remove the fuel tank as described later in this chapter.

2. Remove inspection cover and disconnect fuel tank gauge unit harness connector. Disconnect the vapor lines for the evaporative emissions system and plug them. Label and then disconnect the electrical connectors for the pump power supply and for the gauge.

3. Remove the bolts attaching the top of the pump to the tank. These are located all around the outside diameter of the pump assembly top.

4. Remove the pump assembly from the tank. Replace the O-ring.

5. Install the fuel pump in the reverse order of removal, torquing the mounting bolts to 1.4-1.9 ft. lbs. Make sure all fuel lines are reconnected securely and with clamps situated a short distance from the ends of the hoses. Replace any hoses that are cracked or damaged, using high pressure fuel hose designed for use with fuel injection (not carburetor) type fuel systems. Make sure each electrical connector is fully connected to the proper connector on the pump.

TESTING

NOTE: *To perform this procedure, you will need a pressure gauge capable of reading up to about 25 psi pressure and fittings to effectively tee this gauge into the fuel inlet line.*

1. Release the fuel system pressure as follows:

a. With the ignition switch turned off, remove the fuse from the circuit which supplies the fuel pump.

b. Start the engine and allow it to continue to run until it stalls. Then, crank the engine over several revolutions. Turn the ignition switch off again.

2. Remove the air cleaner and locate it to one side, with all vacuum lines connected. Disconnect the fuel supply (upper) line where it connects with the injection throttle body. Tee in the pressure gauge. Double-check all connections to make sure they are tight.

3. Start the engine and allow it to idle, watching the pressure gauge. The fuel pressure should be approximately 14 psi. If the pressure is significantly below this, depressurize the fuel system and remove and inspect the fuel filter by draining fuel from the inlet side into a metal container. If the fuel drained from the filter has a high concentration of contaminants, replace the filter and repeat the test. If the pressure is still low, make sure the fuel pump connector is supplying 12 volts. If the power supply is okay and fuel pressure is still low, replace the pump.

Throttle Body

REMOVAL AND INSTALLATION

NOTE: *To perform this procedure, you will need a set of Allen type wrenches that you can torque to approx. 20 ft. lbs. Also, make sure to get a complete set of gaskets (for both sides of the mixture heater) before beginning.*

1. Disconnect the negative battery cable. Remove the air cleaner.

2. Disconnect:

a. The large vacuum line that connects the throttle body to the E.G.R./Canister cut solenoid valve at the throttle body.

b. Mixture heater electrical connector at the heater unit.

c. Throttle valve switch sensor at the connector a few inches away from the sensor.

d. Depressurize the fuel system as described above under fuel pressure testing. Then, disconnect the fuel inlet and return lines at the throttle body and plug the opening in the line. Collect any fuel that drains out of the throttle body in a metal container.

e. The airflow meter connector.

d. The injector electrical connector.

3. Remove the four large through-bolts equipped with Allen type heads. Remove the throttle body and mixture heater from the intake manifold.

4. Thoroughly clean all 4 gasket surfaces, being careful not to scratch them. Install a new gasket onto the manifold with the boltholes lined up and then install the mixture heater.

5. Locate the gasket that goes under the throttle body onto the top of the mixture heater. Make sure all 4 of the boltholes line up. Then, locate the throttle body on top of the gasket, again carefully aligning boltholes. Be care-

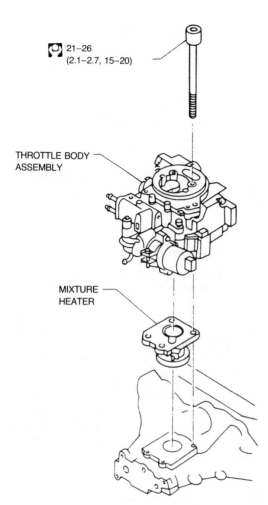

21–26
(2.1–2.7, 15–20)

THROTTLE BODY
ASSEMBLY

MIXTURE
HEATER

Removing the fuel injection throttle body

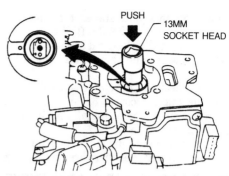

PUSH   13MM
SOCKET HEAD

Installing the injector into the throttle body. Make sure to align the electrical terminals as shown in the inset.

1. Disconnect the negative battery cable. Remove the air cleaner.
2. Depressurize the fuel system as described above under fuel pressure testing.
3. Disconnect the injector electrical connector at the injector cover.
4. Remove the small rubber plug from the injector cover. Remove the small Phillips type screw from the injector.
3. Remove the three large Phillips screws from the injector cover. Remove the injector cover (the top section of the throttle body). Being careful not to scratch any surfaces, remove the large O-ring from the cover.
4. Using a pair of pliers, grasp the flats at the top of the injector carefully so as to avoid grabbing the electrical terminal. Pull the injector straight upward and out of the throttle body.
5. Coat the O-rings with clean engine oil. Gently pull the top cover off the injector. Roll the old O-rings off the top and bottom of the injector.
6. Install the new lower O-ring into the injector bore in the throttle body. Then, turn the injector so the angle of the electrical connector is right (so that it will line up with the corresponding part of the cover). Start it into the throttle body.
7. Install a 13 mm socket (with the drive hole upward) to the top of the injector *so that it will not bend the electrical connectors*. Then, gently force the injector downward until it seats.
8. Position the upper O-ring onto the injector. Then, install a 19 mm socket squarely over the injector and, with it, gently work the O-ring down over the top of the injector and into position. Then, install the white injector top cover.
9. Install both the large and small O-rings into the injector cover. Install the injector cover (which forms the top of the throttle body) onto the throttle body with the screw holes and the electrical connectors squarely lined up.
10. Install the three large attaching screws.

ful to align the throttle body before it rests on top of the gasket to avoid shifting the gasket's position.
6. Install the four through bolts into the throttle body and start them into the manifold. Tighten finger tight. Then torque in 3 stages, in a criss-cross pattern, to 15-20 ft. lbs.
7. Reconnect: the injector electrical connector; airflow meter connector; fuel lines; throttle valve switch; mixture heater electrical connector; and vacuum lines.
8. Install the air cleaner and reconnect the battery cable. Start the engine and make sure it idles smoothly and without fuel leaks.

INJECTOR REPLACEMENT

NOTE: *To perform this procedure, you will need various size Phillips screwdrivers which can be turned with a torque wrench, a complete set of O-rings for the fuel injector, 13 mm and 19 mm sockets and locking type sealer.*

Torque them in several stages, tightening in a criss-cross manner to 2.9-3.6 ft. lbs.

11. Make sure the electrical connector for the injector is secure and then install the rubber plug.

12. Reconnect the injector electrical connector at the injector cover. Reconnect the fuel lines in a secure manner. Install the air cleaner and reconnect the battery.

13. Start the engine and make sure the engine idles smoothly and that there are no fuel leaks.

THROTTLE VALVE SWITCH ADJUSTMENT

1. Run the engine until it reaches operating temperature. Disconnect the throttle valve switch and throttle sensor harness connectors. Connect a tachometer according to manufacturer's instructions.

2. Block the wheels and set the parking brake securely. Set the idle speed to 750 rpm with a manual transmission and 670 in Drive with automatics. Then, put the transmission back into Neutral if it's an automatic. Read the idle speed in Neutral if the car has an automatic.

3. Connect an ohmmeter between the center and right side throttle valve switch connectors on the throttle body. Open the throttle to rev the engine to 2,000 rpm. Then, lower the engine speed slowly until the resistance goes from infinity to 0Ω (indicating that the switch has closed), noting the rpm.

4. The rpm should be 1,000-1,300 rpm on manual transmission cars and just 300 rpm above the neutral rpm for automatics. If the rpm is incorrect, loosen the mounting screws and turn the throttle valve switch. Tighten the screws and repeat Steps 3 and 4 to retest until the rpm is correct.

5. Turn the engine off, remove the instruments, and reconnect the electrical connectors.

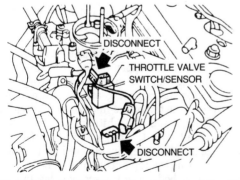

Disconnect the throttle valve switch and throttle sensor harness connectors to adjust the throttle switch (fuel injected Sentras)

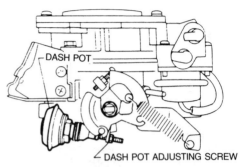

Location of the dashpot adjusting screws on 1987–88 Sentra with electronic injection

DASHPOT ADJUSTMENT

1. Run the engine until it is warmed up. Connect a tachometer according to manufacturer's instructions.

2. Make sure the engine idle speed is correct. Then, watching the tachometer, accelerate the engine to 3,000 rpm turning the throttle shaft by hand. Slowly lower the engine speed, and note the rpm at which the dash pot just touches the adjusting screw on the throttle mechanism.

3. The rpm should be 2,200-3,000 rpm when this happens. If not, adjust the dashpot adjusting screw with a small, open-end wrench and then repeat the test until the adjustment is correct.

DIESEL FUEL SYSTEM

Injection Lines
REMOVAL AND INSTALLATION

CAUTION: *Although diesel fuel is much safer than gasoline, remove all sources of ignition from the area before working on fuel lines and allow the engine to cool thoroughly. Catch spilling fuel in a metal cup and dispose of it safely.*

1. Note the firing order of the injection pump and the line locations for easy reassembly (the lines are held together by clamps to dampen vibration, so it is almost impossible to mix them up unless they are separated). Install a wrench on the flats of each nozzle or injection pump fitting. Then, install a wrench on the injection line flare nut. Turn the flare nut loose while opposing the torque with an equal force in the opposite direction on the pump or nozzle fitting.

2. Remove the tubes, which are clamped together to dampen vibration, as an assembly. *Carefully plug all openings to keep dirt out of the system.* If it is necessary to remove the injector spill tubes, unclamp and slide off the hose at one end. Then, remove the retaining nuts from

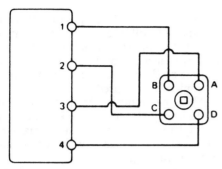

Diesel engine injection line connections

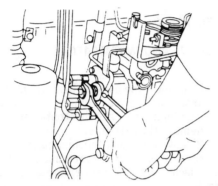

Tighten and loosen injection pump and nozzle fittings with a backup wrench to oppose the torque, as shown

the tops of the injectors and remove the spill tubes, noting the direction of installation.

3. Install the spill tube assembly, install the retaining nuts, and torque them to 29-36 ft. lbs. Inspect the return hose, replacing it if necessary. Install it onto the spill tube assembly and clamp it tightly.

4. Install the injection lines in their original firing order. Torque the flare nuts to the pump and nozzles using a backup wrench to oppose the torque. Torque the flare nuts to 16-18 ft. lbs.

5. Loosen the bleeder cock (equipped with a wingnut) near the top of the filter unit, place a metal cup underneath it, and then activate the priming pump by repeated depressing the top of the unit. When fuel without bubbles comes out, close the cock.

6. Loosen the fuel return hose at the injection pump. Have someone turn the engine over until fuel without bubbles comes out of this fitting. Then, reconnect the hose securely.

7. If the engine will not start, have someone crank the engine as you loosen each injector line at the pump and allow fuel to spray out until it is free of bubbles. Then, retorque the flare nuts.

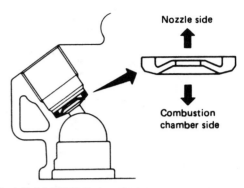

Install the injector nozzle gasket in the direction shown

Injector Nozzles
REMOVAL AND INSTALLATION

1. Remove the lines on the nozzle side and loosen them on the pump side.

2. Remove the spill tube.

3. Unscrew the injector from the engine.

4. Installation is the reverse of removal. Observe the following:

   a. Always use a new injector gasket. Install the gasket in the proper direction.

   b. Torque the injectors to 43-51 ft. lbs.

   c. Torque the lines to 16-18 ft. lbs.

   d. Torque the spill tube to 29-36 ft. lbs.

Injection Pump
REMOVAL AND INSTALLATION

1. Disconnect the battery ground.

2. Drain the coolant.

3. Disconnect and tag the wires and hoses attached to the pump or in the way of pump removal.

4. Remove the pump drive belt.

5. Remove the pump pulley.

6. Disconnect the injection lines at the pump.

7. Unbolt and remove the pump.

8. Installation is the reverse of removal. Observe the following points:

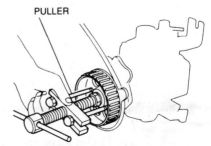

Removing injection pump pulley using puller

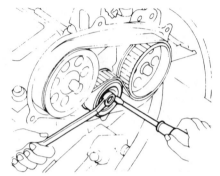

Move the belt tensioner to the free position

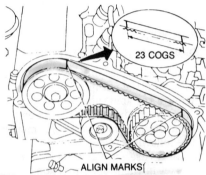

Mark the timing belt before removal

a. Make sure that the engine is at TDC of #1 piston's compression stroke.

b. Adjust the injection timing.

c. Connect the injection lines in a 4-3-2-1 order.

d. Bleed the fuel system.

9. Torque the injection pump nut to 9-13 ft. lbs.; the pump-to-rear bracket bolts to 23-17 ft. lbs.; the injection line nuts to 16-18 ft. lbs.

INJECTION TIMING ADJUSTMENT

NOTE: *Timing adjustment is necessary only if the injection pump or timing belt have been removed.*

1. Remove the air cleaner and duct.

2. Make sure that the #1 piston is at TDC of the compression stroke.

3. If the timing belt is still in position, remove it by freeing the tensioner.

4. If the injection pump was off the engine, install it at this time.

5. Clean the timing belt thoroughly and inspect it for cracks or wear. If any sign of wear exists, replace it.

6. On the outside of the belt, make a paint mark directly over one of the cogs. Count to your right, 23 cogs from the one with the paint mark, and place another paint mark directly over the 23rd cog.

7. If the engine is at TDC of #1 compression, the timing mark on the camshaft pulley should

be roughly at the 1 o'clock position. Turn the injection pump pulley so that its timing mark is in roughly the same position. Install the timing belt so that the paint marks align with the timing marks on the pulleys. Some turning of the pulleys might be required.

8. When the timing marks are aligned, tighten the tensioner. Turn the engine over by hand, two complete revolutions in the normal direction of rotation and make sure that the timing marks are still aligned.

FUEL TANK

REMOVAL AND INSTALLATION

1200

1. Disconnect the battery. Remove the drain plug from the tank bottom and completely drain the tank into a suitable container.

2. Remove the fuel lines.

3. Remove the trunk finishing panel.

4. Remove the four bolts retaining the tank.

5. Disconnect the hose clamp and gauge wire.

6. Remove the fuel tank.

B210 Sedan

1. Disconnect the battery ground cable.

2. Remove the front trunk panel.

3. Remove the spare tire and the plug from the spare housing.

4. Place a pan under the drain plug, remove the plug and drain the gas.

5. Disconnect the filler hose, ventilation lines, and fuel line from the tank.

6. Disconnect the fuel gauge wires from the tank.

7. Remove the rear seat cushion and back. Remove the front mounting bolts.

8. Remove the other two retaining bolts, and lift out the tank.

9. Installation is the reverse of removal.

B210 Coupe

1. Disconnect the battery ground cable.

2. Remove the finish panel from the right side of the trunk.

3. Place a pan under the drain plug, remove the plug, and drain the gas.

4. Disconnect the filler hose, ventilation lines, and fuel line from the tank.

5. Disconnect the evaporative lines from the reservoir tank.

6. Remove the spare tire and then the inspection plate from the rear floor.

7. Disconnect the sending unit wires.

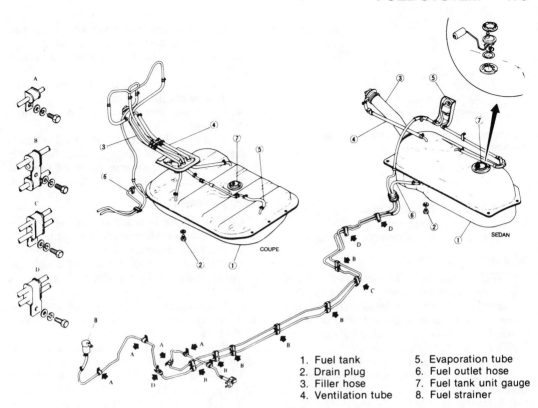

1. Fuel tank
2. Drain plug
3. Filler hose
4. Ventilation tube
5. Evaporation tube
6. Fuel outlet hose
7. Fuel tank unit gauge
8. Fuel strainer

B210 fuel tank and lines

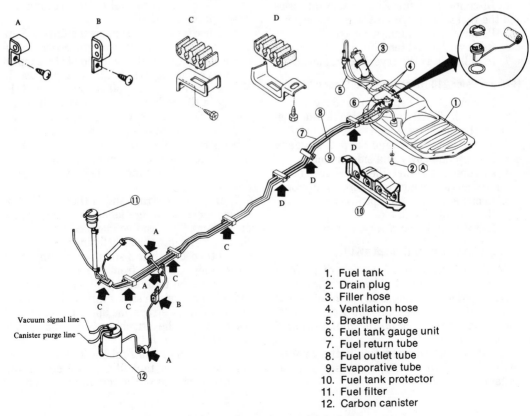

Vacuum signal line

Canister purge line

1. Fuel tank
2. Drain plug
3. Filler hose
4. Ventilation hose
5. Breather hose
6. Fuel tank gauge unit
7. Fuel return tube
8. Fuel outlet tube
9. Evaporative tube
10. Fuel tank protector
11. Fuel filter
12. Carbon canister

210 fuel tank and lines. Sentra similar

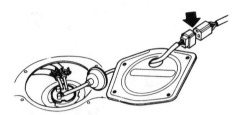

Removing fuel tank gauge unit and harness connection

8. Remove the fuel tank mounting bolts and lift the tank out of the car.

9. Installation is the reverse of removal.

1979 and later 210 Sedan

NOTE: *Install fuel filler hose after fuel tank has been mounted in place. Failure to follow this rule could result in leakage from around the hose connections. Do not twist or smash vent hoses when they are routed. Be sure to retain them securely with clips.*

1. Disconnect the battery ground cable.

2. Drain the fuel from the fuel tank, then disconnect the fuel hose.

3. Remove the filler hose protector and inspection cover in the luggage compartment.

4. Disconnect the fuel filler hose, vent hoses and the fuel tank gauge unit wire connector.

5. Remove the fuel tank protector.

6. Remove the fuel tank.

7. Installation is the reverse of removal.

1979 and later 210 Hatchback and Station Wagon

1. Disconnect the battery ground cable.

2. Drain the fuel from the fuel tank, then disconnect the fuel hose.

3. Remove the luggage carpet, luggage board, inspection cover and side finisher.

4. Disconnect the fuel filler hose, vent hoses and the fuel tank gauge unit wire connector.

5. Remove the fuel tank protector.

6. Remove the fuel tank.

7. Installation is the reverse of removal.

1982 and Later Sentra (Except 4WD)

CAUTION: *Remove all sources of ignition from the area of the car. Make sure the area is well ventilated to remove any fuel fumes that may collect. Make suer you have a safe, enclosed container for the fuel that is drained from the tank.*

1. Disconnect the negative battery cable. Drain fuel into a safe, enclosed, metal container.

2. Remove inspection cover and disconnect fuel tank gauge unit harness connector.

3. Disconnect fuel filler and ventilation tubes.

NOTE: *Plug hose and pipe openings to prevent entry of dust and dirt.*

4. Disconnect fuel outlet, return and evaporation hoses.

5. Remove six bolts attaching fuel tank flange to the body and then take out fuel tank.

6. Install in the reverse order of removal. Torque the tank mounting bolts to 20-27 ft. lbs.

Sentra with 4WD

CAUTION: *Remove all sources of ignition from the area of the car. Make sure the area is well ventilated to remove any fuel fumes that may collect. Make suer you have a safe, enclosed container for the fuel that is drained from the tank.*

1. Disconnect the negative battery cable. Drain fuel into a safe, enclosed, metal container.

2. Remove inspection cover and disconnect fuel tank gauge unit harness connector.

3. Disconnect fuel filler and ventilation tubes.

NOTE: *Plug hose and pipe openings to prevent entry of dust and dirt.*

4. Disconnect the fuel outlet, return and evaporation hoses.

5. Raise the car and support it securely. Support the tank securely from underneath. Remove the bolt from the rear end of the support strap on either side (the bolts screw in upward). You may twist the strap 90° an pull it out of the fitting in the body where it connects, if necessary for clearance or to replace it if damaged.

6. Lower the tank and remove it. If the tank is being replaced, remove the fuel pump mounting bolts and remove the pump. Install it with a a new O-ring, torquing the bolts to 1.4-1.9 ft. lbs.

7. Inspect the straps and, if they are bent or show cracks anywhere along their length, replace them. They can be installed by inserting the inner end into the body fitting with the outer end turned outboard and then turning them 90° so they run from front to rear.

8. Raise the tank into position. Then, raise the rear ends of the straps into position so the boltholes in the straps line up with those in the body. Install the attaching bolts and torque them to 20-27 ft. lbs.

9. Reconnect the fuel lines, evaporative emissions system, tank filler and electrical connectors in reverse of the removal procedure.

Chassis Electrical

6

UNDERSTANDING AND TROUBLESHOOTING ELECTRICAL SYSTEMS

At the rate which both import and domestic manufacturers are incorporating electronic control systems into their production lines, it won't be long before every new vehicle is equipped with one or more on-board computer. These electronic components (with no moving parts) should theoretically last the life of the vehicle, provided nothing external happens to damage the circuits or memory chips.

While it is true that electronic components should never wear out, in the real world malfunctions do occur. It is also true that any computer-based system is extremely sensitive to electrical voltages and cannot tolerate careless or haphazard testing or service procedures. An inexperienced individual can literally do major damage looking for a minor problem by using the wrong kind of test equipment or connecting test leads or connectors with the ignition switch ON. When selecting test equipment, make sure the manufacturers instructions state that the tester is compatible with whatever type of electronic control system is being serviced. Read all instructions carefully and double check all test points before installing probes or making any test connections.

The following section outlines basic diagnosis techniques for dealing with computerized automotive control systems. Along with a general explanation of the various types of test equipment available to aid in servicing modern electronic automotive systems, basic repair techniques for wiring harnesses and connectors is given. Read the basic information before attempting any repairs or testing on any computerized system, to provide the background of information necessary to avoid the most common and obvious mistakes that can cost both time and money. Although the replacement and test-ing procedures are simple in themselves, the systems are not, and unless one has a thorough understanding of all components and their function within a particular computerized control system, the logical test sequence these systems demand cannot be followed. Minor malfunctions can make a big difference, so it is important to know how each component affects the operation of the overall electronic system to find the ultimate cause of a problem without replacing good components unnecessarily. It is not enough to use the correct test equipment; the test equipment must be used correctly.

Safety Precautions

CAUTION: *Whenever working on or around any computer based microprocessor control system, always observe these general precautions to prevent the possibility of personal injury or damage to electronic components.*

● Never install or remove battery cables with the key ON or the engine running. Jumper cables should be connected with the key OFF to avoid power surges that can damage electronic control units. Engines equipped with computer controlled systems should avoid both giving and getting jump starts due to the possibility of serious damage to components from arcing in the engine compartment when connections are made with the ignition ON.

● Always remove the battery cables before charging the battery. Never use a high output charger on an installed battery or attempt to use any type of "hot shot" (24 volt) starting aid.

● Exercise care when inserting test probes into connectors to insure good connections without damaging the connector or spreading the pins. Always probe connectors from the rear (wire) side, NOT the pin side, to avoid accidental shorting of terminals during test procedures.

● Never remove or attach wiring harness

connectors with the ignition switch ON, especially to an electronic control unit.

• Do not drop any components during service procedures and never apply 12 volts directly to any component (like a solenoid or relay) unless instructed specifically to do so. Some component electrical windings are designed to safely handle only 4 or 5 volts and can be destroyed in seconds if 12 volts are applied directly to the connector.

• Remove the electronic control unit if the vehicle is to be placed in an environment where temperatures exceed approximately 176°F (80°C), such as a paint spray booth or when arc or gas welding near the control unit location in the car.

ORGANIZED TROUBLESHOOTING

When diagnosing a specific problem, organized troubleshooting is a must. The complexity of a modern automobile demands that you approach any problem in a logical, organized manner. There are certain troubleshooting techniques that are standard:

1. Establish when the problem occurs. Does the problem appear only under certain conditions? Were there any noises, odors, or other unusual symptoms?

2. Isolate the problem area. To do this, make some simple tests and observations; then eliminate the systems that are working properly. Check for obvious problems such as broken wires, dirty connections or split or disconnected vacuum hoses. Always check the obvious before assuming something complicated is the cause.

3. Test for problems systematically to determine the cause once the problem area is isolated. Are all the components functioning properly? Is there power going to electrical switches and motors? Is there vacuum at vacuum switches and/or actuators? Is there a mechanical problem such as bent linkage or loose mounting screws? Doing careful, systematic checks will often turn up most causes on the first inspection without wasting time checking components that have little or no relationship to the problem.

4. Test all repairs after the work is done to make sure that the problem is fixed. Some causes can be traced to more than one component, so a careful verification of repair work is important to pick up additional malfunctions that may cause a problem to reappear or a different problem to arise. A blown fuse, for example, is a simple problem that may require more than another fuse to repair. If you don't look for a problem that caused a fuse to blow, for example, a shorted wire may go undetected.

Experience has shown that most problems tend to be the result of a fairly simple and obvious cause, such as loose or corroded connectors or air leaks in the intake system; making careful inspection of components during testing essential to quick and accurate troubleshooting. Special, hand held computerized testers designed specifically for diagnosing the EEC-IV system are available from a variety of aftermarket sources, as well as from the vehicle manufacturer, but care should be taken that any test equipment being used is designed to diagnose that particular computer controlled system accurately without damaging the control unit (ECU) or components being tested.

NOTE: *Pinpointing the exact cause of trouble in an electrical system can sometimes only be accomplished by the use of special test equipment. The following describes commonly used test equipment and explains how to put it to best use in diagnosis. In addition to the information covered below, the manufacturer's instructions booklet provided with the tester should be read and clearly understood before attempting any test procedures.*

TEST EQUIPMENT

Jumper Wires

Jumper wires are simple, yet extremely valuable, pieces of test equipment. Jumper wires are merely wires that are used to bypass sections of a circuit. The simplest type of jumper wire is merely a length of multistrand wire with an alligator clip at each end. Jumper wires are usually fabricated from lengths of standard automotive wire and whatever type of connector (alligator clip, spade connector or pin connector) that is required for the particular vehicle being tested. The well equipped tool box will have several different styles of jumper wires in several different lengths. Some jumper wires are made with three or more terminals coming from a common splice for special purpose testing. In cramped, hard-to-reach areas it is advisable to have insulated boots over the jumper wire terminals in order to prevent accidental grounding, sparks, and possible fire, especially when testing fuel system components.

Jumper wires are used primarily to locate open electrical circuits, on either the ground (-) side of the circuit or on the hot (+) side. If an electrical component fails to operate, connect the jumper wire between the component and a good ground. If the component operates only with the jumper installed, the ground circuit is open. If the ground circuit is good, but the component does not operate, the circuit between the power feed and component is open. You can sometimes connect the jumper wire directly from the battery to the hot terminal of the component, but first make sure the component uses

12 volts in operation. Some electrical components, such as fuel injectors, are designed to operate on about 4 volts and running 12 volts directly to the injector terminals can burn out the wiring. By inserting an inline fuseholder between a set of test leads, a fused jumper wire can be used for bypassing open circuits. Use a 5 amp fuse to provide protection against voltage spikes. When in doubt, use a voltmeter to check the voltage input to the component and measure how much voltage is being applied normally. By moving the jumper wire successively back from the lamp toward the power source, you can isolate the area of the circuit where the open is located. When the component stops functioning, or the power is cut off, the open is in the segment of wire between the jumper and the point previously tested.

CAUTION: *Never use jumpers made from wire that is of lighter gauge than used in the circuit under test. If the jumper wire is of too small gauge, it may overheat and possibly melt. Never use jumpers to bypass high resistance loads (such as motors) in a circuit. Bypassing resistances, in effect, creates a short circuit which may, in turn, cause damage and fire. Never use a jumper for anything other than temporary bypassing of components in a circuit.*

12 Volt Test Light

The 12 volt test light is used to check circuits and components while electrical current is flowing through them. It is used for voltage and ground tests. Twelve volt test lights come in different styles but all have three main parts; a ground clip, a probe, and a light. The most commonly used 12 volt test lights have pick-type probes. To use a 12 volt test light, connect the ground clip to a good ground and probe wherever necessary with the pick. The pick should be sharp so that it can penetrate wire insulation to make contact with the wire, without making a large hole in the insulation. The wrap-around light is handy in hard to reach areas or where it is difficult to support a wire to push a probe pick into it. To use the wrap around light, hook the wire to probed with the hook and pull the trigger. A small pick will be forced through the wire insulation into the wire core.

CAUTION: *Do not use a test light to probe electronic ignition spark plug or coil wires. Never use a pick-type test light to probe wiring on computer controlled systems unless specifically instructed to do so. Any wire insulation that is pierced by the test light probe should be taped and sealed with silicone after testing.*

Like the jumper wire, the 12 volt test light is used to isolate opens in circuits. But, whereas the jumper wire is used to bypass the open to operate the load, the 12 volt test light is used to locate the presence of voltage in a circuit. If the test light glows, you know that there is power up to that point; if the 12 volt test light does not glow when its probe is inserted into the wire or connector, you know that there is an open circuit (no power). Move the test light in successive steps back toward the power source until the light in the handle does glow. When it does glow, the open is between the probe and point previously probed.

NOTE: *The test light does not detect that 12 volts (or any particular amount of voltage) is present; it only detects that some voltage is present. It is advisable before using the test light to touch its terminals across the battery posts to make sure the light is operating properly.*

Self-Powered Test Light

The self-powered test light usually contains a 1.5 volt penlight battery. One type of self-powered test light is similar in design to the 12 volt test light. This type has both the battery and the light in the handle and pick-type probe tip. The second type has the light toward the open tip, so that the light illuminates the contact point. The self-powered test light is dual purpose piece of test equipment. It can be used to test for either open or short circuits when power is isolated from the circuit (continuity test). A powered test light should not be used on any computer controlled system or component unless specifically instructed to do so. Many engine sensors can be destroyed by even this small amount of voltage applied directly to the terminals.

Open Circuit Testing

To use the self-powered test light to check for open circuits, first isolate the circuit from the vehicle's 12 volt power source by disconnecting the battery or wiring harness connector. Connect the test light ground clip to a good ground and probe sections of the circuit sequentially with the test light. (start from either end of the circuit). If the light is out, the open is between the probe and the circuit ground. If the light is on, the open is between the probe and end of the circuit toward the power source.

Short Circuit Testing

By isolating the circuit both from power and from ground, and using a self-powered test light, you can check for shorts to ground in the circuit. Isolate the circuit from power and ground. Connect the test light ground clip to a good ground and probe any easy-to-reach test point in the circuit. If the light comes on, there is a short somewhere in the circuit. To isolate the short, probe a test point at either end of the isolated circuit (the light should be on). Leave the test light probe connected and open connectors, switches, remove parts, etc., sequentially, until the light goes out. When the light goes out, the short is between the last circuit component opened and the previous circuit opened.

NOTE: *The 1.5 volt battery in the test light does not provide much current. A weak battery may not provide enough power to illuminate the test light even when a complete circuit is made (especially if there are high resistances in the circuit). Always make sure that the test battery is strong. To check the battery, briefly touch the ground clip to the probe; if the light glows brightly the battery is strong enough for testing. Never use a self-powered test light to perform checks for opens or shorts when power is applied to the electrical system under test. The 12 volt vehicle power will quickly burn out the 1.5 volt light bulb in the test light.*

Voltmeter

A voltmeter is used to measure voltage at any point in a circuit, or to measure the voltage drop across any part of a circuit. It can also be used to check continuity in a wire or circuit by indicating current flow from one end to the other. Voltmeters usually have various scales on the meter dial and a selector switch to allow the selection of different voltages. The voltmeter has a positive and a negative lead. To avoid damage to the meter, always connect the negative lead to the negative (-) side of circuit (to ground or nearest the ground side of the circuit) and connect the positive lead to the positive (+) side of the circuit (to the power source or the nearest power source). Note that the negative voltmeter lead will always be black and that the positive voltmeter will always be some color other than black (usually red). Depending on how the voltmeter is connected into the circuit, it has several uses.

A voltmeter can be connected either in parallel or in series with a circuit and it has a very high resistance to current flow. When connected in parallel, only a small amount of current will flow through the voltmeter current path; the rest will flow through the normal circuit current path and the circuit will work normally. When the voltmeter is connected in series with a circuit, only a small amount of current can flow through the circuit. The circuit will not work properly, but the voltmeter reading will show if the circuit is complete or not.

Available Voltage Measurement

Set the voltmeter selector switch to the 20V position and connect the meter negative lead to the negative post of the battery. Connect the positive meter lead to the positive post of the battery and turn the ignition switch ON to provide a load. Read the voltage on the meter or digital display. A well charged battery should register over 12 volts. If the meter reads below 11.5 volts, the battery power may be insufficient to operate the electrical system properly. This test determines voltage available from the battery and should be the first step in any electrical trouble diagnosis procedure. Many electrical problems, especially on computer controlled systems, can be caused by a low state of charge in the battery. Excessive corrosion at the battery cable terminals can cause a poor contact that will prevent proper charging and full battery current flow.

Normal battery voltage is 12 volts when fully charged. When the battery is supplying current to one or more circuits it is said to be "under load". When everything is off the electrical system is under a "no-load" condition. A fully charged battery may show about 12.5 volts at no load; will drop to 12 volts under medium load; and will drop even lower under heavy load. If the battery is partially discharged the voltage decrease under heavy load may be excessive, even though the battery shows 12 volts or more at no load. When allowed to discharge further, the battery's available voltage under load will decrease more severely. For this reason, it is important that the battery be fully charged during all testing procedures to avoid errors in diagnosis and incorrect test results.

Voltage Drop

When current flows through a resistance, the voltage beyond the resistance is reduced (the larger the current, the greater the reduction in voltage). When no current is flowing, there is no voltage drop because there is no current flow. All points in the circuit which are connected to the power source are at the same voltage as the power source. The total voltage drop always equals the total source voltage. In a long circuit with many connectors, a series of small, unwanted voltage drops due to corrosion at the connectors can add up to a total loss of voltage which impairs the operation of the normal loads in the circuit.

INDIRECT COMPUTATION OF VOLTAGE DROPS

1. Set the voltmeter selector switch to the 20 volt position.
2. Connect the meter negative lead to a good ground.

3. Probe all resistances in the circuit with the positive meter lead.

4. Operate the circuit in all modes and observe the voltage readings.

DIRECT MEASUREMENT OF VOLTAGE DROPS

1. Set the voltmeter switch to the 20 volt position.

2. Connect the voltmeter negative lead to the ground side of the resistance load to be measured.

3. Connect the positive lead to the positive side of the resistance or load to be measured.

4. Read the voltage drop directly on the 20 volt scale.

Too high a voltage indicates too high a resistance. If, for example, a blower motor runs too slowly, you can determine if there is too high a resistance in the resistor pack. By taking voltage drop readings in all parts of the circuit, you can isolate the problem. Too low a voltage drop indicates too low a resistance. If, for example, a blower motor runs too fast in the MED and/or LOW position, the problem can be isolated in the resistor pack by taking voltage drop readings in all parts of the circuit to locate a possibly shorted resistor. The maximum allowable voltage drop under load is critical, especially if there is more than one high resistance problem in a circuit because all voltage drops are cumulative. A small drop is normal due to the resistance of the conductors.

HIGH RESISTANCE TESTING

1. Set the voltmeter selector switch to the 4 volt position.

2. Connect the voltmeter positive lead to the positive post of the battery.

3. Turn on the headlights and heater blower to provide a load.

4. Probe various points in the circuit with the negative voltmeter lead.

5. Read the voltage drop on the 4 volt scale. Some average maximum allowable voltage drops are:

FUSE PANEL – 7 volts
IGNITION SWITCH – 5 volts
HEADLIGHT SWITCH – 7 volts
IGNITION COIL (+) – 5 volts
ANY OTHER LOAD – 1.3 volts
NOTE: *Voltage drops are all measured while a load is operating; without current flow, there will be no voltage drop.*

Ohmmeter

The ohmmeter is designed to read resistance (ohms) in a circuit or component. Although there are several different styles of ohmmeters, all will usually have a selector switch which permits the measurement of different ranges of resistance (usually the selector switch allows the multiplication of the meter reading by 10, 100, 1000, and 10,000). A calibration knob allows the meter to be set at zero for accurate measurement. Since all ohmmeters are powered by an internal battery (usually 9 volts), the ohmmeter can be used as a self-powered test light. When the ohmmeter is connected, current from the ohmmeter flows through the circuit or component being tested. Since the ohmmeter's internal resistance and voltage are known values, the amount of current flow through the meter depends on the resistance of the circuit or component being tested.

The ohmmeter can be used to perform continuity test for opens or shorts (either by observation of the meter needle or as a self-powered test light), and to read actual resistance in a circuit. It should be noted that the ohmmeter is used to check the resistance of a component or wire while there is no voltage applied to the circuit. Current flow from an outside voltage source (such as the vehicle battery) can damage the ohmmeter, so the circuit or component should be isolated from the vehicle electrical system before any testing is done. Since the ohmmeter uses its own voltage source, either lead can be connected to any test point.

NOTE: *When checking diodes or other solid state components, the ohmmeter leads can only be connected one way in order to measure current flow in a single direction. Make sure the positive (+) and negative (-) terminal connections are as described in the test procedures to verify the one-way diode operation.*

In using the meter for making continuity checks, do not be concerned with the actual resistance readings. Zero resistance, or any resistance readings, indicate continuity in the circuit. Infinite resistance indicates an open in the circuit. A high resistance reading where there should be none indicates a problem in the circuit. Checks for short circuits are made in the same manner as checks for open circuits except that the circuit must be isolated from both power and normal ground. Infinite resistance indicates no continuity to ground, while zero resistance indicates a dead short to ground.

RESISTANCE MEASUREMENT

The batteries in an ohmmeter will weaken with age and temperature, so the ohmmeter must be calibrated or "zeroed" before taking measurements. To zero the meter, place the selector switch in its lowest range and touch the two ohmmeter leads together. Turn the calibration knob until the meter needle is exactly on zero.

NOTE: *All analog (needle) type ohmmeters*

must be zeroed before use, but some digital ohmmeter models are automatically calibrated when the switch is turned on. Self-calibrating digital ohmmeters do not have an adjusting knob, but its a good idea to check for a zero readout before use by touching the leads together. All computer controlled systems require the use of a digital ohmmeter with at least 10 meagohms impedance for testing. Before any test procedures are attempted, make sure the ohmmeter used is compatible with the electrical system or damage to the onboard computer could result.

To measure resistance, first isolate the circuit from the vehicle power source by disconnecting the battery cables or the harness connector. Make sure the key is OFF when disconnecting any components or the battery. Where necessary, also isolate at least one side of the circuit to be checked to avoid reading parallel resistances. Parallel circuit resistances will always give a lower reading than the actual resistance of either of the branches. When measuring the resistance of parallel circuits, the total resistance will always be lower than the smallest resistance in the circuit. Connect the meter leads to both sides of the circuit (wire or component) and read the actual measured ohms on the meter scale. Make sure the selector switch is set to the proper ohm scale for the circuit being tested to avoid misreading the ohmmeter test value.

CAUTION: *Never use an ohmmeter with power applied to the circuit. Like the self-powered test light, the ohmmeter is designed to operate on its own power supply. The normal 12 volt automotive electrical system current could damage the meter.*

Ammeters

An ammeter measures the amount of current flowing through a circuit in units called amperes or amps. Amperes are units of electron flow which indicate how fast the electrons are flowing through the circuit. Since Ohms Law dictates that current flow in a circuit is equal to the circuit voltage divided by the total circuit resistance, increasing voltage also increases the current level (amps). Likewise, any decrease in resistance will increase the amount of amps in a circuit. At normal operating voltage, most circuits have a characteristic amount of amperes, called "current draw" which can be measured using an ammeter. By referring to a specified current draw rating, measuring the amperes, and comparing the two values, one can determine what is happening within the circuit to aid in diagnosis. An open circuit, for example, will not allow any current to flow so the ammeter reading will be zero. More current flows

through a heavily loaded circuit or when the charging system is operating.

An ammeter is always connected in series with the circuit being tested. All of the current that normally flows through the circuit must also flow through the ammeter; if there is any other path for the current to follow, the ammeter reading will not be accurate. The ammeter itself has very little resistance to current flow and therefore will not affect the circuit, but it will measure current draw only when the circuit is closed and electricity is flowing. Excessive current draw can blow fuses and drain the battery, while a reduced current draw can cause motors to run slowly, lights to dim and other components to not operate properly. The ammeter can help diagnose these conditions by locating the cause of the high or low reading.

Multimeters

Different combinations of test meters can be built into a single unit designed for specific tests. Some of the more common combination test devices are known as Volt/Amp testers, Tach/Dwell meters, or Digital Multimeters. The Volt/Amp tester is used for charging system, starting system or battery tests and consists of a voltmeter, an ammeter and a variable resistance carbon pile. The voltmeter will usually have at least two ranges for use with 6, 12 and 24 volt systems. The ammeter also has more than one range for testing various levels of battery loads and starter current draw and the carbon pile can be adjusted to offer different amounts of resistance. The Volt/Amp tester has heavy leads to carry large amounts of current and many later models have an inductive ammeter pickup that clamps around the wire to simplify test connections. On some models, the ammeter also has a zero-center scale to allow testing of charging and starting systems without switching leads or polarity. A digital multimeter is a voltmeter, ammeter and ohmmeter combined in an instrument which gives a digital readout. These are often used when testing solid state circuits because of their high input impedance (usually 10 megohms or more).

The tach/dwell meter combines a tachometer and a dwell (cam angle) meter and is a specialized kind of voltmeter. The tachometer scale is marked to show engine speed in rpm and the dwell scale is marked to show degrees of distributor shaft rotation. In most electronic ignition systems, dwell is determined by the control unit, but the dwell meter can also be used to check the duty cycle (operation) of some electronic engine control systems. Some tach/dwell meters are powered by an internal battery, while others take their power from the car battery in use. The battery powered testers usually require calibration much like an ohmmeter before testing.

Special Test Equipment

A variety of diagnostic tools are available to help troubleshoot and repair computerized engine control systems. The most sophisticated of these devices are the console type engine analyzers that usually occupy a garage service bay, but there are several types of aftermarket electronic testers available that will allow quick circuit tests of the engine control system by plugging directly into a special connector located in the engine compartment or under the dashboard. Several tool and equipment manufacturers offer simple, hand held testers that measure various circuit voltage levels on command to check all system components for proper operation. Although these testers usually cost about $300-500, consider that the average computer control unit (or ECM) can cost just as much and the money saved by not replacing perfectly good sensors or components in an attempt to correct a problem could justify the purchase price of a special diagnostic tester the first time it's used.

These computerized testers can allow quick and easy test measurements while the engine is operating or while the car is being driven. In addition, the on-board computer memory can be read to access any stored trouble codes; in effect allowing the computer to tell you where it hurts and aid trouble diagnosis by pinpointing exactly which circuit or component is malfunctioning. In the same manner, repairs can be tested to make sure the problem has been corrected. The biggest advantage these special testers have is their relatively easy hookups that minimize or eliminate the chances of making the wrong connections and getting false voltage readings or damaging the computer accidentally.

NOTE: *It should be remembered that these testers check voltage levels in circuits; they don't detect mechanical problems or failed components if the circuit voltage falls within the preprogrammed limits stored in the tester PROM unit. Also, most of the hand held testers are designed to work only on one or two systems made by a specific manufacturer.*

A variety of aftermarket testers are available to help diagnose different computerized control systems. Owatonna Tool Company (OTC), for example, markets a device called the OTC Monitor which plugs directly into the assembly line diagnostic link (ALDL). The OTC tester makes diagnosis a simple matter of pressing the correct buttons and, by changing the internal PROM or inserting a different diagnosis cartridge, it will work on any model from full size to subcompact, over a wide range of years. An adapter is supplied with the tester to allow connection to all types of ALDL links, regardless of the number of pin terminals used. By inserting an updated PROM into the OTC tester, it can be easily updated to diagnose any new modifications of computerized control systems.

Wiring Harnesses

The average automobile contains about ½ mile of wiring, with hundreds of individual connections. To protect the many wires from damage and to keep them from becoming a confusing tangle, they are organized into bundles, enclosed in plastic or taped together and called wire harnesses. Different wiring harnesses serve different parts of the vehicle. Individual wires are color coded to help trace them through a harness where sections are hidden from view.

A loose or corroded connection or a replacement wire that is too small for the circuit will add extra resistance and an additional voltage drop to the circuit. A ten percent voltage drop can result in slow or erratic motor operation, for example, even though the circuit is complete. Automotive wiring or circuit conductors can be in any one of three forms:

1. Single strand wire
2. Multistrand wire
3. Printed circuitry

Single strand wire has a solid metal core and is usually used inside such components as alternators, motors, relays and other devices. Multistrand wire has a core made of many small strands of wire twisted together into a single conductor. Most of the wiring in an automotive electrical system is made up of multistrand wire, either as a single conductor or grouped together in a harness. All wiring is color coded on the insulator, either as a solid color or as a colored wire with an identification stripe. A printed circuit is a thin film of copper or other conductor that is printed on an insulator backing. Occasionally, a printed circuit is sandwiched between two sheets of plastic for more protection and flexibility. A complete printed circuit, consisting of conductors, insulating material and connectors for lamps or other components is called a printed circuit board. Printed circuitry is used in place of individual wires or harnesses in places where space is limited, such as behind instrument panels.

Wire Gauge

Since computer controlled automotive electrical systems are very sensitive to changes in resistance, the selection of properly sized wires is critical when systems are repaired. The wire gauge number is an expression of the cross section area of the conductor. The most common system for expressing wire size is the American Wire Gauge (AWG) system.

Wire cross section area is measured in circular mils. A mil is $\frac{1}{1000}''$ (0.001"); a circular mil is the area of a circle one mil in diameter. For example, a conductor $\frac{1}{4}''$ in diameter is 0.250 in. or 250 mils. The circular mil cross section area of the wire is 250 squared (250^2) or 62,500 circular mils. Imported car models usually use metric wire gauge designations, which is simply the cross section area of the conductor in square millimeters (mm^2).

Gauge numbers are assigned to conductors of various cross section areas. As gauge number increases, area decreases and the conductor becomes smaller. A 5 gauge conductor is smaller than a 1 gauge conductor and a 10 gauge is smaller than a 5 gauge. As the cross section area of a conductor decreases, resistance increases and so does the gauge number. A conductor with a higher gauge number will carry less current than a conductor with a lower gauge number.

NOTE: *Gauge wire size refers to the size of the conductor, not the size of the complete wire. It is possible to have two wires of the same gauge with different diameters because one may have thicker insulation than the other.*

12 volt automotive electrical systems generally use 10, 12, 14, 16 and 18 gauge wire. Main power distribution circuits and larger accessories usually use 10 and 12 gauge wire. Battery cables are usually 4 or 6 gauge, although 1 and 2 gauge wires are occasionally used. Wire length must also be considered when making repairs to a circuit. As conductor length increases, so does resistance. An 18 gauge wire, for example, can carry a 10 amp load for 10 feet without excessive voltage drop; however if a 15 foot wire is required for the same 10 amp load, it must be a 16 gauge wire.

An electrical schematic shows the electrical current paths when a circuit is operating properly. It is essential to understand how a circuit works before trying to figure out why it doesn't. Schematics break the entire electrical system down into individual circuits and show only one particular circuit. In a schematic, no attempt is made to represent wiring and components as they physically appear on the vehicle; switches and other components are shown as simply as possible. Face views of harness connectors show the cavity or terminal locations in all multi-pin connectors to help locate test points.

If you need to backprobe a connector while it is on the component, the order of the terminals must be mentally reversed. The wire color code can help in this situation, as well as a keyway, lock tab or other reference mark.

NOTE: *Wiring diagrams are not included in this book. As trucks have become more complex and available with longer option lists, wiring diagrams have grown in size and complexity. It has become almost impossible to provide a readable reproduction of a wiring diagram in a book this size. Information on ordering wiring diagrams from the vehicle manufacturer can be found in the owner's manual.*

WIRING REPAIR

Soldering is a quick, efficient method of joining metals permanently. Everyone who has the occasion to make wiring repairs should know how to solder. Electrical connections that are soldered are far less likely to come apart and will conduct electricity much better than connections that are only "pig-tailed" together. The most popular (and preferred) method of soldering is with an electrical soldering gun. Soldering irons are available in many sizes and wattage ratings. Irons with higher wattage ratings deliver higher temperatures and recover lost heat faster. A small soldering iron rated for no more than 50 watts is recommended, especially on electrical systems where excess heat can damage the components being soldered.

There are three ingredients necessary for successful soldering; proper flux, good solder and sufficient heat. A soldering flux is necessary to clean the metal of tarnish, prepare it for soldering and to enable the solder to spread into tiny crevices. When soldering, always use a resin flux or resin core solder which is non-corrosive and will not attract moisture once the job is finished. Other types of flux (acid core) will leave a residue that will attract moisture and cause the wires to corrode. Tin is a unique metal with a low melting point. In a molten state, it dissolves and alloys easily with many metals. Solder is made by mixing tin with lead. The most common proportions are 40/60, 50/50 and 60/40, with the percentage of tin listed first. Low priced solders usually contain less tin, making them very difficult for a beginner to use because more heat is required to melt the solder. A common solder is 40/60 which is well suited for all-around general use, but 60/40 melts easier, has more tin for a better joint and is preferred for electrical work.

Soldering Techniques

Successful soldering requires that the metals to be joined be heated to a temperature that will melt the solder—usually 360-460°F (182-238°C). Contrary to popular belief, the purpose of the soldering iron is not to melt the solder itself, but to heat the parts being soldered to a temperature high enough to melt the solder when it is touched to the work. Melting flux-cored solder on the soldering iron will usually destroy the effectiveness of the flux.

NOTE: *Soldering tips are made of copper for good heat conductivity, but must be "tinned" regularly for quick transference of heat to the project and to prevent the solder from sticking to the iron. To "tin" the iron, simply heat it and touch the flux-cored solder to the tip; the solder will flow over the hot tip. Wipe the excess off with a clean rag, but be careful as the iron will be hot.*

After some use, the tip may become pitted. If so, simply dress the tip smooth with a smooth file and "tin" the tip again. An old saying holds that "metals well cleaned are half soldered." Flux-cored solder will remove oxides but rust, bits of insulation and oil or grease must be removed with a wire brush or emery cloth. For maximum strength in soldered parts, the joint must start off clean and tight. Weak joints will result in gaps too wide for the solder to bridge.

If a separate soldering flux is used, it should be brushed or swabbed on only those areas that are to be soldered. Most solders contain a core of flux and separate fluxing is unnecessary. Hold the work to be soldered firmly. It is best to solder on a wooden board, because a metal vise will only rob the piece to be soldered of heat and make it difficult to melt the solder. Hold the soldering tip with the broadest face against the work to be soldered. Apply solder under the tip close to the work, using enough solder to give a heavy film between the iron and the piece being soldered, while moving slowly and making sure the solder melts properly. Keep the work level or the solder will run to the lowest part and favor the thicker parts, because these require more heat to melt the solder. If the soldering tip overheats (the solder coating on the face of the tip burns up), it should be retinned. Once the soldering is completed, let the soldered joint stand until cool. Tape and seal all soldered wire splices after the repair has cooled.

Wire Harness and Connectors

The on-board computer (ECM) wire harness electrically connects the control unit to the various solenoids, switches and sensors used by the control system. Most connectors in the engine compartment or otherwise exposed to the elements are protected against moisture and dirt which could create oxidation and deposits on the terminals. This protection is important because of the very low voltage and current levels used by the computer and sensors. All connectors have a lock which secures the male and female terminals together, with a secondary lock holding the seal and terminal into the connec-

tor. Both terminal locks must be released when disconnecting ECM connectors.

These special connectors are weather-proof and all repairs require the use of a special terminal and the tool required to service it. This tool is used to remove the pin and sleeve terminals. If removal is attempted with an ordinary pick, there is a good chance that the terminal will be bent or deformed. Unlike standard blade type terminals, these terminals cannot be straightened once they are bent. Make certain that the connectors are properly seated and all of the sealing rings in place when connecting leads. On some models, a hinge-type flap proides a backup or secondary locking feature for the terminals. Most secondary locks are used to improve the connector reliability by retaining the terminals if the small terminal lock tangs are not positioned properly.

Molded-on connectors require complete replacement of the connection. This means splicing a new connector assembly into the harness. All splices in on-board computer systems should be soldered to insure proper contact. Use care when probing the connections or replacing terminals in them as it is possible to short between opposite terminals. If this happens to the wrong terminal pair, it is possible to damage certain components. Always use jumper wires between connectors for circuit checking and never probe through weather-proof seals.

Open circuits are often difficult to locate by sight because corrosion or terminal misalignment are hidden by the connectors. Merely wiggling a connector on a sensor or in the wiring harness may correct the open circuit condition. This should always be considered when an open circuit or a failed sensor is indicated. Intermittent problems may also be caused by oxidized or loose connections. When using a circuit tester for diagnosis, always probe connections from the wire side. Be careful not to damage sealed connectors with test probes.

All wiring harnesses should be replaced with identical parts, using the same gauge wire and connectors. When signal wires are spliced into a harness, use wire with high temperature insulation only. With the low voltage and current levels found in the system, it is important that the best possible connection at all wire splices be made by soldering the splices together. It is seldom necessary to replace a complete harness. If replacement is necessary, pay close attention to insure proper harness routing. Secure the harness with suitable plastic wire clamps to prevent vibrations from causing the harness to wear in spots or contact any hot components.

NOTE: *Weatherproof connectors cannot be replaced with standard connectors. Instruc-*

tions are provided with replacement connector and terminal packages. Some wire harnesses have mounting indicators (usually pieces of colored tape) to mark where the harness is to be secured.

In making wiring repairs, it's important that you always replace damaged wires with wires that are the same gauge as the wire being replaced. The heavier the wire, the smaller the gauge number. Wires are color-coded to aid in identification and whenever possible the same color coded wire should be used for replacement. A wire stripping and crimping tool is necessary to install solderless terminal connectors. Test all crimps by pulling on the wires; it should not be possible to pull the wires out of a good crimp.

Wires which are open, exposed or otherwise damaged are repaired by simple splicing. Where possible, if the wiring harness is accessible and the damaged place in the wire can be located, it is best to open the harness and check for all possible damage. In an inaccessible harness, the wire must be bypassed with a new insert, usually taped to the outside of the old harness.

When replacing fusible links, be sure to use fusible link wire, NOT ordinary automotive wire. Make sure the fusible segment is of the same gauge and construction as the one being replaced and double the stripped end when crimping the terminal connector for a good contact. The melted (open) fusible link segment of the wiring harness should be cut off as close to the harness as possible, then a new segment spliced in as described. In the case of a damaged fusible link that feeds two harness wires, the harness connections should be replaced with two fusible link wires so that each circuit will have its own separate protection.

NOTE: *Most of the problems caused in the wiring harness are due to bad ground connections. Always check all vehicle ground connections for corrosion or looseness before performing any power feed checks to eliminate the chance of a bad ground affecting the circuit.*

Repairing Hard Shell Connectors

Unlike molded connectors, the terminal contacts in hard shell connectors can be replaced. Weatherproof hard-shell connectors with the leads molded into the shell have non-replaceable terminal ends. Replacement usually involves the use of a special terminal removal tool that depress the locking tangs (barbs) on the connector terminal and allow the connector to be removed from the rear of the shell. The connector shell should be replaced if it shows any evidence of burning, melting, cracks, or breaks.

Replace individual terminals that are burnt, corroded, distorted or loose.

NOTE: *The insulation crimp must be tight to prevent the insulation from sliding back on the wire when the wire is pulled. The insulation must be visibly compressed under the crimp tabs, and the ends of the crimp should be turned in for a firm grip on the insulation.*

The wire crimp must be made with all wire strands inside the crimp. The terminal must be fully compressed on the wire strands with the ends of the crimp tabs turned in to make a firm grip on the wire. Check all connections with an ohmmeter to insure a good contact. There should be no measurable resistance between the wire and the terminal when connected.

Mechanical Test Equipment

Vacuum Gauge

Most gauges are graduated in inches of mercury (in.Hg), although a device called a manometer reads vacuum in inches of water (in. H_2O). The normal vacuum reading usually varies between 18 and 22 in.Hg at sea level. To test engine vacuum, the vacuum gauge must be connected to a source of manifold vacuum. Many engines have a plug in the intake manifold which can be removed and replaced with an adapter fitting. Connect the vacuum gauge to the fitting with a suitable rubber hose or, if no manifold plug is available, connect the vacuum gauge to any device using manifold vacuum, such as EGR valves, etc. The vacuum gauge can be used to determine if enough vacuum is reaching a component to allow its actuation.

Hand Vacuum Pump

Small, hand-held vacuum pumps come in a variety of designs. Most have a built-in vacuum gauge and allow the component to be tested without removing it from the vehicle. Operate the pump lever or plunger to apply the correct amount of vacuum required for the test specified in the diagnosis routines. The level of vacuum in inches of Mercury (in.Hg) is indicated on the pump gauge. For some testing, an additional vacuum gauge may be necessary.

Intake manifold vacuum is used to operate various systems and devices on late model vehicles. To correctly diagnose and solve problems in vacuum control systems, a vacuum source is necessary for testing. In some cases, vacuum can be taken from the intake manifold when the engine is running, but vacuum is normally provided by a hand vacuum pump. These hand vacuum pumps have a built-in vacuum gauge that allow testing while the device is still attached to the component. For some tests, an additional vacuum gauge may be necessary.

HEATER AND AIR CONDITIONING

Heater or Heater/Air Conditioner Blower Motor

REMOVAL AND INSTALLATION

1200, B210

1. Disconnect the battery ground cable.
2. Disconnect the heater blower harness connector.
3. Remove the three outer bolts holding the blower motor assembly in place and remove the motor with the fan attached.

NOTE: *Make sure you remove the outer bolts and not the bolts holding the motor to the backing plate.*

4. Installation is the reverse of removal.

1978 and later B210 and Sentra

1. Remove the instrument panel lower cover (this is not required on 1987-88 models).
2. Disconnect the blower motor harness connector.
3. Remove the blower casing attaching screws and drop the casing.
4. Remove the blower motor after removing the retaining screws. Install in the reverse order of removal.

Heater Assembly

REMOVAL AND INSTALLATION

NOTE: *Heater assembly removal is given here because it is necessary to remove the en-tire assembly to remove the heater core on all models.*

1973 1200 and 210 through 1977

1. Remove the package tray and ashtray.
2. Drain the coolant. Disconnect the two hoses between the heater and engine.

CAUTION: *When draining the coolant, keep in mind that cats and dogs are attracted by the ethylene glycol antifreeze, and are quite likely to drink any that is left in an uncovered container or in puddles on the ground. This will prove fatal in sufficient quantity. Always drain the coolant into a sealable container. Coolant should be reused unless it is contaminated or several years old.*

3. Disconnect the cables from the heater unit and heater controls. Disconnect the wiring.
4. Disconnect the two control wires from the water cock and interior valve, and the control rod from the shut valve. Set the heater control upper lever to DEF and lower lever to OFF.
5. Pull off the right and left defroster hoses.
6. Remove the four screws holding the heater unit to the firewall. Remove the control knob and remove the screws holding the control unit to the instrument panel. Remove the heater unit.
7. Install the heater unit into position on the firewall. Install the mounting bolts.
8. Install the control unit and knobs.
9. Install the right and left defroster hoses.
10. Install both defroster hoses.
11. Connect the control rod to the water shut-

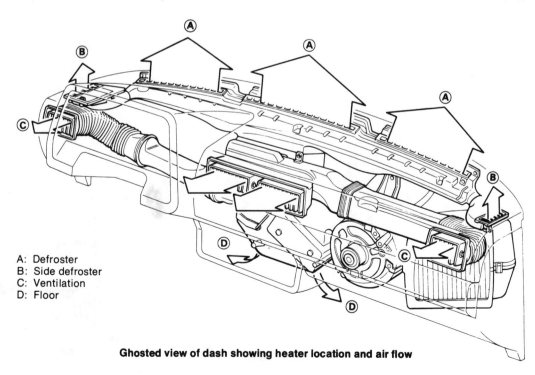

A: Defroster
B: Side defroster
C: Ventilation
D: Floor

Ghosted view of dash showing heater location and air flow

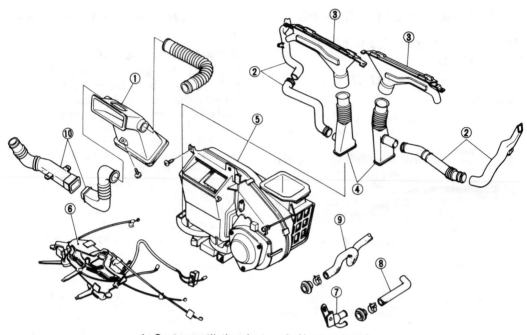

1. Center ventilation duct
2. Side defroster duct
3. Defroster nozzle
4. Defroster duct
5. Heater unit
6. Heater control
7. Water cock
8. Water inlet hose
9. Water outlet hose
10. Air cond. duct

210 heater assembly. Others similar

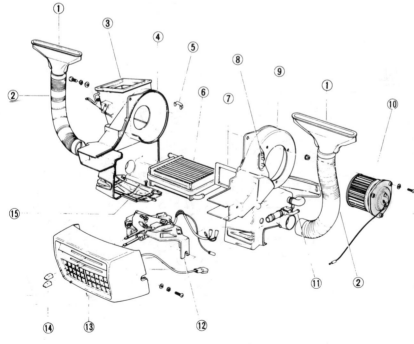

1. Defroster nozzle
2. Defroster hose
3. Air intake box
4. Heater box (L.H.)
5. Clip
6. Heater core
7. Ventilator valve
8. Resistor
9. Heater box (R.H.)
10. Fan and fan motor
11. Heater cock
12. Heater control
13. Center ventilator
14. Knob
15. Heat valve

B210 heater

off valve and the control wires to the water cock and interior valves.

12. Connect the wiring connector to the heater unit. Connect the heater control cables and adjust them so the doors close all the way.

13. Reconnect the heater hoses.

14. Install the package tray and ashtray.

15. Refill the cooling system.

B210 through 1977

1. Disconnect the battery ground cable.

2. Drain all the coolant from the radiator.

CAUTION: *When draining the coolant, keep in mind that cats and dogs are attracted by the ethylene glycol antifreeze, and are quite likely to drink any that is left in an uncovered container or in puddles on the ground. This will prove fatal in sufficient quantity. Always drain the coolant into a sealable container. Coolant should be reused unless it is contaminated or several years old.*

3. Disconnect the coolant inlet and outlet hoses.

4. Remove the heater duct hoses from both sides of the heater unit. Remove the defroster hose or hoses.

5. Disconnect the electrical wires of the heater unit (and air conditioner, if so equipped) at their connections.

6. Disconnect and remove the heater control cables.

7. Remove one attaching bolt from each side and one bolt from the top center of the heater unit (all B210 models).

8. Remove the heater unit.

9. To install the heater unit, first put the unit into position and install the lower bolts on either side and the single bolt at the top.

10. Install the cables. Adjust them so the doors close all the way.

11. Connect the electrical connectors for both heating and air conditioning functions, as required.

12. Reconnect the duct hoses to either side. Reconnect the defroster hoses.

13. Connect the heater hoses to the core. Reconnect the battery. Refill the cooling system. Run the engine for a few minutes (don't forget to top up the radiator with coolant) with the heater on to make sure the system is filled with coolant.

1978 and later 210

1. Disconnect the ground cable at the battery. Drain the coolant.

CAUTION: *When draining the coolant, keep in mind that cats and dogs are attracted by the ethylene glycol antifreeze, and are quite likely to drink any that is left in an uncovered container or in puddles on the ground. This*

will prove fatal in sufficient quantity. Always drain the coolant into a sealable container. Coolant should be reused unless it is contaminated or several years old.

2. Remove the package tray on the 210, if so equipped.

3. Remove the driver's side of the instrument panel. See the section below for instructions.

4. Remove the heater control assembly; remove the defroster ducts, vent door cables at the doors, harness connector and the control assembly.

5. Remove the radio.

6. On air conditioned models, disconnect the cooler ducts at heater unit side.

7. Disconnect the heater ducts, side defrosters and the center vent duct.

8. Remove the screws attaching the defroster nozzle to the unit. Disconnect the blower wiring harness and the heater hoses.

9. Remove the retaining bolts and the heater unit.

10. To install the heater, place it into position on the firewall so the mounting holes in the brackets line up with the holes in the firewall. Then, install the mounting bolts and tighten them.

11. Connect the heater hoses and clamp them securely. Install the defroster nozzle and attaching screws.

12. Connect the heater ducts, side defrosters and the center vent duct.

13. If the car has air conditioning, connect the cooler ducts at the side of the heater unit.

14. Install the radio.

15. Install the heater control assembly; install the defroster ducts, vent door cables at the doors, harness connector and the control assembly.

16. Install the driver's side of the instrument panel.

17. Install the package tray, if so equipped.

18. Connect the negative battery cable. Refill the cooling system. Run the engine for a few minutes (don't forget to top up the radiator with coolant) with the heater on to make sure the system is filled with coolant.

1982-86 Sentra

1. Disconnect the negative battery cable. Set "TEMP" lever to maximum "HOT" position and drain engine coolant.

CAUTION: *When draining the coolant, keep in mind that cats and dogs are attracted by the ethylene glycol antifreeze, and are quite likely to drink any that is left in an uncovered container or in puddles on the ground. This will prove fatal in sufficient quantity. Always drain the coolant into a sealable container.*

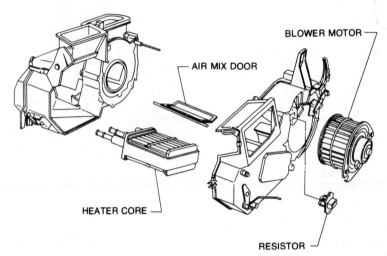

BLOWER MOTOR

AIR MIX DOOR

HEATER CORE

RESISTOR

Typical heater unit showing blower assembly

Coolant should be reused unless it is contaminated or several years old.

2. Disconnect the heater hoses at the engine compartment.

3. Remove the instrument panel assembly as follows:

   a. Disconnect the choke control cable, harness connectors, hood latch control cable, speedometer cable, and radio aerial cable.

   b. Remove the two screws from the lower side of the instrument hood and remove it.

   c. Remove the two screws from the top of the instrument cluster, pull it out to disconnect the electrical connectors, and remove it.

   d. Slide the ash tray out and then unscrew and remove the ash tray slider bracket.

   e. Remove the radio knobs and bezel. Disconnect the antenna and power cable, remove the attaching bolts, and remove the radio.

   f. Remove the heater control bezel. Disconnect the heater cables and electrical connector and remove the heater control from the dash.

   g. Remove the instrument panel section located just above the glovebox drawer by removing the attaching bolt on the right and then unclipping the panel section. Tilt the glove box drawer downward, work the hinge pins out of the dash at top and bottom and remove it.

   h. Remove the small panels out of the top left and top right of the dash by prying them very gently. Remove the two small screw covers from either side of the center of the dash at the top.

   i. Remove the four bolts from the bottom of the instrument panel assembly (one at each corner and two below the radio). Then,

support the assembly (perhaps with the help of an assistant). Remove the four bolts (one under each cover) that support the assembly at the top and remove it from the car.

4. Support the unit and remove the bolt from the mounting bracket located on the top right. Then, loosen the two bolts that support the unit via slotted brackets at the bottom. Lift the unit so the slots clear these bolts and remove it.

5. Install the heater unit to the firewall by positioning it on the two lower bolts and then installing and tightening the upper bolt. Tighten the lower bolt.

6. Reconnect the heater hoses and clamp them securely.

7. With a helper, put the instrument panel into position and hold it there. Then, install the four bolts that fasten the unit at the top.

8. Install the four bolts that fasten the unit at the bottom. Install the bolt covers on the top of the panel.

9. Install the glovebox and adjacent instrument panel section by reversing the removal procedure.

10. Install the heater control, connect the cables, and adjust them. Connect the electrical connector.

11. Install the radio by reversing the removal procedure.

12. Install the ash tray slider and the ashtray.

13. Install the instrument cluster in reverse of the removal procedure. Install the instrument hood.

14. Connect the choke control cable, harness connectors, hood latch control cable, speedometer cable, and radio aerial cable.

15. Refill the engine with coolant. Reconnect the battery. Start the engine and check for

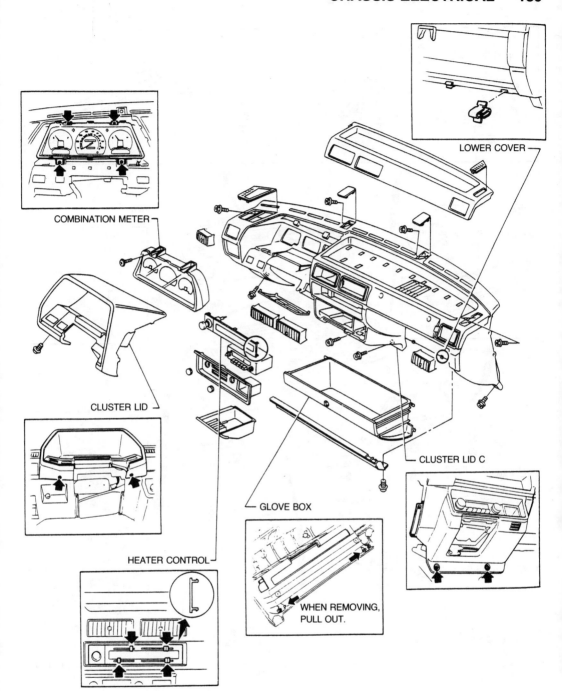

LOWER COVER

COMBINATION METER

CLUSTER LID

CLUSTER LID C

GLOVE BOX

HEATER CONTROL

WHEN REMOVING, PULL OUT.

Removing the dash panel on 1982–86 Sentras

leaks. Refill the cooling system after the engine has reached operating temperature and has then been allowed to cool.

1987-88 Sentra

NOTE: *This is a very lengthy procedure, requiring complete removal of the instrument panel.*

1. Disconnect the negative battery cable. Remove the upper defroster grilles by gently pulling them upward to free the eight clips fastening each of them in place.

2. Slide a thin, flat instrument in to release the clips by depressing the tangs on top and on the bottom of the center and right side air discharge grilles. Then, slide them out of the instrument panel.

3. Remove the four bolts from the top of the

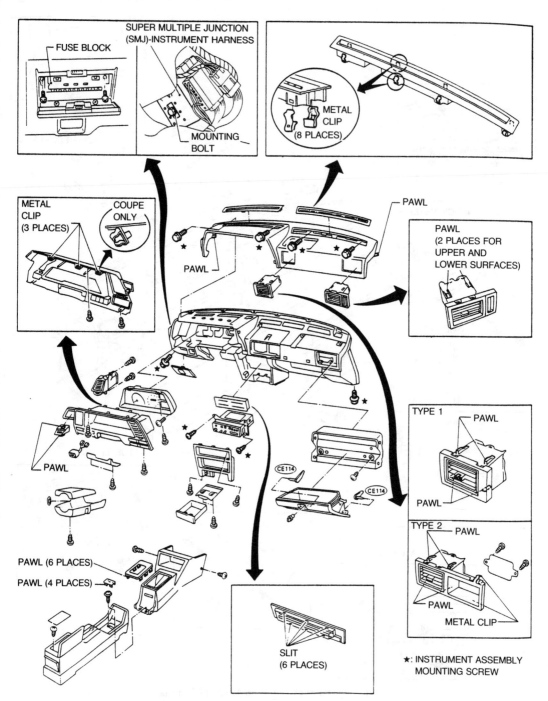

Removing the dash panel on 1987–88 Sentras

instrument panel cover (these are accessible at either end of the slots for the defroster grilles, removed earlier).

4. Remove the two screws from underneath the cluster bezel and the two from the underside of the cluster hood. Then, use a thin, flat object to depress the locking pawl in the fastener located at the top left of the cluster bezel; then, slide this fastener out of the dash. Now, slide the cluster bezel out of the dash.

5. Remove the instrument panel cover from the instrument panel by pulling it straight back so as to disengage the mounting pawls from the panel underneath, and remove it.

6. Remove the mounting screws from the underside and front of the instrument cluster

and then pull it out of the dash panel far enough for you to gain access to the electrical connectors. Disconnect these connectors and then remove the cluster by sliding it out of the dash.

7. Remove the large screw cover from the rear part of the rear console. Remove the console mounting screw located underneath it. Remove the small screw cover from the front of the console and remove the screw underneath that. Remove the rear console.

8. Remove the screw from either side of the front console. Remove the gearshift knob by unscrewing it. Then, remove the forward section of the console.

9. Slide out the ashtray drawer, depress the lock, and then remove it. Remove the two mounting screws (accessible from underneath) and then remove the ashtray slider.

10. Remove the two mounting screws and then remove the radio/heater control bezel. Disconnect the electrical connector for the heater control. Disconnect the air door cables the control actuates.

11. Then, remove the two mounting screws and pull the radio out for access to the electrical connector and antenna cable connector. Disconnect these and remove the radio.

12. Remove its mounting bolt and then disconnect the Super Multiple Junction connector from under the dash.

13. Remove the two mounting screws and remove the fuse block.

14. Remove the hood latch release.

15. Remove the left and right side instrument panel mounting screws, accessible from underneath and located near the corners of the unit. Then, pull the unit outward and remove it from the car.

16. Drain the cooling system into a clean container. Disconnect the heater hoses in the engine compartment.

CAUTION: *When draining the coolant, keep in mind that cats and dogs are attracted by the ethylene glycol antifreeze, and are quite likely to drink any that is left in an uncovered container or in puddles on the ground. This will prove fatal in sufficient quantity. Always drain the coolant into a sealable container. Coolant should be reused unless it is contaminated or several years old.*

17. Loosen the two bolts, located in slots, that support the unit on either side. Then, holding the unit against the firewall, remove the bolt from the hanger at the top. Raise the unit slightly so it will clear the lower mounting bolts and remove it from the firewall.

18. To install, first raise the unit into position and locate it so the grooves in the lower mounts fit over the two lower supporting bolts. Then

install and tighten the upper mounting bolts. Tighten the lower mounting bolts.

19. Install and connect the heater hoses and clamps.

20. Put the instrument panel into position so the mounting pawls line it up and install the right and left side mounting screws.

21. Install the hood release and fuse block. Connect the Super Multiple Junction connector and install its mounting bolt.

22. Install the radio and the heater control.

23. Install the ashtray slider and ashtray.

24. Install the front console and then the rear console. Install the gearshift knob.

25. Put the instrument cluster into position, connect all the electrical connectors and install it.

26. Install the instrument cluster bezel.

27. Install the instrument panel cover.

28. Install the center and right air discharge grilles.

29. Install the upper defroster grilles. Reconnect the battery and refill the cooling system.

Heater Core

REMOVAL AND INSTALLATION

1200, B210

1. Remove the heater from the car.

2. Remove the clip and slide the hose from the heater core cock.

3. Remove the clips and separate the left and right sides of the heater case.

4. Lift out the heater core.

1978 and Later 210 and Sentra

1. Remove the heater unit as outlined earlier.

2. Loosen the hose clamps and disconnect the inlet and outlet hoses.

3. Remove the clips securing the case halves and separate the cases.

4. Remove the heater core.

5. Installation is in the reverse order of removal.

Evaporator Core

REMOVAL AND INSTALLATION

210 Series

1. Disconnect the battery ground cable. Discharge the refrigerant system as described in Chapter 1.

2. *Using two wrenches to avoid placing torque on the lines,* loosen the flare nut connection at each of the two evaporator connections in the engine compartment. Immediately cover the openings with tape or a plastic cap.

3. Unscrew and remove the lower instrument panel pad. Then, remove the glovebox.

4. Disconnect the electrical connectors at both the compressor relay and the thermostat.

5. Remove the four attaching bracket bolts and remove the evaporator by first pulling it straight out to guide the refrigerant tubes through the firewall.

6. Cut the seals where upper and lower halves of the case fit together, using a knife. Then, remove the clips fastening the case halves together and separate the case halves.

7. Remove the evaporator coil. Install the evaporator back into the case and assemble it in reverse of disassembly. Use a sealer at the joints formed by cutting the seal earlier.

8. Begin installing the unit by guiding the tubes through the firewall. Then, situate it against the firewall with the boltholes in the brackets and firewall lined up. Install and tighten the mounting bolts.

9. Connect the electrical connectors for the compressor relay and thermostat.

10. Install the glovebox and lower instrument panel pad. Remove tape or plugs, coat the sealing surfaces of the flare fittings with clean refrigerant oil and tighten both, using a backup wrench.

11. Have the refrigerant system evacuated with a vacuum pump. Reconnect the battery. Have the system charged, or charge it with refrigerant yourself as described in Chapter 1. Check the system for proper operation and for leaks.

1982-86 Sentra

1. Discharge the refrigerant from the system as described in Chapter 1. Disconnect the battery ground cable.

2. Using a backup wrench, disconnect the refrigerant lines running to the evaporator on the engine compartment side of the firewall. Immediately tape or cap the openings. Remove the piping grommet and cover.

3. Remove the lower instrument panel cover from the passenger's side of the dash panel. Remove the glovebox.

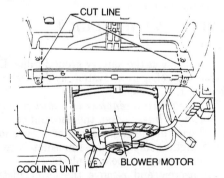

Cut out the section of dash panel between the two lines, using a hacksaw, on 1982–86 Sentras

4. Cover the blower motor vent holes with tape. Then, cut out the section of the lower instrument panel brace between two boltholes that will block removal of the blower and evaporator.

5. Clean all shavings away from the blower motor. Remove the blower motor. Remove the tape covering the blower motor cooling holes. Disconnect the electrical connector for the thermostat.

6. Unbolt the evaporator case from the firewall and remove it.

7. Cut the seals where upper and lower halves of the case fit together, using a knife. Then, remove the clips fastening the case halves together and separate the case halves.

8. Remove the evaporator coil. Install the evaporator back into the case and assemble it in reverse of disassembly. Use a sealer at the joints formed by cutting the seal earlier.

9. Begin installing the unit by guiding the tubes through the firewall. Then, situate it against the firewall with the boltholes in the brackets and firewall lined up. Install and tighten the mounting bolts.

10. Connect the electrical connectors for the thermostat.

11. Install the blower motor.

12. Install a replacement plate for the dash panel.

13. Install the glovebox and lower instrument panel pad. Remove tape or plugs, coat the sealing surfaces of the flare fittings with clean refrigerant oil and tighten both, using a backup wrench.

14. Have the refrigerant system evacuated with a vacuum pump. Reconnect the battery. Have the system charged, or charge it with refrigerant yourself as described in Chapter 1. Check the system for proper operation and for leaks.

1987-88 Sentra

1. Discharge the refrigerant from the system as described in Chapter 1. Disconnect the battery ground cable.

2. Using a backup wrench, disconnect the refrigerant lines running to the evaporator on the engine compartment side of the firewall. Immediately tape or cap the openings. Remove the piping grommet and cover.

3. Remove the lower instrument panel cover from the passenger's side of the dash panel. Remove the glovebox.

4. Cut out the section of the lower instrument panel brace located between the two marks in the illustration that will block removal of the evaporator.

5. Disconnect the electrical connector for the thermostat.

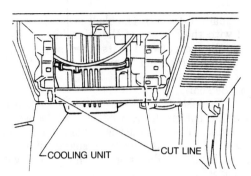

Cut the out section of dash panel between the two lines, using a hacksaw, on 1987–88 Sentras

6. Unbolt the evaporator case from the firewall and remove it.

7. Cut the seals where upper and lower halves of the case fit together, using a knife. Then, remove the clips fastening the case halves together and separate the case halves.

8. Remove the evaporator coil. Install the evaporator back into the case and assemble it in reverse of disassembly. Use a sealer at the joints formed by cutting the seal earlier.

9. Begin installing the unit by guiding the tubes through the firewall. Then, situate it against the firewall with the boltholes in the brackets and firewall lined up. Install and tighten the mounting bolts.

10. Connect the electrical connectors for the thermostat.

11. Install the glovebox and lower instrument panel pad. Remove tape or plugs, coat the sealing surfaces of the flare fittings with clean refrigerant oil and tighten both, using a backup wrench.

12. Have the refrigerant system evacuated with a vacuum pump. Reconnect the battery. Have the system charged, or charge it with refrigerant yourself as described in Chapter 1. Check the system for proper operation and for leaks.

RADIO

REMOVAL AND INSTALLATION

1200, B210

1. Remove the instrument cluster (procedure follows).

2. Detach all electrical connections attaching the radio to the car.

3. Remove the radio knobs and their retaining nuts.

4. Remove the rear support bracket.

5. Remove the radio.

6. Reverse the procedure for installation

210

NOTE: *The dashboard must be first removed on the 210 to gain access to the radio.*

1. Disconnect the battery ground cable.

2. Remove the steering column cover.

3. Remove the lighting control knob assembly.

4. Pull out the heater control knob and remove the heater control panel facing.

5. Remove the screws attaching the heater control assembly to the dash panel, or cluster lid "A" (see illustration).

6. Pull out the ash tray and remove the screws holding the ash tray holder in place.

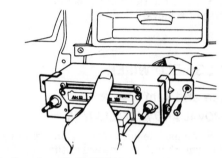

Radio removal, B210, 210

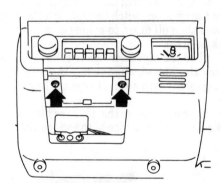

Sentra radio mounting screws under ash tray

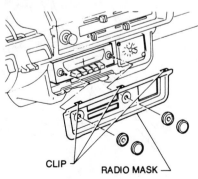

Removing radio mask (cover) for radio access, Sentra

8. Disconnect the harness connector and the antenna feeder cable.

9. Remove the eight screws holding the dashboard in place: three along the bottom, one on the driver's door side and four along the windshield. Remove the dashboard.

10. Remove the radio bracket by loosening the retaining screws.

11. Remove the radio.

12. Installation is the reverse of removal.

Sentra

1. Remove the ash tray and ash tray bracket.

2. Remove the radio mounting bolts.

3. Remove the radio mask (front cover) after removing the tuning knobs.

4. Remove the radio unit. Installation is the reverse of removal.

WINDSHIELD WIPER

Blade and Arm

REMOVAL AND INSTALLATION

1. Some models have covers that are hinged to the arm. Pull these upward at the end of the arm opposite the blade. Other models have covers that fit over the end of the linkage shaft and the arm; simply pull these off. If necessary, turn the ignition switch on and turn the wipers on and then off again to bring them to the full park position.

2. Hold the wiper arm against the torque and loosen the nut which attaches the arm to the linkage shaft with a socket wrench. Remove the nut.

3. Note or measure the distance between the blade and the lower edge of the windshield (this is usually about 1''). The blade is usually parallel with the bottom of the windshield. Then, turn the arm outward on its hinges so its spring pressure is removed from the lower end. Pull the lower end of the arm straight off the splines on the shaft.

4. To install, first line up the wiper blade with the bottom of the windshield at the proper clearance. Then, install the end of the arm over the end of the shaft, turning it slightly, if necessary, in either direction so the splines will engage.

5. Install the attaching nut. Hold the arm to minimize torque on the driveshaft and torque the nut to 9-13 ft. lbs. Install decorative caps or covers in reverse of removal.

Wiper Motor

REMOVAL AND INSTALLATION

All Models

The wiper motor is on the firewall under the hood. The operating linkage is on the firewall inside the car.

1. Detach the motor wiring plug.

2. Inside the car, remove the nut connecting the linkage to the wiper shaft. Slide the linkage off the shaft. If there is a lot of resistance, use a small puller or force the linkage lever off the shaft with a pair of pliers. *Don't tap on the motor shaft with a hammer!*

3. Unbolt and remove the wiper motor from the firewall.

4. Reverse the procedure for installation.

Rear Wiper Motor

REMOVAL AND INSTALLATION

NOTE: *To perform this procedure, you will need a soft material used to seal the plastic*

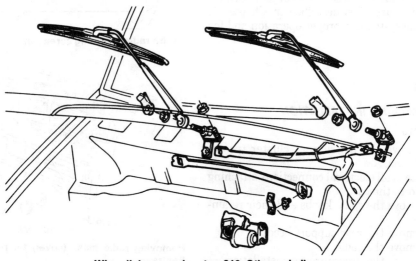

Wiper linkage and motor, 210. Others similar

watershields used in vehicle doors and tailgates.

1. Disconnect the negative battery cable. Bend the wiper arm to raise the wiper blade off the rear window glass. Then, remove the attaching bolt or nut and washers and work the wiper arm off the motor shaft.

2. Remove the attaching screws and remove the tailgate inner finish panel. Carefully peel the plastic water shield off the sealer.

3. Disconnect the electrical connector at the motor. Remove the motor mounting bolts and remove the motor.

4. Install the motor in reverse of the removal procedure. Before installing the water shield, run a fresh ring of sealer around the outer edge.

Wiper Linkage

REMOVAL AND INSTALLATION

1. Open the hood. Remove the mounting screws and remove access panels from the firewall. Then, remove the motor as described just above.

2. Remove the wiper arms as described above.

3. Remove the nut that attaches each wiper arm driveshaft unit to the cowl. Then, work the shaft downward and into the cowl interior.

4. Work the linkage out of the access holes and remove it from the car.

5. Install the linkage in reverse order.

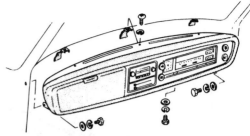

1200 dashboard removal

INSTRUMENTS AND SWITCHES

Instrument Cluster

REMOVAL AND INSTALLATION

1200

1. Disconnect the battery negative lead.

2. Depress the wiper, light switch, and choke knobs, turning them counterclockwise to remove.

3. From the rear, disconnect the lighter wire. Turn and remove the lighter outer case.

4. Remove the radio and heater knobs.

5. Remove the shell cover from the steering column.

6. Remove the screws which hold the instrument cluster to the instrument panel. Pull out the cluster.

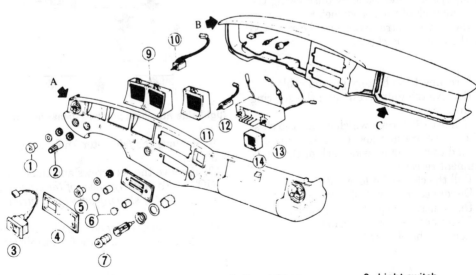

A. Cluster cover	4. Escutcheon	9. Light switch
B. Instrument pad	5. Wiper switch knob	10. Tachometer
C. Instrument panel	6. Radio knob	11. Wiper switch
1. Light switch knob	7. Cigarette lighter	12. Radio
2. Light control knob	8. Gauges	13. Clock
3. Rear window defogger switch		

B210 instrument cluster removal

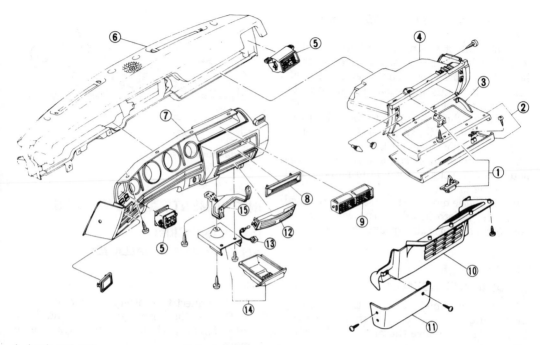

1. Lock and striker
2. Lid finisher
3. Lid stopper
4. Cluster lid B compartment
5. Side vent grille

6. Instrument panel assembly
7. Cluster lid A
8. Radio mask
9. Center vent grille
10. Instrument lower assist cover

11. Instrument lower center cover
12. Heater control finisher
13. Illumination lamp
14. Ash tray
15. Heater control lever bracket

1980 210 instrument panel. Other 210 similar

7. Disconnect the wiring connector. Disconnect the speedometer cable by unscrewing the nut at the back of the speedometer.

8. Individual instruments may be removed from the rear of the cluster.

B210

1. Disconnect the battery ground cable.

2. Remove the four screws and the steering column cover.

3. Remove the screws which attach the cluster face. Two are just above the steering column, and there is one inside each of the outer instrument recesses.

4. Pull the cluster lid forward.

5. Disconnect the multiple connector.

6. Disconnect the speedometer cable.

7. Disconnect any other wiring.

8. Remove the cluster face.

210 instrument panel left side attaching points

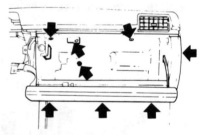

Right side attaching points, 210 instrument panel

9. Remove the odometer knob if the vehicle has one.

10. Remove the six screws and the cluster.
NOTE: *To make removal of the cluster easier, remove the steering wheel and turn signal switch.*

11. Instruments may now be readily replaced.

12. Reverse the procedure for installation.

210

See 210 Radio Removal and Installation for instrument cluster removal and installation procedure.

1982-86 Sentra

NOTE: *If complete instrument panel removal is required, refer to the "Heater Assembly*

Removal and Installation" procedure above. This operation is most commonly performed to remove a leaky heater core.

1. Disconnect the battery negative cable. Remove the two screws from the lower side of the instrument hood and remove it.

2. Remove the two screws from the top of the instrument cluster, pull it out to disconnect the electrical connectors, and remove it.

3. Install the cluster in reverse of the removal procedure.

1987-88 Sentra

NOTE: If complete instrument panel removal is required, refer to the "Heater Assembly Removal and Installation" procedure above. This operation is most commonly performed to remove a leaky heater core.

1. Disconnect the battery negative cable. Remove the two screws from underneath the cluster bezel and the two from the underside of the cluster hood. Then, use a thin, flat object to depress the locking pawl in the fastener located at the top left of the cluster bezel; then, slide this fastener out of the dash. Now, slide the cluster bezel out of the dash.

2. Remove the mounting screws from the underside and front of the instrument cluster and then pull it out of the dash panel far enough for you to gain access to the electrical connectors. Disconnect these connectors and then remove the cluster by sliding it out of the dash.

3. Install the cluster by reversing the removal procedure.

Console

In the case of the 1987-88 Sentra, the console must be removed for clearance in removing the instrument panel. Refer to the "Heater Assembly Removal and Installation" procedure above for this procedure.

Windshield Wiper Switch

The switch for the front wipers is universally part of the combination switch which also operates the turn signal and headlights. Replacement of this switch requires removal of the steering wheel and disassembly of the upper column. It is therefore combined with other steering system operations in Chapter 8.

Rear Window Wiper Switch

The rear wiper switch is mounted near the bottom of the dash. To replace it:

1. Disconnect the negtive battery cable. Disconnect the electrical connector for the switch.

2. Loosen the mounting screw for the knob using an Allen wrench and pull the knob off the switch shaft. Then, use a large, deep well socket to remove the mounting nut from the front of the switch. Remove it by pulling toward the rear and pulling it out from under the dash.

3. Install the switch in reverse order.

Headlight Switch

REMOVAL AND INSTALLATION

The switch for the headlights is universally part of the combination switch which also operates the turn signal and headlights. Replacement of this switch requires removal of the steering wheel and disassembly of the upper column. It is therefore combined with other steering system operations in Chapter 8.

Speedometer Cable

REPLACEMENT

NOTE: *Cable routing varies slightly among the 1200, B210, 210 and Sentra models. Cable replacement procedures for all models are basically the same. On some models it may be easier to remove the instrument cluster to gain access to the cable.*

1. Remove any lower dash covers that may be in the way and disconnect the speedometer cable from the back of the speedometer.

2. Pull the cable from the cable housing. If the cable is broken, the other half of the cable will have to be removed from the transmission end. Unscrew the retaining knob at the transmission and remove the cable from the transmission on extension housing.

3. Lubricate the cable with graphite powder (sold as speedometer cable lubricant) and feed the cable into the housing. It is best to start at the speedometer end and feed the cable down towards the transmission. It is also usually necessary to unscrew the transmission connection and install the cable end to the gear, then reconnect the housing to the transmission. Slip the cable into the speedometer and reconnect the cable housing.

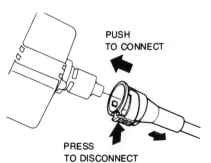

PUSH
TO CONNECT

PRESS
TO DISCONNECT

Sentra speedometer connection to speedometer. 210 similar

SEATBELT SYSTEM

Warning Buzzer and Light

Since 1972, the federal government has required all cars to have a warning system designed to remind the driver to buckle his or her seat belt.

When the ignition switch is turned to the "ON" position, the warning lamp comes on and remains on for 4 to 8 seconds. At the same time, the chime (warning buzzer in 1980 and earlier models) sounds for 4 to 8 seconds intermittently if the driver's seat belt is not properly fastened. The chime or buzzer is also used as a theft warning alarm.

This warning system consists of an ignition switch, a timer unit, a warning lamp, a driver's seat belt switch and a buzzer or chime. The dash board seat belt lights and the buzzer or chime is controlled by pressure-sensitive switches hidden in the front bench or bucket seats. A switch in each of the front seat belt retractors turns off the warning system only when the belt or belts are pulled a specified distance out of their retractors.

Two different types of switches are used to control the system, depending upon the type of transmission used:

On manual transmission equipped cars, the

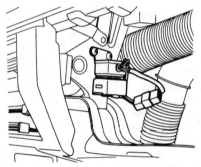

Seat belt warning buzzer unit, 210 (B210 similar). Sentra seat belt timer is under radio

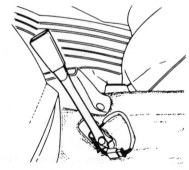

Seat belt warning switch

transmission neutral switch is used to activate the seat belt warning circuit.

Automatic transmissions use the inhibitor switch to activate the seat belt warning circuit.

When removing the seats, be sure to unplug the pressure-sensitive switches at their connections.

SEAT BELT SWITCH DISCONNECTION

1. Disconnect the battery ground cable.
2. Slide the seat all the way forward.
3. Disconnect the harness connector.
4. Remove the inner seat belt by removing the security bolt.
5. Install the inner seat belt in the reverse order of removal.

Seat Belt/Starter Interlock System

As required by law, all 1974 and most 1975 Datsun passenger cars cannot be started until the front seat occupants are seated and have fastened their seat belts. If the proper sequence is not followed, e.g., the occupants fasten the seat belts and then sit on them, the engine cannot be started.

The shoulder harness and lap belt are permanently fastened together, so that they both must be worn. The shoulder harness uses an inertia-lock reel to allow freedom of movement under normal driving conditions.

NOTE: *This type of reel locks up when the car decelerates rapidly, as during a crash.*

The switches for the interlock system have been removed from the lap belt retractors and placed in the belt buckles. The seat sensors remain the same as those used in 1973.

For ease of service, the car may be started from outside, by reaching in and turning the key, but without depressing the seat sensors.

In case of system failure, an override switch is located under the hood. This is a "one start" switch and it must be reset each time it is used.

This system is discontinued after 1975.

LIGHTING

Headlights

REMOVAL AND INSTALLATION

Except 1985-88 Sentra

NOTE: *The 1200 and B210 Datsun have radiator grilles which are unit-constructed to also serve as headlight frames. For these models it will be necessary to remove the grille to gain access to the headlights.*

1. Remove the grille, if necessary.
2. Remove the headlight retaining ring (frame) screws. These are the three or four

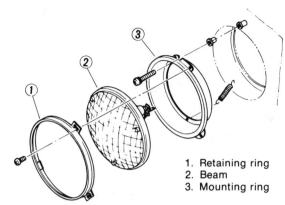

1. Retaining ring
2. Beam
3. Mounting ring

Exploded view of standard headlight. Square headlights similar

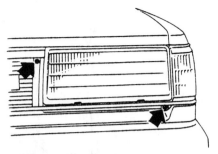

The headlamp on 1987–88 Sentra sedans. The arrowed screws are for adjustment only—leave them alone when working on the headlamps! On coupes, these screws are both at the top.

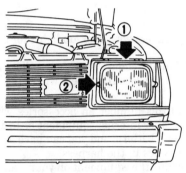

1. Vertical adjustment   2. Horizontal adjustment

210 headlight adjustment. Others similar except Sentra vertical adjustment screw is on bottom of unit

short screws in the assembly; there are also two longer screws at the top and side of the headlight which are used to aim the headlight. Do not tamper with these or the headlights will have to be re-aimed.

3. Remove the ring around the round (pre-1981) headlights by turning it clockwise. The square headlamp assemblies should pull straight out without having to turn them.

4. Pull the headlight bulb from its socket and disconnect the electrical connector.

5. Connect the plug to the new bulb.

6. Position the new headlight in the shell. Make sure the word "TOP" is, indeed, at the top and that the knobs in the headlight lens engage the slots in the mounting shell.

7. Place the retaining ring over the bulb and install the screws.

8. Install the grille, if removed.

1985-88 Sentra

CAUTION: *HANDLE CAREFULLY. The halogen bulbs used in these models contain a high pressure gas. The bulb may burst and*

cause personal injury if it is dropped or scratched. Install the new bulb immediately after removing the old one to keep moisture and dirt out of the reflector.

1. Disconnect the negative battery cable. Open the hood.

2. Reach behind the headlamp assembly and disconnect the electrical connector. Then, turn the retaining ring located around the rear of the bulb counterclockwise until it unlocks from of the reflector and pull it off.

3. Pull the bulb straight out of the headlamp reflector assembly *without either shaking or rotating it.*

4. Install the proper replacement bulb—a 65/45 watt 9004 or equivalent.

5. To install, insert the bulb into the reflector assembly with the flat side of the plastic base facing upward.

6. Slide the retaining ring over the rear of the bulb and relector with the locking tangs lined up with the slots. Then, rotate the ring clockwise until it locks tightly.

7. Install the electrical connector into the plastic base as far as it goes and until it snaps.

8. Connect the battery negative cable and test the headlamp.

Signal and Marker Lights
REMOVAL AND INSTALLATION

Front turn signal lights and rear side marker lights are mounted in the bumper. Remove the two retaining screws from the front of the lens, and pull the lens out of the bumper. Then, turn the light socket counterclockwise until it unlocks and remove it. Depress the bulb in the socket and turn it counterclockwise to remove it. Install in reverse order.

To replace front marker/parking lights, remove the two screws from the outboard surface of the lens and pull the lens/reflector unit out of the edge of the body.

On sedans, replace rear taillights/brakelights

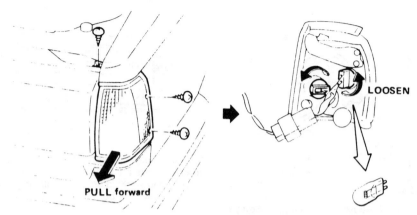

Changing the front marker/parking light

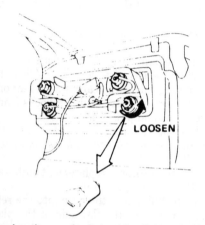

Changing the rear brake/parking light on sedans

by first opening the trunk or tailgate and un-screwing the fasteners and removing the light cover. On coupes, replace rear taillights/brakelights by releasing the catch and then pulling out the small door which covers the light sockets. Then, on both types of cars, turn the light socket counterclockwise until it un-locks and remove it. Depress the bulb in the socket and turn it counterclockwise to remove it. Install in reverse order.

TRAILER WIRING

Wiring the car for towing is fairly easy. There are a number of good wiring kits available and these should be used, rather than trying to de-sign your own. All trailers will need brake lights and turn signals as well as tail lights and side marker lights. Most states require extra mark-er lights for overwide trailers. Also, most states have recently required back-up lights for trail-ers, and most trailer manufacturers have been

building trailers with back-up lights for several years.

Additionally, some Class I, most Class II and just about all Class III trailers will have electric brakes.

Add to this number an accessories wire, to operate trailer internal equipment or to charge the trailer's battery, and you can have as many as seven wires in the harness.

Determine the equipment on your trailer and buy the wiring kit necessary. The kit will con-tain all the wires needed, plus a plug adapter set which included the female plug, mounted on the bumper or hitch, and the male plug, wired into, or plugged into the trailer harness.

When installing the kit, follow the manufac-turer's instructions. The color coding of the wires is standard throughout the industry.

One point to note, some domestic vehicles, and most imported vehicles, have separate turn signals. On most domestic vehicles, the brake lights and rear turn signals operate with the same bulb. For those vehicles with separate turn signals, you can purchase an isolation unit so that the brake lights won't blink whenever the turn signals are operated, or, you can go to your local electronics supply house and buy four diodes to wire in series with the brake and turn signal bulbs. Diodes will isolate the brake and turn signals. The choice is yours. The isola-tion units are simple and quick to install, but far more expensive than the diodes. The diodes, however, require more work to install properly, since they require the cutting of each bulb's wire and soldering in place of the diode.

One final point, the best kits are those with a spring loaded cover on the vehicle mounted socket. This cover prevents dirt and moisture from corroding the terminals. Never let the ve-hicle socket hang loosely. Always mount it se-curely to the bumper or hitch.

CIRCUIT PROTECTION

Fuses

REPLACEMENT

The fuses are located in a fusebox, which is under the left side of the instrument panel. Tilt down the box on older (pre 1980) models using convention fuses. On later models using plug type fuses, slide the cover off the fusebox or un-latch the cover and pull it down, off the dash. Conventional, glass fuses may be gently pried out with a screwdriver, *but be careful not to ground the contacts in which the ends of the fuse are retained.* Pry toward the center of the fuse, only. To replace, first align the ends of the fuse squarely with the contacts and then push it straight in at the center.

The newer, plug type fuses are removed using the special puller retained in the fuse box cover. Note the orientation of the fuse in the socket as you pull it out. Replace the fuse by first orienting it the same way as the one removed and then pushing it firmly in at the center.

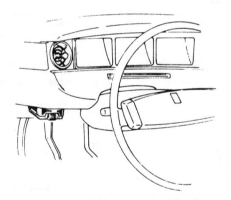

The location of the fuse box in models where conventional, glass cartridge type fuses are used.

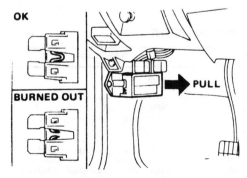

Here's how a fuse that is good looks compared to one that is blown (on the left). Pull the fuse box cover off as shown to gain access to the fuses where plug type fuses are used.

With either type of fuse, the soft metal conductor is visible through the glass cover. With conventional fuses, the conductor runs straight from one side to the other; with plug type fuses, the conductor is curved and visible between the two plastic sections of the fuse body in which the prongs are mounted. In either case, the metal is obviously separated when the fuse blows most of the time.

The cardinal rule of fuse replacement is to replace the blown fuse with one of the same amperage. The reason for this is that the fuse is very precisely sized according to the amount of current the circuit can safely handle. Since the temperature of the wiring and components will rise directly in proportion to the amount of current flowing in it, using a fuse of even 5 amps higher than the rated amperage can easily cause burnt out wiring or components *or even a dangerous vehicle fire.* Proceed as follows:

1. Read the amperage listed for the circuit the fuse protects. It is listed on the fuse box cover or on the fuse box, adjacent to the contacts.

2. Replace the fuse with one of precisely the same amperage. If there is no such fuse on hand, don't try to restore the circuit by using a fuse of higher amperage. It is safe to use a fuse of a lower rating. You may be able to keep the circuit operating by noting the accessories operated by it and then reducing the load by turning some of them off, or by minimizing the load, for example, by running the heater-air conditioning blower on low speed.

Fusible Links

A fusible link is a protective device used in an electrical circuit. When current increases beyond a certain amperage, the fusible metal wire of the link melts, thus breaking the electrical circuit (like a fuse) and preventing further damage to the other components and wiring. Whenever a fusible link is melted because of a short circuit, correct the cause before installing a new link.

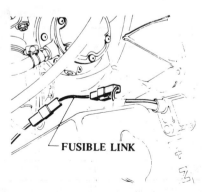

Most fusible links are found beside the battery

Use the following chart to locate the fusible link(s) on your Datsun.

All Datsun fusible links are the plug-in kind. To replace them, simply unplug the bad link and insert the new one.

CAUTION: *Never wrap vinyl tape around a fusible link. Extreme care should be taken with this link to ensure that it does not come into contact with any other wiring harness, vinyl, or rubber parts.*

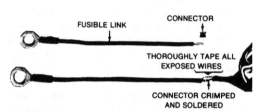

New fusible links are spliced to the wire

Flashers

The flasher units used for the four way and direction signal flashing functions are located as listed in the chart nearby. To replace a flasher, first make sure the ignition switch is off. Then, pull the plug out of the bottom of the flasher. Pull the flasher out of its mounting clip. Replace in reverse order.

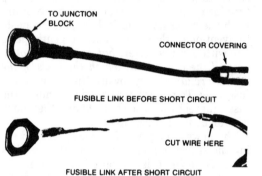

Fusible links before and after a short circuit

Fusible Links

Year	Model	Number	Color/Products	Location
1973	1200	1	Green/Charging system	At positive battery terminal
1974–78	B210	1	Green/Fuse block, electrical systems	At positive battery terminal
1979–82	210	2	Green/Starting, ignition, charging, headlights	At positive battery terminal
1982–86	Sentra	2	Green/Starting, ignition, charging, headlights	At positive battery terminal
1987	Sentra	3	White/Charging system Brown/Red/Ignition/E.C.C. Yellow/E.C.C. Relay	Fusible link holder near coil
1988	Sentra	3	White/Charging system Brown/Red/Ignition accessories Green/Red/Radiator fan relay	Fusible link holder near coil

Fuse Box and Flasher Location

Year	Model	Fuse Box Location	Flasher Location
1973	1200	Under instrument panel, right of steering wheel	Under dash
1974–78	B210	Below hood release knob	Turn signal: Behind radio Hazard: Under driver's side of dashboard
1979–82	210	Below hood release knob	Under driver's side dashboard ①
1982–86	Sentra	Below hood release knob	Under driver's side dashboard ①
1987–88	Sentra	Above hood release knob	To left of steering column

NOTE: The original turn signal flasher unit is pink, and larger than the original hazard flasher unit, which is gold.
① Both the turn signal and the hazard flashers are side by side.

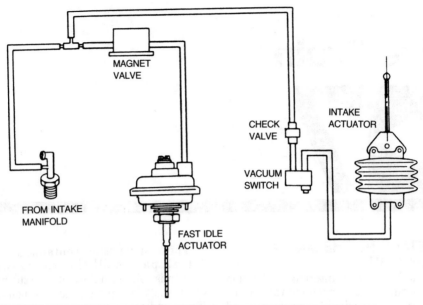

MAGNET
VALVE

CHECK
VALVE

INTAKE
ACTUATOR

VACUUM
SWITCH

FROM INTAKE
MANIFOLD

FAST IDLE
ACTUATOR

A/C vacuum diagram—1980–82 210

Drive Train

7

UNDERSTANDING THE MANUAL TRANSMISSION

Because of the way an internal combustion engine breathes, it can produce torque, or twisting force, only within a narrow speed range. Most modern, overhead valve engines must turn at about 2,500 rpm to produce their peak torque. By 4,500 rpm they are producing so little torque that continued increases in engine speed produce no power increases.

The torque peak on overhead camshaft engines is, generally, much higher, but much narrower.

The manual transmission and clutch are employed to vary the relationship between engine speed and the speed of the wheels so that adequate engine power can be produced under all circumstances. The clutch allows engine torque to be applied to the transmission input shaft gradually, due to mechanical slippage. The car can, consequently, be started smoothly from a full stop.

The transmission changes the ratio between the rotating speeds of the engine and the wheels by the use of gears. 4-speed or 5-speed transmissions are most common. The lower gears allow full engine power to be applied to the wheels during acceleration at low speeds.

The clutch drive plate is a thin disc, the center of which is splined to the transmission input shaft. Both sides of the disc are covered with a layer of material which is similar to brake lining and which is capable of allowing slippage without roughness or excessive noise.

The clutch cover is bolted to the engine flywheel and incorporates a diaphragm spring which provides the pressure to engage the clutch. The cover also houses the pressure plate. The driven disc is sandwiched between the pressure plate and the smooth surface of the flywheel when the clutch pedal is released, thus forcing it to turn at the same speed as the engine crankshaft.

The transmission contains a mainshaft which passes all the way through the transmission, from the clutch to the halfshafts. This shaft is separated at one point, so that front and rear portions can turn at different speeds.

Power is transmitted by a countershaft in the lower gears and reverse. The gears of the countershaft mesh with gears on the mainshaft, allowing power to be carried from one to the other. All the countershaft gears are integral with that shaft, while several of the mainshaft gears can either rotate independently of the shaft or be locked to it. Shifting from one gear to the next causes one of the gears to be freed from rotating with the shaft and locks another to it. Gears are locked and unlocked by internal dog clutches which slide between the center of the gear and the shaft. The forward gears usually employ synchronizers; friction members which smoothly bring gear and shaft to the same speed before the toothed dog clutches are engaged.

The clutch is operating properly if:

1. It will stall the engine when released with the vehicle held stationary.

2. The shift lever can be moved freely between 1st and reverse gears when the vehicle is stationary and the clutch disengaged.

A clutch pedal free-play adjustment is incorporated in the linkage. If there is about 1-2″ (25-50mm) of motion before the pedal begins to release the clutch, it is adjusted properly. Inadequate free-play wears all parts of the clutch releasing mechanisms and may cause slippage. Excessive free-play may cause inadequate release and hard shifting of gears.

Some clutches use a hydraulic system in place of mechanical linkage. If the clutch fails to release, fill the clutch master cylinder with fluid to the proper level and pump the clutch pedal to fill the system with fluid. Bleed the system in the same way as a brake system. If leaks are located, tighten loose connections or overhaul the master or slave cylinder as necessary.

Front wheel drive cars do not have conventional rear axles or drive shafts. Instead, power is transmitted from the engine to a transaxle, or a combination of transmission and drive axle, in one unit. Both the transmission and drive axle accomplish the same function as their counterparts in a front engine/rear drive axle design. The difference is in the location of the components.

In place of a conventional driveshaft, a front wheel drive design uses two driveshafts, sometimes called halfshafts, which couple the drive axle portion of the transaxle to the wheels. Universal joints or constant velocity joints are used just as they would in a rear wheel drive design.

Identification

Various four speed manual transmissions are standard equipment on all 1200, B210 and 210 models covered in this guide, except for the 1981 and later 210 MPG, which is equipped with a five speed transmission as standard. The front wheel drive Nissan Sentra uses either a four or five speed manual transaxle, which is actually a combination transmission and differential. All models feature integral shift linkage, which requires no adjustment.

The 1973 1200, 1974 B210 and 1980 210s use the F4W56 four speed transmission, which is constructed in two sections: a combined clutch and transmission housing, and an extension housing. There is a cast iron adaptor plate between the housings, and no case cover plates. The 1981 and later 210s use the F4W56 four speed.

The 1977-78 B210 uses the model FS5W63A five speed transmission. The 1979 210 has a FS5W60L five speed transmission, while the 1980 and later use the FS5W60A five speed transmissions.

Adjustments
CLUTCH SWITCH

The clutch switch, on those models so equipped, is integral with the stop bolt which sets pedal height. Therefore, it is covered below under "Clutch Adjustments."

REMOVAL AND INSTALLATION
All 1200, B210 and 210 Models

1. Jack up the car and safely support it with jackstands. Disconnect the battery cables. Disconnect the backup light switch, neutral switch, top gear switch, overdrive switch, and any other switches on the transmission after marking their positions with tape for later assembly.

2. On all models (1200, B210 and 210) disconnect the exhaust pipe from the exhaust manifold and bracket. Disconnect the speedometer cable from the speedometer cable drive on the transmission.

3. Scribe or paint matchmarks on the driveshaft flange and transmission flange so the driveshaft can be reinstalled with both flanges in the exact same relationship. Pull the driveshaft out of the rear of the transmission. *Be careful not to damage the seal in doing this!* Quickly plug the end of the transmission extension housing to prevent leakage of transmission oil (which will begin immediately when the driveshaft is removed).

4. Remove the shift lever.

5. Remove the clutch operating cylinder from the clutch housing.

6. Support the engine by placing a jack under the oil pan with a wooden block used between the oil pan and the jack.

CAUTION: *Do not place the jack under the oil pan drain plug.*

7. Support the transmission, preferably with a jack, and unbolt the transmission from the crossmember. Remove the crossmember.

8. Lower the rear of the engine slightly to allow a little clearance.

9. Remove the starter from the engine.

10. Remove the bolts securing the transmission to the engine and mounting brackets.

11. Slide the transmission back away from the engine so the mainshaft will slide out of the pilot bearing and clutch without disturbing the position of the clutch disc. Then, with both engine and transmission still supported, lower the jack supporting the transmission (with the transmission on it) to the rear and away from the engine. Remove the transmission from underneath the car.

NOTE: *When removing the transmission, take care not to strike any adjacent parts, especially the main drive gear and spline.*

12. Before installing, clean all mating surfaces of the engine rear plate and transmission case. Clean the transmission rear flange and front driveshaft flange. Make sure the matchmarks on both flanges are lined up during assembly. Also lightly apply a multi-purpose grease to the splined parts of the clutch disc and main drive gear, and to the moving surfaces of the gear control lever and striking rod.

13. Support the transmission on a jack and move it into position behind the engine. Carefully align the mainshaft with the splined female center of the clutch disc. Turn the mainshaft just slightly, if necessary, so it can be

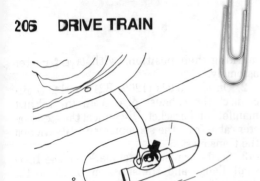

1200, B210 and 210 shift lever removal

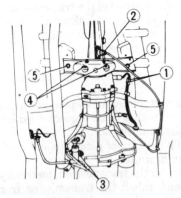

1200 and B210—disconnect the back-up light switch (1), speedometer cable (2), clutch slave cylinder (3), rear engine mount bolts (4), crossmember bolts (5). 210 similar

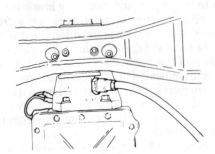

Disconnect speedometer and back-up light switch

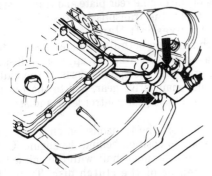

Remove the clutch slave cylinder

easily inserted into the disc. Then, slide the transmission toward the engine so the clutch housing rests against the rear of the engine and all the boltholes line up.

14. Install the transmission mounting bolts into the rear of the engine. Install the bolts which fasten the transmission to the mounting brackets.

15. Install the starter. Then, raise the rear of the engine slightly so it is in its normal position.

16. Install the crossmember. Then, remove the jack which supports the engine via the oil pan.

17. Install the clutch slave cylinder as described below. Install the gearshift.

18. Remove the plug from the rear of the transmission extension housing and insert the driveshaft into the transmission mainshaft, turning it slightly as necessary for the splines to engage easily. Then, match the marks on the rear driveshaft flange and the differential input flange, align the mounting boltholes, and install the mounting bolts and nuts.

19. Connect the exhaust pipe to the exhaust manifold and to its mounting bracket.

20. Connect the speedometer cable. Connect the backup light switch, neutral switch, top gear switch, overdrive switch, and any other switches disconnected in removal. Remove the transmission filler plug and fill the transmission with a gearbox lubricant rated API GL-5 to the level of the filler plug hole.

21. Check the clutch linkage adjustment. Reconnect the battery.

4-Speed Transmission Model F4W56A

This transmission is constructed in 2 sections: a combined clutch and transmission housing and an extension housing. There is a cast iron adapter plate between the housings. There are no case cover plates.

DISASSEMBLY

1. Drain the oil.

2. Remove the dust cover, spring, clutch throwout lever and release bearing.

3. Remove the front cover from inside the clutch housing.

4. Remove the speedometer drive pinion from the extension housing. Remove the striker rod return spring plug, spring, plunger and bushing. Remove the striker rod pin and separate the striker rod from the shift lever bracket.

5. Remove the extension housing. Tap it with a soft hammer, if necessary.

6. Separate the adapter plate from the transmission case, being careful not to lose the countershaft bearing washer.

7. Clamp the adapter plate in a vise with the reverse idler gear up.

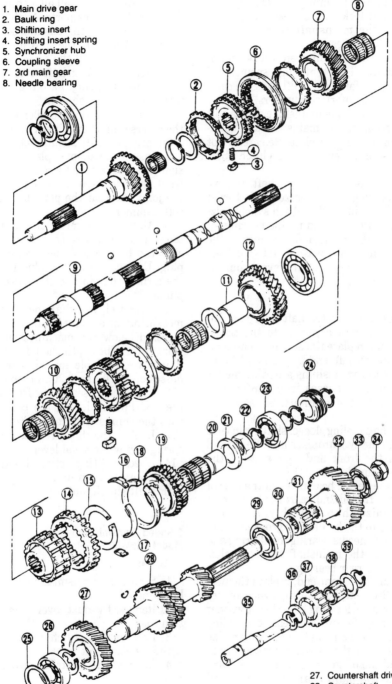

1. Main drive gear
2. Baulk ring
3. Shifting insert
4. Shifting insert spring
5. Synchronizer hub
6. Coupling sleeve
7. 3rd main gear
8. Needle bearing

9. Mainshaft
10. 2nd main gear
11. Bushing
12. 1st main gear
13. OD-reverse synchronizer hub
14. Reverse gear
15. Circlip
16. Thrust block
17. Brake band

18. Synchronizer ring
19. Overdrive main gear
20. Overdrive gear bushing
21. Washer
22. Mainshaft nut
23. Overdrive mainshaft bearing
24. Speedometer drive gear
25. Countershaft front bearing shim
26. Countershaft front bearing

27. Countershaft drive gear
28. Countershaft
29. Countershaft bearing
30. Reverse counter gear spacer
31. Reverse counter gear
32. Overdrive counter gear
33. Countershaft rear bearing
34. Countershaft nut
35. Reverse idler shaft
36. Reverse idler thrust washer
37. Reverse idler gear
38. Reverse idler gear bearing
39. Reverse idler thrust washer

Exploded view of the gear train—FS5W71B and FS5W71C

8. Drive out the retaining pin and remove the reverse shift fork and reverse idler gear.

9. Remove the mainshaft rear snapring, washer and reverse gear.

10. Drive out the remaining shift fork retaining pins. Remove all 3 detent plugs, springs and balls. Remove the forks and shift rods. Be careful not to lose the interlock plungers.

11. Tap the rear of the mainshaft with a soft hammer to separate the mainshaft and countershaft from the adapter plate. Be careful not to drop the shafts. Separate the clutch shaft from the mainshaft.

12. From the front of the mainshaft, remove the needle bearing, synchronizer hub thrust washer, steel locating ball, 3rd/4th synchronizer, baulk ring, 3rd gear and needle bearing.

13. Press off the mainshaft bearing to the rear. Remove the thrust washer, 1st gear, needle bearing, baulk ring, 1st/2nd synchronizer, snapring and bearing.

ASSEMBLY

1. Press on the countershaft bearings. Install the countershaft assembly to the transmission case and replace the adapter plate temporarily. Countershaft end-play should be 0-0.20mm. Front bearing shims are available for adjustment in thicknesses from 0.80mm to 1.30mm. Remove the countershaft assembly from the case.

2. Install the coupling sleeve, shifting inserts and spring on the synchronizer hub. Be careful not to hook the front and rear ends of the spring to the same insert.

3. Install the needle bearing from the rear of the mainshaft. Install 2nd gear, the baulk ring and synchronizer hub assembly. Align the shifting insert to the baulk ring groove. Install the 1st gear side needle bearing, baulk ring and 1st gear. Install the mainshaft thrust washer and press on the rear bearing.

On the mainshaft front end, replace the needle bearing, 3rd gear, baulk ring, synchronizer hub assembly, steel locating ball, thrust washer and pilot bearing. Be sure to grease the sliding surface of the steel ball and thrust washer. The dimpled side of the thrust washer must face to the front and the oil grooved side to the rear.

4. Replace the main bearing, washer and snapring onto the clutch shaft. The web side of the washer must face the bearing. Place the baulk ring on the clutch shaft and assemble the clutch shaft to the mainshaft.

5. Align the mainshaft assembly with the countershaft assembly and install them to the adapter plate by lightly tapping on the clutch shaft with a soft hammer.

6. Place the 1st/2nd and 3rd/4th shift forks on the shift rods, being careful that the forks

are not reversed. Install all 3 shift rods and the detent and interlock parts. Apply locking agent to the detent plug threads and screw the plugs in flush. Make sure the shift forks are in their grooves and drive in the remaining pins.

7. Install the mainshaft reverse gear, thrust washer and snapring. Face the web side of the thrust washer to the gear.

8. Replace the reverse idler gear and pin on the reverse shift fork. Check interlock action by attempting to shift 2 shift rods at once.

9. Install the adapter plate to the transmission case. Make sure to install the countergear front shim selected in Step 1. Use sealant on the joint and seat the plate by tapping with a soft hammer.

10. Align the striker lever and install the extension housing. Use sealant on the joint. Install the bushing, plunger return spring and plug. Use sealant on the plug threads. Install the striker rod pin and the speedometer drive pinion.

11. Select clutch shaft bearing shim(s) by measuring the amount the bearing outer race is recessed below the machined surface for the front cover. The depth should be 5.00-5.15mm. Shims are available for adjustment in thicknesses of 0.010mm, 0.20mm, and 0.50mm.

12. Place the oil seal in the front cover, grease the seal lip and install the cover and O-ring with the shim(s) selected in Step 11.

13. Replace the clutch release bearing, return spring and withdrawal lever.

14. Check shifting action. Rotate the clutch shaft slowly in neutral. The rear of the mainshaft should not turn.

5-Speed Transmission
Model FS5W60A

DISASSEMBLY

1. Secure the transmission and drain the lubricating oil.

2. Remove the dust cover from the transmission case.

3. Remove the clutch release bearing and withdraw the pivot lever.

4. Remove the electrical switches from the case.

5. Remove the speedometer driven gear assembly.

6. Remove the shift selector stopper pin bolt and nut from the boss of the rear extension housing.

7. Remove the shift selector return spring plug, return spring and plunger from the rear extension.

8. Remove the reverse check sleeves assembly.

9. Remove the front bearing cover, O-ring and front cover adjusting shim.

10. Remove the main bearing snapring from the groove in the bearing outer race.

11. Remove the rear extension retaining bolts and turn the shift selector rod clockwise.

12. Using a special puller, remove the rear extension housing from the output shaft.

13. Separate the transmission case from the adapter plate by tapping evenly around the transmission case.

NOTE: *Do not pry the units apart with a prybar. Damage can occur to the mating surfaces.*

14. A special type holding tool should be used to hold the adapter plate so that it can be held in a vise or other holding tool. This plate can be purchased or fabricated.

15. Mount the unit in the holding tool and remove the countergear thrust washer.

16. Using a pin punch, remove the retaining pins from the forks and selector rods.

17. Remove the 3 check ball plugs.

18. Remove the selector rods from the adapter plate and detach the forks from the rods.

CAUTION: *Do not lose the check balls, springs and the 2 interlock plungers.*

NOTE: *Each gear and shaft can be removed from the adapter plate independently of the other shaft and without the removal of the selector rods and forks.*

19. Remove the outer snapring of the mainshaft end bearing with a bearing puller. Remove the 2nd bearing snapring from the shaft.

20. Engage the 1st/reverse speeds so that the gear train is located in 2 gears at the same time. Remove the countergear nut after releasing the staking.

21. From the rear extension side of the adapter plate, remove the mainshaft holding snapring, C-ring holder, C-ring and the thrust washer.

22. Remove the O.D. main gear with the needle bearings and the O.D. countergear together.

23. Remove the synchronizer (baulk) ring, the coupling sleeve, the O.D. and reverse synchronizer hub snapring, the O.D. and reverse synchronizer hub and the reverse gear together with the needle bearing and bushing and the reverse countergear at the same time.

24. Remove the bearing retainer screws from the adapter plate. Remove the bearing retainer.

25. Remove the snapring from the mainshaft rear bearing and remove the mainshaft assembly together with the countergear by lightly tapping on the rear shaft while holding the front of the mainshaft and countergear assembly by hand to avoid dropping the assembly.

26. Remove the snapring and spacer from the reverse idler shaft and tap the idler shaft outward slightly.

27. Using a pin punch, remove the retaining pin from the reverse idler shaft and remove the

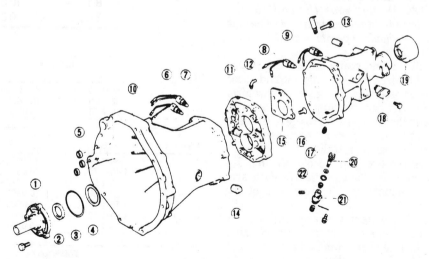

1. Front cover	9. Neutral switch	17. Drain plug
2. Front cover oil seal	10. Transmission case assembly	18. Reverse check sleeve
3. Front cover O-ring	11. Adapter plate	19. Rear extension dust cover
4. Front cover adjusting shim	12. Breather	with oil seal
5. Welch plug	13. Return spring bushing	20. Speedometer pinion
6. Top gear switch	14. Filler plug	21. Speedometer sleeve
7. O.D. gear switch	15. Bearing retainer	22. Retaining pin
8. Reverse lamp switch	16. Rear extension assembly	

Transmission case components, model FS5W60A

shaft. Remove the thrust washers, spacer and reverse idler gear with the needle bearing.

28. Disassemble the mainshaft assembly by removing the snapring from the shaft front end. Remove the 3rd/4th synchronizer assembly, synchronizer (baulk) rings, 3rd gear and the mainshaft needle bearing toward the front side.

29. Remove the mainshaft bearing with a puller.

30. Remove the thrust washer and 1st gear, together with the needle bearing and bushing, synchronizer (baulk) rings, coupling sleeve, 1st/2nd synchronizer hub and the 2nd gear with the needle bearing.

31. Remove the snapring and spacer from the maindrive gear and remove the bearing with a press or puller.

32. The countershaft rear bearing can be removed with the use of a press.

33. The synchronziers can be disassembled for repairs by removing the spread spring and removing the shifting insert. Separate the coupling sleeve from the synchronizer hub.

ASSEMBLY

1. Replace any bearings, seals or worn parts as required.

2. Install the synchronizer hub into the coupling sleeve and fit the shifting inserts into their respective grooves on the assembly.

3. Install the spread springs to the inserts so that the insert is securely attached to the inner side of the coupling sleeve.

CAUTION: *Do not hook the ends of the spread springs to the same insert. The hub and sleeve should operate smoothly when moved by hand.*

4. Install the 2nd gear needle bearing, 2nd gear, synchronizer (baulk) ring, 1st/2nd speed synchronizer assembly, 1st gear synchronizer (baulk) ring, 1st gear bushing, needle bearing, 1st gear and thrust washer onto the mainshaft.

5. Press the bearing onto the mainshaft, using a press or bearing installer.

6. Install the 3rd gear needle bearing, 3rd gear, synchronizer (baulk) ring, 3rd/4th synchronizer assembly on the front side of the mainshaft.

7. Install a selective snapring on the mainshaft so that a minimum clearance exists between the face of the hub and the ring.

CAUTION: *Be sure the snapring is fully seated in its groove.*

8. Install the main drive gear bearing onto the shaft. Install the main drive bearing spacer on the main drive bearing and secure the bearing with a proper sized snapring that will eliminate any end-play.

9. Install the countergear thrust washer and countergear into the transmission case and select the countergear thrust washer of proper thickness, by using a straightedge, from the countergear face to the transmission case, allowing for standard end-play of 0.10mm-0.20mm.

10. Remove the countergear from the transmission and keep the thrust washer with the gear.

11. Install the thrust washers, needle bearing, reverse idler gear and inner thrust washer in place on the reverse idler shaft. Install a new retaining pin in the reverse idler shaft.

12. Install the reverse idler shaft into the adapter plate. Position a thrust washer and install a new snapring so that the minimum clear-

No.	Thickness	
	mm	(in.)
1	1.15	(0.0453)
2	1.02	(0.047)

No.	Thickness	
	mm	(in.)
1	7.87	(0.3098)
2	7.94	(0.3126)
3	8.01	(0.3154)
4	8.08	(0.3181)
5	8.15	(0.3209)
6	8.22	(0.3236)

No.	Thickness	
	mm	(in)
1	1.55-1.60	(0.0610-0.0630)
2	1.60-1.65	(0.0630-0.0650)
3	1.65-1.70	(0.0650-0.0669)

No.	Thickness	
	mm	(in)
1	1.34-1.40	(0.0528-0.0551)
2	1.40-1.46	(0.0551-0.0575)
3	1.46-1.52	(0.0575-0.0598)
4	1.52-1.58	(0.0598-0.0622)
5	1.58-1.64	(0.0622-0.0646)
6	1.64-1.70	(0.0646-0.0669)
7	1.70-1.76	(0.0669-0.0693)

No.	Thickness	
	mm	(in)
1	2.20-2.25	(0.0866-0.0886)
2	2.25-2.30	(0.0886-0.0906)
3	2.30-2.35	(0.0906-0.0925)
4	2.35-2.40	(0.0925-0.0945)
5	2.40-2.45	(0.0945-0.0965)
6	2.45-2.50	(0.0965-0.0984)
7	2.50-2.55	(0.0984-0.1004)
8	2.55-2.60	(0.1004-0.1024)

ance exists between the adapter plate and the thrust washer.

13. Install a synchronizer (baulk) ring on the main drive gear and place with the mainshaft to complete this portion of the assembly.

NOTE: *Install the pilot bearing in place before coupling the main drive gear to the mainshaft.*

14. Combine the mainshaft assembly with the countergear assembly and place them into the adapter plate as a unit.

NOTE: *Use a puller tool to move the mainshaft into the adapter plate. Carefully hold the gears to avoid dropping them until in position.*

CAUTION: *Be sure the snapring grooves on the mainshaft rear bearing clears the adapter plate.*

15. Install the rear bearing snapring into its groove. Install the bearing retainer and install the retaining screws. Torque to 61-86 in. lbs. (6.9-9.8 Nm).

NOTE: *Stake each screw at 2 points with a center punch.*

16. Place the thrust washer, reverse gear bushing, needle bearing and the reverse main drive gear on the end of the mainshaft.

17. Install the reverse countergear on the end of the countershaft.

18. Install the O.D. and reverse synchronizer assembly and install a new snapring so that the minimum amount of clearance exists between the end face of the hub and the snapring.

19. Position the synchronizer (baulk) ring, O.D. gear needle bearing and the O.D. main gear on the end of the mainshaft.

20. Install the O.D. countergear on the end of the mainshaft.

21. Place the thrust washer in place so that a minimum of clearance exists between the C-holder and the ring. Position the C-ring and the C-ring holder and fit a new mainshaft holder snapring.

22. Engage the 1st and reverse gears and tighten the countershaft nut to 36-43 ft. lbs. (49-59 Nm).

23. Stake the countershaft nut to the groove in the countershaft with a punch.

24. Measure the gear end-play. The measurements are as follows:

25. Place a snapring to the front of the mainshaft end bearing, Measuring 1.15mm.

26. Install the mainshaft end bearing using a bearing installer. Fit a snapring to the rear side of the bearing to eliminate any end-play. The available snaprings are as follows:

27. Install the O.D. and reverse fork and selector rod into the adapter plate. Place the rod in the neutral position and install the interlock plunger into its bore in the adapter plate.

1st main gear
  0.15–0.25mm
  (0.0059–0.0098 in.)
2nd main gear
  0.30–0.40mm
  (0.0118–0.0157 in.)
3rd main gear
  0.15–0.35mm
  (0.0059–0.0138 in.)
O.D. (5th) main gear
0.30–0.40mm
  (0.0118–0.0157 in.)
Reverse main gear
  0.30–0.55mm
  (0.0118–0.0217 in.)
Countergear
  0.10–0.20mm
  (0.0039–0.0079 in.)
Reverse idler gear
  0–0.20mm
  (0–0.0079 in.)

28. Install the 3rd/4th selector rod into the fork and install a new snapring. Install the selector rod and fork into the adapter plate.

29. Insert the interlock plunger into the adapter plate with the selector rods in the neutral position.

30. Install the 1st/2nd selector rod into the fork and install both into the adapter plate.

31. Secure all the selector rods and forks with new retaining pins.

IMPORTANT: *Properly align the groove in the assembled selector rod with the interlock plunger, during the assembly. Align the shift forks with their respective coupling sleeves before installing!*

32. Install the check balls and springs into the proper bores. Seal and install the check ball plugs.

33. Align the center notch in each fork selector rod with the check balls, as required.

NOTE: *The selector rod for the 1st/2nd gear is longer than the 3rd/4th or the O.D./reverse selector rods.*

CAUTION: *To make sure the interlock plunger is installed properly, slide the 1st/2nd selector rod into gear and operate the other selector rods. All other gears should not mesh. Check all other rods in the same manner!*

34. Prepare the adapter plate and transmission case by installing a sealer to the mating surfaces.

35. Apply grease to the sliding surface of the thrust washer for the countergear, that was selected previously. The oil groove should face to the front while the dimpled side should face towards the thrust side.

36. Place the clutch housing end of the transmission case flat on a surface and level the

No.	"A" mm	(in.)	Adjusting shim mm	(in.)
1	6.05-6.09	(0.2382-0.2398)	0.50	(0.0197)
2	6.10-6.14	(0.2402-0.2417)	0.55	(0.0217)
3	6.15-6.19	(0.2421-0.2437)	0.60	(0.0236)
4	6.20-6.24	(0.2441-0.2457)	0.65	(0.0256)
5	6.25-6.29	(0.2461-0.2476)	0.70	(0.0276)
6	6.30-6.34	(0.2480-0.2496)	0.75	(0.0295)
7	6.35-6.39	(0.2500-0.2516)	0.80	(0.0315)

housing. Position the adapter plate assembly into the transmission housing and tap the plate into the transmission housing. Line the dowel pin to its proper position.

37. Carefully install the main drive bearing and countergear front needle bearing.

NOTE: *Be sure the mainshaft rotates freely.*

38. Install the main drive bearing snapring in its groove in the bearing.

39. Apply sealant to the mating surfaces of the adapter plate and the rear extension housing.

40. Place the selector rods in the O.D. position on the transmission, while placing the main selector rod in the neutral position. Turn the striking guide clockwise and then adjust the main selector rod and the shift arm. Align the shift arm pin with the groove in the selector rods and assemble the rear extension housing to the adapter plate. Install the retaining bolts and torque to 12-16 ft. lbs. (16-22 Nm).

41. Install grease to the plunger and install it into the rear extension. Install the return spring, apply sealer to the return spring plug and install it.

42. Turn the transmission assembly so that the front is up. Measure the distance from the front end of the transmission case to the main drive bearing outer race with a depth gauge. Select a shim to correspond to the dimension or thickness **A**. The front cover adjusting shim can be 1 of 7 shims.

43. Install the front cover with the adjusting shim and the O-ring in place.

44. Install the speedometer driven gear and install the securing bolt and nut.

45. Install a new O-ring in the groove of the reverse check sleeve and tighten the bolts.

46. Replace the electrical switches that were removed during the disassembly.

47. Install the pivot lever, the release bearing and sleeve. Connect the holding spring and install the dust cover.

MANUAL TRANSAXLE

Identification

Front wheel drive Sentra models use either the RS5F30A, or RS5F31A 5-speed, or the

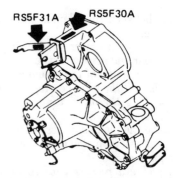

Locations of the identification stampings on RS5F31A and RS5F30A transaxles

RN4F30A or RN4F31A 4-speed transaxle. The RN4 models are 4-speeds and the RS5 models are 5-speeds. The 31 designation, whether for the 4-speed or 5-speed types, use a modified input bearing retainer. Front wheel drive Sentras up to 1986 use either the N4 4-speed or the S5 5-speed 30 type. 1987 models use only 5-speeds, although either the 30 or 31 type bearing retainer can be used. 1988 models use either the RN4F31A four speed or the RS5F31A 5-speed.

Adjustments
CLUTCH SWITCH

The clutch switch, on those models so equipped, is integral with the stop bolt which sets pedal height. Therefore, it is covered below under "Clutch Adjustments."

Transaxle
REMOVAL AND INSTALLATION
Sentra Front Wheel Drive Models

1. Remove battery and battery holding plate.
2. Jack up front of car and safely support with jackstands.
3. Remove the radiator reservoir tank.
4. Drain transmission gear oil.
5. Draw out the drive halfshafts from the

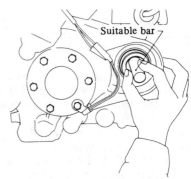

Temporarily insert a bar or dowel into the transaxle after halfshaft is removed

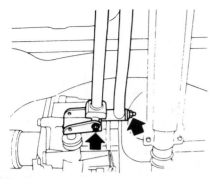

Separating control rod and support rod from Sentra transaxle

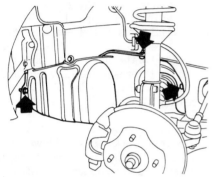

Removing Sentra wheel house protector

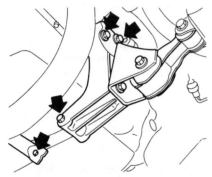

Sentra engine mount and gusset securing bolts

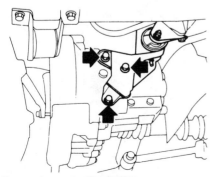

Sentra engine mounting bolts

transaxle. Refer to Driveshaft and U-Joints Removal and Installation, later in this chapter.

NOTE: *When removing halfshafts, use care not to damage the lip of the oil seal. After shafts are removed, insert a steel bar or wooden dowel of the same diameter as the splined portion of the driveshaft into the transmission case to prevent the side gears from rotating and falling into the differential case.*

6. Remove the wheel house protector.

7. Separate the control rod and support rod from the transaxle.

8. Remove the engine gusset securing bolt and the engine mounting.

9. Remove the clutch control cable from the withdrawal lever.

10. Disconnect the speedometer cable from the transaxle.

11. Disconnect the wires from the reverse (back-up) and neutral switches.

12. Support the engine by placing a jack under the oil pan, with a wooden block placed between the jack and pan for protection. *Be careful not to support the pan by the drain plug!*

13. Support the transaxle with a hydraulic floor jack.

14. Remove the engine mount securing bolts.

15. Remove the bolts attaching the transaxle to the engine.

16. Carefully slide the transaxle input shaft straight out of the clutch pilot bearing and driven disc. Then, using the hydraulic floor jack as a carrier, carefully lower the transaxle down and away from the car.

CAUTION: *Be careful not to strike any adjacent parts or the input shaft (the shaft protruding from the transaxle which fits into the clutch assembly) when removing the transaxle from the car.*

17. Before installing, clean the mating surfaces on the engine rear plate and clutch housing. Then, apply a light coat of a lithium based grease (which includes molybdenum-disulfide)

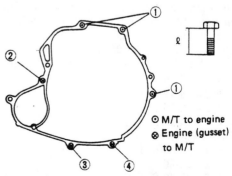

When torquing the bolts on the Sentra 2 WD gasoline powered transaxle, torque numbered bolts to the figures shown in the text

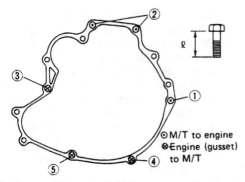

When torquing the bolts on the Sentra 2 WD diesel powered transaxle, torque numbered bolts to the figures shown in the text

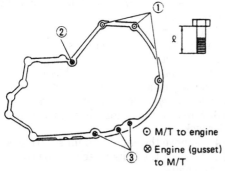

When torquing the bolts on the Sentra 4 WD gasoline powered transaxle, torque numbered bolts to the figures shown in the text

to the spline parts of the clutch disc and the transaxle input shaft. Finally, carefully raise the transaxle into position.

18. Carefully line up the input shaft with the center of the clutch disc. If necessary, turn the input shaft slightly to get the splines to engage. When they do, slide the transmission into position and align the boltholes in the clutch housing with those in the rear of the engine block.

19. Follow the patterns shown in the illustrations and install and torque the transmission-to-engine and transmission-to-transmission mount bolts. Utilize the torque figures according the the number code shown for each bolt in the applicable illustration:

Two Wheel Drive, Gasoline Powered Cars:
- 1 – 12-16 ft. lbs.
- 2 – 14-22 ft. lbs.
- 3 – 12-16 ft. lbs.
- 4 – 14-22 ft. lbs.

Diesel Powered Cars:
- 1 – 22-30 ft. lbs.
- 2 – 22-30 ft. lbs.
- 3 – 33-40 ft. lbs.
- 4 – 12-16 ft. lbs.
- 5 – 12-16 ft. lbs.

4-Wheel Drive, Gasoline Powered Cars:
- 1 – 17-20 ft. lbs.
- 2 – 17-20 ft. lbs.
- 3 – 22-30 ft. lbs.

20. Remove the supporting jacks from the transaxle and then from the engine.

21. Reconnect the wiring to the various transaxle mounted switches.

22. Reconnect the speedometer cable and clutch control cable. Adjust the clutch cable as described later in this chapter.

23. Reconnect the engine mount bolt.

24. Connect the support rod to the transaxle. Connect the control rod to the transaxle.

25. Install the drive halfshafts into the transaxle. Refer to Driveshaft and U-Joints Removal and Installation, later in this chapter.

26. Remove the filler plug and fill the transaxle with 4⅞ U.S. pints (four speed) and 5¾ U.S. pints (five speed) of a quality API GL-4 rating. Fill to the level of the plug hole. Apply a thread sealant to the threads of the filler plug and install the plug in the transaxle case. Tighten the bolts securing the transaxle to the engine to 12-15 ft. lbs.

27. Install the radiator reservoir tank.

28. Remove the jackstands and lower the car to the floor. Install the battery mounting plate and the battery and reconnect the battery.

OVERHAUL

4- and 5-Speed Transaxle
Models RN4F30A, RS5F30A AND RS5F31A

TRANSMISSION CASE DISASSEMBLY

1. Drain the oil from the transmission case.

2. Remove the mounting bolts, tap the case lightly with a rubber mallet and then lift off the transmission case.

NOTE: *When removing the transmission case, tilt it slightly to prevent interference from the 5th gear shift fork.*

3. Disconnect the back-up light switch and then remove the oil gutter.

4. Remove the input shaft bearing.

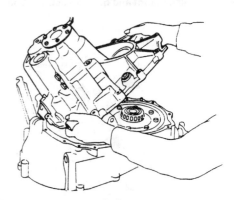

Removing the transmission case

5. Remove the case cover, the mainshaft bearing adjusting shim and the spacer.

6. Remove the mainshaft bearing rear outer race and the differential side bearing outer race.

7. Draw out the reverse idler spacer.

ASSEMBLY

1. Press fit the differential side bearing outer race and the mainshaft rear bearing outer race.

2. Install the input shaft needle bearing. Apply sealant to the welch plug and then install it on the transmission case.

3. Install the oil gutter. Apply sealant to the back-up light switch and install it.

4. If the transmission case has been replaced, adjust the differential side bearing and the mainshaft rotary frictional force (preload) by means of shims.

5. Apply an even coating of sealant to the mating surfaces of the transmission case and the clutch housing. Mount the case on the clutch housing and tighten the mounting bolts to 12-15 ft. lbs.

6. Remove the transmission case cover. Clean the mating surfaces and apply sealant to the transmission case.

7. Install the case cover with the convex side facing outward. Tighten the mounting bolts to 52-72 in. lbs.

8. Check that the gears move freely and then install the drain plug (with sealant) and fill with lubricant.

CLUTCH HOUSING DISASSEMBLY

1. Drain the oil and then remove the transmission case.

2. Draw out the reverse idler spacer and fork shaft, then remove the 5th/3rd/4th shift fork.

NOTE: *Do not lose the shifter caps.*

3. Remove the control bracket with the 1st and 2nd gear shift fork.

NOTE: *Be careful not to lose the select check ball, spring and the shifter caps (5-speed only).*

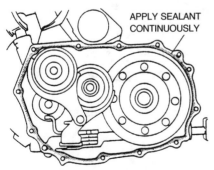

Applying sealer to the mating surfaces of the transmission case and the clutch housing

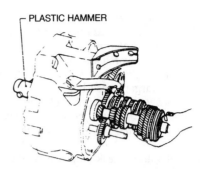

When removing the input shaft, tap lightly on the outer end of the shaft with a plastic hammer to free it

6. Remove the 3 screws and detach the bearing retainer. One of the screws is a special torx type and should be removed using a special torx allen wrench.

7. Turn the clutch housing so that its side is facing down. Lightly tap the end of the input shaft (on the engine side) with a rubber mallet and then remove the input shaft along with the bearing retainer and reverse idler gear.

NOTE: *Don't remove the reverse idler shaft from the clutch housing because these fittings will be loose. Do not scratch the oil seal lip with the input shaft spline while removing the shaft.*

8. Remove the reverse idler gear and final drive assembly.

9. Remove the oil pocket, shift check ball springs and then the check ball plugs.

10. Drive the retaining pins out of the striking lever. Remove the striking rod, lever and interlock.

   a. Select a position where the pin doesn't interfere with the clutch housing when removing it.

   b. When removing the striking rod, be careful not to damage the oil seal lip. It may be a good idea to tape the edges of the striking rod when removing it.

11. Remove the reverse and 5th gear check plug and then detach the check spring and balls. Remove the reverse and 5th gear check assembly.

12. Remove the clutch control shaft, release bearing and clutch lever.

13. Remove the mainshaft bearing outer race. Remove the differential side bearing outer race.

14. Remove the oil channel.

ASSEMBLY

1. Install a new oil channel so that the oil groove in the channel faces the oil pocket.

2. Install the mainshaft bearing and differential side bearing outer races.

3. Install the clutch control shaft, release bearing and clutch lever.

4. Install the oil pocket.

NOTE: *Make sure that oil flows from the oil pocket to the oil channel.*

5. Install the reverse and 5th gear check assembly. The smaller check ball is inserted first and then the larger check ball.

NOTE: *When installing the clutch housing and reverse and 5th gear check assembly, it is necessary to adjust the reverse check force.* 100›

a. Install a used check plug and tighten it to 14-18 ft. lbs.

b. Use a spring gauge to measure the spring check force 139-100 inch lbs. for the 4-speed; 195-239 inch lbs. for the 5-speed.

c. If the reverse check force is not within the above ranges, select another check plug of a different length until the specifications can be met.

6. Installation of the remaining components is in the reverse order of removal. Please note the following:

a. Follow all NOTES listed under the disassembly procedures.

b. Apply a locking sealer to the threads of the torx screw and tighten it to 12-15 ft. lbs.(16.3-20.3 Nm). Use a punch and stake the head of the screw at two points.

c. Tighten the bearing retainer bolts to 12-15 ft. lbs.(16.3-20.3 Nm).

d. Coat the select check ball (5-speed) and shifter caps with grease before installing.

e. Coat the support spring with grease before installing it. This will prevent the spring from falling into the hole for the fork shaft in the clutch housing.

Halfshafts

REMOVAL AND INSTALLATION

Sentra

1. Jack up the car and safely support it with jackstands.

2. Remove the wheel. On 1987-88 models, have someone apply the brakes and loosen the wheel hub nut.

3. Remove the brake caliper assembly (refer to Chapter 9, Brakes, for this procedure).

4. Pry off the cotter pin from the castellated nut on the wheel hub on 1986 and earlier models and remove the castellated locknut on these models.

5. On 1986 and earlier models, loosen, but do not remove, the wheel hub nut from the halfshaft while holding the wheel hub with a suitable tool (for example, with a prybar used as

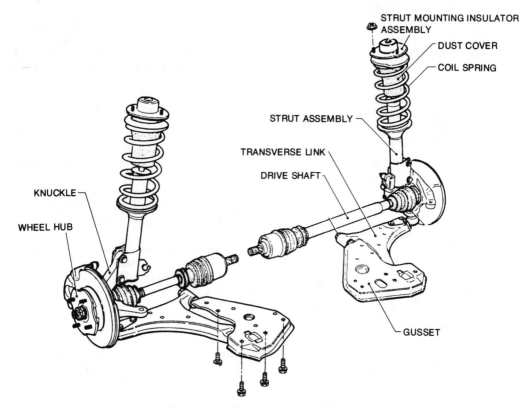

Sentra front drive train and suspension

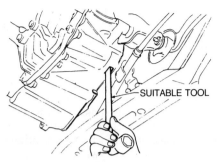

Pry the right side halfshaft out of the Sentra trans-axle as shown

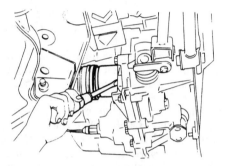

Pry the left side halfshaft out of the Sentra trans-axle as shown

a lever between two nuts installed onto the studs). Turn the nut out so its outer edge is just past the end of the shaft, in order to protect the threads. Then, lightly tap the nut in order to free the shaft from the hub.

6. Make a matchmark to retain the alignment setting and then remove the bolts and nuts which retain the steering knuckle to the bottom of the strut.

7. Remove the tie rod ball joint (see Chapter 8, Suspension, for this procedure). Remove the lower ball joint. Do not reuse the nut once it has been removed; install a new nut during assembly.

8. Drain the gear oil from the transaxle.

9. Using a suitable prybar, gently pry the halfshaft out of the transaxle on either side, as shown. Remove the halfshaft, along with the wheel hub and knuckle.

10. Insert a suitable bar, wooden dowel or similar tool into the transaxle to prevent the side gear from dropping inside (see Manual Transaxle Removal procedures for an illustration).

CAUTION: *When removing the halfshaft, be very careful not to damage the grease seal in the transaxle side.*

11. Coat the transaxle and halfshaft splines with a molybdenum disulfide grease before insertion. Make sure the rubber gaiters on both ends of the halfshaft are in good shape; if not, replace them (use new metal bands to retain the gaiters).

12. Insert the driveshaft outer end through the splined section of the hub. Install the wheel hub and knuckle with the matchmarks made previously aligned, torquing the bolts to 72-87 ft. lbs. Install the lower ball joint with a new nut; and then install the tie rod ball joint, as described in Chapter 8.

13. Install the wheel hub nut and torque it to 87-145 ft. lbs. on 1986 and earlier models. Then, install the adjusting cap and insert a new

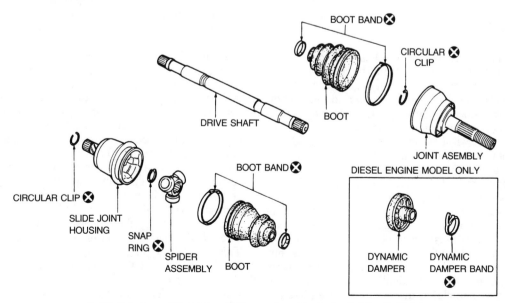

Exploded view of the driveshafts used on front wheel drive Sentras

cotter pin. On 1987-88 models, install the nut and torque it to 145-203 ft. lbs.

14. Install the brake caliper as described in Chapter 9. Install the wheel.

OVERHAUL

Transaxle Side Joint

1. Remove boot bands.
2. Match mark slide joint housing and driveshaft and separate.
3. Match mark spider assembly and then remove snapring and spider assembly. DO NOT disassemble spider assembly.

NOTE: *Cover driveshaft serration with tape so as not to damage the boot.*

4. Remove axle boot from driveshaft.
5. To install reverse the removal procedures.

NOTE: *Always use new snaprings and align all matchmarks. Pack driveshaft and boot assembly with grease.*

Wheel Side Joint

NOTE: *The joint on the wheel side cannot be disassembled.*

1. Match mark the driveshaft and the joint assembly.
2. Separate joint assembly with suitable tool.
3. Remove boot bands.
4. Install boot with new boot bands.
5. Align matchmarks lightly tap joint assembly onto the shaft.
6. Pack driveshaft with grease.
7. Lock both boot band clamps.

NOTE: *There are two different type (transaxle side) front axle joints used on Datsun/Nissan models.*

CLUTCH

The purpose of the clutch is to disconnect and connect engine power from the transmission. A car at rest requires a lot of engine torque to get all that weight moving. An internal combustion engine does not develop a high starting torque (unlike steam engines), so it must be allowed to operate without any load until it builds up enough torque to move the car. Torque increases with engine rpm. The clutch allows the engine to build up torque by physically disconnecting the engine from the transmission, relieving the engine of any load or resistance. The transfer of engine power to the transmission (the load) must be smooth and gradual; if it weren't, drive line components would wear out or break quickly. This gradual power transfer is made possible by gradually releasing the clutch pedal. The clutch disc and pressure plate are the connecting link between the engine and

transmission. When the clutch pedal is released, the disc and plate contact each other (clutch engagement), physically joining the engine and transmission. When the pedal is pushed in, the disc and plate separate (the clutch is disengaged), disconnecting the engine from the transmission.

The clutch assembly consists of the flywheel, the clutch disc, the clutch pressure plate, the throwout bearing and fork, the actuating linkage and the pedal. The flywheel and clutch pressure plate (driving members) are connected to the engine crankshaft and rotate with it. The clutch disc is located between the flywheel and pressure plate, and splined to the transmission shaft. A driving member is one that is attached to the engine and transfers engine power to a driven member (clutch disc) on the transmission shaft. A driving member (pressure plate) rotates (drives) a driven member (clutch disc) on contact and, in so doing, turns the transmission shaft. There is a circular diaphragm spring within the pressure plate cover (transmission side). In a relaxed state (when the clutch pedal is fully released), this spring is convex; that is, it is dished outward toward the transmission. Pushing in the clutch pedal actuates an attached linkage rod. Connected to the other end of this rod is the throwout bearing fork. The throwout bearing is attached to the fork. When the clutch pedal is depressed, the clutch linkage pushes the fork and bearing forward to contact the diaphragm spring of the pressure plate. The outer edges of the spring are secured to the pressure plate and are pivoted on rings so that when the center of the spring is compressed by the throwout bearing, the outer edges bow outward and, by so doing, pull the pressure plate in the same direction - away from the clutch disc. This action separates the disc from the plate, disengaging the clutch and allowing the transmission to be shifted into another gear. A coil type clutch return spring attached to the clutch pedal arm permits full release of the pedal. Releasing the pedal pulls the throwout bearing away from the diaphragm spring resulting in a reversal of spring position. As bearing pressure is gradually released from the spring center, the outer edges of the spring bow outward, pushing the pressure plate into closer contact with the clutch disc. As the disc and plate move closer together, friction between the two increases and slippage is reduced until, when full spring pressure is applied (by fully releasing the pedal), The speed of the disc and plate are the same. This stops all slipping, creating a direct connection between the plate and disc which results in the transfer of power from the engine to the transmission. The clutch disc is now rotating with the pressure plate at engine speed and, because it is splined to the transmission shaft, the shaft now turns at the same engine speed. Understanding clutch operation can be rather difficult at first; if you're still confused after reading this, consider the following analogy. The action of the diaphragm spring can be compared to that of an oil can bottom. The bottom of an oil can is shaped very much like the clutch diaphragm spring and pushing in on the can bottom and then releasing it produces a similar effect. As mentioned earlier, the clutch pedal return spring permits full release of the pedal and reduces linkage slack due to wear. As the linkage wears, clutch free-pedal travel will increase and free-travel will decrease as the clutch wears. Free-travel is actually throwout bearing lash.

The diaphragm spring type clutches used are available in two different designs: flat diaphragm springs or bent spring. The bent fingers are bent back to create a centrifugal boost ensuring quick re-engagement at higher engine speeds. This design enables pressure plate load to increase as the clutch disc wears and makes low pedal effort possible even with a heavy-duty clutch. The throwout bearing used with the bent finger design is 1¼" long and is shorter than the bearing used with the flat finger design. These bearings are not interchangeable. If

the longer bearing is used with the bent finger clutch, free-pedal travel will not exist. This results in clutch slippage and rapid wear.

The transmission varies the gear ratio between the engine and drive wheels. It can be shifted to change engine speed as driving conditions and loads change. The transmission allows disengaging and reversing power from the engine to the wheels.

The clutch used in all 1200, B210 and 210 Datsun models covered in this guide is a hydraulic, single dry disc, diaphragm spring type clutch. The Sentra clutch is conventional (non-hydraulic) singleplate, diaphragm spring type clutch. The major clutch components consist of the flywheel, the clutch disc, the pressure plate, diaphragm springs, the throwout (release) bearing fork, the clutch master cylinder, slave cylinder and connecting line, and the pedal. The flywheel and the clutch pressure plate (driving members) are connected to the engine crankshaft and rotate with it. The clutch disc is located between the flywheel and pressure plate, and is splined to the transmission shaft. A driving member is one that is attached to the engine and transfers engine power to a driven member (clutch disc) on the transmission shaft. A driving member (pressure plate) rotates (drives) a driven member (clutch disc) on contact, and in

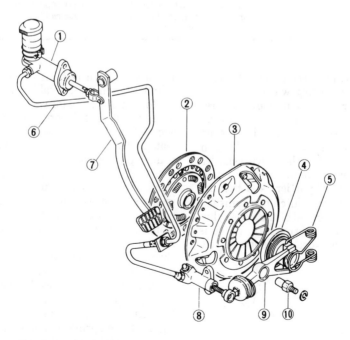

1. Clutch master cylinder
2. Clutch disc assembly
3. Clutch cover assembly
4. Release bearing and sleeve assembly
5. Return spring
6. Clutch line
7. Clutch pedal
8. Operating cylinder
9. Withdrawal lever
10. Withdrawal lever ball pin

1200 and B210 clutch control system. 210 similar

Troubleshooting Basic Clutch Problems

Problem	Cause
Excessive clutch noise	Throwout bearing noises are more audible at the lower end of pedal travel. The usual causes are: · Riding the clutch · Too little pedal free-play · Lack of bearing lubrication A bad clutch shaft pilot bearing will make a high pitched squeal, when the clutch is disengaged and the transmission is in gear or within the first 2″ of pedal travel. The bearing must be replaced. Noise from the clutch linkage is a clicking or snapping that can be heard or felt as the pedal is moved completely up or down. This usually requires lubrication. Transmitted engine noises are amplified by the clutch housing and heard in the passenger compartment. They are usually the result of insufficient pedal free-play and can be changed by manipulating the clutch pedal.
Clutch slips (the car does not move as it should when the clutch is engaged)	This is usually most noticeable when pulling away from a standing start. A severe test is to start the engine, apply the brakes, shift into high gear and SLOWLY release the clutch pedal. A healthy clutch will stall the engine. If it slips it may be due to: · A worn pressure plate or clutch plate · Oil soaked clutch plate · Insufficient pedal free-play
Clutch drags or fails to release	The clutch disc and some transmission gears spin briefly after clutch disengagement. Under normal conditions in average temperatures, 3 seconds is maximum spin-time. Failure to release properly can be caused by: · Too light transmission lubricant or low lubricant level · Improperly adjusted clutch linkage
Low clutch life	Low clutch life is usually a result of poor driving habits or heavy duty use. Riding the clutch, pulling heavy loads, holding the car on a grade with the clutch instead of the brakes and rapid clutch engagement all contribute to low clutch life.

so doing, turns the transmission shaft. There is a circular diaphragm spring within the pressure plate cover (transmission side). In a relaxed state (when the clutch pedal is fully released), this spring is convex, that is, it is dished outward toward the transmission. Pushing in the clutch pedal actuates the slave cylinder (only on hydraulic clutches), which is the smaller of the two hydraulic cylinders and the one that actually operates the clutch mechanism.

Connected to the other end of the slave cylinder rod is the throwout bearing fork, which is also found on the non-hydraulic Sentra clutch.

Sentra clutch control layout

When the clutch pedal is depressed, the slave cylinder (or the clutch cable on Sentra) pushes the fork and bearing forward to contact the diaphragm spring of the pressure plate. The outer edges of the spring are secured to the pressure plate and are pivoted on rings so that when the center of the spring is compressed by the throwout bearing, the outer edges bow outward, and, by so doing, pull the pressure plate in the same direction -- away from the clutch disc. This action separates the disc from the plate, disengaging the clutch from the transmission and allowing the transmission to be shifted into another gear. Releasing the pedal allows the throwout bearing to pull away from the diaphragm spring resulting in a reversal of spring position. As bearing pressure is gradually released from the spring center, the outer edges of the spring bow inward, pushing the pressure plate into closer contact with the clutch disc. As the disc and plate move closer together, friction between the two increases and slippage is reduced until, when full spring pressure is applied (by fully releasing the pedal), the speed of the disc and plate are the same. This

Clutch Specifications

Model	Pedal Height Above Floor (in.)	Pedal Free-Play (in.)
1200	5.6	0.12
B210	6.02	0.04–0.12
210	5.75	0.04–0.20
Sentra	7.9–8.1	0.43–0.83

stops all slipping, creating a direct connection between the plate and disc which results in the transfer of power from the engine to the transmission. The clutch disc is now rotating with the pressure plate at the engine speed and, because it is splined to the transmission shaft, the shaft now turns at the same engine speed.

ADJUSTMENT

Refer to the Clutch Specifications Chart for clutch pedal height above floor and pedal free play.

Since all 1200, B210 and 210 models have a hydraulically operated clutch, pedal height is usually adjusted with a stopper limiting the upward travel of the pedal or a stop combined with a clutch electrical switch. Pedal free play is adjusted at the master cylinder pushrod. The Sentra clutch is adjusted with a pedal stopper and adjusting locknut.

On some models, there is a clutch switch that prevents the engine from cranking unless the

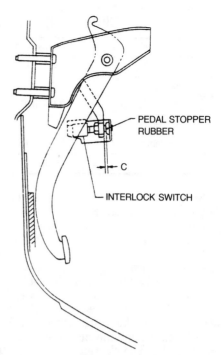

PEDAL STOPPER RUBBER

C

INTERLOCK SWITCH

Adjusting the clutch interlock switch on 1987–88 models

clutch pedal has been depressed. This is combined with and functions as a pedal stop. Adjust it in the same way as the simple bolt and locknut.

1. Adjust pedal height on all models, **H**, with pedal stopper. Then tighten locknut (see illustration).

2. Adjust 1200, B210 and 210 pedal free play with master cylinder pushrod. Then tighten locknut.

3. Adjust Sentra withdrawal lever at the lever tip end (on side of transaxle) with adjusting nut. Play in lever is as shown in the chart. Then, cross-check the adjustment by checking the free play at the pedal.

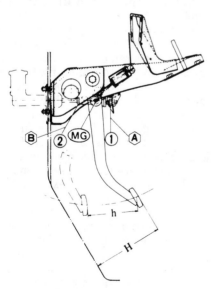

B   2   MG   1   A

h

H

1. Adjust pedal height here
2. Adjust pedal free-play here
MG. Lubricate with multipurpose grease here
H. is pedal height
h. is free-play

Clutch adjusting points

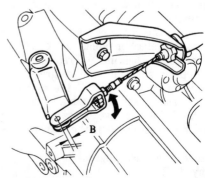

B

Sentra withdrawal lever adjustment. Arrow shows locknut adjustment

Clutch Adjustment Specifications Chart

Model	Pedal Height (in.)	Pedal Free Play (in.)	Lever Free Play (in.)
1980–81 210	5.63–5.87	0.04–0.20	—
1982 Sentra	7.91–8.15	0.43–0.83	0.08–0.16
1983–84 Sentra	7.64–8.03	0.43–0.83	0.08–0.16
1985 Sentra	8.23–8.43	0.492–0.689	0.098–0.138
1986 Sentra	7.76–8.15	0.492–0.689	0.098–0.138
1987–88 Sentra	6.38–6.77	0.492–0.689	0.492–0.689

4. Depress and release clutch pedal (on all models) over its entire stroke to ensure that the clutch linkage operates smoothly without squeak, noise, and interference, or binding.

5. On 1987-88 Sentras only, complete the adjustment by performing the adjustment of the clutch interlock switch (U.S. models only):

6. Have a helper depress the clutch pedal all the way and hold it. Then, adjust the clearance between the end of the clutch interlock switch, which is threaded, and the rubber stop mounted on the pedal. The clearance must be 1.00-2.00mm on 1987 models and 0.10-1.00mm on 1988 models.

REMOVAL AND INSTALLATION

1200, B210, 210 Hydraulic Clutch

CAUTION: *The clutch driven disc contains asbestos, which has been determined to be a cancer causing agent. Never clean the clutch surfaces with compressed air! Avoid inhaling any dust from any clutch surface! When cleaning clutch surfaces, use a commercially available brake cleaning fluid.*

1. Remove the transmission from the engine.

2. Loosen the pressure plate mounting bolts in sequence, a turn at a time. Remove the bolts.

3. Remove the pressure plate and clutch disc.

4. Remove the release mechanism. Apply multi-purpose grease to the bearing sleeve inside groove, the contact point of the withdrawal lever and bearing sleeve, the contact surface of the lever ball pin and lever. Replace the release mechanism.

5. Inspect the pressure plate for wear, scoring, etc., and reface or replace as necessary. Inspect the release bearing and replace as necessary. Apply a small amount of grease to the transmission splines. Install the disc on the splines and slide back and forth a few times. Remove the disc and remove excess grease on hub. Be sure no grease contacts the disc or pressure plate.

6. Install the disc, aligning it with a splined dummy shaft.

7. Install the pressure plate and torque the bolts to 11-16 ft. lbs.

8. Remove the dummy shaft.

9. Replace the transmission.

Sentra

CAUTION: *The clutch driven disc contains asbestos, which has been determined to be a cancer causing agent. Never clean the clutch surfaces with compressed air! Avoid inhaling any dust from any cltuch surface! When cleaning clutch surfaces, use a commercially available brake cleaning fluid.*

1. Remove transaxle from engine.

2. Insert Nissan clutch aligning tool or a similar splined clutch tool (must fit the Sentra's clutch splines) into the clutch disc hub.

3. Loosen the bolts attaching the clutch cover to the flywheel, one turn each at a time, until the spring pressure is released.

NOTE: *Be sure to turn them out in a crisscross pattern.*

4. Remove the clutch disc and cover assembly.

5. Inspect the pressure plate for scoring or roughness, and reface or replace as necessary (slight roughness can be smoothed with a fine emery cloth). Inspect the clutch disc for worn or oily facings, loose rivets and broken or loose springs, and replace. (You probably have the clutch out of the car to replace it anyway).

6. Apply a light coat of a molybdenum disulfide grease to the transaxle input shaft spline. Slide the clutch disc on the input shaft several times to distribute the grease. Remove the clutch disc and wipe off the excess lubricant pushed off by the disc hub.

CAUTION: *Take special care to prevent any grease or oil from getting on the clutch facing. During assembly, keep all disc facings, flywheel and pressure plate clean and dry. Grease, oil or dirt on these parts will result in a slipping clutch when assembled.*

7. Install the clutch cover assembly. Each bolt should be tightened one turn at a time in a crisscross pattern. Torque the bolts to 12-15 ft. lbs.

8. Remove the clutch aligning tool.

9. Reinstall the transaxle.

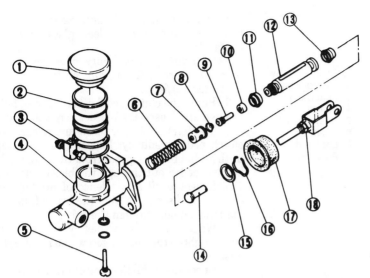

1. Reservoir cap
2. Reservoir
3. Reservoir band
4. Cylinder body
5. Supply valve stopper
6. Return spring
7. Spring seat
8. Valve spring
9. Supply valve rod
10. Supply valve
11. Primary cup
12. Piston
13. Secondary cup
14. Push rod
15. Stopper
16. Stopper ring
17. Dust cover
18. Lock nut

210 clutch master cylinder. 1200 and B210 similar

Clutch Master Cylinder

REMOVAL AND INSTALLATION

Hydraulic Clutch Models

1. Remove snap pin from clevis pin, and pull out clevis pin.

2. Disconnect the clutch pedal arm from the pushrod.

3. Disconnect the clutch hydraulic line from the master cylinder.

NOTE: *Take precautions to keep brake fluid from coming in contact with any painted surfaces.*

4. Remove the nuts attaching the master cylinder and remove the master cylinder and pushrod toward the engine compartment side.

5. Install the master cylinder in the reverse order of removal and bleed the clutch hydraulic system.

OVERHAUL

1. Remove the master cylinder from the vehicle.

2. Drain the clutch fluid (same as brake fluid) from the master cylinder reservoir.

3. Remove the boot and circlip and remove the pushrod.

4. Remove the stopper, piston, cup and return spring.

5. Clean all of the parts in clean brake fluid.

6. Check the master cylinder and piston for wear, corrosion and scores and replace the parts as necessary. Light scoring and glaze can be removed with crocus cloth soaked in clean brake fluid.

7. The cup seal should be replaced each time the master cylinder is disassembled, if there is any evidence of wear, cracking, damage, or fatigue.

8. Check the clutch fluid reservoir, filler cap, dust cover and the pipe for distortion and damage and replace the parts as necessary.

9. Lubricate all new parts with clean brake fluid.

10. Reassemble the master cylinder parts in the reverse order of disassembly, taking note of the following:

    a. Reinstall the cup seal carefully to prevent damaging the lipped portions;

    b. Adjust the height of the clutch pedal after installing the master cylinder in position on the vehicle;

    c. Fill the master cylinder and clutch fluid reservoir and then bleed the clutch hydraulic system (see, Bleeding Clutch Hydraulic System).

Clutch Slave Cylinder

REMOVAL AND INSTALLATION

Hydraulic Clutch Models

1. Remove the slave cylinder attaching bolts and the pushrod from the shift fork.

2. Disconnect the flexible fluid hose from the slave cylinder and remove the unit from the vehicle.

3. Install the slave cylinder in the reverse order of removal and bleed the clutch hydraulic system.

OVERHAUL

1. Remove the slave cylinder from the vehicle.

2. Remove the pushrod and boot.

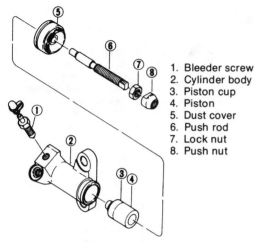

1. Bleeder screw
2. Cylinder body
3. Piston cup
4. Piston
5. Dust cover
6. Push rod
7. Lock nut
8. Push nut

Typical hydraulic clutch slave cylinder

3. Force out the piston by blowing compressed air into the slave cylinder at the hose connection.

NOTE: *Be careful not to apply excess air pressure to avoid possible injury.*

4. Clean all of the parts in clean brake fluid. CAUTION: *Never use mineral solvents such as kerosene or gasoline to clean master cylinder and other brake parts. These solvents will ruin the rubber parts of the hydraulic system.*

5. Check and replace the slave cylinder bore and piston if wear or severe scoring exists. Light scoring and glaze can be removed with crocus cloth soaked in clean brake fluid.

6. Normally the piston cup should be replaced when the slave cylinder is disassembled. Check the piston cup and replace it if it is found to be worn, fatigued or scored.

7. Replace the rubber boot if it is cracked or broken.

8. Lubricate all of the new parts in clean brake fluid and reassemble in the reverse order of disassembly, taking note of the following:

   a. Use care when reassembling the piston cup to prevent damaging the lipped portion of the piston cup;

   b. Fill the master cylinder with brake fluid and bleed the clutch hydraulic system;

   c. Adjust the clearance between the pushrod and the shift fork to ⁵⁄₆₄″.

BLEEDING THE CLUTCH HYDRAULIC SYSTEM

1. Check and fill the clutch fluid reservoir to the specified level as necessary. During the bleeding process, continue to check and replenish the reservoir to prevent the fluid level from getting lower than ½ the specified level.

2. Remove the dust cap from the bleeder screw on the clutch slave cylinder and connect a tube to the bleeder screw and insert the other end of the tube into a clean glass or metal container.

NOTE: *Take precautionary measures to prevent the brake fluid from getting on any painted surfaces.*

3. Pump the clutch pedal several times, hold it down and loosen the bleeder screw slowly.

4. Tighten the bleeder screw and release the clutch pedal gradually. Repeat this operation until air bubbles disappear from the brake fluid being expelled out through the bleeder screw.

5. Repeat until all evidence of air bubbles completely disappears from the brake fluid being pumped out through the tube.

6. When the air is completely removed, securely tighten the bleeder screw and replace the dust cap.

7. Check and refill the master cylinder reservoir as necessary.

8. Depress the clutch pedal several times to check the operation of the clutch and check for leaks.

AUTOMATIC TRANSMISSION

Understanding Automatic Transmissions

The automatic transmission allows engine torque and power to be transmitted to the drive wheels within a narrow range of engine operating speeds. The transmission will allow the engine to turn fast enough to produce plenty of power and torque at very low speeds, while keeping it at a sensible rpm at high vehicle speeds. The transmission performs this job entirely without driver assistance. The transmission uses a light fluid as the medium for the transmission of power. This fluid also works in the operation of various hydraulic control circuits and as a lubricant. Because the transmission fluid performs all of these three functions, trouble within the unit can easily travel from one part to another. For this reason, and because of the complexity and unusual operating principles of the transmission, a very sound understanding of the basic principles of operation will simplify troubleshooting.

THE TORQUE CONVERTER

The torque converter replaces the conventional clutch. It has three functions:

1. It allows the engine to idle with the vehicle at a standstill, even with the transmission in gear.

2. It allows the transmission to shift from range to range smoothly, without requiring

that the driver close the throttle during the shift.

3. It multiplies engine torque to an increasing extent as vehicle speed drops and throttle opening is increased. This has the effect of making the transmission more responsive and reduces the amount of shifting required.

The torque converter is a metal case which is shaped like a sphere that has been flattened on opposite sides. It is bolted to the rear end of the engine's crankshaft. Generally, the entire metal case rotates at engine speed and serves as the engine's flywheel.

The case contains three sets of blades. One set is attached directly to the case. This set forms the torus or pump. Another set is directly connected to the output shaft, and forms the turbine. The third set is mounted on a hub which, in turn, is mounted on a stationary shaft through a one-way clutch. This third set is known as the stator.

A pump, which is driven by the converter hub at engine speed, keeps the torque converter full of transmission fluid at all times. Fluid flows continuously through the unit to provide cooling.

Under low speed acceleration, the torque converter functions as follows:

The torus is turning faster than the turbine. It picks up fluid at the center of the converter and, through centrifugal force, slings it outward. Since the outer edge of the converter moves faster than the portions at the center, the fluid picks up speed.

The fluid then enters the outer edge of the turbine blades. It then travels back toward the center of the converter case along the turbine blades. In impinging upon the turbine blades, the fluid loses the energy picked up in the torus.

If the fluid were now to immediately be returned directly into the torus, both halves of the converter would have to turn at approximately the same speed at all times, and torque input and output would both be the same.

In flowing through the torus and turbine, the fluid picks up two types of flow, or flow in two separate directions. It flows through the turbine blades, and it spins with the engine. The stator, whose blades are stationary when the vehicle is being accelerated at low speeds, converts one type of flow into another. Instead of allowing the fluid to flow straight back into the torus, the stator's curved blades turn the fluid almost 90° toward the direction of rotation of the engine. Thus the fluid does not flow as fast toward the torus, but is already spinning when the torus picks it up. This has the effect of allowing the torus to turn much faster than the turbine. This difference in speed may be compared to the difference in speed between the

smaller and larger gears in any gear train. The result is that engine power output is higher, and engine torque is multiplied.

As the speed of the turbine increases, the fluid spins faster and faster in the direction of engine rotation. As a result, the ability of the stator to redirect the fluid flow is reduced. Under cruising conditions, the stator is eventually forced to rotate on its one-way clutch in the direction of engine rotation. Under these conditions, the torque converter begins to behave almost like a solid shaft, with the torus and turbine speeds being almost equal.

THE PLANETARY GEARBOX

The ability of the torque converter to multiply engine torque is limited. Also, the unit tends to be more efficient when the turbine is rotating at relatively high speeds. Therefore, a planetary gearbox is used to carry the power output of the turbine to the halfshafts.

Planetary gears function very similarly to conventional transmission gears. However, their construction is different in that three elements make up one gear system, and, in that all three elements are different from one another. The three elements are: an outer gear that is shaped like a hoop, with teeth cut into the inner surface; a sun gear, mounted on a shaft and located at the very center of the outer gear; and a set of three planet gears, held by pins in a ring-like planet carrier, meshing with both the sun gear and the outer gear. Either the outer gear or the sun gear may be held stationary, providing more than one possible torque multiplication factor for each set of gears. Also, if all three gears are forced to rotate at the same speed, the gearset forms, in effect, a solid shaft.

Most modern automatics use the planetary gears to provide either a single reduction ratio of about 1.8:1, or two reduction gears: a low of about 2.5:1, and an intermediate of about 1.5:1. Bands and clutches are used to hold various portions of the gearsets to the transmission case or to the shaft on which they are mounted. Shifting is accomplished, then, by changing the portion of each planetary gearset which is held to the transmission case or to the shaft.

THE SERVOS AND ACCUMULATORS

The servos are hydraulic pistons and cylinders. They resemble the hydraulic actuators used on many familiar machines, such as bulldozers. Hydraulic fluid enters the cylinder, under pressure, and forces the piston to move to engage the band or clutches.

The accumulators are used to cushion the engagement of the servos. The transmission fluid must pass through the accumulator on the way to the servo. The accumulator housing contains a thin piston which is sprung away from the discharge passage of the accumulator. When fluid passes through the accumulator on the way to the servo, it must move the piston against spring pressure, and this action smooths out the action of the servo.

THE HYDRAULIC CONTROL SYSTEM

The hydraulic pressure used to operate the servos comes from the main transmission oil pump. This fluid is channeled to the various servos through the shift valves. There is generally a manual shift valve which is operated by the transmission selector lever and an automatic shift valve for each automatic upshift the transmission provides: i.e., 2-speed automatics have a low/high shift valve, while 3-speeds have a 1-2 valve, and a 2-3 valve.

There are two pressures which effect the operation of these valves. One is the governor pressure which is affected by vehicle speed. The other is the modulator pressure which is affected by intake manifold vacuum or throttle position. Governor pressure rises with an increase in vehicle speed, and modulator pressure rises as the throttle is opened wider. By responding to these two pressures, the shift valves cause the upshift points to be delayed with increased throttle opening to make the best use of the engine's power output.

Most transmissions also make use of an auxiliary circuit for downshifting. This circuit may be actuated by the throttle linkage or the vacuum line which actuates the modulator, or by a cable or solenoid. It applies pressure to a special downshift surface on the shift valve or valves.

The transmission modulator also governs the line pressure, used to actuate the servos. In this way, the clutches and bands will be actuated with a force matching the torque output of the engine.

Identification

All models covered in this guide are also available with a 3-speed automatic transmission (Sentras have an automatic transaxle—see below). Except for the various checks and maintenance procedures outlined here, it is recommended that major automatic transmission service be left to an automatic transmission specialist who has the expertise and special tools required to work on these units.

Fluid Pan

REMOVAL AND INSTALLATION

1. Jack up the front of the car and support it safely on stands.
2. Slide a drain pan under the transmission. Loosen the rear oil pan bolts first, to allow most

Automatic transmission pan removal

of the fluid to drain off without making a mess on your garage floor.

3. Remove the remaining bolts and drop the pan.
4. Discard the old gasket, clean the pan, and reinstall the pan with a new gasket.
5. Tighten the retaining bolts in a crisscross pattern starting at the center.

CAUTION: *The transmission case is aluminum and easily stripped, so don't put too much torque on the bolts. Use 36-60 in. lbs.*

6. Refill the transmission through the dipstick tube. Check the fluid level as described in Chapter 1.

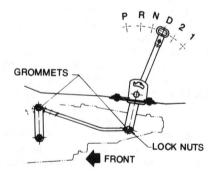

Automatic transmission shift linkage adjustment, 1200, B210 and 210

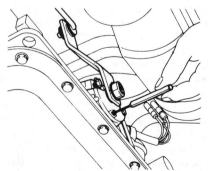

Adjusting neutral (inhibitor) switch using alignment pin

SHIFT LINKAGE ADJUSTMENT

The adjustment of the manual linkage is an important adjustment of the automatic transmission. Move the shift lever from the **P** range into the **1** range. You should be able to feel the detents (stops) in each range.

If the detents cannot be felt or the pointer indicating the range is improperly aligned, the linkage needs adjustment.

1200, B210 and 210

1. Place shift lever in **D** range.
2. Loosen locknuts (see illustration) and move shift lever until **D** is properly aligned and car is in **D** range.
3. Tighten locknuts when lever is in proper position.
4. Recheck **P** and range **1** positions. As a safety measure, be sure you can feel full detent when shift lever is placed in **P**. If you are unable to make an adjustment, grommets may be badly worn or damaged and should be replaced.

DOWNSHIFT SOLENOID/KICKDOWN SWITCH CHECK AND ADJUSTMENT

1200, B210 and 210 Models

The kickdown switch is located at the upper post of the accelerator pedal, inside the car. The downshift solenoid is screwed into the outside of the transmission case.

When the kickdown operation is not made properly or the speed changing point is too high, check the kickdown switch, downshift solenoid and the wiring connection between them.

1. Turn the ignition switch **ON** to the first position.
2. Push the accelerator pedal all the way down to actuate the downshift switch.
3. The downshift solenoid should click when actuated if working properly. If there is no click, loosen the locknut and extend the switch until the pedal lever makes contact with the switch and the switch clicks.

CAUTION: *Do not allow the switch to make contact too soon. This would cause the transmission to downshift on part throttle.*

4. If the switch can be heard clicking even if the transmission is not kicking down, check the electrical continuity of the switch with a continuity tester. Also check to see if current is reaching the switch.

INHIBITOR SWITCH (NEUTRAL SAFETY AND BACKUP LIGHT) ADJUSTMENT

The switch unit is bolted to the left side of the transmission case, behind the transmission shift lever. The switch prevents the engine from being started in any transmission position except Park or Neutral. It also controls the backup lights.

1200, B210 and 210 Models

1. Remove the transmission shift lever retaining nut and the lever.
2. Remove the switch.
3. Remove the machine screw in the case under the switch.
4. Align the switch to the case by inserting a 1.5mm diameter pin through the hole in the switch into the screw hole. Mark the switch location.
5. Remove the pin, replace the machine screw, install the switch as marked, and replace the transmission shift lever and retaining nut.
6. Make sure, while holding the brakes and parking brake on, that the engine will start only in Park or Neutral. Check that the backup lights go on only in Reverse.

Transmission

REMOVAL AND INSTALLATION

1. Disconnect the battery cable.
2. Remove the accelerator linkage.
3. Detach the shift linkage.
4. Disconnect the neutral safety switch and downshift solenoid wiring.
5. Remove the drain plug and drain the torque converter. If there is no converter drain plug, drain the transmission. If there is no transmission drain plug, remove the pan to drain. Replace the pan to keep out dirt.
6. Remove the front exhaust pipe.
7. Remove the vacuum tube and speedometer cable.
8. Disconnect the fluid cooler tubes.
9. Remove the driveshaft and starter.
10. Support the transmission with a jack and wood block under the oil pan and support the engine.
11. Remove the rear crossmember.
12. Mark the relationship between the torque converter and the drive plate with a scribe or grease pencil. Remove the four bolts holding the converter to the drive plate through the hole at the front, under the engine, turning the assembly as necessary to gain access to each bolt. Unbolt the transmission from the engine. Pull the transmission just slightly away from the engine and then lower the transmission and remove it.
13. Make sure that the drive plate is warped no more than 0.5mm by rotating the crankshaft and measuring the runout with a dial indicator. Drive plate-to-crankshaft bolt torque is 101-116 ft. lbs. Check this torque before installing the transmission. Raise the transmission until it is in position just behind the engine and then

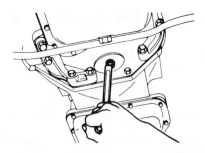

Disconnecting the torque converter bolts through access hole

slide it toward the engine so all boltholes line up. Install the mounting bolts and torque to 29-36 ft. lbs.

14. Align the matchmarks relating the positions of the driveplate and converter. Apply a locking sealer to the bolt threads. Then, install the converter retaining bolts one by one, turning the crankshaft as necessary for access. Torque these too to 29-36 ft. lbs.

15. Install the rear crossmember.

16. Remove the block and jack supporting the transmission. Reconnect the driveshaft, maintaining the original alignment.

17. Refill the transmission and check the fluid level.

AUTOMATIC TRANSAXLE

Identification

The transxle bears a serial number located, as shown, on the housing. Only one type of unit is used in the Sentra, so it is not necessary to refer to codes when ordering parts.

Fluid Pan

REMOVAL AND INSTALLATION

1. Jack up the front of the car and support it safely on stands.

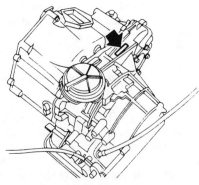

Location of the transaxle serial number

2. Slide a drain pan under the transmission. Loosen the rear oil pan bolts first, to allow most of the fluid to drain off without making a mess on your garage floor.

3. Remove the oil pan guard. Remove the remaining bolts and drop the pan.

4. Discard the old gasket, clean the pan, and reinstall the pan with a new gasket.

5. Tighten the retaining bolts in a crisscross pattern starting at the center. CAUTION: *The transmission case is aluminum and easily stripped, so don't put too much torque on the bolts. Use 36-60 in. lbs.*

6. Refill the transmission through the dipstick tube. Check the fluid level as described in Chapter 1.

Adjustments

SHIFT LINKAGE

The adjustment of the manual linkage (control cable on Sentra) is an important adjustment of the automatic transmission. Move the shift lever from the **P** range into the **1** range. You should be able to feel the detents (stops) in each range.

If the detents cannot be felt or the pointer indicating the range is improperly aligned, the linkage (control cable) needs adjustment.

Sentra

1. Place gear lever in the **P** position.
2. Connect the control cable end to the man-

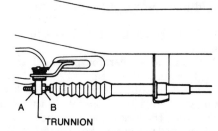

Sentra automatic transaxle cable adjustment

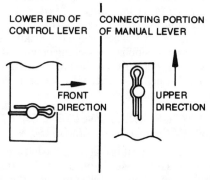

Proper Sentra automatic transaxle spring pin position

ual lever in the transaxle unit, and tighten the control cable securing bolts.

3. Move the gear lever from the **P** position to the **1** position. Make sure that the gear lever can move smoothly and without any sliding noise.

4. Place the gear lever in the **P** range again. Make sure that the control lever locks at the **P** range.

5. Remove the control cable adjusting nut **A** and loosen nut **B**, then connect the control cable to the trunnion. Install nut **A** and **B**, then tighten them.

6. Move the gear lever from **P** to **1** position again. Make sure the lever moves smoothly without any sliding noise.

7. Apply a dab of grease to the spring washer.

8. After properly adjusting the control cable, check the spring pin to see if it is assembled as shown in the illustration. If not, adjust the spring pin.

INHIBITOR SWITCH (NEUTRAL SAFETY AND BACKUP LIGHT) ADJUSTMENT

The switch unit is bolted to the left side of the transmission case, behind the transmission shift lever. The switch prevents the engine from being started in any transmission position except Park or Neutral. It also controls the backup lights.

Sentra

1. Loosen the inhibitor attaching screws (three Phillips head screws).

2. Set the select lever (manual shaft) at the **N** position.

3. Insert a 2.5mm diameter pin into the adjustment hoels in both the inhibitor switch and the switch lever as near vertical as possible.

4. Tighten the screws.

5. Check the inhibitor switch for continuity at the **N**, **P** and **R** ranges. With the gear lever in neutral position, turn the manual lever an equal amount in both directions to see if the current flow ranges are nearly the same.

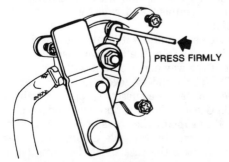

PRESS FIRMLY

Sentra inhibitor switch adjustment

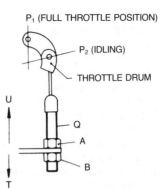

P₁ (FULL THROTTLE POSITION)

P₂ (IDLING)

THROTTLE DRUM

U

Q

A

B

T

Adjusting the throttle cable on the Sentra automatic transaxle

Throttle Cable
ADJUSTMENT

1. Loosen the double locknuts located on either side of the throttle cable bracket. This bracket is located near the throttle body or carburetor and retains the cable housing.

2. Open the throttle wide and hold it there, with the assistance of a helper. Then, grasp the cable housing, **Q**, on the carburetor/throttle body side of the bracket and pull it toward the bracket with a force of about 9 lbs. Hold it there and turn the nut on the transmission side of the bracket **B** toward the bracket, in direction **U**, just until it touches the bracket.

3. Now, turn nut **B** exactly 1-1½ turns back from the point reached in the step above. Finally, tighten nut **A** until it touches the bracket. Use an opposing wrench to keep nut **B** from turning and then tighten nut **A** with another wrench.

4. Relax the tension on the throttle. Mark the position of the throttle innner cable where it enters the cable housing. Then, open the throttle all the way. Measure the distance the mark on the cable moved in direction **U**. The distance must be 27.4-31.4mm. If not, readjust the cable to correct the stroke of the throttle.

Transaxle
REMOVAL AND INSTALLATION

1. Disconnect the battery cable.

2. Disconnect the accelerator linkage.

3. Detach the shift linkage and throttle cable.

4. Disconnect the inhibitor switch.

5. Remove the drain pan and drain the transmission. Replace the pan to keep out dirt, using a new gasket.

7. Disconnect the speedometer cable.

8. Disconnect the fluid cooler tubes and drain them into a convenient container. Cap the openings.

9. Remove the driveshafts as described above under the manual transaxle section.

10. Support the transaxle with a jack and some sort of fixture that will keep the unit from tipping and which will also support it by the bottom of the case rather than the pan.

11. Remove the transaxle support rod bolt.

12. Mark the relationship between the torque converter and drive plate. Then, turn the crankshaft for access to the converter-to-drive plate bolts. Remove each bolt and then turn the crank until the next one is lined up. Remove all four bolts in this manner.

13. Remove all engine-to-transaxle case bolts. Then, carefully pull the unit a very short distance away from the engine so the converter will clear the drive plate.

14. Lower the unit very slowly and carefully so it will not strike any nearby engine or chassis parts and remove it from the car.

15. Make sure that the drive plate is warped no more than 0.50mm by rotating the crankshaft and measuring the runout with a dial indicator. Also measure the distance between the torque converter bolt-up surfaces and the front plane of the transaxle case, as shown. Clearance must be 21mm or more.

16. Raise the transaxle until it is in position just behind the engine and then slide it toward the engine so all boltholes line up. Install the transaxle-to-engine mounting bolts and torque to 12-16 ft. lbs.

17. Align the matchmarks relating the positions of the driveplate and converter. Apply a locking sealer to the bolt threads. Then, install the converter retaining bolts one by one, turning the crankshaft as necessary for access. Torque them to 36-51 ft. lbs.

18. Rotate the crankshaft for several revolutions and make sure it turns wihtout biding to ensure that the converter is properly mounted.

19. Install the transaxle support rod bolt. Then, remove the transmission support.

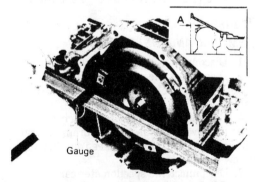

Measure dimension "A" to determine whether or not the converter is correctly installed. It must be 0.831 in. or more.

20. Reinstall the driveshafts as described above in the manual transaxle section.

21. Reconnect the transmission cooling lines.

22. Connect the speedometer cable.

23. Connect the inhibitor switch. Check its operation with a test lamp or careful road test before attempting to drive the car normally.

24. Re-attach the shift linkage, and then adjust it as described above. Make sure the linkage is properly adjusted and puts the transmission in the right shift position before attempting to drive the car normally.

25. Connect the accelerator linkage.

26. Connect the throttle cable and then adjust it as described above.

27. Connect the battery cable.

28. Refill the transmission pan to the proper level with the approved fluid. Recheck the fluid level after the transmission has warmed up.

Halfshafts

REMOVAL AND INSTALLATION

Removing the halfshafts on vehicles equiped with an automatic transaxle is identical to that used on manual transaxle equipped vehicles. Refer to the appropriate procedure under the manual transaxle section, above.

OVERHAUL

Halfshaft overhaul procedures on vehicles equipped with an automatic transaxle are identical to that used on manual transaxle equipped vehicles. Refer to the appropriate procedure under the manual transaxle section, above.

TRANSFER CASE

REMOVAL AND INSTALLATION

1. Drain the gear oil from the transaxle and the transfer case.

2. Disconnect and remove the forward exhaust pipe.

3. Using chalk or paint, matchmark the flanges on the driveshaft and then unbolt and remove the driveshaft from the transfer case.

4. Unbolt and remove the transfer control actuator from the side of the transfer case.

5. Disconnect and remove the right side halfshaft.

6. Unscrew and withdraw the speedometer pinion gear from the transfer case. Position it out of the way and secure it with wire.

7. Unbolt and remove the front, rear and side transfer case gussets (support members).

8. Use an hydraulic floor jack and a block of wood to support the transfer case, remove the transfer case-to-transaxle mounting bolts and then remove the case itself. Be careful when moving it while supported on the jack.

9. Install the transfer case in the vehicle. Tighten the transfer case-to-transaxle mounting bolts and the transfer case gusset mounting bolts to 22-30 ft. lbs. (30-40 Nm).

10. Be sure to use a multi-purpose grease to lubricate all oil seal surfaces prior to reinstallation.

11. Install the speedometer pinion gear.

12. Install the halfshaft.

13. Connect the transfer control actuator to the side of the transfer case.

14. Install the driveshaft to the transfer case.

15. Install the forward exhaust pipe.

16. Refill all fluid levels, the transfer case and

Troubleshooting Basic Driveshaft and Rear Axle Problems

When abnormal vibrations or noises are detected in the driveshaft area, this chart can be used to help diagnose possible causes. Remember that other components such as wheels, tires, rear axle and suspension can also produce similar conditions.

BASIC DRIVESHAFT PROBLEMS

Problem	Cause	Solution
Shudder as car accelerates from stop or low speed	• Loose U-joint • Defective center bearing	• Replace U-joint • Replace center bearing
Loud clunk in driveshaft when shifting gears	• Worn U-joints	• Replace U-joints
Roughness or vibration at any speed	• Out-of-balance, bent or dented driveshaft • Worn U-joints • U-joint clamp bolts loose	• Balance or replace driveshaft • Replace U-joints • Tighten U-joint clamp bolts
Squeaking noise at low speeds	• Lack of U-joint lubrication	• Lubricate U-joint; if problem persists, replace U-joint
Knock or clicking noise	• U-joint or driveshaft hitting frame tunnel • Worn CV joint	• Correct overloaded condition • Replace CV joint

BASIC REAR AXLE PROBLEMS

First, determine when the noise is most noticeable.

Drive Noise: Produced under vehicle acceleration.

Coast Noise: Produced while the car coasts with a closed throttle.

Float Noise: Occurs while maintaining constant car speed (just enough to keep speed constant) on a level road.

Road Noise

Brick or rough surfaced concrete roads produce noises that seem to come from the rear axle. Road noise is usually identical in Drive or Coast and driving on a different type of road will tell whether the road is the problem.

Tire Noise

Tire noises are often mistaken for rear axle problems. Snow treads or unevenly worn tires produce vibrations seeming to originate elsewhere. **Temporarily** inflating the tires to 40 lbs will significantly alter tire noise, but will have no effect on rear axle noises (which normally cease below about 30 mph).

Engine/Transmission Noise

Determine at what speed the noise is most pronounced, then stop the car in a quiet place. With the transmission in Neutral, run the engine through speeds corresponding to road speeds where the noise was noticed. Noises produced with

the car standing still are coming from the engine or transmission.

Front Wheel Bearings

While holding the car speed steady, lightly apply the foot-brake; this will often decease bearing noise, as some of the load is taken from the bearing.

Rear Axle Noises

Eliminating other possible sources can narrow the cause to the rear axle, which normally produces noise from worn gears or bearings. Gear noises tend to peak in a narrow speed range, while bearing noises will usually vary in pitch with engine speeds.

NOISE DIAGNOSIS

The Noise Is	Most Probably Produced By
· Identical under Drive or Coast	· Road surface, tires or front wheel bearings
· Different depending on road surface	· Road surface or tires
· Lower as the car speed is lowered	· Tires
· Similar with car standing or moving	· Engine or transmission
· A vibration	· Unbalanced tires, rear wheel bearing, unbalanced driveshaft or worn U-joint
· A knock or click about every 2 tire revolutions	· Rear wheel bearing
· Most pronounced on turns	· Damaged differential gears
· A steady low-pitched whirring or scraping, starting at low speeds	· Damaged or worn pinion bearing
· A chattering vibration on turns	· Wrong differential lubricant or worn clutch plates (limited slip rear axle)
· Noticed only in Drive, Coast or Float conditions	· Worn ring gear and/or pinion gear

the transaxle. Use the approved types and weights of lubricant, and then road test for proper operation.

DRIVELINE

Driveshaft and Universal Joints

The driveshaft transfers power from the front mounted engine and transmisison to the differential and rear axles and then to the rear wheels to drive the car. All 1200, B210 and 210 Datsun models covered in this guide utilize a conventional rear wheel drive system. The driveshafts in these models have two universal joints at each end, and a slip yoke at the front of the assembly which fits into the back of the transmisison. These U-joints permit the driveshaft to both connect transmission and differential, which are not mounted on the same

plane and to follow the rear axle up and down with the rear suspension movement as it also spins on its axis.

On the front wheel drive Sentras, the entire drive train is bolted in unit with the engine up front. Since the Sentra engine is transversely mounted (across the chassis), its crankshaft is already spinning on the same plane as the front (drive) wheels. Compared to its Datsun cousins, the Sentra transaxle has an easy job -- instead of having to change the direction of the engine torque from a longitudinal plane to the transverse plane of the drive wheels, the Sentra transaxle merely has to connect the two. Instead of one long driveshaft and U-joints carrying the engine torque to the wheels, the Sentra transaxle drives the front wheels directly through two unequal length driveshafts, or halfshafts. Each halfshaft has a U-joint type spider (called a Constant Velocity, or CV joint)

1. Sleeve yoke
2. Spider with four bearing journals
3. Bearing race snap-ring
4. Bearing race with needle rollers
5. Spider with four bearing journals
6. Flange yoke
7. Bearing race snap-ring
8. Bearing race with needle rollers
9. Bolt
10. Lockwasher
11. Nut

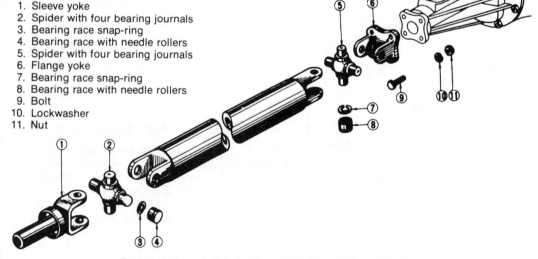

Exploded view of 1200, B210 and 210 driveshaft and U-joints

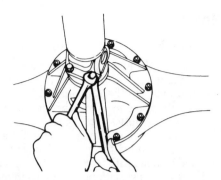

Disconnecting the rear driveshaft flange

on each end, making the wheels independent of one another.

REMOVAL AND INSTALLATION

1200, B210, 210

These driveshafts are all one-piece units with a U-joint and flange at the rear, and a U-joint and a splined sleeve yoke which fits into the rear of the transmission, at the front. Early 1200 and some B210 models generally have U-joints with grease fittings. U-joints without grease fittings must be disassembled for lubrication, usually at 24,000 mile intervals. The splines are lubricated by transmission oil.

1. Jack up car and safely support it with jackstands. Matchmark both the driveshaft and rear flange so that the shaft can be reinstalled in the same position.
2. Be ready to catch oil coming from the rear of the transmission and to plug the extension housing.
3. Unbolt the rear flange (differential end).
4. Pull the driveshaft down and back.
5. Plug the transmission extension housing.
6. Reverse the procedure to install, oiling the splines. Flange bolt torque is 15-20 ft. lbs. (1200), 17-24 ft. lbs. (B210-210).

Sentra 4 Wheel Drive

These models use a driveshaft with 3 U-joints and a center support bearing. The driveshaft is balanced as an assembly. It is not recommended that it be disassembled.

1. Mark the relationship of the driveshaft flange to the differential flange. Also mark the relationship between the front driveshaft flange and the transaxle flange.
2. Remove the nuts from the center bearing bracket, lower the assembly slightly and remove both the upper and lower halves of the bearing retainer. Support the driveshaft at or near the center bearing.
3. Unbolt the driveshaft flange from the differential flange. Support it at the rear. Then, unbolt it at the transaxle.

4. Pull the driveshaft back and out under the rear axle.
5. On installation, align the marks made in Step 1. Torque the flange bolts to 17-24 ft. lbs. Center bearing bracket attaching nut torque is 26-35 ft. lbs.

U-JOINT OVERHAUL

All Rear Wheel Drive Models

DISASSEMBLY

1. Match mark the relationship of all components for reassembly.
2. Remove the snaprings. On early units, the snaprings are seated in the yokes. On later units, the snapring seat in the needle bearing races.
3. Tap the yoke with a rubber hammer to release one bearing cap. The needle rollers are lined up around the inside wall of the caps and may be loose if their grease packing has disappeared. Use care in disassembling the U-joint from this point, as the rollers are easily lost.
4. Remove the other bearing caps. Remove the U-joint spiders from the yokes.

INSPECTION

1. Spline backlash should not exceed 0.5mm.
2. Driveshaft runout should not exceed 0.4mm.
3. On later models with snaprings seated in the needle bearing races, different thicknesses of snaprings are available for U-joint adjustment. Play should not exceed 0.02mm.
4. U-joint spiders must be replaced if their bearing journals are worn more than 0.15mm from their original diameter.

ASSEMBLY

1. Grease the inside diameter of the cap races with enough grease to hold the rollers in place. Line the rollers up tightly, side by side inside the races.
2. Put the spider into place in its yokes.
3. Replace all seals.
4. Tap the races into position and secure them with snaprings.

Sentra

To rebuild the CV joints on the Sentra, refer to the Halfshafts Overhaul procedure above under Manual Transaxle.

Center Bearing (4WD only)

REMOVAL AND INSTALLATION

NOTE: *Performing this operation requires a special locking tool J34311 or equivalent, a puller, a special center bearing tool J22912-01 or equivalent and a large press.*

1. Remove the driveshaft as described above. Mark the relationship between the flanges and then remove the bolts connecting the front and rear sections of the driveshaft at the center U-joint.

2. Matchmark the relationship between the flange next to the center bearing and the shaft. Then, remove the locking nut from the shaft, using J34311 and a socket wrench.

3. Use a puller with the center on the driveshaft and the arms hooked under the companion flange to remove the flange from the driveshaft.

4. Use J22912-01 to support the bearing. Press the shaft out of the bearing with a large press.

5. In installation, position the **F** mark on the center bearing toward the front of the vehicle. Coat the end face of the center bearing and both sides of the washer with a multi-purpose lithium, molybdenum disulphide grease. Start the bearing on the driveshaft, start a new locking nut, and then use the special tool and a torque wrench to torque it to 181-217 ft. lbs.

6. Reassemble the driveshaft, aligning flanges according to the matchmarks. Torque the flange bolts to 25-33 ft. lbs.

7. Install the driveshaft as described above.

Rear Halfshafts (4WD only)
REMOVAL AND INSTALLATION

1. Raise the vehicle and support it securely. Remove the rear wheels.

2. Have someone depress the brake pedal as you remove the wheel bearing locknut. Then, separate the driveshaft from the knuckle. Use a block of wood and hammer to gently tap the shaft inward and out of the knuckle.

3. Matchmark the position of each bolt that fastens the transverse link to the strut—its angle of installation must be restored, or alignment will be affected. Then, remove the nuts and bolts that fasten the radius rod and transverse link to the knuckle.

4. Gently pry the driveshaft out of the rear axle, using a small, flat lever on either side.

5. Install in reverse order, making sure to align matchmarks for the transverse link mounting bolts. Torque the wheel bearing locknut to 174-231 ft. lbs., the transverse link-to-knuckle nut (holding the position of the bolt) to 72-87 ft. lbs. and the radius rod-to-knuckle bolt to 72-87 ft. lbs.

OVERHAUL

This shaft is identical with the front driveshaft covered earlier under Manual Trasaxle.

REAR AXLE
Identification

All 1200, B210 and 210 Datsun models covered in this guide utilize a solid (non-independent) rear axle. On the 1200 and B210 models, the rear axle assembly is attached to the frame through semi-elliptical leaf springs and telescopic shock abosrbers. The rear axle of the 210 models is suspended through coil springs and links, and damped with telescopic shock absorbers. There are no variations or options in terms of axle usage for a given model.

Determining Gear Ratio

Determining the axle ratio of any given axle can be a very useful tool to the contemporary car owner. Axle ratios are a major factor in a vehicle's fuel mileage, so the car buyer of today should know both what he or she is looking for, and what the salesperson is talking about. Knowledge of axle ratios is also valuable to the owner/mechanic who is shopping through salvage yards for a used axle, who is repairing his or her own rear axle, or who is changing rear axle ratios by changing rear axles.

The rear axle ratio is said to have a certain ratio, say 4.11. It is called a 4.11 rear although the 4.11 actually means 4.11 to 1 (4.11:1). This means that the driveshaft will turn 4.11 times for every turn of the rear wheels. The number 4.11 is determined by dividing the number of teeth on the pinion gear into the number of teeth on the ring gear. In the case of a 4.11 rear, there could be 9 teeth on the pinion and 37 teeth on the ring gear ($37 \div 9 = 4.11$). This provides a sure way, although troublesome, of determining your rear axle's ratio. The axle must be drained and the rear cover removed to do this, and then the teeth counted.

A much easier method is to jack up the car and safely support it with jackstands, so BOTH rear wheels are off the ground. Block the front wheels, set the parking brake and put the transmission in Neutral. Make a calk mark on the rear wheel and the driveshaft. Turn the rear wheel one complete revolution and count the number of turns that the driveshaft makes (having an assistant here to count one or the other is helpful). The number of turns the driveshaft makes in one complete revolution of the rear wheel is an approximation of the rear axle ratio.

Differential

NOTE: *All differential service should be performed by a professional mechanic, especially one well versed in differential repair. A great deal of experience and many*

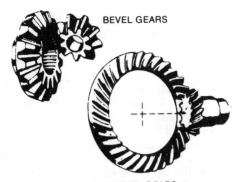

Bevel gears

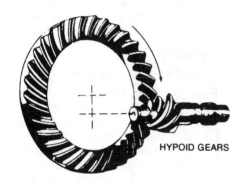

Hypoid gears

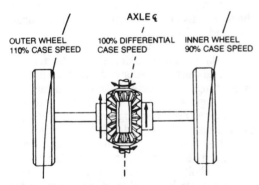

Differential action during cornering

special tools are required in servicing a differential; this is not an area the owner/mechanic should tackle without experience.

The rear axle on the 1200, B210 and 210 models must transmit power through a 90 degree bend. To accomplish this, straight cut bevel gears or spiral cut bevel gears were originally used. This type of gear drive is satisfactory for differential side gears, but since the centerline of the gears must intersect, they are not suitable for ring and pinion gears (main drive gears in all differentials). The lowering of the driveshaft brought about a variation of bevel gears called the hypoid gear. This type of

gear does not require a meeting of the gear centerlines and can therefore be underslung, relative to the centerline of the ring gear.

Operation

The differential is an arrangement of gears which permits the rear wheels to turn at different speeds when cornering and divides the torque between the axle shafts. The differential gears are mounted on a pinion shaft and the gears are free to rotate on this shaft. The pinion shaft is fitted in a bore in the differential case and is at right angles to the axle shafts.

Power flow through the differential is as follows. The drive pinion, which is turned by the driveshaft, turns the ring gear. The ring gear, which is bolted to the differential case, rotates the case. The differential pinion forces the pinion gears against the side gears. In cases where both wheels have equal traction, the pinion gears do not rotate on the pinion shaft, because the input force of the pinion gear is divided equally between the two side gears. Consequently, the pinion gears revolve with the pinion shaft, although they do not rotate on the pinion shaft itself. The side gears, which are splined to the axle shafts, and meshed with the pinion gears, rotate the axle shafts.

When it becomes necessary to turn a corner, the differential becomes effective and allows the axle shafts to rotate at different speeds. As the inner wheel slows down, the side gear splined to the inner wheel axle shaft also slows down. The pinion gears act as balancing levers by maintianing equal tooth loads to both gears while allowing unequal speeds of rotation at the axle shafts. If the vehicle speed remains constant, and the inner wheel slows down to 90 percent of vehicle speed, the outer wheel will speed up to 110 percent.

Axle Shaft, Bearing and Seal
REMOVAL AND INSTALLATION

NOTE: *Bearings must be pressed on and off the shaft with an arbor press. Unless you have access to one, it is inadvisable to attempt any repair work on the axle shaft and bearing assemblies.*

1. Remove the hub cap or wheel cover. Loosen the lug nuts.

2. Raise the rear of the car and support it safely on stands.

3. Remove the rear wheel. Remove the four brake backing plate retaining nuts. Detach the parking brake linkage from the brake backing plate.

4. Attach a slide hammer to the axle shaft and remove it. Use the slide hammer and a two

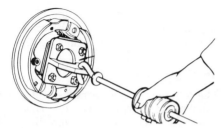

Removing axle on 1200, B210 and 210 models using a slide hammer

pronged puller to remove the oil seal from the housing.

NOTE: *If a slide hammer is not available, the axle can sometimes be pried out using pry bars on opposing sides of the hub. If endplay is found to be excessive, the bearing should be replaced. Shimming the bearing is not recommended as this ignores endplay of the bearing itself and could result in improper seating of the bearing.*

5. Using a chisel, carefully nick the bearing retainer in three or four places. The retainer does not have to be cut, only collapsed enough to allow the bearing retainer to be slid off the shaft.

6. Pull or press the old bearing off and install the new one by pressing it into position.

7. Install the outer bearing retainer with its raised surface facing the wheel hub, and then install the bearing and the inner bearing retainer in that order on the axle shaft.

8. With the smaller chamfered side of the inner bearing retainer facing the bearing, press on the retainer. The edge of the retainer should fully touch the bearing.

9. Clean the oil seal seat in the rear axle housing. Apply a thin coat of chassis grease.

10. Using a seal installation tool, drive the oil seal into the rear axle housing. Wipe a thin coat of bearing grease on the lips of the seal.

11. Determine the number of retainer gaskets which will give the correct bearing-to-outer retainer clearance of 0.25mm.

12. Insert the axle shaft assembly into the axle housing, being careful not to damage the seal. Ensure that the shaft splines engage those of the differential pinion. Align the vent holes of the gasket and the outer bearing retainer. Install the retaining bolts.

13. Install the nuts on the bolts and tighten them evenly, and in a criss-cross pattern, to 20 ft. lbs.

Differential Carrier

REMOVAL AND INSTALLATION

1. Raise the car and support it securely via the outer sections of the axle. Drain the gear lube.

2. Remove the propeller shaft as described above. Remove the axle shafts as also described above.

3. Support the differential carrier (which forms the nose of the axle housing). Loosen and remove the bolts attaching the carrier, pull it out of the axle housing, and remove it. Remove the gasket from the housing.

4. To install the carrier, assemble a new gasket to the differential housing, position the carrier onto the front of the housing so the boltholes line up and then install the bolts finger tight. Tighten alternately in several stages to 12-17 ft. lbs.

5. Complete the installation by installing the propeller shaft and axle shafts as described above.

Axle Housing

REMOVAL AND INSTALLATION

1. Block the front wheels to keep the car from rolling. Support the car by the body on both sides. Also support the center of the differential housing with a floorjack.

2. Remove the rear wheels. Mark the relationship of the U-joint parts and then disconnect the driveshaft at the companion flange by removing the attaching bolts and nuts.

3. Disconnect the brake hydraulic hose at the pipe connection mounted on the body, drain the fluid and cap the openings.

4. Remove the lower shock absorber mounting bolts on either side. Then, shorten the shock and work the lower end out of the bracket by pushing the lower end straight upward.

5. Lower the housing very gradually to control the release of spring pressure. When the coil springs are fully extended, separate them from the mounts located on the axle. Then, raise the axle back to its normal ride height. Remove the bolts, nuts, and washers from the upper and lower links, where they mount to the axle assembly. Then, lower and remove the axle.

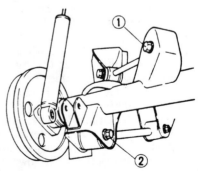

Disconnecting the upper and lower links on coil spring-equipped cars

6. If the car has leaf springs, lower the axle until the springs have lost their tension, unbolt the spring shackles, and then remove the axle assembly.

7. To install the unit if the car has leaf springs, balance it on a floorjack and position it squarely under the springs or spring mounts. Install the leaf spring shackles and nuts.

8. If the car has coil springs, first position the axle where it normally rides and then install the bolts and washers fastening the upper and lower links to the axle. Install the nuts and torque to 51-58 ft. lbs. Then lower the axle until there is sufficient clearance between the spring mounts on the body and axle for installation of the springs.

9. Install coil springs between the axle and body mounts. Raise the axle back up until the lower ends of the shocks will reach the shock mounts located on the axle. Install the lower shock nut and bolt and torque to 51-58 ft. lbs.

10. Uncap the brake tubes and connect the flared fittings, torquing the nut to 11-13 ft. lbs.

11. Reconnect the driveshaft companion flange, torquing the bolts to 17-24 ft. lbs.

12. Install the wheels, torquing the lugnuts to specified torque and lower the car to the ground. Retighten the link bushing nuts at the body and axle now that the axle has reached normal ride height.

13. Thoroughly bleed the brake system.

Suspension and Steering

8

FRONT SUSPENSION

All models covered in this book use MacPherson strut front suspension. In this type of suspension, each strut combines the function of coil spring and shock absorber. The spindle is mounted to the lower part of the strut through a single ball joint. No upper suspension arm is required in this design. The lower suspension arm is bolted to the front subframe assembly.

MacPherson Strut

REMOVAL AND INSTALLATION

1200, B210, 210

1. Jack up the car and support it safely. Remove the wheel.
2. Disconnect and plug the brake hose. Remove the brake caliper as outlined in Chapter 9. Remove the disc and hub as described in this chapter. On some 1200 models and early B210s with drum front brakes, loosen the brake tube connecting nut, remove the brake hose locking spring, withdraw the plate, and remove the brake hose from the strut assembly bracket.
3. Disconnect the tension rod and stabilizer bar from the transverse link.
4. Unbolt the steering arm. Pry the control arm down to detach it from the strut.
5. Place a jack under the bottom of the strut.
6. Open the hood and remove the nuts holding the top of the strut.
7. Lower the jack slowly and cautiously until the strut assembly can be removed.
8. Align the studs on the top of the strut with the boltholes in the wheel house, and work the studs through the boltholes. Then, raise the control arm and attach it to the strut. Install new self-locking nuts onto the top of the strut.
9. Connect the tension rod and stabilizer bar to the transverse link.
10. Install the brake drum or disc, hub, and

caliper in reverse of the above (refer to Chapter 9 for additional detail).
11. Install the wheel. Bleed the brake system thoroughly.

Sentra

1. Raise the vehicle and support it by the body or front suspension crossmember. Remove the wheel.
2. Detach the brake tube where it is mounted to the strut (the tube need not be disconnected).
3. Support the transverse link with a jack. Remove the nuts and washers which retain the strut at the top from the top of the wheelhouse.
4. Make sure the strut is supported at the bottom. Mark the relationship between the through-bolts that attach the steering knuckle to the strut. Then, remove the nuts, washers, and the through-bolts.
5. Back the strut out of the knuckle and work it downward and out of the car.
6. Align the studs on the top of the strut with the boltholes in the wheel house, work the studs through the boltholes, and then slide the bracket on the bottom of the strut over the steering knuckle so all boltholes align.
7. Install the through bolts, turning them to align the matchmarks made earlier. Install the washers and nuts and torque the nuts (without

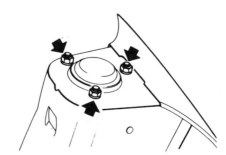

Front top strut mounting bolts. All models similar

Troubleshooting Basic Steering and Suspension Problems

Problem	Cause	Solution
Hard steering (steering wheel is hard to turn)	• Low or uneven tire pressure • Loose power steering pump drive belt • Low or incorrect power steering fluid • Incorrect front end alignment • Defective power steering pump • Bent or poorly lubricated front end parts	• Inflate tires to correct pressure • Adjust belt • Add fluid as necessary • Have front end alignment checked/adjusted • Check pump • Lubricate and/or replace defective parts
Loose steering (too much play in the steering wheel)	• Loose wheel bearings • Loose or worn steering linkage • Faulty shocks • Worn ball joints	• Adjust wheel bearings • Replace worn parts • Replace shocks • Replace ball joints
Car veers or wanders (car pulls to one side with hands off the steering wheel)	• Incorrect tire pressure • Improper front end alignment • Loose wheel bearings • Loose or bent front end components • Faulty shocks	• Inflate tires to correct pressure • Have front end alignment checked/adjusted • Adjust wheel bearings • Replace worn components • Replace shocks
Wheel oscillation or vibration transmitted through steering wheel	• Improper tire pressures • Tires out of balance • Loose wheel bearings • Improper front end alignment • Worn or bent front end components	• Inflate tires to correct pressure • Have tires balanced • Adjust wheel bearings • Have front end alignment checked/adjusted • Replace worn parts
Uneven tire wear	• Incorrect tire pressure • Front end out of alignment • Tires out of balance	• Inflate tires to correct pressure • Have front end alignment checked/adjusted • Have tires balanced

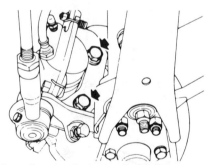

Brake caliper-to-strut mounting bolts

turning the bolts) to 51-65 ft. lbs. on 1982-83 models and 72-87 ft. lbs. on later models.

8. Install the washers and nuts onto the wheelhouse studs and torque the nuts to 11-17 ft. lbs. on 1982 models, and 46-53 ft. lbs. on 1983-88 models.

9. Attach the brake tube, remove the supports and lower the car.

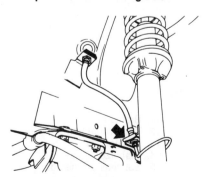

Disconnect brake hose before removing struts

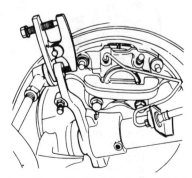

Removing side rod ball joint using ball joint puller. Forked ball joint tool may also be used

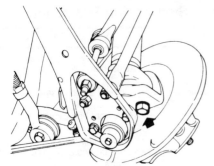

1200 and B210 strut-to-control arm/steering knuckle bolts. 210 similar

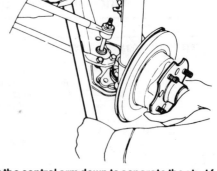

Pry the control arm down to separate the strut from the knuckle

MacPherson Strut Coil Spring and Shock Absorber

REMOVAL AND INSTALLATION

CAUTION: *The coil springs are under considerable tension, and can exert pressure to cause serious injury. Disassemble the struts only if the proper tools are available, and use extreme caution.*

Coil springs on all models must be removed with the aid of a coil spring compressor. If you don't have one, don't try to improvise by using something else; you could risk injury. The Nissan coil spring compressor is Special Tool ST3565S001 or variations of that number. Ba-

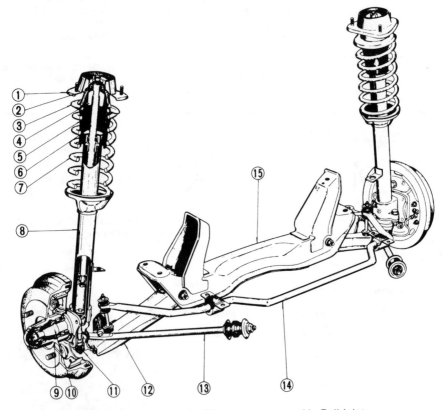

1. Strut mounting insulator	6. Piston rod
2. Strut mounting bearing	7. Front spring
3. Upper spring seat	8. Strut assembly
4. Bumper rubber	9. Hub assembly
5. Dust cover	10. Spindle

11. Ball joint
12. Transverse link
13. Tension rod
14. Stabilizer
15. Suspension member

1200, B210 and 210 series front suspension

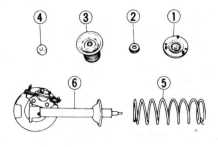

1. Strut mounting insulator
2. Bearing
3. Spring upper seat and dust cover
4. Damper rubber
5. Coil spring
6. Strut assembly

Exploded view of 1200 and B210 strut, others similar

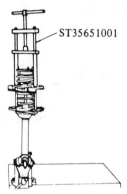

ST35651001

Datsun spring compressor correctly mounted on coil spring

sically, they are all the same tool. These are the recommended compressors, although they are probably not the only spring compressors which will work. Always follow manufacturer's instructions when operating a spring compressor. You can now buy cartridge type shock absorbers for many Nissans and Datsuns. However, installation procedures are not the same as those given here. In the case of these after-market shocks, always follow the instructions that come with the shock absorbers.

To remove the coil spring(s), you must first remove the strut assembly from the vehicle. See above for procedures and follow the caution.

1. Secure the strut assembly in a vise.

2. Attach the spring compressor to the spring, leaving the top few coils free.

3. Remove the dust cap from the top of the strut to expose the center nut, if a dust cap is provided.

4. Compress the spring just far enough to permit the strut insulator to be turned by hand. Remove the self-locking center nut.

5. Take out the strut insulator, strut bearing, oil seal, upper spring seat and bound bumper rubber from the top of the strut. Note their sequence of removal and be sure to assemble them in the same order.

6. Remove the spring with the spring compressor still attached.

NOTE: *If the replacement of any strut component parts is found to be necessary, make sure that parts are the same brand as those used in the strut assembly.*

7. Reinstall the spring fully compressed. Make sure you assemble the unit with the shock absorber piston rod fully extended. Then, install the strut insulator, bearing, oil seal, upper spring seat and bumper rubber in the correct sequence of installation (opposite the removal sequence).

8. Install the strut insulator and self-locking center nut. Torque the nut to 47-53 ft. lbs. Install the dust cap, if there is one. When assembling, take care that the rubber spring seats, both top and bottom, and the spring are positioned in their grooves before releasing the spring.

9. To remove the shock absorber: Remove the dust cap, if equipped, and push the piston rod down until it bottoms. With the piston in this position, loosen and remove the gland packing shock absorber retainer. This calls for Nissan Special Tool ST35500001, but you should be able to loosen it with a pipe wrench (very carefully) or by tapping it around with a drift.

NOTE: *If the gland tube is dirty, clean it before removing it to prevent dirt from contaminating the fluid inside the strut tube.*

9. Remove the O-ring from the top of the piston rod guide and lift out the piston rod together with the cylinder. Drain all of the fluid from the strut and shock components into a suitable container. Clean all parts; do not use a mineral based solvent on any of the rubber parts.

10. After installing the cylinder and piston rod assembly (the shock absorber kit) in the outer casing, remove the piston rod guide, if equipped, from the cylinder and pour the correct amount of fresh fluid into the cylinder and strut outer casing. Shock absorber kits list the correct amount of fluid to use, or check the following chart. Use only a high quality fluid made specifically for hydraulic struts (Nissan Strut Oil or equivalent).

NOTE: *When tightening the gland packing, extend the piston rod about 3 to 5 inches from the end of the outer casing to expel most of the air from the strut.*

11. After the kit is installed, bleed the air from the system in the following manner: Hold the strut with its bottom end facing down. Pull

Shock Strut Refill Capacities

Year	Model	Shock Make	Capacity
1973	1200	AMPCO (ATSUGI)	280cc (17.1 cu. in.)
1974–78	B210	AMPCO (ATSUGI)	325cc (19.83 cu. in.)
1979 and later	210 (U.S.)	ATSUGI	325cc (19.83 cu. in.)
	210 (1.2L Canadian)	ATSUGI	260cc (16 cu. in.)
		TOKICO	230cc (14.5 cu. in.)

the piston rod out as far as it will go. Turn the strut upside down and push the piston in as far as it will go. Repeat this procedure several times until an equal pressure is felt on both the

Removing the shock absorber from the gland tube

Filling the shock assembly with oil

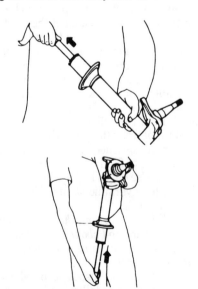

Bleeding air from strut unit

pull-out and the push-in strokes of the piston rods.

TESTING SHOCK ABSORBER ACTION

Shock absorbers require replacement if the vehicle fails to recover quickly after a large bump is encountered, if there is a tendency for the vehicle to sway or nose dive excessively, or, sometimes, if the suspension is overly susceptible to vibration.

A good way to test the shocks is to intermittently apply downward pressure to one corner of the vehicle until it is moving up and down for almost the full suspension travel, then release it and watch the recovery. If the vehicle bounces slightly about one more time and then comes to rest, the shock absorbers are serviceable. If the vehicle goes on bouncing, the shocks require replacement.

Ball Joint

INSPECTION

The lower ball joint should be replaced when play becomes excessive. Nissan does not publish specifications on just what constitutes excessive play, relying instead on a method of determining the force (in inch pounds) required to keep the ball joint turning. This method is not very helpful to the owner mechanic since it involves removing the ball joint, which is what we are trying to avoid in the first place. An effective way to determine ball joint play is to jack up the car until the wheel is just a couple of inches off the ground and the ball joint is unloaded (meaning you can't jack directly underneath the ball joint). Place a long bar under the tire and move the wheel and tire assembly up and down. Keep one hand on top of the tire while you are doing this. If there is over ¼inch of play at the top of the tire, the ball joint is probably bad. This is assuming that the wheel bearings are in good shape and properly adjusted. As a double check on this, have someone watch the ball joint while you move the tire up and down with the bar. If you can see considerable play, besides feeling play at the top of the wheel, the ball joint needs replacing.

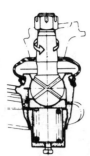

Cross section of a ball joint. Note plug at the bottom for grease nipple

REMOVAL AND INSTALLATION

All Models Except Sentra

The ball joint should be greased every 30,000 miles. There is a plugged hole in the bottom of the joint for the installation of a grease fitting.

1. Raise and support the car so that the wheels hang freely. Remove the wheel.

2. Unbolt the tension rod and stabilizer bar from the transverse link.

3. Remove the bolt and press the ballstud for the steering rod out of the steering arm.

4. Unbolt the strut from the steering arm.

5. Unbolt the ball joint from the transverse link.

6. Remove the cotter pin and ball joint stud nut. Press the ball joint from the steering arm.

7. Install the new balljoint stud through the steering arm. Install the nut and torque to 40 ft. lbs. Then, torque further very gradually, watching for alignment of the castellations on the nut with the cotter pin hole in the ballstud up to a maximum of 72 ft. lbs. Install a new cotter pin.

8. Bolt the balljoint to the transverse link, torquing the bolts to 37-44 ft. lbs. Bolt the steering arm to the strut, torquing the bolts to 53-72 ft. lbs. (33-44 ft. lbs. on Canadian 1.2 L cars).

9. Reconnect the steering rod to the steering arm. Torque the nut to 37 ft. lbs. Then, turn the nut farther just enough to install the cotter pin into the ballstud and install the cotter pin (maximum torque 44 ft. lbs.).

10. Grease the joint after installation, forcing grease in until the old grease begins to squeeze out of the joint.

Sentra

The Sentra lower ball joints can be unbolted from the lower control arm. The ball joint is attached to the arm by a plate with three bolts through it, from the top of the lower arm. The nuts screw up onto these bolts from underneath the joint.

1. Remove the driveshaft (refer to Driveshaft Removal for procedures).

2. Remove the lower ball joint by removing the three nuts and separating the ball joint from the steering knuckle using a ball joint removal tool.

3. Install the new ball joint in the reverse order of removal. Torque the balljoint stud nut to 25-36 ft. lbs. and the nuts fastening the balljoint assembly to the transverse link to 40-47 ft. lbs.

4. Lubricate the ball joint after assembly.

Sway Bar

REMOVAL AND INSTALLATION

1. Raise the car and support it securely. Remove the wheels for additional working room.

2. Disconnect the connecting rods that link both ends of the stabilizer bar to the transverse link. Disconnect each link at both ends. On 1987-88 Sentras, in doing this, place a wrench on the flats located near the center of the link to oppose torque applied to the lower attaching nut.

3. Have someone hold the stabilizer bar in position. Remove the bolts that retain the brackets fastening the stabilizer bar to the car body. Remove the stabilizer bar.

4. Inspect all brackets, bushings, spacers and washers and replace parts as necessary.

5. Bolt the stabilizer bar to the car body. Then, assemble the links and their related parts, installing bolts or nuts attaching them to both the stabilizer bar and to the transverse link. Torque the bolts fastening the stabilizer bar to the body to 12-15 ft. lbs. On 1986 Sentras, torque the link nut to 72-96 in. lbs. On 1987-88 Sentras, torque the upper attaching nut for this link to 25-33 ft. lbs. and the lower attaching nut to 12-16 ft. lbs.

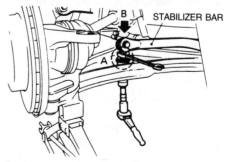

When disconnecting the link connecting the stabilizer bar with the transverse link on 1987-88 Sentras, oppose the torque on the link at "B" with an opposing wrench installed at "A"

Tension Rod

REMOVAL AND INSTALLATION

Model 210s use a tension rod to handle fore and aft torque on the lower control arm, which uses a single inner mounting point.

1. Raise the car and support it securely. Remove the front wheels.

2. Remove the nut from the front end of the tension rod, whcih is located on a body mount, collecting the washer and bushing underneath and *carefully noting their locations.*

3. Remove the two bolts which fasten the rod to the control arm. Then, slide the rod rearward and out of the body mount.

4. Disassemble all remaining spacers, bushings, and washers *carefully noting their locations.* Inspect all carefully for cracks, breakage, or brittleness and replace as necessary.

5. Reassemble the inner washers, bushings and spacer. Insert the rod through the body mount. Install the mounting nut and torque it to 33-37 ft. lbs. Install the mounting bolts connecting the rod to the lower control arm and torque them to 37-44 ft. lbs. Install the wheels and lower the car.

Lower Control Arm (Transverse Link) and Ball Joint

REMOVAL AND INSTALLATION

NOTE: *A ball joint removal tool of either the forked type or the puller type is needed.*

1. Jack up the vehicle and support it with jackstands; remove the wheel.

2. Remove the splash board, if so equipped. If the car has front wheel drive, remove the driveshaft as described in Chapter 7.

3. Remove the cotter pin and castle nut from the side rod (steering arm) ball joint and separate the ball joint from the side rod.

4. Separate the steering knuckle arm from the MacPherson strut.

5. Disconnect the tension rod and stabilizer bar from the lower arm, if the car has them.

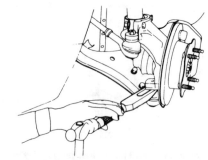

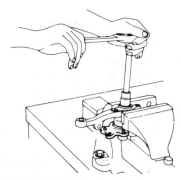

Separating ball joint from the knuckle using forked ball joint tool

Removing the ball joint

6. Remove the nuts and bolts connecting the lower control arm (transverse link) to the suspension crossmember on all models.

7. Remove the lower control arm (transverse link) with the suspension ball joint and knuckle arm still attached.

8. Check all rubber parts, such as tension rod and stabilizer bar bushings, to be sure they are not deteriorated or cracked, and replace if necessary. Also examine tension rod and stabilizer bar for evidence of damage and replace if necessary.

9. Assemble the control arm, temporarily tighten the nuts and/or bolts securing the control arm to the suspension crossmember. Tighten them fully only after the car is sitting on its wheels.

10. Install the stabilizer bar as described above, tightening nuts loosely. Be sure the bar is not closer to either side, but is located at the middle. Then, final tighten the mounting bolts and nuts. If the car has a tension rod, install that as described above.

11. Bolt the steering knuckle arm to the strut as described above. Install the balljoint stud to the steering knuckle as described above.

12. If the car has front wheel drive, reinstall the driveshaft.

13. Install the splashboard, if so equipped. Lubricate the ball joints after assembly.

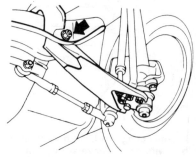

Removing bolt connecting control arm to crossmember—210

Knuckle and Spindle

REMOVAL AND INSTALLATION

On the 210 and B210, the knuckle and spindle are integral with the MacPherson Strut. Remove the strut as described above to remove the knuckle.

1982-86 Sentra

1. Raise the vehicle and support it securely. Remove the wheels. Refer to Chapter 9 and remove the brake caliper as described there.

2. Remove the cotter pin from the outer end of the driveshaft. Install two nuts on the studs of the wheel hub. Use a prybar between them to keep the hub from turning; loosen the hub nut.

3. Remove the cotter pin and nut from the steering rod balljoint stud that connects with the steering knuckle. Then, use a ball joint remover to press the stud out of the steering knuckle.

4. Remove the three nuts attaching the balljoint to the transverse link. Discard the old nuts and supply new ones.

5. Drain the transaxle fluid. Then, gently pry the driveshaft out of the transaxle, being careful not to damage the grease seal. Insert a bar of about the same diameter as the driveshaft into the transaxle to keep the side gear in position.

6. Support the hub. Remove the nuts and bolts attaching the hub to the bottom of the strut. Then, remove the hub, knuckle, and driveshaft as a unit. Remove the driveshaft attaching nut and use a puller to pull the hub off the driveshaft.

7. Remove the circlip that retains the driveshaft in the transaxle and replace it with a new one.

8. Insert the driveshaft into the wheel hub and start the nut. Assemble the driveshaft/hub and knuckle assembly to the strut with the nuts and bolts, torquing to 51-65 ft. lbs.

9. Remove the bar inserted into the transaxle earlier. Align the splines and then insert the driveshaft. Tap it lightly at the flange of the slide joint cover to insert it into the transaxle side gear until the circlip locks securely. Test to make sure the circlip has locked by pulling outward by hand.

10. Refill the transaxle to the correct level with the approved fluid. Bolt the ball joint to the transverse link, torquing the bolts to 40-47 ft. lbs.

11. Install the balljoint stud into the steering knuckle. Install the nut and torque to 31 ft. lbs. Turn the nut further until castellations align with the cotter pin hole up to a maximum torque of 40 ft. lbs.

12. Torque the nut on the outer end of the driveshaft to pull the shaft through the hub and tighten the nut. Use the same method to hold the wheel hub still as in removal and torque the nut to 87-145 ft. lbs. Torque to the minimum figure and then turn the nut just enough farther to align castellations and the cotter pin hole. Install a new cotter pin.

13. Install the steering rod balljoint nut into the steering knuckle. Torque the nut to 22 ft. lbs. Then, turn the nut just enough farther to align castellations and the cotter pin hole (maximum torque it 36 ft. lbs. Install a new cotter pin.

14. Install the brake caliper as described in Chapter 9. Install the wheels.

1987-88 Sentra

1. Raise the vehicle and support it securely. Remove the wheels. Have a helper depress the brake pedal as you loosen the locknut for the wheel bearing.

2. Refer to Chapter 9 and remove the brake caliper as described there (without disconnecting the hydraulic line). Then, remove the cotter pin and castellated nut and press the ball joint for the steering tie rod out of the steering knuckle.

3. Turn the wheel bearing locknut until it is flush with the end of the driveshaft. Then, tap the nut lightly with a soft hammer to force the driveshaft to begin sliding out of the wheel hub. Cover the rubber boots with a rag to protect them. Then remove the driveshafts as described in Chapter 7. Note that, for automatic transmission models, the right driveshaft *must* be removed first.

4. Matchmark the upper nut and bolt where the steering knuckle is bolted to the bottom of the MacPherson strut (to maintain front end alignment). Then, remove the bolts and nuts.

5. Loosen the lower ball joint nut a few turns. Press the ball joint stud so it becomes loose in the transverse link with a ball joint removal tool (J25730-A or equivalent). Then, remove the ball joint attaching nut and remove the steering knuckle from the transverse link.

6. Position the steering knuckle and fit the lower balljoint ballstud through it. Start the nut onto the ballstud and then torque it to 43-54 ft. lbs.

7. Position the steering knuckle onto the bottom of the strut, install the attaching bolts, and align the matchmarks. Then, carefully hold the bolts in position and install and torque the nuts to 72-87 ft. lbs.

8. Install the driveshaft as described in Chapter 7.

9. Install the brake caliper as described in Chapter 9. Install the steering tie rod balljoint stud into the knuckle, install the nut, and torque it to 22 ft. lbs. Then, turn it farther, to

the point where the first castellation lines up with the cotter pin hole (maximum torque 29 ft. lbs.) and install the cotter pin.

10. Have someone apply the brakes and torque the wheel bearing locknut to 145-203 ft. lbs.

Front Wheel Bearings
WHEEL BEARING PACKING AND REPLACEMENT

It is important to remember that wheel bearings, although basically very durable, are subject to many elements that can quickly destroy them. Grit, misalignment, and improper preload are especially brutal to any roller bearing assembly. And like any bearing (ball, roller, needle, etc.), lubrication is extremely important.

1. Loosen the lug nuts on the wheel you intend to fix. Jack up the car and safely support it with jackstands.

2. Remove the wheel and tire. Remove the brake drum or brake caliper, following the procedure(s) in Chapter 9.

3. It is not necessary to remove the drum or disc from the hub. The outer wheel bearing will come off with the hub. Simply pull the hub and disc or drum assembly toward you and off the spindle. (Follow hub removal procedures for Sentra). Be sure to catch the bearing before it falls to the ground.

4. From the inner side of the hub, remove the inner grease seal, and lift the inner bearing from the hub. Discard the grease seal, as you will be replacing it with a new one.

5. Clean the bearings carefully in solvent, and allow them to air dry (or blow them out with compressed air, if available). You risk leaving bits of lint in the races if you dry them with a rag. Clean the grease caps, nuts, spindle, and the races in the hub thoroughly, and allow the parts to dry.

6. Inspect the bearings carefully. If they show any signs of wear (pitting, cracks, scoring, brinelling, burns, etc.), replace them along with the bearing cups in which they run in the hub. Do not mix old and new parts; you won't regret replacing everything if the parts look marginal.

7. If the cups are worn at all, remove them from the hub, using a brass rod as a drift. Use care not to damage the cup seats with the drift.

8. If the old cups were removed, install the new inner and outer cups into the hub, using either a tool made for the purpose, or a socket or piece of pipe of a large enough diameter to press on the outside rim of the cup only.

CAUTION: *Be careful not to cock the bearings in the hub. If they are not fully seated,* *the bearings will be impossible to adjust properly.*

9. Pack the inside of the hub and cups with grease. Pack the inside of the grease cap while you're at it, but do not install the cap into the hub.

10. Pack the inner bearing with grease. Place a large glob of grease into the palm of one hand and push the inner bearing through it with a sliding motion. The grease must be forced through the side of the bearing and in between each roller. Continue until the grease begins to ooze out the other side through the gaps between the rollers; the bearing must be completely packed with grease. Install the inner bearing into its cup in the hub, then press a new grease seal into place over it.

11. Install the hub and rotor or drum assembly onto the spindle. Pack the outer bearing with grease in the same manner as the inner bearing, then install the outer bearing into place in the hub.

12. Apply a thin coat of grease to the washer and the threaded portion of the spindle, then loosely install the washer and adjusting nut. Refer to the bearing preload adjustment in Chapter 1 and adjust the bearings.

Front Hub and Bearing
REMOVAL, REPACKING AND INSTALLATION
Sentra

The Sentra front wheel bearings are fitted using spacers, which fit between the bearing race in the steering knuckle and the outer wheel bearing. The spacers are available from Nissan dealers and parts stores, and are numbered as to their size. New spacers must be installed whenever the knuckle is replaced, or when the bearings and/or their races are worn to an extent that end play is noticeable at the front wheel. When new grease seals or bearings are installed, new spacers should be installed. Make sure they have the same mark as the spacers you have removed. If there is not much wear in your bearings, etc., and you are just repacking bearings, the old spacer can be reused.

1. With the front hub and halfshaft disassembled, install the outside grease seal and bearing into the wheel hub with a suitable drift.

2. Pack the seal lip with a quality multi-purpose wheel bearing grease. Be sure that the grease seal is facing in the proper direction. Press the bearing into the inner race to install. Do not force the bearing.

3. Install the spacer. Spacer numbering ranges from number 05 to number 22, with each succeeding spacer being 0.06mm thicker.

4. Tighten the bolts securing the hub to the disc rotor.

5. Assemble the halfshaft into the knuckle and wheel hub. Install the rotor and hub assembly.

6. Tighten the hub nut to 87-145 ft. lbs.

7. Spin the wheel several times in both directions.

8. Measure wheel bearing preload. The rotation starting torque of the wheel bearings is ½-2 lbs. Measured at the wheel hub bolt, you should obtain a reading of 3.1 to 10.8 lbs. on a pull scale.

9. If the bearing preload is not in accord with the specifications, reselect the spacer. When any axial endplay is present in the wheel bearing, replace the spacer with a smaller one. If bearing preload is greater and endplay is present, replace spacer with a larger one.

Front End Alignment

The major front end adjustments for the Nissan are given here: caster/ camber, toe, and steering angle. However, we recommend that a professional shop, specializing in front end alignment handle the work. Shops such as this are fully equipped for these procedures, and get the alignment correct the first time, which is something the average owner/mechanic may not do (especially if you do not have access to a hydraulic lift). The usually modest cost of a professional front end alignment job is well worth it when compared to the prospect of an improperly aligned (and unsafe) front end.

CASTER AND CAMBER

Caster is the forward or rearward tilt of the upper end of the kingpin, or the upper ball joint, which results in a slight tilt of the steering axis forward or backward. Rearward tilt is referred to as a positive caster, while forward tilt is referred to as negative caster.

Camber is the inward or outward tilt from the vertical, measured in degrees, of the front wheels at the top. An outward tilt gives the wheel positive camber. Proper camber is critical to assure even tire wear and safe handling.

Since caster and camber are adjusted traditionally by adding or subtracting shims behind the upper control arms, and the Nissans covered in this guide have replaced the upper control arm with the MacPherson strut, the only way to adjust caster and camber is to replace bent or worn parts of the front suspension on most models. On 1987-88 Sentras, the attachment for the steering knuckle, located at the bottom of the strut, has been modified to per-

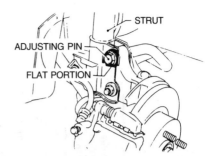

Adjustable camber type strut used on 1987–88 Sentras

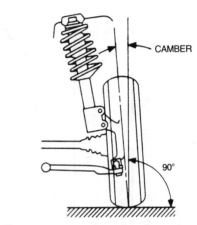

Camber refers to the inward or outward tilt of the wheel. It is adjustable only on 1987–88 Sentras

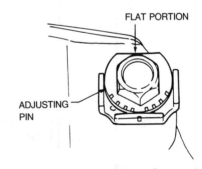

Camber adjustment on 1987–88 Sentras is performed by turning the adjusting pin. See text.

mit adjustment of the camber only. To adjust camber:

1. Raise the vehicle and support it. Remove the wheel.

2. Remove the adjusting pin, which is factory installed with a flat facing downward. Turn the pin 180°—so the flat faces up and reinstall it.

Wheel Alignment Specifications

Year	Model	Caster		Camber		Toe-In (in.)	Steering Axis Inclination (deg.)	Wheel Pivot Ratio (deg)	
		Range (deg)	Preferred Setting (deg.)	Range (deg.)	Preferred Setting (deg.)			Inner Wheel	Outer Wheel
1973	1200	40'–1°40'	1°10'	35'–1°35'	1°05'	0.16–0.24	7°55'	42–44	35–37
1974	B210	1°15'–2°15'	1°45'	40°–1°40'	1°10'	0.079–0.157	7°47'–8°47'	37–39	31–33
1975–78	B210	1°00'–2°30'	1°45'	0°25'–1°55'	1°10'	0.08–0.16	7°32'–9°02'	37–39	31–33
1979–82	210 Sedan, Hatchback	1°40'–3°10'	2°25'	0°–1°30'	0°45'	0.04–0.12	7°50'–9°20'	38–42	31°30'–35°30'
	210 Station Wagon	1°55'–3°25'	2°40'	0°–1°30'	0°45'	0.04–0.12	7°50'–9°20'	38–42	31°30'–35°30'
1982–86	Sentra	45'–2°15'	1°30'	–35'–1°05' ①	0°15'	0.12–0.20	12°10'–13°40'	40–44	31–35
1987	Sentra	1°05'–2°35'	1°47'	–55'–35'	0°15'	–0.04–0.04	13°15'–14°45'	21°30'	20°
1987	Sentra Coupe	1°15'–2°45'	1°57'	–1°05'–25'	–0°37'	–0.04–0.04	13°35'–15°05'	21°36'	20°
1988	Sentra	45°–2°15'	1°30'	–55'–35'	0°45'	–0.020–0.059	13°15'–14°45'	21°36'	20°
1988	Sentra Coupe	55'–2°25'	0°47'	–1°05'–25'	–0°37'	–0.028–0.051	13°35'–15°05'	21°36'	20°
1988	4WD Wagon	0°10'–1°40'	0°55'	–0°50'–0°40'	–0°5'	–0.020–0.059	12°50'–44°20'	22°12'	20°

① 1984–86 (–25–1°05')

3. Reinstall the wheel and lower the vehicle to the floor. Now, the camber may be adjusted by rotating the position of the pin. Each marked increment represents about 15' of camber change.

TOE-IN

Toe is the amount, measured in a fraction of an inch, that the wheels are closer together at one end than the other. Toe-in means that the front wheels are closer together at the front than the rear; toe-out means the rears are closer than the front. Nissans are adjusted to have a slight amount of toe-in. Toe-in is adjusted by turning the tie rod, which has a right hand thread on one end and a left hand thread on the other.

You can check your vehicle's toe-in yourself without special equipment if you make careful measurements. The wheels must be straight ahead.

1. Toe-in can be determined by measuring the distance between the center of the tire treads, at the front of the tire and at the rear. If the tread pattern of your car's tires makes this impossible, you can measure between the edges of the wheel rims, but make sure to move the car forward and measure in a couple of places to void errors caused by bent rims or wheel runout.

2. If the measurement is not within specifications, loosen the locknuts at both ends of the tie rod (the driver's side locknut is left hand threaded).

3. Turn the top of the tie rod toward the front of the car to reduce toe-in, or toward the rear to increase it. When the correct dimension is reached, tighten the locknuts and check the adjustment.

NOTE: *The length of the tie rods must always be equal to each other.*

STEERING ANGLE ADJUSTMENT

The maximum steering angle is adjusted by stopper bolts on the steering arms. Loosen the locknut on the stopper bolt, turn the stopped bolt in or out as required to obtain the proper maximum steering angle and retighten the locknut.

SUSPENSION HEIGHT

Suspension height is adjusted by replacing the springs. Various springs are available for adjustment.

REAR SUSPENSION

There are four basic rear suspension types used on the Nissans and Datsuns covered in this guide. All 1200 and B210 models are equipped with solid (non-independent) rear axles suspended by leaf springs and telescopic shock absorbers. The 1979 and later 210s, including wagons, are equipped with four-link type solid rear axles suspended by coil springs and telescopic shock absorbers. The 1982-86 2WD Nissan Sentras utilize an independent

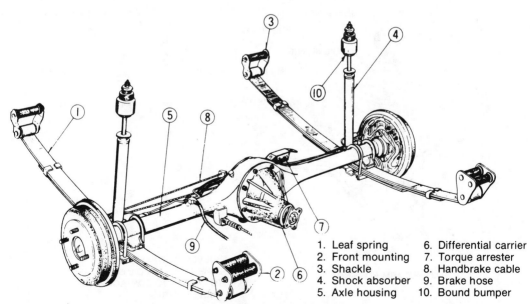

1. Leaf spring	6. Differential carrier
2. Front mounting	7. Torque arrester
3. Shackle	8. Handbrake cable
4. Shock absorber	9. Brake hose
5. Axle housing	10. Bound bumper

1200 and B210 rear suspension

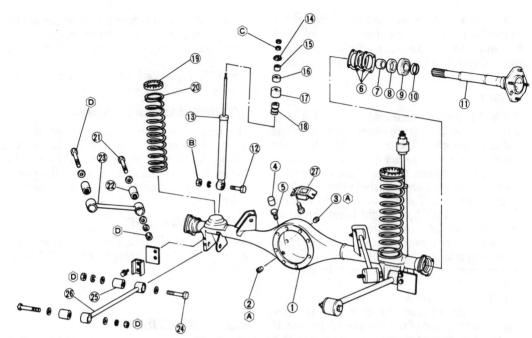

1. Rear axle case
2. Drain plug
3. Filler plug
4. Breather cap
5. Breather
6. Rear axle case end shim
7. Bearing collar
8. Oil seal
9. Rear axle bearing (wheel bearing)
10. Bearing spacer
11. Rear axle shaft
12. Shock absorber lower end bolt
13. Shock absorber assembly
14. Special washer
15. Shock absorber mounting bushing A
16. Shock absorber mounting bushing B
17. Bound bumper cover
18. Bound bumper rubber
19. Shock absorber mounting insulator
20. Coil spring
21. Upper link bushing bolt
22. Upper link bushing
23. Upper link
24. Lower link bushing bolt
25. Lower link bushing
26. Lower link
27. Torque arrester

Tightening torque (ft-lb)
Ⓐ (43–72)
Ⓑ (51–58)
Ⓒ (11–14)
Ⓓ (51–58)

210 rear axle and suspension

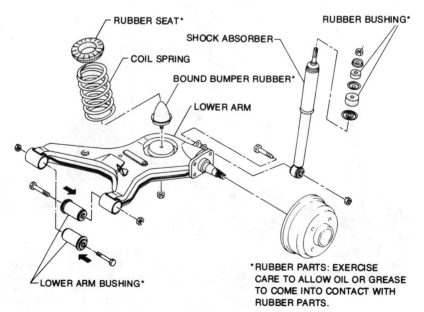

RUBBER SEAT*
RUBBER BUSHING*
SHOCK ABSORBER
COIL SPRING
BOUND BUMPER RUBBER*
LOWER ARM
LOWER ARM BUSHING*

*RUBBER PARTS: EXERCISE CARE TO ALLOW OIL OR GREASE TO COME INTO CONTACT WITH RUBBER PARTS.

Sentra rear suspension—1982–86

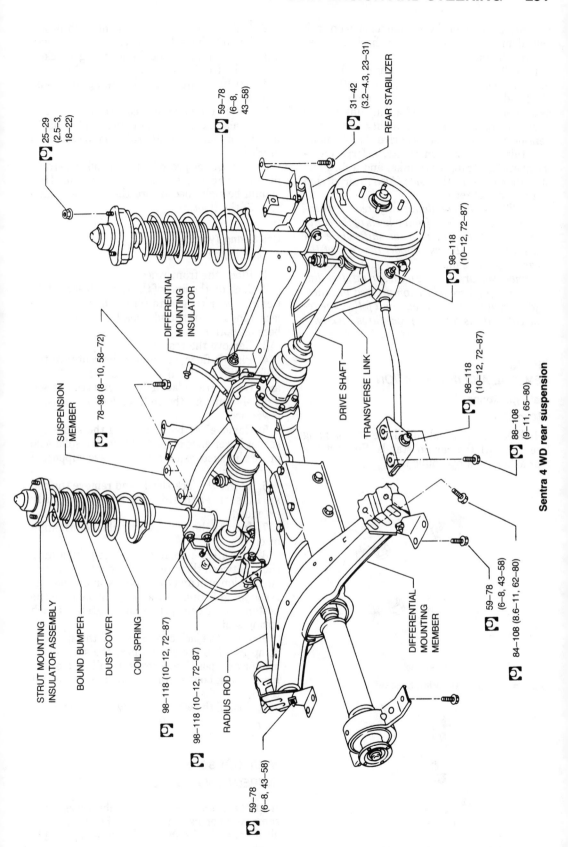

25–29
(2.5–3,
18–22)

59–78
(6–8,
43–58)

31–42
(3.2–4.3, 23–31)

REAR STABILIZER

98–118
(10–12, 72–87)

DIFFERENTIAL
MOUNTING
INSULATOR

78–98 (8–10, 58–72)

SUSPENSION
MEMBER

DRIVE SHAFT

TRANSVERSE LINK

98–118
(10–12, 72–87)

88–108
(9–11, 65–80)

Sentra 4 WD rear suspension

STRUT MOUNTING
INSULATOR ASSEMBLY

BOUND BUMPER

DUST COVER

COIL SPRING

98–118 (10–12, 72–87)

98–118 (10–12, 72–87)

RADIUS ROD

59–78
(6–8, 43–58)

59–78
(6–8, 43–58)

84–108 (8.6–11, 62–80)

DIFFERENTIAL
MOUNTING
MEMBER

rear suspension: one lower control arm on each side, dampened by a telescopic shock absorber and coil spring.

1987-88 models utilize two rear parallel links on either side, combined with a MacPherson strut and a radius rod. The radius rod acts both as a stabilizer bar and as a locating link to help maintain the fore and aft stability of the suspension system. Four wheel drive 1987-88 models utilize: MacPherson struts; a large crossmember; two transverse links; and a fore and aft radius rod on either side. Also incorporated is a rear stabilizer bar.

CAUTION: *Before doing any rear suspension work, block both front wheels of the car to insure that it won't move or shift while you are under it. Always support the rear of the car with jackstands, NOT a jack. Also, remember you are dealing with spring steel that has enough force when compressed to injure you (when released) if you don't follow the removal and installation procedures exactly.*

Springs
REMOVAL AND INSTALLATION
Leaf Type Spring
1200 and B210

1. Raise the rear axle until the wheels hang free. Support the car on stands. Support the rear axle with a hydraulic jack.

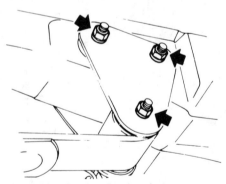

1200 and B210 front spring bracket

1200 and B210 rear spring shackle

2. Unbolt the bottom end of shock absorber.
3. Unbolt the axle from the spring leaves. Unbolt and remove the front spring bracket. Lower the front of the spring to the floor.
4. Unbolt and remove the spring rear shackle.
5. Before reinstallation, coat the front bracket pin, bushing, shackle pin, and shackle bushing with a soap and water solution to serve as a lubricant.
6. Reverse the procedure to install. The front pin nut and the shock absorber mounting should be tightened before the vehicle is lowered to the floor.

Coil Spring Type
210 AND SENTRA

1. Block the front wheels.
2. Jack up the rear of the car high enough to permit working underneath, and place jackstands securely underneath the body members on both sides.
3. Remove the rear wheels.
4. Place a floor jack under the center of the differential carrier if the car has a solid rear axle. On Sentras, place a floor jack so that it will securely support the independent suspension lower arm.
5. Remove the bolts securing the shock absorber lower ends on each side with a solid axle or on the suspension arm you have supported on Sentras.
6. Lower the jack slowly and remove the coil springs on each side after they are fully extended.
7. Inspect the springs for yield, deformation or cracks.
8. Install the springs by first positioning them between their seats on the differential or suspension arm and the rubber seat and its corresponding fitting on the body. Make sure the bottom of the coil springs sit squarely on each spring seat.
9. Raise the jack carefully until the spring is compressed to the point where the suspension arm or axle position permits installation of the lower shock bolt. Install this bolt and torque it to 26-35 ft. lbs.
10. Install the wheels and lower the car to the floor.

Shock Absorber
INSPECTION AND TESTING

Inspect and test the rear shock absorbers in the same manner as outlined for the front shock absorbers. Shocks should always be replaced in pairs.

REMOVAL AND INSTALLATION
Leaf Spring Type
1200 AND B210

1. Jack up the rear of the car and support the rear axle on two stands.
2. Disconnect the lower shock mounting bolt at the spring plate (plenty of penetrating oil is often useful here).
3. From inside the car, remove the rear seat back and disconnect the upper mounting nut.
4. Remove the shock absorber.
5. Install the replacement shock in the reverse of the removal procedure.

210 AND SENTRA

1. Open the trunk and remove the nuts securing the shock absorber upper end to the wheel house panel. Pry off the shock mount covers on the station wagon.
2. Remove the bolt securing the shock absorber lower end to the lower control arm and remove the shock absorber (using penetrating oil if necessary).

NOTE: *When removing the shock absorber lower end from the bracket, squeeze the shock absorber and lift it out to accommodate the embossment inside bracket.*

3. Test the shock absorber action by slowly pulling the piston rod out to full extension. Check for a steady pull with plenty of resistance and no sticking. Now begin to push the rod back, with a steady motion until the shock is fully compressed. The feel of the damping should not be grabby, weak or loose. There should be no evidence of the shock leaking ei-

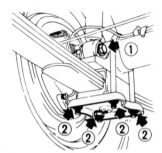

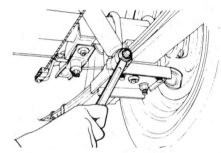

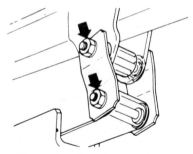

Detach lower shock absorber mount (1) and spring U-bolts (2)—1200 and B210 sedan shown

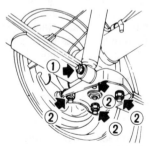

Removing the lower shock absorber nut

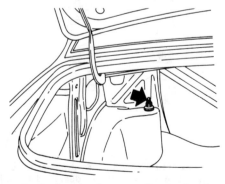

Remove the spring shackle

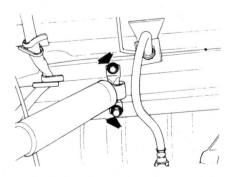

Detach lower shock absorber mount (1) and spring U-bolts (2)—1200 and B210 coupe shown

Rear shock absorber top mounting (sedans)

Upper shock absorber retaining bolts

ther air or oil (or both). Check the piston rod for straightness, and all rubber parts (including mount bushings) for wear, cracks, damage or deformation. Replace entire shock unit if necessary (usually replaced in pairs).

4. Install the shock absorbers in the reverse order of removal.

NOTE: *Tighten shock absorber upper end nut to 11-14 ft. lbs. until it is fully tightened to thread end of piston rod. Then securely tighten lock nut. Tighten lower shock mounting nut to 51-58 ft. lbs.*

MacPherson Struts
REMOVAL AND INSTALLATION
2 WD and 4 WD Sentra

1. Raise the car and support it securely by the body.

2. Remove the nuts and bolts attaching the rear wheel hub to the bottom of the strut.

3. Support the strut underneath. Then, go into the trunk and remove the attaching nuts for the strut upper spring seat. Then, lower the strut and remove it from the car.

4. To install the strut, first position it in its normal orientation and work the studs in the upper spring seat through the mounting holes in the body. Support the strut in this position and then go in and install the attaching nuts to the spring seat, torquing them to 18-22 ft. lbs.

5. Line up the wheel hub assembly boltholes with those in the lower strut and then install the through bolts and nuts attaching the hub to the strut. Torque the bolts to 72-87 ft. lbs.

6. Lower the car to the floor.

Control Arms
REMOVAL AND INSTALLATION
210

The 210 solid rear axle is located by two links on either side. The downward travel is normally limited by the shock absorbers. Replace one or more links as follows:

1. Raise the car and support it securely by the body. Place a floorjack under the rear axle assembly so as to support it in an even and secure manner.

2. Remove the nuts, washers, and bolts from the lower shock absorber mounts. Then, gradually lower the axle until all spring tension is removed. Remove the springs.

3. Make sure the axle continues to be evenly supported. Remove the appropriate nuts and bolts at either end of the link or links to be removed. Remove the link.

4. Replace each link removed in reverse order. Install the bolt and then the washers and

the nut. Hold the bolt still and torque the nut at either end of each link to 51-58 ft. lbs.

5. Locate the springs on the spring seats on the axle and with the upper mounting insulators in proper position on the body. Then, carefully raise the axle until the springs assume their proper mounting positions and the shock absorbers will reach their lower mounts on the axle.

6. Install the shock through-bolts and then the nuts, torquing to 51-58 ft. lbs. Remove the floor jack from under the axle and then lower the car.

1982-86 Sentra

1. Carefully follow the procedure above for removing the springs. Loosen the flare nut at the connection in the brake line and disconnect it. Plug the openings.

2. Unclip the handbrake wire from the control arm. Then, remove the nuts from the control arm. Support the arm and, finally, remove the bolts from the bushings. Remove the arm from the car.

3. Inspect the bushings for wear, cracks, or actual breakage. If they need replacement, grind the flanges that retain the bushings off the arm. Then, using a C-clamp and drift, press the bushing out of the arm.

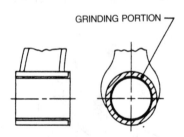

To replace the bushings on the 1982–86 Sentra rear suspension arms, grind off the crosshatched area

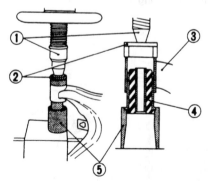

In replacing the bushings on Sentra rear suspension arms, use special fittings designed for this purpose

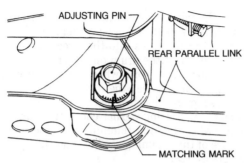

Matchmark the relationship between the mounting bolt and suspension crossmember to maintain toe-in on 1987–88 Sentras

4. Press new bushings into the arm with a C-clamp and appropriate tools. Install the arm and the bolts and nuts. Just tighten until snug.

5. Carefully position the spring on the seats at top and bottom and then raise the arm until the shock can be reconnected. Install and tighten the lower shock mounting bolt just until it is snug.

6. Install the wheel and lower the car to the floor. Torque the control arm bushing bolts to 43-51 ft. lbs. and the shock absorber lower mounting bolt to 26-35 ft. lbs.

1987-88 Sentra

1. Raise the vehicle and support it securely. Remove the rear wheels.

2. Mark the adjustment of the toe-in on both rear parallel links by matchmarking the position of the bolt angle scale on the crossmember.

3. Unbolt and remove the links. It will be easier to remove and replace one link at a time, as this will maintain the position of the steering knuckle and make it easier to reinstall bolts.

4. Install the (rear) bolts, which adjust rear toe, at the proper angle so the matchmarks align. Tighten bolts just snug. Then, lower the car and final torque to 72-87 ft. lbs.

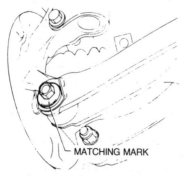

Matchmark the installation angle of the rear/outboard suspension arm mounting bolt on 4WD Sentras

1988 Sentra 4WD

1. Raise the vehicle and support it securely by the body. The rear outboard bolt adjusts rear wheel alignment. Carefully matchmark the installation angle of this bolt on either side.

2. Remove the outboard bolts and nuts as well as the washer which indicates installation angle on the rear bolt. Allow the control arm to hang downward.

3. Remove the nut, through-bolt and washers from inner end of the arm and remove it from the crossmember.

4. Install the control arm in reverse order, starting by installing the inner bolt, spacer and nut, and making sure to align the matchmarks for the rear/outboard bolts.

5. Install the outboard bolts securely, but final torque them to 72-87 ft. lbs. with the weight of the car on the wheels.

Sway Bar/Radius Rod
REMOVAL AND INSTALLATION
1987-88 2WD Sentras

This system is used only on these models. The rod minimizes fore and aft movement of the suspension struts and parallel links while limiting body roll.

1. Raise the car and support it securely by the body. Remove the nut at the rear of each side of the radius rod. Then, remove the split and whole washers and bushings from the rear ends of the rod, noting their order of installation.

2. Support the rod at the front end. Remove the bolt from either end of both rod brackets and remove the brackets.

3. Lower the rod slightly, hold the rear arms of the rod up to prevent bushings, washers and spacers from falling off, and pull the rod forward and out of the knuckle spindles.

4. Remove the spacer, bushing and washer from either arm of the rod, noting their order of installation.

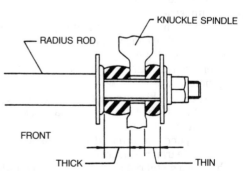

Install bushing liinking the sway bar/radius rod on 1987–88 Sentras as shown

5. Inspect all bushings for cracks or crushing. In general, rubber parts should be replaced unless the car is very new. Split the bushings which separate the bar from the forward moutning brackets to replace them.

6. Install the washer, bushing, and spacer on the sway bar, and then install the bar, holding its rear arms upward to retain these parts. Insert the bar through the knuckle spindles on either side. Then, locate the bar on the body and install the brackets over the bushings. Install bolts and torque to 65-80 ft. lbs.

7. Install bushings, washers and nuts on the rear threads of the bar and torque to 47-61 ft. lbs.

1988 4 WD Sentras

1. Raise the car and support it securely via the body. Remove this rod by simply removing the nut, washers and through-bolts at either end.

2. Inspect the bracket located at the forward end of the rod. If it is cracked, replace it by removing the two mounting bolts. Torque the bolts to 72-87 ft. lbs. when replacing the bracket.

3. Install the radius rods in reverse order, tightening the bolts and nuts just sung. Allow the car to rest on the rear wheels and final torque the bolts to 72-87 ft. lbs.

Rear Wheel Bearings

REMOVAL AND INSTALLATION

1982-86 Sentra

CAUTION: *Since brake lining contains asbestos, A CARCINOGEN, don't use compressed air to remove brake dust from these parts. Use of compressed air can cause you to inhale asbestos fibers.*

1. Raise the rear of the vehicle and support it securely. Remove the rear wheels. Release the parking brake.

2. Pry off the hub cap. Straighten the ends of the cotter pin, slide it out, and discard it. Then, unscrew the adjusting cap and the wheel bearing nut underneath.

3. Slide the brake drum off the spindle. Remove the wheel bearing washer and the bearing from the brake drum.

4. Remove the bearing and grease seal from the spindle.

5. Inspect the bearing races for cracks, pits, or brinnelling. If they are worn or damaged, replace them. To do this:

   a. Suspend the brake drum on blocks so there is clearance underneath.

   b. Use a metal rod and a hammer to knock the race out, toward the outside of the drum, on both sides.

c. Install new races with a cone shaped tool such as KV401021S0 or equivalent an a hammer. Tap the races into their recesses from the outside of the drum on either side.

6. Thoroughly work wheel bearing grease into the areas between the rollers of each bearing. Also grease the threaded part of the wheel spindle, the bearing washer contacting surface of the wheel bearing retaining nut, the inner surface of the retaining washer, and the lips of the grease seal.

7. Install the inner bearing into the brake drum with a new grease seal. Install the drum onto the spindle.

8. Install the outer bearing, washer, and wheel bearing nut. Then, adjust preload as follows:

   a. Spin the brake drum as you torque the wheel bearing nut to 29-33 ft. lbs. Hold this torque and turn the drum several turns in either direction to make sure the bearing is seated and properly preloaded.

   b. Install the adjusting cap nut over the bearing nut just until it touches the bearing nut. Then, turn the bearing nut and cap nut counterclockwise *just* until one of the castellations lines up with the cotter pin hole in the spindle (this must not be more than 90°). Install a new cotter pin and bend over the ends.

9. It should be possible to start the brake drum rotating using a spring scale at 90° to a line running between opposite wheel studs with less than 6.9 in. lbs. with a new grease seal and less than 3.5 in. lbs. with an old seal.

10. Check for wheel bearing axial play. There should be zero axial play.

11. Pack the hub cap with wheel bearing grease. Coat its O-ring with grease and then install the cap. Install the wheel.

1987-88 2WD Sentra

NOTE: *To perform this procedure, a large (3-ton) press and special tools ST33220000, J25804-01 and J26082 or equivalent are required. The press must be able to measure pressure. You might be able to engage the services of a machine shop to perform this procedure.*

CAUTION: *Since brake lining contains asbestos, A CARCINOGEN, don't use compressed air to remove brake dust from these parts. Use of compressed air can cause you to inhale asbestos fibers.*

1. Raise the car and support it securely via the body. Remove the rear wheels.

2. Remove the wheel bearing locknut. Then, remove the brake drum/hub and bearing assembly from the spindle.

3. Invert the brake drum and carefully pry

the circlip out of the inside diameter of the drum. Then, utilize ST33220000 J25804-01 and a press to force the bearing assembly down and out of the brake drum by pressing it toward the inside of the drum with the drum suspended on blocks.

4. Check the circlip for cracks or any sign that it has been sprung (bent inward). Have the hub inspected for cracks by a machine shop equipped with a magnetic or dye test. Do the same with the spindle.

5. Apply multipurpose grease to the seal lip. Then, press a new bearing assembly into the hub from the inside using the press and ST33220000 J26082. *Be sure not to press the inner race of the wheel bearing assembly and to carefully avoid damaging the grease seal.* If the bearing cannot be pressed in with a pressure of 3 tons, replace the hub.

6. Install a new circlip into the groove in the drum/hub.

7. Install the hub onto the spindle. Install the wheel bearing locknut and torque it to 137-188 ft. lbs.

1988 Sentra 4WD

NOTE: *To perform this procedure, you will need special tools designed to be used with a hammer to drive inner and outer bearing races from the rear knuckles of 4 WD Sentras. You will also need a large press, and a tool designed to transfer the power of that press to the bearing to install it. Also neded is a special tool to transfer the power of a 5.5 ton press to the bearing and such a press to apply pressure to the bearing to test preload.*

CAUTION: *Since brake lining contains asbestos, A CARCINOGEN, don't use compressed air to remove brake dust from these parts. Use of compressed air can cause you to inhale asbestos fibers.*

1. Raise the car and support it by the body. Remove the rear wheels.

2. Disconnect the brake line at the connection and plug the openings.

3. Cover the driveshaft rubber boots with rags. Tap the end of the driveshaft very lightly with a hammer, block of wood, and a suitable broad ended punch to free the driveshaft from the knuckle.

4. Matchmark the rear bolt installation angle to retain alignment. Then, remove the nuts and bolts fastening the control arm to the knuckle. Unbolt the radius rod from the knuckle. Unbolt the knuckle from the strut and remove it.

5. Mount the knuckle in a vise and drive the hub out of the knuckle via the inner race with a tool such as J25804-01 and hammer.

6. Use a press to force the outboard bearing

inner race from the hub. You will need blocks, a press, and ST30031000. Remove the other grease seal.

7. With the knuckle in a vise, drive the bearing inner race and grease seal out of the knuckle. Use an appropriate, cone shaped special tool and hammer.

8. *Cautiously* remove the inner and outer circlips from the knuckle with pointed instruments.

9. Drive the bearing outer race out of the knuckle with a hammer and appropriate, cone shaped special tool.

10. Have a machine shop inspect the knuckle for cracks with a magnetic or dye process. Replace radius rod or transverse link bushings, if necessary. Inspect the C-clips and replace if they are cracked or sprung.

11. Install the inner C-clip into the knuckle, making sure it seats in its groove. Then, press a new bearing outer race into the into the knuckle with a suitable tool and press without using any lubricant.

12. Apply wheel bearing grease to each bearing, working the grease thoroughly into the areas between the rollers. Also apply the grease to the lip of the grease seal. Install the bearings into the knuckle. Install the grease seal into the knuckle.

13. Install the outer C-clip into the groove in the knuckle. Then, use an appropriate tool to apply the pressure to the outer race and tap it to install the race into the hub.

14. Now, install a special tool onto the top of the hub that will drive the hub onto the knuckle by applying pressure on the inner race only. Support the hub at the center only. Then, place the assembly in a press and press the hub into the knuckle with about 3 tons force. Now, increase the pressure on the press to 5.5 tons. Spin the knuckle several turns in each direction to make sure the wheel bearing operates smoothly (preload is not excessive).

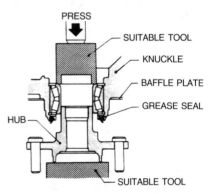

Pressing the wheel hub back into the steering knuckle (4WD)

15. Coat the lips of the inner grease seal with bearing grease and then install it into the knuckle.

16. Slide the driveshaft splines through the center of the wheel hub. Bolt the knuckle onto the strut and torque the bolts to 72-87 ft. lbs.

17. Install the bolts attaching the transverse link to the steering knuckle. Align the matchmarks made earlier to maintain rear wheel alignment. Install the nuts and torque them to 72-87 ft. lbs.

18. Connect the brake line. Thoroughly bleed the brake system as described in the next chapter. Then, install the wheel bearing locknut, have a helper hold the brake pedal down, and torque the locknut to 174-231 ft. lbs. Check wheel bearing axial (end) play with a dial indicator. It should be 0.05mm or less. Install the wheels.

Rear End Alignment

Rear wheel alignment does not usually require adjustment, but on 1987-88 Sentras, toe-in can be changed in case of unusual wear.

On 2WD models, toe-in is adjusted at the front bolt attaching the parallel link to the crossmember. The nut is loosened and the attaching bolt is turned to change its angle in relation to the crossmember, as shown.

On 4WD models, toe-in is adjusted at the outer end of the transverse link, by turning the rear attaching bolt. The nut is loosened and the attaching bolt is turned to change its angle in relation to the link, as shown.

STEERING

Steering Wheel

REMOVAL AND INSTALLATION

1. Position the front wheels in the straight ahead direction. The steering wheel should be right side up and level.

2. Disconnect the battery ground cable.

3. Look at the back of your steering wheel. If there are countersunk screws in the back of the spokes, remove the screws and pull off the horn pad. Some models have a horn wire running from the pad to the steering wheel. Disconnect it. On the 3-spoke "sport" steering wheel on some 210s and the Sentra wheel, the central horn pad simply pulls off.

4. You may need to remove the rest of the horn switching mechanism, noting the relative location of the parts. Remove the mechanism only if it hinders subsequent wheel removal procedures.

5. Matchmark the top of the steering column shaft and the steering wheel flange.

6. Remove the attaching nut and remove the steering wheel with a puller.

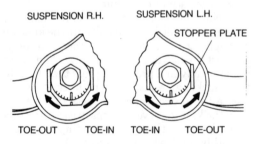

FRONT VIEW ON VEHICLE

Adjusting rear wheel alignment on 2WD 1987–88 Sentras

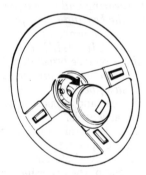

Removing horn pad—210

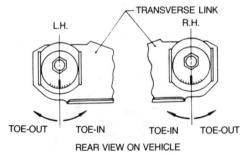

REAR VIEW ON VEHICLE

Adjusting rear wheel alignment on 4WD 1988 Sentras

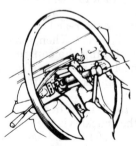

Using puller to remove the steering wheel

CAUTION: *Do not strike the shaft with a hammer, which may cause the column to collapse.*

7. Carefully and thoroughly grease the entire surface (both sides) of the turn signal canceling pin and and the horn contact slipring. Install the steering wheel in the reverse order of removal, aligning the punch marks. Do not drive or hammer the wheel into place, or you may cause the collapsible steering column to collapse; in which case you'll have to buy a whole new steering column unit.

8. Tighten the steering wheel nut to 22-25 ft. lbs. on the 1200 and B210, and to 27-38 ft. lbs.

9. Reinstall the horn pad and button.

Turn Signal Switch
REMOVAL AND INSTALLATION

On the 1979 and later 210s, and 1982 and later Sentra, the turn signal switch is part of a combination switch (which includes lights, wipers, etc.). The entire unit is removed together. The turn signal switch on the B210 and 1200 models does not include any other functions (other than the high beam).

Combination Switch
210 AND SENTRA

1. Disconnect the battery ground cable.
2. Remove the steering wheel as previously outlined. Observe the caution on the collapsible steering column.
3. Remove the steering column covers.
4. Disconnect the electrical plugs from the switch.
5. Remove the retaining screws and remove the switch.
6. Installation is the reverse of removal. Some turn signal switches have a tab which must fit into a hole in the steering shafts in order for the system to return the switch to the neutral position after the turn has been made. Be sure to align the tab and the hole when installing.

Turn Signal Switch
1200 AND B210 MODELS

1. Disconnect the battery ground cable.
2. Remove the steering wheel.
3. Remove the four screws securing the upper and lower shell covers to each other. Shell covers can then be taken out easily.
4. Disconnect the lead wires of the turn signal switch at the two connectors.
5. Loosen the two screws holding the switch assembly to the steering column jacket. The switch assembly can now be easily taken out.
6. Installation is the reverse of removal.

Make sure that the location tab of the switch fits in the hole of the steering column jacket.

Steering Lock
REMOVAL AND INSTALLATION

The steering lock/ignition switch/warning buzzer assembly is attached to the steering column by special screws whose heads shear off when installed at the factory (so the lock cannot be removed easily). The screws must be drilled out to remove the assembly. The ignition switch or warning switch can be replaced without removing the assembly. The ignition switch is on the back of the assembly, and the warning switch on the side. The warning buzzer, which sounds when the driver's door is opened with the steering unlocked, is located behind the instrument panel.

Steering Column
REMOVAL AND INSTALLATION

1. Remove the steering wheel as described above. On 210 and B210, remove the through-bolts from the steering shaft rubber coupling. On Sentra, remove the bolt that passes through the upper end of the steering coupling and locks it to the bottom of the column.

2. Remove the combination or turn signal switch as described above, if the column is being replaced. Otherwise, refer to the removal procedure for this switch and disconnect the wiring. Remove the heater ducts if they will be in the way.

3. Remove the screws that attach the flange at the bottom of the jacket to the floor panel. Sentras have spacers between the upper bracket and dash panel. Be careful not to lose these. Then, support the column and remove the bolts attaching the upper bracket to the dash panel. If there are nuts attaching the lower column to the dash panel, as on late model Sentra, remove them as well.

4. Tilt the column downward and remove it from the car.

5. To install the column, first position it inside the the car, align the rubber steering shaft coupling or the coupling that links the column to the steering box. Then, slide the column into position and install the two spacers. Support it during the next step.

6. Install the 2 or 4 bolts that attach the column to the dash and then tighten them.

7. Install the lower column bracket bolts.

8. Install the bolts linking the column to the steering box, and those that attach the flange at the bottom of the jacket to the floor panel, but tighten them only slightly. Once all these bolts are installed, retighten them securely.

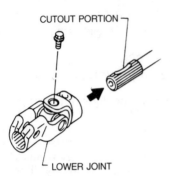

CUTOUT PORTION

LOWER JOINT

Attaching the steering column to the coupling on late model Sentras. Make sure the cutout area in the splined portion of the column is turned so the bolt will pass through it when it is installed.

9. Install the combination or turn signal switch, or reconnect it, as necessary, in reverse of removal. Install the heat ducts as necessary.

10. Install the bolt or bolts attaching the steering column to the steering box though the rubber flexible coupling or U-joint. On later models using a splined joint with a flat at the bottom of the column, make sure the flat is turned to permit the bolt to pass through the top section of the U-joint before installing the U-joint bolt.

11. Make sure the column turns smoothly from lock to lock.

Steering Linkage
REMOVAL AND INSTALLATION
Tie Rod Ends (Steering Side Rods)

NOTE: *You will need either type of ball joint remover for this operation.*

1. Jack up the front of the vehicle and support it on jackstands.

2. Locate the faulty tie rod end. It will have a lot of play in it and the dust cover will probably be ripped.

3. Remove the cotter key and nut from the tie rod stud. Note the position of the tie rod end in relation to the rest of the steering linkage.

4. Loosen the locknut holding the tie rod to the rest of the steering linkage.

5. Free the tie rod ball joint from either the relay rod or steering knuckle by using the ball joint remover.

6. Unscrew and remove the tie rod end, counting the number of turns it takes to completely free it.

7. Install the new tie rod end, turning in exactly as far as you screwed out the old one. Make sure it is correctly positioned in relation to the rest of the steering linkage and tigheten the nut.

8. Fit the ball joint and nut. Torque the nut to 22-29 ft. lbs. Then, tighten it just far enough to align the cotter pin hole in the stud with the next set of castellations using a torque wrench,

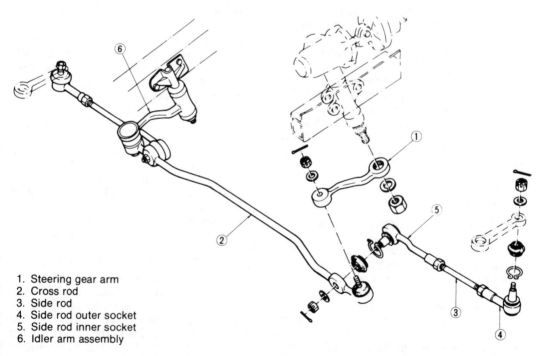

1. Steering gear arm
2. Cross rod
3. Side rod
4. Side rod outer socket
5. Side rod inner socket
6. Idler arm assembly

Steering linkage—toe-in adjustment is made at the side rod (tie rod)

limiting the torque to 36 ft. lbs. Install a new cotter pin.

9. Have the the toe-in of the vehicle checked and adjusted, if necessary.

Center Link (210 and B210 Only)

1. Raise the vehicle and support it securely via the body. Remove the cotter pins from the two nuts attaching the center link to the tie rods. Then, loosen these nuts about two turns. Use a ball joint remover to pull the tie rod studs out of the center link.

2. Remove the cotter pin from the nut attaching the center link to the steering box arm. Do the same for the nut attaching it to the idler arm. Then, support the link and loosen these nuts about two turns. Pull the studs for the link out of the idler arm and steering arm with a balljoint remover. Then, remove the nuts.

3. Install the center link studs into the steering shaft arm and idler arm. Install the attaching nuts and torque them to 22-51 ft. lbs. Then, turn the nuts just enough farther to install the cotter pins (aligning the cotter pin holes in the studs with the next castellations in the nuts) and install them.

4. Repeat this process for the two nuts attaching the center link to the tie rods.

Manual Steering Gear

ADJUSTMENTS

210, B210

1. Remove the steering gear from the car as described below.

2. Using a torque wrench, measure the initial turning torque of the worm shaft assembly (the shaft operated by the steering column when the box is in the car) at the center of its rotating range. Torque should be 3.5-7.8 inch lbs. Maximum is 9.5 inch lbs.

3. If the figure is outside specification, loosen the locknut located at the bottom of the worm shaft, rotate the adjusting screw, and retighten the locknut. Recheck the torque figure.

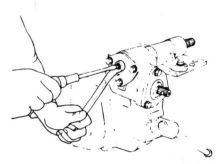

Adjusting the worm shaft assembly on 210 Series cars

1982-86 Sentra

1. Remove the steering gear from the car as described below. Disconnect the tie rod ends and remove boots.

2. Turn the pinion shaft to neutral (centered) position. This puts the spacer at $-38.3°$ to $-25,3°$ on 1982-84 models and $-33.5°$ to $-46.5°$ on 1985 models; and sets the guide chip to 43.5° to 56.5° on 1986 models.

3. On 1982-84 models, measure pinion rotating torque with an inch lb. torque wrench working on the pinion shaft. It must be 13 inch lbs. or less. Measure rack starting force with a spring scale. Rack starting force must be 18-40 lb. Loosen the locknut and adjust the retainer adjusting screw as necessary.

4. On 1985 and 1986 models, measure the pinion shaft rotating torque with an inch lb. torque wrench on the pinion shaft. Rotate the shaft slowly from its neutral or centered position 180° in both directions, watching for the spot where torque is at its greatest level. Loosen the adjusting screw with the pinion at this position and then hand tighten the adjusting screw until its end touches the retainer. Hold the adjustment and tighten the locknut.

5. On 1985 and 1986 models, now rotate the pinion from its centered position to the end of the rack and make sure torque is no more than 13 inch lbs. on 1985 models and 16 inch lbs. on 1986 models.

6. Reassemble the steering gear linkage and install the gear in the car.

1987-88 Sentra

1. Remove the steering gear from the car as described below. Disconnect the tie rod ends and remove boots.

2. Turn the pinion shaft to neutral (centered) position. This puts the guide chip at neutral position (6° either side of center).

3. Loosen the locknut. Tighten the adjusting screw to 43. inch lbs. Then, loosen it and tighten it to this torque again.

4. Loosen the adjusing screw and torque it to 1.7 inch lbs.

5. Rotate the pinion to move the rack back and forth all the way through two full cycles. Then, return it to neutral position.

6. Slowly rotate the pinion and measure rotating torque through the entire 180° range either side of neutral. Find the point where rotating force is at its maximum. Loosen the adjusting screw at this point. Then, torque it to 26 inch lbs.

7. Now check the pinion rotating torque. Traveling 100° either side of neutral position, should average 6.1-10.4 inch lbs. It must not fluctuate more than 2.6 inch lbs.

8. If necessary, loosen the adjusting screw until the pinion rotating torque is within specification. Hold the adjusting nut in this position and torque the locknut to 29-43 ft. lbs. If this will not correct the rotating torque, it will be necessary to replace the retaining spring.

REMOVAL AND INSTALLATION

B210, 210 (Worm Gear Steering Box)

1. If the car has a manual transmission, remove the clutch master cylinder as described in Chapter 7, but do not disconnect the hydraulic line. Instead, set the cylinder aside and support it so the hose will not be under stress.
2. Raise the car and support it securely via the body. Remove the nuts attaching the exhaust pipe to the exhaust manifold. Also remove the bolts that attach the exhaust pipe clamps to the brackets. Then, disconnect the exhaust pipe from the manifold and move it out of the way.
3. Remove the bolt that secures the steering worm shaft to the steering column rubber coupling.
4. Remove the nut and lockwasher that attach the steering gear to the sector shaft of the steering box. Use an appropriate puller to pull the arm off the shaft.
5. Unbolt the steering gear housing from the body member. Pull the steering gear out of the engine compartment.
6. To install, first position the steering gear on the body with boltholes and the rubber coupling lined up. Then, install the mounting bolts and torque them to 51-58 ft. lbs.
7. Install the steering arm to the sector shaft of the steering box with the four grooves in the arm serrations lined up with the four projections on the sector shaft. Install the nut and lockwasher. Torque the nut to 94-108 ft. lbs.
8. Install the coupling bolt that links the steering worm shaft to the sector shaft.
9. Reattach the exhaust pipe and install mount bolts. Install the clutch master cylinder.

SENTRA (Rack & Pinion Steering)

1. Raise the car and support it securely by the body. Remove the cotter pins and the nuts that fasten the tie rod ball joints to the the arms of the steering knuckles.
2. Use a suitable puller to press the ballstuds out of the arms.
3. Slightly loosen the steering gear mounting bolts without removing them. Then, remove the bolt which fastens the lower steering column U-joint to the bottom of the steering column shaft.
4. Support the steering gear and then re-move the attaching bolts. Remove the gear and rubber mounts from the car.
5. Pull the brackets off the mounting rubber bushings. Inspect the bushings and replace them if they are cracked, worn or brittle. They may be removed and installed by splitting them at the crack.
6. Install the mounting bushings with arrows pointing upward. Install brackets with their arrows pointing upward as well.
7. Position the steering gear on the body with boltholes lined up and install the mounting bolts loosely.
8. Align the steering joint so the bolt will pass directly through the cutout portion of the shaft. Then, insert the spined portion of the shaft through the coupling and install the bolt, torquing it to 22-29 ft. lbs.
9. Torque the mounting bolts for the steering box to 43-58 ft. lbs. on 1982-86 models and 54-72 ft. lbs. on 1987-88 models. Install the tie rod ends to the steering knuckle arms. Torque the nuts to 22 ft. lbs. Then, torque the nut farther (maximum of 36 ft. lbs.) until the castellations align with the cotter pin hole and install a new cotter pin. Lower the car.

Power Steering Gear
ADJUSTMENTS

Only the power rack and pinion steering system used on 1987-88 models is adjustable. Adjustment is usually performed only after overhaul and replacement of major parts. A special socket wrench KV48100700 must be used with an inch lb. torque wrench in performing this work.

1. Disconnect the unit and remove it from the car as described below.
2. Rotate the pinion shaft from lock to lock, counting turns. Then, divide the number of turns in half, and turn the shaft that distance from either lock to center it.
3. Loosen the locknut and loosen the adjust-

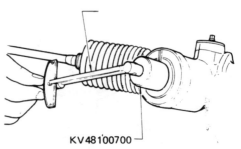

KV48100700

Adjusting the power steering gear on 1987–88 Sentra. The adjusting screw for pinion rotating torque is visible at the top of the unit.

ing screw. Then, torque it to a torque of 43 inch lbs. Loosen it and torque it again to that figure.

4. Loosen the adjusting screw and torque it to 0.43-1.74 inch lbs. Loosen the locknut and apply locking sealer to the lower threads of the adjusting screw as well as the retainer cover surrounding it. Then, tighten the locknut to 29-43 ft. lbs.

5. Move the rack through its entire stroke several times. Then, install the torque wrench and special socket and measure the rotating torque of the pinion 100° either side of the neutral position. The torque should be 6.9-11.3 inch lbs. with a maximum of 16 inch lbs.

6. If the torque is incorrect, readjust the screw appropriately. When the rotating torque is correct, reapply sealer and retorque the locknut as necessary.

REMOVAL AND INSTALLATION

1982-86 Sentra

1. Raise the vehicle and support it securely by the body. Place a metal container under the power steering hydraulic line connections at the unit.

2. Loosen the hose clamp and flare nut (with a flare nut wrench) and disconnect both the high and low pressure lines from the unit. Plug the openings of both the lines and the unit to keep dirt out.

3. Remove the cotter pins and nuts fastening the the tie rod ballstuds to the steering knuckle arms. Use a balljoint remover to press the studs out of the arms.

4. Securely support the transaxle with a floorjack. Unbolt the exhaust pipe at the exhaust manifold and at the clamp located just to the rear of the engine oil pan. Remove this section of the exhaust system. Then, remove the rear engine mount.

5. Support the steering gear securely and then remove the four steering gear mounting bolts.

6. Remove the bolt that fastens the lower steering column shaft U-joint to the pinion shaft. Then, remove the steering gear and tie rod assembly by pulling it out over the suspension transverse link.

7. Inspect the mounting rubber bushings and replace them if cracked or worn. Install new ones with the arrows facing upward.

8. To install the unit, first work it into position over the suspension transverse link and support it there. Then, align the flattened portion of the splined end of the pinion shaft with the boltholes in the lower steering column U-joint so the bolt will pass right over the flat. Install the bolt and torque it to 22-29 ft. lbs.

9. Install the steering unit into position and install the mounting brackets with the arrows pointing upward. Torque the bolts to 43-58 ft. lbs.

10. Install the rear engine mount. Remove the floorjack. Install the exhaust pipe removed earlier.

11. Remove the plugs and connect both the high and low pressure lines to the unit. Torque the high pressure line flare nut to 11-18 ft. lbs.

12. Reconnect the tie rod ballstuds to the steering knuckle arms. Install and torque the stud nuts and cotter pins as described earlier under Steering Linkage.

13. Refill the power steering pump with an approved fluid and bleed the system as described below. If the tie rod ends have been removed from the assembly, check the wheel alignment and adjust if necessary.

1987-88 Sentra

1. Raise the car and support it securely. Turn the steering wheel so the wheels are in straight ahead position. Place a metal container under the power steering hydraulic line connections at the unit.

2. Loosen the hose clamp and flare nut (with a flare nut wrench) and disconnect both the high and low pressure lines from the unit. Plug the openings of both the lines and the unit to keep dirt out.

3. Remove the cotter pins and nuts fastening the tie rod ballstuds to the steering knuckle arms. Use a balljoint remover to press the studs out of the arms.

4. Support the steering gear securely and then remove the four steering gear mounting bolts.

6. Remove the bolt that fastens the lower steering column shaft U-joint to the pinion shaft. Before completely disconnecting the U-joint from the pinion shaft, matchmark the pinion shaft and pinion housing to mark the neutral position for reassembly. Then, remove the steering gear and tie rod assembly by pulling it out over the suspension transverse link.

7. Inspect the mounting rubber bushings and replace them if cracked or worn. Install new ones with the arrows facing upward.

8. Center the steering gear, if necessary, by turning the pinion shaft until the tie rod boots are equal in length and the matchmarks made earlier line up. Then, align the flattened portion of the splined end of the pinion shaft with the boltholes in the lower steering column U-joint so the bolt will pass right over the flat. Install the bolt and torque it to 17-22 ft. lbs.

9. To install, put the steering unit into position and install the mounting brackets with the arrows pointing upward. Torque the bolts to 54-72 ft. lbs.

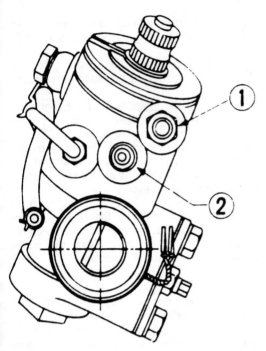

Connect the low pressure line to 1 and the high pressure line to 2 on the 1987–88 Sentra power steering unit

10. Connect the low and high pressure hydraulic lines, installing new O-rings (note that the low pressure connection is larger). Torque the low pressure line to 20-29 ft. lbs. and the high pressure line to 11-18 ft. lbs.

11. Reconnect the tie rod ballstuds to the steering knuckle arms. Install and torque the stud nuts to 25 ft. lbs. Then, tighten farther until the castellation in the nut lines up with the cotter pin hole, checking the torque (maximum 36 ft. lbs). Install the cotter pins and bend them over securely.

12. Refill the power steering pump with an approved fluid and bleed the system as described below. If the tie rod ends have been removed from the assembly, check the wheel alignment and adjust if necessary.

Power Steering Pump
REMOVAL AND INSTALLATION

1. Loosen the belt adjustment lockbolt. Then, turn the pump belt tension adjusting bolt clockwise and loosen and remove the pump belt.

2. Place a pan under the area of the pump to collect draining fluid. Disconnect the high pressure line at the pump. Then, loosen the low pressure hose clamp and disconnect the low pressure hose.

3. Remove the mounting bolts and remove the pump.

4. Put the pump into position and install all mounting bolts loosely.

5. If O-rings are used on the connections, replace them and coat with with ATF. Reconnect the low pressure hose and tighten the clamp. Connect the high pressure hose and torque the connection to 22-36 ft. lbs.

6. Install the belt, adjust it with the adjusting bolt, and torque the mounting bolts to 12-16 ft. lbs.

7. Refill the reservoir with approved power steering fluid. Then, bleed the system as follows:

   a. Raise the car and support it securely so the front wheels are off the ground.

   b. Have someone remove the reservoir top and fill it to the proper level with the approved fluid. Have that person watch the level and refill it as necessary as air is bled out.

   c. Turn the wheel to the right and left locks (engine off).

   d. Make sure the transmission is in neutral (manual) or Park (automatics) and that the parking brake is securely applied. Start the engine and allow it to idle. Repeat Step C until the level no longer drops.

Brakes

BRAKE SYSTEM

Adjustments

Front disc brakes are used on all models covered in this guide except some early 1200 models. All 1200, B210 and 210 Datsuns and Nissan Sentras are equipped with independent front and rear hydraulic systems with a warning light to indicate loss of pressure in either system. All models have rear hydraulic drum brakes.

The 1973 1200 is the only model covered here that does not have a power booster system to lessen the required brake pressure. The parking brake on all models operates the rear brakes through a cable system.

NOTE: *All front disc brakes covered in this guide are self-adjusting, needing no external adjustment. The drum brakes on the 1200 and B210 models require adjustment; 210 model drum brakes are automatically adjusted when the parking brake is applied (parking brake adjustment is also covered here).*

To adjust the brakes, jack up the car, remove the wheels, and safely support the rear with jackstands. Disconnect the parking brake linkage from the rear wheels, apply the brakes hard a few times to center the drums, and proceed as follows:

FRONT DRUM BRAKES

1. With the brake drum installed, insert the brake adjusting spoon through the backing plate. Tighten the cam adjusting stud clockwise until the brake shoes contact the brake drum (you will be unable to turn the drum freely).

2. Now turn the cam adjusting stud counterclockwise until the brake shoes separate slightly from the drums. The drums should turn freely.

3. Turn the brake drum, and if the brake shoe interferes (drags) on the drum, readjust

the clearance. Depress the brake pedal and make sure the brake operates correctly.

REAR BRAKES

1200

1. Remove the rubber grommets from the backing plate, and insert a brake adjusting spoon through the backing plate. Tighten the brake adjuster wedge clockwise, moving the brake shoes against the brake drum. You should now be unable to turn the brake drum.

2. Back off the adjuster just enough that the brake drum will turn freely without dragging. Depress the brake pedal to make sure the brake operates effectively.

B210, 210 and Sentra

1. Make sure the hand brake lever assembly returns properly to its original position (down all the way).

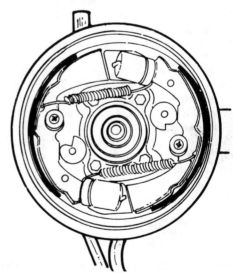

1200 front drum brake. All rear drums similar except utilize one wheel cylinder

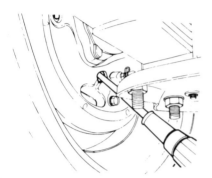

Rear brake adjustment. Brake adjusting spoon is recommended

2. Remove the rubber grommets from the adjuster holes in the backing plates.

3. Using a brake adjusting spoon or conventional screwdriver, turn the toothed adjusting nut to expand the brake shoes. Stop turning the adjusting nut when the shoes have made contact with the drum (drum won't turn).

4. Back off the adjusting nut several notches until the brake shoes are slightly away from the drum, with no drag. Test the brakes and make sure the operation is effective.

BRAKE PEDAL ADJUSTMENT

Before making this adjustment, make sure that the wheel brakes are properly adjusted. On all but 1987-88 models: Adjust the pedal free play by means of the pedal pushrod locknut (on the floor side of the pedal). Adjust the pedal height by adjusting the brake lamp switch locknut (and operating rod if equipped with a brake booster).

On 1987-88 models: Adjust pedal free height with the brake booster input rod, making sure not to adjust so the rod moves outside the car interior; then tighten the locknut. Next, adjust the clearance between the pedal stop and the threaded end of the stoplight switch to be 0.30-1.00mm. Tighten the locknuts. Next, check pedal free play and *make sure* the stop lamp is off when the pedal is released. Finally, with wheels securely blocked, automatic transmission in "Park", manual transmission in Neutral and parking brake off, check the brake pedal depressed height. Have a helper depress the pedal with normal, moderate pressure. Pedal height should be as shown in the chart. If not, check for a leak-free and properly bled brake system.

Brake Light Switch

REMOVAL AND INSTALLATION

The brake light switch is situated just behind the pedal lever on a bracket. To remove it, disconnect the battery and then unplug the switch. Then, loosen the locknut and remove the switch. Install the switch in reverse order, adjusting it as described above. Tighten the locknut, replug the electrical connector and reconnect the battery.

Master Cylinder

REMOVAL AND INSTALLATION

Clean the outside of the cylinder thoroughly, particularly around the cap and fluid lines. Disconnect the fluid lines and cap them to exclude dirt (Be careful not to allow any dirt into the system). Remove the clevis pin connecting the pushrod to the brake pedal arm inside the car. This pin need not be removed with the vacuum booster, if equipped. Unbolt the master cylinder from the firewall and remove. The adjustable pushrod is used to adjust brake pedal freeplay (see Brake Pedal Adjustment above). To install, first bolt the master cylinder onto the booster or its mounting bracket. Uncap and connect the hydraulic lines. Bleed the system thoroughly, as described below. After installation, check the pedal free-play on cars without a brake booster.

NOTE: *Ordinary brake fluid will boil and cause brake failure under high temperatures developed in disc brake systems. Use only DOT 3 or 4 fluid developed for disc brake systems.*

OVERHAUL

CAUTION: *Master cylinders are supplied to Datsun by two manufacturers: Nabco and Tokico. Parts between these two manufacturers are not interchangeable. Be sure you obtain the correct rebuilding kit for your master cylinder.*

The master cylinder can be disassembled using the illustrations as a guide. Clean all parts in clean brake fluid. Replace the cylinder or piston as necessary if clearance between the two exceeds 0.15mm. Lubricate all parts in clean brake fluid on assembly. Master cylinder rebuilding kits, containing all the necessary parts, are available to simplify and cheapen the expense of overhaul.

Power Brake Booster

REMOVAL AND INSTALLATION

1. Remove the master cylinder as described above. Unclamp and then disconnect the vacuum line at the booster.

2. Remove the lockpin and then the clevis pin from inside the passenger compartment.

3. Remove the mounting nuts from behind the mounting bracket in the engine compartment and slide the unit off.

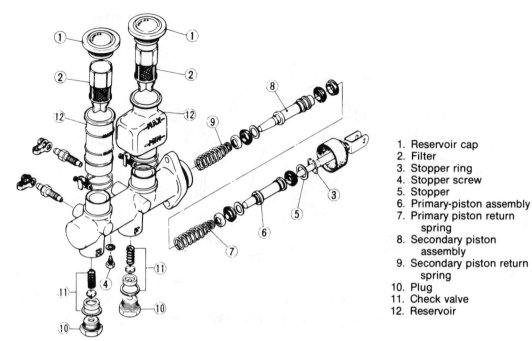

1. Reservoir cap
2. Filter
3. Stopper ring
4. Stopper screw
5. Stopper
6. Primary-piston assembly
7. Primary piston return spring
8. Secondary piston assembly
9. Secondary piston return spring
10. Plug
11. Check valve
12. Reservoir

Exploded view of 1200, B210 and 210 master cylinder. Sentra similar

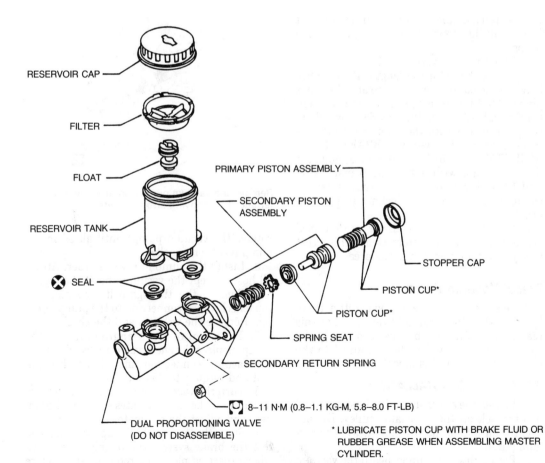

RESERVOIR CAP

FILTER

FLOAT

RESERVOIR TANK

SEAL

PRIMARY PISTON ASSEMBLY

SECONDARY PISTON ASSEMBLY

STOPPER CAP

PISTON CUP*

PISTON CUP*

SPRING SEAT

SECONDARY RETURN SPRING

8–11 N·M (0.8–1.1 KG-M, 5.8–8.0 FT-LB)

DUAL PROPORTIONING VALVE (DO NOT DISASSEMBLE)

* LUBRICATE PISTON CUP WITH BRAKE FLUID OR RUBBER GREASE WHEN ASSEMBLING MASTER CYLINDER.

The master cylinder used on 1987–88 Sentras

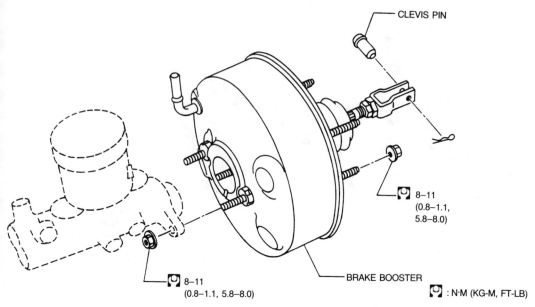

CLEVIS PIN

8–11
(0.8–1.1,
5.8–8.0)

8–11
(0.8–1.1, 5.8–8.0)

BRAKE BOOSTER

: N·M (KG-M, FT-LB)

The brake booster installed on 1987–88 Sentra

4. Install the unit onto the mounting bracket and install the mounting nuts, torquing to 5-8 ft. lbs.

5. Reconnect the vacuum line.

6. Adjust the input rod length (the distance between the booster rear surface and the clevis pin hole) to 135mm on 210, and 150mm on Sentra through 1984. On 1985-86 Sentras, adjust the pedal height with the input rod to the dimension specified above under BRAKE PEDAL ADJUSTMENT. On 1987-88 Sentra, adjust it to 164-174mm with automatic transmission and 160-168mm on manual transmission equipped cars. Torque the locknut to 12-16 ft. lbs.

7. Install the master cylinder as described above and bleed the system thoroughly. Test the system thoroughly in a safe area.

Diesel Vacuum Pump

Since the diesel engine has no throttle, there is very little intake manifold vacuum. For this reason, a vacuum pump is used to supply the vacuum necessary for the standard brake booster to work on this model.

REMOVAL AND INSTALLATION

1. Loosen the alternator belt adjustment and pull the belt off the alternator pulley. Disconnect the air intake and vacuum lines at the vacuum pump.

2. Place a drain pan underneath the vacuum pump. Rotate the alternator drive pulley (this

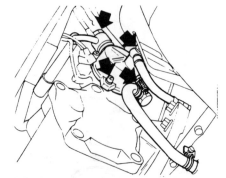

Remove the vacuum pump from the rear of the alternator by removing arrowed bolts

rotates the vacuum pump) until all oil in the pump has been expelled.

3. Install the pump in reverse order. Attach all hoses except the vacuum line at the top.

4. Remove the through-bolt attaching the top (check valve) connection to the pump at the top. Remove the washers and the check valve.

5. Pour 6ml of clean engine oil into the pump. Replace the check valve and washers and the vacuum connection, install the through-bolt and torque it to 22-25 ft. lbs.

6. Turn the vacuum pump over several revolutions to make sure it rotates smoothy. Reconnect and adjust the alternator drive belt.

7. Start the engine, build up vacuum, and test the brake system thoroughly in an area where there is plenty of room to stop before driving the car on the road.

Brake Proportioning Valve

All Datsuns covered in this guide are equipped with brake proportioning valves of several different types. The valves all do the same job, which is to separate the front and rear brake lines, allowing them to function independently, and preventing the rear brakes from locking before the front brakes. Damage, such as brake line leakage, in either the front or rear brake system will not affect the normal operation of the unaffected system. If, in the event of a panic stop, the rear brakes lock up before the front brakes, it could mean the proportioning valve is defective. If tire pressures and condition are as they should be and the brasic brake components are in good working order, it may be necessary to replace the entire proportioning valve.

REMOVAL AND INSTALLATION

NOTE: *Since leakage in a brake system is a critical problem, you should have a flare nut wrench that can be adapted to a torque wrench to properly torque the proportioning valve connections.*

1. Place a drain pan under the brake proportioning valve.
2. Note the routing of the connections to the valve and the orientation of the valve in the engine compartment. If necessary, mark the lines or the new valve.
3. Using a flare nut wrench, disconnect all 4 or 6 connections.
4. Remove the mounting bolt from the body of the car. Then, install the new valve in the original orientation, but do not torque the mounting bolt yet.
5. Install the brake tubes into the correct connections on the valve and start the flare nuts (you may have to change the angle of the valve slightly to do this). Once the tubes are properly started, tighten them and then torque them to 11-13 ft. lbs.
6. Torque the mounting bolt to 35-43 in. lbs.
7. Refill the master cylinder with approved fluid. Bleed the system as described below.

ADJUSTMENT/CENTERING

The proportioning valve is not adjustable and is inherently self-centering. Make sure all brake system parts are in proper mechanical and hydraulic condition and fully bled. Then, apply the brakes hard repeatedly. The valve should center itself. If it does not, there may be air or leakage (either internal or external) in one part of the system. These problems must be corrected before condemning or replacing the valve.

Brake Hoses
REMOVAL AND INSTALLATION

NOTE: *You should have a torque wrench that will operate a flare nut wrench in order to torque flared connections to perform this operation.*

1. Place a drain pan under the fitting to be disconnected. Using a flare-nut wrench, remove the flare nut from the tubing end of the hose. Cap both openings.
2. Pull off the spring that fastens the connection to the body mount. Place the drain pan under the connection at the other end of the flexible hose. Then, use a wrench on the flats at the other end and disconnect the hose there. Plug open ends.
3. Install hose in reverse order, torquing the flare nut connections to 11-13 ft. lbs. Bleed the system thoroughly as described below. Then, road test the car in a safe area before driving it on the road.

System Bleeding

Bleeding the brake system is required whenever air gets into the hydraulic fluid, causing a spongy feeling at the pedal and slow brake response. Air may find its way into the system through a worn master cylinder, worn wheel cylinders, a loose or broken brake line, or if any brake system component is removed from the system for repair.

NOTE: *The brake system must always be*

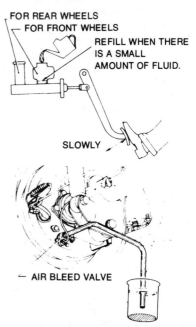

FOR REAR WHEELS
FOR FRONT WHEELS
REFILL WHEN THERE IS A SMALL AMOUNT OF FLUID.
SLOWLY
AIR BLEED VALVE
REFILL UNTIL NEW FLUID APPEARS

Bleeding the brakes

bled if a component is removed or the system disconnected in any way. The sequence in the procedure below applies to all models through 1982. On 1983 models, bleed in this sequence: Right rear wheel cylinder; left front caliper; left rear wheel cylinder; right front caliper. On 1984-88 models, bleed in this sequence: Left rear wheel cylinder; right front caliper; right rear wheel cylinder; left front caliper.

1. Top up the master cylinder reservoir with the proper brake fluid. Make sure the fluid you use is approved for disc brakes (unless your car is a 1200 model with front drum brakes). All brake systems should use DOT 3 or 4 brake fluid.

2. Jack up the rear of the car and safely support it with jackstands.

3. Begin with the wheel farthest from the master cylinder. Clean all dirt off of the bleeder nipple. Fit a rubber hose over the bleeder nipple on the inside (facing underneath the car) of the brake backing plate. Submerge the other end of the hose in clean brake fluid in a clear glass jar.

NOTE: *Do not reuse any brake fluid that has been bled from the system.*

4. Have an assistant pump the brake pedal three or four times. On the bottom of the fourth stroke (pedal all the way down), loosen the bleeder screw behind the nipple (while your assistant keeps the pedal depressed) and allow the air bubbles to escape in the fluid. Quickly tighten the bleeder screw.

NOTE: *Continue to check the fluid level in the master cylinder during the bleeding procedure. Refill as necessary.*

6. Proceed to the other rear wheel and perform the same operation. When this wheel is bled, take the car down off of the jackstands, jack up the front end and support it with the stands. Bleed the front wheel farthest from the master cylinder then the wheel closest.

7. After bleeding all four wheels, check that the brake pedal is now firm. If not, repeat the bleeding operation.

FRONT DRUM BRAKES

CAUTION: *Brake shoes contain asbestos, which has been determined to be a cancer causing agent. Never clean the brake surfaces with compressed air! Avoid inhaling any dust from any brake surface! When cleaning brake surfaces, use a commercially available brake cleaning fluid.*

Brake Drums
REMOVAL AND INSTALLATION

1. Jack up the front of the vehicle so that the wheel which is to be serviced is off the ground. be sure to loosen the lug nuts before the wheel comes off the ground.

2. Remove the wheel and tire assembly.

3. Pull the brake drum off the hub. If the drum cannot be easily removed, back off on the brake adjustment.

NOTE: *Never depress the brake pedal while the brake drum is removed.*

4. Install the brake drum in the reverse order of removal and adjust the brakes.

Brake Shoes
REMOVAL AND INSTALLATION

CAUTION: *Brake shoes contain asbestos, which has been determined to be a cancer causing agent. Never clean the brake surfaces with compressed air! Avoid inhaling any dust from any brake surface! When cleaning brake surfaces, use a commercially available brake cleaning fluid.*

1. Jack up the vehicle until the wheel which is to be serviced if off the ground two or three inches. Remove the wheel and brake drum.

NOTE: *It is not absolutely essential to remove the hub assembly from the spindle, but it makes the job much easier. If you can work with the hub in place, skip down to Step 7.*

2. Remove the hub dust cap.

3. Straighten the cotter pin and remove it from the spindle.

Brake Pedal Adjustments

	1200	B210	210	1983–86 Sentra	1987–88 Sentra
Pedal free play (in.)	0.20–0.50	0.04–0.20	0.04–0.20	0.40–0.20	.04–.12
Pedal height (in.) ①	5.65–5.87	6.18	5.65–5.87	② ③	6.46–6.85 ⑤
Depressed height (in.)	1.00	2.76	2.76	④	3.35 ⑥ or more

① Pedal height measured from floorboard to pedal pad
② Manual transaxle—1982 (7.53–7.76), 1983–86 (7.64–8.03)
③ Automatic transaxle—1982 (7.60–7.83), 1983–86 (7.76–8.15)
④ Gasoline engine—3.35 or more, Diesel engine—3.15 or more
⑤ Applies to automatic. Manual—6.30–6.61
⑥ Applies to automatic. Manual—3.15 or more

4. Unscrew the spindle nut and remove the adjusting cap, spindle nut, and spindle washer.

5. Wiggle the hub assembly until the outer bearing comes unseated and can be removed from the hub. Remove the outer bearing.

6. Pull the hub assembly off the spindle.

7. Unlock the brake shoe retainers. Unhook the return springs on the brake shoes and remove the shoes.

8. Apply brake grease to the adjuster assemblies and back the adjusters off the whole way using the bolts on the backing plate. Apply brake grease to the areas on the brake backing plate where the brake shoes make contact.

9. Install the brake shoes by first putting them into postion and then locking the retainers. Install the return springs.

10. Install the hub, brake drum and wheel in the reverse order of removal. Adjust the wheel bearings as described in Chapter 1. Then, adjust the brakes as described above.

Wheel Cylinders
REMOVAL AND INSTALLATION

CAUTION: *Brake shoes contain asbestos, which has been determined to be a cancer causing agent. Never clean the brake surfaces with compressed air! Avoid inhaling any dust from any brake surface! When cleaning brake surfaces, use a commercially available brake cleaning fluid.*

1. Jack up the wheel to be serviced.

2. Remove the wheel, brake drum, hub assembly, and brake shoes.

3. Disconnect the brake hose from the wheel cylinder.

4. Unscrew the wheel cylinder securing nut and remove the wheel cylinder from the brake backing plate.

5. Install the wheel cylinder in the reverse order of removal, assemble the remaining components, and bleed the brake hydraulic system.

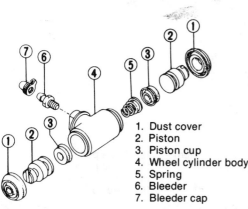

1. Dust cover
2. Piston
3. Piston cup
4. Wheel cylinder body
5. Spring
6. Bleeder
7. Bleeder cap

Typical wheel cylinder

OVERHAUL

NOTE: *Datsun obtains parts from two manufacturers: Nabco and Tokico. Parts are not interchangeable. The name of the manufacturer is usually on the wheel cylinder. Replacement wheel cylinder parts and complete rebuilt wheel cylinders are available from most auto parts stores under other names. Those parts must be replacements for the Tokico and Nabco originals, however.*

1. Remove the wheel cylinder form the backing plate.

2. Remove the dust boot and take out the piston. Discard the piston cup. The dust boot can be reused, if necessary, but it is better to replace it.

3. Wash all of the components in clean brake fluid.

4. Inspect the piston and piston bore. Replace any components which are severely corroded, scored, or worn. The piston and piston bore can be polished lightly with crocus cloth. Move the crocus cloth around the piston bore; not in and out of the piston bore.

5. Wash the wheel cylinder and piston thoroughly in clean brake fluid, allowing them to remain lubricated for assembly.

6. Coat all of the new components to be installed in the wheel cylinder with clean brake fluid prior to assembly.

7. Install the pistons with new cups. Install the new boots. Install the wheel cylinder in the reverse order of removal. Assemble the remaining components and bleed the brake hydraulic system.

FRONT DISC BRAKES

CAUTION: *Brake shoes contain asbestos, which has been determined to be a cancer causing agent. Never clean the brake surfaces with compressed air! Avoid inhaling any dust from any brake surface! When cleaning brake surfaces, use a commercially available brake cleaning fluid.*

Disc Brake Pads
INSPECTION

You should be able to check the pad lining thickness without removing the pads. Check the Brake Specifications Chart at the end of this chapter to find the manufacturer's pad wear limit. However, this measurement may disagree with your state inspection laws. When replacing pads, always check the surface of the rotors for scoring or wear. The rotors should be removed for resurfacing if badly scored.

REMOVAL AND INSTALLATION

CAUTION: *Brake shoes contain asbestos, which has been determined to be a cancer causing agent. Never clean the brake surfaces with compressed air! Avoid inhaling any dust from any brake surface! When cleaning brake surfaces, use a commercially available brake cleaning fluid.*

NOTE: *All four front brake pads must always be replaced as a set.*

Annette Type

1. Raise and support the front of the car with jackstands. Remove the wheels.

2. Remove the clip, pull out the pins, and remove the pad springs.

3. Remove the pads by pulling them out with pliers.

4. To install, first lightly coat the yoke groove and end surface of the piston with grease. Do not allow grease to contact the pads or rotor.

5. Open the bleeder screw slightly and push the outer piston into the cylinder until its end aligns with the end of the boot retaining ring. Do not push too far; if you do, the caliper will have to be disassembled. Install the inner pad.

6. Pull the yoke toward the outside of the car

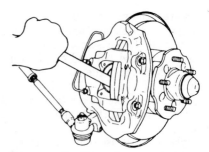

Pushing the inner piston in to install new brake pads, 1200, B210 and 210 calipers

to push the inner piston into place. Install the outer pad.

7. Apply the brakes a few times to seat the pads. Check the master cylinder and add fluid if necessary. Bleed the brakes if necessary.

Sentra Pad

1. Jack up the front of the car and safely support it with jack stands.

2. Remove the caliper lock pin.

3. The caliper cylinder body swings upward for pad replacement. Remove the pad retainers and pads.

CAUTION: *When the cylinder body is in the*

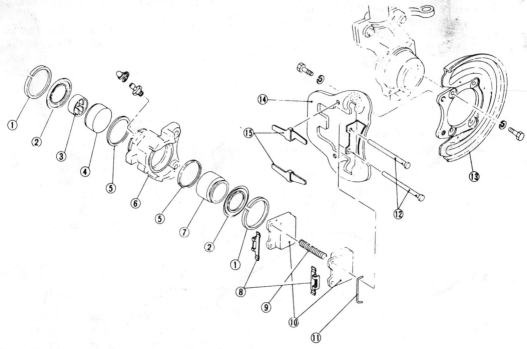

1. Retaining ring	6. Cylinder body	11. Clip
2. Boot	7. Piston B (outer piston)	12. Clevis pin
3. Bias ring	8. Hanger spring	13. Buffle plate
4. Piston A (inner piston)	9. Spring	14. Yoke
5. Piston seal	10. Pad	15. Yoke spring

Typical Annette-type disc brake

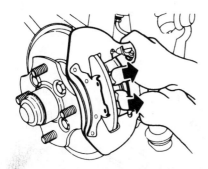

Make sure you don't push the piston in too far

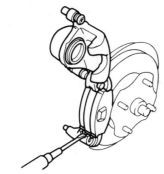

Swing the Sentra cylinder body up for pad access

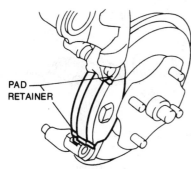

PAD
RETAINER

Sentra brake pad retainer location

"up" position, DO NOT depress the brake pedal, or the piston will jump out!

4. Before installation, clean the piston end and the pin bolts.

5. Apply a coat of PBC grease or equivalent to the pad-to-torque member clearance.

NOTE: *DO NOT get any grease on the pads or brake rotor (disc).*

6. Install the inner pad. Swing the cylinder body down and to the other side.

7. Install the outer pad, then the pad retainers. Install the lock pin.

Calipers

NOTE: *Use the Brake Identification Chart in this section to find the brake system your car uses. This information will be useful in buying replacement brake parts.*

OVERHAUL

CAUTION: *Brake shoes contain asbestos, which has been determined to be a cancer causing agent. Never clean the brake surfaces with compressed air! Avoid inhaling any dust from any brake surface! When cleaning brake surfaces, use a commercially available brake cleaning fluid.*

Annette Type

1. Remove the pads.
2. Disconnect the brake tube.
3. Remove the two bottom strut assembly installation botls to provide clearance.
4. Remove the caliper assembly mounting bolts.
5. Loosen the bleeder screw and press the pistons into their bores.
6. Clamp the yoke in a vise and tap the yoke head with a hammer to loosen the cylinder. Be careful that primary piston does not fall out.
7. Remove the bias ring from primary piston. Remove the retaining rings and boots from both pistons. Depress and remove the pistons from the cylinder. Remove the piston seal from the cylinder carefully with the fingers so as not to mar the cylinder wall.
8. Remove the yoke springs from the yoke.
9. Wash all parts with clean brake fluid (do not use gasoline, kerosene, thinners or any other mineral solvent).
10. If the piston or cylinder is badly worn or scored, replace both. The piston surface is plated and must not be polished with emery paper. Replace all seals. The rotor can be removed and machined if scored, but final thickness must be at least 8.5mm. Runout must not exceed 0.025mm.
11. Lubricate the cylinder bore with clean brake fluid and install the piston seal.
12. Insert the bias ring into primary piston so that the rounded ring portion comes to the bottom of the piston. The primary piston has a small depression inside, while the secondary does not.
13. Lubricate the pistons with clean brake fluid and insert into the cylinder. Install the boot and retaining ring. The yoke groove of the bias ring of primary piston must align with the yoke groove of the cylinder.
14. Install the yoke springs to the yoke so the projecting portion faces to the disc (rotor).
15. Lubricate the sliding portion of the cylinder and yoke. Assemble the cylinder and yoke by tapping the yoke lightly.
16. Replace the caliper assembly and pads. Torque the mounting bolts to 33-41 ft. lbs. Ro-

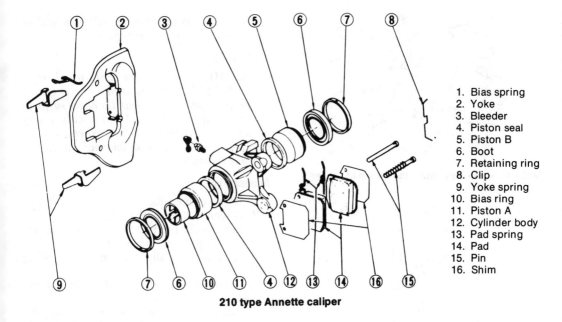

1. Bias spring
2. Yoke
3. Bleeder
4. Piston seal
5. Piston B
6. Boot
7. Retaining ring
8. Clip
9. Yoke spring
10. Bias ring
11. Piston A
12. Cylinder body
13. Pad spring
14. Pad
15. Pin
16. Shim

210 type Annette caliper

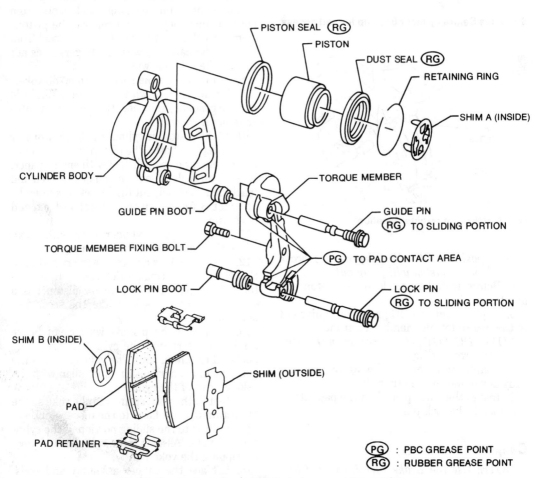

PG : PBC GREASE POINT
RG : RUBBER GREASE POINT

Sentra disc brake caliper exploded view—gasoline engine

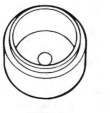

PISTON A
(INNER PISTON)

PISTON B
(OUTER PISTON)

Piston comparison (inner and outer)

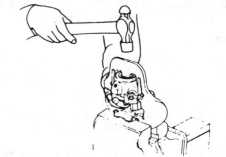

Tapping the yoke head with a hammer

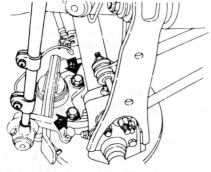

Caliper removal

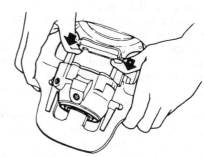

Assembling the yoke and cylinder (Annette type)

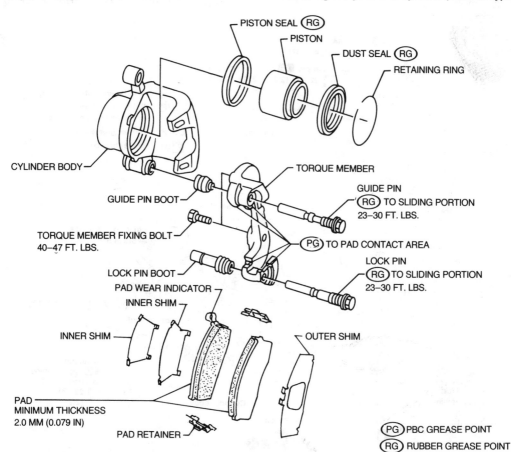

PISTON SEAL (RG)

PISTON

DUST SEAL (RG)

RETAINING RING

CYLINDER BODY

TORQUE MEMBER

GUIDE PIN BOOT

GUIDE PIN
(RG) TO SLIDING PORTION
23–30 FT. LBS.

TORQUE MEMBER FIXING BOLT
40–47 FT. LBS.

(PG) TO PAD CONTACT AREA

LOCK PIN BOOT

LOCK PIN
(RG) TO SLIDING PORTION
23–30 FT. LBS.

PAD WEAR INDICATOR

INNER SHIM

INNER SHIM

OUTER SHIM

PAD
MINIMUM THICKNESS
2.0 MM (0.079 IN)

PAD RETAINER

(PG) PBC GREASE POINT
(RG) RUBBER GREASE POINT

Sentra disc brake caliper exploded view—diesel engine

tor bolt torque is 20-27 ft. lbs. Strut bolt torque is 33-44 ft. lbs. Bleed the system of air.

Sentra Type

1. Separate cylinder body of caliper from the torque member by unbolting the two, swinging the cylinder body up (as in pad replacement) and sliding the pin out of the hole.

2. Remove the brake hose. Press out the piston with the dust seal and retainer ring.

3. Remove the piston seal.

4. Remove the guide pin, lock pin, guide pin boot and lock pin boot.

5. Clean and check all parts. Clean parts with clean brake fluid only (never use solvents). Check the inside surface of the cylinder for rust, ear, damage or foreign material. Minor rust damage may be removed with crocus cloth soaked in clean brake fluid. Check the torque member for wear, cracks or damage. Check the piston for scoring, rust, wear or damage. Replace if any fault is detected.

CAUTION: *The piston sliding surface is plated. Do not attempt to polish the surface with even crocus cloth or fine emery cloth.*

6. Replace the piston seal and dust seal during assembly.

7. Check the guide pin for wear, cracks or damage.

8. Install the piston seal, applying rubber grease or brake fluid to the seal groove and seal.

9. Apply rubber grease or brake fluid to the sliding portions and the inside of the dust seal.

10. With the dust seal fitted to the piston, insert the dust seal into the groove on the cylinder body and install the piston.

11. Install the retainer ring and properly secure the dust seal.

12. Apply a coat of rubber grease to the guide pin and lock pin sliding surfaces. Install the lock pin boot, guide pin boot, lock pin and guide pin.

13. Attach the torque member to the cylinder body, and connect the brake hose.

Disc Brake Rotor

REMOVAL AND INSTALLATION

CAUTION: *Brake shoes contain asbestos, which has been determined to be a cancer causing agent. Never clean the brake surfaces with compressed air! Avoid inhaling any dust from any brake surface! When cleaning*

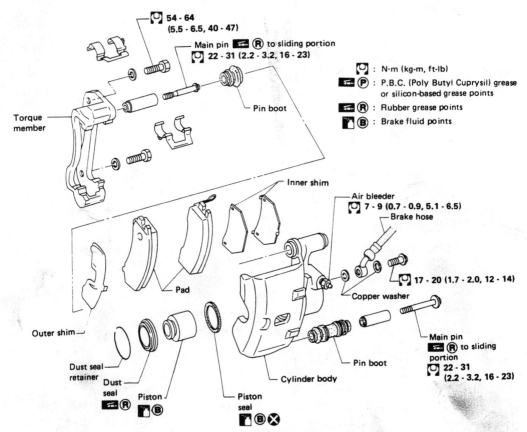

Exploded view of the AD18V caliper used on 1987–88 Sentras

brake surfaces, use a commercially available brake cleaning fluid.

1200, B210 and 210

1. Block rear wheels with chocks, and firmly apply parking brake.

2. Jack up front of car and safely support it with jackstands.

3. Remove wheel and tire assembly.

4. Remove the brake hose, plug the openings and then remove the brake caliper assembly.

5. Work off the small hub cap from the hub using thin screwdrivers or pry bars. If necessary, tap around it with a soft hammer while removing cap.

NOTE: *Use care while removing the cap, as there is an O-ring underneath that must not be damaged.*

6. Remove the cotter pin from the castellated nut and discard it (assemble the hub with a new cotter pin). Take out the adjusting cap and the wheel bearing locknut.

7. Remove the wheel hub with the disc brake rotor from the spindle with the bearing installed. Be careful not to drop the outer bearing cone out of the hub when removing the knuckle from the knuckle spindle.

8. Remove the outer bearing cone.

9. Loosen the four bolts securing the brake disc; remove the brake disc rotor from the wheel hub assembly.

10. Install the rotor to the wheel hub. Torque rotor bolts to 20-38 ft. lbs. Make sure wheel bearings are properly greased and install a new hub grease seal. Install the hub and rotor onto the spindle. Adjust the wheel bearings by following the procedure outlined in Chapter 1. Install a new cotter pin.

1983-86

1. Remove the front hub and halfshaft as a unit, as described in Chapter 7 Drive Train.

2. Remove the hub nut and then separate the halfshaft from the hub assembly.

3. Separate the wheel hub from the steering knuckle using a slide hammer.

4. Remove the bolts securing the wheel hub to the disc rotor and remove the rotor.

5. Install the rotor onto the hub and install the bolts. The rotor bolts should be torqued to 18-25 ft. lbs. Grease the end of the halfshaft before installing it into the front hub. Install a new hub grease seal., and torque the halfshaft to hub bolt to 87-145 ft. lbs. Install the front hub and halfshaft as described in Chapter 7.

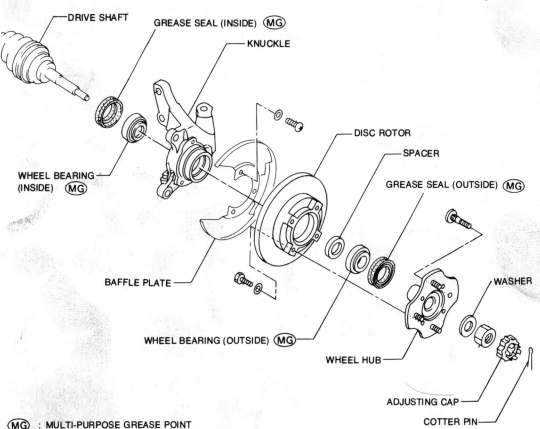

(MG) : MULTI-PURPOSE GREASE POINT

Sentra front disc and hub assembly

Sentra 1987-88

1. Raise the car and support it securely. Remove the front wheel or wheels involved.

2. Remove the caliper as described above. Hang the caliper near its normal position so the brake hose will not be stretched.

3. Remove the rotor from the studs on the wheel hub.

4. Installation is the reverse of removal.

REAR DRUM BRAKES

CAUTION: *Brake shoes contain asbestos, which has been determined to be a cancer causing agent. Never clean the brake surfaces with compressed air! Avoid inhaling any dust from any brake surface! When cleaning brake surfaces, use a commercially available brake cleaning fluid.*

Brake Drums

REMOVAL AND INSTALLATION

ALL MODELS EXCEPT 1987-88 Sentra 2 WD

1. Raise the rear of the vehicle and support it on jackstands.

2. Remove the wheels.

3. Release the parking brake.

4. Pull off the brake drums. On some models there are two threaded service holes in each brake drum. If the drum will not come off, fit two correct size bolts in the service holes and screw them in; this will force the drum away from the axle.

5. If the drum cannot be easily removed, back off the brake adjustment.

NOTE: *Never depress the brake pedal while the brake drum is removed.*

6. Installation is the reverse of removal.

1987-88 Sentra (2 WD only)

On the latest Sentras, the brake drum and rear wheel hub and bearing are combined.

1. Raise the rear of the vehicle and support it on jackstands.

2. Remove the wheels.

3. Release the parking brake.

4. Remove the hub cap. Remove the wheel bearing locknut and the washer behind it.

5. Remove the drum, wheel bearing and hub by sliding them off the spindle. If the drum fails the inspection, it must be machined or replaced. If necessary to remove and replace the wheel bearing to machine or replace the drum, refer to Chapter 7.

6. To install the drum/hub assembly, first slide it onto the spindle. Install the washer and the wheel bearing nut. Torque the wheel bearing nut to 137-188 ft. lbs. Rotate the drum and make sure the wheel bearing rotates smoothly.

7. Install the hub cap. Install the wheel and torque the nuts.

INSPECTION

1. After removing the brake drum, wipe out the accumulated dust with a damp cloth.

CAUTION: *Brake shoes contain asbestos, which has been determined to be a cancer causing agent. Never clean the brake surfaces with compressed air! Avoid inhaling any dust from any brake surface! When cleaning brake surfaces, use a commercially available brake cleaning fluid.*

2. Inspect the drum for cracks, deep grooves, roughness, scoring, or out-of- roundness. Replace any brake drum which is cracked.

3. Smooth any slight scores by polishing the friction surface with a fine emery cloth. Heavy or extensive scoring will cause excessive brake lining wear and should be removed from the brake drum through resurfacing (most auto re-

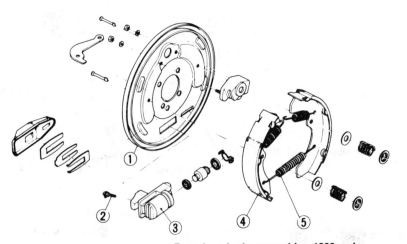

1. Brake disc
2. Bleeder
3. Wheel cylinder
4. Shoe assembly
5. Return spring

Rear drum brake assembly—1200 series

Brake Identification Chart

Match the numbers on the chart with those below to identify your brake system

Model	1973	1974	1975	1976	1977	1978	1979	1980	1981	1982	1983	1984	1985	1986	1987	1988
1200	① ② ⑤															
B210		① ②	① ②	① ②	① ③	① ③										
210							① ④	① ④	① ④	① ④						
Sentra										⑥ ④	⑥ ④	⑥ ④	⑥ ④	⑥ ④	⑥ ④	⑦ ④

① Annette Type front disc brakes
② Rear drum brakes with bolt-type adjuster
③ Rear drum brakes with internal, toothed adjusting nut
④ Rear drum brakes with automatic adjustment
⑤ Front drum brakes with top and bottom bolt-type adjusters
⑥ CL18B front disc brakes—Gasoline engine, AD20V front disc brakes—Diesel engine
⑦ CL18B or AD18V front disc brakes

pair shops and machine shops provide this service).

Brake Shoes and Wheel Cylinders
REMOVAL AND INSTALLATION

CAUTION: *Brake shoes contain asbestos, which has been determined to be a cancer causing agent. Never clean the brake surfaces with compressed air! Avoid inhaling any dust from any brake surface! When cleaning brake surfaces, use a commercially available brake cleaning fluid.*

All models

1. Jack up the rear of the car and safely support it with jackstands.
2. Loosen the handbrake cable, remove the clevis pin from the wheel cylinder lever, disconnect the handbrake cable, and remove the return pull spring.
3. Remove the brake drum as described above. Loosen the brake adjusters if the drums are difficult to remove. Remove the return springs, shoe retainers, and brake shoes. Place a heavy rubber band around the cylinder to prevent the pistons from coming out.
4. Clean the backing plate and check the wheel cylinder for leaks. To remove the wheel cylinder, remove the brake line, dust cover, securing nuts or plates and adjusting shims. Clearance between cylinder and piston should not exceed 0.15mm.
5. The drums must be machined if scored or out-of-round more than 0.20mm on cars built

through 1986. On 1987-88 models, the drums must not be more than 0.30mm out of round and radial runout must not exceed 0.03mm. The drum inside diameter must not be machined beyond 204.2mm on those models built before 1987. On 1987-88 models, the maximum machined diameter is 204.5mm for 203mm drums and 230mm for 228mm drums. Minimum safe lining thickness is 1.5mm (1.0mm for the F10).

6. Install the new wheel cylinder into position with any shims or plates and install the mounting bolts. Then, install the dust cover and brake line.
7. Install the shoes, install the shoe retainers and lock them by turning 90°, and then install the return springs.
8. Retract the adjusters all the way. Install the drum as described above. Reconnect the handbrake, install the wheels, and lower the car. If the wheel cylinder was removed, bleed the system thoroughly. Then, for all cars, make sure to apply the brakes hard repeatedly to activate the adjuster until a good hard pedal is available.

Wheel Cylinder

See the section just above "Brake Shoes Removal and Installation" for wheel cylinder removal and installation procedures. See the "Front Drum Brake Wheel Cylinder Overhaul" for overhaul procedures for the rear drum brake cylinders, as they are identical. Observe

Brake Specifications

All measurements given are in inches unless noted

Model	Year	Lug Nut Torque (ft. lbs.)	Master Cylinder Bore	Brake Disc		Drum		Minimum Lining Thickness	
				Minimum Thickness	Maximum Run-Out	Diameter	Max. Wear Limit	Front	Rear
1200	1973	58–65	0.6875	0.3307	0.0012	8.000	8.051	0.0630 (disc) 0.0591 (drum)	0.0591
B210	1974–78	58–65	0.750	0.331	0.0047	8.000	8.051	0.063	0.059
210	1979–82	58–72	0.8125	0.331	0.0047	8.000	8.050	0.063	0.059
Sentra	1982–84	58–72	0.750	0.433 ①	0.0047 ②	7.09	7.13	0.079	0.059
	1985–86	58–72	③	0.433 ④	0.0028	8.000	8.05	0.079	0.059
	1987–88	72–87	¹⁵⁄₁₆ ⑤	0.394 ⑥	0.0028	8.00	8.05 ⑦	0.079	0.059

NOTE: Minimum lining thickness is as recommended by the manufacturer. Due to variation in state inspection regulations, the minimum allowable thickness may be different than recommended by the manufacturer.
① 0.394 in. (1983–86)
② 0.0028 in. (1983–86)
③ E165—¹⁵⁄₁₆ in.
   CD17—1.0 in.
④ With AD20V calipers, 0.63 in.
⑤ With 4WD—1.0 in.
⑥ With AD18V calipers—0.630 in.
⑦ For 9 in. drums—9.06 in.

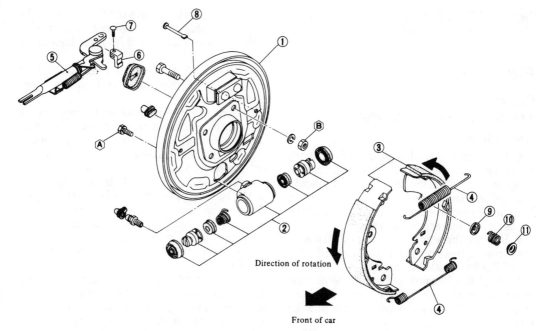

1. Brake disc
2. Wheel cylinder assembly
3. Brake shoe assembly
4. Return spring
5. Adjuster assembly
6. Stopper
7. Stopper pin
8. Anti-rattle pin
9. Spring seat
10. Anti-rattle spring
11. Retainer

Direction of rotation

Front of car

Exploded view of drum brake assembly—210 series

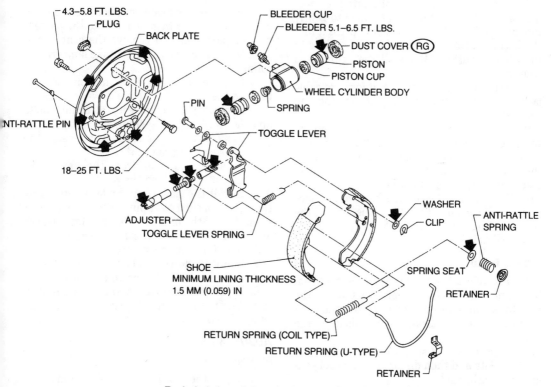

4.3–5.8 FT. LBS.
PLUG
BACK PLATE
BLEEDER CUP
BLEEDER 5.1–6.5 FT. LBS.
DUST COVER RG
PISTON
PISTON CUP
WHEEL CYLINDER BODY
PIN
SPRING
ANTI-RATTLE PIN
TOGGLE LEVER
18–25 FT. LBS.
ADJUSTER
TOGGLE LEVER SPRING
WASHER
CLIP
ANTI-RATTLE SPRING
SHOE
MINIMUM LINING THICKNESS
1.5 MM (0.059) IN
SPRING SEAT
RETAINER
RETURN SPRING (COIL TYPE)
RETURN SPRING (U-TYPE)
RETAINER

Exploded view of drum brake assembly—Sentra

the "NOTE" about different manufacturers of wheel cylinder components.

PARKING BRAKE

Cables

REMOVAL AND INSTALLATION

1987-88 Sentra

1. Working inside the passenger compartment, remove the console (as described in Chapter 10) and the insulator pad underneath.

2. Release the brake lever. Remove the two brake lever mounting bolts and lift the brake lever assembly upward for access.

3. Remove the adjusting nuts and then slide the threaded front portion of the forward cable out of the handbrake assembly.

4. Twist the forward fittings of the rear cables appropriately to release them from the equalizer. The forward cable may now be removed.

5. To remove the rear cable, raise the vehicle and support it securely. Remove the nuts attaching the forward, middle, and rearward cable jacket slides to the body for both rear cables.

6. Remove the rear wheels and rear brake drums. Disconnect the cables at the adjusters on both sides. Then, pull the cable jackets out of the rear brake backing plates and remove them.

7. To install, insert the cables into the backing plates. Use a hammer and punch to gently tap the flange on the cable jacket to press it into the backing plate. Connect the inner cables to the brake adjusters. Reinstall the drums and wheels.

8. Install the rear, center, and forward cable jacket mounts on both sides by bolting them to the body.

9. Working inside, clip the forward ends of the inner cables to the equalizer. Install the forward, threaded portions of the inner cables through the holes in the handbrake mechanism and then install the adjusting nuts.

10. Bolt the handbrake mechanism in place and torque the bolts to 5.8-8 ft. lbs. Install the console. Adjust the handbrake mechanism as described below.

210 and B 210

1. Disconnect the electrical connector from the handbrake warning light switch on the handbrake mechanism. Then, remove the bolts mounting the handbrake mechanism to the floor.

2. Then, raise and support the car. Remove the lockplate and then disconnect the cable adjuster on either side.

3. Pull the front cable into the passenger compartment and remove it with the brake lever. If the cable must be replaced, break the attaching pin and separate it from the handbrake mechanism.

4. To remove the center and rear cables, first disconnect the cable adjuster from the front cable.

5. Remove the lockplate and strap located near the axle housing, at the rear of the center cable. Then, pull off the return spring and disconnect the rear cable at the lever by pulling out the clevis pin.

6. Connect the rear cable to the apply lever on the backing plate by installing the clevis pin. Connect the rear cable to the center cable at the rear axle by installing the clevis pin and lock plate. Install the return spring.

7. Connect the adjuster between the center and front cables.

8. Connect the front attaching pin of the front cable to the handbrake mechanism. Reinstall the handbrake in reverse of the removal procedure. Adjust the mechanism as described below.

1982-86 Sentra

1. To remove the rear cable, first raise the car and support it securely. Then, unscrew the locknuts that attach the front of either rear cable to the equalizer. Then, remove the rear wheel and brake drum and disconnect the cable at the adjuster.

2. If the forward cable needs to be replaced, next lower the car to gain access to the passenger compartment and remove the center console. Disconnect the parking brake lamp switch connector.

3. Remove the bolts that anchor the seat belts to the body.

4. Remove the brake lever attaching bolts and the front cable attaching screws.

5. Remove the front cable from inside the passenger compartment.

6. Separate the cable from the handbrake mechanism by breaking the pin.

7. Install the new front cable by attaching the clevis pin and cotter pin to the brake mechanism. Install the brake mechanism into the car and reconnect the electrical connector.

8. Install the center console.

9. Connect the rear cables at the adjusters and then install the drums and wheels.

10. Attach the rear cables to the equalizer by installing the locknuts. Adjust the mechanism as described below.

ADJUSTMENT

All Models 1973-86

1. Adjust the rear brake shoe-to-drum clearance before adjusting hand brake.

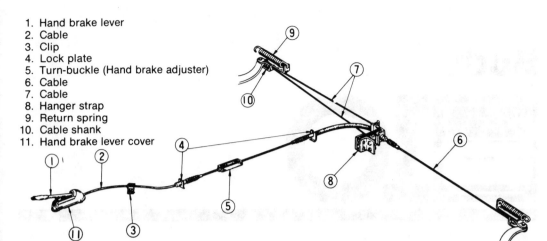

1. Hand brake lever
2. Cable
3. Clip
4. Lock plate
5. Turn-buckle (Hand brake adjuster)
6. Cable
7. Cable
8. Hanger strap
9. Return spring
10. Cable shank
11. Hand brake lever cover

1200 and B210 parking brake assembly. 210 and Sentra similar

Parking brake adjustment turnbuckle

2. Turn the adjusting nut on the front (short) end of the turnbuckle so that the operating stroke is 78.5mm, pulled by a force of 24-33 lbs. This corresponds to the sixth notch from the completely released lever position.

3. After the above adjustment is made, operate the lever twice at a force of 55 to 66 lbs. so as to seat it properly.

4. Adjust again as described above in number 2.

5. Tighten the locknut securely (see illustration).

6. If the adjustment is no longer effective on its threaded end, replace the front cable.

1987-88 Sentra

1. Pull the brake up with standard application force—about 45 lbs., counting the notches.

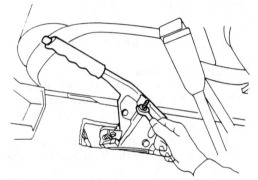

Adjusting the handbrake on 1987–88 Sentra

It should come up 7-11 notches. If the brake comes up too far, lower the handle and tighten the nuts. If it does not come up enough notches, lower the handle and loosen the nuts. This force must bring the handle up 7-11 notches when the adjustment is complete (the adjustment will last longer if it is 8-9 notches).

2. Bend the brake warning lamp switch plate so the light will come on as the handle is raised 1-2 notches.

Body

10

Exterior

Doors

REMOVAL AND INSTALLATION

Front

1. Remove the windshield wiper blades and cowl top grille.
2. Remove the front fender.
3. With the door in the full open position, place a garage jack or stand under the door to support its weight. Place a rag on top of the jack to protect the paint.
4. Loosen the bolts attaching the door hinge to the body and remove the front door from the car.
5. Use the jack (covered with a rag) to position the door so door hinge boltholes line up with those in the body. Install the bolts loosely.
5. Align the door so the striker will latch properly and the front edge of the door will lay flush with the adjoining edge of the body. Then, torque the mounting bolts to 15-20 ft. lbs.
6. Install the front fender, cowl top grille, and wiper blades.

Rear

1. Open the front door and keep it open.
2. Open the rear door to the full open position, and place a support under it. Protect the paint with a rag between the support and the door.
3. Loosen the bolts attaching the rear door hinges to the center pillar and remove the rear door from the body.
4. Use the jack (covered with a rag) to position the door so door hinge boltholes line up with those in the body. Install the bolts loosely.
5. Align the door so the striker will latch properly and the front edge of the door will lay flush with the adjoining edge of the body. Then, torque the mounting bolts to 15-20 ft. lbs.

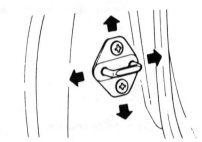

Adjusting door lock striker

ADJUSTMENT

Front and Rear

Proper door alignment can be obtained by adjusting the door hinge and door lock striker. The door hinge and striker can be moved up and down fore and aft in enlarged holes by loosening the attaching bolts.

NOTE: *The door should be adjusted for an even and parallel fit for the door opening and surrounding body panels.*

Hood

REMOVAL AND INSTALLATION

1. Open the hood and protect the body with covers to protect the painted surfaces.
2. Mark the hood hinge locations on the hood for proper reinstallation.
3. Holding both sides of the hood, unscrew the bolts securing the hinge to the hood. This operation requires a helper.
4. Install the hood with a helper, aligning boltholes. Install the bolts loosely.
5. Carefully shift the position of the hood to align the matchmarks positioning the hood on the hinges. Then, tighten the bolts. If installing a new part, align the hood as described below.

ALIGNMENT

The hood can be adjusted with bolts attaching the hood to the hood hinges, hood lock

CHILTON'S
AUTO BODY REPAIR TIPS

Tools and Materials • Step-by-Step Illustrated Procedures
How To Repair Dents, Scratches and Rust Holes
Spray Painting and Refinishing Tips

With a little practice, basic body repair procedures can be mastered by any do-it-yourself mechanic. The step-by-step repairs shown here can be applied to almost any type of auto body repair.

TOOLS & MATERIALS

You may already have basic tools, such as hammers and electric drills. Other tools unique to body repair — body hammers, grinding attachments, sanding blocks, dent puller, half-round plastic file and plastic spreaders — are relatively inexpensive and can be obtained wherever auto parts or auto body repair parts are sold. Portable air compressors and paint spray guns can be purchased or rented.

Auto Body Repair Kits

The best and most often used products are available to the do-it-yourselfer in kit form, from major manufacturers of auto body repair products. The same manufacturers also merchandise the individual products for use by pros.

Kits are available to make a wide variety of repairs, including holes, dents and scratches and fiberglass, and offer the advantage of buying the materials you'll need for the job. There is little waste or chance of materials going bad from not being used. Many kits may also contain basic body-working tools such as body files, sanding blocks and spreaders. Check the contents of the kit before buying your tools.

BODY REPAIR TIPS

Safety

Many of the products associated with auto body repair and refinishing contain toxic chemicals. Read all labels before opening containers and store them in a safe place and manner.

• Wear eye protection (safety goggles) when using power tools or when performing any operation that involves the removal of any type of material.

• Wear lung protection (disposable mask or respirator) when grinding, sanding or painting.

Sanding

1 Sand off paint before using a dent puller. When using a non-adhesive sanding disc, cover the back of the disc with an overlapping layer or two of masking tape and trim the edges. The disc will last considerably longer.

2 Use the circular motion of the sanding disc to grind *into* the edge of the repair. Grinding or sanding away from the jagged edge will only tear the sandpaper.

3 Use the palm of your hand flat on the panel to detect high and low spots. Do not use your fingertips. Slide your hand slowly back and forth.

WORKING WITH BODY FILLER

Mixing The Filler

Cleanliness and proper mixing and application are extremely important. Use a clean piece of plastic or glass or a disposable artist's palette to mix body filler.

1 Allow plenty of time and follow directions. No useful purpose will be served by adding more hardener to make it cure (set-up) faster. Less hardener means more curing time, but the mixture dries harder; more hardener means less curing time but a softer mixture.

2 Both the hardener and the filler should be thoroughly kneaded or stirred before mixing. Hardener should be a solid paste and dispense like thin toothpaste. Body filler should be smooth, and free of lumps or thick spots.

Getting the proper amount of hardener in the filler is the trickiest part of preparing the filler. Use the same amount of hardener in cold or warm weather. For contour filler (thick coats), a bead of hardener twice the diameter of the filler is about right. There's about a 15% margin on either side, but, if in doubt use less hardener.

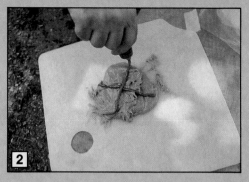

3 Mix the body filler and hardener by wiping across the mixing surface, picking the mixture up and wiping it again. Colder weather requires longer mixing times. Do not mix in a circular motion; this will trap air bubbles which will become holes in the cured filler.

Applying The Filler

1 For best results, filler should not be applied over 1/4" thick.

Apply the filler in several coats. Build it up to above the level of the repair surface so that it can be sanded or grated down.

The first coat of filler must be pressed on with a firm wiping motion.

Apply the filler in one direction only. Working the filler back and forth will either pull it off the metal or trap air bubbles.

REPAIRING DENTS

Before you start, take a few minutes to study the damaged area. Try to visualize the shape of the panel before it was damaged. If the damage is on the left fender, look at the right fender and use it as a guide. If there is access to the panel from behind, you can reshape it with a body hammer. If not, you'll have to use a dent puller. Go slowly and work the metal a little at a time. Get the panel as straight as possible before applying filler.

1 This dent is typical of one that can be pulled out or hammered out from behind. Remove the headlight cover, headlight assembly and turn signal housing.

2 Drill a series of holes ½ the size of the end of the dent puller along the stress line. Make some trial pulls and assess the results. If necessary, drill more holes and try again. Do not hurry.

3 If possible, use a body hammer and block to shape the metal back to its original contours. Get the metal back as close to its original shape as possible. Don't depend on body filler to fill dents.

4 Using an 80-grit grinding disc on an electric drill, grind the paint from the surrounding area down to bare metal. Use a new grinding pad to prevent heat buildup that will warp metal.

5 The area should look like this when you're finished grinding. Knock the drill holes in and tape over small openings to keep plastic filler out.

6 Mix the body filler (see Body Repair Tips). Spread the body filler evenly over the entire area (see Body Repair Tips). Be sure to cover the area completely.

7 Let the body filler dry until the surface can just be scratched with your fingernail. Knock the high spots from the body filler with a body file ("Cheese-grater"). Check frequently with the palm of your hand for high and low spots.

8 Check to be sure that trim pieces that will be installed later will fit exactly. Sand the area with 40-grit paper.

9 If you wind up with low spots, you may have to apply another layer of filler.

10 Knock the high spots off with 40-grit paper. When you are satisfied with the contours of the repair, apply a thin coat of filler to cover pin holes and scratches.

11 Block sand the area with 40-grit paper to a smooth finish. Pay particular attention to body lines and ridges that must be well-defined.

12 Sand the area with 400 paper and then finish with a scuff pad. The finished repair is ready for priming and painting (see Painting Tips).

Materials and photos courtesy of Ritt Jones Auto Body, Prospect Park, PA.

REPAIRING RUST HOLES

There are many ways to repair rust holes. The fiberglass cloth kit shown here is one of the most cost efficient for the owner because it provides a strong repair that resists cracking and moisture and is relatively easy to use. It can be used on large and small holes (with or without backing) and can be applied over contoured areas. Remember, however, that short of replacing an entire panel, no repair is a guarantee that the rust will not return.

1 Remove any trim that will be in the way. Clean away all loose debris. Cut away all the rusted metal. But be sure to leave enough metal to retain the contour or body shape.

2 Grind away all traces of rust with a 24-grit grinding disc. Be sure to grind back 3-4 inches from the edge of the hole down to bare metal and be sure all traces of paint, primer and rust are removed.

3 Block sand the area with 80 or 100 grit sandpaper to get a clear, shiny surface and feathered paint edge. Tap the edges of the hole inward with a ball peen hammer.

4 If you are going to use release film, cut a piece about 2-3" larger than the area you have sanded. Place the film over the repair and mark the sanded area on the film. Avoid any unnecessary wrinkling of the film.

5 Cut 2 pieces of fiberglass matte to match the shape of the repair. One piece should be about 1" smaller than the sanded area and the second piece should be 1" smaller than the first. Mix enough filler and hardener to saturate the fiberglass material (see Body Repair Tips).

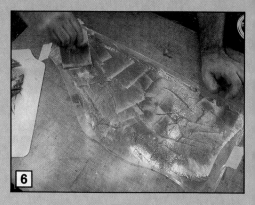

6 Lay the release sheet on a flat surface and spread an even layer of filler, large enough to cover the repair. Lay the smaller piece of fiberglass cloth in the center of the sheet and spread another layer of filler over the fiberglass cloth. Repeat the operation for the larger piece of cloth.

7 Place the repair material over the repair area, with the release film facing outward. Use a spreader and work from the center outward to smooth the material, following the body contours. Be sure to remove all air bubbles.

8 Wait until the repair has dried tack-free and peel off the release sheet. The ideal working temperature is 60°-90° F. Cooler or warmer temperatures or high humidity may require additional curing time. Wait longer, if in doubt.

9 Sand and feather-edge the entire area. The initial sanding can be done with a sanding disc on an electric drill if care is used. Finish the sanding with a block sander. Low spots can be filled with body filler; this may require several applications.

10 When the filler can just be scratched with a fingernail, knock the high spots down with a body file and smooth the entire area with 80-grit. Feather the filled areas into the surrounding areas.

11 When the area is sanded smooth, mix some topcoat and hardener and apply it directly with a spreader. This will give a smooth finish and prevent the glass matte from showing through the paint.

12 Block sand the topcoat smooth with finishing sandpaper (200 grit), and 400 grit. The repair is ready for masking, priming and painting (see Painting Tips).

Materials and photos courtesy Marson Corporation, Chelsea, Massachusetts

---

PAINTING TIPS

Preparation

1 SANDING — Use a 400 or 600 grit wet or dry sandpaper. Wet-sand the area with a ¼ sheet of sandpaper soaked in clean water. Keep the paper wet while sanding. Sand the area until the repaired area tapers into the original finish.

2 CLEANING — Wash the area to be painted thoroughly with water and a clean rag. Rinse it thoroughly and wipe the surface dry until you're sure it's completely free of dirt, dust, fingerprints, wax, detergent or other foreign matter.

3 MASKING — Protect any areas you don't want to overspray by covering them with masking tape and newspaper. Be careful not get fingerprints on the area to be painted.

4 PRIMING — All exposed metal should be primed before painting. Primer protects the metal and provides an excellent surface for paint adhesion. When the primer is dry, wet-sand the area again with 600 grit wet-sandpaper. Clean the area again after sanding.

Painting Techniques

Paint applied from either a spray gun or a spray can (for small areas) will provide good results. Experiment on an old piece of metal to get the right combination before you begin painting.

SPRAYING VISCOSITY (SPRAY GUN ONLY) — Paint should be thinned to spraying viscosity according to the directions on the can. Use only the recommended thinner or reducer and the same amount of reduction regardless of temperature.

AIR PRESSURE (SPRAY GUN ONLY) — This is extremely important. Be sure you are using the proper recommended pressure.

TEMPERATURE — The surface to be painted should be approximately the same temperature as the surrounding air. Applying warm paint to a cold surface, or vice versa, will completely upset the paint characteristics.

THICKNESS — Spray with smooth strokes. In general, the thicker the coat of paint, the longer the drying time. Apply several thin coats about 30 seconds apart. The paint should remain wet long enough to flow out and no longer; heavier coats will only produce sags or wrinkles. Spray a light (fog) coat, followed by heavier color coats.

DISTANCE — The ideal spraying distance is 8"-12" from the gun or can to the surface. Shorter distances will produce ripples, while greater distances will result in orange peel, dry film and poor color match and loss of material due to overspray.

OVERLAPPING — The gun or can should be kept at right angles to the surface at all times. Work to a wet edge at an even speed, using a 50% overlap and direct the center of the spray at the lower or nearest edge of the previous stroke.

RUBBING OUT (BLENDING) FRESH PAINT — Let the paint dry thoroughly. Runs or imperfections can be sanded out, primed and repainted.

Don't be in too big a hurry to remove the masking. This only produces paint ridges. When the finish has dried for at least a week, apply a small amount of fine grade rubbing compound with a clean, wet cloth. Use lots of water and blend the new paint with the surrounding area.

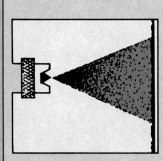

WRONG

Thin coat. Stroke too fast, not enough overlap, gun too far away.

CORRECT

Medium coat. Proper distance, good stroke, proper overlap.

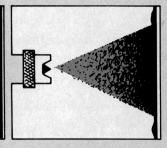

WRONG

Heavy coat. Stroke too slow, too much overlap, gun too close.

mechanism and hood bumpers. The gaps between the hood and fenders should be equal all around. The hood should sit level with the fenders on both sides.

1. Adjust the hood fore and aft by loosening the bolts attaching the hood to the hinge and repositioning hood.

2. Loosen the hood bumper lock nuts and lower bumpers until they do not contact the front of the hood when the hood is closed.

3. Set the striker at the center of the hood lock, and tighten the hood lock securing bolts temporarily.

4. Raise the two hood bumpers until the hood is flush with the fenders.

5. Tighten the hood lock securing bolts after the proper adjustment has been obtained.

Trunklid

REMOVAL AND INSTALLATION

1. Open the trunk lid and position a cloth or cushion to protect the painted areas.

2. Mark the trunk lid hinge locations or trunk lid for proper reinstallation.

3. Support the trunk lid securely. *Planning carefully ahead for the release of force, cau-*

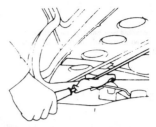

Removing/installing trunk lid supporting torsion bars safely

tiously pry the torsion bar that supports the trunk lid out of its locking grooves so that all torsional force will be released.

4. Support the trunk lid by hand and remove the bolts attaching the trunk lid to the hinge. Then remove the trunk lid.

5. Install the trunklid with a helper, aligning boltholes. Install the bolts loosely.

6. Carefully shift the position of the lid to align the matchmarks positioning it on its hinges. Then, tighten the bolts. If installing a new part, align the lid as described below.

7. Support the lid and reinstall the torsion bars, *working cautiously to avoid allowing them to slip and release force.*

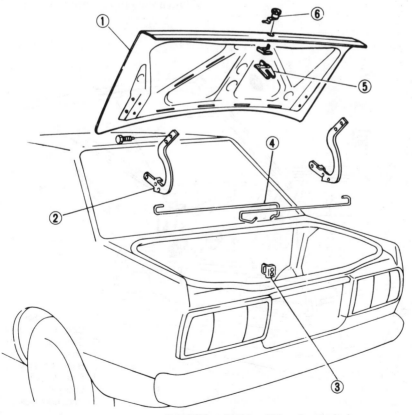

1. Trunk lid
2. Trunk lid hinge
3. Striker
4. Torsion bar
5. Trunk lid lock
6. Lock cylinder

Trunk lid assembly—210 series, typical

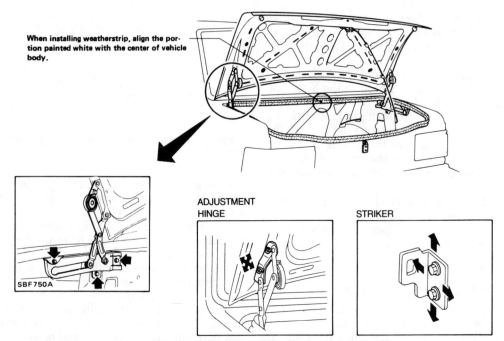

When installing weatherstrip, align the portion painted white with the center of vehicle body.

ADJUSTMENT HINGE

STRIKER

SBF750A

Trunk lid assembly—Sentra series, typical

ALIGNMENT

1. Loosen the trunk lid hinge attaching bolts until they are just loose enough to move the trunk lid.

2. Move the trunk lid for and aft to obtain a flush fit between the trunk lid and the rear fender.

3. To obtain a snug fit between the trunk lid

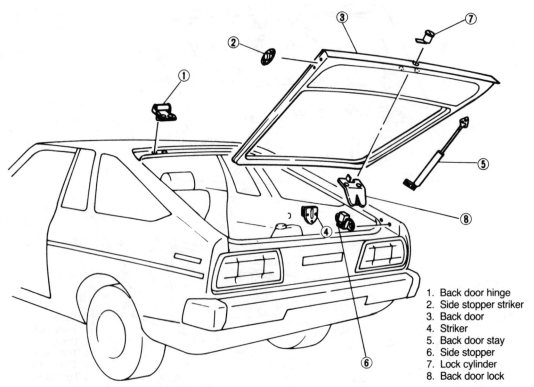

1. Back door hinge
2. Side stopper striker
3. Back door
4. Striker
5. Back door stay
6. Side stopper
7. Lock cylinder
8. Back door lock

Hatchback door assembly—210 series typical

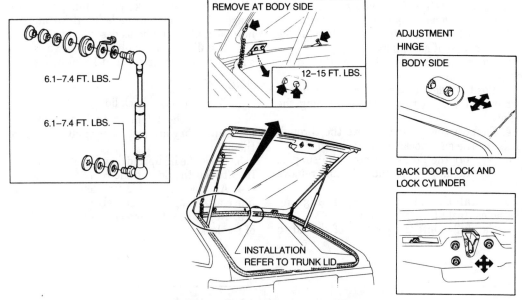

Hatchback door assembly—Sentra series

REMOVE AT BODY SIDE

6.1–7.4 FT. LBS.

6.1–7.4 FT. LBS.

12–15 FT. LBS.

ADJUSTMENT HINGE

BODY SIDE

BACK DOOR LOCK AND LOCK CYLINDER

INSTALLATION REFER TO TRUNK LID

and weatherstrip, loosen the trunk lid lock striker attaching bolts enough to move the lid, working the striker up and down and from side to side as required.

4. After the adjustment is made tighten the striker bolts securely.

Hatchback or Tailgate Lid
REMOVAL AND INSTALLATION

CAUTION: *The shocks which support the hatchback or tailgage lid are gas pressurized. Avoid applying heat or excessive mechanical*

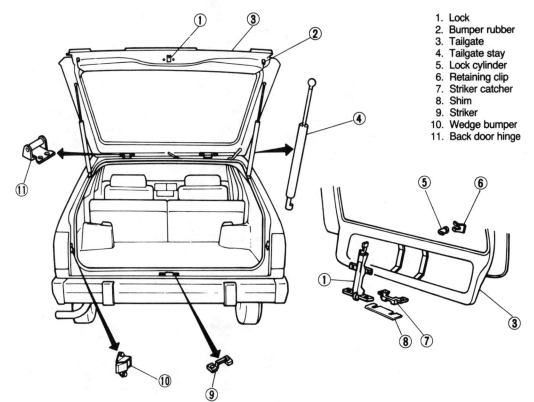

1. Lock
2. Bumper rubber
3. Tailgate
4. Tailgate stay
5. Lock cylinder
6. Retaining clip
7. Striker catcher
8. Shim
9. Striker
10. Wedge bumper
11. Back door hinge

Tailgate assembly—210 series

force, or severe injury may result. Avoid scratching them, or gas may be released!

1. Open the lid and disconnect the rear defogger harness if so equipped.

2. Mark the hinge locations on the lid for proper relocation.

3. Position rags between the roof and the upper end of the lid to prevent scratching the paint.

4. Support the lid and remove the through bolts for the gas shocks, if so-equipped.

5. Support the lid and remove the support bolts for the hinge retaining bolts and remove the lid.

6. Install the lid with a helper, aligning boltholes. Install the bolts loosely.

7. Carefully shift the position of the lid to align the matchmarks positioning it on its hinges. Then, tighten the bolts. If installing a new part, align the lid as described below.

8. Install the through-bolts for the gas shock supports and torque them to 15-20 ft. lbs.

ALIGNMENT

1. Open the hatchback lid.

2. Loosen the lid hinge to body attaching bolts until they are just loose enough to move the lid.

3. Move the lid up and down to obtain a flush fit between the lid and the roof.

4. After adjustment is completed tighten the hinge attaching bolts securely.

5. Adjust the striker so it fits into the center of the lock.

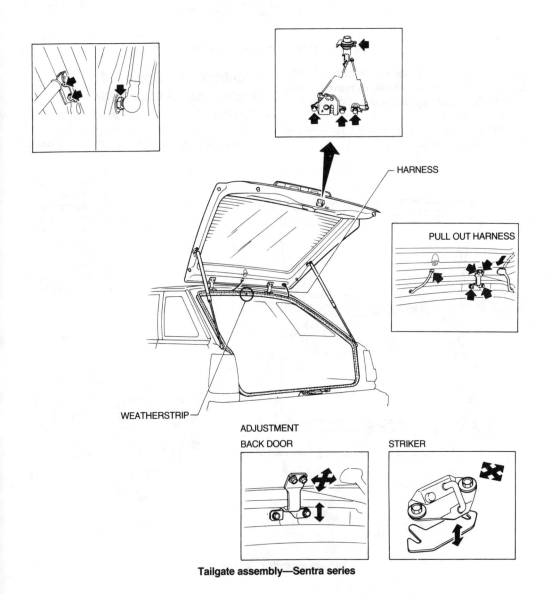

Tailgate assembly—Sentra series

Windshield Glass

REMOVAL

1. Place a protective cover over the hood, front fenders, instrument panel and front seats.
2. Remove the windshield wiper arm assemblies.
3. Remove the windshield moldings.
4. On the inside of the body, loosen the lip of the weatherstrip from the body flange along the top and the sides of the windshield opening. Use an appropriate tool and carefully put the weatherstrip over the body flange.
5. After the windshield weatherstrip is free from the body flange, with the aid of a helper, carefully lift the windshield from the opening. There are special suction cup tools available especially made for this purpose.

INSTALLATION

1. Check the windshield weatherstrip for irregularities.
2. Clean off the old sealer around the winshield opening and check the entire body opening flange for irregularities.
3. With the aid of a helper carefully position the replacement glass on the windshield opening.

CAUTION: *Be careful not to chip the edge of the glass during installation. Edge chips can lead to future breaks.*

4. With the windshield glass supported and centered in the body opening, check the relationship of the glass to the body opening around the entire perimeter of the glass.

   a. The inside surface of the glass should completely lap to body flange.

   b. The curvature of the glass should be uniform to that of the body opening.

5. Mark any sections of the body to be reformed. Remove the glass, and reform the opening as required.
6. Clean out the old sealer in the glass cavity of the windshield weatherstrip and around the base of the weatherstrip.
7. Install the weatherstrip to the glass.

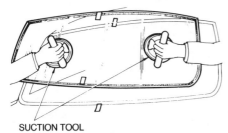

SUCTION TOOL

Removing windshield glass with the aid of special suction tools

8. Insert a strong cord in the groove of the weatherstrip where the body flange fits. Apply soapy water to it, so it will fit into the weatherstrip groove easily. Tie the ends of the cord and tape to the inside surface of the glass at the bottom center of the glass.
9. With the aid of a helper, carefully position and center the windshield assembly in the body opening.

NOTE: *Do not tap or hammer on the glass at any time.*

10. When the glass and weatherstrip are properly positioned in the opening, slowly pull the ends of the cord, starting at the lower center of the windshield to seat the lip of the weatherstrip over the body flange. The cord should be pulled first across the bottom of the windshield, then up each side and finally across the windshield top.
11. Using a pressure type applicator, seal the inner and outer lips of the weatherstrip to the glass with an approved weatherstrip adhesive. Seal completely around the weatherstrip.

CAUTION: *The car should not be driven on rough roads or surfaces until the sealant has properly vulcanized. Also it is a good idea to leave one window open slightly for a few days to reduce the chance of pressure induced leaks before the seal has completelty vulcanized.*

NOTE: *The rear glass on most sedan models is removed and installed in the manner as as the windshield glass. Most rear glass on hatchbacks and and wagons are replaced as an assembly only. Check with the manufacturer.*

Bumpers

REMOVAL AND INSTALLATION

210 Series and 1982-86 Sentra

CAUTION: *These bumpers use fluid and gas filled shock absorbers. Be careful not to puncture, heat, or attempt to disassemble these units. Failure to observe this caution can result in severe injury.*

1. The bumpers are retained to the body via shock absorbers. The easiest way to remove the bumper is to remove the single vertical bolt and corresponding nut on either side that retain the bumper to the shock. If the parking lights are retained in the bumper, first disconnect both electrical connectors. Then, support the bumper, remove the bolts, and remove the bumper from the shocks.
2. If it is necessary to replace the shocks, unbolt the 3 or 4 bolts that retain the shocks to the car body and remove the shocks.
3. Bolt the shocks to the body by locating

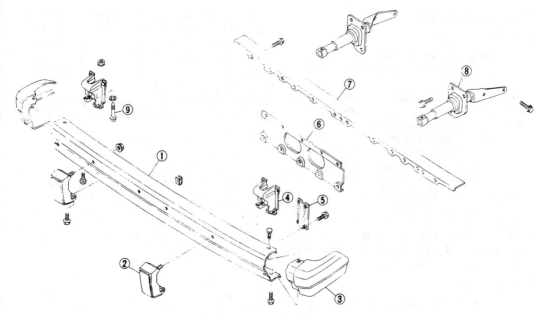

Bumper removal—210 Series

them and installing the mounting bolts securely.

4. Install the bumper to the shocks with the two vertical bolts, and the washers and nuts.

1987-88 Sentra

On these models, the shock absorber is replaced by a plastic energy absorbing element. To remove the bumper:

1. Support the bumper. Remove the vertical bolts that fasten the retainer to the bottom of the bumper. Remove the vertical bolts that attach the fascia to the body.

2. Remove the nuts from the horizontal studs that retain the bumper via the metal bracket to the reinforcement. Then, remove the bumper fascia from the reinforcement bracket and the energy absorber form along with it.

3. If the reinforcement bracket has been damaged, remove the four vertical attaching bolts from the body and remove it.

4. If necessary, bolt a new or repaired bumper reinforcement bracket to the body.

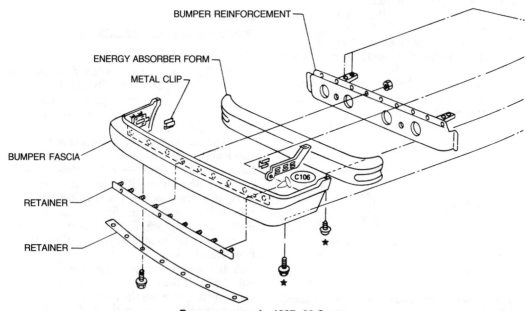

Bumper removal—1987–88 Sentra

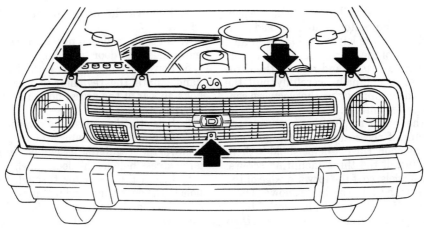

Removing the 210 grille

5. Position the fascia onto the absorber form. Align the assembly with the boltholes in the renforement and then install the studded retainer so the studs pass through the fascia and reinforcement. Then, install all the mounting nuts and tighten them securely.

6. Install the vertical bolts that retain the lower retainer and tighten them evenly.

Grille

REMOVAL AND INSTALLATION

The grille is attached through either bolts or special fasteners. On the 210, just remove the mounting bolts. On the 1982 Sentra, remove the screws at the corners with a Phillips screwdriver before removing the special fasteners. On later Sentras, and for most areas of th 1982 grille, the "CG101" fastener has a diamond shaped front. Simply turn the diamond 45° in either direction, so it looks like an ordinary square and then gently pull it out.

If the grille is of plastic, be careful to avoid allowing it to come in contact with oil or grease. Installation is the reverse of removal. During installation of the special fasteners, remember to turn them to a position that would permit removal, insert them, and then turn them 45° to the locking position.

Mirrors

REMOVAL AND INSTALLATION

The door mirror is mounted at the right front corner of the left side door glass. If the mirror is a manual design, remove the setscrew from underneath and remove the handle. Then, on either electrical or manual mirrors, remove the finish panel. Note that on 1987-88 models, this

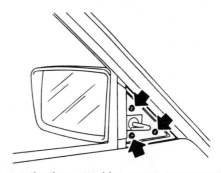

Remove the three attaching screws to remove the door mirror

Removal   **Installation**

Rotate 45°
to remove.

Removal

Removing CG101 type fasteners are used to fasten many Sentra grilles

Butyl seal

Apply butyl sealer to the corner door finish panel before replacing it must be done by first pulling or prying the panel outward at the bottom and then sliding it downward and to the left to pull tangs located at top right out of the doorframe. Next, support the mirror from outside and remove the three mounting screws. Finally, carefully pull the unit off the door, unplugging the electrical connector on power mirrors.

Install the mirror by plugging in the electrical connector, if necessary, and then positioning it on the door. Have a helper hold it there while you install the three mounting screws. On earlier models, coat the forward edge of the finish panel with a butyl sealer as shown. Then, install it. On 1987-88 models, be careful to install the tangs into the doorframe first and then snap the locking pin into the door by forcing the right lower edge toward the mirror. Install the handle on manual models.

INTERIOR

Door Panel, Glass and Regulator
REMOVAL AND INSTALLATION

Front and Rear

1. Remove the regulator handle by pushing the set pin spring.
2. Remove the arm rest, door inside handle escutcheon and door lock.

3. Remove the door finisher and sealing screen.
4. On some models it may be necessary to remove the outer door moulding.
5. Lower the door glass with the regulator handle until the regulator-to-glass attaching bolts appear at the access holes in the door inside panel.
6. Raise the door glass and draw it upwards.
7. Remove the regulator attaching bolts and remove the regulator assembly through the large access hole in the door panel.
8. Install the regulator through the access hole in the door panel and install the mounting and adjusting bolts loosely. Adjust the regulator until the galss mounts are accessible and install the glass by reversing Steps 5 and 6.
9. Refer to the arrows in the accompanying illustrations. These show where the regulator or tracks are adjustable. Where a track is adjustable, move it for and aft or up and down so the window is pinned between front and rear tracks just tightly enough that it will not try to escapt the track groove in moving all the way from top to bottom of its travel. Then, tighten the mounting bolts securely and retest.
10. Where regulator mounting bolts are adjustable, raise the window all the way and then rock the regulator to ensure that the window touches the top of the door frame all along in an

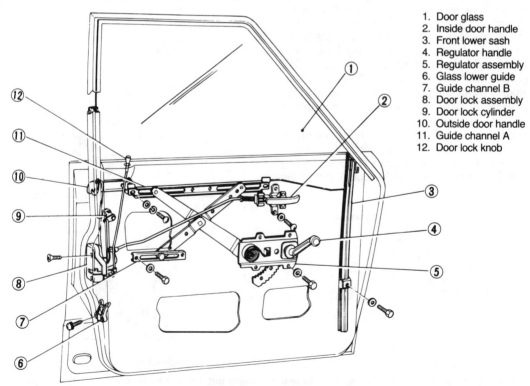

1. Door glass
2. Inside door handle
3. Front lower sash
4. Regulator handle
5. Regulator assembly
6. Glass lower guide
7. Guide channel B
8. Door lock assembly
9. Door lock cylinder
10. Outside door handle
11. Guide channel A
12. Door lock knob

Front door assembly—4 dr. models—210 series

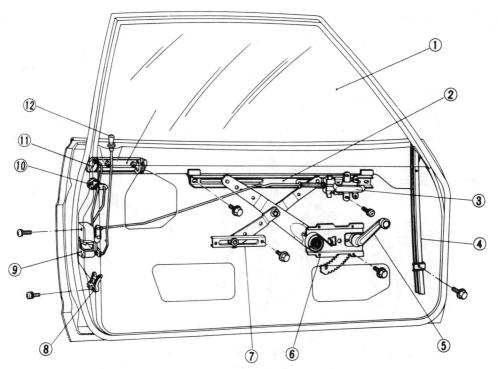

1. Door glass	5. Regulator handle	9. Door lock assembly
2. Guide channel A	6. Regulator assembly	10. Door lock cylinder
3. Inside door handle	7. Guide channel B	11. Outside door handle
4. Front lower sash	8. Glass lower guide	12. Inside door lock knob

Front door assembly—2 dr. models—210 series

1. Door glass
2. Inside door lock knob
3. Inside door handle
4. Guide channel A
5. Regulator handle
6. Regulator assembly
7. Lower sash
8. Center sash
9. Door lock assembly
10. Outside door handle

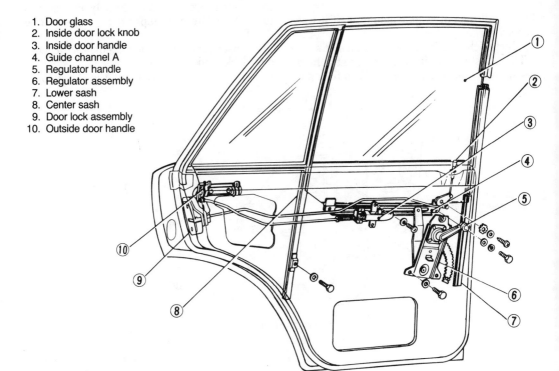

Rear door assembly—210 series

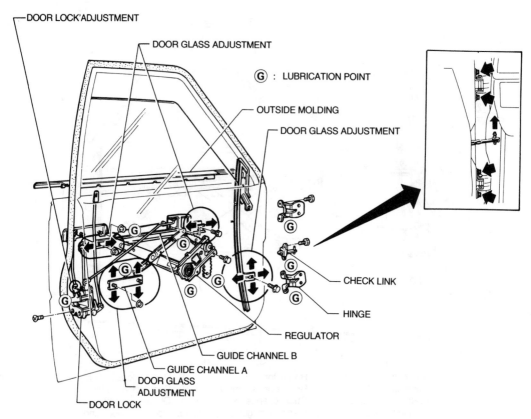

DOOR LOCK ADJUSTMENT

DOOR GLASS ADJUSTMENT

ⓖ : LUBRICATION POINT

OUTSIDE MOLDING

DOOR GLASS ADJUSTMENT

CHECK LINK

HINGE

REGULATOR

GUIDE CHANNEL B

GUIDE CHANNEL A

DOOR GLASS ADJUSTMENT

DOOR LOCK

Front door assembly—Sentra series

even manner. Then, tighten the mounting bolts.

11. Install the outer door moulding, if it was removed earlier.

12. Install the sealing screen with a soft sealer. Then, install the finish panel by attaching the clips over the door frame and then fitting it tightly against the frame. Line up the clips and then gently force the panel directly over each to lock it in the corresponding hole in the doorframe.

13. Install the door inside handle escutcheon, door lock, and arm rest.

14. Install the set spring and the gently force

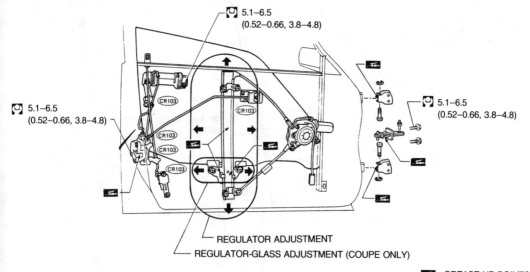

5.1–6.5 (0.52–0.66, 3.8–4.8)

5.1–6.5 (0.52–0.66, 3.8–4.8)

5.1–6.5 (0.52–0.66, 3.8–4.8)

CR103

REGULATOR ADJUSTMENT

REGULATOR-GLASS ADJUSTMENT (COUPE ONLY)

: GREASE-UP POINTS

: N·M (KG-M, FT-LB)

Front door interior—1987–88 Sentra

DOOR GLASS ADJUSTMENT

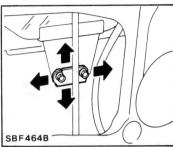

SBF464B

G : LUBRICATION POINT

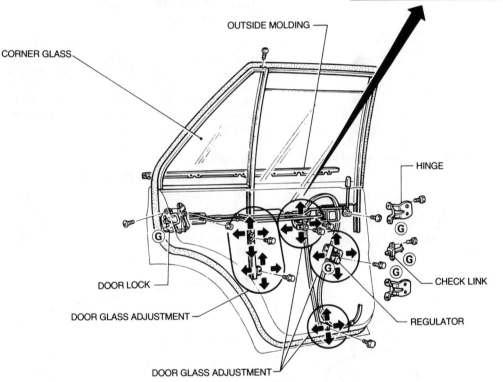

OUTSIDE MOLDING

CORNER GLASS

HINGE

DOOR LOCK

DOOR GLASS ADJUSTMENT

DOOR GLASS ADJUSTMENT

CHECK LINK

REGULATOR

Rear door assembly—Sentra series

the door handle over the splined shaft of the regulator to lock the spring in the retaining grooves.

Door Locks

REMOVAL AND INSTALLATION

1. Turn the interior lock button and escutcheon counterclockwise to unscrew them from the lockrod and remove them.

2. Remove the door finisher and sealing screen.

3. Remove the lock cylinder from the rod by turning the resin clip.

4. Loosen the nuts attaching the outside door handle and remove the outside door handle.

5. Remove the screws retaining the inside door handle and door lock, and remove the door

lock assembly from the hole in the inside of the door.

6. Remove the lock cylinder by removing the retaining clip.

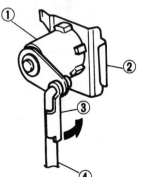

1. Door lock cylinder
2. Retaining clip
3. Resin clip
4. Lock cylinder rod

Removing the lock cylinder rod

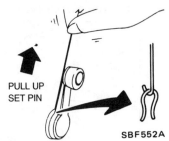

SBF552A

Install regulator handle as shown below, using set pins. Door should be closed

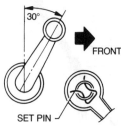

30°

FRONT

SET PIN

Regulator handle and set pin removal and installation

7. Install The lock cylinder with the retaining clip. Then, install the lock assembly via the hole in the inside of the door.

8. Install the inside door handle and lock and install their attaching screws.

9. Attach the locking rod to the cylinder with the resin clip.

10. Install the sealing screen with soft adhesive and then remount the finish panel. Line up the clips and then gently force the panel directly over each to lock it in the corresponding hole in the doorframe.

11. Install the interior lock button by reversing the removal procedure.

Inside Rear View Mirror
REPLACEMENT

The roof mounted mirror is retained to the roof with a central attaching screw. On deluxe models, there is a base which is screwed into the mounting bracket from above. Make sure to remove the attaching screw from the top and move the base to the replacement mirror before installing it.

Headliner
REMOVAL AND INSTALLATION

1. Remove the lamp, assist grip, coat hangers, inside rear view mirror and sun visors.

2. Remove the body side welts and remove the roof side garnishes and tail rail garnish.

3. Remove the rear side finishers.

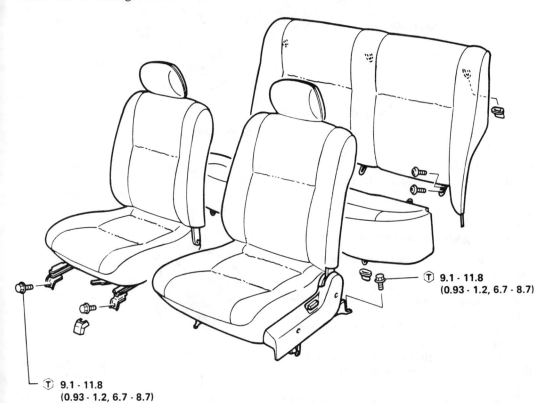

Ⓣ 9.1 - 11.8
(0.93 - 1.2, 6.7 - 8.7)

Ⓣ 9.1 - 11.8
(0.93 - 1.2, 6.7 - 8.7)

Sentra sedan front and rear seat mounting

4. Draw out the roof headlining from the windshield weatherstrip.

5. Installation is the reverse of removal.

Seats

REMOVAL AND INSTALLATION

Front Seats

The seats are attached to sliding brackets. These, in turn, are bolted to the floor via angled bolts at the front and bolts that screw straight into the floor at the rear. Remove all four of the mounting bolts and simply pull the seat out the door to remove it.

210 rear bench seat lower cushions are fastened by a bolt on either side that runs fore and aft and is located under the front of the cushion. Simply remove these and remove the cushion. On Sentras with a straight backrest, the attaching bolts for the lower cushion are located at the top rear of the cushion, just below the backrest. Remove these, lift the cushion to disengage the locating tangs, and remove the cushion from the car.

On Sentras with a solid backrest, remove the retaining bolts from under the rear cushion and lift it to free the tangs on the back face of the cushion from the locators. Where the backrest folds down, remove the bolts from the hinge brackets at right and left sides and at the center, unlock the seat lock at the top rear, and remove it.

For all seats, installation is simply a matter of reversing the removal procedure. Note that with hinged backrests, it will be necessary to engage the hinge pins of the brackets with the corresponding holes in the sides of the seats, move the seats and brackets in position, line up the boltholes, and then install the bolts.

Mechanic's Data

1":254mm
10.16mm
TAX
Liter
Parts
Overhaul

11

General Conversion Table

Multiply By	To Convert	To	
		LENGTH	
2.54	Inches	Centimeters	.3937
25.4	Inches	Millimeters	.03937
30.48	Feet	Centimeters	.0328
.304	Feet	Meters	3.28
.914	Yards	Meters	1.094
1.609	Miles	Kilometers	.621
		VOLUME	
.473	Pints	Liters	2.11
.946	Quarts	Liters	1.06
3.785	Gallons	Liters	.264
.016	Cubic inches	Liters	61.02
16.39	Cubic inches	Cubic cms.	.061
28.3	Cubic feet	Liters	.0353
		MASS (Weight)	
28.35	Ounces	Grams	.035
.4536	Pounds	Kilograms	2.20
—	To obtain	From	Multiply by

Multiply By	To Convert	To	
		AREA	
.645	Square inches	Square cms.	.155
.836	Square yds.	Square meters	1.196
		FORCE	
4.448	Pounds	Newtons	.225
.138	Ft./lbs.	Kilogram/meters	7.23
1.36	Ft./lbs.	Newton-meters	.737
.112	In./lbs.	Newton-meters	8.844
		PRESSURE	
.068	Psi	Atmospheres	14.7
6.89	Psi	Kilopascals	.145
		OTHER	
1.104	Horsepower (DIN)	Horsepower (SAE)	.9861
.746	Horsepower (SAE)	Kilowatts (KW)	1.34
1.60	Mph	Km/h	.625
.425	Mpg	Km/1	2.35
—	To obtain	From	Multiply by

Tap Drill Sizes

National Coarse or U.S.S.		
Screw & Tap Size	Threads Per Inch	Use Drill Number
No. 5	40	39
No. 6	32	36
No. 8	32	29
No. 10	24	25
No. 12	24	17
1/4	20	8
5/16	18	F
3/8	16	5/16
7/16	14	U
1/2	13	27/64
9/16	12	31/64
5/8	11	17/32
3/4	10	21/32
7/8	9	49/64

National Coarse or U.S.S.		
Screw & Tap Size	Threads Per Inch	Use Drill Number
1	8	7/8
1 1/8	7	63/64
1 1/4	7	1 7/64
1 1/2	6	1 11/32

National Fine or S.A.E.		
Screw & Tap Size	Threads Per Inch	Use Drill Number
No. 5	44	37
No. 6	40	33
No. 8	36	29
No. 10	32	21

National Fine or S.A.E.		
Screw & Tap Size	Threads Per Inch	Use Drill Number
No. 12	28	15
1/4	28	3
6/16	24	1
3/8	24	Q
7/16	20	W
1/2	20	29/64
9/16	18	33/64
5/8	18	37/64
3/4	16	11/16
7/8	14	13/16
1 1/8	12	1 3/64
1 1/4	12	1 11/64
1 1/2	12	1 27/64

Drill Sizes In Decimal Equivalents

Inch	Decimal	Wire	Letter	mm
1/64	.0156			.39
	.0157			.4
	.0160	78		
	.0165			.42
	.0173			.44
	.0177			.45
	.0180	77		
	.0181			.46
	.0189			.48
	.0197			.5
	.0200	76		
	.0210	75		
	.0217			.55
	.0225	74		
	.0236			.6
	.0240	73		
	.0250	72		
	.0256			.65
	.0260	71		
	.0276			.7
	.0280	70		
	.0292	69		
	.0295			.75
	.0310	68		
1/32	.0312			.79
	.0315			.8
	.0320	67		
	.0330	66		
	.0335			.85
	.0350	65		
	.0354			.9
	.0360	64		
	.0370	63		
	.0374			.95
	.0380	62		
	.0390	61		
	.0394			1.0
	.0400	60		
	.0410	59		
	.0413			1.05
	.0420	58		
	.0430	57		
	.0433			1.1
	.0453			1.15
3/64	.0465	56		
	.0469			1.19
	.0472			1.2
	.0492			1.25
	.0512			1.3
	.0520	55		
	.0531			1.35
	.0550	54		
	.0551			1.4
	.0571			1.45
	.0591			1.5
	.0595	53		
	.0610			1.55
1/16	.0625			1.59
	.0630			1.6
	.0635	52		
	.0650			1.65
	.0669			1.7
	.0670	51		
	.0689			1.75
	.0700	50		
	.0709			1.8
	.0728			1.85
	.0730	49		
	.0748			1.9
	.0760	48		
	.0768			1.95
5/64	.0781			1.98
	.0785	47		
	.0787			2.0
	.0807			2.05
	.0810	46		
	.0820	45		
	.0827			2.1
	.0846			2.15
	.0860	44		
	.0866			2.2
	.0886			2.25
	.0890	43		
	.0906			2.3
	.0925			2.35
	.0935	42		
3/32	.0938			2.38
	.0945			2.4
	.0960	41		
	.0965			2.45
	.0980	40		
	.0981			2.5
	.0995	39		
	.1015	38		
	.1024			2.6
	.1040	37		
	.1063			2.7
	.1065	36		
	.1083			2.75
7/64	.1094			2.77
	.1100	35		
	.1102			2.8
	.1110	34		
	.1130	33		
	.1142			2.9
	.1160	32		
	.1181			3.0
	.1200	31		
	.1220			3.1
1/8	.1250			3.17
	.1260			3.2
	.1280			3.25
	.1285	30		
	.1299			3.3
	.1339			3.4
	.1360	29		
	.1378			3.5
	.1405	28		
9/64	.1406			3.57
	.1417			3.6
	.1440	27		
	.1457			3.7
	.1470	26		
	.1476			3.75
	.1495	25		
	.1496			3.8
	.1520	24		
	.1535			3.9
	.1540	23		
5/32	.1562			3.96
	.1570	22		
	.1575			4.0
	.1590	21		
	.1610	20		
	.1614			4.1
	.1654			4.2
	.1660	19		
	.1673			4.25
	.1693			4.3
	.1695	18		
11/64	.1719			4.36
	.1730	17		
	.1732			4.4
	.1770	16		
	.1772			4.5
	.1800	15		
	.1811			4.6
	.1820	14		
	.1850	13		
	.1850			4.7
	.1870			4.75
3/16	.1875			4.76
	.1890			4.8
	.1890	12		
	.1910	11		
	.1929			4.9
	.1935	10		
	.1960	9		
	.1969			5.0
	.1990	8		
	.2008			5.1
	.2010	7		
13/64	.2031			5.16
	.2040	6		
	.2047			5.2
	.2055	5		
	.2067			5.25
	.2087			5.3
	.2090	4		
	.2126			5.4
	.2130	3		
	.2165			5.5
7/32	.2188			5.55
	.2205			5.6
	.2210	2		
	.2244			5.7
	.2264			5.75
	.2280	1		
	.2283			5.8
	.2323			5.9
	.2340		A	
15/64	.2344			5.95
	.2362			6.0
	.2380		B	
	.2402			6.1
	.2420		C	
	.2441			6.2
	.2460		D	
	.2461			6.25
	.2480			6.3
1/4	.2500		E	6.35
	.2520			6.
	.2559			6.5
	.2570		F	
	.2598			6.6
	.2610		G	
	.2638			6.7
17/64	.2656			6.74
	.2657			6.75
	.2660		H	
	.2677			6.8
	.2717			6.9
	.2720		I	
	.2756			7.0
	.2770		J	
	.2795			7.1
	.2810		K	
9/32	.2812			7.14
	.2835			7.2
	.2854			7.25
	.2874			7.3
	.2900		L	
	.2913			7.4
	.2950		M	
	.2953			7.5
19/64	.2969			7.54
	.2992			7.6
	.3020		N	
	.3031			7.7
	.3051			7.75
	.3071			7.8
	.3110			7.9
5/16	.3125			7.93
	.3150			8.0
	.3160		O	
	.3189			8.1
	.3228			8.2
	.3230		P	
	.3248			8.25
	.3268			8.3
21/64	.3281			8.33
	.3307			8.4
	.3320		Q	
	.3346			8.5
	.3386			8.6
	.3390		R	
	.3425			8.7
11/32	.3438			8.73
	.3445			8.75
	.3465			8.8
	.3480		S	
	.3504			8.9
	.3543			9.0
	.3580		T	
	.3583			9.1
23/64	.3594			9.12
	.3622			9.2
	.3642			9.25
	.3661			9.3
	.3680		U	
	.3701			9.4
	.3740			9.5
3/8	.3750			9.52
	.3770		V	
	.3780			9.6
	.3819			9.7
	.3839			9.75
	.3858			9.8
	.3860		W	
	.3898			9.9
25/64	.3906			9.92
	.3937			10.0
	.3970		X	
	.4040		Y	
13/32	.4062			10.31
	.4130		Z	
	.4134			10.5
27/64	.4219			10.71
	.4331			11.0
7/16	.4375			11.11
	.4528			11.5
29/64	.4531			11.51
15/32	.4688			11.90
	.4724			12.0
31/64	.4844			12.30
	.4921			12.5
1/2	.5000			12.70
	.5118			13.0
33/64	.5156			13.09
17/32	.5312			13.49
	.5315			13.5
35/64	.5469			13.89
	.5512			14.0
9/16	.5625			14.28
	.5709			14.5
37/64	.5781			14.68
	.5906			15.0
19/32	.5938			15.08
39/64	.6094			15.47
	.6102			15.5
5/8	.6250			15.87
	.6299			16.0
41/64	.6406			16.27
	.6496			16.5
21/32	.6562			16.66
	.6693			17.0
43/64	.6719			17.06
11/16	.6875			17.46
	.6890			17.5
45/64	.7031			17.85
	.7087			18.0
23/32	.7188			18.25
	.7283			18.5
47/64	.7344			18.65
	.7480			19.0
3/4	.7500			19.05
49/64	.7656			19.44
	.7677			19.5
25/32	.7812			19.84
	.7874			20.0
51/64	.7969			20.24
	.8071			20.5
13/16	.8125			20.63
	.8268			21.0
53/64	.8281			21.03
27/32	.8438			21.43
	.8465			21.5
55/64	.8594			21.82
	.8661			22.0
7/8	.8750			22.22
	.8858			22.5
57/64	.8906			22.62
	.9055			23.0
29/32	.9062			23.01
59/64	.9219			23.41
	.9252			23.5
15/16	.9375			23.81
	.9449			24.0
61/64	.9531			24.2
	.9646			24.5
31/32	.9688			24.6
	.9843			25.0
63/64	.9844			25.0
1	1.0000			25.4

GLOSSARY OF TERMS

AIR/FUEL RATIO: The ratio of air to gasoline by weight in the fuel mixture drawn into the engine.

AIR INJECTION: One method of reducing harmful exhaust emissions by injecting air into each of the exhaust ports of an engine. The fresh air entering the hot exhaust manifold causes any remaining fuel to be burned before it can exit the tailpipe.

ALTERNATOR: A device used for converting mechanical energy into electrical energy.

AMMETER: An instrument, calibrated in amperes, used to measure the flow of an electrical current in a circuit. Ammeters are always connected in series with the circuit being tested.

AMPERE: The rate of flow of electrical current present when one volt of electrical pressure is applied against one ohm of electrical resistance.

ANALOG COMPUTER: Any microprocessor that uses similar (analogous) electrical signals to make its calculations.

ARMATURE: A laminated, soft iron core wrapped by a wire that converts electrical energy to mechanical energy as in a motor or relay. When rotated in a magnetic field, it changes mechanical energy into electrical energy as in a generator.

ATMOSPHERIC PRESSURE: The pressure on the Earth's surface caused by the weight of the air in the atmosphere. At sea level, this pressure is 14.7 psi at 32°F (101 kPa at 0°C).

ATOMIZATION: The breaking down of a liquid into a fine mist that can be suspended in air.

AXIAL PLAY: Movement parallel to a shaft or bearing bore.

BACKFIRE: The sudden combustion of gases in the intake or exhaust system that results in a loud explosion.

BACKLASH: The clearance or play between two parts, such as meshed gears.

BACKPRESSURE: Restrictions in the exhaust system that slow the exit of exhaust gases from the combustion chamber.

BAKELITE: A heat resistant, plastic insulator material commonly used in printed circuit boards and transistorized components.

BALL BEARING: A bearing made up of hardened inner and outer races between which hardened steel ball roll.

BALLAST RESISTOR: A resistor in the primary ignition circuit that lowers voltage after the engine is started to reduce wear on ignition components.

BEARING: A friction reducing, supportive device usually located between a stationary part and a moving part.

BIMETAL TEMPERATURE SENSOR: Any sensor or switch made of two dissimilar types of metal that bend when heated or cooled due to the different expansion rates of the alloys. These types of sensors usually function as an on/off switch.

BLOWBY: Combustion gases, composed of water vapor and unburned fuel, that leak past the piston rings into the crankcase during normal engine operation. These gases are removed by the PCV system to prevent the build-up of harmful acids in the crankcase.

BRAKE PAD: A brake shoe and lining assembly used with disc brakes.

BRAKE SHOE: The backing for the brake lining. The term is, however, usually applied to the assembly of the brake backing and lining.

BUSHING: A liner, usually removable, for a bearing; an anti-friction liner used in place of a bearing.

BYPASS: System used to bypass ballast resistor during engine cranking to increase voltage supplied to the coil.

CALIPER: A hydraulically activated device in a disc brake system, which is mounted straddling the brake rotor (disc). The caliper contains at least one piston and two brake pads. Hydraulic pressure on the piston(s) forces the pads against the rotor.

CAMSHAFT: A shaft in the engine on which are the lobes (cams) which operate the valves. The camshaft is driven by the crankshaft, via a belt, chain or gears, at one half the crankshaft speed.

CAPACITOR: A device which stores an electrical charge.

CARBON MONOXIDE (CO): a colorless, odorless gas given off as a normal byproduct of combustion. It is poisonous and extremely dangerous in confined areas, building up slowly to toxic levels without warning if adequate ventilation is not available.

CARBURETOR: A device, usually mounted on the intake manifold of an engine, which mixes the air and fuel in the proper proportion to allow even combustion.

CATALYTIC CONVERTER: A device installed in the exhaust system, like a muffler, that converts harmful byproducts of combustion into carbon dioxide and water vapor by means of a heat-producing chemical reaction.

CENTRIFUGAL ADVANCE: A mechanical method of advancing the spark timing by using flyweights in the distributor that react to centrifugal force generated by the distributor shaft rotation.

CHECK VALVE: Any one-way valve installed to permit the flow of air, fuel or vacuum in one direction only.

CHOKE: A device, usually a moveable valve, placed in the intake path of a carburetor to restrict the flow of air.

CIRCUIT: Any unbroken path through which an electrical current can flow. Also used to describe fuel flow in some instances.

CIRCUIT BREAKER: A switch which protects an electrical circuit from overload by opening the circuit when the current flow exceeds a predetermined level. Some circuit breakers must be reset manually, while other reset automatically

COIL (IGNITION): A transformer in the ignition circuit which steps of the voltage provided to the spark plugs.

COMBINATION MANIFOLD: An assembly which includes both the intake and exhaust manifolds in one casting.

COMBINATION VALVE: A device used in some fuel systems that routes fuel vapors to a charcoal storage canister instead of venting them into the atmosphere. The valve relieves fuel tank pressure and allows fresh air into the tank as fuel level drops to prevent a vapor lock situation.

COMPRESSION RATIO: The comparison of the total volume of the cylinder and combustion chamber with the piston at BDC and the piston at TDC.

CONDENSER: 1. An electrical device which acts to store an electrical charge, preventing voltage surges.
2. A radiator-like device in the air conditioning system in which refrigerant gas condenses into a liquid, giving off heat.

CONDUCTOR: Any material through which an electrical current can be transmitted easily.

CONTINUITY: Continuous or complete circuit. Can be checked with an ohmmeter.

COUNTERSHAFT: An intermediate shaft which is rotated by a mainshaft and transmits, in turn, that rotation to a working part.

CRANKCASE: The lower part of an engine in which the crankshaft and related parts operate.

CRANKSHAFT: The main driving shaft of an engine which receives reciprocating motion from the pistons and converts it to rotary motion.

CYLINDER: In an engine, the round hole in the engine block in which the piston(s) ride.

CYLINDER BLOCK: The main structural member of an engine in which is found the cylinders, crankshaft and other principal parts.

CYLINDER HEAD: The detachable portion of the engine, fastened, usually, to the top of the cylinder block, containing all or most of the combustion chambers. On overhead valve engines, it contains the valves and their operating parts. On overhead cam engines, it contains the camshaft as well.

DEAD CENTER: The extreme top or bottom of the piston stroke.

DETONATION: An unwanted explosion of the air fuel mixture in the combustion chamber caused by excess heat and compression, advanced timing, or an overly lean mixture. Also referred to as "ping".

DIAPHRAGM: A thin, flexible wall separating two cavities, such as in a vacuum advance unit.

DIESELING: A condition in which hot spots in the combustion chamber cause the engine to run on after the key is turned off.

DIFFERENTIAL: A geared assembly which allows the transmission of motion between drive axles, giving one axle the ability to turn faster than the other.

DIODE: An electrical device that will allow current to flow in one direction only.

DISC BRAKE: A hydraulic braking assembly consisting of a brake disc, or rotor, mounted on an axle, and a caliper assembly containing, usually two brake pads which are activated by hydraulic pressure. The pads are forced against the sides of the disc, creating friction which slows the vehicle.

DISTRIBUTOR: A mechanically driven device on an engine which is responsible for electrically firing the spark plug at a predetermined point of the piston stroke.

DOWEL PIN: A pin, inserted in mating holes in two different parts allowing those parts to maintain a fixed relationship.

DRUM BRAKE: A braking system which consists of two brake shoes and one or two wheel cylinders, mounted on a fixed backing plate, and a brake drum, mounted on an axle, which revolves around the assembly. Hydraulic action applied to the wheel cylinders forces the shoes outward against the drum, creating friction and slowing the vehicle.

DWELL: The rate, measured in degrees of shaft rotation, at which an electrical circuit cycles on and off.

ELECTRONIC CONTROL UNIT (ECU): Ignition module, module, amplifier or igniter. See Module for definition.

ELECTRONIC IGNITION: A system in which the timing and firing of the spark plugs is controlled by an electronic control unit, usually called a module. These systems have not points or condenser.

ENDPLAY: The measured amount of axial movement in a shaft.

ENGINE: A device that converts heat into mechanical energy.

EXHAUST MANIFOLD: A set of cast passages or pipes which conduct exhaust gases from the engine.

FEELER GAUGE: A blade, usually metal, of precisely predetermined thickness, used to measure the clearance between two parts. These blades usually are available in sets of assorted thicknesses.

F-Head: An engine configuration in which the intake valves are in the cylinder head, while the camshaft and exhaust valves are located in the cylinder block. The camshaft operates the intake valves via lifters and pushrods, while it operates the exhaust valves directly.

FIRING ORDER: The order in which combustion occurs in the cylinders of an engine. Also the order in which spark is distributed to the plugs by the distributor.

FLATHEAD: An engine configuration in which the camshaft and all the valves are located in the cylinder block.

FLOODING: The presence of too much fuel in the intake manifold and combustion chamber which prevents the air/fuel mixture from firing, thereby causing a no-start situation.

FLYWHEEL: A disc shaped part bolted to the rear end of the crankshaft. Around the outer perimeter is affixed the ring gear. The starter drive engages the ring gear, turning the flywheel, which rotates the crankshaft, imparting the initial starting motion to the engine.

FOOT POUND (ft.lb. or sometimes, ft. lbs.): The amount of energy or work needed to raise an item weighing one pound, a distance of one foot.

FUSE: A protective device in a circuit which prevents circuit overload by breaking the circuit when a specific amperage is present. The device is constructed around a strip or wire of a lower amperage rating than the circuit it is designed to protect. When an amperage higher than that stamped on the fuse is present in the circuit, the strip or wire melts, opening the circuit.

GEAR RATIO: The ratio between the number of teeth on meshing gears.

GENERATOR: A device which converts mechanical energy into electrical energy.

HEAT RANGE: The measure of a spark plug's ability to dissipate heat from its firing end. The higher the heat range, the hotter the plug fires.

HUB: The center part of a wheel or gear.

HYDROCARBON (HC): Any chemical compound made up of hydrogen and carbon. A major pollutant formed by the engine as a byproduct of combustion.

HYDROMETER: An instrument used to measure the specific gravity of a solution.

INCH POUND (in.lb. or sometimes, in. lbs.): One twelfth of a foot pound.

INDUCTION: A means of transferring electrical energy in the form of a magnetic field. Principle used in the ignition coil to increase voltage.

INJECTION PUMP: A device, usually mechanically operated, which meters and delivers fuel under pressure to the fuel injector.

INJECTOR: A device which receives metered fuel under relatively low pressure and is activated to inject the fuel into the engine under relatively high pressure at a predetermined time.

INPUT SHAFT: The shaft to which torque is applied, usually carrying the driving gear or gears.

INTAKE MANIFOLD: A casting of passages or pipes used to conduct air or a fuel/air mixture to the cylinders.

JOURNAL: The bearing surface within which a shaft operates.

KEY: A small block usually fitted in a notch between a shaft and a hub to prevent slippage of the two parts.

MANIFOLD: A casting of passages or set of pipes which connect the cylinders to an inlet or outlet source.

MANIFOLD VACUUM: Low pressure in an engine intake manifold formed just below the throttle plates. Manifold vacuum is highest at idle and drops under acceleration.

MASTER CYLINDER: The primary fluid pressurizing device in a hydraulic system. In automotive use, it is found in brake and hydraulic clutch systems and is pedal activated, either directly or, in a power brake system, through the power booster.

MODULE: Electronic control unit, amplifier or igniter of solid state or integrated design which controls the current flow in the ignition primary circuit based on input from the pickup coil. When the module opens the primary circuit, the high secondary voltage is induced in the coil.

NEEDLE BEARING: A bearing which consists of a number (usually a large number) of long, thin rollers.

OHM: (Ω) The unit used to measure the resistance of conductor to electrical flow. One ohm is the amount of resistance that limits current flow to one ampere in a circuit with one volt of pressure.

OHMMETER: An instrument used for measuring the resistance, in ohms, in an electrical circuit.

OUTPUT SHAFT: The shaft which transmits torque from a device, such as a transmission.

OVERDRIVE: A gear assembly which produces more shaft revolutions than that transmitted to it.

OVERHEAD CAMSHAFT (OHC): An engine configuration in which the camshaft is mounted on top of the cylinder head and operates the valve either directly or by means of rocker arms.

OVERHEAD VALVE (OHV): An engine configuration in which all of the valves are located in the cylinder head and the camshaft is located in the cylinder block. The camshaft operates the valves via lifters and pushrods.

OXIDES OF NITROGEN (NOx): Chemical compounds of nitrogen produced as a byproduct of combustion. They combine with hydrocarbons to produce smog.

OXYGEN SENSOR: Used with the feedback system to sense the presence of oxygen in the exhaust gas and signal the computer which can reference the voltage signal to an air/fuel ratio.

PINION: The smaller of two meshing gears.

PISTON RING: An open ended ring which fits into a groove on the outer diameter of the piston. Its chief function is to form a seal between the piston and cylinder wall. Most automotive pistons have three rings: two for compression sealing; one for oil sealing.

PRELOAD: A predetermined load placed on a bearing during assembly or by adjustment.

PRIMARY CIRCUIT: Is the low voltage side of the ignition system which consists of the ignition switch, ballast resistor or resistance wire, bypass, coil, electronic control unit and pick-up coil as well as the connecting wires and harnesses.

PRESS FIT: The mating of two parts under pressure, due to the inner diameter of one being smaller than the outer diameter of the other, or vice versa; an interference fit.

RACE: The surface on the inner or outer ring of a bearing on which the balls, needles or rollers move.

REGULATOR: A device which maintains the amperage and/or voltage levels of a circuit at predetermined values.

RELAY: A switch which automatically opens and/or closes a circuit.

RESISTANCE: The opposition to the flow of current through a circuit or electrical device, and is measured in ohms. Resistance is equal to the voltage divided by the amperage.

RESISTOR: A device, usually made of wire, which offers a preset amount of resistance in an electrical circuit.

RING GEAR: The name given to a ring-shaped gear attached to a differential case, or affixed to a flywheel or as part a planetary gear set.

ROLLER BEARING: A bearing made up of hardened inner and outer races between which hardened steel rollers move.

ROTOR: 1. The disc-shaped part of a disc brake assembly, upon which the brake pads bear; also called, brake disc.
2. The device mounted atop the distributor shaft, which passes current to the distributor cap tower contacts.

SECONDARY CIRCUIT: The high voltage side of the ignition system, usually above 20,000 volts. The secondary includes the ignition coil, coil wire, distributor cap and rotor, spark plug wires and spark plugs.

SENDING UNIT: A mechanical, electrical, hydraulic or electromagnetic device which transmits information to a gauge.

SENSOR: Any device designed to measure engine operating conditions or ambient pressures and temperatures. Usually electronic in nature and designed to send a voltage signal to an on-board computer, some sensors may operate as a simple on/off switch or they may provide a variable voltage signal (like a potentiometer) as conditions or measured parameters change.

SHIM: Spacers of precise, predetermined thickness used between parts to establish a proper working relationship.

SLAVE CYLINDER: In automotive use, a device in the hydraulic clutch system which is activated by hydraulic force, disengaging the clutch.

SOLENOID: A coil used to produce a magnetic field, the effect of which is produce work.

SPARK PLUG: A device screwed into the combustion chamber of a spark ignition engine. The basic construction is a conductive core inside of a ceramic insulator, mounted in an outer conductive base. An electrical charge from the spark plug wire travels along the conductive core and jumps a preset air gap to a grounding point or points at the end of the conductive base. The resultant spark ignites the fuel/air mixture in the combustion chamber.

SPLINES: Ridges machined or cast onto the outer diameter of a shaft or inner diameter of a bore to enable parts to mate without rotation.

TACHOMETER: A device used to measure the rotary speed of an engine, shaft, gear, etc., usually in rotations per minute.

THERMOSTAT: A valve, located in the cooling system of an engine, which is closed when cold and opens gradually in response to engine heating, controlling the temperature of the coolant and rate of coolant flow.

TOP DEAD CENTER (TDC): The point at which the piston reaches the top of its travel on the compression stroke.

TORQUE: The twisting force applied to an object.

TORQUE CONVERTER: A turbine used to transmit power from a driving member to a driven member via hydraulic action, providing changes in drive ratio and torque. In automotive use, it links the driveplate at the rear of the engine to the automatic transmission.

TRANSDUCER: A device used to change a force into an electrical signal.

TRANSISTOR: A semi-conductor component which can be actuated by a small voltage to perform an electrical switching function.

TUNE-UP: A regular maintenance function, usually associated with the replacement and adjustment of parts and components in the electrical and fuel systems of a vehicle for the purpose of attaining optimum performance.

TURBOCHARGER: An exhaust driven pump which compresses intake air and forces it into the combustion chambers at higher than atmospheric pressures. The increased air pressure allows more fuel to be burned and results in increased horsepower being produced.

VACUUM ADVANCE: A device which advances the ignition timing in response to increased engine vacuum.

VACUUM GAUGE: An instrument used to measure the presence of vacuum in a chamber.

VALVE: A device which control the pressure, direction of flow or rate of flow of a liquid or gas.

VALVE CLEARANCE: The measured gap between the end of the valve stem and the rocker arm, cam lobe or follower that activates the valve.

VISCOSITY: The rating of a liquid's internal resistance to flow.

VOLTMETER: An instrument used for measuring electrical force in units called volts. Voltmeters are always connected parallel with the circuit being tested.

WHEEL CYLINDER: Found in the automotive drum brake assembly, it is a device, actuated by hydraulic pressure, which, through internal pistons, pushes the brake shoes outward against the drums.

ABBREVIATIONS AND SYMBOLS

A: Ampere

AC: Alternating current

A/C: Air conditioning

A-h: Ampere hour

AT: Automatic transmission

ATDC: After top dead center

μA: Microampere

bbl: Barrel

BDC: Bottom dead center

bhp: Brake horsepower

BTDC: Before top dead center

BTU: British thermal unit

C: Celsius (Centigrade)

CCA: Cold cranking amps

cd: Candela

cm^2: Square centimeter

cm^3, cc: Cubic centimeter

CO: Carbon monoxide

CO_2: Carbon dioxide

cu.in., in^3: Cubic inch

CV: Constant velocity

Cyl.: Cylinder

DC: Direct current

ECM: Electronic control module

EFE: Early fuel evaporation

EFI: Electronic fuel injection

EGR: Exhaust gas recirculation

Exh.: Exhaust

F: Fahrenheit

F: Farad

pF: Picofarad

μF: Microfarad

FI: Fuel injection

ft.lb., ft. lb., ft. lbs.: foot pound(s)

gal: Gallon

g: Gram

HC: Hydrocarbon

HEI: High energy ignition

HO: High output

hp: Horsepower

Hyd.: Hydraulic

Hz: Hertz

ID: Inside diameter

in.lb.; in. lb.; in. lbs: inch pound(s)

Int.: Intake

K: Kelvin

kg: Kilogram

kHz: Kilohertz

km: Kilometer

km/h: Kilometers per hour

kΩ: Kilohm

kPa: Kilopascal

kV: Kilovolt

kW: Kilowatt

l: Liter

l/s: Liters per second

m: Meter

mA: Milliampere

mg: Milligram

mHz: Megahertz

mm: Millimeter

mm^2: Square millimeter

m^3: Cubic meter

MΩ: Megohm

m/s: Meters per second

MT: Manual transmission

mV: Millivolt

μm: Micrometer

N: Newton

N-m: Newton meter

NOx: Nitrous oxide

OD: Outside diameter

OHC: Over head camshaft

OHV: Over head valve

Ω: Ohm

PCV: Positive crankcase ventilation

psi: Pounds per square inch

pts: Pints

qts: Quarts

rpm: Rotations per minute

rps: Rotations per second

R-12: A refrigerant gas (Freon)

SAE: Society of Automotive Engineers

SO$_2$: Sulfur dioxide

T: Ton

t: Megagram

TBI: Throttle Body Injection

TPS: Throttle Position Sensor

V: 1. Volt; 2. Venturi

μV: Microvolt

W: Watt

∞: Infinity

$<$: Less than

$>$: Greater than

Index

Chilton's Repair & Tune-Up Guides

The Complete line covers domestic cars, imports, trucks, vans, RV's and 4-wheel drive vehicles.

RTUG Title	Part No.	RTUG Title	Part No.
AMC 1975-82	7199	**Corvair 1960-69**	6691
Covers all U.S. and Canadian models		Covers all U.S. and Canadian models	
Aspen/Volare 1976-80	6637	**Corvette 1953-62**	6576
Covers all U.S. and Canadian models		Covers all U.S. and Canadian models	
Audi 1970-73	5902	**Corvette 1963-84**	6843
Covers all U.S. and Canadian models.		Covers all U.S. and Canadian models	
Audi 4000/5000 1978-81	7028	**Cutlass 1970-85**	6933
Covers all U.S. and Canadian models including turbocharged and diesel engines		Covers all U.S. and Canadian models	
Barracuda/Challenger 1965-72	5807	**Dart/Demon 1968-76**	6324
Covers all U.S. and Canadian models		Covers all U.S. and Canadian models	
Blazer/Jimmy 1969-82	6931	**Datsun 1961-72**	5790
Covers all U.S. and Canadian 2- and 4-wheel drive models, including diesel engines		Covers all U.S. and Canadian models of Nissan Patrol; 1500, 1600 and 2000 sports cars; Pick-Ups; 410, 411, 510, 1200 and 240Z	
BMW 1970-82	6844		
Covers U.S. and Canadian models		**Datsun 1973-80 Spanish**	7083
Buick/Olds/Pontiac 1975-85	7308	**Datsun/Nissan F-10, 310, Stanza, Pulsar 1977-86**	7196
Covers U.S. and Canadian full size rear wheel drive models		Covers all U.S. and Canadian models	
Cadillac 1967-84	7462	**Datsun/Nissan Pick-Ups 1970-84**	6816
Covers all U.S. and Canadian rear wheel drive models		Covers all U.S and Canadian models	
Camaro 1967-81	6735	**Datsun/Nissan Z & ZX 1970-86**	6932
Covers all U.S. and Canadian models		Covers all U.S. and Canadian models	
Camaro 1982-85	7317	**Datsun/Nissan 1200, 210, Sentra 1973-86**	7197
Covers all U.S. and Canadian models		Covers all U.S. and Canadian models	
Capri 1970-77	6695	**Datsun/Nissan 200SX, 510, 610, 710, 810, Maxima 1973-84**	7170
Covers all U.S. and Canadian models		Covers all U.S. and Canadian models	
Caravan/Voyager 1984-85	7482	**Dodge 1968-77**	6554
Covers all U.S. and Canadian models		Covers all U.S. and Canadian models	
Century/Regal 1975-85	7307	**Dodge Charger 1967-70**	6486
Covers all U.S. and Canadian rear wheel drive models, including turbocharged engines		Covers all U.S. and Canadian models	
		Dodge/Plymouth Trucks 1967-84	7459
Champ/Arrow/Sapporo 1978-83	7041	Covers all $^1/_2$, $^3/_4$, and 1 ton 2- and 4-wheel drive U.S. and Canadian models, including diesel engines	
Covers all U.S. and Canadian models			
Chevette/1000 1976-86	6836	**Dodge/Plymouth Vans 1967-84**	6934
Covers all U.S. and Canadian models		Covers all $^1/_2$, $^3/_4$, and 1 ton U.S. and Canadian models of vans, cutaways and motor home chassis	
Chevrolet 1968-85	7135		
Covers all U.S. and Canadian models		**D-50/Arrow Pick-Up 1979-81**	7032
Chevrolet 1968-79 Spanish	7082	Covers all U.S. and Canadian models	
Chevrolet/GMC Pick-Ups 1970-82 Spanish	7468	**Fairlane/Torino 1962-75**	6320
Chevrolet/GMC Pick-Ups and Suburban 1970-86	6936	Covers all U.S. and Canadian models	
Covers all U.S. and Canadian $^1/_2$, $^3/_4$ and 1 ton models, including 4-wheel drive and diesel engines		**Fairmont/Zephyr 1978-83**	6965
		Covers all U.S. and Canadian models	
		Fiat 1969-81	7042
Chevrolet LUV 1972-81	6815	Covers all U.S. and Canadian models	
Covers all U.S. and Canadian models		**Fiesta 1978-80**	6846
Chevrolet Mid-Size 1964-86	6840	Covers all U.S. and Canadian models	
Covers all U.S. and Canadian models of 1964-77 Chevelle, Malibu and Malibu SS; 1974-77 Laguna; 1978-85 Malibu; 1970-86 Monte Carlo; 1964-84 El Camino, including diesel engines		**Firebird 1967-81**	5996
		Covers all U.S. and Canadian models	
		Firebird 1982-85	7345
		Covers all U.S. and Canadian models	
		Ford 1968-79 Spanish	7084
Chevrolet Nova 1986	7658	**Ford Bronco 1966-83**	7140
Covers all U.S. and Canadian models		Covers all U.S. and Canadian models	
Chevy/GMC Vans 1967-84	6930	**Ford Bronco II 1984**	7408
Covers all U.S. and Canadian models of $^1/_2$, $^3/_4$, and 1 ton vans, cutaways, and motor home chassis, including diesel engines		Covers all U.S. and Canadian models	
		Ford Courier 1972-82	6983
		Covers all U.S. and Canadian models	
Chevy S-10 Blazer/GMC S-15 Jimmy 1982-85	7383	**Ford/Mercury Front Wheel Drive 1981-85**	7055
Covers all U.S. and Canadian models		Covers all U.S. and Canadian models Escort, EXP, Tempo, Lynx, LN-7 and Topaz	
Chevy S-10/GMC S-15 Pick-Ups 1982-85	7310	**Ford/Mercury/Lincoln 1968-85**	6842
Covers all U.S. and Canadian models		Covers all U.S. and Canadian models of FORD Country Sedan, Country Squire, Crown Victoria, Custom, Custom 500, Galaxie 500, LTD through 1982, Ranch Wagon, and XL; MERCURY Colony Park, Commuter, Marquis through 1982, Gran Marquis, Monterey and Park Lane; LINCOLN Continental and Towne Car	
Chevy II/Nova 1962-79	6841		
Covers all U.S. and Canadian models			
Chrysler K- and E-Car 1981-85	7163		
Covers all U.S. and Canadian front wheel drive models			
Colt/Challenger/Vista/Conquest 1971-85	7037		
Covers all U.S. and Canadian models			
Corolla/Carina/Tercel/Starlet 1970-85	7036		
Covers all U.S. and Canadian models		**Ford/Mercury/Lincoln Mid-Size 1971-85**	6696
Corona/Cressida/Crown/Mk.II/Camry/Van 1970-84	7044	Covers all U.S. and Canadian models of FORD Elite, 1983-85 LTD, 1977-79 LTD II, Ranchero, Torino, Gran Torino, 1977-85 Thunderbird; MERCURY 1972-85 Cougar,	
Covers all U.S. and Canadian models			

continued on next page

RTUG Title	Part No.	RTUG Title	Part No.
1983-85 Marquis, Montego, 1980-85 XR-7; LINCOLN 1982-85 Continental, 1984-85 Mark VII, 1978-80 Versailles		**Mercedes-Benz 1974-84** Covers all U.S. and Canadian models	6809
Ford Pick-Ups 1965-86 Covers all ½, ¾ and 1 ton, 2- and 4-wheel drive U.S. and Canadian pick-up, chassis cab and camper models, including diesel engines	6913	**Mitsubishi, Cordia, Tredia, Starion, Galant 1983-85** Covers all U.S. and Canadian models	7583
Ford Pick-Ups 1965-82 Spanish	7469	**MG 1961-81** Covers all U.S. and Canadian models	6780
Ford Ranger 1983-84 Covers all U.S. and Canadian models	7338	**Mustang/Capri/Merkur 1979-85** Covers all U.S. and Canadian models	6963
Ford Vans 1961-86 Covers all U.S. and Canadian ½, ¾ and 1 ton van and cutaway chassis models, including diesel engines	6849	**Mustang/Cougar 1965-73** Covers all U.S. and Canadian models	6542
		Mustang II 1974-78 Covers all U.S. and Canadian models	6812
GM A-Body 1982-85 Covers all front wheel drive U.S. and Canadian models of BUICK Century, CHEVROLET Celebrity, OLDSMOBILE Cutlass Ciera and PONTIAC 6000	7309	**Omni/Horizon/Rampage 1978-84** Covers all U.S. and Canadian models of DODGE omni, Miser, 024, Charger 2.2; PLYMOUTH Horizon, Miser, TC3, TC3 Tourismo; Rampage	6845
GM C-Body 1985 Covers all front wheel drive U.S. and Canadian models of BUICK Electra Park Avenue and Electra T-Type, CADILLAC Fleetwood and deVille, OLDSMOBILE 98 Regency and Regency Brougham	7587	**Opel 1971-75** Covers all U.S. and Canadian models	6575
		Peugeot 1970-74 Covers all U.S. and Canadian models	5982
		Pinto/Bobcat 1971-80 Covers all U.S. and Canadian models	7027
GM J-Car 1982-85 Covers all U.S. and Canadian models of BUICK Skyhawk, CHEVROLET Cavalier, CADILLAC Cimarron, OLDSMOBILE Firenza and PONTIAC 2000 and Sunbird	7059	**Plymouth 1968-76** Covers all U.S. and Canadian models	6552
		Pontiac Fiero 1984-85 Covers all U.S. and Canadian models	7571
GM N-Body 1985-86 Covers all U.S. and Canadian models of front wheel drive BUICK Somerset and Skylark, OLDSMOBILE Calais, and PONTIAC Grand Am	7657	**Pontiac Mid-Size 1974-83** Covers all U.S. and Canadian models of Ventura, Grand Am, LeMans, Grand LeMans, GTO, Phoenix, and Grand Prix	7346
		Porsche 924/928 1976-81 Covers all U.S. and Canadian models	7048
GM X-Body 1980-85 Covers all U.S. and Canadian models of BUICK Skylark, CHEVROLET Citation, OLDSMOBILE Omega and PONTIAC Phoenix	7049	**Renault 1975-85** Covers all U.S. and Canadian models	7165
		Roadrunner/Satellite/Belvedere/GTX 1968-73 Covers all U.S. and Canadian models	5821
GM Subcompact 1971-80 Covers all U.S. and Canadian models of BUICK Skyhawk (1975-80), CHEVROLET Vega and Monza, OLDSMOBILE Starfire, and PONTIAC Astre and 1975-80 Sunbird	6935	**RX-7 1979-81** Covers all U.S. and Canadian models	7031
		SAAB 99 1969-75 Covers all U.S. and Canadian models	5988
Granada/Monarch 1975-82 Covers all U.S. and Canadian models	6937	**SAAB 900 1979-85** Covers all U.S. and Canadian models	7572
Honda 1973-84 Covers all U.S. and Canadian models	6980	**Snowmobiles 1976-80** Covers Arctic Cat, John Deere, Kawasaki, Polaris, Ski-Doo and Yamaha	6978
International Scout 1967-73 Covers all U.S. and Canadian models	5912	**Subaru 1970-84** Covers all U.S. and Canadian models	6982
Jeep 1945-87 Covers all U.S. and Canadian CJ-2A, CJ-3A, CJ-3B, CJ-5, CJ-6, CJ-7, Scrambler and Wrangler models	6817	**Tempest/GTO/LeMans 1968-73** Covers all U.S. and Canadian models	5905
		Toyota 1966-70 Covers all U.S. and Canadian models of Corona, MkII, Corolla, Crown, Land Cruiser, Stout and Hi-Lux	5795
Jeep Wagoneer, Commando, Cherokee, Truck 1957-86 Covers all U.S. and Canadian models of Wagoneer, Cherokee, Grand Wagoneer, Jeepster, Jeepster Commando, J-100, J-200, J-300, J-10, J20, FC-150 and FC-170	6739	**Toyota 1970-79 Spanish**	7467
		Toyota Celica/Supra 1971-85 Covers all U.S. and Canadian models	7043
		Toyota Trucks 1970-85 Covers all U.S. and Canadian models of pickups, Land Cruiser and 4Runner	7035
Laser/Daytona 1984-85 Covers all U.S. and Canadian models	7563	**Valiant/Duster 1968-76** Covers all U.S. and Canadian models	6326
Maverick/Comet 1970-77 Covers all U.S. and Canadian models	6634	**Volvo 1956-69** Covers all U.S. and Canadian models	6529
Mazda 1971-84 Covers all U.S. and Canadian models of RX-2, RX-3, RX-4, 808, 1300, 1600, Cosmo, GLC and 626	6981	**Volvo 1970-83** Covers all U.S. and Canadian models	7040
		VW Front Wheel Drive 1974-85 Covers all U.S. and Canadian models	6962
Mazda Pick-Ups 1972-86 Covers all U.S. and Canadian models	7659	**VW 1949-71** Covers all U.S. and Canadian models	5796
Mercedes-Benz 1959-70 Covers all U.S. and Canadian models	6065	**VW 1970-79 Spanish**	7081
Mereceds-Benz 1968-73 Covers all U.S. and Canadian models	5907	**VW 1970-81** Covers all U.S. and Canadian Beetles, Karmann Ghia, Fastback, Squareback, Vans, 411 and 412	6837

Chilton's Repair & Tune-Up Guides are available at your local retailer or by mailing a check or money order for **$13.95** plus **$3.25** to cover postage and handling to:

Chilton Book Company
Dept. DM
Radnor, PA 19089

NOTE: When ordering be sure to include your name & address, book part No. & title.